June 5   ch 5 +6
  6-13 Ch 7, 8, 9, 11
  16-17 Ch 13 + 14

Fiscal Administration

Analysis and Applications for the Public Sector

Fiscal Administration
Analysis and Applications
for the Public Sector

John L. Mikesell
Professor of Public and Environmental Affairs
Indiana University

Second Edition

The Dorsey Press

Chicago, Illinois   60604

© THE DORSEY PRESS, 1982 and 1986

ISBN 0-256-03392-7
Library of Congress Catalog Card No. 85–073806

Printed in the United States of America

1 2 3 4 5 6 7 8 9 0 MP 3 2 1 0 9 8 7 6

To Karen, Amy, Tom, and Daniel

Preface

The period since the first edition of *Fiscal Administration* has been laden with change for public finance and budgeting. To mention only a few of the developments that had to be captured in this edition, the federal deficit continued to rage out of control, the congressional budget process apparently cannot meet even its own internal standards for performance, federal general revenue sharing seems doomed, states have developed a great taste for lottery revenue, and federal tax system reform has caught the fancy of Congress, the president, and the public. Keeping up with public finance practice certainly is no simple task!

In the face of these changes in practice, this edition sticks to the same principles that guided its predecessor. Two in particular should be noted. First, a public affairs student has to have some idea about where the money comes from. The revenue system is the Achilles' heel of modern government; if armies move on their stomachs, then certainly governments crawl on their purses! Anyone without some concept of that system will be left out of many interesting and crucial policy discussions. The second is the belief that many principles of public financial administration and budgeting cannot fully be understood without working through the numbers, tedious though that may be. That is why the questions and exercises—moved to the end of each chapter in this edition—stress the application of procedures and techniques, not speculation about logic or philosophy. They are an attempt to bring the student directly to the heart of fiscal administration as quickly as possible.

Several changes beyond an updating of all data in the text have been made in this edition. The largest changes have been in Part 1 (budgeting) and Part 3 (debt and cash management), but revisions have been made throughout. Chapters 2 through 4 have been revised to reflect current budget debates and structures. There are more illustrations from budget materials, both in the text and in accompanying appendixes. Chapter 5 now includes material on opportunity cost and discounting that formerly appeared in the appendix to the text. Chapters 7 and 8 are the result of placing the coverage of income and consumption taxes in two separate chapters. Chapter 11 now adds government enterprise and lottery revenue to its prior consideration of user charges. Chapter 12 encompasses the Reagan administration's restructuring of federal aid. The treatment of cash management, Chapter 14, is completely rewritten. I have tried to focus on the fiscal issues of greatest enduring importance.

Some people have been particularly helpful with this revision. My students, undergraduate and graduate alike, at Indiana University have taken great pleasure in pointing out ambiguities, confusions, and errors in the first edition. For their attention to detail, I am appreciative. I also thank my public finance colleagues, especially C. Kurt Zorn and Jeanne Patterson at Indiana, Eric B. Henzik at Texas A&M University, and Anthony Kwasi Antwi at Sam Houston State University, who have offered both encouragement and suggestions. Two others, however, deserve particular mention and special appreciation. With good spirits, Alice Eads typed the manuscript from often strange and obscure drafts, for which I am grateful. And my graduate assistant through much of this revision process, Jacqueline Thiell, not only helped keep this and other projects alive but, more importantly, made sure that we all kept a reasonable perspective and worked in good cheer. For all of you, many thanks.

John L. Mikesell

Preface to the First Edition

Fiscal administration encompasses a wide range of activities vital to the operation of any government, including all portions of the budget cycle, the tax, charge, and aid processes of revenue generation, administration of the government debt, and management of idle cash, the topics examined through this book. Fiscal officers are likewise involved in collective bargaining, in developing policies for risk management and insurance, in managing purchasing and inventory policies, and so on. Those other activities are assigned because the fiscal officer is best able to integrate the effects of decisions made in those areas with the financial conditions of the government. Furthermore, the fiscal officer is not likely to be overwhelmed by quantitative manipulations needed to protect the interests of the government in such discussions. In sum, those in fiscal administration are necessarily a crucial link between policy formation and the process by which services are delivered. A world of scarcity, either severe or minimal, requires that the practitioners of fiscal administration be at the heart of the action.

This text evolved from my frustrated search of almost 10 years for a book appropriate for public finance and budgeting courses in a public affairs–public administration program. Material from economics, my academic discipline, usually ignored the practicalities of public agency operations, frequently required theoretical background beyond that of the typical student, and gave cursory attention to budget systems. Material from political science, generally limited to budgeting, concentrated on process outcomes and organizational dynamics without much development of analytic framework. Material from finance both emphasized corporate operations and required substantial theoretical background. No single approach was enough. No text or group of texts integrated all that students needed exposure to in a coherent conceptual framework with the appropriate analytical tools.

The needs of future practitioners are diverse. They need to learn about budget systems and their operation, revenue policies and their administration, public debt management, and idle fund management—because those are the responsibilities of the people doing fiscal administration. That is what this text examines—integrating materials, concepts, and approaches from several academic disciplines.

The structure of the text similarly emerges from almost 10 years of developing an integrated view of public financial administration. It seemed to me that the appropriate textbook should (1) introduce an analytic framework for public financial administration; (2) develop an understanding of fiscal institutions and the political constraints on their operation; (3) provide as many concrete examples of principles developed as possible; and (4) develop some technical skills that could be useful both immediately and over a career in public management. To put those views into action, the book contains short cases and related selections which illustrate and expand on principles developed in the chapters. Questions after each case or selection are designed only to start discussion; there is sufficient conflict in most of them to generate substantial debate. Each major section also has a series of homework exercises that require application of technical skills developed in the text. A number of the exercises are difficult and time-consuming. They will cause fewer problems, however, than would being unprepared on the job.

Chapters develop the environment of fiscal administration, cultivate the mindset appropriate for fiscal administration, and introduce a number of techniques used in fiscal administration. While it is true that the financial mechanisms—the forms, deadlines, system labels, etc.—of every government are different from that of every other, the objectives and analytic approaches are consistent. These chapters chart a path that may be followed through the cloud of institutional peculiarities regardless of local jargon.

The first chapter examines why governments exist and why there is any need for public financial administration, separate and distinct from business finance. The arguments developed there are based on the logic of public choice, an academic discipline which brings several tools of modern economics to the study of political science questions. It is a robust field of inquiry which comes as close as anything to presenting a general theory of budgeting.

The next chapters, gathered as Part 1, examine how (and why) the budget process operates, what its logic is, and how practitioners try to improve that process. The chapters, along with cultivating the attitudes requisite to roles in the budget process, provide several analytic techniques used by participants in the process. The chapters do not replicate special studies of behavior in the budgetary process; some instructors will want to supplement coverage in the text with their favorite from that group.

The second major part, six chapters, focuses on the means of financing the services provided through budgetary decisions. Four chapters cover taxes, the compulsory extractions that are the foundation of government finance. One chapter is devoted to user charges, a much-discussed but little-used revenue source. Such revenue is attractive because of feared resistance to tax increases, although services provided seldom are good candidates to yield substantial charge revenue. A final chapter in the section outlines intergovernmental fiscal relations, an area including division of responsibilities between governments, tax relationships, mandates, and grant systems.

The third section contains two chapters on important areas of government finance: debt administration and cash management.

Some may argue that the revenue section ought to come before the budgeting section because government budgeting involves allocation of whatever the revenue system can produce. Others would agree that budgeting should come first because the financing function serves to acquire sufficient resources to accommodate the provision of services adopted through the budget process. It is a judgment call and makes for a lively discussion. Instructors may pursue their personal preference here, for the sections are designed to be used in either sequence. What is certain is that neither can be ignored.

ACKNOWLEDGMENTS

I owe special thanks to Jerry McCaffery of Indiana University and John Bowman of Virginia Commonwealth University. Our many discussions improved my understanding of public finance, defined what ought to be taught about public budgeting and finance, and contributed illustrations and examples used here. Thanks also to reviewers of an earlier version of the manuscript (John R. Gist of Virginia Polytechnic Institute, Marcia W. Taylor of The University of South Carolina, and series editor Samuel Patterson of The University of Iowa) for comments that improved both the logic and the clarity of the final product. Students at Indiana University tested earlier versions of the material here, probably in violation of regulations against cruel treatment of human subjects—some of the early material was really bad. Thanks are also due Mrs. Karen Evans, who miraculously converted almost incomprehensible drafts into a manuscript.

J. L. M.

Contents

Part 2
Revenue Sources, Structure, and Administration, 229

Part 3
Administration of Public Debt and Idle Fund Management, 429

List of Figures

List of Tables

1

Fundamental Principles of Public Finance

Governments budget, businesses budget, and, although often unconsciously, individuals budget. Budgeting, a method for selecting an action to be taken from available options, is a nearly universal activity. Efforts to finance those actions are likewise universal; few valued resources are free, so any government, business, or individual must figure out some way to pay for the resources it uses. Because governments, businesses, and individuals must budget and finance these budgets in order to exist, the important first questions for public fiscal administration pertain to why governments exist and what distinguishes them from businesses and individuals, not why budgeting and finance should be studied.

Modern public financial administration, including budgeting, borrows liberally the tools and concepts of business management.[1] That transfer of techniques cannot be complete, however, because of the basic nature of services provided by government. Private enterprise has failed to provide the appropriate level of these government services, so some feature must distinguish them from goods and services provided privately. (The feature certainly is not importance to life, as virtually all governments, foreign and domestic, leave provision of food, clothing, and usually shelter, to the private sector.) This feature—shortly to be described as nonappropriability—both prevents private provision

---

[1]That is not new. Woodrow Wilson wrote in 1887: "The field of administration is a field of business. It is removed from the hurry and strife of political life only as the methods of the counting house are part of the life of society." ["The Study of Administration," *Political Science Quarterly* 2 (1887) as reprinted in *Classics of Public Administration*, ed. Jay M. Shafritz and Albert C. Hyde (Oak Park, Ill.: Moore Publishing, 1978), p. 3]. The borders and distinctions have, however, grown more interesting as the following chapters will demonstrate, particularly when mechanics surrender to analysis.

and limits the extent to which business management techniques can be applied in fiscal administration. Thus, this initial section examines the nature of public services that renders them the unique province of government.

THE BASIS FOR GOVERNMENT ACTION: NONAPPROPRIABILITY

Governments exist to provide to people valuable services which businesses or individuals are unwilling or unable to provide independently. Richard Musgrave identifies three economic functions of government.[2] The first function, stabilization and growth, involves the combat against unemployment and inflation and provision for increases in the standard of living for the citizenry. The second function is distribution, the correction of perceived injustices in the distribution of wealth in society. That presumably means taking from the well-to-do and improving the conditions of the less well-to-do. The third function is allocation, the provision of public or collective goods. These are goods or services which are socially desirable but which ordinary business firms cannot be expected to provide in desirable amounts. The reasons for their reluctance to provide public goods will become apparent shortly.

Such market failure, "the failure of a more or less idealized system of price-market institutions to sustain 'desirable' activities or to stop 'undesirable' activities," is the logical basis of government actions in market economies, so our essential concern is with this allocation function.[3] What about these goods makes them public? Why can private action not be relied on to provide police and urban fire protection, primary education, national defense, and so on? Individuals do demand these services, and we expect businesses to provide services demanded. Quite simply, a business would not provide them because it would be unable to charge a price for the service sufficient to cover the cost of resources used to provide that service (including a normal profit for the firm).

The public good problem is one of excluding those who have not paid for the good from receipt of services from that good.[4] If someone

---

[2]Richard A. Musgrave, *The Theory of Public Finance* (New York: McGraw-Hill, 1959), p. 5.

[3]Francis M. Bator, "The Anatomy of Market Failure," *Quarterly Journal of Economics,* August 1958, p. 351. Public goods are only one type of market failure, but they are the basis for budgeting, taxation, and other parts of fiscal administration. Other failures create the need for government regulation of electric utilities, railroads, and so on. Those will not be considered here.

[4]A more complete analysis of public goods may be found in "The Welfare Foundations of Public Finance Theory," the first chapter of John G. Head, *Public Goods and Public Welfare* (Durham, N.C.: Duke University Press, 1974).

pays for a public good, everyone in the immediate area will receive the services of that public good. Thus, if Lombardi in apartment 10A pays for fire protection, Banks in adjoining apartment 10B receives some of that protection, regardless of any payment by Banks. That illustrates the nonappropriability feature: the inability of a provider to receive all returns from the purchase of a service. Nonappropriability includes two elements, as diagramed in Figure 1-1, which distinguishes private goods, public goods, and two intermediate kinds of goods—toll goods and common-property resources. The initial element is **failure of exclusion**: there is no way to prevent people from receiving the service even though they have not paid for it. The other element is **nonexhaustion** or **nonrivalry**: one person's use of the service does not preclude anyone else from concurrent full use of the service. Private goods do not have appropriability problems: one person's use eliminates the possibility of anyone else using it, and exclusion is feasible. Obviously, the full range of ordinary commodities and services (bread, milk, etc.) fall into this private good class. The only way an individual can receive the benefits from a private good is by paying for it; there are no effects on others, and it is possible to separate payers from nonpayers.

Public goods include services, such as national defense, mosquito abatement, pollution control, and disease control. The common characteristics of these services are that once they are made available, separation of those who have paid from those who haven't paid is impossible, and any number of people can consume the same good at the same time without diminishing the amount of good available for anyone else to consume. The most obvious example of a pure good is national defense. If one person in Detroit is protected against thermonuclear attack now, others in Detroit would be protected as well. In fact, most people in the midwestern United States and part of Canada would have exactly the same level of protection. The service, once provided, can be consumed by a large number of people without diminishing the amount of service

FIGURE 1-1 The Elements of Nonappropriability

		Exhaustion	
		Alternate use	Joint use
Exclusion	Feasible	Private goods	Toll goods
	Not feasible	Common pool resources	Public goods

available to others, and no mechanism is available to deny service to those not paying for it.

Some goods have one characteristic of the public good but not both (as shown in Figure 1–1) and are not public goods. These are toll goods and common pool resources. Toll goods have a nonexhaustion characteristic: one person can consume the service to its fullest while leaving the same amount of the service for someone else to consume. For these goods, however, exclusion is feasible; boundaries can separate payers and nonpayers. Examples include drive-in movies and toll roads: up to a congestion point, a larger number of people can consume these services without exhausting the service concurrently available to others. Neither are public because those not paying can be prevented from receiving the service—by fences or toll barriers.

Common pool resources are goods or services for which exclusion is not feasible, but there are competing and exhaustive uses. Examples include water from underground pools or aquifers, oil and gas deposits, and fisheries. There are no normal barriers allowing people to exercise normal property or ownership rights on the resource, but the resource, when used, becomes unavailable for others to use. Left to private processes, these resources may be rapidly used because the resource is valuable and in its natural state is not subject to normal ownership controls. (First come, first served is a normal allocation principle.)

Within the range of exclusion failure, if someone provides the service, all receive that service. When one structure in an urban area receives fire protection, nearby structures receive protection as well, given the propensity of fires to spread.[5] The public good is fire protection, not fire fighting; when the equipment is putting out the fire at Smith's house, it is not available to put out the fire anywhere else. But extinguishing that fire provides fire protection equally to many neighbors. Obviously there are geographic limits to that range of nonappropriability: fire protection provided in Bloomington, Indiana, will not extend to the people in Jackson, Mississippi. Within that geographic area, however, all receive the service regardless of payment made for it, whether they want it or not. Such is the special monopoly position of governments: not only are alternate providers unavailable, but residents do not have the option of not paying for the service because revenue systems operate independently from service delivery. A governor of Kentucky recognized the difference between operating the state and operating his successful business: "Hell, governing Kentucky is easier

---

[5]Private firms sell fire protection to individuals in parts of Arizona. Neighbors are distant and fires seldom spread, so the service is a private good in the environment. Roger S. Ahlbrandt, Jr., *Municipal Fire Protection Services: Comparison of Alternative Organizational Forms* (Beverly Hills and London: Sage Professional Papers in Administration and Policy Studies 03-002, 1973).

than running Kentucky Fried Chicken. There's no competition."[6] There is no competition because only one state governs in Kentucky and because no private firms will provide the services provided by the state. The former occurs because American rules of government define geographic boundaries for government; the latter, because those services are nonappropriable and, hence, cannot feasibly be sold at market. Paying regardless of preference or consumption is, of course, a unique feature of government provision.

Provision of a good or service by a government does not render that good or service a public good; whether the good is public depends on its appropriability. Furthermore, government provision does not necessarily require government production. Provision ensures that the good is available for consumption, generally at no direct charge to the user. Private production could be through contract with the providing government. The production choice should be made according to which producer would produce the desired quantity and quality of service at least cost to the providing government.

Some cities, especially in California, have provided a full range of services entirely by contract. Such an arrangement is called the Lakewood Plan after an early contract city.[7] Production by contract is probably limited by the ability to design a contract specifying the service qualities to be delivered more than by anything else. Even parts of the judicial system may be privately produced: California permits litigants to hire private jurists when court congestion or special expertise makes such procedure attractive to both parties.[8]

Our focus primarily is with public goods, the class of goods and services for which private action will fail to provide the desired service because the private supplier cannot effectively charge for the service. Business firms provide goods and services because they intend to make money, not for the sheer enjoyment of providing the goods or services. If it is not possible to charge people for the use of the good or service, a business firm will seldom provide the service. Occasionally governments will provide private goods and almost always do a very bad job of it. Organizational problems, particularly lack of appropriate production incentives, cause high cost, undesirable production strategies, and a bland product designed by an uneasy consensus. Governments do provide toll goods (highways, bridges, etc.), and sometimes they do about as well as the private producer would do. Evidence is, however, that fewer resources will be wasted if government avoids provision of private goods.

---

[6]Governor John Y. Brown, Jr., quoted in *Newsweek*, March 30, 1981.

[7]Robert Bish, *The Public Economy of Metropolitan Areas* (Chicago: Markham Publishing, 1971), p. 85.

[8]"California Is Allowing Its Wealthy Litigants to Hire Private Jurists," *The Wall Street Journal*, August 6, 1980.

Some observers of public fiscal problems have suggested that privatization, allowing private enterprise to take over activities currently undertaken by government, will relieve pressures on government finances. That is a realistic response if the service being privatized in fact lacks substantial public good features; one wonders why, in such a case, the government got involved in its provision. On the other hand, to expect private firms to provide public goods at desirable levels is folly. At best, the private firm may be contracted to *produce* the public good provided (paid for) by the government. It is clear that privatization cannot be a general and complete cure for fiscal problems, no matter how inefficient a troubled government might be. For public goods, efficient private provision cannot substitute for inefficient government provision of public goods.

PUBLIC CHOICES AND PUBLIC FINANCE

Building Social Decisions from Individual Preferences

The logic of moving from individual choice to choices made by society as a whole is built on a few fairly simple tenets. First, individuals are the best judges of their own well-being and will generally act to improve that well-being as they see it. There is no scientific principle which leads us to reject or accept the judgments made by individuals about their own lives. Second, the welfare of the community depends on the welfare of the individuals in that community. In other words, communities are made up of the people in them. From that comes the third tenet, judging the impact of a social action on the welfare of the community. The Pareto criterion, named after a 19th-century economist, holds that if at least one person is better off from a policy action and no person is worse off, then the community as a whole is unambiguously better off for that policy.[9] Does a social action harming anyone, despite improving the condition of many individuals, improve the welfare of society as a whole? It cannot be indisputably argued that such an action improves the well-being of society, regardless of the numbers made better off, because the relative worth of those harmed cannot scientifically be compared with those helped. Such a proposed policy would fail the Pareto criterion for judging social action.[10]

---

[9]Vilfredo Pareto, *Manuel d'economie politique*, 2d ed. (Paris: M. Giard, 1927), pp. 617–18.

[10]Benefit-cost analysis, an analytic technique which will be discussed in a later chapter, employs a less restricting and somewhat less logically appealing rule than the Pareto criterion. This is the Kaldor criterion, which holds that a social action improves community welfare if those benefiting from a social action could hypothetically compensate in full the losers from that action and still have gain left over. Because no compensation need actually occur, losers can remain, and the Pareto criterion would not be met.

TABLE 1-1

Individual	Individual Benefit
A	4,000
B	2,000
C	2,000
D	5,000
E	2,500

With those standards we can analyze the implications of nonappropriability on public provision. Suppose that only five people are influenced by construction of a harbor on a lake. The cost of that harbor is $7,500. Each individual in this community knows the maximum sacrifice that he or she would be willing to make to have that harbor as compared to having no harbor at all. These are the individual benefit numbers in Table 1-1. The harbor, we assume, would be a public good: each individual could use it without using up capacity available for anyone else, and exclusion of nonpayers is not feasible.

First, would the harbor get built without public action (by individual action only)? The cost of the harbor is $7,500, the most that any single individual (individual D) will pay to get the harbor built is $5,000. Thus, the harbor would not be produced by any single individual. If the harbor only costs $4,200 to construct, however, we suspect individual D would build the harbor for his benefit and four other people in the community would receive benefits from the harbor without payment. (The four would be "free-riders.") Once the harbor is there, it is available for all because it has the public good features. The initially presumed construction cost is, however, such that the maximum individual benefit is less than the cost of the project, so the harbor will not be built by private action.

Is the harbor socially desired, in the sense that the value of the harbor is greater than the resources going into the construction of the harbor? The social cost, the value of the resources being used up in the construction of the harbor, equals $7,500. The social benefit of the harbor, the sum of the improved welfares of the individuals with the harbor, equals $15,500. Thus, social benefits are greater than social costs, so it is a desirable project for the community.[11] A responsive government would act to provide the harbor and would raise sufficient funds through the revenue structure to finance the project. Should the government levy an equal per capita tax on the community to finance the

---

[11] A small number of people may construct the harbor without the full coercion of government. Individuals A, B, and D could form a little yacht club: the sum of benefits to those three exceeds the cost. Those people might agree privately to build the harbor for their use, and the benefits would spill over to C and E.

harbor ($1,500 each), all individuals would still be better off with the harbor and the tax than without either. Government can thus provide a desired service which public good features prevent private action from providing.

A second example yields additional insights. Presume that the community receives benefits from a project as in Table 1-2. The project is a public good. The cost of the project is $7,000. Because the sum of individual benefits ($6,200) is less than the cost of the project, the resources going into the project would be worth more in other uses than they are in the particular use being considered. Suppose, however, that the project decision will be made at a referendum among the people in the community, with a simple majority required for passage. The referendum also includes the method to be used to finance the project: by an equal per capita tax (project cost divided by number of people in the community, or $1,400 per person). If the people in the community vote according to their individual net gain or loss from the project (as computed in Table 1-2), it will be approved (three for, two against). Does voter approval make the project desirable for the community? Not at all, because the project misallocates resources: it consumes resources that have a greater value in other use. The majority vote may misallocate resources when used for public decisions, as may any technique that does not involve comparisons of social cost and social return.

A third example further illustrates the limits of scientific principles in public decision making. Table 1-3 presents individual benefits from a project with a total cost of $8,000 and an equal per capita tax method of distributing the tax burden. Total benefits do exceed total cost, so the project apparently represents an appropriate way to use scarce resources—and the project would be approved by majority vote if the people voted according to their individual gains or losses. The project does, however, leave an individual worse off. Is the loss to E less important to the community than the gains of A, B, C, and D? That takes a value judgment about the worth of individuals to society, one with which science and Pareto cannot help.[12] Politicians make such choices frequently, but not with the benefit of science.

One voting rule would ensure that only projects that pass the Pareto criterion would be approved. That rule is unanimity, because we presume that people will not vote for policies contrary to their own best interest. This rule is seldom used because of the substantial cost of reaching decisions which would often result. James Buchanan and Gordon

---

[12]For the project presented in Table 1-3, it is possible to rearrange individual cost shares to compensate those losing from the project (one option: increase the payments made by A and C by $500 and reduce those made by D and E by the same amount). That is a general situation for any project in which total benefits exceed total cost. There is no possible reallocation of cost which will allow the project in Table 1-2 to pass the criterion.

TABLE 1–2

Individual	Individual Benefit	Cost Share	Individual Gain
A	$2,000	$1,400	$ 600
B	1,500	1,400	100
C	2,000	1,400	600
D	500	1,400	− 900
E	200	1,400	− 1,200

TABLE 1–3

Individual	Individual Benefit	Cost Share	Individual Gain
A	$ 3,000	$1,600	$1,400
B	4,000	1,600	2,400
C	2,000	1,600	400
D	1,700	1,600	100
E	100	1,600	− 1,500
Total	$10,800	$8,000	

Tullock identify two elements constituting the full cost of making a community decision.[13] The first, the cost of reaching the decision, the "time and effort . . . which is required to secure agreement,"[14] rises as the percentage agreement required for the decision rises. As more of the group must agree on any issue, the investment of effort in bargaining, arguing, and discussion normally rises. That investment is a real cost because the effort could have been directed to other uses. The second element, the external costs or the cost from group "choices contrary to the individual's own interest"[15] falls as the agreement percentage rises. (These are the costs imposed by a simple majority choice on individuals D and E in Table 1–2. Those costs could have been prevented by requiring a higher vote for approval.) The optimal choice percentage—the lowest combination of the two cost elements—usually would require neither unanimity nor one-person rule, as the former has excessive decision costs and the latter, excessive external costs. Certain decisions are more dangerous to minorities (the losers in decisions) than others. For instance, many juries must reach a unanimous verdict because of the very high external costs that juries can place on people.

[13]James M. Buchanan and Gordon Tullock, *The Calculus of Consent* (Ann Arbor: University of Michigan Press, 1962), chaps. 6–8.

[14]Ibid., p. 68.

[15]Ibid., p. 64.

For similar reasons, constitutional revision has high-percentage vote requirements because of that danger of external costs.[16]

The Paradox of Voting

A further problem, the cyclical majority, infects the voting process. Kenneth Arrow demonstrated that individual preferences may not be combinable into a unique collective choice.[17] In other words, there may be no single "people's choice." For example, assume a three-person group; each person has an equal vote, with decisions made by majority rule. Suppose that there are three alternatives open (a school, a library, and a museum) and that each person has the specific preferences shown in Figure 1-2. The voting paradox emerges when options are considered two at a time. In a comparison of the library against the museum, the library is the preferred alternative of two of the three individuals (Table 1-4). If the library then competes against the school, the school is the choice of two of the three people. To test the consistency of the result: if now the school competes with the museum, the museum is the choice of two of the three people. Thus, there is no alternative which is

FIGURE 1-2

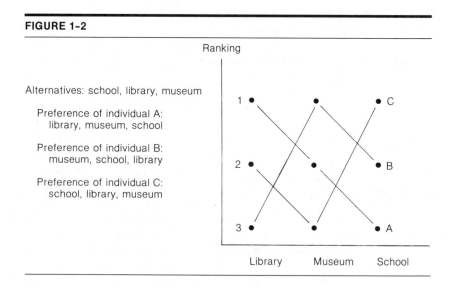

Ranking

Alternatives: school, library, museum

Preference of individual A:
library, museum, school

Preference of individual B:
museum, school, library

Preference of individual C:
school, library, museum

---

[16]Majority votes can be structured to approve only projects that meet the social benefits greater than social cost criterion if projects are financed solely from benefit-base charges.

[17]Kenneth J. Arrow, *Social Choice and Individual Values* (New York: John Wiley & Sons, 1951).

TABLE 1-4 Voting Results

Library versus museum—Library chosen.
Library versus school—School chosen.
School versus museum—Museum chosen.

the consistent choice, and there is no clearly preferable collective outcome: the majority choice cycles among the alternatives.

Obviously the absence of a clear winner creates a problem for the logic of democracy. If individual choices cannot be combined to generate a unique community choice, voting—the decision tool of a democracy—loses much of its attractiveness. All is not lost, however: the cyclical majority noted in the example occurs because the preference pattern of one individual is multipeaked, individual C as the options are ordered in Figure 1-2. In other words, that voter prefers either extreme policy to an intermediate policy. (Should the options be rearranged in the figure, C would no longer have multipeaked preferences, but another of the three would.) Only if preferences are multipeaked does the problem arise.

The cyclical majority will not arise if voters do not prefer the extreme policies to an intermediate policy. In other words, it will not arise if preferences are **single peaked** (individuals A and B as the options are arranged in Figure 1-2). That property may be further illustrated by the following example: suppose the alternatives being considered are (*a*) raise teachers' salaries by $1,000, (*b*) raise teachers' salaries by $500, (*c*) no raise for teachers' salaries. In this instance, there is a natural ordering for preferences. The ordering *a*, *b*, *c*, and *c*, *b*, *a*, are clearly plausible (more to some to none; none to some to more). Other rankings, for instance *c*, *a*, *b*, seem less plausible because they would rank the intermediate position lower than either of the two extremes. When that apparently illogical ranking is excluded, the cyclical majority will not emerge. It should also be noticed that in any voting condition based on majority rule, the alternative finally chosen will be that preferred by the individual whose preferences are median for the group (50 percent above, 50 percent below). The effect of majority rule decision making is thus to convert the person with median preferences into the decisive party in the community.

Complications from Representation

Decisions on public expenditure and taxation typically occur through a representative process, not direct election. An understanding of some elements of the representative process is needed to understand the budget and financing functions. Anthony Downs's works

provide insights into the process of representation.[18] He argues that political parties in a democracy operate to obtain votes to retain the income, power, and prestige that come with being in office. Parties are
not units of principle or ideals but are primarily seekers of votes. A second presumption is lack of perfect knowledge in the system: parties
don't always know what citizens want; citizens don't always know
what the government in power or its opposition has done, is doing, or
should be doing to try to serve their interests. Further, information
that would reduce this ignorance is expensive to acquire. The scarcity
of knowledge obscures the path from citizen preferences to their votes.

Several consequences for the representative process result. First,
some people are politically more important than others because they
have influence over government action. Democratic government won't
treat everyone with equal deference in a world of imperfect knowledge.
Second, specialists in influencing people will appear, and some will
emerge as representatives for the people. These individuals will try to
convince government that the policies they support, and which directly
benefit them, are good for and desired by the electorate. A rational government will discount these claims, but it cannot ignore them. Information provided will reasonably be filtered to provide only data consistent
with the supported cause. Third, imperfect information makes a government party susceptible to bribery simply because the party in power
needs resources to persuade voters to return it to power. Parties out of
power are susceptible as well, but they currently have nothing to sell.
Political influence is a necessary result of imperfect information combined with the unequal distribution of income and wealth in society.
Parties have to use economic resources to provide and obtain information.

Lobbying is a rational response to the lack of perfect information,
but an important imbalance of interests influences the lobbying process. Suppose a direct subsidy to industry is being considered. This
subsidy is of great total value to that industry. The total subsidy paid
by taxpayers, of course, exactly equals the subsidy received by the industry. However, each taxpayer bears a small individual share of that
total subsidy. Who will undertake the expense of lobbying on the measure? The industry will, not the taxpayer, because the net benefit to
lobbying is positive for the industry (comparing the substantial cost of
lobbying with the substantial direct benefit to the industry) and negative for any taxpayer (as the substantial lobbying cost overwhelms the
small individual share of the subsidy which could be saved).

A related influence on representative government is the principle
of rational ignorance. Citizen effort to acquire information to cast an in-

---

[18]Anthony Downs, *An Economic Theory of Democracy* (New York: Harper & Row,
1956).

formed vote is usually irrational.[19] Although the cost of obtaining information may be low, the expected return of an informed vote is even lower. If others vote in an informed manner, a citizen's uninformed vote is irrelevant because the informed majority choice wins. If others vote in an uninformed manner, a citizen's informed vote is irrelevant because the choice of the uninformed majority wins. In either case, the action of the majority produces the election result, so individual effort to become informed yields no return. Thus, electorate choices produce indivisible benefits or costs. Information gathering to cast informed votes will produce no electoral benefits for an individual. That, of course, is a crucial problem in any democratic society. Fortunately, many individuals become informed for other motives, including pure enjoyment.

A final important point in the process of representation deals with the intensity of preference. In ordinary voting, there is no method of representing intensity of preference on particular issues. Each vote has equal weight. In a legislative body, however, trading of votes presents a method of recognizing preference intensity because a series of votes occurs on multiple issues, not just single votes. Legislators, thus, can trade votes according to intensity of preference. For example, a member of Congress may be particularly interested in the outcome on issue B but may have little concern about issue A. That representative may trade his vote on issue A for some other congressman's vote on issue B. This process, "logrolling," can produce wasteful spending (a water project yielding benefit to a small area at great national cost, for instance), but it also can make it possible to improve the responsiveness of government by ensuring that intense preferences get recognized. Furthermore, the representative process has special devices for protecting the interests of minorities. These do not appear in the general referendum process.

> The required majority of those voting (in a referendum) can inflict severe costs on the rest of society with dramatic consequences for the social fabric. Their major disadvantage must emerge from the absence of minority power in the direct legislation system. An initiated referendum has no provision for executive veto, creation of political stalemates in the legislative process, or changed negotiating positions in committees, all vital positions of lawmaking which can serve to protect minorities.[20]

THE CONSTRAINTS OF FEDERALISM

Three layers of relatively independent governments, not a single government, provide public services in the United States. The federal

[19]Ibid., chap. 13.

[20]John L. Mikesell, "The Season of Tax Revolt," in *Fiscal Retrenchment and Urban Policy*, ed. John P. Blair and David Nachmias (Beverly Hills, Calif.: Sage Publications, 1979), p. 128.

system, featuring an independent state level, appears here and in Canada, West Germany, Switzerland, and Australia, to list the major federal countries. Others use unitary systems, which have central and local governments, but lack the independent middle layer. Some understanding of the federal legal powers and limits is fundamental to understanding the prevailing fiscal processes. Relations among the levels are governed by national and state constitutions. The United States Constitution delimits federal authority: Article 1, Section 8 lists available powers; Section 9 lists the powers denied the federal government. Of course, court decisions over time specifically define the extent of those powers. The federal constitution likewise enumerates in Article 1, Section 10 the powers specifically denied the states. These forbidden powers are primarily in the area of conduct of foreign affairs, production of a medium of exchange (printing money), and interference with interstate commerce. The commerce clause is particularly significant for its limitations on the taxing abilities and regulatory powers of states. Other sections of the constitution apply requirements of due process and equal protection on the states. These requirements have had substantial impact on service provision processes of states, particularly as the federal constitutional requirement has often been copied in state constitutions. For instance, the dramatic change in school finance in California generated by the court case *Serrano* v. *Priest*[21] resulted from state constitutional requirements copied after the federal requirement.

The major constitutional provision for states appears in the 10th Amendment of the U.S. Constitution (Rights reserved to states or people): "the powers not delegated to the United States by the Constitution, nor prohibited by it to the states, are reserved to the states respectively, or to the people." The states, thus, have residual powers. The Constitution does not need to provide specific authority for a state government to have a particular power: constitutional silence implies that the state can act in the area in question. States are the unique "middle layer" in the federal system. In unitary governments, the middle layer between the national government and cities may not exist, or it may be simply a department of the central government. In the United States, states exist as an independent layer of government with full powers (including independent financial authority) and all residual powers.

Local governments in the United States typically appear as captive creatures of their states, unless that relationship has been specifically altered by state action. The principle was defined by Judge J. F. Dillon of Iowa:

> It is general and undisputed proposition of law that a municipal corporation possesses and can exercise the following powers and no others: First, those granted in express words; second, those necessarily or fairly implied

---

[21]Cal. 3d 584, 487 P.2d 1241, 97 Cal. Reptr. 601 (1971).

in or incident to the powers expressly granted; third, those essential to the declared objects and purposes of the corporation—not simply convenient, but indispensable. Any fair, reasonable, substantive doubt concerning the existence of power is resolved by the courts against the corporation, and the power denied.[22]

Dillon's rule thus holds that if state law is silent about a particular local power the presumption is that the local level lacks power. In state-local relationships, state government holds all powers. That is a critical limitation on local government fiscal activity.

Several states have altered Dillon's rule by granting home rule charter powers to particular local governments. Such powers are particularly prevalent in states containing a small group of large metropolitan areas with conditions substantially different from the environment in other areas of the state. The special conditions of such large cities can be handled by providing them home rule charter power to govern their own affairs. State law can thus proceed without being cluttered by numerous special enactments for the larger units. When charter powers have been provided, local governments can act in all areas unless state law specifically prohibits those actions. Many times, however, fiscal activities are included in the range of areas that are prohibited under charter powers. Thus it is better to presume limits than to presume local freedom to choose in fiscal affairs. That presumption is accurate if Dillon's rule applies or if charter powers have been constrained in fiscal activities.

CONCLUSION

An overview of the basis for government action certainly indicates that government choices made in budgeting and revenue raising will not be simple. Government will be unable to sell its services because these services are nonappropriable (neither excludable nor exhaustible). That means that government won't have normal market tests available to help it with choices.

Governments surely don't want to waste resources—after all, resources are scarce and most things used by government do have alternative uses—so the benefits to society from government action ought to exceed the cost to society from that action. Determining whether actions really improve the conditions of the community gets complicated, however, when there is no basis for making comparisons of the worth of individuals. The Pareto criterion for judging—the welfare of a community is improved if some members are made better off by an action and

---

[22]John F. Dillon, *Commentaries on the Law of Municipal Corporations*, 5th ed. (Boston: Little, Brown, 1911), vol. 1, sec. 237. See *City of Clinton v. Cedar Rapids and Missouri Railroad Company* (1868).

no one is made worse off by it—has no logical flaws and does not require interpersonal judgments, but it leaves many choices open to political decision. Despite sophistication and rigor, science and analysis will not provide definitive answers to many government choices.

Votes, either on issues or for representatives, will settle many decisions. Direct votes will not, however, guarantee no wasteful public decisions or choices which satisfy the Pareto criterion for improving society and can impose substantial costs on minorities. Further, the cyclical majority property can prevent a clear public choice from emerging from individual preferences. Some problems of direct choice are reduced when representatives make decisions, but there will remain imbalances of influence and posturing to continue in office rather than to follow clearly defined principles.

Finance in a representative democracy is not simple. Success ought to be judged on its general responsiveness to public preferences and on its refusal to ignore minority positions. Not all governments can meet those simple standards, and not all budget systems used in the United States do much to contribute to those objectives. The U.S. structure delivers and finances services using three tiers of government—federal, state, and local. Although independent in some respects, there are important mutual constraints. The federal level has powers delimited in the U.S. Constitution; the states have residual powers. Local governments—under Dillon's rule—have only powers expressly granted by their states. Some states grant local home rule, giving localities all powers save those expressly prohibited them. Few home rule authorizations are complete, however. Thus, budget and finance functions vary widely across the country.

Questions and Exercises

1. A community project (a public good) will cost $1,500 and will benefit the five members of the community as follows:

Resident	Individual Benefit	Cost Share
A	$500	$300
B	500	300
C	100	300
D	250	300
E	250	300

   a. Is the project economically feasible?

   b. Would the project be approved by a majority at a referendum?

   c. Does the project meet the Pareto criterion?

   d. If possible, revise the cost shares to allow the project to meet the Pareto criterion and to pass a referendum.

2. Smith, Jones, and Baker are the arrangements committee for the an-

nual Old Timers Club visit to a Cincinnati Reds game. They must thus decide what team (besides the Reds) they will see play. Smith's preferences are the Cubs, Cardinals, and Mets, in that order; Jones's are Cardinals, Mets, and Cubs; Baker's are Mets, Cubs, and Cardinals. If they vote between pairs of teams (Cubs or Cardinals, Cubs or Mets, etc.), which team will emerge as the clear preference of the three?

3. Determine for your state the budget and finance constraints that the state places on local government. Does Dillon's rule apply? Do some units have home rule powers? What is the extent of any such powers?

Case for Discussion

This article, excerpted from *The Wall Street Journal*, appeared early in New York City's battle to gain control over its finances. Use the article and the fundamentals outlined in Chapter 1 to appraise the situation.

Consider These Questions

1. *What can business principles provide public financial management?*
2. *What choices must be left to elected officials?*
3. *Are there any guides to drawing that important line?*

Penney's Ken Axelson Finds Running a City Is Figures and People

By Frederick Andrews

NEW YORK—Kenneth S. Axelson is the very model of a corporate money man. As the senior vice president and chief financial officer of J. C. Penney Company his life flows with calculated precision. "You plan, you organize, and you program accordingly—and it all works," he says.

But since last September Ken Axelson has been experiencing a very different kind of life. It is a world that would seem to defy planning and controls and where agonizing choices have to be made that will affect the lives of millions.

Mr. Axelson is a businessman in city government. As New York's deputy mayor for finance, on loan for a year from his company, he has been working night and day to help stave off the city's financial collapse and to scale down the city's swollen (and often chaotic) operations to help it live within its means. In the process he has become a man in the middle, caught between the disparate worlds of business and politics.

Trying to organize a city's finances has little relation to the closed, secure corporate world, he is finding. "You get to the office at 8 A.M., and by five after the whole day is shot. The mayor is calling, the governor is calling . . . and in public life there are so many different people coming at you all the time, all with legitimate demands on your time."

New York's highly unusual action in turning to the business world for help in sorting out its tangled financial affairs is not only promising to bring order to the city's accounts but also is beginning to restore the financial world's and the public's badly shaken confidence in the effectiveness of the nation's largest municipal administration.

But should other businessmen similarly be attracted to helping out struggling city administrations, Mr. Axelson would warn them that municipal budget-cutting, unlike corporate belt-tightening, poses the most agonizing social choices. Already, with the city's financial crisis far from over, thousands of city employees have lost their jobs, all new city construction has been stopped, libraries are being closed, centers for preschoolers shut down, police patrols cut back, support for foster children frozen, and fire stations closed.

"It's a terrible responsibility making these judgments," he frets. "When you are in a position to wield enormous power, it's very easy to make enormous mistakes."

DEFERRING TO THE MAYOR

Not surprisingly, the unprecedented exercising of influence by non-elected officials has stirred fears in New York of "economic czars" riding roughshod over the democratic process and slashing services vital to the city's poor.

But the businessmen [brought into New York City government], to the disappointment of their critics, have not done this. Certainly they have pushed the city hard to meet its cost-cutting goals. But, observers say, they have consistently shown caution and have deferred to Mayor Abraham Beame and his aides in deciding which programs to cut. And because they are not politicians they try to ignore the pressures from interest groups to dictate to the mayor.

"It isn't clear that the businessmen have done any more than provide an image and some tough language," says Gary Sperling, executive director of the Citizens Union, a civic group.

Three of the most talented of these businessmen sit on the Emergency Financial Control Board, which was created by the state last September to take over the city's fiscal powers.

Although the control board has final authority over New York City's spending, it is up to the 53-year-old Mr. Axelson, the city's main spokesman before the board, to push the city to bring its spending into line. At the same time, he must protect the city from what he views as the occasionally excessive demands of the board.

THE SUPER BOOKKEEPER

Mr. Axelson didn't volunteer for this exhausting job. He was brought in to placate the financial community, which had lost faith in the city's ability to organize its affairs (in fact, Mayor Beame's closest aide, James A. Cavanagh, became an anathema on Wall Street and was forced to resign).

So far, New York's creditors are mostly happy with Mr. Axelson's performance as a super bookkeeper threading his way through a morass of detail without getting bogged down. It was this ability to master fine details that won him a reputation as a meticulous money strategist during Penney's period of greatest growth. A certified public accountant, he joined the $7 billion retail company in 1963 after working for Peat, Marwick, Mitchell & Company. (Penney is continuing to pay his salary, which is in the $150,000 range, during his year with the city.)

One of his greatest assets, say his admirers, is his candor. It is generally agreed that he made Penney's annual report a model of disclosure by providing information on areas that many companies prefer to keep hidden, such as details on minority hiring. "He would get up at analysts' meetings and talk about bad news without burying it," observes one veteran financial reporter.

A major job during this year with the city has been to assemble what amounts to a massive blueprint for balancing the city's budget by 1977–78. The control board's major function is to supervise this plan. To get it under way, two deadlines were set. By last September 30 the board had to give Mr. Axelson estimates of the city's future revenues. By October 15 he had to give the board a plan for bringing the city's spending into line with these projected revenues.

(At the same time, Mr. Axelson had to develop a "doomsday" plan: the exact steps the city would follow if it fell into default. He decided he would take the pragmatic approach of shutting down much of the city, including schools, and then resuming services only as money came in.)

The three-year spending plan the city submitted to the board last October was a job of forecasting probably never before attempted by any other city. Just to predict one portion of the city's future cash needs required checking thousands of contracts to see when payments were due. Using computers to project tax revenues, it was calculated that the city's annual spending of about $12 billion had to be cut by $724 million over three years.

None of this information has been easy to get. Mr. Axelson found he had inherited an antiquated and crazy-quilt accounting system (the city's published financial reports, many say, were barely comprehensible). The city also lacked any internal machinery for matching actual outlays and receipts against budgeted amounts.

And just to add complications, no single official is responsible for the city's finances. The mayor controls the budget and thus the pace of spending. The city controller, Harrison J. Goldin (also as elected official) keeps the books, manages the cash, and pays the bills.

Before Mr. Axelson returns to Penney he feels his most important accomplishment as deputy mayor will have been to launch a modern accounting system to monitor the city's finances and to bridge the gap between mayor and controller. To help in this, American Management Systems, of Arlington, Virginia, and Touche Ross & Company, the international accounting firm, have been brought in at a cost of $600,000.

Despite his candor and transparent goodwill (one city councilman calls him "a gentle soul") Mr. Axelson has proved a keen disappointment to those city critics who want upheaval, not mind-numbing financial plans. In their view, the deputy mayor fell too readily into traditional City Hall thinking. When he gave a speech pointing out how little room the city had to maneuver, one banker declared, "I was aghast. He gave a speech that could just as easily been given by Beame or Cavanagh." Another prominent financial figure asserts that "he should have gone in and taken hold much more vigorously."

Mr. Axelson replies that it is so much easier to criticize from the outside. He recalls that before he took over the job, "my wife, the doorman, and I, between us, thought we had all the city's problems solved." His major role, he insists, "is to see that the decisions are made." The decisions themselves should be left to elected officials, he says.

Part of the problem is that Mr. Axelson and the business members of the control board are being pressed to rule on the funding of many major social programs, decisions they feel unqualified to make. Thus they prefer to defer to Mayor Beame. (In fact the control board, unwilling to be caught up in politics, won't even force funding decisions on areas, such as the city university and hospitals, which are included in the city's new financial plan but are not directly controlled by Mayor Beame.)

Perhaps Mr. Axelson can't be blamed for veering away from these decisions because of the inevitable occasions when he has been exposed as a political neophyte. Early on, he became caught up in one of the most emotional issues in New York: the funding of the city university and its bitterly debated free tuition and open enrollment. Mr. Axelson sought to end the argument by pointing out the city simply couldn't afford to continue spending $100 million a year on the university.

In the corporate boardroom that observation would have brought applause and immediate action. In the city, he was faced with stubborn resistance from the university's supporters. And though the university seems destined to run out of money this spring, no final decisions on funding have yet been made.

On another occasion Mr. Axelson urged that the state legislature increase city taxes on commuters to the city. But the idea was swiftly blocked by legislators from the suburbs.

This lack of teamwork (teamwork being the essence of corporate life), still mystifies Mr. Axelson. He is shocked at the changing alliances and the cross-purposes of politics. Last fall, for example, he discovered that Gov. Carey apparently planned to propose harsher city tax increases than those agreed on only the previous evening by city and state officials. "The damn games they play," he fumed. "They never said *anything*. The world collapsing around us—you would think people would go out of their way to pull together. I just don't understand it."

Nor did Mr. Axelson appreciate being lectured by congressmen at Washington hearings on federal aid for the city last fall. "I haven't been spoken to like that since I was a kid," he says.

He considers the effort worth it. For in the process of helping change the city, he feels the city is also helping to change him and to enable him to step back from his insulated corporate world.

Recently, late in the afternoon of the final day before the state housing agency was about to default, an alarmed U.S. Treasury official told him that default would also create several problems for the city. Mr. Axelson recalls simply saying, "Relax, there are six hours yet to go." And, in fact, the state legislature passed bills to save the agency at 11:19 that night.

But, says Mr. Axelson, if that incident had happened three months before, "my heart would have stopped beating."

PART 1

Budgeting, Budget Structures, and Budget Reform

2

The Logic and Process of Budgets

The budget process—a formalized routine involving legislative and executive branches of government—plays a key role in the provision of public goods and services. This process fulfills tasks similar to those of an economic market as it determines what government services will be provided, what individuals will receive these services, and how these services will be provided. Except for the limited number of town meeting and referendum decisions, elected representatives make the primary spending decisions. In budget preparation, nonelected public employees make many crucial decisions. While these employees enjoy employment security and may be less responsive to public demands for service than those elected, the logic of representative government presumes that such bureaucrats can be made to respond to executive or legislative dictates flowing from the citizenry. A complete understanding of public expenditures obviously requires an understanding of the budget process.

Public agencies can operate with a haphazard budget process. An effectively operating system that includes incentives for officials to respond to public demands is, however, more likely to produce consistently good decisions. A good public decision will provide citizens with the quantity and quality of public services they desire, at times and locations they desire them, at least cost to society. At a minimum, the process must recognize competing claims on resources and should focus directly on the questions of alternatives and options. A major portion of the process will involve presentation of accurate and relevant information to individuals making budget decisions.

25

BUDGET LOGIC AND FORM

The market process allocates private resources without a need for outside intervention; price movements serve as an automatic signaling device for resource flows. In the public sector, decisions about resource use cannot be made automatically because of the special features of services typically provided by government. First, there can be no sale of government service and consequently profit can neither measure success nor serve as an incentive. The nonappropriability of public goods effectively destroys the possibility of profit. Second, public and private resource constraints differ dramatically. While individual earnings constrain spending of private entities, governments are limited only by the total resources of the society.[1] There are obviously political limits to tax extractions, but those limits differ dramatically from resource limits on a private firm. Third, governments characteristically operate as perfect monopolies. Consumers cannot purchase from an alternate supplier and, more importantly, the consumer must pay whether or not the good provided is used. And finally, public actions are undertaken in an environment of mixed motives. In many instances, not only the service provided but also the recipients of the service (redistribution) or the mere fact of provision (stabilization) are important. For example, free school lunches may be provided to improve the living standard of families with school children or to increase the income of food producers, even though more economical methods may be available to achieve these objectives. Accordingly, more may matter in the provision of a public service than simply the direct return from the service compared to its cost. Because these multiple and mixed objectives cannot be weighted scientifically, the budget process will be political, involving both pure bargaining or political strategies and scientific analysis.

Budgeting allocates resources among government activities and between government and private use. While these allocations are being made, the budget process erects a framework for control, accountability, and evaluation of government activity. Systems of budget and revenue raising are separable planning processes because nonappropriability ensures that payment of a service cannot be a precondition of receipt of service. Budgeting is a process of allocating resources to prevent waste of scarce resources: setting the size of the public sector and deciding what government activities are supported from that pool of public resources. The budget process establishes what gets produced,

---

[1]Few have dared suggest natural limits to the ability of governments to extract resources from society since Colin Clark's proposition of several years ago: "25 percent of the national income is about the limit for taxation in any nontotalitarian community in times of peace." ["Public Finance and Changes in the Value of Money," *The Economic Journal* 55 (December 1945), p. 380.] That limit has been exceeded by Western nations for years, although in fairness to Clark, his limit was based on zero inflation—so it may not have been truly tested.

FIGURE 2-1 Service Delivery and Revenue Systems as Separate Planning Processes

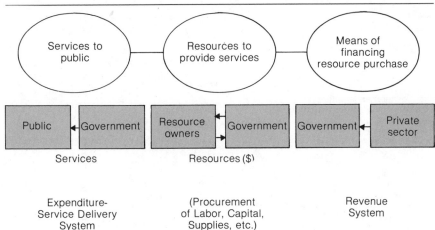

how it gets produced, and who gets the production. Revenue raising, then, is a planning process that determines how private individuals will share the burden of the public sector. Revenue planning determines whose real income will be reduced by extraction of resources to deliver the budgeted services.[2] The total resources used must equal total resources raised, but the profile of government expenditure does not establish the appropriate distribution of the cost of government services. Figure 2-1 notes how dollars, resources, and public services flow from the revenue system to the procurement process to service delivery. The public procurement process involves exchange transactions (purchase on the open market) and, with few exceptions, is much like procurement by private firms. The basic issues are the same. The unique public sector features involve revenue production and service delivery decisions, the concerns of the following chapters. Our first focus is on the expenditure and service delivery process. Revenue planning will be examined in later chapters. As a backdrop to further discussion, however, a quick review of public expenditures in the United States is appropriate.

The Size and Growth of Government Expenditure

Direct expenditure includes all payments made by a government except those to other governments (intergovernmental expenditures). Direct general expenditure includes all such expenditure except that classified as liquor store expenditure (spending by government alcoholic

[2]John L. Mikesell, "Government Decisions in Budgeting and Taxing: The Economic Logic," *Public Administration Review* 38 (November/December 1978).

TABLE 2-1 Government Expenditures in the United States 1960–Early 1980s
($ millions)

| | 1960 | | 1969–70 | |
| | Federal | State and Local | Federal | State and Local |
Fiscal Year				
Direct general expenditure				
National defense and international relations	47,464	-0-	84,253	-0-
Nondefense				
Education and libraries	685	18,980	3,053	53,418
Transportation	1,937	10,007	2,975	17,998
Public welfare, hospitals, health	1,508	8,199	6,756	24,348
Police protection, fire protection, corrections	217	3,530	492	8,144
Sewerage, sanitation	-0-	1,727	-0-	3,413
Parks, recreation, natural resources	7,225	1,959	8,737	4,620
Housing, urban renewal	284	858	1,051	2,138
Administration	982	2,959	2,709	6,738
Interest on general debt	7,662	1,670	14,037	4,374
Other	8,761	1,987	19,722	6,140
Total nondefense	29,261	51,876	59,432	131,331
Total direct general expenditure	76,725	51,876	143,685	131,331
Insurance trust expenditure	13,565	4,031	41,248	7,273
Utility expenditure	-0-	4,066	-0-	7,820
Liquor store expenditure	-0-	1,022	-0-	1,627
Domestic direct expenditure, federal	42,826	-0-	100,680	-0-
Total direct expenditure	90,290	60,995	184,933	148,051

SOURCE: U.S. Bureau of Census, *Governmental Finances* (various years).

beverage distribution facilities), utility expenditure (spending by government owned and operated water, electric, gas, or transit systems), and insurance trust expenditure (payments to government insurance or retirement program beneficiaries). As Table 2–1 shows, direct expenditure in 1982–83 totaled more than $1,350,000 million: 58.2 percent by the federal government. The total constituted around 40 percent of gross national product (GNP), the total value or production in the nation. Direct general expenditure was $1,002,051 million: 53.5 percent by the federal government and about 30 percent of GNP. Almost 17 percent of total expenditure was for national defense and international relations; the function with the next largest identifiable importance was 13 percent for education. Insurance trust expenditures—the various elements of federal old-age, survivors, disability, and health insurance; public employee retirement programs; veterans' life insurance; unemployment compensation; and the like—constitute 22 percent of total expenditure, an even larger chunk than the other elements. Its many dissimilar elements, however, make treatment of the category as if it were a single function unwarranted. The size of insurance trust programs in total does make such spending a major concern of government finance, even though many of these operations lie outside the

1979–80		1982–83		Rate of Compound Growth from 1960		Percent of Expenditures 1982–83	
Federal	State and Local	Federal	State and Local	Federal	State and Local	Total	General
149,459	-0-	228,763	-0-	7.1%	—%	16.9	22.8
10,951	134,905	13,059	166,089	13.7	9.9	13.2	17.9
5,114	37,323	5,006	41,581	4.2	6.4	3.4	4.6
30,348	79,462	37,126	104,602	14.9	11.7	10.5	14.1
2,126	25,660	2,802	35,299	11.8	10.5	2.8	3.8
-0-	13,214	-0-	15,603	—	10.0	1.2	1.6
29,734	12,029	49,105	15,132	8.7	9.3	4.8	6.4
6,080	6,062	10.017	8,505	16.8	10.5	1.4	1.8
7,858	20,443	10,486	26,981	10.8	10.1	2.8	3.7
61,286	14,747	108,735	24,136	12.2	12.2	9.8	13.3
52,798	25,242	70,532	28,492	9.5	12.3	7.3	9.9
206,295	369,087	306,868	466,420	10.8	10.0	57.2	77.2
335,754	369,087	535,631	466,420	8.8	10.0	74.1	100.0
170,576	28,797	250,094	47,335	13.5	11.3	22.0	X
-0-	33,599	-0-	49,995	—	11.5	3.7	X
-0-	2,591	-0-	2,816	—	4.5	0.2	X
376,871		556,962		11.8	—	41.2	X
526,330	434,074	785,725	566,566	9.9	10.2	100.0	X

normal budget process. More details of federal and state-local expenditures by function appear in Table 2–1.

The table presents the average annual growth rate from 1960 to the present to allow comparisons of rates between expenditure categories.[3] Total direct general expenditure by the federal government grew at an

rate of growth

---

[3]The compound rate of growth is computed according to the formula

$$r = \{\text{antilog}[(\ln Y - \ln X)/n]\} - 1$$

where r = the growth rate, Y = the end value, X = the beginning value, and n = the number of periods. For instance, the growth rate for national defense and international relations expenditure from 1960 to 1983 is computed as follows:

$$r = \{\text{antilog}[(\ln 228763 - \ln 47464)/23]\} - 1$$
$$= \text{antilog}[(12.340 - 10.768)/23] - 1$$
$$= 1.071 - 1 = 0.071$$

Thus, the expenditure category increased at an annual rate of 7.1 percent from 1960 to 1983.

Concerning the notation used in the equation: "The logarithm of a positive number p to the base a (>1) is defined as the index of that power of a which equals p. In symbols:

$$\text{If } p = a^q, \text{ then } q = \log_a p.$$

[R. D. G. Allen, *Mathematical Analysis for Economists* (London: Macmillian, 1964), p. 213.] Logarithms can be computed for any base, but common logarithms (base 10) and

annual rate of 8.8 percent over those years. State and local government expenditure grew at a 10 percent rate over the same period. When insurance trust expenditures are added to both groups and defense expenditure is removed from federal expenditure to limit the analysis to domestic expenditure, the federal expenditure growth rate was somewhat higher: 11.8 percent to 10.2 percent. Many expenditure categories grew at rates around 10 percent per year, although there is much variation by function.

Government expenditure can take many forms, including purchase of goods and services from private suppliers (including payment of wages to public employees), transfer payments made to individuals, grants to other governments, interest paid on debt, and subsidies given to government-operated businesses. Table 2-2 presents government expenditures from 1960 to 1984 broken down by major form of expenditure, rather than by function. The totals do not exactly coincide with those of Table 2-1 because the Table 2-2 figures use national income and product accounts concepts for measurement and are on a calendar-year basis; they are generally consistent, however.

Special attention should be given to the difference between price and physical effects on purchases. For example, aggregate federal government purchases of goods and services increased from $197,180 million in 1980 to $295,400 million in 1984. Two forces produced this increase: (1) the greater purchases of physical goods and services and (2) their purchase at higher prices. The components of change in total expenditure in current dollars equals movements in physical (real) purchases and movement in prices. The table shows that the implicit price deflator for federal purchases of goods and services, a measure of prices in that year relative to prices in another, rose from 185.2 to 241.2 (1972 prices as base equal to 100), a 30.2 percent increase. Converting the purchases to the standard price level produces real purchases of $106,469 million in 1980 and $122,471 million in 1984, an increase of 15 percent.[4] Thus, the total increase from 1980 to 1984 of 49.8 percent resulted from a 30.2 percent increase in prices of goods and services

---

natural logarithms (base 2.71828 or "e") are most frequently found in fiscal analysis. Typically, but not always, "log" designates common and "ln" designates natural (most pocket calculators follow that convention). The antilog reverses the logarithm. Examples:

$$2 = \log 100 \text{ because } 10^2 = 100$$
$$3.163 = \log 1455.5 \text{ because } 10^{3.163} = 1455.5$$
$$4.605 = \ln 100 \text{ because } e^{4.605} = 100$$

Logarithms will be used in the analysis of revenue adequacy (elasticities), in evaluating tax equity, and in revenue forecasting later in the text, as well as in the computation of growth rates.

[4]The conversion formula: real value in subject year in base year prices = current dollar value in subject year divided by deflation index and result times 100 or $106,469 = ($197,180/185.2) × 100.

TABLE 2-2 Government Expenditures and Price Deflators in National Income and Product Accounts, 1960–1984 ($millions)

	1960	1970	1980	1984	Annual Rate of Compound Growth from 1960
Government expenditures (millions)					
Federal expenditures					
Purchases of goods and services	53,711	95,737	197,180	295,400	7.4
Defense	44,451	73,565	131,360	221,500	6.9
Nondefense	9,260	22,172	65,820	73,900	9.0
Transfer payments	23,448	63,532	251,443	353,000	12.0
Grants to state-local government	6,526	24,447	88,675	93,200	11.7
Total	93,106	204,306	602,092	880,500	9.8
State and local expenditures					
Purchases of goods and services	46,548	124,408	341,195	452,000	9.9
Transfer payments	5,404	14,735	39,637	54,800	10.1
Total	49,822	133,546	357,767	470,700	9.8
Implicit price deflators for government purchases of goods and services (1972 = 100)					
Federal purchases	59.4	86.6	185.2	241.2	6.0
National defense	—	—	187.5	247.2	7.2
Nondefense	—	—	180.8	224.7	5.6
State and local purchases	56.5	88.6	191.5	251.7	6.4
Constant dollar government purchases (1972 = 100)					
Federal	90,423	110,551	106,469	122,471	1.3
Defense	74,833	84,948	70,059	89,604	0.8
Nondefense	15,589	25,603	36,405	32,888	3.2
State and local purchases	82,386	140,415	178,170	179,579	3.3
Population (July 1) (thousands)	180,671	205,052	225,055	235,535	1.1
Gross national product (billions)	506.5	992.7	2631.7	3662.8	8.6

SOURCE: *Survey of Current Business* (various issues).

purchased and a 15.0 percent increase in physical or real purchases.[5] A similar analysis may be applied to the other government purchase

---

[5]The real and price change rates do not add to the total change, but they are related. If X84, X80, and t are total expenditure in 1984, total expenditure in 1980, and the percentage increase in total expenditure between the years; if D84, D80, and g are the similar concepts for deflated (real or constant dollar) expenditure; and if P84, P80, and p are similar concepts for price levels, then

$$X84 = X80 + (X80 \times t) = X80(1 + t)$$
$$D84 = D80 + (D80 \times g) = D80(1 + g)$$
$$P84 = P80 + (P80 \times p) = P80(1 + p).$$

Total expenditure in 1984 equals real expenditure in 1984 times the 1984 price level:

$$X84 = D84 \times P84$$

Thus, substituting into the equation: (*continued*)

categories; this is the procedure followed to produce the constant dollar (or real) expenditure statistics at the foot of the table.[6]

Some Terminology of the Budgeting and Spending Process

Budgets are simply plans denominated in dollar terms. They get developed as a means (1) for establishing executive branch plans, (2) for providing legislative branch approval of those plans, and (3) for providing a control and review structure for executive implementation of approved plans. The language of budgeting and spending includes a number of concepts which often get confused, with resulting errors in understanding. These concepts need to be clarified before starting formal consideration of the budget process. Budgets begin as *agency requests.* The agency request is built on an agency *plan* for service in an upcoming year (the agency response to public demands for service) and an agency forecast of conditions in the upcoming year (the group of conditions influencing the agency but not subject to agency control).[7] For example, a state department of highways' request for funds for snow removal would involve a *forecast* of the number of snowy days and a *planned response* for handling that snow. For any forecast of snow conditions, agency request will vary depending on how promptly the agency responds to snowfall (after trace snowfall, after 1 inch, after 3 inches, etc.), what roadways will be cleared (arterials, secondary, residential, etc.), and so on. The forecast does not dictate the request. Some agencies build their plans on inputs (the highway department bought 120 tons of road salt last year so it will request about that amount for the budget year); this approach makes changes in service delivery difficult. The public service demands will be forecasts, but agency responses will be plans formulated from decisions and forecasts.

$$X80(1+t) = D80(1+g) \times P80(1+p) \text{ and rearranging terms}$$
$$X80(1+t) = D80 \times P80(1+g)(1+p)$$

Because $X80 = D80 \times P80$, then

$$(1+t) = (1+g)(1+p).$$

For the data in the text,

$$(1+0.498) = (1+0.15)(1+0.302).$$

[6]Price index base years may be easily converted. For instance, with 1972 = 100, the implicit deflator for state and local government purchases in 1960 equals 56.5. If 1960 is to be selected as the base year, then the 1960 index would be 100 and the 1972 index would be 177.0 (100/56.5). The absolute difference in the index differs according to what base year is used, but the percentage change remains the same. Price indexes and deflated (constant or real) values have meaning *only* in a relative sense.

[7]These are forecasts, or best estimates of conditions in the future; they are not necessarily projections, or simple extensions of prevailing conditions to the future.

The *budget document,* or executive budget, incorporates all agency requests into a government-wide request or plan. The requests by the agencies have been accumulated and aggregated according to the policy directives of the chief executive. Agency requests will almost always be reduced by the chief executive to produce an overall executive plan. As will be discussed later, the substantial changes made in agency requests even before the proposals are seen by the legislature reflect differences in attitudes and service clienteles of the agencies and chief executive.

The budget document is transmitted to the legislature for debate and consideration. **Appropriations** are the outcome of the legislative process. These laws provide funds for operating agencies to spend in a specified fashion in the budget year. The initial requests by the agency reflect the plans of that agency; appropriation converts these plans (or portions of them) into legal intentions of the government.

Appropriations provide agencies with resources to make **expenditures,** the acquisition of resources by the agency during the year. Expenditure occurs when the unit pays for goods or services delivered by some supplier. Expenditure (or spending) is the direct result of appropriations made to carry out the service delivery envisioned in the agency's initial budget plan. Because, however, expenditures can involve the acquisition of resources for use both in the present period and in the future, it would not generally be correct to view the amount of expenditure to be exactly equal to the current cost of providing government services. Some of the expenditure now will provide services in later periods. (In simplest terms, part of the road salt purchased this year may be used next year, but much of the difference between expenditure and service cost will be caused by capital assets, such as buildings, trucks, computers, and so on.) The cost of government would equal the amount of resources used or consumed during the period, some resources coming from expenditure in that period and some from expenditures made in earlier periods. Focus on expenditure will thus not render an entirely accurate view of the cost of government. Figure 2–2 on p. 34 outlines the flow of transactions and accompanying management information requirements between budget authority and service cost.

Expenditures are not, however, recorded in the same manner by all accounting systems. Under a *cash accounting* system, money is considered spent or "disbursed" only when a check is written. Under a *modified accrual* system, the system that is required as part of generally accepted accounting procedures (GAAP), "expenditure" is recorded when liability is recognized, generally meaning when a good or service is delivered to the purchaser and normally well before any check is written. From the view of budget control, however, money must be reserved or "encumbered" when the order is placed. From the modified accrual

---

FIGURE 2–2 Financial Information for Management

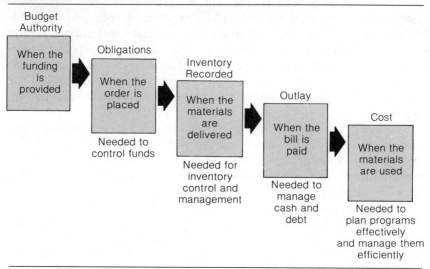

SOURCE: General Accounting Office. *Managing the Cost of Government: Building an Effective Financial Management Structure.* Vol. II, *Conceptual Framework* (GAO/AFMD–85–35–A).

---

accounting view, expenditure would be recorded when delivery occurs and the government becomes obligated to pay; disbursement occurs when the check is mailed. A cash accounting system obviously could provide a misleading view of a government's financial status, but much of the accounting hazard can be corrected with modified accrual. Budget control through the fiscal year, however, requires encumbrance control as well. More about encumbrances will appear in the next chapter.

Some reference to the federal structure may help clarify. Budget authority—provided by appropriation, through borrowing authority, or through contract authority—allows agencies to enter into commitments that will ultimately result in spending, immediate or future.[8] That authority usually is not the amount the agency will spend during the fiscal year, but is the upper limit on new spending without obtaining additional authority. Figure 2–3 illustrates the relationship between budget authority and outlays envisioned in the 1986 federal budget. While a major portion of planned outlays for the year ($754.3 billion) are based on proposals in the 1986 budget, almost $220 billion (23 percent of the total) is based on unspent authority enacted in prior years. That clearly shows that budget authority in a particular year is substantially different from outlays for the year; outlay analysis requires consideration of both present and past authority timing.

---

[8]Borrowing authority permits a federal agency to borrow funds and to spend the proceeds for specified purposes. Contract authority allows an agency to make obligations before appropriations have been passed.

FIGURE 2-3 Relation of Budget Authority to Outlays—1986 Budget

$ billions

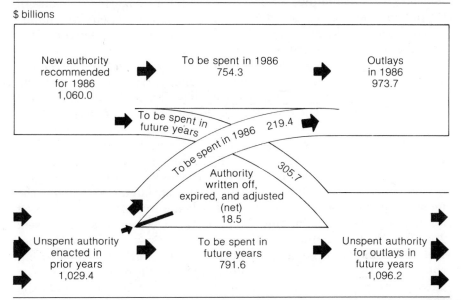

SOURCE: *Budget of the U.S. Government,* Fiscal Year 1986.

At the federal level, only appropriation and historical reports of spending and revenue are mentioned in the Constitution:

> Article 1. Sec. 9 [7] No money shall be drawn from the treasury, but in consequence of appropriations made by law; and a regular statement and account of the receipts and expenditures of all public money shall be published from time to time.

Budgeting procedures have developed in practice and through a handful of laws passed to improve the decision process.

Orientations of a Budget

Governments exist to provide services. The budget period provides a time for examination of the public services desired by the public and of the options available to the government for providing these services. If governments budget simply to prevent public officials from stealing (a traditional attitude toward budgeting), the implication is that government does nothing useful and is little more than an expensive nuisance. A mental inventory of services to individuals, business, and the environment should lead to rejection of that implication and the associated attitude toward budgeting. Public financial managers recognize that properly designed budget procedures serve three important functions: (1) expenditure control; (2) management and efficiency; and (3) planning for service requirements.[9] Methods for the first function differ little from techniques used in private sector budgeting. Because of output measurement and valuation problems associated with public goods, however, the government approaches in the latter two functions are substantially different from their private sector counterparts.

The expenditure control function in budgeting involves restraining expenditures to the limits of available finance and preserving the legality of transactions conducted by the agency. Expenditures must agree with appropriation. They must coincide with the intent of the legislature. The control function helps develop information for cost estimates used in preparation of new budgets and in preserving audit trails after budget years are over. An audit trail is a sequence of documents—invoices, receipts, canceled checks, and so forth—which allows an outside observer to trace transactions involving appropriated money: when the money was spent and who received it, when purchases were delivered and what price was paid, how the purchases were cared for and used, and what the final disposition of those purchases was. Much of the control will come from within the spending unit, although monitoring through the year and postexpenditure audit will be external to the agency. Budgets were initially developed at the municipal level in the United States to prevent thievery, pure and simple. Budgeting and appropriating given amounts of dollars for the purchase of given quantities of inputs simplified the determination of whether legislative intent had been implemented during the year: does the agency have resources to make the appropriation and were purchases by the agency made according to appropriation? If the appropriation was for the purchase of 10 tons of gravel, was that gravel actually purchased and delivered? Questions of that simple but critical nature served as the impetus for development of public budgeting.

Budgets also serve as a tool to increase managerial control of operating units and to improve efficiency in agency operations. This function focuses on the performance activities of governments and does not dwell on inputs or resources purchased by the unit. The important concern is the relationship between the resources used by a department and the public services performed by that department. The public budget—as in an ordinary business—serves as the control device for the government and points up the efficiency in operation of departments. For this purpose, the agency must consider what measurable activities it performs—an often difficult, but seldom impossible, task.

The final budget function recognizes that governments face many opportunities for provision of services and that present actions both influence and are influenced by development of the community. The bud-

---

[9] Allen Schick, "The Road to PPB: The Stages of Budget Reform," *Public Administration Review* 26 (December 1966), p. 243–58.

get formulation period presents an ideal opportunity to consider these implications in an organized framework. Any budget item that has clear implications for spending patterns in the future (a new sewage treatment plant that will require operating expenses in the future, for instance) ought to be considered as an element of long-range plans during budget deliberation. The planning orientation uses the budget as a decision tool concerning continuation of activities, development of new programs, and allocation of resources between activities of government.

All of these are potential uses of a public budget and each can have a role in the budget procedures of public units. The processes used by state, local, and federal governments are subject to substantial individual peculiarities. The treatment here will focus on elements common to most public budget processes with special mention only of the most important peculiarities.

Budget Decisions and the Provision Flow

Governments seek to improve the general standard of living of the citizenry by using resources in reasonable fashion. Their operations in this respect are not dissimilar to those of private business: resources are acquired for their use in a process to produce a valued output. Budgets can focus on three different points in the flow of government activity from the purchase of resources through the provision of the services desired by the general public. Figure 2–4 on p. 38 outlines that flow of service provision. The government buys asphalt, crushed stone, and so on. These inputs are used to fill chuckholes and resurface streets. Those activities improve road quality to reduce commuting time, lessen damage to vehicles from driving over roads in poor condition, and reduce vehicle accidents. That output improves the well-being of members of the community. Thus, the inputs acquired are used to the ultimate benefit of the community.

Some budget structures and procedures focus on inputs (the resources—labor, machines, supplies, buildings, etc.—acquired) in the flow of service provision. Object-of-expenditure, or line-item, budget classifications are structured for that focus. The budget in Figure 2–5 on p. 39—the agency request for St. Paul's Como Zoo, part of that city's Division of Parks and Recreation—illustrates that classification. All request entries are for items to be purchased by the organizational unit. Not all possible object classifications are included in the unit request, because no purchase will be planned in many input areas. (An example of object classification structure appears in an appendix to this chapter.) This is the basic structure for budget preparation, serving as the starting point for all budget classifications. Other classifications will be examined in later chapters.

FIGURE 2-4

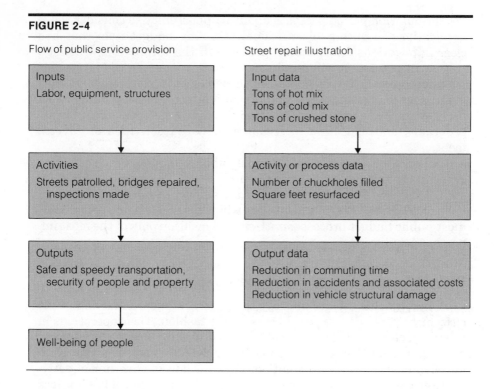

Flow of public service provision

Inputs
Labor, equipment, structures

Activities
Streets patrolled, bridges repaired,
  inspections made

Outputs
Safe and speedy transportation,
  security of people and property

Well-being of people

Street repair illustration

Input data
Tons of hot mix
Tons of cold mix
Tons of crushed stone

Activity or process data
Number of chuckholes filled
Square feet resurfaced

Output data
Reduction in commuting time
Reduction in accidents and associated costs
Reduction in vehicle structural damage

THE BUDGET CYCLE

A cycle is a complete set of events or phenomena recurring in the
same sequence. Recurring (and overlapping) events in the budgeting
and spending process constitute the budget cycle. While specific activities differ among governments, any government with separation of
powers between the executive and legislative branches shows many
elements outlined here.[10] The four major stages of the cycle—executive
preparation, legislative consideration, execution, and audit/evaluation—
are considered in turn. The cycles are, in fact, linked across the years,
because the findings of audit/evaluation are important data for preparation of future budgets. The four phases recur, so at any time, an operating agency will be in different phases of different budget years.
Suppose an agency is on a July 1 to June 30 fiscal year, and present
date is March 1988. That agency would be in the execution phase of the
fiscal year 1988. It would likely be in the legislative consideration
phase of the fiscal year 1989, in the preparation phase of fiscal year

---

[10]A parliamentary government would not fit this cycle, for instance, because there is no
real separation between executive and legislative roles—the legislative leader is the chief
executive.

FIGURE 2-5 1984 Department of Budget Request for Como Zoo, Division of Parks and Recreation, Saint Paul, Minnesota

Object Code	Title	1984 Budget Department Request
111	Full-time certified personnel	$302,150
141	Overtime	7,700
	Subtotal	309,850
215	Fees—medical	5,000
211	Postage	500
222	Telephone	3,500
234	Type I—occasional ($3/day and 15)	1,300
235	Type II—regular ($3/week and 15)	700
242	Duplicating—all processes	1,500
271	Building—repair service	1,000
274	Self-propelled vehicle—repair	200
276	Office equipment and furniture repairs	200
277	Other equipment repairs	700
279	Other—repair and maintenance	300
285	Rental of duplicating equipment	200
389	Rentals—miscellaneous	5,500
299	Other miscellaneous services	1,000
	Subtotal	21,600
341	Motor fuel	1,500
343	Oils and lubricants	
344	Parts for vehicles	400
352	Medical supplies	1,000
353	Chemical or laboratory	5,000
356	Safety supplies	100
369	Other—office supplies	300
371	Electricity	42,000
373	Gas including bottle	27,500
381	Books, periodicals, pictures, records	100
383	Small tools	200
384	Food for zoo animals	60,000
385	Food service supplies	100
386	Clothing—uniforms	1,000
389	Other miscellaneous supplies	1,000
	Subtotal	146,950
	Total	$478,400

1990, and in the audit phase for fiscal 1987 and prior years. Thus, the budget cycle is both continuous and overlapping, as illustrated in Figure 2-6 on p. 40. The federal fiscal year begins in October; many local governments have fiscal years beginning January; all state governments except Alabama, Michigan, New York, and Texas start fiscal years in July. The fiscal year in Alabama and Michigan coincides with the federal, but New York has an April start and Texas has a September start. By convention, fiscal years are named after the year in which they end. Thus, the federal fiscal year that starts on October 1, 1987, would be the 1988 fiscal year.

FIGURE 2-6 Phases of a Budget Cycle

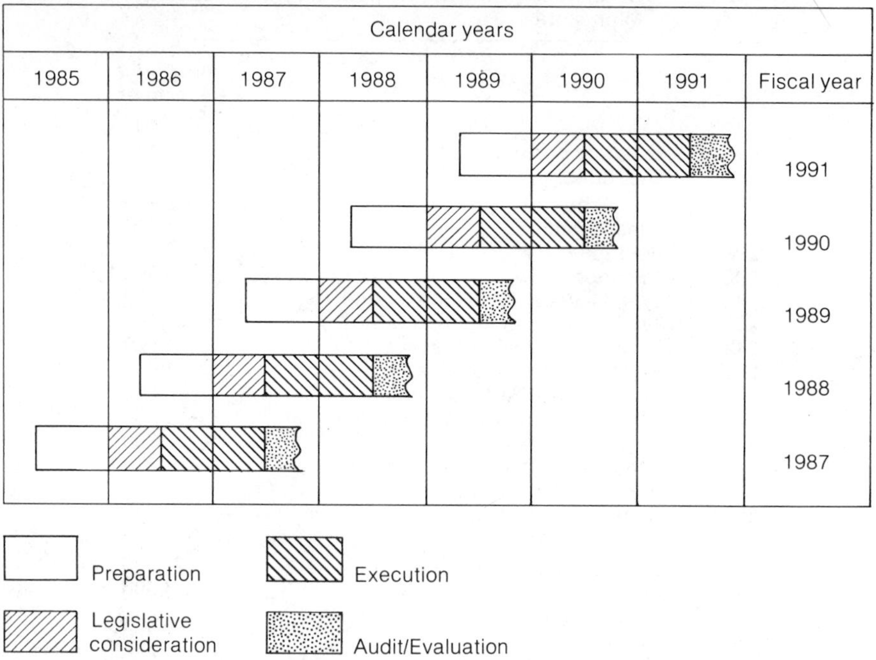

Calendar years							
1985	1986	1987	1988	1989	1990	1991	Fiscal year
							1991
							1990
							1989
							1988
							1987

☐ Preparation   ▨ Execution

▨ Legislative consideration   ▨ Audit/Evaluation

Executive Preparation

Several separate and distinct steps constitute the executive prep-aration phase. At the start of the preparation phase, the chief executive transmits general directions for agency request preparation. These instructions (sometimes labeled the "call for estimates") include a time-table for submissions, instructions for developing requests, and some overall priority directions to spending agencies. (For the federal gov-ernment, these instructions are Circular A–11 issued by the Office of Management and Budget.) They may also provide forecasts of input price increases, service population trends, and so on, but not necessar-ily. Agencies develop an estimate of the cost of providing services it plans to deliver during the upcoming spending period and a narrative justification for the requests. These reflect the large number of pro-gram decisions that the agency has made. As Douglas Lee points out, a "budget, after all, is only an accounting of the financial cost of many political and social decisions."[11] The budget agency of the chief execu-tive gathers the requests made by the operating agencies and consoli-

---

[11]L. Douglas Lee, "How Congress Handles the Budget," *The Wharton Magazine* 4(Winter 1980), p. 29.

dates these requests. The office reviews budget requests for consistency with the policies of the chief executive, for reasonableness of cost and logical content of the budget, and for total consistency with spending directions. Often there will be administrative hearings for reconciliations of the agency request and budget office adjustments. Finally, the executive budget document is transmitted to the legislature for its consideration. Law often establishes the date of transmission to the legislature.

Table 2–3 on p. 42 presents a budget summary from the 1986 federal budget. That display brings together intentions for budget authority, receipts to the government, outlays, credit programs supported by the government, and levels of federal debt. This is the point in the structure where spending intentions must confront the financing realities: the intent of the 1986 budget is a deficit of $179,996 million.[12] Although the budget represents the plan for programs to be carried out in fiscal year 1986, the document includes fiscal figures for other years as well. In particular, it includes a *final report* for the most recently completed year (1984 actual), a *progress report* for the current fiscal year (1985 estimated), and the *budget year* itself (1986 estimated or requested). The 1986 federal budget also includes estimates for two years after the budget year (1987 and 1988, years that would be *out years* or years beyond the budget year in the request cycles). The longer horizon reflects a growing concern with future implications of fiscal choices. Budgets at all levels of government will normally include final report, progress report, and request years, regardless of other formats dictated.

Legislative Consideration

After the executive has submitted the budget to the legislature, the legislature typically splits that budget into as many parts as appropriation bills will be finally passed and submits those parts to legislative subcommittees. At the federal level, there are normally 13 major appropriation bills. A recent tally of the states shows that 25 usually have a single budget bill and 25 usually have multiple budget bills. Those multiples range from 2 to 450.[13] This consideration usually begins with the lower house of a bicameral legislature. In subcommittee hearings, agencies defend their requests in the budget document, often calling attention to differences between their initial request and what appears in the executive budget. After the lower house has approved the appropriation, the upper house goes through a similar hearing process. When both houses have approved appropriations, a conference

---

[12]The last presidential budget that intended balance (or surplus) was the 1971 fiscal year budget proposed by Richard Nixon.

[13]James H. Bowhay and Virginia D. Thrall, *State Legislative Appropriations Process* (Chicago: Midwestern Office, Council of State Governments, 1975), p. 81.

TABLE 2-3 Federal Budget Summary, Fiscal Year 1986 ($ millions)

Description	1984 Actual	1985 Estimate	1986 Estimate	1987 Estimate	1988 Estimate
		The Budget			
Budget authority (largely appropriations):					
Available through current action by Congress:					
Enacted and pending*	544,936				
Proposed in this budget		548,371	554,213	609,350	670,509
To be requested separately		6,628	−9,635	−3,421	−3,751
Available without current action by Congress	572,820	691,288	708,017	734,226	791,505
Deductions for offsetting receipts†	−168,005	−183,207	−192,612	−197,144	−205,271
Total budget authority	949,751	1,064,870	1,059,983	1,143,011	1,252,992
(On-budget under current law)	(927,397)	(1,042,666)	(1,052,351)	(1,138,931)	(1,249,364)
(Off-budget under current law)‡	(22,354)	(22,204)	(7,632)	(4,080)	(3,628)
Budget receipts, outlays, and surplus or deficit:					
Receipts:					
Budget receipts	666,457	736,859	793,929	861,676	950,376
Outlays:					
Budget outlays	851,781	959,085	973,725	1,026,625	1,094,761
(On-budget under current law)	(841,815)	(946,626)	(972,224)	(1,029,865)	(1,099,095)
(Off-budget under current law)‡	(9,966)	(12,459)	(1,501)	(−3,240)	(−4,334)
Surplus or deficit (−):					
Budget deficit (−)	−185,324	−222,226	−179,996	−164,949	−144,385
(On-budget under current law)	(−175,358)	(−209,767)	(−178,495)	(−168,189)	(−148,719)
(Off-budget under current law)‡	(−9,966)	(−12,459)	(−1,501)	(−3,240)	(−4,334)
		The Credit Budget			
New obligations and commitments:					
New direct loan obligations	39,093	51,904	24,240	22,745	19,856
New guaranteed loan commitments§	70,798	74,018	77,208	78,538	80,908
Total	109,892	125,923	101,448	101,283	100,763

	1983 Actual					
Change in outstandings:						
Direct loans		6,323	15,234	−276	−3,730	−5,470
(On-budget under current law)		*(−1,334)*	*(4,344)*	*(−584)*	*(−692)*	*(−1,616)*
(Off-budget under current law)‡		*(7,658)*	*(10,890)*	*(−308)*	*(−3,038)*	*(−3,854)*
Guaranteed loans§		20,110	20,224	31,902	32,583	32,114
Total		26,433	35,458	31,626	28,853	26,643
Federal Debt						
Debt outstanding, end of year:						
Gross Federal debt	1,381,886	1,576,748	1,841,077	2,074,231	2,308,278	2,546,388
Held by						
Government agencies	240,114	264,159	327,110	387,642	457,468	552,006
The public	1,141,771	1,312,589	1,513,967	1,686,589	1,850,810	1,994,382
Federal Reserve System	155,527	155,122				
Others	986,244	1,157,467				
MEMORANDUM‖						
Debt subject to statutory limitation	1,377,953	1,572,975	1,837,414	2,070,714	2,305,006	2,543,946
Debt not subject to statutory limitation	3,933	3,973	3,663	3,517	3,272	2,442

*Includes an imputed charge ($16,503 million) for accruals for military retirement contributions in 1984 to adjust data for comparability with the military retirement presentation beginning in 1985. Offsetting receipts equal to the imputed charge for accruals are included as deductions for offsetting receipts in 1984.

†These consist of intragovernmental transactions and proprietary receipts from the public.

‡Proposed to be included on-budget.

§To avoid double counting, excludes guarantees (or commitments) of loans previously guaranteed or guarantees (or commitments) by one Government account of direct loans made by another Government account.

‖For additional information on the Federal debt subject to statutory limitation, see Table 12 of this part, Part 6 of this volume, and Special Analysis E, "Borrowing and Debt."

SOURCE: Budget of the United States Government, Fiscal Year 1986.

committee from the two houses prepares a unified version for final passage by both houses and approval by the chief executive.

At the federal level, the president's options are to approve or to veto the entire appropriation. Some governors have item veto powers; they can veto certain parts of an appropriation bill and approve the remainder. Some observers feel that the item veto provides a useful final screening of projects which political clout, not vitality of the project, has inserted in the appropriation bill. Others are skeptical about such power because of its possible use for executive vendettas against selected groups or agencies.

Appropriations are normally *annual* and agency funds revert to the general treasury for reappropriation if not spent during the budget year. Other appropriation forms are, however, used. (Note that in Table 2–3, $708,017 million in budget authority for fiscal 1986 is "Available without current action by Congress.") *Permanent* appropriations continue indefinitely without current legislative action. To add greater certainty to public capital markets, interest on the federal debt is such an appropriation. *No year* appropriations provide specific amounts of money until the money is exhausted, without restriction placed on the year of use. Most construction funds, some funds for research, and many trust fund appropriations have been handled on that basis. *Multiple year* appropriations provide funds for a particular activity for several years at once, specifying both the fiscal year and amount for that year. General revenue sharing was established on that basis. Finally, *advance* appropriation provides agencies with funds for fiscal years in future. This structure is seldom used, although it can facilitate planning and has been strongly argued for use in defense system procurement. All appropriation types but annual reduce the ability of legislative and executive branches to realign fiscal policy when economic or social conditions change while increasing the ability of agencies to develop long-range program plans. The trade is not an easy one, but responsibility and accountability chains probably weigh the balance toward annual appropriation.

Budget authority not obligated within the time period for which it was appropriated expires and is not held over for future use. Congress may act to extend the availability of funds, either before or after their scheduled expiration, through *reappropriation.* The federal budget structure counts these amounts as new budget authority for the fiscal year of reappropriation. At other levels of government, unspent appropriations normally revert to the treasury of the government.

Two other methods of providing agency funds, in addition to these normal appropriations, should be mentioned. A *continuing resolution* allows agencies to function when a new fiscal year begins before agency appropriations have been made. The resolution—simply an agreement between both legislative houses—authorizes the agencies to continue operations. The resolution level may be the same as the prior year, may entail certain increases, or may encompass the appropriate bill as it has emerged from one house of Congress; the resolution may be for part of the fiscal year or the entire year. Without some action, however, the agency without appropriation could not spend and would not be able to provide services. The Congressional budget process establishes a timetable for appropriations which would eliminate the need for continuing resolutions—all appropriation bills must be passed before seven days after Labor Day. That deadline has not always been met, so federal continuing resolutions continue in use.[14] For example, the continuing resolution for fiscal 1985, approved on October 11, 1984, to cover the remainder of the fiscal year after the passage of four interim resolutions from October 1 to October 11, reportedly was the largest and most sweeping in history. It provided funding for Defense, Foreign Assistance, Interior, Military Construction, Transportation, Agriculture, Labor–Health–Human Services–Education, Treasury–Postal Service, and District of Columbia. Each would normally have been included in a separate appropriation; the continuing resolution remains significant.[15]

Such a large omnibus continuing resolution, although having many trappings of appropriation, raises some special issues. First, the continuing resolution in theory would have few if any new programs. A steady pattern of such funding for an agency could hinder the development of programs and the response to changing service conditions. Second, the omnibus continuing resolution may partly impede the veto power of the president. Special pressure to accept programs is apparent because of the time pressures of continuing the flow of service and the omnibus package makes the pressure even worse. Finally, the omnibus package may tempt members of Congress to add special favors for their constituencies, causing the funding result to have an inordinate number of pet projects, well above those in a smaller appropriation bill more easily open to scrutiny and rejection. The continuing resolution deserves an uneasy life.

A second special form of providing funds is the **supplemental appropriation,** an appropriation of funds for spending during the current budget year. (Requests are normally for future budget years.) Thus, the budget request for fiscal 1986 (Table 2–3) which is considered during fiscal 1985 contains a request for $6,628 million in additional budget authority for fiscal 1985. For the federal budget, details on the supplemental requests appear in the budget appendix volume. The request

---

[14]States occasionally end legislative sessions with neither appropriations nor continuing resolutions passed. Until a special session is held the state cannot operate.

[15]Dale Tate, "Stop Gap Measure Was Biggest, Most Complex," *Congressional Quarterly,* October 20, 1984, p. 2732.

would ordinarily result because events have caused some agencies to spend more than anticipated during planning and consideration of that budget. Typical reasons include the need (1) to cover the cost of programs newly enacted by the legislature, (2) to provide for higher than anticipated prices, or (3) to cope with surprise developments. The request is for appropriation in addition to funds previously approved by the legislature. Because of forecasting problems, most budgets will have requests for supplemental appropriation, but large supplements raise questions about the capability of those initially preparing and considering the budget.

Execution

During execution, agencies carry out their approved budgets: appropriations are spent and services are delivered. The approved budget becomes an important device to monitor spending activity. While there are other important managerial concerns during execution, spending must proceed in a manner consistent with the appropriation laws. Law typically forbids—often with criminal sanctions—agencies from spending more money than has been appropriated.[16] Spending less than the appropriation, while a possible sign of efficient operation, may well mean that anticipated services have not been delivered or that agency budget requests were needlessly high. Finance officers must thus continuously monitor the relationship between actual expenditures and planned-approved expenditures (the appropriation) during the fiscal year.[17] Most governments have some preexpenditure audit system to determine the validity of expenditures, according to appropriation, before the expenditure occurs.

Audit and Evaluation

An audit is an "examination of records, facilities, systems, and other evidence to discover or verify desired information. Internal audits are those performed by professionals employed by the entity being audited; external audits are performed by outside professionals who are independent of the entity."[18] Information will be documented on the basis of a sample of transactions and other activities of the entity—a judgment about purchasing practices, for instance, will be made from a review of a sample of transactions, not from an examination of all invoices. Post-

---

[16]The Anti-Deficiency Act of 1906 is the governing federal law; similar laws apply at state and local levels.

[17]The Office of Management and Budget handles that monitoring at the federal level.

[18]Peter F. Rousmaniere, *Local Governments Auditing—A Manual for Public Officials* (New York: Council on Municipal Performance, 1980), p. 83.

expenditure audits determine compliance with appropriations and report findings to the legislature (or to a judicial body if laws have been violated).[19] At the federal level, the General Accounting Office supervises audits of agencies, although the actual auditing is done by agency personnel. States frequently have elected auditors or independent agencies which audit state agencies and local governments. Local governments sometimes have audits done by independent accounting firms as well as by governmental bodies, although some such governments have not frequently had independent audits.[20]

Audits take different forms, depending on their orientation as determined by the expected use of that budget. The first, a *financial audit*, checks financial records to determine whether the funds were spent legally, whether receipts were properly recorded and controlled, and whether financial records and statements are complete and reliable. This audit concentrates on establishing compliance with appropriation law and on determining whether financial reports prepared by the operating agency are accurate and reliable. The financial audit still must determine, however, whether or not there has been theft by government employees or their confederates, although this part of the task will be minor for modern governments because of internal control methods.

A second type of audit is a *management or operations audit.* This audit focuses on efficiency of operation, including utilization and control of resources. The stress is on managerial aspects, including such concerns as duplication of effort, utilization of resources, and mismanagement of equipment, supplies, stocks, etc. The audit is more concerned with waste of government resources than on the theft aspects of a financial audit.

Program audits, a third emphasis, examine the extent to which desired results are being achieved and whether there might be lower cost alternatives to reach the desired results. An important focus of the program is whether objectives of the program are being met.

The fourth variety, a *performance audit,* assesses the total operations of an agency, including compliance, management, and program audits. Sunset reviews are one opportunity for such audits. Sunset legislation establishes "a set schedule for legislative review of programs and agencies unless affirmative legislative action is taken to reauthorize them. Thus, the 'sun sets' on agencies and programs."[21] States with

---

[19]A preaudit within an agency prior to expenditure ascertains the legality or appropriateness of making payment. Such an analysis often occurs, for instance, prior to the delivery of payroll checks.

[20]Federal general revenue sharing required since 1976 an audit at least once in three years for general-purpose governments receiving such money.

[21]Advisory Commission on Intergovernmental Relations, "Sunset Legislation and Zero-Based Budgeting," *Information Bulletin* no. 76–5 (December 1976), p. 1.

such legislation typically include a performance audit as part of the preparation for action on agencies or programs eligible for termination.

A simple example may illustrate the focus of each audit. Consider a state highway department appropriation to purchase road salt for snow and ice removal. A financial audit would consider whether the agency had an appropriation for salt purchased, whether salt purchased was actually delivered, whether approved practices were followed in selecting a supplier, and whether agency reports showed the correct expenditure on salt. A management audit would consider whether the salt inventory is adequately protected from the environment, whether the inventory is adequate or excessive, and whether other methods of selecting a supplier would cause cost to be lower. A program audit would consider whether the prevailing level of winter highway clearing is an appropriate use of community resources and whether approaches other than spreading salt would be less costly to the community. Finally, a performance audit would examine all operations of the highway department.

When all audit work is completed, the budget cycle is complete for that fiscal year. In a complementary fashion the federal inspector general system in 16 departments or agencies works within units to identify fraud or waste and, under 1976 and 1978 legislation, reports findings to department or agency heads and, eventually, to Congress. The system has potential as an adjunct to the audits conducted for Congress by the General Accounting Office.

The Federal Cycle

The general budget cycle may be illustrated by a brief review of federal budget timing. Because the federal government is a continuing institution, its budget cycle operates across several calendar years. The flow of events confuses neophytes, but the pieces are arranged on the four-phase logic previously outlined. An abbreviated federal timetable appears in Table 2-5 on pp. 50–51; more complete detail appears in Appendix B at the end of this chapter.

Three organizations constitute the primary professional budgeting establishment for the United States government and play a major role in the federal budget cycle. These are the two units formed by the Budget and Accounting Act of 1921 (the Office of Management and Budget and the General Accounting Office) and the Congressional Budget Office (established by the Congressional Budget and Impoundment Act of 1974). Table 2–4 notes the major elements of the acts. The offices work with the agency budget staff and appropriation committee staff to produce the budgets, appropriations, and expenditures of the federal government. The Office of Management and Budget (OMB) is a part of the Executive Office of the President. (It initially was part of the Trea-

TABLE 2-4 Highlights of the Acts Establishing the Federal Budget Process

	Budget and Accounting Act of 1921	Congressional Budget and Impoundment Control Act of 1974
Fiscal year start	July 1*	October 1
Institutions created	1. Bureau of Budget (Office of Management and Budget, OMB) 2. General Accounting Office	1. Congressional Budget Office 2. House and Senate Budget Committees
Requires	President's Budget Message	1. Current Services Budget 2. Congressional Budget Resolutions
Other	Supplemental appropriations	Functional Classification in President's Budget Tax Expenditure Analysis Recission/Deferral Process
Citation	Sixty-seventh Congress, Session I, Ch. 18, 47 Stat. 20	Public Law 93–344

*Not established in the act.

sury Department, but became part of the newly established Executive Office in 1939). The president appoints its director, and its staff is expected to carry out the policies of the president. The office develops the executive budget by consolidating agency requests for appropriations within the guidelines provided by the president. Initial agency requests are usually reduced by OMB; an administrative process within OMB considers protests of these reductions before transmission of the budget to Congress. After congressional appropriation, OMB meters the flow of spending to ensure that agencies do not spend more than the amount appropriated. Most states and many local governments have budget agencies which function like OMB, although not all have the skilled staff required for review and analysis of requests.[22]

The General Accounting Office (GAO) is the congressional agency which holds accountable the operations of federal departments and agencies. In most instances, it supervises the accounting done by others and emphasizes investigations to improve the effectiveness of government. Much of the audit detail is, in fact, done by the audit staff of the agency itself. The head of GAO, the comptroller general, is appointed by the president with consent of the Senate for a single 15-year term;

[22]Complete views of the agency appear in Percival Flack Brundage, *The Bureau of the Budget* (New York: Praeger Publishers, 1970) and Larry Berman, *The Office of Management and Budget and the Presidency, 1921–1979* (Princeton, N.J.: Princeton University Press, 1979). Brundage was Budget Director for President Eisenhower, after a career with a national accounting firm.

TABLE 2-5 Federal Budget Timetable

1. Executive preparation:

Key Events in Executive Branch Budget Process

	March (or earlier)	April/May	June	July–September 30	October/November	December/January
	Budget Policy Development		Preparation and Submission of Agency Budgets to OMB		OMB and Presidential Review Decisions	Budget Prepared and Submitted to Congress
Agencies/departments	Reviews major programs and budget issues	Submits projection of future needs to OMB	Issue internal budget guidance	Prepare and submit budget to OMB for review	Defend budget to OMB, revise to meet president's decisions	Final agency appeals to president
Office of Management and Budget (OMB)	Develops economic assumptions, fiscal projections	Issues policy guidance economic assumptions	Issues budget planning, targets to agencies	Economic, fiscal assumptions updated	Reviews agency budgets, advises president, reexamines economic, fiscal assumptions	Final review of economic, fiscal assumptions; budget prepared for Congress
President	Discusses budget outlook/policy with OMB and others		Establishes overall budget policy and targets		Decides agency budgets and final economic fiscal assumptions	Decides final appeal, revises and approves budget

During this same time supplemental budget requests for the current budget year are prepared and sent to Congress and the current year's budget is being executed.

2. Legislative consideration:

Key Events in Legislative Branch Budget Process

	January/February	May 15	September 15	September 25	October 1
Legislative activity	President's budget submitted	First budget resolution adopted	Second budget resolution adopted†	Reconciliation bill enacted	New fiscal year begins / (Possible continuing resolution enacted)*
Budget committees	Hearings and report first budget resolution	Work on second budget resolution			
Authorizing committees	Hearings, views, and estimates reports on budget, report authorization bills	Authorization bills enacted	Reconciliation		
Appropriation committees	Hearings, views, and estimates reports on budget, work on appropriation bills	(Debt ceiling raised)*	Appropriations bills enacted		
Tax committees	Hearings, views, and estimates reports on budget, work on possible revenue bills		Revenue bills enacted / Reconciliation		
Congress	Debate and floor votes	Debate and floor votes	Debate and floor votes	Debate and floor votes	Debate and floor votes

*If necessary

†In recent years, reconciliation has occurred after the adoption of the first budget resolution.

3. Execution: October 1–September 30
4. Audit: from October 1

the comptroller general is almost unremovable.[23] Much of the current emphasis of GAO work is on evaluation of government programs, sometimes at the request of a single member of Congress, sometimes at the request of a committee. Some states have similar agencies working for their legislatures, but many have elected state auditors. Skills and emphases differ dramatically among the states, but many limit their work to accounting for funds. Other state and local governments employ private accounting firms for audit. The important element is that the audit be external, not whether done by private or public entity, so long as accepted audit standards are applied.

The third federal organization is the Congressional Budget Office (CBO), a unit established to provide Congress with staff having expertise similar to that of OMB. Before CBO, there appeared to be an imbalance: the president had a permanent, professional budget staff with well-honed abilities and continuing knowledge about the mechanics and content of the budget; Congress had only appropriation committee staff, none of whom maintained a view of the budget as a whole. Legislation in 1974 provided the CBO, a professional director, and a professional staff. That supplied Congress with an independent source of budget information and expertise, although there remains doubt whether Congress can truly have a single slate of priorities in light of the many interests of its individual members.

In the first phase, executive preparation and submission, the Office of Management and Budget collects agency estimates of expenditures for the fiscal year and consolidates these requests. The overall requests are compared with presidential program objectives, expenditure ceilings set by the president, Department of Treasury revenue estimates, and economic forecasts from the Council of Economic Advisers and the Federal Reserve System. The economic estimates—the rate of inflation, the level of unemployment, the level of gross national product—are especially important for the federal budget because many budget totals are sensitive to the economy. In other words, Congress has passed laws which provide expenditures that depend on the level of economic activity: unemployment assistance depends on the level of unemployed workers qualifying for assistance, food stamp assistance depends on the number of eligibles and prices of food, and so on. Furthermore, federal revenues are particularly sensitive to economic activity. As a result, the forecast of economic activity used to prepare the

---

[23]Two major recent studies provide a detailed view of the GAO: Frederick C. Mosher in *The GAO: The Quest for Accountability in American Government* (Boulder, Colo.: Westview Press, 1979) traces the development of the GAO to the end of the 1970s, and Erasmus H. Kloman, ed., *Cases in Accountability: The Work of the GAO* (Boulder, Colo.: Westview Press, 1979) collects several cases which illustrate the kind of audits or evaluations done by the GAO.

budget can substantially alter the spending and revenue plans the budget encompasses.

The OMB transmits broad policy decisions back to the agencies for final expenditure estimates. Any remaining excess requests by agency are defended before OMB hearing examiners. Transmission of the final document—the president's budget message—occurs 15 days after Congress meets in a new session (about mid-January). This document presents the president's program plans, with price tags attached, for the upcoming fiscal year. For a fiscal year beginning on October 1, 1986, for instance, the message would be delivered late in January 1986; first work on this budget message began in the spring of 1985.

The period between delivery of the budget message and the end of its fiscal year is long. Not only can there be economic and social surprises to upset plans but Congress may not agree with the presidential agenda. Nevertheless, differences between presidential plans and actual spending have been surprisingly small in relative terms. Table 2–6 traces those differences from 1971 to 1984: the median difference is only 2.25 percent of the initial request and, to the extent there is a difference, actual outlay exceeds the initial proposal in all but three of the reported years. In pragmatic terms, this suggests the key role of the executive in aggregate expenditure control. There are, of course, greater differences in individual programs than appear in these aggregates.

TABLE 2-6 Initial Budget Outlay Proposals and Actual Federal Outlays, 1971–1985

Fiscal Year	Outlays Proposed in Initial Budget Message ($billions)		Actual Outlays ($billions)		Percent Differences	
	On Budget Only	On and Off Budget	On Budget	On and Off Budget	On Budget	On and Off Budget
1971	$200.8		$211.4		5.3	
1972	229.2		231.9		1.2	
1973	246.3		246.5		0.1	
1974	268.7		268.4		−0.1	
1975	304.4		324.6		6.6	
1976	349.4		366.5		4.9	
1977	394.2		401.9		2.0	
1978	440.0	$449.1	450.8	$461.2	2.5	2.7
1979	500.2	512.7	493.7	506.1	−1.3	−1.3
1980	531.6	543.5	579.6	593.9	9.0	9.3
1981	615.8	633.9	657.2	678.2	6.7	7.0
1982	739.3	757.6	728.4	745.7	−1.5	−1.6
1983	757.6	773.3	796.0	808.3	5.1	4.5
1984	848.5	862.5	841.8	841.8	0.8	−2.4
1985	925.5	940.3	n.a.*	n.a.	—	—
1986	972.2	973.7	n.a.	n.a.	—	—
			Mean:		2.95	2.6
			Median:		2.25	2.7

*n.a. = Not available.
SOURCE: *Budget of the United States* for 1971 through 1986.

Present budget legislation requires an earlier budget message to Congress. The current services budget is delivered to Congress on November 10, prior to the budget message (or president's budget request). The current services budget estimates what the cost would be to continue current programs at their current level without additions or deletions. If this report has any use, it would be to help gauge the effects of price change on public spending and to help sort out program expansions from program continuations. It is not a request for money, and its usefulness or role have not been proven.

The second phase of the cycle, legislative review and authorization, has been revised significantly since 1974. Before the 1974 Congressional Budget and Impoundment Control Act, the federal budget was considered only as split into the several appropriation bills; Congress did not consider the budget as a whole. The budget was fragmented back to general administrative department chunks, with each chunk considered by a separate appropriation committee. That procedure might give greater scrutiny to individual department requests, but it certainly did not permit the overall comparison of revenue, expenditures, and accompanying surplus or deficit. More importantly, that practice did not permit consideration of government-wide priorities—transportation versus defense, etc.—that effective budget formulation requires.

The new process, used initially for the 1977 budget, produced a dual flow through Congress: while the appropriations committees work as before, separate budget committees consider federal spending as a whole. Figure 2–7 diagrams that dual path. The budget committees produce a budget resolution which sets ceilings for total taxes and expenditure, a debt or surplus target, and broad spending priorities among major functions. The First Concurrent Resolution is approved by both houses of Congress in May, before appropriation consideration begins in earnest. Congress can change ceilings in a second resolution passed shortly before the start of a new fiscal year, but Congress is not supposed to adjourn before reconciliation of appropriation totals and ceilings. (Congress frequently violates that requirement.) The congressional budget process permits Congress to develop its own spending priorities, particularly with the assistance of the Congressional Budget Office, and to consider the appropriate macroeconomic impact for its spending actions. Without this element, the process emphasizes presidential priorities; the element allows a congressional view, an important part in the American system of separation of powers. Many states and local governments have but a single appropriation bill, not the dozen or so that this federal government has, so there is less significance in the distinction between budget consideration and appropriation consideration.

FIGURE 2-7 Budget Reconciliation Process

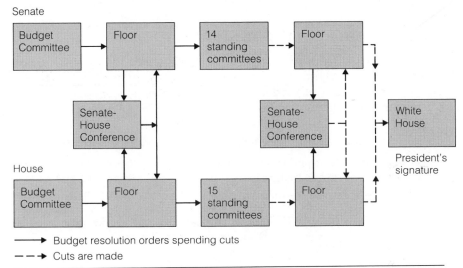

Senate

House

———▶ Budget resolution orders spending cuts

– – ▶ Cuts are made

3rd stage   The end points of the fiscal year presumably set the bounds for execution, the third stage of the process. This is the period in which appropriated moneys are spent and public services are provided. The fact that money is appropriated for a purpose, however, does not automatically and immediately lead to public expenditure. To prevent agencies from exhausting funds before the end of the fiscal year and to use expenditure timing for macroeconomic purpose, the OMB divides total money to agencies into sums for distribution over the year (apportionments). Current law makes is difficult for the president to direct OMB to delay scheduled expenditure (deferral), and even more difficult to cancel expenditure of funds appropriated (rescission). Congress can reject deferral by disapproving them; either house of Congress may reject a rescission.

4th phase   The audit phase of the federal cycle, supervised by the General Accounting Office, formally begins at the end of the fiscal year. Some audit functions do, however, continue through the fiscal year as agencies themselves work to prevent illegal and irregular transactions by various approval stages. In an important sense, the audit phase ensures that everything else in the budget process matters: unless the decisions made elsewhere in the process get carried through, the process is irrelevant. The audit phase determines whether those directions were followed. The General Accounting Office reports to the House and Senate Committees on Government Operations.

BUDGETS AND POLITICAL STRATEGIES

The incrementalist view maintains that budgeting is heavily, if not exclusively, a process of political strategy. It rejects the public service delivery orientation of models from public finance economics and rejects budgeting techniques that attempt to make the process more rational. Budgeting, appropriating, and spending is a process of strategies and role playing. As Aaron Wildavsky diagnoses the process,

> Budgeting is incremental. The largest determining factor of the size and content of this year's budget is last year's budget. Most of the budget is a product of previous decisions. . . . The budget may be conceived of as an iceberg with by far the largest part below the surface, outside the control of anyone. Many items in the budget are standard and are simply reenacted every year unless there is a special reason to challenge them.[24]

Budget making and appropriating becomes a process of percentage monetary adjustments to existing programs, that is, the application of rule-of-thumb percentage increases to the budget base of agencies, the base being the prior year budget. Analysis during budget construction is not a mechanism for consideration of basic policy choices. Agencies and legislatures use strategies within the context of anticipated roles. Budgets are built from percentage increments to the historic budget base in accord with some notion of fair shares to each agency.

Roles

Service delivery choices in the budget process involve several different roles, each with different approaches and biases. Participants in the budget process recognize and expect those approaches in the budget process, being aware of the errors, incentives, and organizational blindspots inherent in each. The major orientations of attitude are those of operating agencies, the office of the chief executive, and the position of the legislator. All participants in the budget process seek to provide service to the public without waste. Each, however, works from different perspectives, resulting in differences of incentives and different definitions of that objective in practice. A full understanding of the budget process obviously requires recognition of those roles.

Operating agencies.   Operating agencies are the units which spend money for the delivery of government services. These agencies focus on

---

[24]Aaron Wildavsky, *The Politics of the Budgetary Process*, 3d ed. (Boston: Little, Brown, 1979), p. 13. Treatment here of roles and strategies relies heavily on work by him.

the clientele they serve. It is unreasonable to expect an agency to be concerned with services provided by other agencies or to be interested in relative priorities among services of agencies. The agency probably will not be much concerned with comparisons of the cost of service with the value of that service. They recognize the value of the services they provide to their clients and will ordinarily try to increase those services, regardless of overall budget conditions of the government. There will be a virtually limitless expanse of service opportunities, many of which will go unfunded simply because other uses of public resources yield a greater social return. Agencies, however, seldom recognize those competing uses and complain about their own lack of resources. Large agencies will have both operating people who have little direct contact with the budget and budget people who have little direct contact with service delivery. Both groups of people, however, can be expected to have essentially the same point of view and clientele orientation.

Chief executive.   The Office of the Chief Executive, whether it be president, governor, mayor, or whatever, has budget specialists acting on its behalf. The agencies will have different names (federal: Office of Management and Budgeting; state: state budget agencies, etc.), but their function and role are the same regardless of name and level. Analysts in that agency will operate with the priorities of the chief executive, not their own, and will have the constraint of available revenue in mind. The analysts will cut requests in line with the executive priorities until total spending fits within that constraint. Reductions will be typical for items not adequately justified, items which are not closely related to achieving the objective of the agency, and items not consistent with the priorities of the chief executive. While agencies have a clientele orientation, the chief executive (selected by the entire population) must balance the interests of the total population. Thus, priorities for an individual agency should not be expected to coincide with those of the chief executive, because specific client group priorities seldom match those of the general public. The interests of corn belt farmers, for instance, are not the same as those of the general population. The chief executive's priorities will dominate in the reductions done by these budget analysts.

Legislature.   The priorities of elected representatives can be expected to follow those of their constituencies. They will be concerned with programs and projects serving the people who elect them. It is not reasonable to expect them to consistently take an overall view of agencies or of programs of agencies. Their focus will be on a specific subset of the population, as is the case for operating agencies. Their subset, however, will be regionally oriented rather than specific client group oriented. Most electoral regions will, of course, contain numerous client groups.

Strategies

Wildavsky has identified group strategies employed within the roles pursued in the budget process on the basis of an analysis of the United States Congress.[25] Many of these strategies—"links between intentions and perceptions of budget officials and the political system that imposes restraints and creates opportunites for them"[26]—are transferable to other governments. Two agency strategies are *ubiquitous.* The first is cultivation of an active clientele for help in dealing both with the legislature and with the chief executive. The clientele may be those directly served (as with farmers in particular programs provided by the Department of Agriculture) or those selling services to the particular agency (as with highway contractors doing business with a state department of highways). Agencies unable to identify and cultivate such clientele will find budget hearings difficult, as active support may be difficult to identify and mobilize.

A second ubiquitous strategy is the development of confidence of other government officials. Agency administrators must avoid being surprised in hearings or by requests for information. Officials must show results in the reports they make and must tailor the complexity of their message to their audience. If results themselves are not directly available, proxies from procedure and processes are substituted. Confidence is critical because in the budget process many elements of defense must derive from the judgments of the administrators, not on hard evidence. If confidence has been developed, those judgments will be trusted; if not, those judgments will be suspect.

Another group of strategies—*contingent* strategies—depend on the budget circumstances. The crucial circumstance is what is being proposed with respect to the agency's programs from the prior year (its base). In defending its base for cuts, an agency may: (1) suggest that the politically popular program be cut, as with reduction in athletic and band programs when school districts face fiscal problems; (2) argue that the program is an all-or-nothing choice: any reduction would make the program impossible, so it might as well be eliminated; (3) take advantage of a strong clientele on individual projects within the program by listing those projects separately to prevent across-the-board reductions; or (4) force the representative to choose what programs ought to be cut rather than attempting the difficult choice within the agency.

In an effort to increase the agency base (increase the scope of existing programs), the agency may (1) argue that the program is really nothing new but is simply a continuation of existing effort; (2) round all cost estimates upward: agencies round at different levels, ranging from $100 million to $10, but any agency can make at least small expansions by rounding; or (3) maintain an expenditure category dollar amount,

---

[25] Ibid., chap. 3.
[26] Ibid., p. 63.

but move the duties elsewhere, using released funds to increase the scope of a particular program.

Efforts to expand the agency base require different tactics. Among them are the following: (1) the agency may practice "foot-in-the-door finance" by starting small and gradually expanding through the base-increasing process; (2) the program may start on a "temporary" basis, with interim extensions until it is made permanent; (3) the program may be sold on the basis of its "paying for itself," and thus has no net budget impact; and (4) the activity may be sold on the basis of a crisis (energy, environment, etc.), preferably advertised using some catchy name for the ensuing programs. Base expansion is generally difficult because of the lack of developed clienteles. Base expansion should continue to be difficult because of the difficulty of cutting back or eliminating a program once it is started.

The Uses of Incrementalism

Few developments in society occur without warning, without building gradually over the years. In that environment, agencies reasonably prepare their budgets in an incremental fashion: what better guide can there be toward the next year than the recent past, even in a rational world? The forecasting models of rational analysts are based on recent history, so building from the recent past cannot be tagged as an attribute of rationalism or incrementalism. It is simply a reasonable tool to use in budget construction. Similarly, the nature of roles and strategies in the budget process contributes important insights into incentives motivating budget behavior.

It is not clear, however, that appropriations follow the pattern of small adjustments implicit in the incrementalist view.[27] Bailey and O'Connor examined the pattern of budget results from one year to the next for agencies in the federal government (appropriations and expenditures), in the state of Virginia (expenditures), and in Columbia (expenditures). They computed for each agency of the government the change in expenditure (or appropriation) from one year to the next over the time period studied. Table 2–7 on p. 60 reports the distribution of those changes. The striking result of the analysis is the large number of changes well above 10 percent—and in periods not characterized by substantial inflation in the United States. (Comparable Columbian results are those adjusted for inflation). Agencies were in fact capable of major increases in their operations. In more recent times, inflation has caught up with the United States, and substantial annual changes

---

[27]In a generic sense, any change—large or small—is an increment. The change is limited to small ones simply to give the view meaning. The continuing argument about the meaning and applicability of budget incrementalism is examined in Harvey J. Tucker, "Incremental Budgeting: Myth or Model?" *Western Political Quarterly* 35 (September 1982), p. 327–38.

TABLE 2-7 Distribution of Annual Percentage Changes in Expenditure or Appropriation by Agencies

	Incremental (change from 0 to 10 percent)	Intermediate (11 to 30 percent)	Nonincremental (31 percent and above)
Congressional appropriation (12-year period, pre-1960?)	52.5%	34.2%	15.2%
Federal expenditures (1961–71)	49.1	32.1	19.8
Columbian central government expenditures:			
Actual (1961–71)	22.7	34.5	42.8
Adjusted for inflation	43.9	25.9	30.2
Virginia expenditures (1967–70)	34.7	52.1	13.1

SOURCE: John J. Bailey and Robert J. O'Connor, "Operationalizing Incrementalism: Measuring the Muddles," *Public Administration Review* 35 (January/February 1975), pp. 60–66. Reprinted with permission from Public Administration Review © 1975 by The American Society for Public Administration, 1225 Connecticut Avenue, N.W., Washington, D.C. All rights reserved.

could be expected for that reason alone. Over the 1972 through 1984 period, the annual compound growth rate of deflators for government purchases, an index or prices that governments must pay, was 8.06 percent for state and local government purchases, 7.85 percent for federal defense purchases, and 7.07 percent for federal nondefense purchases. That inflation improves the prospects for cutting into the service base of an agency: increases in spending power less than that rate of growth will reduce real spending power of the agency.

CONCLUSION

Budgets serve as the choice mechanism for allocation of public resources. The flow of budget decisions from plan to expenditure is accomplished in a four-phase cycle involving legislative and executive branches of government. The phases: executive preparation, legislative consideration, execution, and audit. While budgets are constructed and approved in a political environment, it is not clear that appropriations are the simple product of adding a small increment to the prior year appropriation. There is at least some room for attempts at rational choice in budget structures.

Questions and Exercises

1. The relative size of government has been a continuing concern for public policy. Size and growth questions have been important at the

state and local level, as demonstrated by the several state referenda to limit state and/or local expenditure, and at the federal level. Some evidence for those discussions can be drawn from data on trends of spending activity, using information from the Department of Commerce's *Survey of Current Business* (monthly), the Census Bureau's *Governmental Finances* (annual), and the Advisory Commission on Intergovernmental Relations' *Significant Features of Fiscal Federalism* (biennial). From those sources, prepare answers to these questions about the size of government in the United States.

a. Has the public sector grown relative to the private sector? How does the size of the federal government compare with that of state and local government? (Some benchmarks for comparison are the percentage of gross national product or personal income accounted for by the sectors.)

b. Which sectors have been fastest growing? Compare growth of the public sector in your state with that of its neighbors and of the nation. Why might a comparison based on expenditure growth differ from one based on employment?

c. Which functions account for the greatest share of federal, state, and local government expenditure? Does the pattern differ much among states?

d. What is the relative significance of local government compared to state government expenditure in your state? (Make the comparison first counting state aid to local government as state expenditure. Then, omit that portion from state expenditure.) How does your state compare with its neighbors and the nation?

2. Identify these key elements of your state budget process:
   a. Does your state have an annual or biennial budget?
   b. What units direct the preparation of the executive budget? (Not all states have an executive budget.)
   c. How many appropriation bills are usually passed?
   d. How much object-of-expenditure detail appears in these bills?
3. Use these data to answer the three questions.

Calendar Year Data from *Survey of Current Business*

	1980	1983
Federal government		
Purchase of goods and services ($ billions)		
Defense	131.7	200.3
Nondefense	67.2	74.5
Implicit price deflator (1972 = 100)	185.6	DRM
National defenses	~~135.6~~	237.7
Federal nondefense purchases	180.6	222.0

a. Compute the total, real, and price growth rates of defense and nondefense purchases from 1980 through 1983.

b. Convert the price deflator to 1980 = 100 and recompute the rates. Are they the same?

c. Suppose prices from 1983 to 1986 are expected to change at exactly the same rate that they did from 1980 to 1983. What levels of defense and nondefense purchases would leave real purchasing power the same in 1986 as it was in 1983?

Cases for Discussion

 This selection requires no additional comment.

Spending for B1s and MXs Is Rising, So the Tubas Got an Increase, Too

By Richard L. Hudson

WASHINGTON—Military spending is going up. So spending for military bands is going up. What could be more natural?

It isn't fair, say outraged partisans of the arts, to spend more money on Sousa oompahs when spending for genuine classical music is being cut. They note balefully that the National Endowment for the Arts has been targeted by the administration for a 50 percent budget cut this year, to $77 million, while the Army, Navy, Air Force and Marine bands are in line for a 2 percent increase, to $89.7 million.

The discrepancy has arts hawks in Congress seething. "There are three full (military) bands in the Washington area, and each of them has a larger budget than the National Symphony Orchestra," says Rep. Fred Richmond, a New York Democrat and a leading congressional Medici. "I don't think it's fair," he says, that civilian arts should suffer while military music prospers.

NONCOMBAT TROOPS

Such cries draw a sympathetic audience among legislators worried about Pentagon "waste." One is Republican Sen. Mark Hatfield of Oregon, whose Appropriations Committee scrutinizes defense spending. He recently lambasted the military brass for budgeting bands, historians, museum curators and 1,605 "recreation specialists and sports technicians," all of whom "contribute little or nothing to our military strength."

Democratic Rep. Dan Glickman of Oklahoma calls the band budget "a sacred cow that has waded" through prior spending debates with insufficient scrutiny.

PRESERVING MORALE

"It looks like everybody's trying to chop our heads off," complains an Army band official, Sgt. Major Donald Young. The bands "wave the flag" and "stir patriotism," he says. A Pentagon spokesman says the 5,335 military-band members are needed to help lure recruits, preserve morale at foreign bases and burnish the military image.

It remains to be seen if critics of the military band buildup can torpedo Mr. Reagan's plans to raise funding. But arts lobbyists say the sniping has at least helped protect the arts endowment from the full 50 percent cut pushed by the White House. The Senate last Tuesday backed a 25 percent cut, and the House approved a token 1 percent reduction.

The critics aren't denying that a good military band plays a rousing tune. It does, says Representative Richmond. But "it's sure as heck not the National Symphony."

B   Once the budget justifications and numbers have been prepared, agencies face the task of marketing the package to the legislature. Conditions vary from year to year; the tactics applicable in one session may not be at all appropriate in the next. The changing approaches are described in the following review of the strategies used by Secretary of Defense Caspar Weinberger in selling budgets for fiscal 1982 through 1986.

Identify the budget strategies used. Is there a common logic running through them or is each independent of the others? To what extent would they be transferable to other budget environments?

Weinberger Finds His Well-Worn Strategies Always Succeed in Blunting Defense Budget Ax

By Tim Carrington

WASHINGTON—Defense Secretary Caspar Weinberger has privately referred to his campaign for a bigger defense budget as Kabuki, a highly ritualized Japanese art form in which all movements are tightly choreographed in advance.

Despite the furor surrounding the Reagan administration's push to add $29 billion to the military budget for the next fiscal year, many aspects of the contest seem to follow a set script. And after four years in the fray, the tireless Mr. Weinberger is nothing if not well-rehearsed.

Since President Reagan launched his military buildup, Congress has provided the Pentagon with about 95 percent of the spending authority it has sought. A look at the defense budget debate over the past four years bears out Mr. Weinberger's observations that it's less a political brawl than one of Washington's most stylized dramas. And the past could well foreshadow what happens this year.

1982

In March 1981, Congress granted the Pentagon a startling 20 percent increase, bringing its budget for the fiscal 1982 to $216.5 billion, just below the $222 billion the administration sought. However, five months later Mr. Weinberger faced dissent from within the Reagan administration. David Stockman, director of the Office of Management and Budget, proposed rescinding part of that increase and scaling back the projected military expansion for future years.

The budget chief had just learned that the fiscal 1982 federal budget deficit was likely to rise to $62.6 billion, small in relation to today's deficits of more than $200 billion, but for that time a record. Mr. Stockman recognized that Mr. Reagan's goal of showing a balanced budget by 1984 was in jeopardy, and he considered the defense buildup part of the program.

In staving off Mr. Stockman's assault on the planned buildup, Mr. Weinberger turned to a tactic for which he has since become famous, the chart and easel. The defense secretary's charts, presented in a meeting with the president, showed large soldiers bearing large weapons, which were labeled "Reagan budget." They towered above small soldiers with small weapons labeled "OMB budget." President Reagan went along with the "Reagan budget."

1983

In preparing the fiscal 1983 plan, Mr. Weinberger was again confronted with the budget slashing demands of Mr. Stockman. The defense chief had many allies within the administration but by now government officials began to refer to the hegemony of the "majority of two," Mr. Weinberger and President Reagan.

With unwavering White House support, the defense secretary shot down an OMB attempt to chop $20 billion from the proposed defense budget, then offered an unusual set of cuts himself. In what became a recurring feature of the budget process, the Pentagon stripped billions from its budget simply by adjusting the inflation assumptions. Weapons programs remained intact.

In defending the budget on Capitol Hill, Mr. Weinberger emphasized "the Soviet threat" and insisted that economic and fiscal concerns shouldn't influence the Pentagon's spending. But deficit concerns were mounting nonetheless and world financial markets were unusually jittery. When the administration sought $257 billion for defense in fiscal 1983, Rep. Joseph Addabbe (D-N.Y.), chairman of the defense appropriations subcommittee, declared that "defense is not sacrosanct" in the deficit-cutting effort.

In the Senate, Chairman Pete Domenici (R-N.M.) opened Budget Committee hearings with the declaration that "the hemorrhage of the budget deficit must be alleviated." The committee pressed Secretary Weinberger to suggest modest cuts from the proposed Pentagon budget, but the secretary refused. He said he hoped Congress wouldn't be "unwise enough" to reduce the budget request at all.

Congress, while hammering away at the Pentagon to offer up cuts, was loath to impose its own set of reductions. When the face-off ended, Congress gave the Pentagon budget authority of $245 billion, $12 billion less than the $257 billion the administration asked for but still 13 percent, or $29 billion, more than it got the previous year.

1984

Preparations of the defense budget for fiscal 1984 brought another confrontation with Mr. Stockman, who demanded that Mr. Weinberger take $11 billion out of his planned $284.7 billion budget.

The Pentagon, expert at protecting weapons programs through what observers call "cut insurance," was ready to meet these demands almost painlessly. Inflation assumptions were lowered, fuel-price calculations adjusted, and some military-construction projects postponed. In addition, a planned pay increase was dropped. In presenting a new budget request for $273.4 billion, Mr. Weinberger declared: "We have reached the bone."

Many legislators expressed outrage at Mr. Weinberger's refusal to consider other cuts despite mounting economic worries over the government's budget deficit. Sen. Don Riegle, a Democrat from badly pressed Michigan, asserted that the United States had a defense secretary "whose basic judgment is dangerous to our country." Mr. Weinberger replied: "You have accomplished your principal purpose, which is to launch a demogogic attack on me in time for the afternoon and evening editions.

The debate had become more rancorous, but the Pentagon's tactics still produced results. When the war of words ended, Congress granted the Pentagon 93 percent of the spending authority it sought—a $262.2 billion budget, up 8 percent, or $20.2 billion, from the previous year.

1985

Deficit-reduction efforts in early 1984 centered on making a "down payment" against the deficit in fiscal 1985. After another skirmish with Mr. Stockman, Mr. Weinberger agreed to seek a 15 percent increase that would bring the Pentagon's spending authority to $305 billion.

House Democrats assailed the plan, but as in the past, they wanted Mr. Weinberger to suggest the cuts, rather than slash on their own initiative politically popular military programs in an election year. Mr. Weinberger refused, saying: "We need it all."

Congress didn't give him the full $305 billion he sought, but again provided 93 percent of that; it approved a fiscal 1985 military budget of $284.7 billion, up 7 percent, or $19.5 billion, from the previous year.

1986

The contest over the fiscal 1986 budget is following the pattern of early years. Mr. Weinberger called for a 13 percent increase in a budget he said had been "scrubbed" down to the basics. After Mr. Stockman's demands for cuts gathered support from other cabinet members, Mr. Weinberger made accounting adjustments to produce $6.2 billion in reductions.

Further cuts? Mr. Weinberger asserts that the budget he presented is the "bare minimum." When pushed to suggest some cuts. Mr. Weinberger recently resorted to what's called "the Washington Monument strategy"—for "cut my budget and I'll close the Washington Monument" (or something equally visible).

During Senate hearings, the defense secretary warned that if Congress cuts the Pentagon budget, there would be a slowdown in the B-1 bomber project, elimination of two Trident submarines, and cancellation of a multiple-launch rocket system—all considered high-priority programs.

Some participants say the ritual is getting tiring. "It's the same Kabuki dance," says one Senate Budget Committee aide, "but Domenici is getting extremely frustrated with it."

C   Agencies without a specific clientele face special problems in defending their budget requests against budget cutters. A classic illustration of agency strategy appears in the following case, reproduced in entirety from *The Wall Street Journal.*

Consider These Questions

1. *What budget strategies did NASA use in defense of ERTS?*
2. *At what stage of the budget cycle were the reductions made?*
3. *How might other agencies use similar approaches? For instance, suggest explicitly how a state university might adopt those strategies in dealing with a legislature.*

How Backers of a Technology Satellite Induced Ford to Overrule His Advisers, Provide Money

By Arlen J. Large

WASHINGTON—Frank Moss is an ERTS nut, in a world of people who aren't.

So he considers it his duty to spread the gospel about his pet project. It helps that he is a U.S. Senator from Utah and chairman of the Senate Space Committee.

Daniel Evans may not be a nut on the subject, but he is an ERTS fan. As governor of the state of Washington, he wrote Senator Moss an unspontaneous letter saying that the "Earth Resources Technology Satellite has provided valuable information to both the agriculture and forestry industries and to the state of Washington.

Gerald Ford may not even be an ERTS fan, but he is a friend. Not long ago, he overruled his White House advisers and put $11 million in the new budget to start work on a third ERTS satellite, which will be launched in the fall of 1977.

So some very heavy politicians have been rallying around this little-known and unglamorous project of the National Aeronautics and Space Administration. The backstage tugging over the money for the third satellite is the kind of thing that goes on all over town during preparation of a new budget, and it provides a good case study of how budget winners win.

The loser was the president's Office of Management and Budget, which for months had urged that the third satellite be deferred to some future budget. Roy Ash, the just-departed OMB director who was overruled by Mr. Ford, observed with sarcasm that "one must congratulate NASA for its notable job of mobilizing outside opinion" on behalf of the new satellite.

THE SHOW-BIZ PROBLEM

However, it would be hard to pin the whole mobilizing effort on the space bureaucrats at NASA. There's something called "the ERTS community"—geographers, foresters, pollution fighters and land-use planners—that lobbied heavily for the new satellite. For its part, NASA has tried to tackle the show-biz problem caused by the satellite's grating, uncommunicative name. The agency is trying to get people to call it Landsat, but even space officials sometimes forget, and the names are used interchangeably.

The first satellite in the series was shot into polar orbit in 1972. It still is there but is running down. The second went up last January 22 with similar equipment for looking at the earth in four wavelengths of light and sending images back to ground stations for analysis by computers. Computer-processed pictures are sold by the Interior Department at Sioux Falls, S.D., to anyone who wants to use them to count crops, spot oil, see insect-chewed forests, trace earthquake-producing faults, and do a lot of other things.

All this really turns Senator Moss on, making him a self-admitted "virtual zealot" for these satellites. "ERTS was the first thing I could see where you have a very distinct and obvious applications return," he says. "It's a great example of the benefits coming out of the space program." People who appreciate the down-to-earth value of the ERTS pictures, he says, are more likely to embrace the space agency's flightier doings, such as the exploration of Mars.

The satellite launched last month is expected to work for two years. Congress last year authorized a third ERTS to take its place in 1977. NASA was more than willing to start building it, and so, of course, was General Electric Co., the main contractor for the first two. Plans were made to upgrade the new model with a heat-measuring sensor.

Mr. Ash's OMB, the government-wide spending monitor, demurred. A third satellite shouldn't go up, budget officials argued, until NASA succeeded in developing cameras with sharper vision. Without that, ERTS satellites would never be useful in making good crop-production forecasts, forest surveys, or pollution maps.

The space agency intends to double the sharpness of vision of one of the cameras on the third satellite. The other equipment, officials contend, sees sharply enough on the second and third satellites to undertake a large-scale survey of U.S. wheat production. And with a little practice, space officials think that they will get a better notion of the size of each year's Soviet wheap crop, thus giving a more accurate forewarning of export market demand.

NASA and its allies argued all last year that a third satellite should be on duty in 1977 to take over when the second one dies; otherwise, there would be a gap in the data that would discourage picture buyers in "the ERTS community."

The trick was to bring this argument to OMB's attention in an impressive way. An important part of the lobbying blitz was orchestrated on Capitol Hill by Senator Moss and his ally, Arizona's Senator Barry Goldwater.

LETTERS TO THE STATES

Hoping to show that the ERTS community had plenty of political muscle, Senator Moss wrote every governor, asking if state agencies had made use of ERTS and whether the federal government should sell the pictures on a permanent basis.

The senator got replies from 25 governors, plus some top officials in other states. Vermont's Thomas Salmon said ERTS pictures will be used to trace pollution in Lake Champlain. In California, said then Governor Ronald Reagan, ERTS had helped outline land-use patterns. Missouri's Christopher Bond said the pictures have been used to spot flood-prone areas. Only Delaware's Sherman Tribbitt replied bluntly that the pictures didn't prove useful.

One by one, Senator Moss dribbled the gubernatorial letters into the Congressional Record in the closing months of last year. "It was like the drop-of-water technique, day by day," he says.

Besides that, Senator Moss waved letters of support from the Society of Photographic Scientists and Engineers, the American Society of Photogrammetry, the Association of American Geographers, the American Forestry Association, and various distinguished professors. Meanwhile, on the scientific-seminar circuit, General Electric's people were forever turning up with ERTS displays. Daniel Fink, general manager of GE's space division, preached the need to keep those space photos coming in.

Nevertheless, OMB last December turned down NASA's request to put money for the third satellite, called Landsat-C, into the budget being prepared for the new Congress. Word spread along the ERTS community's grapevine. OMB got letters from the National Academy of Science and the National Academy of Engineering, both quasi-government bodies. Letters came from important scientists.

APPEALING THE DECISION

The budget keepers still said no. Under the rules, an agency can go over OMB's head and appeal directly to the president. So ERTS was kicked around at a meeting between Mr. Ford, Mr. Ash, and James Fletcher, the NASA boss. "It was not a confrontation," Mr. Fletcher insists.

He says his agency kept explaining to OMB that the third satellite didn't represent an "operational" earth-scanning system but would remain an experimental instrument. Then in early January the remaining differences between the two agencies were reduced to an "issue paper" that went to Mr. Ford. The satellite money was approved.

Mr. Ash appeared to see a connection between NASA's victory and a praise-filled article on ERTS in the February issue of *Fortune* magazine.

The article portrayed OMB as the villain in trying to block the third satellite, concluding: "To cripple or kill this program, after the millions of words spewed out about the coming 'fallout' from space research, would certainly be foolhardy."

NASA had indeed been eager for *Fortune* to do the article. "It was Fletcher who put this bug in my bonnet about a year ago," recalls Robert Lubar, the magazine's managing editor. John Donnelly, the agency's assistant administrator for public affairs, also remembers writing Mr. Lubar about the ERTS project. "I tried to plant the seed of an idea for a story I thought was of quite legitimate interest to businessmen," he says. Editor Lubar says that he doesn't remember seeing that letter and that the decision to have the article written was his. Anyway, he says, the February *Fortune* didn't hit the streets until the last week in January, after Mr. Ford had made his decision.

Illustration of Object-of-Expenditure Classification

An agency would be required to classify its budget into the following resource classes. It would, of course, use only the classes in which it intended to make purchases.

Expenditure Classifications:

1. Personal services.
    1.1   Head of department.
    1.2   Classified positions.
    1.3   Unclassified positions (temporary).
    1.4   Overtime, shift differentials.
    1.5   Vacation, sick relief.
2. Contractual services.
    2.1   Freight, express, deliveries.
    2.2   Travel.
    2.3   Telephone, telegraph.
    2.4   Repairs.
    2.5   Subscriptions and dues.
    2.6   Printing, binding, advertising.
    2.7   Postage and postal supplies.
    2.8   Water, heat, light, power.
    2.9   Professional and other fees (consultants, physicians, lawyers, etc.).
    2.10   Other contractual services.
3. Supplies.
    3.1   Food.
    3.2   Fuel.
    3.3   Feed and veterinary supplies.
    3.4   Office.
    3.5   Household, laundry, janitorial.

      3.6   Medical.
      3.7   Educational, playground, recreational.
      3.8   Motor vehicle supplies.
      3.9   Agricultural supplies.
      3.10   Clothing and dry goods.
      3.11   Maintenance supplies.
      3.12   Data processing supplies.
      3.13   Other supplies.

4. Rents and insurance.
      4.1   Rents—privately owned properties.
      4.2   Rents—publicly owned properties.
      4.3   Rents—data processing equipment.
      4.4   Rents—other equipment.
      4.5   Rents—other.
      4.6   Insurance.

5. Equipment.
      5.1   Office equipment.
      5.2   Medical equipment.
      5.3   Household equipment.
      5.4   Motor vehicles and equipment.
      5.5   Agricultural equipment and livestock.
      5.6   Aircraft equipment.
      5.7   Educational, playground, recreational.
      5.8   Data processing equipment.
      5.9   Library books.

6. Land and buildings.
      6.1   Purchase lands.
      6.2   Buildings.
      6.3   Nonstructural improvements.

7. Employee benefits.
      7.1   State retirement.
      7.2   Police-fire retirement.
      7.3   Social security.
      7.4   Workers' compensation.
      7.5   Health insurance.

8. Contingencies.

APPENDIX B

Overview of the Federal Budget Process

The federal budget, like all public budgets, reflects what is proposed to be done for a specific period of time in the future, usually 12 months. It is a plan concerned with managing public funds, and it deals with how much government will spend and how those expenditures will be financed. When passed by Congress and signed by the president, the budget becomes law. The amount of funds specified in the legislation is then legally binding for all federal agencies for a given fiscal year. Agencies cannot spend more than is specified unless they are able to get supplemental or deficiency appropriations through the same legal channels as the original budget.

The budget, of course, is much more than a legally binding financial plan. Since funds are always limited, the act of budgetmaking becomes a process of choosing among alternative expenditures, and the budget document itself becomes a description of national goals and priorities. The budget process, then, entails political decisions (choices) as well as financial and economic analyses. In the United States that process is lengthy and complex. What our federal budget actually contains in any given fiscal year is the result of the interplay between the executive branch, and its many departments and agencies, and Congress, with its system of committees and subcommittees.

Although the Constitution (Article I, Sect. 1) gives Congress the responsibility for budget decisions, by law the executive branch is charged with preparing and submitting the budget. Under the Budget and Accounting Act of 1921, every year the president transmits a proposed federal budget to Congress within 15 days after it convenes in the new calendar year. Until 1976, the president's annual budget message contained the proposed budget for the fiscal year that began July 1 and ended June 30. The Congressional Budget and Impoundment

Source: Adapted from *A Glossary of Terms Used in the Federal Budget Process*, 3d ed., PAD-81-27 (Washington, D.C.: U.S. General Accounting Office, 1981).

Control Act of 1974 (P.L. 93–344) changed those dates. The federal fiscal year now runs from October 1 through September 30. The act has not directly altered the executive budget process—agency officials continue to channel their budget requests through the cabinet level, and in turn through the Office of Management and Budget which reviews the requests in light of the president's proposed budget initiatives (See Table 1)—but the act has strengthened the legislative side of budgetmaking by introducing changes that have helped Congress form a clearer perspective of fiscal policy requirements.

Although federal budgeting is a continuous process, it can be understood and studied in terms of four phases: (1) executive preparation and submission, (2) congressional action or the congressional budget process, (3) implementation and control of the enacted budget, and (4) review and audit. Our discussion of these phases augments Figure 1, on p. 76, which describes and identifies the activities and actors in the federal budget process. Most of our discussion is devoted to phase 2 because, with the passage of the 1974 Budget Act, Congress acquired a new budget process. Rather than acting on the executive's budget proposals in a piecemeal fashion, as had been done in the past, Congress now has a system for looking at the budget as a unified proposal early in the budget cycle. The act has given both Houses the opportunity to determine if the budget is consistent with national priorities.

TABLE 1 Executive Branch Budget Timetable

Timing	Action to Be Completed
April–June (March)	Conduct spring planning review to establish presidential policy for the upcoming budget.
June	OMB sends policy letters to the agencies.
September 1	Smaller agencies submit initial budget request materials.
September 15	Cabinet departments and major agencies submit initial budget request materials.
October 15	Legislative branch, judiciary, and certain agencies submit initial budget request materials.
September–January (September)	OMB and the president review agency budget requests and prepare the budget documents.
January	The president transmits the budget during the first 15 days of each regular session of Congress.
January–February	OMB sends allowances letters to the agencies.
April 10 (February)	The president transmits an update of the budget estimates. (Note: transmittal is often requested to be made earlier than the required date.)
July 15 (June)	The president transmits an update of the budget estimates. (Note: transmittal is often requested to be made earlier than the required date.)

SOURCE: OMB Circular no. A-11, rev., June 3, 1980.

PHASE 1: EXECUTIVE PREPARATION AND SUBMISSION

Preparing the president's budget starts many months before it is submitted to Congress in late January. Formulation begins at the agency level, where individual organizational units review current operations, program objectives, and future plans in relation to the upcoming budget. Throughout this preparation period, there is a continuous exchange of information among the various federal agencies, OMB, and the president. Agency officials receive help in the form of revenue estimates and economic outlook projections from the Treasury Department, the Council of Economic Advisers, the Departments of Commerce and Labor, and OMB. The budget timetable (included here) highlights the key steps involved in preparing the president's budget and transmitting it to Congress. The months in parentheses indicate when agencies are expected to submit review materials to OMB.

PHASE 2: THE CONGRESSIONAL BUDGET PROCESS (AN ILLUSTRATIVE OVERVIEW)

The Budget of the United States Government, published early January, contains the president's proposals for the federal government's outlays and budget authority for the ensuing fiscal year. Congress can act as it wishes on these proposals. It can change funding levels, modify or eliminate programs, or add new ones not requested by the president, and it can act on legislation determining tax rates. The final outcome of Congress' actions is the expenditure (outlay) of federal funds. However, Congress does not act (vote) on outlays directly, but rather on requests for budget authority. Through the appropriations bills it passes, Congress grants budget authority to agencies, which permits them to incur obligations and hence to spend federal funds.

Before a request for budget authority can be considered, Congress must first enact legislation authorizing an agency to carry out a particular program, such as revenue sharing or food stamps. Authorizing legislation can set a limit on the funds for a given program or call for "such sums as may be necessary," but it cannot stipulate the dollar amount to be spent on the program. Some major programs, like space, defense procurement, and foreign affairs, are reauthorized by the standing legislative committee every year, while other programs are authorized for several years in advance.

How much money each department, agency, or program receives is determined by the House and Senate Appropriations Committees and their subcommittees, each of which has jurisdiction over specific numbers of federal agencies. Money bills (i.e., appropriations) may be for

FIGURE 1 The Federal Budgetmaking Process

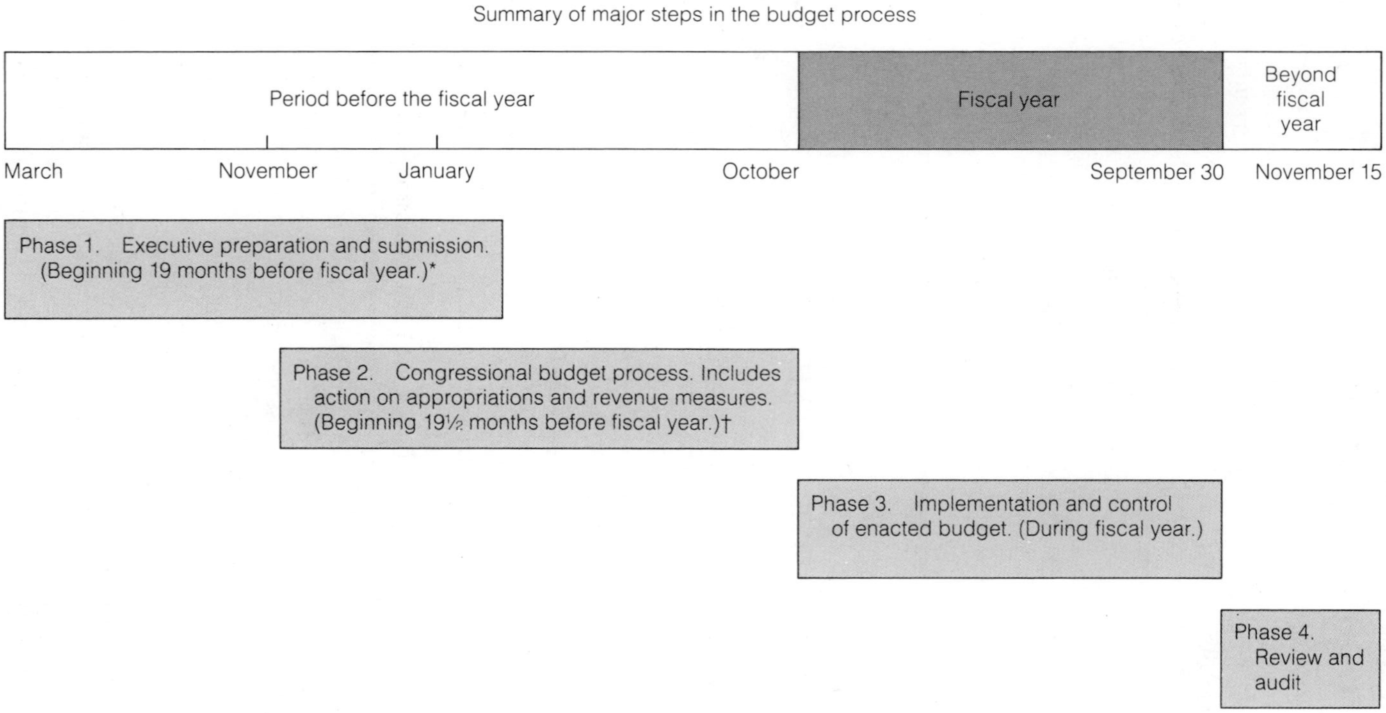

Summary of major steps in the budget process

Period before the fiscal year		Fiscal year	Beyond fiscal year
March	November	January	October	September 30	November 15

Phase 1. Executive preparation and submission. (Beginning 19 months before fiscal year.)*

Phase 2. Congressional budget process. Includes action on appropriations and revenue measures. (Beginning 19½ months before fiscal year.)†

Phase 3. Implementation and control of enacted budget. (During fiscal year.)

Phase 4. Review and audit

FIGURE 1 (*continued*)

Phase 1-Executive preparation and submission

Approximate timing	Agency	Office of Management and Budget	The president

Budget policy development

Approximate timing	Agency	Office of Management and Budget	The president
March (or earlier in some agencies)	Reviews current operations, program objectives, issues, and future plans in relation to upcoming annual budget. Submits projections of requirements that reflect current operations and future plans, supporting memoranda and related analytic studies that identify major issues, alternatives for resolving issues, and comparisons of costs and effectiveness.	Develops economic assumptions. Obtains forecasts of international and domestic situations. Prepares fiscal projections.*	
April May		Issues policy guidance on material to be developed for spring planning review.	Discusses budgetary outlook and policies with the director of OMB and with the Cabinet as appropriate.
May		Discusses program developments and management issues, and resulting budgetary effects, with agencies. Compiles total outlay estimates for comparison with revenue estimates. Develops recommendations for president on fiscal policy*, program issues, and budget levels.	Discusses with the director of OMB and others as necessary, general budget policy, major program issues, budgetary planning targets, and projections. Establishes general guidelines and agency planning targets for annual budget.
June	Issues internal instructions on preparation of annual budget estimates.	Issues technical instructions for preparation of annual budget estimates.	

Compilation and submission of agency estimates

Approximate timing	Agency	Office of Management and Budget	The president
		Conveys president's decisions to agency heads on government-wide policies and assumptions, the application of policies, and budgetary planning targets to individual agencies.	
July– September 30	Allocates budgetary planning target to agency programs. Develops and compiles detailed estimates.	Advises and assists agencies on preparation of budget submissions.	

Office of Management and Budget review and presidential decisions

Approximate timing	Agency	Office of Management and Budget	The president
September October November	Submits formal estimates for annual budget, including projections of requirements for future years and supporting materials.	Analyzes budget submissions. Holds hearings with agency representatives on program, budget, and management issues in preparation for director's review. Reexamines economic assumptions and fiscal policies. *Discusses program developments with agencies. In light of outlook and policy discussion with president, prepares budget recommendations for the president.	Reviews budget recommendations and decides on agency budget amounts and on overall budget assumptions and policies.
	Revises estimates to conform to president's decisions.	Notifies agency heads of president's decisions.	
December January February		Again reviews economic outlook and fiscal policy for discussion with president of economic policies.* Drafts president's budget message; prepares budget with summary tables, budget appendix, special analyses, and budget-in-brief. Arranges printing of budget documents.	Revises and approves budget message. Transmits recommended budget to Congress within 15 days after Congress convenes.
			Congress

*In cooperation with the Treasury Department and Council of Economic Advisers.
SOURCE: Office of Management and Budget, January 1977.

FIGURE 1 (continued)

Phase 2. Congressional Budget Process

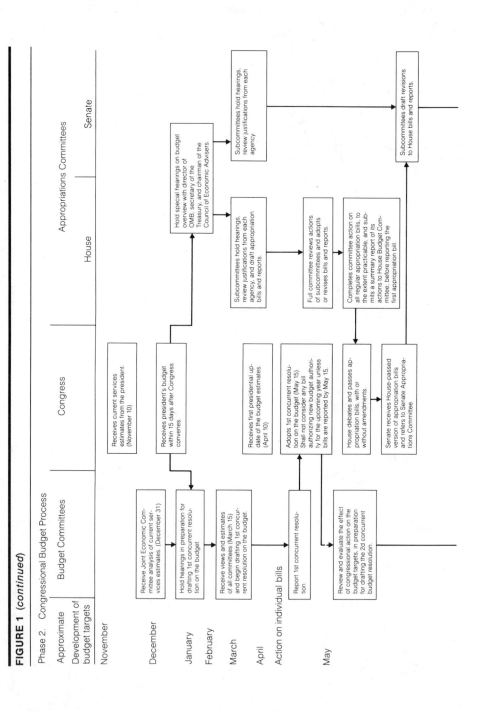

Approximate	Development of budget targets			
	Budget Committees	Congress	Appropriations Committees	
			House	Senate

November

Congress: Receives current services estimates from the president. (November 10)

December

Budget Committees: Receive Joint Economic Committee analysis of current services estimates. (December 31)

Budget Committees: Hold hearings in preparation for drafting 1st concurrent resolution on the budget.

Congress: Receives president's budget within 15 days after Congress convenes.

House Appropriations: Hold special hearings on budget overview with director of OMB, secretary of the Treasury, and chairman of the Council of Economic Advisers.

January

February

Budget Committees: Receive views and estimates of all committees (March 15) and begin drafting 1st concurrent resolution on the budget.

March

House Appropriations: Subcommittees hold hearings, review justifications from each agency, and draft appropriation bills and reports.

Senate Appropriations: Subcommittees hold hearings, review justifications from each agency.

April

Congress: Receives first presidential update of the budget estimates. (April 10)

Action on individual bills

Budget Committees: Report 1st concurrent resolution.

Congress: Adopts 1st concurrent resolution on the budget (May 15). Shall not consider any bill authorizing new budget authority for the upcoming year unless bills are reported by May 15.

House Appropriations: Full committee reviews actions of subcommittees and adopts or revises bills and reports.

May

Budget Committees: Review and evaluate the effect of congressional action on the budget targets, in preparation for drafting the 2d concurrent budget resolution

Congress: House debates and passes appropriation bills, with or without amendments.

House Appropriations: Completes committee action on all regular appropriation bills, to the extent practicable, and submits a summary report of its actions to House Budget Committee, before reporting the first appropriation bill

Congress: Senate receives House-passed version of appropriation bills and refers to Senate Appropriations Committee.

Senate Appropriations: Subcommittees draft revisions to House bills and reports.

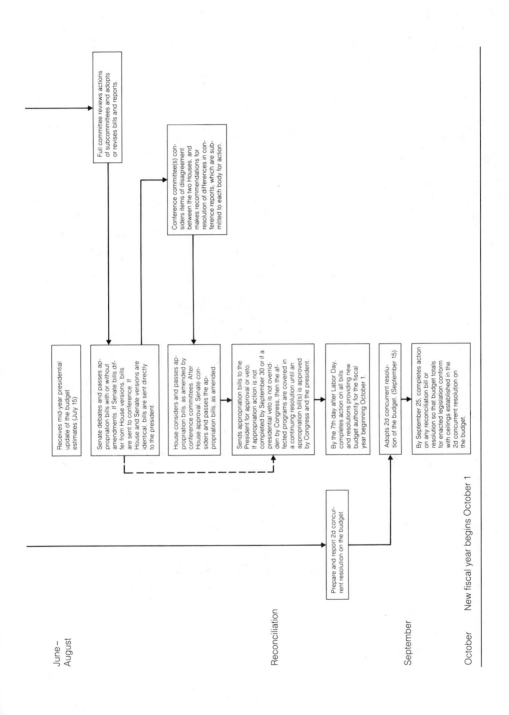

June–
August

Reconciliation

September

October   New fiscal year begins October 1

Full committee reviews actions of subcommittees and adopts or revises bills and reports.

Conference committee(s) considers items of disagreement between the two Houses, and makes recommendations for resolution of differences in conference reports, which are submitted to each body for action.

Receives mid-year presidential update of the budget estimates (July 15)

Senate debates and passes appropriation bills with or without amendments. If Senate bills differ from House versions, bills are sent to conference. If House and Senate versions are identical, bills are sent directly to the president.

House considers and passes appropriation bills, as amended by conference committees. After House approval, Senate considers and passes the appropriation bills, as amended

Sends appropriation bills to the President for approval or veto. If appropriation action is not completed by September 30 or if a presidential veto is not overridden by Congress, then the affected programs are covered in a continuing resolution until an appropriation bill(s) is approved by Congress and the president.

By the 7th day after Labor Day, completes action on all bills and resolutions providing new budget authority for the fiscal year beginning October 1.

Adopts 2d concurrent resolution of the budget. (September 15)

By September 25, completes action on any reconciliation bill or resolution so that budget totals for enacted legislation conform with ceilings established in the 2d concurrent resolution on the budget.

Prepare and report 2d concurrent resolution on the budget

FIGURE 1 *(concluded)*

Phase 3. Implementation and control of enacted budget

Approximate timing

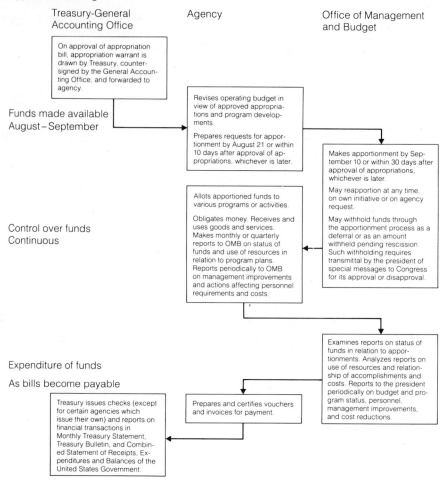

Treasury-General Accounting Office	Agency	Office of Management and Budget

On approval of appropriation bill, appropriation warrant is drawn by Treasury, countersigned by the General Accounting Office, and forwarded to agency.

Funds made available
August – September

Revises operating budget in view of approved appropriations and program developments.

Prepares requests for apportionment by August 21 or within 10 days after approval of appropriations, whichever is later.

Makes apportionment by September 10 or within 30 days after approval of appropriations, whichever is later.

May reapportion at any time, on own initiative or on agency request.

Allots apportioned funds to various programs or activities.

Obligates money. Receives and uses goods and services. Makes monthly or quarterly reports to OMB on status of funds and use of resources in relation to program plans. Reports periodically to OMB on management improvements and actions affecting personnel requirements and costs.

May withhold funds through the apportionment process as a deferral or as an amount withheld pending rescission. Such withholding requires transmittal by the president of special messages to Congress for its approval or disapproval.

Control over funds
Continuous

Expenditure of funds

As bills become payable

Examines reports on status of funds in relation to apportionments. Analyzes reports on use of resources and relationship of accomplishments and costs. Reports to the president periodically on budget and program status, personnel, management improvements, and cost reductions.

Treasury issues checks (except for certain agencies which issue their own) and reports on financial transactions in Monthly Treasury Statement, Treasury Bulletin, and Combined Statement of Receipts, Expenditures and Balances of the United States Government.

Prepares and certifies vouchers and invoices for payment.

Phase 4—Review and audit

Approximate timing

Treasury-General Accounting Office	Agency	Office of Management and Budget

Program evaluation, management appraisal, and independent audit

Periodic

General Accounting Office performs independent audit of financial records, transactions, and financial management, generally. "Settles" accounts of certifying and disbursing officers. Makes reports to Congress including reports on special messages on deferrals and proposed rescissions.

Reviews compliance with established policies, procedures, and requirements. Evaluates accomplishment of program plans and effectiveness of management and operations.

Reviews agency operations and evaluates programs and performance. Conducts or guides agencies in organization and management studies. Assists president in improving management and organization of the executive branch.

one year (the most common form), which allows an agency to spend only during one fiscal year, or they may be multiyear appropriations. The Constitution requires that all revenue (tax) bills originate in the House, and by custom the House also originates appropriations measures.[1]

Since appropriations are not usually considered until authorizing legislation is passed, in recent years many federal agencies have received their appropriations after the new fiscal year has begun. When an agency does not receive its appropriation before the old one lapses, it operates under a continuing resolution passed by Congress. A continuing resolution usually allows an agency to spend at the previous year's rate.

The 1974 Budget Act has introduced the following changes into the congressional budget process:

1. It requires Congress, before it enacts any appropriation bills, to adopt concurrent budget resolutions. The first resolution sets target totals for budget authority, outlays, receipts, and the public debt. These targets serve as a guide for Congress' subsequent considerations of appropriations and tax measures. The resolution also subdivides the targets into 17 functional spending categories, such as defense and health, which represent broad national priorities.

2. It established the House and Senate Budget Committees and has charged them with the responsibility of reporting the concurrent budget resolutions. The committees also keep track of individual authorization, appropriations, and revenue decisions that Congress makes during the budget process.

3. By creating the Congressional Budget Office (the congressional counterpart of OMB) and granting it broad authority to obtain data from executive agencies, the act has provided Congress with a mechanism for obtaining impartial policy and cost analyses and five-year budget projections. CBO provides Congress with all available information related to the budget and conducts budget-related studies at Congress' request. It also monitors individual spending bills and issues periodic scorekeeping reports showing the status of congressional action on these bills.

4. It has provided Congress with a firm budget timetable that coordinates the authorization and appropriations cycles with the overall congressional budget as embodied in the concurrent budget resolutions.

---

[1]Passage of revenue bills follows the same general procedure as appropriation bills, except that revenue measures are reported by the Ways and Means Committee in the House and by the Finance Committee in the Senate.

5. It has changed the rules on presidential impoundment of funds by establishing a procedure for congressional involvement. The act requires that any money not spent must be reported to Congress in rescission or deferral messages. Impoundments take effect unless they are disapproved by both Houses within 45 days of the president's notification. Deferrals (temporary withholding of funds from obligation) are effective until overturned by either House.

The congressional timetable laid down in Title III of the act is illustrated in Figure 1. Congress' activities with respect to the timetable are summarized below.

CONGRESSIONAL BUDGET TIMETABLE

November 10

Congressional review of the budget begins when the president submits estimates of the current services budget, a five-year projection of federal spending based on current programs and existing funding levels, exclusive of any news programs. The Joint Economic Committee assesses these estimates, spelling out the economic assumptions (inflation, unemployment, rate of economic growth) that underlie them, and reports its evaluation to Congress by December 31. Congress uses the current services budget as a basis for examining the president's January budget submission.

January (15 Days after Congress Convenes)

Following the submission of the president's budget, the Senate and House Budget Committees begin hearings to examine the president's economic assumptions and spending priorities in preparation for drafting the first concurrent resolution on the budget.

March 15

Authorization and appropriations committees report to the Budget Committees their views and estimates of new budget authority to be enacted for the ensuing fiscal year. Some committees hold formal markup sessions to draft these views and estimates. The reports are used by the Budget Committees to gauge the total and functional spending estimates contained in the first concurrent budget resolution.

April 1

The Congressional Budget Office submits its report detailing alternative spending patterns and revenue levels associated with different budget options and their budgetary implications to the Budget Committees. The CBO report, which in theory is used in drafting the first budget resolution, presents Congress with spending scenarios above and below the president's.

April 15

The Budget Committees of both Houses report the final concurrent budget resolution to Congress. This initial resolution establishes targets for: (a) the appropriate level of total outlays (money to be spent in the ensuing fiscal year) and total new budget authority (money to be spent in the ensuing fiscal year and in future fiscal years) both in the aggregate and by functional category, (b) the appropriate budget surplus or deficit, (c) the recommended level of federal revenues, and (d) the appropriate level of public debt.

May 15

Budget Committees report legislation proposing new budget authority to the House and Senate. If a committee fails to meet this deadline, the legislation cannot be considered by the House or Senate unless a waiver is reported by the House Rules Committee or the Senate Budget Committee.

May 15

Congress completes action on the first budget resolution. Until the first budget resolution has been finalized, setting a "target" spending ceiling and revenue floor for the fiscal year, neither House can consider any spending or revenue measures that would take effect in that fiscal year.

September (7th Day after Labor Day)

Congress completes action on all regular authorization and appropriation measures. The only exception to this rule is consideration of bills that have been delayed because necessary authorizing legislation has not been enacted in time. When this happens, federal departments and agencies exist on "continuing resolutions"—the prior year's funding levels—until their regular appropriations are passed.

September 15

There is no deadline for reporting the second budget resolution, but it normally occurs before the annual August recess (or immediately after), and it must be made final by September 15. In the first resolution, the total and functional spending levels are "binding." This has the effect of "locking in" a congressional spending ceiling and revenue floor. Once the second budget resolution is in place, no legislation can be passed that would breach these limits, unless Congress passes a subsequent budget resolution.

September 25

Congress completes final actions on reconciliation for second budget resolution, which either affirms or revises the budget targets set in the first resolution. The House and Senate Budget Committees report any changes to the floor in the form of a reconciliation bill. Congress cannot adjourn for the year until the reconciliation legislation is passed.

October 1

The fiscal year begins.

PHASE 3: IMPLEMENTATION AND CONTROL OF THE ENACTED BUDGET

After the budget is approved by Congress, the president is responsible for executing it. Under law, most of the budget authority granted to the agencies of the executive branch is converted into outlays through an apportionment system regulated by the Office of Management and Budget. The director of OMB apportions (distributes) budget authority to each agency by time periods (usually quarters) or by activities over the duration of the appropriation. This ensures both the economical and effective use of funds and obviates the need for agencies having to ask for supplemental authority. However, changes in law or economic conditions during the fiscal year may necessitate the enactment of additional budget authority. When this happens, supplemental requests are sent to Congress for its consideration. On the other hand, the executive branch, under the Antideficiency Act (31 U.S.C. 665), may establish reserves to fund contingencies or to effect savings made possible by more efficient operations or by changes in requirements.

Title X of the 1974 Budget Act permits the president to withhold appropriated funds for fiscal or other policy reasons, or because the president has determined that all or part of an appropriation is not needed to carry out a program. When these circumstances arise, the president sends a special message to Congress requesting that the budget authority be rescinded. If Congress does not pass a rescission bill within 45 days of continuous session, the budget authority is made available for obligation.

In order to defer—temporarily withhold—budget authority, the president must also send a special message to Congress indicating the reasons for the proposed delay in spending. Either House may, at any time, pass a resolution disapproving the president's request for deferral of budget authority, thus requiring that the funds be made available for obligation. When no congressional action is taken, deferrals may remain in effect until, but not beyond, the end of the fiscal year. If continued deferal is desired into the new fiscal year, the president must transmit a new special message to Congress.

PHASE 4: REVIEW AND AUDIT

Individual agencies are responsible—through their own review and control systems—for making sure that the obligations they incur and the resulting outlays adhere to the provisions in the authorizing and appropriations legislation, as well as to other laws and regulations governing the obligation and expenditure of funds. OMB exercises its review responsibility by appraising program and financial reports and by keeping abreast of agencies' efforts to attain program objectives.

In addition, the General Accounting Office, as an agency responsible to Congress, regularly audits, examines, and evaluates Government programs. Its findings and recommendations for corrective action are made to Congress, to OMB, and to the agencies concerned. GAO also monitors the executive branch's reporting of messages on proposed rescissions and deferrals. It reports to Congress any differences it may have with the classifications (i.e., rescissions or deferrals) of the president's requests for withholding funds. Should the president fail to make budget authority available in accordance with the 1974 Budget Act, GAO may bring civil action to obtain compliance.

THE FEDERAL BUDGET DOCUMENTS, FISCAL YEAR 1986[2]

Budget of the United States Government, 1986 contains the budget message of the president and presents an overview of the president's budget proposals. It includes explanations of spending programs in terms of national needs, agency missions, and basic programs, and an

---

[2]Source: *Budget of the United States Government, 1986.*

analysis of receipts, including a discussion of the president's tax program. This document also contains a description of the budget system and various summary tables on the budget as a whole.

United States Budget in Brief, 1986 is designed for use by the general public. It provides a more concise, less technical overview of the 1986 budget than the above volume. Summary and historical tables on the federal budget and debt are also provided, together with graphic displays.

Budget of the United States Government, 1986—Appendix contains detailed information on the various appropriations and funds that comprise the budget. The *Appendix* contains more detailed information than any of the other budget documents. It includes for each agency: the proposed text of appropriation language, budget schedules for each account, new legislative proposals, explanations of the work to be performed and the funds needed, and proposed general provisions applicable to the appropriations of entire agencies or groups of agencies. Supplementals and rescission proposals for the current year are presented separately. Information is also provided on certain activities whose outlays are not part of the budget totals.

Special Analyses, Budget of the United States Government, 1986 contains analyses that are designed to highlight specified program areas or provide other significant presentations of federal budget data. This document includes information about alternative views of the budget, i.e., current services and national income accounts; economic and financial analyses of the budget covering government finances and operations as a whole; and government-wide program and financial information for federal civil rights and research and developmental programs.

Historical Tables, Budget of the United States Government, 1986, is a new volume. It provides data on budget receipts, outlays, surpluses or deficits, and federal debt covering extended time periods—in many cases from 1940–1990. These are much longer time periods than those covered by similar tables in other budget documents. The tables include various aggregations of budget components in current prices, constant prices, and as percentages of the budget totals and of the gross national product. The document includes, for example, data on receipts by major source from 1940 to 1990; and federal debt from 1940 to 1990. The data for the years prior to 1986 have, where necessary, been restructured to be consistent with the concepts and presentation used in the 1986 budget, so these data series are comparable over time. The documents may be purchased from the Superintendent of Documents, U.S. Government Printing Office Washington, D.C. 20402.

Drug Enforcement Administration
Budget Request, Fiscal Year 1986[1]

Author's Comment—*The following is the fiscal year 1986 budget request for the Drug Enforcement Administration, as included in the president's budget. Note (1) the classification by activity and by object, (2) the three budget year presentation, (3) the personal summary, and (4) the extensive workload data presented. The Part 2 reference footnoted is to a supplemental appropriation request for salaries to implement new legislation (that request is included here as well).*

GENERAL AND SPECIAL FUNDS: FEDERAL FUNDS

Salaries and Expenses[2]

For necessary expenses of the Drug Enforcement Administration, including not to exceed $70,000 to meet unforeseen emergencies of a confidential character, to be expended under the direction of the Attorney General, and to be accounted for solely on his certificate; purchase of not to exceed [five hundred seventeen] *five hundred fifty-two* passenger motor vehicles of which four hundred eighty-nine are for replacement only for police-type use without regard to the general purchase price limitation for the current fiscal year; and acquisition, lease, maintenance, and operation of aircraft; [$329,988,000] *$345,671,000*, of which not to exceed $1,200,000 for research shall remain available until expended and not to exceed $1,700,000 for purchase of evidence and payments for information shall remain available until September 30, [1986] *1987. (Reorganization Plan No. 2 of 1973; Reorganization Plan No. 1 of 1968; 21 U.S.C. 801–966 as amended; 40 U.S.C. 304j; 41 U.S.C. 11(a); 49 U.S.C. 783; Department of Justice and Related Agencies Appropriation Act, 1985; additional authorizing legislation to be proposed.)*

---

[1]*Budget of the United States Government, Fiscal Year 1986—Appendix.*
[2]See Part II for additional information.

Program and Financing (thousands of dollars)

Identification Code 15-1100-0-1-751	1984 Actual	1985 Estimate	1986 Estimate
Program by activities:			
Direct program:			
Enforcement of federal law and investigations:			
00.01 Domestic enforcement	121,215	162,484	162,956
00.02 Foreign cooperative investigations	29,619	36,012	37,069
00.03 Diversion control	15,185	17,319	27,756
00.04 State and local assistance	15,661	16,878	17,158
00.05 Intelligence	16,443	17,199	17,324
00.06 Research and engineering	1,942	2,594	2,349
00.07 Support operations	65,953	59,785	60,680
00.08 Program direction	25,883	22,642	20,379
00.91 Total direct program	291,901	334,913	345,671
01.01 Reimbursable program	36,018	5,775	3,250
10.00 Total obligations	327,919	340,688	348,921
Financing:			
Offsetting collections from:			
11.00 Federal funds	−35,168	−4,925	−2,400
14.00 Nonfederal sources	−850	−850	−850
21.40 Unobligated balance available, start of year	−2,061	−243	—
24.40 Unobligated balance available, end of year	243	—	—
25.00 Unobligated balance lapsing	540	—	—
39.00 Budget authority	290,623	334,670	345,671
Budget authority:			
40.00 Appropriation	290,623	329,988	345,671
44.20 Supplemental for civilian pay raises	—	4,682	—
Relation of obligations to outlays:			
71.00 Obligations incurred, net	291,901	334,913	345,671
72.40 Obligated balance, start of year	34,152	35,451	42,441
74.40 Obligated balance, end of year	−35,451	−42,441	−49,642
77.00 Adjustments in expired accounts	−8,794	—	—
90.00 Outlays, excluding pay raise supplemental	281,808	323,393	338,318
91.20 Outlays from civilian pay raise supplemental	—	4,530	152

Summary of Budget Authority and Outlays (thousands of dollars)

	1984 Actual	1985 Estimate	1986 Estimate
Enacted/requested:			
Budget authority	290,623	334,670	345,671
Outlays	281,808	327,923	338,470
Supplemental under existing legislation:			
Budget authority	—	2,700	—
Outlays	—	2,700	—
Rescission proposal:			
Budget authority	—	−876	—
Outlays	—	−876	—
Total:			
Budget authority	290,623	336,494	345,671
Outlays	281,808	329,747	338,470

The mission of the Drug Enforcement Administration (DEA) is to control abuse of narcotics and dangerous drugs by restricting the aggregate supply of those drugs. At the Federal level, DEA is the lead drug law enforcement agency. DEA accomplishes its objectives through coordination with state, local, and other federal officials in drug enforcement activities; development and maintenance of drug intelligence systems; regulation of legitimate controlled substances activities; and enforcement coordination and intelligence-gathering activities with foreign government agencies.

Cooperation among federal law enforcement agencies is extensive, especially within the 13 organized crime drug enforcement (OCDE) task forces. DEA's involvement is integral to this nationwide coordinated enforcement strategy. When coupled with the expansion of DEA/FBI cooperative efforts, overall drug enforcement capabilities have been significantly strengthened in recent years.

The means by which DEA performs its mission are summarized by the following activities:

Enforcement of Federal Law and Investigations

Domestic enforcement.   This activity aims to eliminate or immobilize major drug trafficking organizations and thereby reduce the domestic supply of illicit drugs. The measures below indicate the level of activity performed by this program.

	1984 Actual	1985 Estimate	1986 Estimate
DEA initiated arrests	7,820	7,900	7,900
Other Federal referral arrests	1,086	1,100	1,100
DEA cooperative arrests	1,725	1,750	1,750
Drug related assets seized ($ millions)	$83	$88	$88
Clandestine labs seized	162	165	170
DEA/OCDE arrests	1,817	1,900	2,099
Assets seized ($ millions)	$65	$70	$75

Foreign cooperative investigations.   This activity encompasses efforts to reduce at the source, illicit opium production, heroin, illicitly produced and diverted legitimate dangerous drugs, cocaine and marihuana destined for the United States, and the collection and dissemination of intelligence.

	1984 Actual	1985 Estimate	1986 Estimate
Foreign cooperative arrests	1,072	1,100	1,150
Intelligence reports	146	140	140
Special field intelligence programs	30	53	53

Diversion control.   By authority of the Controlled Substances Act and the Comprehensive Crime Control Act (CCCA) of 1984 (Public

Law 98–473), this activity addresses the problem of the diversion of controlled substances from the legitimate channels in which they are manufactured, distributed, and dispensed. Under the CCCA, the DEA has been given expanded authority to administratively revoke or suspend the registration of any practitioner, manufacturer, or distributor whose actions have resulted in the diversion of controlled substances, if such revocation or suspension is deemed to be in the public interest. The measures below indicate the level of activity performed by this program:

	1984 Actual	1985 Estimate	1986 Estimate
Investigations:			
Periodic	667	750	750
Targeted	226	320	320
Preregistrant (nonpractitioners)	1,185	1,200	1,200
Administrative revocations	—	50	769

State and local assistance.   This activity encompasses cooperative law enforcement activities with state, county, and local authorities. Included are training programs; laboratory analysis and expert testimony; and federal/state and local task forces. Workload measures are provided below:

	1984 Actual	1985 Estimate	1986 Estimate
Task force initiated arrests	2,476	2,600	2,600
Laboratory exhibits analyzed	9,154	7,000	7,000

Intelligence.   This activity encompasses the collection, analysis, and dissemination of drug intelligence in support of DEA, other federal, and state and local agencies. The measures below indicate the level of activity performed by this program.

	1984 Actual	1985 Estimate	1986 Estimate
Intelligence reports	1,111	1,200	1,200
Special field intelligence programs	12	9	9
Enforcement support activity	6,676	6,700	6,700
Information responses	19,159	19,100	19,100
El Paso Intelligence Center (EPIC) watch transactions	282,757	290,000	290,000

Research and engineering.   This activity encompasses research programs directly related to the DEA law enforcement and intelligence functions.

Support operations.   This activity encompasses laboratory analysis of evidence and expert testimony in support of investigation and prosecution of drug traffickers; training programs for all levels of DEA operational personnel; a technical equipment program, including aircraft operations; provision of ADP and record communications support; analysis and review of all records management systems; and the provision of responses to requests made pursuant to the Freedom of Information and Privacy Act (FOIPA).

	1984 Actual	1985 Estimate	1986 Estimate
Laboratory exhibits analyzed	26,228	25,200	25,200
Students trained	15,423	13,913	12,338

Program direction. This program encompasses the overall management and direction of DEA.

Reimbursable program. A reimbursable program providing primarily for the training of foreign drug law enforcement officials is conducted by DEA and funded by the Department of State. Schools are held each year, both in the United States and host countries.

	1984 Actual	1985 Estimate	1986 Estimate
Foreign officers trained	1,052	1,000	1,000

Object Classification (thousands of dollars)

Identification code 15-1100-0-1-751	1984 Actual	1985 Estimate	1986 Estimate
Direct obligations:			
Personnel compensation:			
11.1 Full-time permanent	121,775	148,340	152,160
11.3 Other than full-time permanent	1,337	788	813
11.5 Other personnel compensation	12,118	14,768	14,893
11.9 Total personnel compensation	135,230	163,896	167,866
12.1 Personnel benefits: civilian	22,636	28,998	30,637
13.0 Benefits for former personnel	116	—	—
21.0 Travel and transportation of persons	13,556	12,519	13,099
22.0 Transportation of things	3,251	2,757	2,762
23.1 Standard level user charges	15,670	23,561	23,075
23.2 Communications, utilities, and other rent	19,506	19,844	21,558
24.0 Printing and reproduction	707	1,220	1,325
25.0 Other services	45,840	54,222	55,239
26.0 Supplies and materials	9,100	9,071	9,611
31.0 Equipment	26,156	18,700	20,374
42.0 Insurance claims and indemnities	133	125	125
99.0 Subtotal, direct obligations	291,901	334,913	345,671
99.0 Reimbursable obligations	36,018	5,775	3,250
99.9 Total obligations	327,919	340,688	348,921

Personnel Summary			
Direct:			
Total number of full-time permanent positions	4,083	4,430	4,564
Total compensable workyears:			
Full-time equivalent employment	3,854	4,282	4,428
Full-time equivalent of overtime and holiday hours	470	570	590
Reimbursable:			
Total number of full-time permanent positions	367	30	30
Total compensable workyears:			
Full-time equivalent employment	340	25	25
Full-time equivalent of overtime and holiday hours	30	3	3

TRUST FUNDS

Drug Abuse Prevention and Control Gift Fund

Program and Financing (thousands of dollars)

Identification code 15-8906-0-7-751		*1984 Actual*	*1985 Estimate*	*1986 Estimate*
	Program by activities:			
10.00	Total obligations (object class 25.0)	—	2	—
	Financing:			
21.40	Unobligated balance available, start of year	—	−2	—
24.40	Unobligated balance available, end of year	2	—	—
60.00	Appropriation (trust fund) (permanent, indefinite)	2	—	—
	Relations of obligations to outlays:			
71.00	Obligations incurred, net	—	2	—
90.00	Outlays	—	2	—

These amounts will be transferred to the Drug Enforcement Administration in 1985.

PART II: PROPOSED SUPPLEMENTALS AND RESCISSION PROPOSALS

Salaries and Expenses[3]

For an additional amount for "Salaries and expenses", $2,700,000.

Program and Financing (thousands of dollars)

Identification code 15-1100-1-1-751	1984 Actual	1985 Estimate	1986 Estimate
Program by activities:			
10.00 Total obligations	—	2,700	—
Financing:			
10.00 Budget authority (appropriation)	—	2,700	—
Relation of obligations to outlays:			
11.00 Obligations incurred, net	—	2,700	—
11.00 Outlays	—	2,700	—

Supplemental funding is requested to permit initial implementation of the Diversion Control Amendments contained in the Comprehensive Crime Control Act of 1984.

Object Classification (thousands)

Identification code 15-1100-1-1-751	1984 Actual	1985 Estimate	1986 Estimate
Personnel compensation:			
13.1 Permanent positions	—	1,040	—
13.5 Other personnel compensation	—	80	—
13.9 Total personnel compensation	—	1,120	—
12.1 Personnel benefits: Civilian	—	130	—
12.1 Travel and transportation of persons	—	117	—
12.1 Transportation of things	—	25	—
12.1 Communications, utilities, and other rent	—	374	—
12.1 Other services	—	556	—
12.1 Supplies and materials	—	40	—
12.1 Equipment	—	338	—
12.1 Total obligations	—	2,700	—

---

[3]Supplemental now requested, existing legislation.

Personnel Summary			
Total number of permanent positions	—	156	—
Total compensable workyears:			
Full-time equivalent employment	—	39	—
Full-time equivalent of overtime and holiday hours	—	4	—

3

Budget Methods and Practices

Many tasks in the budget cycle can be learned only by dealing nose to nose against, and elbow to elbow with, other participants. There are some methods and perspectives important to understand, however, before that first crunch. This chapter provides an initial introduction to some methods and activities in each phase of the budget cycle.

PREPARATION OF AGENCY BUDGETS

A budget request includes both the estimated cost of planned activities and a written justification of those activities. Both elements are critical for successful operation of any government because they provide the "how much" and "what it does" information needed for public decisions. The estimates may be developed and organized through one or more of the following approaches. First, the cost may be grouped by the organization (branch, section, division, etc.) incurring the cost. The estimates originate in the offices where the costs occur. The costs thus follow the organization chart. For example, if a city has organizational units called the mayor's office, the comptroller's office, and departments of streets, of public safety, of public works, and of recreation, cost estimates would be prepared for each of those six units on the organization chart. The estimates would, of course, entail that unit's planned response to the forecast operating conditions. Second, they may be grouped by program, purpose, or budget activity. What is the cost of cleaning streets, controlling traffic, collecting garbage, and so on? Sometimes the organization breakdown will coincide with these program breakdowns, but often organization costs are attributable to several different programs. Third, the cost may be broken down by object class, that is, by the nature of goods and services to be purchased.

Agencies will use the uniform object classification required and provided by the budget office of that particular government. An example of such an object classification appeared as Appendix A in Chapter 2.

The foundation of any budget, regardless of eventual focus on performance or program accomplishment, is the object class estimates. This is the basis for estimates of requirements for organization programs or budget activity. Ideally, the agency would determine what it intends to do, determine what resources are needed to get it done, estimate the price of those resources, and multiply price by number of input units to get a total cost of the request. Budget routine does in fact implicitly use this process.

Elements of Cost Estimation

Costs for budgeting purposes occur as agencies acquire resources (personnel, materials, and facilities) to provide public services. Somewhat different estimating techniques apply to each class, with a particular distinction between personnel and nonpersonnel costs.

Compensation of personnel.   Personal services usually are the largest single cost element in budget requests of government agencies. The problem is to determine the kind and amount of personal services needed and to apply prevailing wage and salary rates to compute the total cost. A standard procedure works from personnel data on individuals in each pay step, adjusted for anticipated movements to the next pay step in the budget year. Thus, if there are 50 people in the Tax Auditor I category with five years' experience this year, there likely will be 50 people in the Tax Auditor I category with six years' experience next year. The budget estimate for them would be 50 times the annual pay of a Tax Auditor I with six years' experience. Figure 3–1, budget detail for the Chicago Commission on Animal Care and Control, shows the link between the personnel complement, salaries, and the total personnel component of the budget. The total for positions in the lower part of the display, $1,641,408, equals the sum of the first two elements of the total request (salaries and wages plus salary schedule adjustments). Further, it should be noted that this portion represents over 80 percent of the total budget. The request must be supplemented by lapses that reduce total cost: turnover (retirement, quits, and terminations) with replacement at lower pay grades or with personnel not replaced, delays in filling vacant positions, and so on. Such lapses may be estimated from experience on position turnover. Requests for new personnel ordinarily would be based on changes in expected workload, including new programs.

Associated with ordinary compensation are substantial costs for personnel benefits (pensions, insurance, uniform allowances, social security, etc.) These benefits are usually a separate object class but must

FIGURE 3–1 City of Chicago Budget Display

Commission on Animal Care and Control: It is the function of the Commission, in cooperation with private humane agencies, to protect domestic animals from inhumane treatment, to protect the public from stray and possibly dangerous animals by impoundment, to confine or humanely dispose of stray animals, and to enforce all sections of the Municipal Code relevant to animal care and control.

Code			Amounts Appropriated
	.005	Salaries and wages-on payroll	$1,613,200
	.015	Schedule salary adjustments	28,208
	.025	Vacation relief	
	.096	Uniform allowance	28,350
#4710	.000	For personal services	1,659,758
	.130	Postage and postal charges	2,400
	.150	Publications	11,000
	.157	Rental of equipment and services	7,000
	.160	Repair or maintenance of property	1,200
	.162	Repair or maintenance of equipment	14,000
	.166	Subscriptions and dues	200
	.169	Technical meeting costs	700
	.173	State vehicle license plates	100
	.176	Maintenance and operation—city-owned vehicles	35,000
	.186	Telephone	1,000
#4710	.100	For contractual services	72,600
	.245	Reimbursement to travelers	
#4710	.200	For travel	
	.320	Gasoline	42,000
	.330	Food	30,000
	.340	Material and supplies	35,000
	.342	Drugs, medical, and chemical materials and supplies	26,500
	.350	Stationery and office supplies	7,000
	.360	Repair parts and materials	7,500
#4710	.300	For commodities	148,000
	.410	Equipment for buildings	6,000
	.423	Communication devices	4,000
#4710	.400	For equipment	10,000
#4710	.700	For contingencies	1,500
		*Organization total	$1,901,858

Code	Positions	Number	Rate
	Animal Care and Control–4710		Positions and Salaries
9632	Chairman	1	$
9633	Member	8	
9650	Executive Director	1	45,000
3493	Operations manager—animal control	1	29,844
3494	Assistant operations manager—animal control	1	31,320
3313	Supervising veterinarian	1	40,824
3310	Veterinarian	1	35,796
3310	Veterinarian	1	29,844
3310	Veterinarian	1	25,392

FIGURE 3-1 (concluded)

Code	Positions	Positions and Salaries Number	Rate
	Animal Care and Control–4710		
3492	Veterinary assistant	3	13,020
3487	Supervisor of pavillion maintenance aides	1	20,184
3487	Supervisor of pavillion maintenance aides	2	19,224
3491	Animal control inspector	1	20,184
3491	Animal control inspector	1	19,224
3491	Animal control inspector	1	17,412
3495	Supervisor of animal control officers	1	23,388
3495	Supervisor of animal control officers	1	22,260
3495	Supervisor of animal control officers	1	21,180
3495	Supervisor of animal control officers	2	20,184
3496	Animal control officer	1	22,260
3496	Animal control officer	1	20,184
3496	Animal control officer	4	19,224
3496	Animal control officer	5	18,312
3496	Animal control officer	7	17,412
3496	Animal control officer	3	16,608
3496	Animal control officer	11	15,072
3498	Animal control officer aide	2	16,608
3498	Animal control officer aide	1	15,072
3498	Animal control officer aide	1	14,352
3498	Animal control officer aide	1	13,688
3498	Animal control officer aide	2	12,396
3499	Pavillion maintenance aide	18	11,844
1301	Administrative services officer I	1	24,528
0308	Staff assistant	1	27,080
0303	Administrative assistant III	2	18,312
7102	Dispatch clerk	3	12,398
0415	Inquiry aide III	1	13,020
0413	Inquiry aide I	7	11,844
0403	Senior clerk	1	10,272
0205	Cashier	2	12,396
0797	Receptionist	2	10,272
1815	Principal storekeeper	1	14,352
1754	Statistical clerk	1	11,316
	Schedule salary adjustments		28,208
	Activity total	100	1,060,232
		100	1,595,232
	Less turnover	—	54,824
	Total		$1,641,408

be considered for estimation purposes in association with compensation itself. The total cost of labor to the government includes both direct compensation and fringe benefits, regardless of the budget categorization used. Most such benefits are computed by application of formulas established by law or labor contract that relate the benefit to work force size or to total compensation of the labor force. For instance, state law may require city government payment into a pension fund equal to 20 percent of wages and salaries paid. Such computations, once requirements of the law are worked out, are simple.

Nonpersonnel costs.   Other object costs may be more difficult to estimate for the request than are personnel costs. They are often computed using estimating ratios, as adjusted by recent experience. Much information for the request can be located in prior year budget materials. Five estimation techniques are frequently used in these computations: (1) volume times unit price, (2) workload times average unit cost, (3) work force ratios, (4) ratios to another object class, and (5) adjustment to prior year cost.

First is the volume-times-unit-price method, an attractive approach when a particular quantity and single average price are applicable to a relatively high-ticket object class. Items such as typewriters or automobiles may be estimated, fairly homogeneous categories making up a large part of a cost in an object class. Unit cost, the second approach, is taken from recent cost experience adjusted for inflation and/or productivity changes. For instance, food expenses for a training class could be estimated by such a method (300 trainee days at $20 per trainee day, for a request of $6,000). Third, some categories of cost, particularly small categories of miscellaneous costs, may be estimated by relating them to the work force. For example, office supply expenses for a district office could be related to the size of staff stationed there. Fourth, when there is some relationship between certain categories and other resources used in the production process, that expense group may be estimated by use of ratios to that nonpersonnel object class. As an example, a parts inventory for motor vehicles may be linked to the number of vehicles in the motor fleet. The final method, best suited for small, heterogeneous cost categories, makes estimates by adjustments to prior year lump sums. Prior cost is adjusted to reflect anticipated changes in qualities in the budget year. This method may be necessary when other means are not feasible or economical, but it lacks the precision of other techniques.

No formula or ratio can be automatically applied without hazard. Cost ratios and other relationships may change if operating methods are altered, if prices of inputs change, or if production technologies change. All of these change in a dynamic economy, often with great impact on operating cost.

Budget estimates must be carefully prepared because the quality of the presentation shapes the impressions that budget analysts develop about agencies. Analysts are less likely to trust judgments of budget officers who prepare sloppy budget requests. Several simple errors are particularly frequent, although they ought never occur. First, budgets may not coincide with current budget instructions, budget guidelines, and forms. A budget may be developed using the prior year budget as a guide, but the submission must coincide with current regulations.

Failure to follow instructions produces needless embarrassment. Second, budget submissions may lack required supplemental documents or the documents may not be properly identified. Budget examiners seldom give the benefit of doubt to budgets with missing material. And finally, cost estimate detail columns may not add to totals carried forward in the presentation. Continuous cross-checking must be maintained to preserve the internal consistency of the budget request.

Budget Justification

Program status reports, requests for supplemental funding, supporting explanation for increased staff, budget increases, and so on, require justification for any planned agency action. Well-developed justifications are the important key to attainment of agency budget objectives. There are several general and specific guidelines for the effective writing of budget justifications, beyond the standard rules of English prose. The justification must avoid jargon and uncommon abbreviations, because the justification's purpose is to communicate to individuals less familiar with the details of the proposed activity than are personnel in the operating agency. Neither budget agency examiners nor legislators are likely to approve poorly described projects. The justifications must be factual and must provide documented sources. And the justifications must go through ordinary review and revision to produce a polished presentation.

In terms of structure, the justification will address the current situation, the additional needs, and the expected results from honoring the request. One section describes the current program in terms of measurable workloads, staffing, funding, or productivity trends. It will briefly and specifically inform the budget examiner of existing conditions, without extraneous detail which might misdirect the examiner's attention. Another section of the justification will describe the additional needs. It must specifically identify additional funds, personnel, and materials needed for the budget activity at issue. The reason for the need must be explicitly developed. Common reasons include:

1. Mandates from higher levels of government, the courts, or legislative requirements.
2. Improvement of methods of operation.
3. Increased workload.
4. Higher prices of resources to be purchased.
5. Development of new programs.

The third section describes expected results from the proposal and tries to convince the budget office and the legislature of the need for the proposed activity. It will describe the results that will occur if the requested resources are or are not provided. Because the reviewer will want to know whether partial funding will help, whether critical pro-

---

TABLE 3-1 Checklist for Budget Justification

Completeness—Are the major elements (objective of program, magnitude of need, benefits or accomplishments) covered?

Explicitness—Are program benefits and related funding increases clearly stated?

Consistency—Are the statements or data appearing in several places the same or easily reconcilable?

Balance—Are the most important programs and issues given the most prominence? Do the programs' objectives adequately support the budget level requested?

Quantitative data—Is optimum use made of available quantitative data?

Organization—Is the material well-organized to bring out only the significant matters? Are appropriate headings or titles used? Is introductory or summary material used appropriately?

SOURCE: U.S. Office of Personnel Management, *Budget Presentation and Justification*, 1982.

---

gram objectives will be endangered without funding, whether workload can be backlogged to get around the problem, and what the implications of the request will be for future requests, answers to those questions should be available and defensible. The justification should make a solid case for a realistic increase. There is no reason to spread a justification thin to defend a large increase when a solid case for a smaller increase is possible. Table 3-1 presents a brief checklist for elements to include in a sound justification.

REVIEW OF BUDGETS

Agency requests are reviewed by a central budget office before inclusion in the government budget and by legislative committees after inclusion in the budget. Two features are common to both reviews: The reviewer probably will reduce some items in the proposal and the reviewer will be less informed about agency operations than are those who prepared the budget. Those features dominate budget review. Meltsner has examined budget operations in Oakland, California, in some detail, finding patterns in the way budget analysts review budgets:

> Inexperience in itself forces upon the budget analyst the use of a set of rules of thumb. The analyst first looks at last year's appropriations to identify any significant changes. It is the changes or incremental requests which get his attention. Without going into detail, here is an outline of the rules of cutting:
>
> 1. Cut all increases in personnel.
> 2. Cut all equipment items which appear to be luxuries.
> 3. Use precedent—cut items which have been cut before.
> 4. Recommend repair and renovation rather than replacement of facilities.
> 5. Recommend study as a means of deferring major costs.

6. Cut all nonitem operating costs by a fixed percentage (such as 10 percent).
7. Do not cut when safety or health of staff or public is obviously involved.
8. Cut departments with "bad" reputations.
9. When in doubt ask another analyst what to do.
10. Identify dubious items for the manager's attention.

The analyst, by looking for enough items to cut, proceeds until the budget is balanced within the existing revenue constraint.[1]

Beyond those rules of thumb, is there anything that a budget analyst—always less knowledgeable about the program under review than those who run the program, always looking for budget reductions—can do? There are some points that must be considered in each instance. First, the reviewer must verify the arithmetic used to produce program requests. Overambitious rounding and errors seem to increase requests more often than they reduce them. Second, reviewers should check linkages between justifications and dollar requests. Is there reason to believe that the request will have the result or will things stay about the same, regardless of the money requested? Requests in the latter category are good candidates for elimination, regardless of budget conditions. Third, the reviewer must determine whether the agency proposes changes in its programs or changed directions in existing programs. If changes are contemplated, they should be consistent with legislative (and executive) intent. Fourth, the reviewer must seek omissions from the budget requests. Some years ago, a major university constructed a large center for performing and creative arts, but neglected to request money to cover utilities (electricity, and so on) needed for its operation. That created significant budget problems during the first year, as major reductions had to be imposed on other university activities to cover that utility bill. Finally, the analyst must use all resources available for analysis, particularly the prior year budget and actual expenditure, the current year budget and reported expenditure to date, and the proposed budget. A comparison of these documents can be made without special trouble. The analyst should establish the cause of any deviations from trends apparent in those comparisons. Refer to Appendix B, instructions to budget analysts in Oregon, for more about budget analysis.

The final budget document, like that delivered to Congress by President Reagan early in February 1985 for the 1986 federal fiscal year or those presented by governors, mayors, and other public executives to their legislative bodies each year, will typically contain four basic elements:

---

[1] Arnold J. Meltsner, *The Politics of City Revenue* (Berkeley: University of California Press, 1971), p. 178.

1. *The Budget Message.* An introduction from the chief executive that highlights the major conditions surrounding the preparation of the budget (economic conditions, perceived social problems, service priorities, etc.) and the primary changes proposed in the budget. The message sets the tone for the budget ("hard times," "new beginnings and new challenges," "emerging from severe fiscal crisis," etc.); in simple budgets, this may be the only narrative in the entire document.[2]

2. *Summary Schedules.* Several schedules, the type and number of which will vary by budget, gather together the major aggregates planned in the full document. These include both revenue and expenditure categories, each organized by classification schemes seen as important by the government (revenue by source, expenditure by object class, expenditure by organizational unit, expenditure by function, etc.). Schedules will ordinarily include the budget year amounts, along with comparable figures for the current and most recently completed year.

3. *Detail Schedules.* Detail schedules present the heart of the budget, in terms of why the administrative departments seek the money they hope to spend. The details will be presented in at least one and usually more of the following organization structures: by administrative unit (the department, division, etc., responsible for spending and delivering services), by program or function (type of service delivered), or object of expenditure (input classes to be purchased). These schedules may also include information on performance by the various agencies and may outline performance targets for the upcoming year.

4. *Supplemental Data.* The budget document may also include a wide variety of supplemental materials, depending on the information requirements placed on the executive by the legislative body and on the special problems or opportunities encountered by the subject government. A good illustration of such supplemental data is the special analysis volume of the federal budget. A review of the material here shows that it is useful and interesting, but has no direct bearing on the key tasks of the budget. Other examples of displays that governments use include detailed historical tables on tax rates, analysis done of grant revenue, debt schedules, and special detail on pension and other trust funds.

Phantom Balance

Governments may find it politically convenient or legally necessary to produce a balanced operating budget when reasonably produced

---

[2]For more about the strategy of that message, see Henry W. Maier, *Challenge to the Cities: An Approach to a Theory of Urban Leadership* (New York: Random House, 1966). Maier is the long-time mayor of Milwaukee.

figures would show a deficit.[3] Governments have developed a number of pragmatic devices to produce such an artificial balance. A frequently encountered handful includes: high revenue estimates, shifting requests among budgets, changed revenue or expenditure timing, low requests for high priorities, and unlikely assumptions. Because of their use by governments in trouble, the strategies are worth some attention.

Any budget must be constructed with estimates of revenue for the upcoming fiscal year. Phantom budget balance can therefore be developed through use of artificially high revenue estimates for that year. Such estimates can be produced then by assuming unrealistically high economic activity (state and federal taxes, as well as many local non-property taxes, are sensitive to the level of economic activity), impossibly diligent administration of the tax, or by presuming that the linkage between revenue collections and economic activity has changed in an improved fashion. Local property taxes ordinarily could not be overestimated, as rates are set on the basis of assessed value on a prior valuation date. (More about this in a later chapter.) Thus, the property tax base is not estimated, but is actual. The estimated revenue can be manipulated, however, by assuming unrealistically low delinquency (or noncollection) levels: if 90 percent of the levy historically has been actually collected, a budget boost is possible by assuming 95 percent collection. During the late 1970s, New York City apparently got such boosts toward budget balance by presuming 100 percent collection, a completely unrealistic basis for budgeting. Similar inflation of revenue estimates can be produced by making unrealistic assumptions about the process of intergovernmental assistance from either federal or state sources. A similar unsustainable revenue boost can be produced by sale of property or other aspects held by the government—a "one-time revenue crutch."[4] So long as that revenue is not regarded as a long-term boost to the fiscal base, that sort of boost is not damaging. If it merely is applied to conceal a continuing problem, the danger is clear. An eastern state took the crutch to its ridiculous extreme. A state hospital was declared surplus, was appraised at a handsome value, advertised for sale, and the anticipated revenue from that sale was included in the state revenue estimate. It helped balance a tight budget. Unfortunately, the facility did not sell, but that was not tragic for seekers of phantom balance. The anticipated sales revenue then was included as part of revenue expected for the next budget year! So long as the property remained for sale, the state felt justified in including appraised proceeds as anticipated revenue.

---

[3] An operating budget would include the expenditures to be made for services delivered within the year; the resources purchased from the operating budget would largely be used up within the year.

[4] Karl Nollenberger, "It's More Than Balancing the Budget," *Public Management*, April 1980, p. 3.

A second device involves manipulation among budgets. State and local governments often have capital budgets in addition to and separate from operating budgets. Capital budgets finance purchase of assets with long useful life (as will be discussed in Chapter 5) and often have no requirement for balance, because such long-life assets may logically be financed on a pay-as-you-use basis through the issuance of debt. Some governments have shifted activities which would ordinarily be included in the operating budget to the capital budget to produce the desired balance in the operating budget. For instance, services of the city planning department have a long lifetime, so why not finance them through the capital budget, even though the expenditure flow is continuous? The shift can destroy the logic of the capital budget and, more importantly, can endanger the capability to finance the government's capital infrastructure.

Third, single-year deficits may be managed by accelerated collection of revenue to create a cash "bubble" in the year of acceleration. The advantage is one-shot, yielding gains only in the acceleration year without influencing the fundamental revenue base. The "bubble" can be duplicated in forthcoming fiscal years only by further accelerating collections, an unlikely possibility. Two examples show how acceleration works. In 1969, Illinois state expenditures seemed destined to exceed revenue. The problem was reduced by acceleration of sales tax collections. Retailers had been required to pay sales tax collections to the state at the end of the month following the month of collection: December collections would be due at the end of January. The accelerated schedule required them to remit collections by the end of the business month: December collections were due at the end of December. That change of schedule created a year with 13 months of sales tax collections: December 1968 (remitted in January 1969) through December 1969 (remitted at the end of December 1969).[5] Future collection profiles were not influenced; each year had collections from 12 months. A second example comes from the Philadelphia property tax. Businesses willing to pay estimated 1978 taxes along with their 1977 taxes were given a special discount on their 1978 tax bill, a method of obtaining greater 1977 revenue by reducing the flow available in 1978.[6] Both accelerations create a bubble for the problem year by altering future collections flows.

The balance problem may also be concealed by manipulating when expenditures occur. One approach loads the cost of multiyear programs

---

[5] Illinois accelerated sales tax collections in 1969 and corporate income, retail sales, and individual income withholdings in 1976. Robert M. Whitler, "Accelerated Tax Collection in Illinois," *Revenue Administration, 1977,* Proceedings of the 45th Annual Meeting of the National Association of Tax Administrators, pp. 55–58.

[6] Estimated 1978 property taxes were to be borrowed in May 1977 to ease a city revenue problem without going to banks for financing. ("Early Taxpayers Can Get a Break in Philadelphia," *Louisville Courier Journal,* April 3, 1977.)

in later fiscal years rather than in a sequence consistent with normal project development flow. The low request in the current budget year may help achieve balance in that year; the result, however, may well be greater problems in achieving balance in further budget years. A somewhat different method of expenditure manipulation, particularly within a fiscal year, uses delayed payment for purchases made toward the end of a fiscal year until the next fiscal year (and the next year's appropriations). The technique conceals a short-term operating deficit and amounts to short-term borrowing from suppliers across the two fiscal years.[7] It obviously reduces funds available for the next year. Unless the imbalance is corrected, similar problems will result in following years and the operating deficit carry-over will expand with time.

A fourth device is delivery of a balanced executive budget which omits some activities which political pressures will prevent the legislature from excluding. The executive can thus claim a balanced budget, but the hard choices have not been made, and appropriations actually made will likely produce a deficit or proposals will be radically realigned before appropriation. An illustration: Texas requires that its Legislative Budget Board, the body responsible for preparing the budget document, submit a balanced budget. In the fall of 1984, after substantial work had been done on the document for presentation to the 1985 session, the state comptroller substantially reduced the official revenue estimate because of weak oil and natural gas tax collections. The revision occurred just before the board reviewed higher education requests, the last item on its schedule. Rather than alter recommendations for all state agencies, the board opted to balance the budget entirely through reductions in higher education and recommended a 26 percent appropriation decrease. Possibly the board intended to stimulate efficiency in higher education, but it is probably more likely that it was practicing phantom balance. In any case, the legislature made substantial readjustments; virtually all the reductions were restored and some institutions received increases.[8]

An artificially balanced budget may even be passed, relying on supplemental appropriation in the next year to provide required funds.[9]

---

[7]For example, the city of Chicago in 1980 delayed payments to vendors who regularly did business with the city to avoid bank loans in a cash crisis. The problem emerged because property tax bills were not mailed as scheduled because of a judicial challenge of a homestead exemption program. The city had short-term borrowing authority but feared it was insufficient to cover the shortage. ("City May Delay Payment to Suppliers," *Chicago Tribune*, August 19, 1980.) Because the taxes were actually levied, there is no borrowing across fiscal years in this instance; the strategy is simply one of cash flow management.

[8]Lawrence Biemiller, "How the University of Texas, Flexing Its Political Muscle, Foiled Budget Cutters," *The Chronicle of Higher Education* 30 (June 19, 1985), pp. 12–15.

[9]Regular appropriations are passed before the start of a budget year. Those appropriations may prove inadequate because of unforeseen events. Supplemental appropriations provide additional funds within a current budget year.

Such proceedings may go largely unnoticed, because emphasis traditionally focuses on the budget presentation and consideration, not on what actually happens during the budget year. In a similar fashion, the imbalance may be handled in some budget years by shifting expenditures normally planned for the early part of that budget year into a supplemental request for the current year.

A final mechanism exploits the nature of a budget as an operating plan based on a forecast. Budget results can be managed by use of unlikely environmental assumptions concerning, for instance, state assumption of local welfare responsibilities, major new intergovernmental assistance programs, artificially low employment or inflation conditions, or other conditions which favorably influence expenditures or revenue. Those assumptions may allow a balanced budget presentation with no real potential that those conditions will actually occur. If deficits can readily be accommodated in capital markets, such manipulations may scarcely be noticed.

MANAGING BUDGET EXECUTION

An approved budget becomes an important managerial tool, both to guide agency operations according to plan and to ensure that expenditure does not exceed appropriation. Ordinarily budgets are approved for an entire fiscal year; execution of the budget occurs on a day-to-day, week-to-week basis. How can the budget be a useful device for control of this execution activity? Well-functioning fiscal systems divide the total budget appropriation to operating units for the year into quarterly (or monthly) allotments on agreement with the central budget office. Suppose the department of streets and storm sewers has an appropriation of $4 million for the fiscal year from January 1 to December 31 and relatively constant expenditure rates are anticipated during the year. An allotment plan adopted by the department and the city budget office could then be as follows:

	Allotment to Quarter	Cumulative Allotments
January 1	$1,000,000	$1,000,000
April 1	1,000,000	2,000,000
July 1	1,000,000	3,000,000
October 1	1,000,000	4,000,000
Total	$4,000,000	

A comparison of actual expenditure at each quarter end with the allotment provides an early warning for control of department activity to prevent overspending or unnecessary underprovision of service. If reports of spending plus commitments to spend (encumbrances) through the end of June exceed $2 million, activity (spending) curtailment is needed; if the total is less than $2 million, the activity may be accelerated.[10]

Service delivery and, hence, spending profiles for many agencies will not spread equally through the year. A typical outdoor swimming pool in the northern United States will be in service during the summer months only, so its operating expenditures will concentrate in these months; equal quarterly allotments would not be useful for control and management. Activities that produce uneven expenditure flows during the year (seasonal needs, major capital equipment acquisitions, opening or closing of new facilities, etc.) require uneven allotments. The schedule must be consistent with both the approved budget and activity flow expectations if it is to be usable for control and management.

Comparisons of the allotments and expenditures to date can suggest (1) areas in which expenditure may have to be curtailed, (2) areas in which surpluses may be available for use against deficits in other areas, (3) patterns that may be helpful in preparation of future budgets, and (4) possible need to request a supplemental appropriation (funds beyond those initially appropriated for the fiscal year). Some spending faster than allotment may simply be accelerated acquisition, transfer between quarters to take advantage of low prices, for instance, not anticipated when the budget was prepared. Other spending may imply spending above the approved appropriation. These latter overruns require spending unit action to control the flow, generally according to budget office direction. Both agencies and finance officers can thus maintain better control of budget execution with these periodic allotment-to-expenditure comparisons. While the objective of execution is delivery of services to the public, funds must not be spent in a fashion contrary to the appropriation.

Some units find that there is no special seasonal pattern to their major expenditure categories. That allows them to use more simple budget status reports: they need only compute the percent of total budget used (spent and obligated) at a particular date and compare that with the percent of the fiscal year expired. If the percent of budget used exceeds the percent of year expired, a problem may exist in that portion of the agency operations. Such a budget status report for a transit agency appears as Figure 3-2 on pp. 110-11. The managerial consequences of this report style are the same as for allotment-expenditure reports. There are, however, dangers in being lulled into inattention by percentages: a small percentage variance in a large budget line can be more disastrous than a large percentage variance in a small line.

---

[10]The comparison between expenditure plan and spending activity must include both payments made and contractural commitments made that will involve payment later. These latter totals have different titles in different political jurisdictions (encumbrances and obligations are two) but, regardless of title, they reduce the available spending authority and must be included in the comparison against the expenditure plan.

AUDIT AND EVALUATION

Many audits will be conducted using a prescribed checklist of steps to establish uniformity in the conduct of a class of audits by several different auditors. Much of the audit will focus on controls built into the systems of the agency. If the system operates satisfactorily the audit agency need not be concerned with tracing the body of individual transactions because the system will produce substantial compliance. Accounting controls prevent fraud and waste and ensure the accuracy of operations, ensure compliance with applicable laws, and promote adherence to stated policies (including legislation). The audit determines whether those control systems work. In their audit, examiners look for errors and abuses such as those listed in Table 3–2. Much of the audit will employ statistical sampling to permit probabilistic inferences about the extent of error in the full record population. There is seldom reason to scrutinize all records.

Regardless of their relative importance, thefts from government receive extensive publicity when discovered. Thus, it is worthwhile to review some of the methods that have historically been used to steal from government: phantom resources, procurement fixing, honest graft, straightforward theft, shoddy materials, and kickbacks.

1. *Ghosting.* Theft through phantom resources—receiving payment for resources not actually delivered—can take several different forms. One method, the ghost employee, involves placing on an agency payroll individuals who do no work for that agency. The person receives pay but provides no service. A second method is payment for supplies or services which are not actually delivered. Invoices sent by the firm show delivery, but the agency never receives the supplies or services.

TABLE 3–2 Some Errors or Abuses Sought by Auditors

Year-end accounting manipulations that push revenues and expenditures from one year to the next.
Unrecorded liabilities: commitments to vendors that are suppressed by withholding written agreements and purchase orders from the paperwork system.
Overestimation of revenues, to keep down tax rates.
Failure to reserve adequately for nonpayment of taxes.
Miscalculation of utility, hospital, and other service bills.
Unauthorized transfer of funds between appropriation accounts.
Recording of grant receipts in the wrong funds.
Use of a commingled cash account to disguise use of restricted funds for unauthorized purposes.
Failure to observe legal requirements for review and approval of budgets.
Failure to compile and submit financial reports to state and federal agencies punctually.
Improper computation of state aid claims.

SOURCE: Peter F. Rousmaniere, *Local Government Auditing—A Manual for Public Officials* (New York, N.Y.: Council on Municipal Performance, 1980), p. 10.

FIGURE 3-2 Example of Budget Status Report

BEN FRANKLIN TRANSIT
Expenditure Budget Report
as of
June 30, 1983

% Time Expended 50.00

Account Number	Account Name	Budget	Expended	Obligated	Expended and Obligated	Balance	%
100	Transportation Fund						
41	Operations and maintenance						
	Operations						
11	Salaries and wages						
01	Salaries and wages—operators	800,000.00	454,671.21		454,671.21	525,328.74	46
02	Salaries and wages—others	109,000.00	46,223.94		46,223.94	62,776.06	42
12	Overtime—operators						
01	Overtime operators	27,000.00	27,690.72		27,690.72	690.72 –	103
13	Benefits	474,000.00	197,323.60		127,323.60	276,676.40	42
14	Uniforms	10,000.00	4,280.14		4,280.14	5,719.86	43
	Total personal services	1,600,000.00	730,109.61		730,149.61	069,010.39	46
21	Office supplies						
01	Office supplies	10,000.00	1,501.52	125.00	1,626.52	0,323.40	16
02	Copier supplies	2,000.00	547.50		547.50	1,452.50	27
22	Operating supplies						

Code	Item						
01	Transfers	5,000.00	990.74	865.20	1,655.94	3,144.06	37
04	Other	2,600.00	2,329.10	29.01	2,350.11	241.89	91
	Total supplies	19,600.00	5,368.06	1,019.21	6,300.07	13,211.93	33
31	Professional services						
04	Other	3,600.00	88.52		88.52	3,511.48	2
05	Janitorial	3,600.00	1,195.73	400.00	1,575.73	2,004.27	44
32	Communication						
01	Radio system	2,000.00	2,850.44		2,050.44	850.44	143
02	Common carrier	300.00	55.93		55.93	244.07	19
04	Other	200.00	865.17		865.17	665.17	433
33	Transportation						
01	Living expenses	2,000.00	579.17		579.17	1,420.83	29
02	Common carrier	500.00	564.77		564.77	64.77 –	113
03	Personal vehicle mileage	500.00				500.00	
04	Other	500.00				500.00	
34	Advertising						
01	Printer	3,000.00				3,000.00	
35	Printing and binding						
04	Other	5,000.00	2,029.10		2,029.18	2,770.02	41
36	Utilities						
01	Franklin County Public Utility District one quarter	2,000.00	417.66		417.66	1,582.34	21
02	Cascade Natural Gas one quarter	2,000.00	600.53		608.53	1,391.47	30
03	Water one quarter	200.00	144.40		144.40	55.60	72
04	Other one quarter	200.00	60.58		60.50	132.42	30
05	Heating oil four quarters	6,000.00	3,605.36		3,605.36	2,394.64	60

Closely related is double payment for supplies or services. The services are performed once, but invoices show delivery of two shipments. Each method causes government to pay for resources not delivered and each artificially increases the cost of public service.

2. *Bid rigging.* The procurement fix involves the rigging of bids on supply contracts. Suppose a section of highway is to be repaved. Potential suppliers would establish beforehand the bid winner and the winning price; other firms would submit noncompetitive bids for show alone. Firms would cooperate in the collusion because their turn to win would come on another project. The collusion increases the profits of the firms and increases the cost of government. Government employees may or may not profit from the procurement fix, depending on the arrangements of the bid rigging.

3. *Honest graft.* "Honest" graft uses advance information to produce private profit for the individual employee. The reminiscenes of George Washington Plunkitt, Tammany Hall leader of the early 20th century, describe the process:

> There's an honest graft, and I'm an example of how it works. I might sum up the whole thing by sayin': I seen my opportunities and I took 'em.
>
> Just let me explain by example. My party's in power in the city, and it's goin' to undertake a lot of public improvements. Well, I'm tipped off, say, that they're going to lay out a new park at a certain place.
>
> I see my opportunity and I take it. I go to that place and I buy up all the land I can in the neighborhood. Then the board of this or that makes its plan public, and there is a rush to get my land, which nobody cared particular for before.
>
> Ain't it perfectly honest to charge a good price and make a profit on my investment and foresight.[11]

That profit measures the extent to which the honest grafter, through use of inside information, steals from the public by forcing excess payments for a resource. Honest graft may likewise involve acquisition or establishment of companies to do business with a government. Bid specifications may be written so that company would be the only one qualified. Prices for the commodity or service would be artificially increased for the enrichment of the government employee.

4. *Diversion.* Public assets or the service of employees may be stolen for private use. Office supplies, equipment, gasoline, and so on are as usable for private purposes as for government activities. Public employees may be diverted to private uses, including construction or maintenance projects on property owned by government officials. Employees are sometimes used as workers in political campaigns while on government time—a special illegal advantage of incumbency. These ac-

---

[11] Recorded by William L. Riordon, *Plunkett of Tammany Hall* (New York: E. P. Dutton, 1963), pp. 3–4.

tivities involve straightforward stealing as individuals use assets owned by government without payment.

5. *Shoddy material.* Because low quality supplies and material can generally be delivered at lower cost than can higher quality supplies and material, government contract specifications require delivery of one quality material. A contractor who provides lower than specified quality ("shoddy material") can thus profit at public expense.

6. *Kickbacks.* Public officials who have power to select who receives contracts to do business with governments, what banks receive public deposits, and who works for government agencies may profit by arranging for artificially high contract awards or artificial wage payments with a portion of that payment kicked back to the government official. The favored individual or firm receives higher than the appropriate price for the contracted service, so is able to profit even after making the payment to the contracting agent.

SOME SPECIAL PROBLEMS OF PUBLIC EMPLOYEE COMPENSATION

Governments ordinarily purchase resources on the open market. Occasionally they use powers of condemnation or draft to acquire resources, but these practices generally conflict with prevailing views of freedom and property ownership. The resources are acquired not because of their individual attributes, but because they can be used to provide desired services to the general public. A very large percentage of the total cost of providing those services does in fact consist of wage and salary payment to individuals. Table 3-3 indicates the share of direct wage and salary payments in total expenditure by governments in 1982–83. The percentage for the federal government is much lower

TABLE 3-3 Relative Expenditure on Wages and Salaries, 1982–1983

	Wages and Salaries as Percent of Total Direct Expenditures	Wages and Salaries as Percent of Current Operating Expenditure
Federal government	13.95	37.71
State governments	25.93	41.90
Local governments	43.37	55.82
Cities	35.59	48.64
Counties	40.00	52.75
Independent public schools	62.58	68.17

SOURCES: Bureau of Census, *Governmental Finances in 1982–83* (GF 83 no. 5); *City Government Finances in 1982–83* (FG83 no. 4); *Finances of Public School Systems in 1982–83* (GF83 no. 10); and *County Government Finances in 1982–83* (GF 83 no. 8).

than for the other levels presented there because the federal government does much spending by contract. The contracted service is produced by private employees receiving salaries from private employers, but the resources are being produced for federal provision. Compensation to those employees, however, is established by the private firms for whom they work. The percentage for local government is much higher—55 percent of current operating expenditure for wages and salaries—and even higher for school districts independent of other local governments. Those data clearly demonstrate that much of the cost of modern government will be determined by the compensation paid to employees. The tendency over the years, however, has been for the wage and salary component to decline as a percentage of expenditure at each level.

Wages and Salaries

A reasonable objective of an employee compensation program is to ensure delivery of public service at least cost to the taxpayer. The key question is whether the government can obtain and retain employees with desired skills, balancing the interests of taxpayers/service recipients against the interests of public employees. If employees are overpaid, the taxpayer pays too much for services provided; if employees are underpaid, the taxpayer receives artificial subsidization at the expense of those employees, and government must bear the disruption and cost of high employee turnover. Neither situation is healthy for the survival of the community, and both artificially increase the full cost of government.

With that background, it is reasonable to question how the appropriate wage rates might be established. Although some salaries continue to be set by law passed by higher units of government or by tradition, a large number of governments now establish payment through classification and wage comparability studies or through collective bargaining with employee unions. Both structures will be considered here because they have somewhat different implications for finance officers.

There are, however, problems with the logic of salary comparability. First, some public sector positions have no business equivalents in the relevant market area. It is difficult, for instance, to establish a comparable position to fire fighters (duty hours, danger, special skills, etc.) in most localities and any positions actually found may be occupied by off-duty fire fighters, a circumstance not likely to produce reasonable full-time pay equivalents. That would not be a problem for secretaries, data processing personnel, and other general-skill personnel found working for government, but is a problem not easily solved for other positions.

Second, government is the predominant employer of numerous employment skills in some labor markets. Actions resulting from comparability studies will bring compensating private employer reactions which then feed through comparability, in a continuing cycle. In that circumstance, private local markets simply are not especially helpful and private markets in other areas do not provide usable guidance because regional peculiarities can influence prevailing wages. (Some areas are generally desirable to live in and others are not, according to the reactions of individual families.)

Third, wage comparisons are complicated by differences in employment stability and by differences in fringe benefits provided public and private employees. Public employment tends to be more stable than employment in business. Business employment depends on product and service sales, which fluctuate with general economic conditions. When the economy slumps, employees are laid off. That employment instability does not occur with public employment—the work force remains stable during economic decline. Because of the difference in employment stability, positions paying the same rate will, over time, yield the public employee greater income than is received by the private employee. Just as work stability varies between private and public employment, so too does the extent of employer-financed fringe benefits.[12] Unless care is taken to adjust compensation levels for fringe benefits, true comparability will not be attained. While adjustments for fringe benefits are frequently made—with uneven success—there is no satisfactory adjustment for stability differences presently available.

Finally, public and private employees typically work with dramatically different capital endowments. Thus, secretaries in private business often work with word processing equipment which enables them to make rapid draft changes, to produce perfect copy quickly and to make multiple copies easily. Secretaries in many local governments continue to use nonelectric typewriters. As a result, output per day differs dramatically between the two secretaries (regardless of how skilled the secretaries are, in fact). If the two secretaries are paid comparable rates, the cost of the public service is artificially high—to the detriment of citizens/taxpayers. It is not clear what adjustments could appropriately be made to allow properly for those productivity differences.

Such pay classification is attractive for budget makers because it makes budget estimation relatively simple, particularly in comparison to the uncertainty produced by salaries established through collective bargaining. (Some of those uncertainties will be discussed shortly.) The budget officer determines the personnel classification of individuals to

---

[12]Roy W. Bahl and Bernard Jump, "The Budgetary Implications of Rising Employee Retirement System Costs," *National Tax Journal* 27 (September 1974), pp. 479–90.

be handling the workload during the budget year, determines the salary for each classification, and multiplies the number of people in the classification by the salary of that classification to obtain the budget requirement. Many units will structure their compensation schedules so that personnel receive automatic increments with each year on the job. That situation is handled by adding one year to the experience of those currently working and using that experience factor in the schedules. There is thus a permanence of structure that is convenient in classified schedules.

The second method of public-sector salary establishment is through collective bargaining with employee unions. Salaries are determined by bargaining skills and relative power; comparisons with private employers are not directly relevant. A former budget director of the city of New York reports that public sector union militancy

> has made the job of the budget director more difficult and more complex. More accurately, it has made the job, at least in the city of New York, almost impossible. In smaller and simpler governments, the diagnosis is not likely to be that dismal.[13]

His reasons for that extreme observation hinge around the reduced ability of the budget director to manage the budget within a collective bargaining environment. That is because (1) the municipal labor relations director and the union leaders are comfortable with each other and not with questions of budgets and resource constraints; (2) salary changes for one employee group create disruptions in historic relationships with other groups (sanitation with police and fire fighters, for instance) which bring demands for more changes; (3) work rules prevent changes to introduce new technologies or otherwise improve productivity; and (4) unsettled union contracts make budget preparation and approval uncertain, because salaries, a major component of total expenditure, remain undetermined.

The relationship between the budget process and the collective bargaining process is interesting because of the importance of spending on employee wages and salaries relative to total spending. Derber and colleagues point out: "Collective bargaining introduces considerations that may not be entirely compatible with traditional budget-making practices."[14] The budget process presumably establishes the size of the government and the allocation of finances among various activities; bargaining establishes labor cost of the government. Participants in a budget process occurring before bargaining will have to guess the out-

---

[13]Frederick O. R. Hayes, " Collective Bargaining and the Budget Director," in *Public Workers and Public Unions,* ed. Sam Zagoria (Englewood Cliffs, N.J., Prentice-Hall, 1972), p. 89.

[14]Milton Derber et al., " Bargaining and Budget Making in Illinois Public Institutions," *Industrial and Labor Relations Review* 27 (October 1973), p. 49.

come of that bargaining to use in the personnel cost ceiling for bargaining. Bargaining then becomes only a process for dividing the funds approved in the budget. On the other hand, bargaining before budgeting will determine a large fraction of the total budget. In sum, a failure to integrate the two processes reduces the significance of whichever process occurs last.

There are some ways that governments have devised to accomodate the failure to synchronize budgeting and bargaining. They all involve adding flexibility to one process or the other. Bargaining can be made flexible by providing for retroactive pay or supplemental negotiation if bargaining occurs before budget passage. Budgets can be made more flexible through transfer of funds between accounts or supplemental appropriations. If they are not conducted simultaneously, it is critical that the process occurring first have some provision for revision after the other has occurred. Otherwise, participants in the second process will claim—and with some justification—that their hands have been tied by the other process.

Public sector bargaining grows, even as bargaining covers a continually smaller fraction of private employment. Several analysts argue that public sector bargaining is not desirable:

> In private sector bargaining two responsible parties meet with power to represent themselves. But when public service unions demand collective bargaining rights and ultimate arbitration, they do not contemplate dealing with taxpayers, who, responsibly, are saddled with paying the bills. Instead, the public service union hopes to wrangle it out with other public employees who in many cases happen to be dependent on union votes and union money. Market considerations are far away, and mayors are just other hired hands.[15]

The problem is described as the Hanslowe effect, "a neat mutual back scratching mechanism, whereby public employee representatives and politicians reinforce the other's interest and domain."[16] In that circumstance, the personnel cost share will expand, with little the public can do. The crunch ultimately comes when service cost encounters limits imposed by referenda. What happens then is not clear, but public service delivery will undoubtedly suffer during the transition.

Retirement Programs

Public employee retirement programs—the delayed, but often lucrative, portion of employee compensation—typically include two elements:

[15]John Chamberlin, "When Cops and Teachers Strike," *The Wall Street Journal,* October 22, 1975, p. 16.

[16]Kurt L. Hanslowe, *The Emerging Law of Labor Relations in Public Employment* (Ithaca, N.Y.: New York School of Industrial and Labor Relations, Cornell University, 1967), p. 268.

social security coverage financed through a federal trust fund and a retirement plan provided by the employer. Payroll taxes on employer and employee finance the social security system; payments by the employer and, usually, by the employee finance the latter. State and local governments can, however, choose to be excluded from the social security system, a choice not available to private employers. There are several separate retirement systems for federal government employees. Those for civil service and the military are the two largest. A number of governments outside the system and, in the past few years, a handful left the system, feeling that equivalent or better coverage could be provided employees at lower cost. To leave is now forbidden.

Social Security

There are fundamental differences between social security for public employees and public employee pension systems, even though both are payments made by government to a government employee. Most significant is the fact that the pension is part of an employer-employee exchange; it is a contractural or insurance relationship involving an agreement about delayed compensation. Social security is a relationship between government and a claimant on that government; it is not an employer-employee relationship and, possibly unfortunately, there is no delayed compensation agreement involved. With that system, the federal government supports politically determined benefits with politically determined taxes—there is no employer-employee contractual agreement involved.

Taxes on payrolls finance social security benefits—half legally from the employer, half legally from the employee. Many analysts believe that a much larger share, possibly all, of that burden actually rests on the employee as employers adjust rates of wages or other compensation to allow for the payroll tax owed. If the tax is shifted to the employee, the two parts combined would currently equal a flat rate of over 12 percent on wages and salaries, by far the largest tax burden on many people. Receipts from the tax go to the Social Security Trust Fund, a special fund the federal government uses for social insurance transactions. Any money in the fund is invested in U.S. government securities to provide financing for general government activities. When individuals become eligible for social security assistance, money from the fund (contributions and interest earned) or from payroll taxes paid by those in the current work force cover the expenditure. Levels of benefits and eligibility for them are legislatively determined, although regular benefits are normally based on earnings during the last 10 years worked before retirement. After retirement, benefits can increase by legislative decision.

For many years, there were relatively large numbers of people in the workforce contributing to the fund and relatively few people receiving benefits from it. (The system only began in the mid-1930s.) As a result, the trust fund grew in size as inflow substantially exceeded outflow. In recent years, more eligible people have retired and, at the same time, retirees have been living longer. Fund accumulation has reversed and payroll taxes have increased substantially to cover promised payments. Unfortunately, the payroll tax is significantly regressive (it is a flat tax, it covers only wage and salary income, and it does not apply to income above specified limits) and legislators are reluctant to use it more heavily. Congress continues liberalization of benefits, including the addition of automatic benefit increases tied to the consumer price index. Unfortunately, the rate of increase of payrolls seldom keeps pace with the consumer price index, so the outflow accelerated with inflation. Tax increases and coverage changes in the early 1980s generally restored the position of the fund at least for a decade or so, but the system will eventually require more attention.

Pensions

The other piece of retirement compensation, public employee pensions, are in worse condition than the social security system and responsibility for repair rests primarily with state and local government. Public employee pension funds have not accumulated sufficient reserves during employee work careers to cover the benefits to which they will be entitled through their retirement. Thus, the government will have to pay from its current revenue in later years part of the compensation promised in earlier years. For example, in fiscal 1990, the government would pay the wages and salaries of the 1990 work force and 1990 pension payments to all prior employees whose work in earlier years entitled them to pensions.

For many years, governments and employees seemed content with this financing approach. There appeared to be little danger of missed payments to employees, because governments do not go out of business or get acquired by conglomerates, the dangers faced by private employees. Payments can easily be made by raising taxes on the future tax base. Jump aptly summarizes the traditional view of state and local employee pensions:

> The pension, along with a degree of job security not generally associated with employment in the private sector, was assumed to be a fair offset for lower wages in public sector jobs. Commonly, public pension administration encountered few problems that required more than perfunctory attention from governments' top elected and professional officials. Each year, legislatures appropriated whatever was needed to cover the year's share of

pension costs. In some jurisdictions, appropriations simply equalled the actual benefits to be paid during the year; in other instances, appropriations reflected at least nominally the actuarial cost of benefits accrued during the year by active employees. As long as work force size, benefit levels, and the number of retirees did not grow too rapidly and the jurisdiction's financial condition remained stable, the fiscal implications of the pensions did not appear to be significant.[17]

That easy approach to pensions was battered in the 1970s. Expenditures for employee retirement suddenly increased, absolutely and relative to current personnel cost, as many employees started drawing lucrative pensions. State and local governments began encountering impressive resistance to tax increases, including new constitutional restrictions against rate increases, and some governments teetered on the brink of default on contractual obligations in the midst of fiscal crisis. Credit rating firms, bond underwriters, and investors all became aware of the risk associated with loans to governments whose sizable long-term pension liabilities could endanger repayment of debt. And, possibly most important, investigators discovered an important incentive problem with traditional pension finance: elected officials could seek public employee support with generous pension promises now, knowing that when the payments were made, those officials would not be part of the governing team required to raise those funds. From those influences came a major effort to switch public pension finance from the traditional pay-as-you-go basis to an actuarial funding basis.

Actuarial funding is "a procedure where the estimated cost—the actuarial present value—of pension benefits accruing to active employees is systematically paid by the employer into a fund (perhaps with a share paid in by the employee as well). In turn, the retirement fund makes payments to retirees and invests surplus funds."[18] Thus, the anticipated future cost of pension payments to an employee will be handled while the employee is working. Pension payments on retirement will come from money set aside during the years of employment plus interest on that accumulation. Funding will be on the basis of estimates computed on several assumptions: whether and when the employee will retire, when the retired employee will die, the progression of employee salary, and the rate of interest earned on invested pension funds. None of those factors will be known; all must be reviewed and revised on a reasonable schedule if funding is to be meaningful.

---

[17]Bernard Jump, Jr., "Public Employment, Collective Bargaining, and Employee Wages and Pensions," in *State and Local Government Finance and Financial Management: A Compendium of Current Research,* ed. John E. Petersen et al., (Washington, D.C: Government Finance Research Center, Municipal Finance Officers Association, 1978), p. 78.

[18]Bernard Jump, Jr., *State and Local Employee Pension Plans: Watching for Problems* (Columbus, Ohio: Academy for Contemporary Problems, 1976), p. 9.

TABLE 3-4 Aggregates of State and Local Government Employee Retirement Systems, 1982–1983

Item	All Systems	State Administered Systems	Locally Administered Systems	Percentage Change since 1972–73, All Systems
Receipts	57,906	45,127	12,779	289.2
Employee contribution	8,699	7,196	1,503	108.8
Government contributions	22,936	17,197	5,739	245.0
From states	9,862	9,611	251	229.5
From local governments	13,271	20,734	5,489	257.6
Earnings on investments	26,271	20,734	5,537	546.4
Payments	19,788	14,604	5,183	240.5
Benefits	17,484	12,757	4,727	253.4
Withdrawals	1,770	1,447	323	104.9
Cash and security holdings at end of fiscal year				
Total	289,731	229,685	60,046	269.5
Cash and deposits	8,983	6,063	2,920	722.6
Governmental securities	71,953	55,826	16,128	1343.4
Federal government	69,471	55,066	14,405	1908.4
United States Treasury	44,672	33,982	10,690	n.a.*
Federal agency	24,798	21,083	3,715	n.a.
State and local government	2,483	760	1,723	62.7
Nongovernmental	208,795	167,796	40,999	188.6
Corporate bonds	78,723	62,305	16,418	81.7
Corporate stocks	70,415	55,858	14,557	312.7
Mortgages	25,457	23,983	1,475	273.4
Other securities	22,405	15,202	7,204	n.a.
Other investments	11,795	10,448	1,345	n.a.

*n.a. = Not available.

SOURCE: U.S. Bureau of Census, *Finances of Employee—Retirement Systems of State and Local Governments in 1982–83* (GF83 no. 2).

Table 3–4 shows that public employee retirement systems have made progress toward funding in the aggregate. In fiscal 1983, payments from state-administered systems were covered by earnings on pension fund investments, so did not rely on current contributions. Locally administered funds were not, however, so fortunate; earnings did not cover pay outs. Also in that table should be noted: (1) the high contributions by government to the funds relative to contributions made by the employee; (2) the relatively heavy investment of system holdings in corporate bonds; (3) the small holdings of state and local securities by the funds (and such holdings at all are probably a mistake, in light of the low net yields on them); (4) the growth in federal government security holdings over the decade; and (5) the greater increase in receipts than in payments to move toward actuarial soundness. Of course, much variation among systems is submerged in these aggregate data.

When pension funds accumulate, they become attractive and lucrative targets for abuse.[19] First, some governments have used employee

---

[19]Louis M. Kohlmeier, *Conflicts of Interest: State and Local Pension Fund Asset Management* (New York: Twentieth Century Fund, 1976).

pension funds as guaranteed markets for their own debt. The debt yields an artificially low rate of return because interest on state and local debt is excluded from federal taxation—a benefit of no value to the public employee pension fund because it is not subject to federal tax. Second, pension fund management is sometimes restrained to local firms in an effort to assist those firms, even though they may lack the expertise or scale for high quality, low-cost management. Both actions cause pension participants to lose potential return. Whether these actions are questionable depends on the role of pensions: are they compensation for work rendered or are they gratuities given past employees? If the former, those actions clearly represent mismanagement as they sacrifice net earnings of funds owned by pension participants. If the latter, the funds may be regarded as fair game for any public purpose because they belong to the host government. Governments and employees may have different answers to the role of pensions, although logic is stronger for the compensation and employee ownership view.

CONCLUSION

Budget skills combine techniques which can be taught and cunning which develops with experience. The start for all budgets must be a sound understanding of what the agency request intends to accomplish. Without that foundation, no amount of tricks can help much. As in many government operations, the great problem is information—those who have that information and are able to communicate it will have greater than average success. Beyond that, there are few general truths.

Questions and Exercises

1. The following information about the Marshall Fire Department for fiscal year July 1, 19X5, to June 30, 19X6, is to be used for the questions.

Personnel:

Employee Grade	Number in Grade	Salary
Chief	1	$43,000
Shift commander	3	40,000
Firefighter 1	12	25,000
Firefighter 2	24	20,000
Clerical (part-time)	2	9,000

The city is part of the federal social security system. For calendar year 19X5, the city and the employee each pay 7.05 percent of all salaries up to $39,600 paid to an employee in the year. For 19X6, the rate will be 7.15 percent on the first $42,000 of earnings. For calendar 19x4, the rate was 7.00 percent on salaries up to $37,800. (The salary paid the chief in the 19X5 fiscal year was $40,000; shift commanders received $36,000.)

The city pays a portion of the cost of hospital insurance for each full-time employee, an amount equal to $80 per month. The insurance rate will increase to $90 per month on January 1, 19X6.

Employees on the payroll, regardless of hiring date, after June 30, 19X5 are part of a new pension system, financed by city payment of 20 percent of the employee's salary and employee payment of 5 percent of the employee's salary on pay received after that date. Payments up to that date were made by state appropriations from state tobacco tax revenue.

Full-time employees receive an allowance for uniforms of $600 per year.

Questions:

a. Compute the full cost to the city of fire department labor during the 19X6 fiscal year assuming no change in the personnel complement. Separate that cost into salary and fringe benefit components.

b. What would be the annual cost impact of hiring one additional firefighter 2 in fiscal 19X6?

2. A midwestern city has contracted with a solid-waste and disposal firm for service during the five years from January 1, 19X7, to December 31, 19Y1. Selected provisions of the contract state:

THE BIDDER HEREBY PROPOSES to furnish all required materials, supplies, solid-waste disposal facilities and equipment; to provide and perform all necessary labor and supervision; and to perform all work stipulated in, required by, and in accordance with, the proposed contract documents and the specifications, and other documents referred to therein (as altered, amended, or modified by addenda), in the manner and time prescribed, and to accept in full payment sums determined by the bid plus the following unit price plus or minus any special payments and adjustments provided in the specifications.

Proposition 1

For the complete performance of all the terms, conditions, and provisions of Proposition 1, as per specifications, namely:

A five (5) year contract providing for total solid waste (including garbage, rubbish, and household rubbish) collection and disposal on a weekly schedule from:

a. Curb or alley location for each household unit.
b. Proper storage area for apartment complexes.
c. Approved curb location for mobile home courts.

Also, daily collection (five days per week) and disposal of garbage from commercial food service establishments, all in accordance with regulations described herein.

Total base amount per year, $1,598,888.33, subject to adjustments provided in the specifications.

Proposition 2

Adjustments in the contract price for the providing of collection and disposal of solid waste caused by changes in the total number of residences or commercial food service establishments and active fire stations referred to herein, resulting from annexation, deannexation, new construction, or demolition.

Per collection unit change $34.89

The contract also contains an escalator cause to handle changes in the cost of doing business. The clause states:

The compensation payable to the contractor for the second and subsequent years of the term hereof shall be adjusted upward or downward to reflect changes in the cost of doing business as measured by fluctuations in the consumer price index, published by the U.S. Department of Labor, Bureau of Labor Statistics, for "All items" in the "U.S. City Average" category. At the start of the second year and every year thereafter, the compensation to the contractor shall be increased or decreased in a percent amount equal to one fourth of the net percentage changes in the said consumer price index computed as follows: Beginning with the first month of the second year, the net change shall be the difference between the said consumer price index during the month immediately prior to the beginning of the first contract year and the last month of said year, and said percentage change shall be computed annually in like manner for each subsequent year of the contract.

In addition to the above, the following evaluation will be made:

Ten (10) days after the beginning of the second and each subsequent contract year, a determination shall be made of the then existing status of the wage scale of regular drivers and laborers of the City Street Department. For each 1 percent of average rate change over or under the rate prevailing at bid time, the contractor's yearly compensation shall be adjusted up or down by 3/4 of 1 percent of his total bid, effective at the beginning of each succeeding contract year. The wage rate at the time of bidding for fully qualified men with over 15 months' experience in the City Street Department of the city is $5.01 per hour for drivers and $4.74 per hour for laborers.

Additional Information

a. The consumer price index (1967 = 100) has behaved in the following fashion in recent years:

19X5:

December	166.3

19X6:		19X7:	
January	166.7	January	175.3
February	167.1	February	177.1
March	167.5	March	178.2
April	168.2	April	179.6
May	169.2	May	180.6
June	170.1	June	181.8
July	171.1	July	182.6
August	171.9	August	183.3
September	172.6	September	184.0
October	173.3	October	184.5
November	173.8	November	185.4
December	174.3	December	186.1

Annual:

19X4	147.7
19X5	161.2
19X6	170.5
19X7	186.1

b. The street department signed a two-year contract for 19X8–X9 with an 8 percent wage increase.

c. The national pattern of wages and salaries per full-time equivalent state-local government employee (noneducation) has been:

19X3	$ 9,170
19X4	9,822
19X5	10,517
19X6	11,126

Questions

a. Compute the payment to the contractor for 19X8 if 278 units are annexed and 13 are demolished.

b. The city is proposing to annex an area with 45 collection units. What is the garbage collection charge for this area likely to be in 19X9, 19Y0, and 19Y1?

3. Write budget request and justifications for each of the following program conditions. Start your request by categorizing each request as (a) new service, (b) other continuing, (c) workload change, (d) change in service level, (e) price change, (f) full financing, or (g) methods improvement. The program conditions:

- The agency sends about 275,000 pieces of mail each year. The postal rate has increased by two cents per ounce.

- The division travel appropriation has been $7,000 per year short of actual expenditure for the last three years, after internal transfers of funds.

- Fifteen account examiners process 115,000 assistance files per year. Client growth estimates indicate that, in the next budget biennium, files will increase to 125,000 in the first year and 130,000 in the second. (Account examiners' salaries are $1,775 per month plus fringe benefits of 22 percent.)
- The city council appropriated $18,000 for a program to track down those not paying traffic fines. The program began in the second quarter of fiscal year and has produced fine revenue far greater than its cost. The legal affairs division wants to continue the program through the entire new fiscal year.
- The division wants to replace one typewriter with a microcomputer, letter quality printer, and wordprocessing software.

4. From records maintained over several years, the local water utility finds that its monthly purchases of raw water from the state water authority follow these patterns:

Gallons (000s)		Gallons (000s)	
January	35,000	July	125,000
February	35,000	August	100,000
March	50,000	September	85,000
April	65,000	October	60,000
May	68,000	November	50,000
June	100,000	December	40,000

Presume that the city pays a flat rate per thousand gallons of water purchased and that the fiscal year begins on July 1. Payment is made in the month after use. Prepare quarterly allotments for $4 million appropriated for water purchase.

5. A progress report for the division of streets and roads prepared for transactions through March 31 shows:

	Appropriation	Allotment by Quarter					
Object Class	July 1–June 30	I	II	III	IV	Encumbrance	Expenditure
Utilities	$ 57,000	$ 11,000	$17,000	$ 17,000	$ 12,000	$15,000	$ 38,000
Travel	3,000	800	750	600	850	700	1,400
Materials	300,000	90,000	50,000	100,000	60,000	20,000	225,000
Equipment	175,000	30,000	30,000	85,000	30,000	30,000	115,000
Total	$535,000	$131,800	$97,750	$202,600	$102,850	$65,700	$379,400

What is the status of each object class? What managerial actions are appropriate?

6. Analyze this budget justification:

Workload Change—19X5–X7 Biennial Cost: $84,300

Because of the recognition of new social procedures, our psychometricians are now able to obtain valid test results and scores, enabling our evaluators to make sociological recommendations which are re-alistic and not stereotyped views of battering. Our evaluation professionals plus specialty counselors with special training, in con-junction with their statewide supervisors, have made great strides in bringing together battered spouses throughout the state. In order to achieve maximum effectiveness, an additional four counselor teams to be strategically located are essential. This success factor which we have experienced has also brought about an increase in the referral of abused children, which will also require additional case service funds.

a. List the questions you would raise about the jurisdiction if you were a budget analyst.

b. Rewrite the justification.

Cases for Discussion

A   In 1984, the city of Chicago began an experimental garbage col-lection program in five wards of the city. The new system would replace the 55-gallon garbage drums distributed by elected aldermen with 90-gallon wheeled carts issued by the city. The carts would reduce cost by cutting one worker from each sanitation crew. The following article de-tails the experiment from the standpoint of the aldermen, sanitation workers, and citizens. It is a fine illustration of the inertia than can de-velop in public service delivery systems.

Consider These Questions

1. *Identify the viewpoint of each person in the process.*
2. *How could use of a private sanitation service provider change the decision process?*
3. *How does the traditional budget process based on line-item appropriation to departments create inertia in the way services are provided?*

Trial Garbage System Littered with Tales

By Howard Witt

Seldom has the aldermanic mind exerted as much creative energy as has been devoted to debunking Chicago's experimental 90-gallon garbage carts.

To hear a chorus of aldermen tell it, the black plastic carts, which have now replaced all the traditional 55-gallon steel drums in five wards across the city, have been gnawed through by squirrels and infested by rats; crushed, blown over and vandalized; frozen in ice; and stolen by gang members.

Senior citizens have had trouble moving them; sanitation workers have been injured trying to lift them; and some of the carts might even have exploded in the dead of night.

"There is," Ald. Frank Damato (37th) pronounces, "no possible way this system can work."

But interviews with city officials, sanitation workers, residents of the experimental wards and even a few renegade aldermen suggest that the new system is working, that it's saving money and that it's a long-overdue innovation.

"I love this better than I do my wife," exulted 8th Ward sanitation worker Thomas Bibbs, 50, as he rolled a cart onto a lifting device on the back of a garbage truck one frigid morning last week. "There's no more lifting those heavy cans."

The system "gives us the opportunity to move into the next century on garbage," said Ald. Marian Humes (8th), whose South Side ward was the first to receive the experimental carts last September.

So successful have the carts proven that plans now call for using them in about 35 wards, sanitation officials say, with an alternate system that would employ much larger containers in the more densely populated lakefront wards.

The Road to the cart experiment has been strewn with vigorous opposition. More than two years ago, sanitation department officials began studying a more efficient replacement for the city's traditional four-man garbage crews, who for years have been straining to hoist rusting, 55-gallon steel drums into the back of their trucks.

Streets and Sanitation Commissioner Lester Dickinson said most major cities long ago outlawed the drums because of injuries they caused sanitation workers, such as muscle strains and broken feet. Lids for the drums, when available, never stay on; dogs knock the drums over; and scattered garbage attracts rodents, foes of the drums argue.

Source: *Chicago Tribune,* December, 1984. Reprinted by courtesy of The Chicago Tribune.

A year ago, the sanitation department recommended switching to the carts, used by a number of large cities, including Washington, D.C., and Milwaukee. The carts, with wheels and attached lids, are dumped into the garbage trucks by hydraulic lifters and require only three-man crews: two people behind the truck and a driver.

Labor savings in the experimental wards, Dickinson said, are estimated to be $2.4 million in 1985.

The Chicago City Council, unmoved by Dickinson's estimates that the cart system would save up to $20 million over five years, resisted the change, motivated at least in part by the traditional importance of doling out the steel drums as a vote-getting device. Aldermen finally approved an experimental use of the carts in the 6th, 8th, 34th, 39th and 41st Wards.

By far the most popular refrain now being heard, as the council debates appropriating $4.5 million to expand the program into seven more wards, is that the plastic carts will not survive a Chicago winter. Sanitation officials counter that the carts have withstood winters in Milwaukee.

Beyond the fear of winter, there remain a number of old familiar concerns—and a few new ones:

The plastic carts could explode. Ald. Bernard Hansen (44th), who favors the council majority bloc's plan to continue the cart experiment in the five wards for a year before expanding the program, has suggested this as a danger because the cart lids could trap combustible gases inside.

"Those containers are sort of vacuum-tight," Hansen said. "Maybe they could drill little holes in them to let off any pressure that might build up."

There have been no reports of explosions, Dickinson said.

Squirrels are gnawing little holes into the carts. Other aldermen voice complaints similar to those of Ald. Robert Kellam (18th) who said: "The containers are being eaten by squirrels."

There have in fact been some cases of squirrels gnawing at the tops of the plastic carts, but none has been serious enough to warrant replacement, sanitation officials say. They add that such gnawing means the squirrels must be quite hungry, which they take as a sign that the carts are keeping garbage out of alleys and streets.

Rats are crawling through the holes caused by the squirrels and then jumping out at sanitation workers when they empty the carts. This did happen, Dickinson said—once. In fact, he added, rat populations have dropped in many areas of the experimental wards because incidences of open garbage have decreased.

Street gang members will steal the carts and then "rent" them to frightened residents. Damato has raised this fear, echoed by other aldermen. There have been no reports of this happening, however, Dickinson said. Of the 75,000 carts in the five wards, only 307 have been reported stolen and, of those, 122 have been recovered just down the alley or up the street.

The carts will be vandalized. "What if I'm a neighbor and I throw a heavy piece of concrete in your cart and it cracks?" Damato suggested. "Who's going to replace it.?"

The city would, answered Dickinson, who added that he has had no reports of vandalism or unneighborly acts to the carts.

Senior citizens will have trouble moving the 90-gallon carts. "Take a senior citizen, a widow," Kellam suggested. "Can she handle getting that thing out to the curb?"

No problem, answered Altha Corbins, an 8th Ward resident. "I'm 70 years old, and it's fine to wheel it. They're wonderful. I'm so angry (the aldermen) are trying to make an issue out of these carts when there are so many more important things to concern them."

Sanitation workers will be injured. "Suppose it's cold out," said Ernest Kumerow, president of Local 1001 of the Laborers International Union of North America, which represents all city sanitation workers. "Some of these fellows are getting anxious, so they want to tip the container before (the hydraulic lift) is all the way up. There's going to be injuries and disabilities."

"How can you get injured with this?" asked sanitation worker Walter Jones, 34, as he demonstrated how it takes only about 10 seconds to roll the cart to the truck, empty it and roll it back to a resident's yard. "There's less of a chance of being injured because we don't have to lift anything."

No workers have reported being injured by the carts, Dickinson said, and the city could save $2 million annually in disability payments if it were expanded.

Damato, one of the stauchest doomsayers, said he nevertheless would want the system if it is expanded to other wards. "If you're going to give it to other aldermen, then I want it. . . . If they're going to do it, then put it in my ward and let it be a total failure."

There have been some whispers of optimism in the wilderness. More than 90 percent of 8th Ward residents surveyed by the sanitation department said they liked the system, Dickinson said, adding that he has received requests from a dozen aldermen who want to be included in the program.

So what's really standing in the way? Dickinson speculated that the Laborers union is exerting pressure on the city council to resist a system that reduces the number of union members. (There have been and will be no layoffs as a result of the program, Dickinson said; the reduction in force of 103 workers so far has been achieved by attrition.)

And a number of those interviewed said they believe the council's majority bloc is resisting the cart system precisely because it appears to be so successful. They said the aldermen do not want Mayor Harold Washington to be able to take credit for it.

B   Budgeting would be easier if rules could be established to eliminate the need for human decisions and if incentives could be established which would induce individuals to behave in a desirable fashion.
Those rules and incentives are, however, difficult to invent for public
agencies. If they were simple to create, they would have been enacted
years ago.

The following case, excerpted from *The Wall Street Journal*, illustrates what can happen when a desirable goal is approached by a broad,
general rule.

Consider These Questions

1. *What orientation toward budgeting does the approach applied by
   Senator Sasser represent?*
2. *What is the senator's objective? Is it worthwhile?*
3. *How might the desired effect be achieved without the unexpected
   results of the approach used here?*

Federal Travel Cuts Can Take a Big Slice Out of Unrelated Pies

by Brooks Jackson

WASHINGTON—To some people, the skies appear dark with federal
employees flying about unncessarily. "There are probably more than
20,000 government employees in the air at any one time." Sen. James
Sasser once declared. "I think 18,000 would be sufficient."

Senator Sasser, a Tennessee Democrat, played a lead role in per-
suading Congress to slash $500 million from last year's federal travel
and transportation budget. Then he asserted the action had saved
that much in "unnecessary travel."

Ronald Reagan no doubt was similarly concerned about needless
travel when he signed an executive order, within 48 hours of becoming
president, aimed at cutting $300 million from the year's $3.7 billion
travel budget.

Yet the evidence is that last year's cuts went well beyond frivolous
government travel, into such things as law enforcement, military
training, and safety inspections in factories and mines.

OMB's Study

The cut did help prompt the White House Office of Management and Budget to look for more ways to save money in government travel. And in sampling travel vouchers for the first time, the OMB found to its amazement that there really are an average of 20,000 one-way commercial flights each day by civilian and military federal employees.

But OMB also found that only about 14.5 percent of government travel is for speeches, conferences, and meetings—the sort of travel most often criticized as excessive. Most goes for operations, training, or relocation.

As a result of last year's travel cut, law enforcement by federal park rangers literally came to a standstill for three months on the Natchez Trace Parkway, which winds through federal parklands in Tennessee, Mississippi, and a corner of Alabama. On the parkway, and at many other national parks as well, government trucks and cars are leased and therefore show up as "travel" under federal accounting procedures.

So to meet their share of the travel reduction, Natchez park rangers ceased patrolling and responded only to emergency calls. "We didn't chase any violators," recalls David L. Tomlinson, chief ranger. "People were really hotfooting it there for a while."

Increase in Road Deaths

Ranger Tomlinson says fatalities on the road doubled from five in 1979 to 10 last year, and vandalism increased at remote campsites. Collections of litter and garbage, using the leased vehicle, were cut to one day a week from five, and road repairs were deferred.

At the Defense Department, which accounts for roughly 70 percent of federal travel money, military training was affected. Some maneuvers were scrubbed for lack of funds to get troops to the scene, and summer reserve training was especially hard hit. "For the reserve forces it very nearly amounted to a training disaster," asserts the Association of the U.S. Army. "Units had funds to pay for special schooling, but no money to get students to the training."

Operations were curtailed at some agencies whose employees must travel to accomplish their jobs. The Occupational Safety and Health Administration cut the number of job-safety inspections from about 60,000 in 1979 to 50,000 in 1980. For several months, OSHA couldn't send any inspectors to its special training academy in Illinois.

Mine-safety inspections also were reduced. The federal Mine Safety and Health Administration got rid of 200 leased vehicles from its fleet of 1,700. Officials began taking appeals of fines over the telephone, rather than meeting personally with mine operators. The agency also cut back its on-the-scene technical help to mine operators.

Sometimes the cut actually cost taxpayers money. At Shenandoah National Park in Virginia, for example, patrols weren't curtailed, because the park owns its own cars, which are thus charged to "operations" and not to travel. But the travel cut left the park without enough money to pay lodging and carfare for sending six rangers to Roanoke, Virginia, for a five-day course in fighting forest fires.

So the park asked the rangers to commute each day, 150 miles each way, in park-owned cars. The resulting overtime pay showed up as salary, not travel. "We had to pay more and use our own cars to do the same job," said Bill Loftis, assistant park administrator. "We can't believe this is what Congress had in mind."

Indeed, congressional concern about federal travel, typically is directed at bureaucrats the Congressmen view as living it up at public expense as they travel to needless conferences and meetings. "I find two or three people from the same department at a small meeting in Anchorage or Fairbanks," said Alaska's Republican Senator Ted Stevens during consideration of last year's cut. "Of course, a lot of it depends on whether it is the fishing season or not."

A Deceptive Cut

What did the cut accomplish? "I think you can make a good case that it did in fact save $500 million," Senator Sasser insists. Yet the government actually spent more for travel last year than it had budgeted before the cut.

Senator Sasser says the supplemental appropriations were needed because of such unexpected events as the big increase in oil prices and U.S. military operations in the Persian Gulf following seizure of American hostages in Iran and the Soviet invasion of Afghanistan. But Pentagon officials say the supplemental appropriations included enough extra money to wipe out much of the "saving" from Senator Sasser's cut.

Without the extra money, military officials say, shipments of arms and ammunition to Europe and the Mideast would have been curtailed. More than half the $500 million "saving" was scheduled to come not from the $3 billion budgeted for travel, but from the $5 billion budgeted for costs of shipping such things as military equipment and the household goods of transferred federal employees.

The lesson many federal budget officials draw from all this is that meat-ax cuts in travel don't save much money but do make it harder for the government to do its job. "It's the kind of mentality that makes you eliminate one helicopter from a rescue mission to Iran," says one civil servant at the OMB.

Recommended Approach

Wayne Granquist, who headed the OMB's management-improvement efforts in the Carter administration, says that cutting the size of federal programs is the only way to achieve savings in overhead costs of the size claimed by Senator Sasser and predicted by President Reagan. "Politicians are saying you can save huge sums by cutting out things that nobody thinks are important, such as travel, says Mr. Granquist. "That isn't true. There's no free lunch."

Nonetheless, some travel economies are possible. Indeed, the government says it saved $5.4 million in the last half of 1980 through a new program of bargaining for airline discounts. A new round of discounted fares is expected to yield savings of $12 million in the first six months of this year. The OMB estimates savings from discounts could eventually reach $72 million a year if promoted vigorously.

Another suggested way to save money would be through *looser* regulation of travel. Detailed accountings and audits of travel expenses add $400 million a year to costs associated with travel, the General Accounting Office estimates. Millions could be saved through fewer audits.

It remains to be seen whether savings of $300 million a year, as President Reagan has ordered, are possible without hurting basic government and military operations again.

4

Selected Budget Reform Techniques

Budget processes can help allocate government resources, control agency operations, and manage service delivery. They can be clear statements of plans, priorities, performance, and costs as well as the basic template for administrative control. Unfortunately, prevailing practices often impede the full use of budgeting for planning and analysis to guide public choices. Traditional budgets historically emphasize control of fund use and have not been appropriately structured for resource allocation decisions. That emphasis exists largely because public budgeting emerged in a period when the concern was, purely and simply, prevention of theft. Hence, budgets focused on control of inputs and little else. Modern governments have moved beyond that stage. Governments do provide valued services, so keeping a lid on their actions is not sufficient: budgets no longer are simply devices for restraining thieves. Decision makers must control waste and make allocation choices, so governments need budget structures that permit planning and management for efficiency.

BUDGETS AS A TOOL FOR DECISION MAKING

Traditional budgets embody several impediments to public management and planning. These include (1) the administrative department basis for budget requests and appropriation, (2) the short-period concept for costs in budget considerations, (3) the focus on agency inputs rather than products or outputs, and (4) the absence of comparison of project costs with project benefits. The federal government also has problems with uncontrollability, the problem of spending outside the annual appropriation process. Each will be considered because most reform techniques seek to reduce one or more of these barriers.

135

First, public decisions require meaningful measurement of the total cost of achieving a desired objective. Traditional budget processes do not provide that information. Budgets are proposed and appropriations are made on an administrative department basis, not on the basis of what departments actually intend to achieve. Such categorizations blur the allocation process and impede consideration of alternatives, the essence of resource allocation. Categories of administration—defense, justice, public works, and so forth—are too broad for judgment about the appropriate relative amounts for spending. Further, the agency titles include activity conglomerations that are often more related to the work of other agencies than to each other. In many instances the work of the agency has little to do with what its title sounds like. In short, intelligent resource allocation decisions are unlikely to emerge from budget considerations based on administrative departments. Budgets and appropriations that go through organization charts complicate identification of the cost of achieving a particular objective because most agencies have multiple outputs. Weiss notes the "fallacy of appellation . . . the rhetorical act of obscuring the distinction between the name of a budget category and the actual phenomenon generally associated with that name."[1]

Second, traditional budgets are developed and considered on a single-year basis without development of cost profiles over time. Budgets usually cover a single year of agency operation[2]—an appropriate period for control purposes—even though many activities proposed by an agency have significant future cost implications. The single-year cost often is little more than a program down payment with many installments ahead. Reasonable decision making requires that total cost of a project be examined, not just the single-year project cost. Because such data are seldom a part of the budget process, budget choices must be made without appropriate information.

Third, reasonable choice requires that alternative methods of reaching a desired objective be compared. Agencies traditionally build budgets from existing input combinations. The agencies lock themselves into "normal" operating techniques and alternative methods don't get considered. An important cause is the general focus on what public agencies *buy* (inputs) to the near exclusion of what the agencies *provide* (services or outputs). Ordinary reviews emphasize changes in the objects of expenditure, that is, the personnel to be hired (or fired) and their pay grades, changes in the pay of current staff, and the supplies and equipment to be purchased. An input orientation produces the following logic: if the price of gasoline increases by 25 percent,

---

[1] Edmond H. Weiss, "The Fallacy of Appellation in Government Budgeting," *Public Administration Review* 34 (July/August 1974), p. 377.

[2] Some governments have biennial budgets, but these are essentially single-year budgets times two. Only by accident will the complete cost of a project be captured in a biennial budget.

agency operation requires an increase in the appropriation of those purchases of 25 percent. Otherwise, the agency must cut back its services. That logic implies that the objective of the agency is the purchase of given amounts of specific inputs. A budget process should induce consideration of alternative production strategies to economize on the use of resources which have become relatively more expensive. Seldom is there but a single way to provide a service, and budget processes need to consider alternatives, especially when the price of some inputs has increased dramatically. The reviewers too infrequently consider the public services to be provided with these inputs or the alternative combinations of inputs which could produce those services. A simple analogue to traditional budgeting would be a baker who purchases flour, milk, and sugar, without considering the number of cakes, cookies, breads, and so on to be sold and without considering the alternative recipes for their production. These physical input requirements get selected before any cost estimation and without reference either to alternative production methods or to the programs sacrificed if a particular choice is made.[3]

Fourth, meaningful public decisions must weigh the cost of programs relative to their worth. The line-item costs in traditional budgets are financial, out-of-pockets costs. They exclude social costs not directly paid; they reflect financial transactions, not the value of opportunities not chosen; and they do not distinguish between sunk and incremental costs of actions. Thus, the cost data presented may not be entirely appropriate for making decisions, but budget costs do get reported. Worth of programs delivered, however, seldom is reported or formally considered. That comparison between cost and program value, vital to intelligent resource allocation, is not a regular component of budget processes. Unless some point of the budget process regularly compares total benefits of a program to its cost, poor public decisions are likely. Public decisions based only on program cost—either because costs are high or low—will not consistently lead to a wise use of scarce resources; neither would consideration based solely on project worth to the exclusion of cost. A society with scarcity must require consideration of worth against cost, if only in the sense of considering how society would be poorer in the absence of the service. Regardless of whether worth is easily measurable, no choices are possible solely on a cost basis.

Finally, governments have trouble controlling expenditure from one year to the next in response to changed priorities or to needs for macroeconomic stabilization. At the federal level, a large percentage of

---

[3]Niskanen, Tullock, and others point out that government agency administrators have individual incentives to spend as much as possible (conduct any project at the highest feasible cost). [Gordon Tullock, *The Politics of Bureaucracy* (Washington, D.C.: Public Affairs Press, 1965) and William A. Niskanen, Jr., *Bureaucracy and Representative Government* (Chicago: Aldine Publishing, 1971).]

TABLE 4-1 Controllability of Federal Budget Outlays, 1976–86

Relatively uncontrollable under present law: Open-ended programs and fixed costs:	1976	TQ	1977	1978
Payments for individuals*	162.9	41.2	177.9	190.6
Net interest	26.7	6.9	29.9	35.4
General revenue sharing	6.2	1.6	6.8	6.8
Farm price supports (CCC)	1.1	.5	3.8	5.7
Other open-ended programs and fixed costs	− .3	− .2	− 2.0	− .5
Total, open-ended programs and fixed costs	196.6	50.0	216.4	238.1
Outlays from prior-year contracts and obligations:				
National defense	17.9	7.7	18.5	28.2
Civilian programs	35.8	13.4	40.3	48.7
Total, outlays from prior-year contracts and obligations	53.7	21.1	58.8	76.9
Total, relatively uncontrollable outlays	250.3	71.1	275.2	314.9
Relatively controllable outlays:				
National Defense	53.8	8.9	56.9	55.9
Civilian programs:	72.1	17.1	80.9	91.0
Total, relatively controllable outlays	125.9	26.0	137.8	146.9
Total budget outlays	371.8	96.0	401.2	458.7
Percent of total outlays relatively uncontrollable under present law:	67.3%	74.0%	67.2%	68.7%

*Includes social security and railroad retirement, federal employees' retirement and insurance, unemployment assistance, medical care, assistance to students, food and nutrition assistance, public assistance, etc.
SOURCE: *The Budget of the United State Government, Fiscal Year 1986,* pp. 9–44 and 9–45.

total expenditure is legally *uncontrollable* in the short run.[4] As the federal budget states: "Outlays in any one year are considered to be relatively uncontrollable when the program level is determined by existing statutes or by contracts or other obligations. Outlays for these programs generally depend on factors that are beyond administrative control under existing law at the start of the fiscal year."[5] These outlays include two major categories. First, open-ended programs and fixed costs are mandated by law. These include social security and railroad retirement (the largest of these), federal employees' retirement and insurance, unemployment compensation, medical care, student assistance, interest on the public debt, farm price supports, general revenue sharing, and so on. Many of these outlays are from entitlement pro-

---

[4]The concept of relative controllability comes from Murray L. Weidenbaum, "On the Effectiveness of Congressional Control of the Public Purse," *National Tax Journal* 18 (December 1965), pp. 370–74.

[5]Executive Office of the President, Office of Management and Budget, *Budget of the United States Government, FY1986* (Washington, D.C.: U.S. Government Printing Office, 1985), p. 6–33.

		Actual through 1984				Estimated	
1979	1980	1981	1982	1983	1984	1985	1986
209.5	246.6	287.6	320.1	353.8	357.4	382.7	403.1
42.6	52.5	68.7	85.0	89.8	111.1	130.4	142.9
6.8	6.8	5.1	4.6	4.6	4.6	4.6	4.6
3.6	2.8	4.0	11.7	18.9	7.3	15.0	12.3
−2.6	2.0	2.3	−1.4	−2.3	−1.6	−3.6	−4.0
259.9	310.7	367.8	419.9	464.8	478.8	529.1	558.9
30.9	36.5	`41.4	56.9	68.3	79.5	91.3	109.2
54.4	66.7	67.2	64.5	60.4	65.8	75.7	78.0
85.3	103.2	108.6	121.5	128.7	145.3	167.0	187.1
345.3	413.8	413.8	476.4	541.4	624.1	696.1	746.1
61.9	67.6	90.5	120.8	149.6	147.8	162.4	176.3
98.0	111.0	108.2	86.0	76.4	95.2	115.1	78.8
159.9	178.7	198.7	206.8	226.0	243.0	277.5	255.1
503.5	490.9	678.2	745.7	808.3	851.8	959.1	973.7
74.0%	70.0%	70.2%	72.6%	73.4%	73.3%	72.6%	76.6%

grams. Second are payments from prior-year contracts and obligations. Deobligation is both difficult and expensive; rescission is particularly difficult since the 1974 legislation.

Another variety of contractual obligation generates similar expenditure outside the normal appropriation process. Here, a substantive
committee bypasses appropriation committees by authorizing an agency
to enter into contracts or spend the proceeds of agency borrowing. The
contractual obligations have to be met, so spending occurs without
normal appropriation scrutiny. This procedure, called "backdoor
spending," emerged in the period when the substantive committees
had a dramatically different political viewpoint than did the appropriations committees. Backdoor spending was seen as a way of getting action on socially important policies, even though it seriously bent control processes in public expenditure. This spending is outside the scope
of ordinary budget summaries.

Table 4–1 shows the pattern of uncontrollable budget outlays from
1976 to 1984, with 1985 and 1986 estimates. The percentage relatively
uncontrollable has drifted upward from 67.3 percent in 1976 to 73.3

percent in 1984, heavily driven by increased payments to individuals. That category more than doubled over that period. Of course, the problem of uncontrollability introduces short-term rigidity into federal expenditure, but no federal expenditure is beyond the ultimate control of Congress and the president. These institutions can change entitlement formulas, can alter grant systems, can reduce debt levels, and can deobligate funds. The point is that those actions are difficult in any single year, not that Congress and the president have no options available. What has been enacted can be changed. Uncontrollability cannot be a legitimate reason for inaction. Uncontrollability, however, can limit quick changes in direction and strong countercyclical policy; it clearly suggests the need for multiyear budget planning. Neither the legislature nor the administration should be permitted the political luxury of hiding behind uncontrollability in rough times.

Reform philosophy.   Budget reforms typically seek systems which deliver the right information at the right time to decision makers or which erect an incentive structure directing individuals in agencies to work toward the social interests. Many new budget reform techniques are consistent with the classical principles for appraising budgets.[6]

1. *Comprehensiveness.* The budget should include all receipts and outlays of the government. The single process would thus include all activities of the government.
2. *Unity.* All spending and revenue collecting parts should be related to each other. Consistent evaluation criteria should be applied to any expenditure, regardless of the part of the government in which it is located.
3. *Exclusiveness.* Only financial matters should be in the budget. (Modern analysts recognize, however, that almost every governmental action has financial implications.)
4. *Specification.* The budget should be executed as it is enacted. There should not be cavalier changes made during the budget year.
5. *Annuality.* The budget should be prepared every year for the next year of agency existence.
6. *Accuracy.* Forecasts should be as reasonable as possible and the document should be internally consistent.
7. *Clarity.* The budget should describe what is proposed in understandable fashion.
8. *Publicity.* The budget in a representative democracy ought not be secret. The budget contains the expenditure plan (as well as the revenue estimates) of the government. It is clearly contrary

---

[6]S. Kenneth Howard, *Changing State Budgeting* (Lexington, Ky.: Council of State Governments, 1973), pp. 5–8.

TABLE 4-2 Alternative Budget Formats and Associated Features

Format	Characteristics	Primary Organization Feature	Orientation
Line-item	Expenditure by commodity or resource purchased.	Resources purchased.	Control.
Performance	Expenditure by workload or activity. Presentation of unit cost by activity.	Tasks or activities performed.	Management.
Program	Expenditure related to public goals. Cost data cross organization lines.	Achievements (product or output).	Planning.
Zero-Base	Expenditure by workload or activity. Cost centers differ from organization lines. Alternative service lacks rankings.	Alternate activity levels.	Management.

SOURCE: Adapted from Edward A. Lehan, *Simplified Governmental Budgeting* (Chicago: Municipal Finance Officers Association, 1981), p. 79.

to the underlying principles of a democracy that such important choices be made without a complete public consideration of them.

The particular budget reform systems considered here are performance budgets, program budgets, and zero-base budgets. Most particular budget reform systems mix elements of these systems. Table 4-2 identifies four frequently discussed budget formats—line-item, performance, program, and zero-base—in an introductory comparison of their fundamental features. The first three focus on different stages of the expenditure delivery system, from resources purchased (line-item), through activities performed (performance), to service delivered (program). Line-item, performance, and zero-base systems maintain traditional department structures in the organization of expenditure plans; program budgets classify government outputs (or services provided) without regard for the administrative unit charged with their provision. All seek to improve the job done by government; their fundamental concern does differ: line-item budgets have as their foremost concern expenditure control and accountability, performance budgets seek to improve internal management and to control cost of services provided, program budgets emphasize arranging details in a manner to improve decision capacity for rational choice, and zero-base budgets attempt to augment managerial control and to improve flexibility of fiscal choices. More about each follows.

PERFORMANCE BUDGETS

Performance budgets emphasize agency performance objectives and accomplishments, not the purchase of resources used by the agency. Budgets present the cost of performing measured accomplishment units during the budget year. The budget process then has the dual role of providing funds and establishing performance objectives. Performance budgeting dates to the mid-1910s in New York City; similar efforts continue in state and local governments to the present. The primary impact of performance budgeting on the service delivery process, however, dates from the first Hoover Commission (Commission on Organization of the Executive Branch of the Government) report of 1949.[7]

1. Budget choices and budget information would be structured in terms of activities (repairing roads, treating water, sweeping streets, etc.) rather than individual line-items.
2. Performance measurements would be collected, associated cost should be reported for those performance categories, and efficiency in use of resources should be evaluated.
3. Performance reports comparing deviation of actual cost and accomplishment from planned levels would be monitored for each agency to focus management attention on problems which might arise.

The performance classification promises better services at lower cost from more accountable officials, improved legislative review as attention and debate shift away from issues of personnel, salaries, supplier contracts, etc., toward activity issues more related to how resources are used, and decentralized decision making to allow top management to concentrate its attention on policy matters. Classification of requests follows the activities of the agency, not the inputs it purchases nor the services it provides. The presentation links cost with activities to permit unit cost comparisons across agencies and over time within agencies to emphasize improvements in operating efficiency.

Figure 4–1 illustrates the performance classification further with the performance budget material for snow removal from the 1981–82 Salt Lake City budget. Note the following elements:

1. The *demand* section, a section which defines the expected operating environment for the budget year, presenting prior and current year levels for comparison.
2. The *workload* section, a section which establishes how the operating unit intends to respond to that expected demand by allocation of staff time.
3. The *productivity* section, a section that presents the cost per activity unit that emerges from the budgeted costs. This is the special identifying feature of full performance budgets. Most

---

[7]Commission on Organization of the Executive Branch of the Government, *Budgeting and Accounting* (Washington, D.C.: U.S. Government Printing Office, 1949).

budget documents will not, for instance, allow easy identification of either historic or proposed cost of dealing with snow removal after a snowstorm; the performance classification does.

4. The *effectiveness* section, a section that shows the units performance against criteria that indicate whether the unit is accomplishing its intended objectives.

To present a complete government budget in performance classification is a remarkable undertaking. The budget shown here is remarkable for its faithfulness to that classification.

The performance structure has some special implications. First, the budget becomes a powerful analytic tool for management responsibility and accountability. Budgeting must be a central management responsibility because activity levels and their costs are specifically presented in a document which will guide agency operation. Operating supervisors can no longer permit separate budget personnel to prepare budget requests because those budget requests now become detailed operating plans for the budget year.[8] Many agency managers often do not like the performance budgeting concept because it exposes the details of agency operation (demand estimates, workload trend, etc.) to the scrutiny of external observers, like taxpayers and legislators. Second, legislatures have to change their review and appropriations from the traditional line items to agency activities. The legislature may feel uncomfortable considering something other than objects of expenditures, particularly where there is no apparent linkage to revenue and budget balancing. Finally, a performance budget can make a management by objectives program easier to operate. The objectives would be the performance measures (activities) appearing in the budget. Performance and budget attainment can thus be monitored through the fiscal year.

The performance budget hinges on the quality of the measures and construction of such a budget is not inexpensive. Some performance measures may be misleading or irrelevant: audit quality, for instance, may be more important than audit volume. The number of audits could well be the performance measure, however, simply because it is more easily quantified. Furthermore, the performance budget does not ask whether the performance being measured is the service the public actually wants. And, of course, there is no necessary consideration of alternative ways of doing a particular task. The drive to lower unit cost of performance should induce development of improved methods, not sacrifice of unit quality, but the technique is not geared to handle that problem.

---

[8]Traditional budgets are operating plans as well, except they do not contain identifiable operating objectives. That addition provides the new constraint on the agency.

FIGURE 4-1

PUBLIC PROTECTION	TRAFFIC REGULATION

Program: Snow Removal   *Department:* Public Works

Program Description: To remove snow and ice from city streets for safe travel during inclement weather conditions.

Program Operating Expense

Resource requirements	1979–80 Actual	1980–81 Budget	1980–81 Estimated	1981–82 Recommended
Personnel/personal services	19.5/$279,318	16.90/$325,358	11.35/$190,618	4.7/$111,975
Operating and maintenance supplies	39,081	48,300	29,763	47,720
Charges and services	61,774	193,169	111,864	199,379
Capital outlay	-0-	17,596	12,570	-0-
Work order credits	(212)	-0-	-0-	-0-
Total	$379,961	$584,423	$344,815	$359,074

Program Resources

	1979–80 Actual	1980–81 Budget	1980–81 Estimated	1981–82 Recommended
General fund	$379,961	$584,423	$344,815	$359,074
Total	$379,961	$584,423	$344,815	$359,074

Program Budget Highlights

The 1980–81 budget indicators had an over allocation of man hours in the snow and ice program which have been rectified by mid-year adjustments and are now correctly reflected in the 1981–82 request. During 1980–81, a study was conducted analyzing the past five winters. It was obvious as a result of this study that our projections for the 1980–81 budget year were unrealistic, so we reassigned employees' time to other programs causing other program expenditure levels and personnel allocations to rise.

Performance Objectives:
1. To review "scale" of snow fighter program.
2. To develop an expanded U.D.O.T. and S.L.C. responsibilities exchange where practical.
3. To evaluate an "exceptional storm" emergency backup system.

Performance Review	1979–80 Actual	1980–81 Budget	1980–81 Estimated	1981–82 Recommended
Demand:				
1. Lane miles of priority snow routes	400	400	460	460
2. Inches of snowfall	63	68	45	68
3. Storms requiring crew mobilization	15	19	16	19
4. Storms requiring salt only	7	10	10	10
5. Storms requiring snow plowing	8	9	6	9
Workload:				
1. Man hours salting streets	n.a.*	12,640	1,000	2,060
2. Man hours plowing streets	n.a.	18,960	1,400	3,090
3. Tons of salt applied	7,410	8,000	4,900	8,000
Productivity:				
1. Cost/priority lane mile	962	1,418	874	765
2. Average cost/storm	25,663	29,864	25,138	18,513
Effectiveness:				
1. Vehicle accidents in which snow and ice are a contributing factor	253	250	135	250
2. Complaints received	49	50	35	50

*n.a. = Not applicable.

Curiously enough, advocates of performance budgeting come from two ends of the political spectrum. Some public officials see performance budgets as a way to justify their contribution to the community and possibly to expand their budgets. Others see performance budgets as a tool to expose waste of money and, hence, as a guide for expenditure reduction to permit tax cuts. The performance budget structure does not question whether objectives are appropriate or whether a service is worth its cost of production. Performance budgets consider whether the activity is being done at low cost; it does not consider whether the activity is worth doing.

PROGRAM BUDGETS

The program budget format organizes proposed expenditure according to output or contribution to governmental objectives. Programs are constructed on the basis of contribution to those objectives. The focus is neither on what governments buy nor on activities in which the government is engaged, but on, as nearly as can be defined, the outputs of government. The budget places together programs which contribute to a similar objective so that competition for funds occurs among real alternatives. In an ordinary budget, agencies or departments compete for funds, as do programs within agencies or departments, so similar programs may receive different treatment simply because different agencies house them. In a program budget, similar approaches for handling a public problem will compete with each other, not with dissimilar programs housed in an administrative agency.

Program budgeting defines the goals of an agency and classifies organization activities contributing to each goal. Grouping is by end product, regardless of the administrative organization functions, to focus competition for resources among objectives and alternative programs for achieving objectives. The program structure identifies agency products; it does not focus on the inputs used by the agency. Table 4–3 illustrates the program budget classification used by the state of Pennsylvania and Table 4–4 on p. 148 illustrates the structure used by Park Ridge, Illinois. Notice that the format classifies by service provided to the public. It does not classify by individual department (several services would in fact be provided in more than one department), it does not classify by input purchased, and it does not classify by departmental activity. The structure seeks a product orientation. The nonsubstantive direction and support (Pennsylvania) and policy formulation and management (Park Ridge) classifications are normal in program classifications; those functions provide unallocable inputs to the provision of the other services.

The approach of program budgeting may be illustrated by indicat-

TABLE 4-3 Program Budget Classification, Pennsylvania

	Percent of All Funds
I. Direction and support services—	4.8%
To provide an effective administrative system through which major substantive goals of the Commonwealth can be achieved.	
II. Protection of persons and property—	6.5
To provide an environment and social system in which the lives of individuals and the property of individuals and organizations are protected from natural and man-made disasters, and from illegal and unfair action.	
III. Health, physical, and mental well-being—	19.2
To provide an environment in which hazards to physical and mental health are minimized; to provide means for the prevention of physical and mental disabilities; and to support a system of health care which will assure the availability of health services to those in need of them.	
IV. Intellectual development and education—	30.6
To provide a system of learning experiences and opportunities that will permit each individual to achieve maximum potential intellectual development.	
V. Social development—	8.4
To provide a system of services for reinforcing the capacity of individuals, children, and families for effective adjustment to society and for minimizing socially aberrant behavior.	
VI. Economic development and income maintenance—	14.9
To provide a system in which the employment opportunities of individuals, the economic growth and development of communities, and the overall economic development of the Commonwealth will be maximized, including optimum use of natural resources to support economic development.	
VII. Transportation and communication—	14.4
To provide a system for the fast, efficient, and safe movement of individuals, cargo, and information within the Commonwealth which is interfaced with a national-international system of transportation and communication.	
VIII. Recreation and cultural enrichment—	1.2
To provide a system of service and support functions to make available opportunities for individual and group recreation and cultural growth, including the use of natural resources to support a recreational system.	

ing how a particular item might be classified under three alternative budget structures. Suppose that the item in question is the salary of an instructor employed by a high school operated in a state prison. With a traditional budget, that salary would appear as a part of the personal service (wage and salary) line of the budget of the state department of corrections. It would thus compete for funds, in the first instance, within the priorities of that department. Money received could well depend on how the governor and legislature viewed the overall prison system. If that budget were to be classified according to performance, that expenditure would appear as part of the cost of achieving a target number of

TABLE 4-4 Program Budget Structure Used by Park Ridge, Illinois

Key objective 1—policy formulation and management.
   To interpret and define the needs of the community, to establish policies to meet those needs, and to provide supportive services to administer those policies.
   Service area 1—public representation:
      To serve the citizens of the city of Park Ridge in the capacity of elected officials through a system of public participation and debate.
   Service area 2—executive management:
      To administer the needs of the city in accordance with the city code and policies, ordinances and resolutions adopted by the city council; to advise the city council about current and future financial, manpower and program needs; to establish and implement administrative policies which will enhance the effectiveness and efficiency of city government in carrying out its service commitments to the citizens; and to provide the legal framework for implementing policies of the city council.
   Service area 3—management services:
      To provide a comprehensive, timely and responsive fiscal management system to reflect past, current and future financial conditions; to obtain goods and services required by city departments in an efficient and economical manner; to provide modern data processing facilities where needed; to administer an effective program of personnel recruitment and development; and to maintain all official records of the city.
Key objective 2—protection of persons and property.
   To reduce the frequency and severity of external harm to persons and property; to help people to live peaceably together, and to maintain an atmosphere of personal security.
   Service area 1—police protection:
      To provide individual and public safety through effective patrol, investigation, and preventive law enforcement programs.
   Service area 2—fire and ambulance protection:
      To provide life and property protection through fire prevention, fire fighting, and emergency ambulance service programs.
   Service area 3—public safety communications:
      To provide for prompt communication and response to requests for fire and police service.
   Service area 4—emergency preparedness:
      To provide preplanning for the coordination of emergency services in the event of a major catastrophe.
Key objective 3—maintenance and construction of public facilities.
   To provide safe and efficient public ways for vehicular and pedestrian traffic; prompt disposal of storm drainage, wastewater, refuse, and trash; a pure and adequate water supply; and clean, well-maintained public buildings.
   Service area 1—administration and support:
      To provide general planning, coordination, supervision, and control of the activities necessary to accomplish this key objective.
   Service area 2—public ways:
      To provide and adequately maintain vehicular and pedestrian access to private property while maintaining a safe, efficient flow of traffic on collector and arterial streets; and provide and maintain the optimum of parking facilities considering long-term and short-term needs.
   Service area 3—storm drainage and wastewater:
      To provide a system for disposition of all storm water and wastewater in order to minimize the frequency and severity of flooding and pollution.
   Service area 4—solid wastes collection and disposal:
      To provide a system for regular and efficient collection and disposition of all solid wastes.
   Service area 5—water supply and distribution:
      To provide and maintain facilities for storing, treating, transporting, and measuring water.

TABLE 4-4 (*concluded*)

Service area 6—public buildings maintenance and construction:
  To provide for maintenance and construction of city-owned buildings not used
  and budgeted specifically for one service area.
Key objective 4—community preservation and development.
  To preserve and develop the physical and economic environment of Park Ridge so
  as to enhance its character as an attractive, well-planned, high quality residential
  community.
Service area 1—administer and support:
  To provide general direction, coordination, supervision, and control within the
  objective of preserving a residential community that will remain an attractive,
  pleasant, well-built place to live.
Service area 2—growth management:
  To establish a continuing process for formulating and evaluating the long-range
  objectives of the community, and for appraising the physical, economic, and
  fiscal implications of private development.
Service area 3—code enforcement:
  To regulate the use of private land, the construction of buildings thereon, and the
  continued observance of acceptable levels of property maintenance in order to
  ensure a safe, healthy, and pleasing environment throughout the community.
Service area 4—beautification:
  To preserve and enhance the natural beauty of public properties.
Service area 5—public transportation:
  To assure that necessary public transportation opportunities are available to the
  residents of the city.
Key objective 5—cultural and civic services.
  To provide informational, educational, and recreational services reflective of the
  needs and desires of the citizens of Park Ridge.
Service area 1—library services:
  To select, purchase, organize, and maintain books, films, records, and other
  materials that will meet most of the general needs of the community; assist
  patrons in making use of the various collections of materials; and make
  available the services of the North Suburban Library System and the Illinois
  Regional Library Council.
Service area 2—leisure time opportunities:
  To provide opportunities for the citizens to enrich their leisure time through
  community activities.

SOURCE: Annual Budget of Park Ridge, Illinois, for the fiscal year ending April 30, 1986.

instruction hours by that department. Again, competition for resources would be with other activities of that department. A program structure, however, could well classify that expenditure as a part of a human development program, separating it from its link to incarceration and causing it to be considered with training and education activities. The salary expenditure is the same dollar amount, but the different budget classifications cause it to be treated differently to accommodate different purposes of the budget. The manner of classification undoubtedly would influence the questions asked about the expenditure and, possibly, the size of its appropriation.

Program budgeting requires careful definition of programs. That exercise in taxonomy is the essence of such budgets. While a good understanding of government operations is vital for program classification, the logical criteria for program design provided by Arthur Smithies a number of years ago remain generally helpful:

1. Design programs so that they "permit comparison of alternative methods of pursuing an imperfectly defined policy objective."[9] If there are competing ways of reducing some social problem, make certain they end up in the same program. That breakdown can clarify issues for analysis.

2. Programs must include complementary components which cannot function separately. Thus, health programs require doctors, nurses, physical facilities, and the like in appropriate proportions—and those elements must all be in the program.

3. When one part of a government serves several others, separate supporting service programs may be needed. Thus, central electronic data processing, personnel administration, and so forth may permit operating economies not possible if each agency handles them separately. These activities can be handled as programs, even though their outputs are not governmental objectives. (Recall the direction and support program in Pennsylvania for example.)

4. Governments may have to have overlapping program structures to achieve their objectives. Many revenue departments, for instance, have structures arranged both functionally and geographically. That approach appears when both regional and national (or statewide) objectives are important.

5. Finally, some activities involving research, development, or long-term investment may be considered as separate subprograms because of the long time span over which the expenditure takes effect. That is because of the uncertainties which preclude reasonably reliable estimates of resource requirements beyond relatively short portions of their life.

It can be presumed that all government activities seek to improve the general welfare. The goal of programming is to identify the components of that broad objective so that choices can be made among those components and among alternative approaches to their achievement.

Program construction is the identifying feature, but program budgets often have other elements accompanying them. First, budget time horizons expand beyond an annual appropriation to the lifetime of the program. While appropriation remains annual, decision makers are presented the total cost of the program considered, not simply a down payment. Second, steps in preparation induce agencies to consider alternate operating methods and to propose only those which require least

---

[9]Arthur Smithies, "Conceptual Framework for the Program Budget," in *Program Budgeting,* 2d ed., ed. David Novick (New York: Holt, Rinehart & Winston, 1969), p. 42.

cost to achieve the desired results. Because agency administrators traditionally have incentives toward larger budgets for prestige or advancement, such steps are difficult to enforce. Finally, program budgets often include some benefit-cost analysis of the resource use of programs proposed.[10] Programming brings together costs for achieving particular objectives, so an important piece of the data needed for such analysis is provided.

All these elements appeared in the federal planning programming budgeting system (PPBS) experiment, applied initially to the Department of Defense in 1961, expanded to other federal agencies in 1965, and officially terminated in 1971. Elements of that system remain in budget frameworks of many federal agencies and of many state and local governments.[11] In fact, many of the major features of zero-base budgeting were included in the old PPBS structure.[12] (Note also the federal functional classification required by the 1974 Congressional Budget and Impoundment Control Act; it is described in the appendix to this chapter.)

Program budgets create one important complication for large organizations. Without accompanying reorganization of administrative agencies to match programs, budgets in program form must have an accompanying "crosswalk" to translate program costs to administrative unit appropriations. Without an easy, quick, and understandable crosswalk, the program format yields numbers which are not usable by budget decision makers and choices will continue to be made in the familiar setting of the traditional budget. That problem heavily contributed to the demise of federal PPBS.

Even where used, program budgets cannot cure all budgetary illnesses. Three problems merit special attention. First, many public activities contribute to more than one public objective and the best programmatic classification for them is not always apparent. Whatever choice is made will emphasize one set of policy choices at the expense of another set. Thus, federal expenditures on military academies might be attributed to higher education elements or to defense objectives. The placement of that expenditure will establish the analysis which it faces, so it must depend on the most important issues it currently raises. It should be apparent that any long-maintained program structure will produce the bureaucratic blindness associated with continued examination of the same issues from the same approach. Furthermore, difficult interrelationships among public programs remain. Thus, highway

---

[10]Benefit-cost analysis is discussed in Chapter 5.

[11]See Allen Shick, *Budget Innovation in the States* (Washington, D.C.: Brookings Institution, 1971) for a review of state use of program and performance structures. About 35 states have implemented modified PPB systems at one time or another.

[12]The federal zero-base budget process does, however, involve line managers more and central budget staff less than did the planning programming budget.

transportation activities may influence urban redevelopment or complicate environmental protection. These interrelationships can baffle any budget navigator.

Second, cost estimates for programs may be less meaningful for public decisions than imagined. There is no scientifically defensible method for allocating the substantial joint costs appearing in agencies. Because most units work with several programs, many resources used by the agency are shared and not clearly attributable to a single program. Furthermore, public decisions require concern for social implications—not simply money out of pocket—while program budgets still focus on agency cost alone. Thus, the program cost data are unlikely to be directly usable for guiding choices.

Finally, program budgets may have little impact on decisions. Legislatures, lobbyists, and governmental departments have experience with the traditional budget format. All are familiar with that construction and have developed general guides for analysis for that format. New presentations require new guides and extra effort by all. Unless the major participants in the budget process actually want the improved presentation, it will be ignored in favor of the format to which they are accustomed.

ZERO–BASE BUDGET

A zero-base budget (ZBB) system annually challenges and requires defense of all agency programs. The system does not presume that an agency will receive at least its prior year's appropriation level. (It is not clear, however, that any budget system formally makes that presumption.) At least in theory, the budget must be defended in its entirety, just as if it were the start of a new program. The Advisory Commission on Intergovernmental Relations notes that ZBB has two crucial steps:

> (1) designing and ranking packages of decisions that reflect several possible levels of activity of the organization concerned, the financial requirements needed to support each possible level of activity, and other relevant management data; and (2) establishing priorities for these decision packages.[13]

Zero-base budgeting seeks to make government more flexible, to eliminate low-yield programs, to improve government effectiveness by forcing administrators to consider the total program annually, and to ease shifts of government spending in response to changed service demands without government reorganization or loss of the familiar line-item format. In sum, ZBB attempts to prevent a budget process focused only on program increases.

---

[13]Advisory Commission on Intergovernmental Relations, *The Question of State Government Capability* (Washington, D.C.: ACIR, 1985), p. 179.

The Office of Management and Budget reported the following objectives of zero-base budgeting:

- Involve all managers at all levels in the budget process.
- Justify the resource requirements for existing activities as well as for new activities.
- Focus the justification on the evaluation of discrete programs or activities of each decision unit.
- Establish, for all managerial levels in an agency, objectives against which accomplishments can be identified and measured.
- Assess alternative methods of accomplishing objectives.
- Analyze the probable effects of different budget amounts or performance levels on the achievement of objectives.
- Provide a credible rationale for reallocating resources, especially from old activities to new activities.[14]

The systems used by different governments have individual peculiarities, but many include elements of the system adopted by the federal government and diagramed in Figure 4–2 on p. 154. In the first stage, unit managers prepare decision packages, which are alternatives for performing a particular function with different amounts of money. The package includes funding levels and increments, a description of the activity, compilation of resource requirements, description of the short-term objective of the package, and a statement of its impact on major objectives of the agency. It also describes the implications of not providing funds for the package; the unit manager must be engaged in analysis of objectives, operational planning, consideration of alternatives, and cost estimation.

As the chart shows, unit managers submit their ranked decision packages to agency heads. Agency heads consolidate the packages received from the various unit managers, rank the packages, and transmit the packages ahead in the hierarchy. The packages flow through successive consolidation and ranking to the departmental level. The final consolidation and ranking produces the budget request transmitted to the Office of Management and Budget for eventual inclusion in the presidential budget. Each program element will have survived a number of rankings if it ends up in the request.

The process has numerous potential strengths. It will develop much operating data—workloads, performance measures, and so on—for use in management and should induce consideration of alternative delivery devices. Furthermore, it will require formal consideration of priorities throughout the organization. When taken seriously, budget constructing works from the bottom of the organization up, not from

---

[14]Office of Management and Budget, "Zero Base Budgeting," Bulletin no. 77-9, April 19, 1977.

FIGURE 4-2 The Flow of Zero-Base Budgets

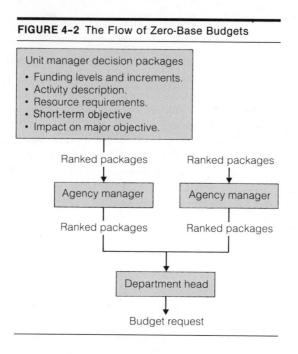

---

the top down, as PPBS (and most other processes) worked. Finally, it forces thought about the objectives of agency activities. Along with the benefits, there are, however, substantial problems. First, package development generates massive volumes of paper. Administrators must be serious about the system if they choose to inflict it on agencies, because even under the best of circumstances, some of that paper will not be serious. Several programs cannot realistically be considered candidates for zeroing out, some packages will never be realistically considered for funding, and some production alternatives may be less than serious alternatives. Many capable administrators simply won't take the ZBB system seriously. Second, performance information may be contrived and not especially germane to the operation of an agency. Measured performance may be accurate, but the performance measured may be trivial to agency purpose. Third, many spending activities won't be amenable to zero-base treatment. Several such categories are mandates on the state and local level, activities controlled by earmarking, contractual relations (debt and pension), or formula entitlements. Unfortunately, these account for a sizable proportion of total spending (as was shown in Table 4–1). Finally, the ZBB process does not compare service worth with service costs. Systems seldom identify whose priorities are to be used in ranking, even though unit manager priorities will quite possibly differ from the social priorities.

Most analysts of ZBB doubt that it has had much impact. Shick says zero-base budgeting "changed the terminology of budgeting, but little more."[15] Zero-base budgeting probably directs too much attention to the routine details of the budget process and away from the tough questions of that process—the questions of program objectives and social value. Zero-base budgeting is not a magic solution to government decision making. Whether it contributes to or hinders the decision process is uncertain, but some key elements have survived a presidential transition. The Carter administration introduced federal ZBB, and the Reagan administration ended the name, but decision units, variable funding level documentation, and priority rankings remain. As with PPB, the name died, but useful practices continue in the budget system.[16]

CONCLUSION

Performance budgets, program budgets, and zero-base budgets all try to increase the rationality of budget choices. None provide the complete solution to the budget problem—it is wrong to expect any system to provide decisions which must be made by people. Each system, however, tries to organize information in a fashion allowing decision makers to make those choices in reasonable fashion. All arrange information in a more usable way than do traditional budgets and, in varying degrees, seek to increase the flexibility of action open to decision makers. People will continue to make budget decisions, and that is appropriate; useful organization of information and erection of reasonable organizational incentives are the role of budget systems. Each of the structures described here can represent significant improvements over the traditional, line-item, administrative unit structure—if executive, bureaucratic, and legislative branches choose to use them. Reluctance to participate on the part of any group can doom any structure.

Questions and Exercises

1. The following sections are narrative from the 1973–74–1974–75 budget request for the South Carolina Department of Social Services.

---

[15]Allen Shick, "The Road from ZBB," *Public Administration Review* 38 (March/April 1978), p. 178.

[16]Some of the ZBB logic likewise appears in "decremental budgeting," an approach to greater flexibility through imposing request reduction constraints on managers. See Jerry McCaffery, "Revenue Budgeting: Dade County Tries a Decremental Approach," *Public Administration Review* 41 (January 1981), p. 179–89. Continued use of ZBB by federal agencies is reviewed in Stanley B. Botner, "Utilization of Decision Units and Ranking Process in Budgetary Decision-Making by Federal Departments and Agencies," *Government Accountants Journal* 33 (Fall 1984), pp. 18–23.

They are part of a nicely prepared and presented line-item budget which requests funds for organizational units.

Goals

In our opinion there are only two reasonable goals for any governmentally supported welfare or social service agency—these are (1) to assist the citizenry in achieving through self-sufficiency a living standard which eliminates the need for public support and (2) to meet the needs for societal service within society and the family unit without the public provision thereof.

Means of achieving these goals

These are generational goals. It is not feasible this year or this decade to achieve "self-sufficiency" for aged, blind, or disabled adults or dependent children who have insufficient income to provide the basic necessities of life. Further, as technological changes occur the demand for unskilled labor decreases. It becomes increasingly difficult for an illiterate or semieducated person to obtain employment paying wages sufficient to enable him/her to support the family. But the basic sexual drive remains, and children are born into families or to women who probably did not want them and have no means to support them. Many of them see no books, papers, or pencils until school. There is little or no home training or "push" for achievement in school. And the cycle repeats itself.

It seems to us that the means of achieving the stated goals are as follows:

a. Social and moral guidance through churches, civic groups, and other interested parties. It can only be effective when it comes through peer groups—outside forces can encourage and guide but cannot force acceptance.

b. Family planning to assure that no unwanted child is conceived. We are of the opinion that family limitation is a personal matter, but we also believe that most persons will gladly accept assistance in this regard, and few have any desire to bring additional children into a deprived setting.

c. Adequate nutrition and medical care to the prospective mother to assure, insofar as possible, a mentally and physically healthy baby.

d. Adequate "preschool" training for socially deprived children to enable them to enter school on a level comparable to that of other children. We support the Department of Education's continuing emphasis on kindergartens, but we also believe that this preschool training should be for the "whole" child and thereby be comprehensive in social services to enable both the child and his/her family to integrate into society.

e. Adequate and enforced educational opportunities and standards. Illiterate high school graduates may end up on welfare rolls. Many children should be directed to vocational opportunities which do not require a high level of academic achievement.

f. Adequate scale of living and housing distributed so that "pockets" of persons living on welfare do not form, thereby giving people a sense of belonging to society and a desire to contribute thereto, and thus eliminating the "welfare" mentality, if indeed such exists.

g. Adequate medical care so that physical deficiencies and disease can be early detected and treated, thereby contributing a healthy individual to society and maintaining him therein.

h. Adequate varied job opportunities so that the individual can be productive.

i. Adequate industrial safeguards, highway standards, and public safety enforcement, to reduce the occurrence of accidental disability.

j. Adequate employer pensions and health insurance plans to provide for an adequate living standard upon retirement and medical care treatment during and after retirement.

Objectives

Many of the objectives of the department have been stated in the "means" section. Also, over many of the means this department has no control. The following list of objectives are those which we feel are more urgent in alleviating current conditions and assisting in moving toward the stated goals.

a. Provision of adequate means of living to those persons in South Carolina unable to provide such for themselves.

b. Provision of "protective services" to those adults and children who are unable to fend for themselves. Neglect of older and disabled adults, abuse and neglect of children should not be tolerated. Our social service program is geared toward these persons now but much additional work needs to be done.

c. Provision of adequate medical care to these persons.

d. Provision of family planning services to those individuals willing to accept such services.

e. Provision of comprehensive social services in a fashion which will prevent dependency and/or encourage persons to become self-sufficient. Such services include but are not limited to early childhood development (including day care), emergency home-making assistance, transportation, adoptions, counseling, foster care, assistance in obtaining information or aid from other groups, locating suitable housing, developing community aid resources, self-support services, etc.

f. Provision of prenatal medical care to unwed mothers.

Measures of success in meeting these objectives

a. Provision of adequate means of living.
   (1) Adults—Effective January 1, 1974, the categorical aid (welfare payment) program for the aged, totally and permanently disabled, and blind will be transferred, along with major funding responsibility, to the Social Security Administration under a new program entitled "supplemental security income (SSI)." The assistance payments which will be made under this program are nationwide in application. These payments are set at a maximum of $130 for an individual and $195 for a couple.

   These payments, while inadequate, are far better than the present payment made by this agency. It is estimated by the Social Security Administration that approximately 50,000 additional persons will be covered under this program. For this reason we are not requesting funding to supplement payments made by SSI. We must, however, under the legislation, provide certain mandatory supplements to this program in the areas of nursing service and boarding home payments. This will be discussed later.

   (2) Children—The General Assembly provided funds for a 10 percent increase in payment levels for FY 73–74. This increase was badly needed; however, we will pay only 50 percent of the budget deficit for dependent children and their mothers. An example of items included in the budget is rent, which is budgeted at $44 per family per month—of which we pay a maximum of 50 percent ($22). We submit that this payment level is not sufficient to allow any individual or family unit to live within our society. There will be little upward mobility of persons coming from this environment. As a matter of interest there is no valid welfare payment in this state made to, or on behalf of, an able-bodied male under the age of 65. They are not covered under our operational plans. Food stamps may be purchased by such an individual, but only upon registration with Employment Security Commission for employment. Our long-range goal is that bonus value of food stamps plus our payment level equal the poverty level in South Carolina.

We are requesting for FY74–75 funds to raise the payment level to the maximum for federal matching purposes—approximately 75 percent of the budget deficit.

b. Protective services to adults and children.

There are service units in each county office dedicated to providing at least a minimum of these services to children. There are, however, children who are unwanted, abused, and neglected because of lack of adequate care arrangements, lack of proper legal attention, and lack of legal ability to take action. Further, most people will not report instances of child abuse. A child in South Carolina is effectively a chattel—to be treated as the owner sees fit. There must be a revulsion by society and adequate legal authority granted to eliminate the "battered child syndrome." Additionally there must be adequate provision for emergency placement of abused, unwanted, or neglected children until adequate long-term care can be arranged or the family situation resolved. The case of the neglected (and often abused) older adult is becoming more prevalent. With our present mobile society and our peculiar youth orientation, in-home care for the aged parent is becoming a thing of the past. "Grandma" or "Grandpa" is in the way. Many of our older citizens become the living dead, eking out only a marginal existence. Many are placed as long-term terminal residents of substandard, unlicensed, unofficial boarding or nursing homes where they may be treated as animals if the attendants so desire. We owe the people who made this country great more than this.

There are social service units in each county office working with these problems. We license and enforce boarding and foster home standards. We have initiated a bedside audit of persons in nursing homes and an examination of patients' records to ascertain the proper level of care and to monitor the care they receive. We are not this year requesting major additional funds for this program—we believe adequate staff is available to enable continuation of implementation.

c. Provision of adequate medical care.

Under the present state medicaid plan, medical care is available only to welfare recipients. During fiscal years 73, 74, and 75 services are being expanded (by virtue of federal directive) to include health screening, diagnosis, and treatment of all children receiving aid under the financial assistance program. Many of these services were not provided under the state plan. This program is estimated to cost an additional $6 million annually. We are requesting in the budget for FY 74–75 funds to implement a categorically related medically indigent program. Because of our low AFDC payment level, such a program would be on a "spend down" basis and would be available only after a disabled, blind, or aged adult or mother with dependent children had spent for medical costs funds sufficient to reduce their income to the AFDC payment level. This coverage would not be available to what is normally termed the "working poor." Coverage for other low-income families can only be provided with full state funds.

d. Provision of family planning services.

We have a contract with the Board of Health to provide these services to former, current, or potential welfare recipients. For this purpose we receive 90 percent federal matching funds. Adequate family planning services are necessary to prevent a continued increase in welfare rolls. We provide all interested persons with a referral to the Board of Health and pay the Board of Health for the provision of this service.

e. Provision of comprehensive social services.

There is a social service unit within each county department of social services charged with the responsibilities outlined in this objective. The services provided by this staff are those which assist the individual in daily living, adoptions, foster care, licensing, and so forth. For certain "hard" services such as day care and clinical service for family planning we must rely on other agencies to provide either the service or the "state" share of the funds. We have not requested major funding increases in this area. We have entered into contracts with many state and local agencies to use their funds to match federal funds for the provision of social services. The total amount of these contracts cannot exceed the federal allocation, and it appears that the usable amount for this program will not exceed $200 million. We will be better able to judge our position as to social service delivery upon the final determination by HEW as to what these funds can be used to provide.

We have not shown in the budget the full impact of the possibilities of these contracts. Federal regulations and approvals are at this time far too nebulous for us to draw any conclusion as to what will finally be determined. If regulations are approved by HEW, which enable use to generate an appreciable amount of these social services funds, the funds must be used to expand services. They may not revert to the general fund of the state. Nor may state funding decrease as a result of these funds.

f. Provision of prenatal medical care to unwed mothers.

The General Assembly provided funds in this year's appropriation to enable us to provide an AFDC award and medical assistance to the unwed woman who is pregnant with her first child. We deplore such a situation but know that adequate medical care and nutrition will increase the probability of delivery of a mentally and physically healthy child. On behalf of the child let me express appreciation for this program. We believe you have resolved this problem if the AFDC award is raised to an adequate level.

Conclusion

We have discussed the goals, means, and objectives of the department. It is important to emphasize that this is our plan of action as best we have been able to formulate it to date.

From this information, prepare a program budget classification for the department.

2. An important piece of zero-base budgeting is the identification of agency decision units. Decision units should have measurable accomplishments and represent a level where policy decisions can be made. They may or may not coincide with the present budget structure. While governments selecting the ZBB technique use various instructions, the federal Office of Management and Budget Bulletin 77–9 defines the decision unit as:

> The program or organizational entity for which budgets are prepared and for which a manager makes significant decisions on the amount of spending and the scope or quality of work to be performed.

The OMB provides further guidance in the selection of decision units:

> Agencies should ensure that the basic decision units selected are not so low in the structure as to result in excessive paperwork and review. On the other hand the units selected should not be so high as to mask important consideration and prevent meaningful review of the work being performed.

Use these criteria in questions which relate to a state department of taxation. Divisions of that department follow:

- The *administrative division* provides direction and administrative supporting services including personnel, research and statistics, purchasing, legal counseling, and collection enforcement.
- The *income tax division* administers income tax laws as they relate to the individuals, corporations, fiduciaries, and partnerships, including withholding tax.

- The *property tax division* assists in programs of reassessment and equalization of real property valuations in counties requesting assistance. It also assesses real and personal property of all manufacturers and public utilities and all personal property held by commercial establishments.
- The *sales and use tax division* administers the sales and use tax laws.
- The *data processing division* processes all returns, deposits all receipts, maintains account files, and performs mathematical checks on all returns.

Some additional detail about the department:

Division	Employees	Budget	Collected
Administrative	90	$1,526,692	—
Income tax	155	1,842,647	$592,657,202
Property tax	34	467,140	—*
Sales and use tax	156	1,761,465	471,555,323
Data processing	75	799,475	—

*The property tax is levied only at the local level.

a. Would each of the five divisions be a decision unit? Why or why not? If not, would the decision units be larger or smaller than a division? Indicate what some decision units would be.

b. Should the costs of the administrative division be prorated to the other divisions or kept separate in preparing decision package costs? Why or why not? If prorated, what basis could be used that is sensible for the purposes of the budget?

Case for Discussion

Zero-base budgeting emerged as the budget fashion of the latter years of the 1970s. The following article appeared in the *The Wall Street Journal*, just as that system was adopted for federal budget preparation.

Consider These Questions

1. *Why did Professor Anthony (a member of the Harvard Business School faculty) view ZBB as a fraud?*
2. *In this application, could a fraud still serve a useful purpose?*

Zero-Base Budgeting Is a Fraud

By Robert N. Anthony

Zero-base budgeting is supposed to be a new way of preparing annual budgets, which contrasts with the current way, which is called incremental budgeting. Incremental budgeting, it is correctly said, takes a certain level of expenses as a starting point and focuses on the proposed increment above that level.

By contrast, if the word "zero" means anything, it signifies that the budgeting process starts at zero and that the agency preparing the budget request must justify every dollar that it requests.

There is only one recorded attempt to take such an approach to budgeting in a government organization of any size. In 1971, the governor of Georgia hired a consultant to install such a system. He did so because of an article the consultant had written for *Harvard Business Review*.

A casual reader of that article could easily get the impression that the author had successfully installed a zero-base budgeting system in a large industrial company. A more careful reader would learn that the author had installed a system in certain staff and research units of that company, comprising an unspecified fraction, but less than 25 percent of the company's annual expenditures, and that the judgment that the system was a great success was entirely the author's and based on a single year's experience.

Anyway, the consultant started to work for the state of Georgia. He was well-intentioned and probably sincere in his belief that it is possible to prepare and analyze a budget from scratch. This belief did not last long. Well before the end of the first budget cycle, it was agreed that expenditures equal to approximately 80 percent of the current level of spending would be given only a cursory examination and that attention would be focused on the increment.

Thus, even before one go around of the new system, the "zero" bench mark was replaced by 80 percent. Moreover, amounts above this floor were in fact "increments" despite the claim that the process is the opposite of incremental budgeting. Eighty percent is a long way from zero and increments above 80 percent are just as much increments as increments above some other base. To put it bluntly, the name zero-base budgeting is a fraud.

Facts Don't Support

The facts don't even support the glowing reports about what happened with respect to the amounts above the 80 percent. In 1974, 13 heads of Georgia departments were interviewed, and only two went so far as to say that zero-base budgeting "may" have led to a reallocation of resources. (The whole idea of budgeting is to allocate resources.) None of 32 budget analysts reported that the system involved a "large" shifting of financial resources, and only 7 said it caused "some" shifting: 21 said there was no apparent shifting, and four were uncertain.

People experienced in budgeting know that zero-base budgeting won't work. Basically, the idea is that the entire annual budget request is to be broken down in "decision packages." These packages are to be ranked in order of priority, and budget decisions are made for each package according to the justification contained therein and its relative priority ranking. There are several things wrong with this approach.

Most important is that large numbers of decision packages are unmanageable. In Georgia, there were 11,000 of them. If the governor set aside four hours every day for two months he could spend about a minute on each decision package, not enough time to read it let alone analyze the merits. If he delegated the job to others, the whole idea of comparing priorities is compromised.

In the Defense Department, whose budget is 30 times as large as Georgia's, top management makes budget judgments on a few hundred items, certainly not as many as a thousand.

Even if the numbers of decision packages were reduced to a manageable size, it is not possible to make a thorough analysis during the time available in the annual budget process. In a good control system, basic decisions are made during the programming process, which precedes the budget process. And the annual budget process is essentially one of fine tuning the financial plan required to implement these decisions during the budget year; there is not time to do anything else.

In zero-base budgeting, there is no mention of a programming process. The assumption evidently is that program decisions are made concurrently with budget decisions. This simply can't be done in an organization of any size; there isn't time.

Experience also shows that the idea of ranking decision packages according to priority doesn't work. Such rankings have been attempted from time to time in government agencies, as far back as 1960. They have been abandoned. Honest agency heads will admit that program priority is influenced by the amount of funds likely to be available, rather than the other way around. If they are less than honest, they will deliberately structure priorities so that essential or politically popular decision packages are given low priority, knowing they will probably be approved and that their approval will automatically constitute approval of packages listed as having a higher priority. Only quite naive people would not expect this to happen.

The budget process is not primarily a ranking process. It is primarily the fine tuning of an approved program. The worth of programs can't be determined by reading words on a two-page form. Judgments about new programs are based on discussions with people involved, in which words on paper play some but not a dominant part. The budget analyst has a whole set of techniques for squeezing water out of budget requests for continuing programs; reading "decision packages" is not one of them.

Compared with the antiquated budget process which Georgia had at the time, zero-base budgeting was probably an improvement—almost any change would have been. Compared with the procedures that already are used in the federal government, it has nothing of substance to offer. The new parts are not good, and the good parts are not new.

Nevertheless, zero-base budgeting is rapidly becoming a highly prestigious term. I think there is a way of capitalizing on this prestige so as to give impetus to improvements in the budget process that really need to be made.

First, by a slight change in wording, the push behind the phrase might be transferred to a process called "zero-base review." This is an extremely valuable part of the control process. It is used by some agencies, but it is not widely used in a systematic way. It should be made systematic and extended throughout the government.

Time Consuming and Traumatic

In a zero-base review, outside experts go into an agency, or some part of it, and carefully examine its reason for being, its methods of operation and its costs. It is a time consuming and traumatic process, so it cannot conceivably be conducted annually. Instead, each agency should be examined about once every five years. It is by far the best way of controlling ongoing programs, just as benefit/cost analysis is the best way of making decisions on proposed new programs.

Next, the "decision packages" discussed so glibly could be used to give renewed emphasis to program budgeting, in contrast to the old-fashioned line-item budgeting that persists in some agencies. Decision packages actually are what are called program elements in a program budget system. Budgeting by programs was a central part of what was called the PPB system, installed by Robert S. McNamara and Charles Hitch in the Defense Department in the early 1960s.

In 1965, an effort was made to extend this system to the entire government, but the extension was made without adequate preparation. Partly for this reason, and partly because it was developed in a Democratic administration, PPB was officially killed by the Republicans in 1969. [sic]

The basic idea of program budgeting remains sound, however. Indeed, in many agencies the basic idea continues to be used under other labels. The zero-base budgeting rhetoric could well be used to push for the complete installation of program budgeting throughout the government.

Third, the emphasis on stating measurable results in the budget proposal, which is implied in the form used to describe the decision packages, is a good one even though there is nothing new about it except the label. Under the term "management by objectives," this idea has been common in industry and in certain parts of the government for years. Zero-base budgeting could be used to strengthen it, particularly to focus more serious attention on the development of better output measures.

So, even though zero-base budgeting is a fraud, and even though the good parts of it are not new, experienced budget people should not let the phrase make them nauseous. They should disregard the rhetoric and latch onto the term as a way of accomplishing what really needs to be accomplished anyway.

CHAPTER 4

APPENDIX

The Federal Functional Classification

The functional classification arranges budget resources so that budget authority and outlays, loan guarantees, and tax expenditures can be related to the national need they address. The congressional budget resolutions establish budget targets for each function.

According to the *Budget of the U.S. Government, Fiscal Year 1986*, these criteria are used in assigning activities to functions:

A function must have a common end or ultimate purpose addressed to an important national need. (The emphasis is on what the federal government seeks to accomplish rather than the means of accomplishment, what is purchased, or the clientele or geographic area served.)

A function must be of continuing national importance and the amounts attributable to it must be significant.

Each basic unit of classification (generally the appropriation or fund account) is classified into the single best or predominant purpose and assigned to only one subfunction. However, when an account is large and serves more than one major purpose, it may be subdivided into two or more subfunctions.

Activities and programs are normally classified according to their primary purpose (or function) regardless of which agencies conduct the activities.

The following material presents the functional classifications, associated descriptions, and programs and departments in the functions.

FUNCTIONAL CLASSIFICATION CODES AND PROGRAM CATEGORIES

FUNCTION 050: NATIONAL DEFENSE
051: Department of Defense—Military
053: Atomic Energy Defense Activities
054: Defense-Related Activities

Description of Function:

Funds in this function are provided to develop, maintain, and equip the military forces of the United States, and to finance defense-related activities of the Department of Energy. Major areas of funding include pay and benefits for military and civilian personnel including an accrual charge for the costs of future military retirement benefits; research, development, testing, and evaluation; procurement of weapons systems and supporting equipment; military construction including family housing; and operations and maintenance of the defense establishment. Funding is also provided for the development and procurement of nuclear weapons and naval reactors.

Major Federal Programs in This Function:

Department of Defense—Military

Atomic Energy Defense Activities

Defense-Related Activities

Major Federal Departments and Agencies in This Function:

Department of Defense

Department of Energy
(Nuclear Weapons and Naval Reactors)

FUNCTION 150: INTERNATIONAL AFFAIRS

151: Foreign Economic and Financial Assistance

152: International Security Assistance

153: Conduct of Foreign Affairs

154: Foreign Information and Exchange Activities

155: International Financial Programs

Description of Function:

Funds in this function are provided to finance the foreign affairs establishment including embassies and other diplomatic missions abroad; sale of U.S. commodities under the Food for Peace programs; foreign aid loan and technical assistance activities in the less-developed countries; security assistance to foreign governments; foreign military sales made through the Foreign Military Sales Trust Fund, U.S. contributions to the international financial institutions, Export-Import Bank activities, and refugee assistance.

Major Federal Programs in This Function:

Foreign Affairs

Foreign Aid

Food for Peace

Security Assistance

Foreign Military Sales

Export Promotion

U.S. Contributions to International Financial Institutions

Refugee Assistance

Major Federal Departments and Agencies in This Function:

Department of State

Department of Defense

Department of the Treasury

Department of Agriculture

Agency for International Development

United States Information Agency

Export-Import Bank

FUNCTION 250: GENERAL SCIENCE, SPACE AND TECHNOLOGY

251: General Science and Basic Research

253: Space Flight

254: Space Science, Applications, and Technology

255: Supporting Space Activities

Description of Function:

This function includes space research and technology, general science, and basic research not specifically covered by other functional areas. The programs in this function are the primary source of funding for the physical and engineering sciences. The budgets for the National Science Foundation [NSF], certain research programs of the Department of Energy [DOE], and the National Aeronautics and Space Administration [NASA]—except for its air transportation programs—are within this category.

Major Federal Programs in This Function:

General Science and Basic Research

Space Flight, Research, Technology, and Application

Major Federal Departments and Agencies in This Function:

National Science Foundation [NSF]

National Aeronautics and Space Administration [NASA]

Department of Energy (high energy physics programs)

FUNCTION 270: ENERGY

271: Energy Supply

272: Energy Conservation

274: Emergency Energy Preparedness

276: Energy Information, Policy, and Regulation

Description of Function:

This function represents a consolidation of nearly all federal energy and energy-related programs.

Major Federal Programs in This Function:

Energy Supply

Energy Research, Development, and Demonstration

Synthetic Fuels Program

Energy Conservation

Strategic Petroleum Reserve

Nuclear Regulation

TVA Power Program

Bonneville Power Administration Programs

Major Federal Departments and Agencies in This Function:

Department of Energy

Nuclear Regulatory Commission

Tennessee Valley Authority

FUNCTION 300: NATURAL RESOURCES AND ENVIRONMENT

301: Water Resources

302: Conservation and Land Management

303: Recreational Resources

304: Pollution Control and Abatement

306: Other Natural Resources

Description of Function:

Programs in this function are primarily designed to develop, manage, and maintain the Nation's natural resources and protect public health by ensuring a clean environment.

Major Federal Programs in This Function:

Conservation, Forestry, and Land Management Programs

Water Resources Program

Sewage Treatment Plant Construction Grant Program

Protection of the Environment

Development, Regulation, and Conservation of Minerals

Management and Preservation of the Public Lands

Weather and Oceanic Research and Information Programs

Major Federal Departments and Agencies in This Function:

Department of the Interior

Department of Agriculture

Army Corps of Engineers

Environmental Protection Agency

National Oceanic and Atmospheric Administration

FUNCTION 350: AGRICULTURE

351: Farm Income Stabilization

352: Agricultural Research and Services

Description of Function:

Federal agricultural programs are intended primarily to limit economic harm to farmers from price fluctuations and to maintain farm income. Programs in this function are designed to assist food producers, provide market information and services, and support food research. Food producers are assisted through deficiency payments, disaster payments, product purchases, insurance, nonrecourse loans, and regular loans. Market information and services include Department of Agriculture administration, animal disease prevention, distribution of market information, and numerous regulatory activities. Research provides for direct support of federal biological research facilities, grants for state-supported facilities and economic analyses.

Major Federal Programs in This Function:

Price Support and Related Programs (Commodity Credit Corporation)

Federal Crop Insurance

FmHA Farm Loans

Research Programs

Extension Programs

Consumer Protection, Marketing, and Regulatory Programs

Economic Intelligence

Major Federal Departments and Agencies in This Function:

Department of Agriculture

FUNCTION 370: COMMERCE AND HOUSING CREDIT
371: Mortgage Credit and Thrift Insurance
372: Postal Service
376: Other Advancement of Commerce

Description of Function:

This function, which is highly volatile from year to year because of changing economic conditions and transactions like mortgage asset sales, provides support to mortgage credit markets, deposit insurance, the Postal Service, and other forms of commerce, including small business.

Major Federal Programs in This Function:

Mortgage Insurance Programs

Rural Housing Loans

Loans and Financing to Support Subsidized Housing

Subsidy Payment to the Postal Service

Small Business Loans

Thrift and Deposit Insurance

Regulatory Activities

Major Federal Departments and Agencies in This Function:

Department of Housing and Urban Development: FHA and GNMA

Department of Agriculture: FmHA

Department of Commerce

Postal Service

Small Business Administration

Regulatory Agencies

Federal Deposit Insurance Corporation

Federal Home Loan Bank Board

Federal Savings and Loan Insurance Corporation

FUNCTION 400: TRANSPORTATION
401: Ground Transportation
402: Air Transportation
403: Water Transportation
407: Other Transportation

Description of Function:

This function provides assistance for transportation activities including ground (highway, railroads, and mass transportation), air and water transportation programs. The transportation activities include major grant-in-aid programs to support State and local activities.

Major Federal Programs in This Function:

> Highway and Bridge Construction, Repair, and Safety
> Mass Transit
> Railroad Assistance
> Airways and Airports
> Maritime Subsidies
> Coast Guard

Major Federal Departments and Agencies in This Function:

> Department of Transportation
> NASA: Aeronautical Research and Development

FUNCTION 450: COMMUNITY AND REGIONAL DEVELOPMENT

> 451: Community Development
> 452: Area and Regional Development
> 453: Disaster Relief and Insurance

Description of Function:

This function provides for urban and rural economic assistance, area and regional development programs, and disaster assistance programs. Community development block grants account for almost half of the outlays in this function. The balance is made up of a wide variety of urban and rural development, Indian assistance, and other grant and loan assistance programs.

Major Federal Programs in This Function:

> Community Development Block Grants
> Urban Development Action Grants
> Rental Development Grants
> Rural Development Assistance
> Economic Development Assistance
> Appalachian Regional Commission
> Indian Assistance Programs
> Disaster Relief and Disaster Loans
> Flood Insurance

Major Federal Department and Agencies in This Function:

Department of Housing and Urban Development

Department of Agriculture: Farmers Home Loan Administration

Department of Commerce: Economic Development Administration

Department of the Interior: Bureau of Indian Affairs

Small Business Administration

FUNCTION 500: EDUCATION, TRAINING, EMPLOYMENT, AND SOCIAL SERVICES

501: Elementary, Secondary, and Vocational Education

502: Higher Education

503: Research and General Education Aids

504: Training and Employment

505: Other Labor Services

506: Social Services

Description of Function:

This function includes programs designed to promote the general extension of knowledge and skills and to assist individuals to become self-supporting members of society: child development, elementary, secondary, vocational, and higher education programs; employment and training programs; and grants to states for general social services and rehabilitation services. Funds in the function may be available as income support directly related to training or education; cash payments (scholarship, loans or stipends) to persons to enable them to participate in education or training programs; grants to states, local governments, Indian tribes, or public and private institutions to operate local educational, employment, training, social service programs; and direct research and departmental management expenditures:

Major Federal Programs in This Function:

Elementary and Secondary Education [ESEA]

Occupational, Vocational, and Adult Education

Higher Education Student Assistance

Higher and Continuing Education

Job Training Partnership Act [JTPA]

Grants to States for Social and Child Welfare Services

Human Development Services

National Endowment for the Arts

National Endowment for the Humanities

Major Federal Departments and Agencies in This Function:

Department of Education

Department of Health and Human Services

Department of Labor

Department of the Interior

ACTION, and Various Other Independent Agencies

FUNCTION 550: HEALTH

551: Health Care Services

552: Health Research

553: Education and Training of Health Care Work Force

554: Consumer and Occupational Health and Safety

Description of Function:

The major purpose of programs in this function is to promote the physical and mental health of the population. Programs include financing of health care for certain population groups such as American Indians, low-income Americans, migrants, grants to states, localities, and community groups to support health services programs. The function also includes research into the causes and cures of diseases; promotion of consumer and occupational health and safety; training support for health workers and researchers; and food, drug, and other product safety and inspection programs.

Major Federal Programs in This Function:

Grants to States for Medical Assistance Program (Medicaid)

Block Grants to States

National Institutes of Health [NIH]

Alcoholism, Drug Abuse and Mental Health Research, and Training

Health Resources Development

Health Services to Designated Population Groups

Disease Prevention and Control

Major Federal Departments and Agencies in This Function:

Department of Health and Human Services

Department of Labor

Office of Personnel Management

Department of Agriculture: Food Safety and Quality Service

FUNCTION 570: MEDICARE
572: Medicare

Description of Function:
The major purpose of the programs in this function is to provide health benefits to one in every six aged and disabled Americans.

Major Federal Programs in This Function:

Hospital Insurance Trust Fund

Supplementary Medical Insurance Trust Fund

Major Federal Departments and Agencies in This Function:

Department of Health and Human Services

Health Care Financing Administration

FUNCTION 600: INCOME SECURITY
601: General Retirement and Disability Insurance

602: Federal Employee Retirement and Disability

603: Unemployment Compensation

604: Housing Assistance

605: Food and Nutrition Assistance

606: Other Income Security

Description of Function:
Programs in this function help meet the needs of individuals by insuring against loss of income resulting from retirement, disability, death, or unemployment of a wage earner, and by assisting those who are unable to provide for themselves. This function includes retirement and disability programs for federal civilian workers and military personnel, railroad employees, and coal miners. This function also includes programs for unemployment compensation, food and nutrition assistance, housing assistance, and other income security.

Major Federal Programs in This Function:

Railroad Retirement

Special Benefits for Disabled Coal Miners

Federal Civilian and Military Retirement

Federal Employee Disability

Unemployment Compensation

Supplemental Security Income [SSI]

Grants to States for Assistance Payments (Primarily AFDC)

Housing Assistance
Food Stamps
Child Nutrition
Child Support Enforcement
Special Supplemental Food [WIC]
Refugee Assistance
Low-Income Energy Assistance
Earned Income Tax Credit

Major Federal Departments and Agencies in This Function:

Office of Personnel Management
Department of Agriculture: Food and Nutrition Service
Department of Health and Human Services
Department of Housing and Urban Development
Department of Labor
Railroad Retirement Board
Department of State

FUNCTION 650: SOCIAL SECURITY
651: Social Security

Description of Function:
The major purpose of the programs in this function is to provide income security to one in every six aged and disabled Americans.

Major Federal Programs in This Function:

Old Age and Survivors' Insurance Trust Fund
Disability Insurance Trust Fund

Major Federal Departments and Agencies in This Function:

Department of Health and Human Services
Social Security Administration

FUNCTION 700: VETERANS BENEFITS AND SERVICES
701: Income Security for Veterans
702: Veterans Education, Training, and Rehabilitation
703: Hospital and Medical Care for Veterans
704: Veterans Housing
705: Other Veterans Benefits and Services

Description of Function:

Most programs in this function are administered by the Veterans Administration in support of former members of the armed services and their survivors and dependents. Over half of the outlays in this function are for income security programs: compensation, pensions, and life insurance, and slightly more than one third of the outlays are targeted at hospital and medical care for veterans. Veterans education, training, rehabilitation, housing, and other benefits comprise the remainder. Nearly the entire function requires current action by Congress, yet most of these outlays are virtually uncontrollable because of the entitlement nature of the major programs.

Major Federal Programs in This Function:

Veterans Disability Compensation

Veterans Pensions

Veterans Education and Training (GI Bill)

Veterans Hospital and Medical Care

Veterans Guaranteed Housing Loans

Veterans Life Insurance

Major Federal Department and Agencies in This Function:

Veterans Administration

FUNCTION 750: ADMINISTRATION OF JUSTICE

751: Federal Law Enforcement Activities

752: Federal Litigative and Judicial Activities

753: Federal Correctional Activities

754: Criminal Justice Assistance

Description of Function:

This function includes law enforcement operations of the Federal Bureau of Investigation, Customs Service, Immigration and Naturalization Service, the Drug Enforcement Administration, and other agencies which together constitute 57 percent of total outlays in this function. Approximately 32 percent of total outlays is used by federal litigative and judicial activities. The balance of outlays, 11 percent, is used for criminal justice assistance and correctional activities.

Major Federal Programs in This Function:

Alcohol, Tobacco, and Firearms Investigation [ATF]

Federal Bureau of Investigation [FBI]

Drug Enforcement Assistance [DEA]

Immigration and Naturalization Service [INS]

Legal Services Corporation

U.S. Customs Service

U.S. Prisons

Federal Judiciary System

Law Enforcement Assistance

Juvenile Delinquency Prevention

Secret Service

Major Federal Departments and Agencies in This Function:

Department of Justice

Department of the Treasury

Legal Services Corporation

FUNCTION 800: GENERAL GOVERNMENT

801: Legislative Functions

802: Executive Direction and Management

803: Central Fiscal Operations

804: General Property and Records Management

805: Central Personnel Management

806: Other General Government

809: Deductions for Offsetting Receipts

Description of Function:

This function covers the general overhead costs of the federal Government. By far the largest proportion of new budget authority and outlays are attributable to operations of the Treasury Department (including the Internal Revenue Service). The balance is distributed among a large number of relatively small accounts. The Legislative Branch typically accounts for about one-fifth of the net total.

Major Federal Programs in This Function:

Legislative Branch Activities

Federal Buildings Fund

Income-Tax Administration

Major Federal Departments and Agencies in This Function:

Congress and Its Agencies

Executive Office of the President

Department of the Treasury
General Services Administration
Office of Personnel Management
Department of the Interior: Office of Territories

FUNCTION 850: GENERAL PURPOSE FISCAL ASSISTANCE

851: General Revenue Sharing
852: Other General Purpose Fiscal Assistance

The General Revenue Sharing program accounts for about 70 percent of this function. The balance of the function is comprised of payments and loans to the District of Columbia, along with the return of a portion of certain taxes and other charges to states, local governments, and territories.

Major Federal Programs in This Function:

General Revenue Sharing
District of Columbia Federal Payment
Payments in Lieu of Taxes to States and Countries [PILT]
Payments to Territories

Major Federal Departments and Agencies in This Function:

Department of the Treasury
Department of the Interior

FUNCTION 900: NET INTEREST

901: Interest on the Public Debt
902: Interest Received by Trust Funds
908: Other Interest

Description of Function:

This function is composed principally of interest on the public debt, to which are added minor amounts of other interest paid by the Federal Government (interest on income tax refunds, for example) and from which are deducted offsetting interest receipts, such as interest received by trust funds and interest paid by the Federal Financing Bank on its off-budget borrowings from the Treasury. The Treasury Department accordingly accounts for almost all of the transactions in this function.

Major Federal Programs in This Function:

Interest on the Public Debt

Interest Received by Trust Funds

Interest Received from Federal Fina᾽ʾcing Bank

Major Federal Departments and Agencies in This Function:

Department of the Treasury

FUNCTION 920: ALLOWANCES

Description of Function:

This function includes an amount for the civilian agency pay raises which are assumed for the budget year and projected for future years. It also may include amounts for contingencies or other budget initiatives, where the specific funding levels, by function, have not yet been determined.

Major Federal Programs in This Function:

Civilian Agency Pay Raise

Contingencies for Other Requirements

FUNCTION 950: UNDISTRIBUTED OFFSETTING RECEIPTS

951: Employer Share Employee Retirement

953: Rents and Royalties on the Outer Continental Shelf

Description of Function:

Undistributed offsetting receipts involve financial transactions that are deducted from budget authority and outlays of the Government as a whole. The two items in this function are the employer's share of employee retirement programs, composed of the federal government's contribution to its employee retirement plans, receipts from the sale of leases on Outer Continental Shelf [OCS] lands, from annual rental fees, and from royalties on oil and gas production from leased Federal lands.

5

Capital Budgeting and Project Evaluation

Capital expenditures purchase assets that are expected to provide services for several years. More technically, "a capital expenditure can be defined as an outlay that produces benefits . . . in periods beyond the current accounting period."[1] That includes the public physical infrastructure, which encompasses "streets, highways, bridges, water systems, sewers, roads, airports, jails, and other public buildings and facilities."[2] It likewise includes equipment, motor vehicles, computers, and the like, all yielding services well beyond the fiscal year of their purchase. Therefore, special care is appropriate in decisions about the purchase of all of them. Furthermore, the price tag on most of these items tends to be high and purchases typically occur at irregular intervals. For those reasons, most governments prepare and maintain a capital budget separate from the current service expenditures in an operating budget. The distinct capital budget focuses decisions, facilitates financial planning, and regularizes the provision of such projects.

Capital budgeting by state and local government requires integration of physical and financial planning. That combination has not always been found in the provision of government capital assets:

> During one phase of development of municipalities, there was a tendency to consider the capital improvement program as the exclusive domain of the Public Works Department. It was assumed that since capital improvements were largely in the nature of construction projects, the planning was

---

[1] Maynard Comiez, *A Capital Budget Statement for the U.S. Government* (Washington, D.C.: Brookings Institution, 1966), p. 4.

[2] Advisory Commission on Intergovernmental Relations, *Financing Public Physical Infrastructure*, Report A–96 (Washington, D.C.: ACIR, 1984), p. 5.

of an engineering nature. After all the planning was complete, then a price tag could be established and proper plans made for the obtaining of funds necessary to carry out the program.[3]

That simple engineering approach seems terribly primitive today as urban mobility and socioeconomic change can render facilities obsolete in a handful of years, as the strings of intergovernmental assistance complicate many financial arrangements, and as governments operate near their legal or economic debt limits. Thus, the designers of a facility must integrate their plans with the social, economic, and financial environment. In fact, that environment will usually be of greater consequence to the capital expenditure profile than the construction plans. The capital budget process establishes the formal mechanism for consideration and adoption of construction plans within prevailing constraints. This chapter describes government capital budgets and introduces cost-benefit analysis, a powerful tool which can help guide capital budget and other public decisions.

WHY HAVE SEPARATE CAPITAL BUDGETS?

A budget process is a complex set of mechanisms in which decision makers select individual projects for funding while simultaneously trying to keep total expenditures within a revenue constraint. Maintaining two different budgets certainly seems to increase complexity of an already complex process. For capital budgets to be defensible, they must make a substantial contribution to improved fiscal choice. At state and local levels, that contribution is substantial.

First, separate consideration can improve both the efficiency and equity of provision and finance of nonrecurrent projects with long-term service flows. These projects will serve, for good or bad, the citizenry for many years beyond the year of purchase. Separate consideration in a budget where deficits may be financed rather than balanced provides important opportunities to improve equity between generations and between local citizenry pools.[4] If a local government project with a 30-year service life is constructed and paid for this year, all the costs will be borne by those paying taxes to that government this year—no construction cost will be paid during the rest of the life of the project. Anyone entering the area taxpaying pool after the construction year (by moving into the area or by growing up) will receive project service with-

---

[3]Morris C. Matson, "Capital Budgeting—Fiscal and Physical Planning," *Governmental Finance* 5 (August 1976), p. 42.

[4]In other words, the spending program in a capital budget can be covered either by revenue raised currently (taxes, charges, grants, etc.) or by borrowing on the promise to repay from future revenues. Thus, the budget is financed (the money is raised from current revenue or debt sources), not balanced (total expenditures equals current revenue). Operating budgets typically must be balanced; capital budgets, financed.

out appropriate contribution. Thus, handling high-price, long-life projects through a debt-financed capital budget has strong equity advantages. Furthermore, the use of capital budgets can improve decision efficiency as well. In a single budget, there may well be a bias against big-ticket items. Separate consideration can avoid that bias and improve the chances for more reasonable response to service demand.[5] Dual budgets—a balanced operating budget and a financed capital budget—thus can make important improvements in the equity and efficiency of provision of projects and producing long-term service flow.

Second, capital budgets can stabilize tax rates when individual capital projects are large relative to the tax base of the host government. If a city with a tax base of $150 million decided to construct a $15 million reservoir for water supply, it would undoubtedly be dissuaded if it were required to collect in one year sufficient revenue for construction. The cost would be 10 percent of the total city tax base, hardly leaving enough for police and fire protection, street operation, and so on. The reservoir may have a service life of 50 years, however. It is reasonable, then, to divide the construction cost over the service life, thus reducing the burden on the tax base each year and, accordingly, preventing the dramatic fluctuation in tax rates which would result from financing the project in the construction year. The case for a regular capital budget process is strong whenever projects are likely to be large enough to significantly influence tax rates.[6]

Third, the special reviews of capital budgeting are appropriate because of the permanence of capital projects—mistakes will be around for many years. Howard illustrates the problem:

> If a new state office building is built today, it will stay there for a long time. Everybody may know by next year that it is in the wrong place, but not much can be done about moving it then. Perhaps it is disrupting the development of a downtown business district; perhaps it is affecting traffic flows and parking facilities in a most undesirable way; or perhaps its location makes it psychologically, if not geographically, far removed from certain segments of the population. Whatever these effects may be, they are real, and they will endure awhile. They should be anticipated to the fullest extent possible *before* the project is undertaken.[7]

---

[5]In a related vein, Moak and Hillhouse suggest that governments having financial trouble may find that identifiable capital projects are more easily postponed than are expenditures for operating agencies. A capital budget separately considered can improve the chances for preservation of those projects when the operating budget is under great pressure. Lennox L. Moak and Albert M. Hillhouse, *Concepts and Practices in Local Government Finance* (Chicago: Municipal Finance Officers Association, 1975), p. 98.

[6]Projects in a capital budget need not automatically be debt-financed. As will be discussed in the debt administration chapter, capital projects that recur can and should be financed from current revenue.

[7]Kenneth Howard, *Changing State Budgeting* (Lexington, Ky.: Council of State Governments, 1973), p. 241.

The capital budget reviews will not prevent all mistakes, but they can provide as much opportunity as possible for reduction of costly errors. On the positive side, those reviews and associated planning processes can produce the orderly provision of public capital facilities to accommodate economic development. Thus, the capital budget process serves to reduce errors both of commission and omission in public infrastructure construction.

Finally, capital budgets are valuable tools for management of limited fiscal resources, particularly in light of the special care required to plan activities which necessitate long-term drains on those resources. Items in this budget tend to be "lumpy." A capital budget provides a mechanism to smooth out peaks and valleys, to regularize construction activity in an effort to avoid local bottlenecks that can delay projects and inflate their cost, to avoid excessive drains on the tax base when projects must be paid for, and to balance spending with the resources available within political, economic, and legal tax and debt limits. Thus, the capital budget is an important resource management tool.

The reasons supporting a separate capital budget are strongest for local and state governments. They are less strong at the federal level. First, the federal government is charged with economic stabilization responsibilities which, according to many proponents of fiscal policy, require periods of net deficit and net federal surplus to induce appropriate macroeconomic stimulus. Dual budgets—one balanced, one not— would unnecessarily hinder federal stabilization efforts. Second, the federal government is so large that no single project is likely to influence tax rates. Third, the federal government does not need the careful planning of project financing inherent in capital budgeting to preserve its debt rating. It has, after all, the ultimate power of printing money to cover deficits. And finally, skeptics say that another budget would simply provide federal bureaucrats, already insulated from public scrutiny by existing spending and personnel mechanisms, with another way to conceal fiscal conditions. Thus, the gains from capital budgeting at lower government levels, particularly local, cannot be translated to a similar federal case.[8]

Capital budgeting promises a significant contribution to the fiscal operation of state and local government.

---

[8]As an aside, it should be pointed out that governments work with capital budgets as a device for managing their capital assets. Contrary to the practice of businesses, governments do not use depreciation accounting, nor do they need to. Businesses depreciate so that they can estimate what their profit (or loss) is in any particular year. Governments do not sell products, so they simply cannot produce such estimates. Their capital management task involves deciding whether particular projects are worth undertaking or continuing; there is no need for annual cost judgments. More discussion of this point appears in Jesse Burkhead, *Government Budgeting* (New York: John Wiley & Sons, 1963), p. 205.

The capital budget . . . provides a vehicle for financial planning and for the regulation of local tax rates. It thus contributes to financial solvency, and at the same time assures that over a period of years needed improvements will be constructed.[9]

A Capital Budget Process

Governments apply capital budgeting processes in many different ways, using various terms, steps, and staging of those steps. The process described here amalgamates several processes for illustration; most operating systems can easily be identified with this outline. In broad strokes, capital budgeting processes are concerned with (1) the selection of capital projects from the multitude of possible alternatives, (2) the timing of expenditure on the projects selected, and (3) the impact on total government finances of various plans which might be used to finance that spending. The steps outlined here encompass both physical planning and financial emphasis.

A capital budget process involves both planning and financial officers; Figure 5-1 provides a rough view of the flow and relationships in the process. The initial stage in the process is the preparation of a capital improvement program, a listing of capital expenditure projects appropriate for the next six years or so. That list is proposed by government agencies and sometimes private organizations as well; each project proposal includes justifying narrative along with cost data. These project proposals are screened by a city planning department or a similar body to evaluate costs, to locate interrelationships, and to establish initial priorities. This screening is particularly concerned with scheduling: projects should be timed to avoid waste (the sewers should be put in before the streets are resurfaced), predetermined program emphases should be implemented, and postponable projects should be identified.[10] Part of this priority review may be linked to a community master plan—a long-term (10- to 25-year), broad gauge estimate of community growth encompassing estimated needs for public improvements and controls on private use of property. (Because long-term forecasts of social, demographic, and economic behavior are so bad, however, that plan ought not be taken too seriously as a guide to actions.) The final capital improvement program will thus have a segment scheduled for each year of its span. The capital budget proposal includes the current year's work from the capital improvement program.

---

[9]Ibid., p. 185.

[10]Moak and Hillhouse, *Concepts and Practices,* pp. 104–5.

FIGURE 5-1

Capital improvement program			
	Projects ($000s)		
Year	Fire station	Library	Sewer expansion	Park
19X0...	185	0	15	15
19X1...	10	0	20	0
19X2...	0	20	30	0
19X3...	0	100	50	0
19X4...	0	0	75	0
19X5...	0	0	40	0

Capital budget	
Projects for 19X0	($000s)
Fire station	185
Sewer expansion.	15
Park	15

Operating budget	
	($000s)
Personnel costs.	640
Supplies and equipment	140
Other	20
	800

Capital expenditures	Operating expenditures
$215,000	$800,000

Total expenditures
$1,015,000

The second stage of the process coordinates a financial analysis of the government with the facility additions envisioned in the capital improvement program. This interrelationship is vital because of the long-term fiscal commitments that such facilities can involve: just as a poorly conceived structure can disrupt a city for many years, so too can a poorly conceived financing approach disrupt that city's fiscal condition. Finance officers must examine the present and anticipated revenue and expenditure profile to determine the financial cushion available for new projects. Particularly important are the status of existing debt issues (Will any issues be retired soon? Will funds be available to meet contractual debt service—principal and interest—payments? Are there needs for extra funds for early bond retirement?), the estimated growth profile of the tax base, and the potential for new revenue sources. This fiscal profile, year by year, can be then related to the priority list of projects, again scheduled by years. In this analysis, fiscal officers usually consider the financing alternatives available for specific projects (special assessments for sidewalks, user charges for water utilities, state or federal aid for highways, etc.) and further reports will have sources attached to projects.[11] From those considerations, the project list is revised in preparation for its insertion into the annual budget process. The financial analysis may permit the project schedule to remain intact, but it may well require changes based on financial conditions. In the latter instance, budget officers must devise priorities for funding, often in consultation with the chief executive (mayor or governor). One set of ranking has been used in Wisconsin:

1. Hazard to safety.
2. To fully utilize present facilities.
3. For present program expansion.
4. For future program expansion.[12]

Other projects may be evaluated with cost-benefit analysis, as described later in this chapter. Ordinarily, some choices must get made even before the projects are proposed for legislative approval.

Capital items, thus, typically are reviewed for inclusion in the capital budget before they are proposed for legislative review and approval. An illustration of the classes of projects often included appears in Figure 5-2, the groupings used in Pennyslvania. Because capital items have implications for many future years, it is appropriate that they receive that special review in the decision process. Furthermore, the CIP review is typically by planners, not budgeting personnel, so the two reviews won't emphasize the same questions. In addition, the CIP may have been prepared some years before and economic or demographic conditions may not match those earlier forecasts. The process thus provides a timely review of the project.

Finally, the surviving projects envisioned in the capital improvement program become the capital budget section of the annual budget. The projects will be reviewed by the legislature and sometimes are substantially modified. When projects are approved, provision must also be made in the operating budget for operation and maintenance of the facility when it is complete: the new civic arena won't do much good if the operating budget has no money for its interior lighting. The capital portion of the budget document usually provides a distribution of projects by function and agency, shows prior and estimated future cost of the project (initial appropriations may well have been annual—each

---

[11]Furthermore, the fiscal officers make choices about the financing policy selected for each project: borrowing (general obligation or revenue bond), use of capital reserve funds (special funds accumulated over time for future capital spending), or pay as you go. These choices are examined in the debt administration chapter.

[12]Howard, *Changing State Budgeting,* p. 257. The system does bias against new programs.

FIGURE 5-2 Groups for the Capital Budget: Pennsylvania

For the purpose of the Capital Budget, capital projects are grouped into the following categories:

- Public improvement projects—Includes all types of new buildings and renovation projects, nonstructural improvements and land acquisition.
- Public improvements—original furnishing and equipment—Includes purchase of initial furniture and equipment for furnishing completed public improvement projects.
- Transportation assistance projects—Includes (a) the purchase of rolling stock, equipment, and construction or improvement of facilities operated by mass transportation agencies throughout the commonwealth, and (b) the acquisition, construction, and equipping of rural and intercity common carrier surface transportation systems or any components thereof as authorized in Act 10 of 1976.
- Highway projects—Includes the design, purchase of right-of-way, and construction of the following improvements to highways and bridges on the state highway system:
  a. New road and bridge construction.
  b. All bridge replacements greater than 20 feet.
  c. Improvements to existing trafficways which increase capacity or ingress/egress.
  d. Highway safety projects which constitute an improvement.

SOURCE: Office of the Budget, Commonwealth of Pennsylvania, *The Budget Process in Pennsylvania*, June 1983, p. 20.

---

year's construction plan requires a new appropriation), and summarizes sources of financing (type of debt, aid, etc.). The capital improvement program thus feeds the capital budget on an annual basis: next year's segment of the capital plan becomes the capital budget proposal for next year, subject to revisions produced by the environmental conditions and the legislative process.

Total expenditures by the government include both the operating expenditures from the operating budget and capital purchases from the capital budget. The former expenditures will normally be financed by current revenue (taxes, grants, charges, etc., collected in the current year). Part of the capital budget will likely be handled on a current basis as well. The balance of capital project cost, however, will undoubtedly be debt-financed, so revenue to liquidate that debt will be raised in later years. Thus, the revenue to be generated in any budget year will equal the operating budget plus a capital project component. The latter equals capital items purchased without debt plus the debt service requirements (interest and repayment of principal) on borrowing for capital items purchased in prior years. Those debt costs would ideally approximate a depreciation charge for capital assets that have been acquired in the past; serial bonds (bonds in a single project issue which are to be paid off at various dates through the life of the project) are a rough approximation of that cost distribution.

Problems in Capital Budgeting

As is always the case with mechanisms to assist in making public decisions, there are problems in the application of capital budgeting. First, the capital improvement–capital budget process presumes a continuous cycle of reappraisal and revaluation of project proposals. That is necessary because the world changes, bringing substantial changes in the need for public projects. Unfortunately, many processes regard priorities, once established, to be unchangeable, even in the face of different project cost and different project demand. As Howard points out: "Too often cost fluctuations do not generate a reassessment of priority rankings; original rankings are retained *despite* the fluctuations."[13] Thus, many state highway construction plans are based on traffic patterns assuming 50-cent-per-gallon gasoline—they need to be revised. In a related manner, the time a project has spent in the priority queue sometimes establishes its priority rank: all old project proposals have higher rankings that any new ones. That approach makes no sense, because time alone does not improve the viability of a project which was marginal when it was first proposed. Furthermore, items entering the priority queue some years ago may have outlived their usefulness by the time they reach the funding point. Again, the problem can be resolved by maintaining reviews of projects in the capital improvement program.

Second, there can be questions about what projects or programs belong in the capital budget because, in the strictest sense, more than capital assets provide future benefit flows. Planning and zoning departments, educational institutions, training programs, and so on all provide benefits which extend beyond the year in which the service expenditure is made. Most generally, however, these activities would properly be excluded from the capital budget because spending for them is *recurrent:* it is not the single-year spending situation, the kind that needs special capital treatment. Further, most processes will establish dollar-size limits for capital budget treatment: a $500 typewriter, useful life of eight years, would be part of the operating budget, whereas an $8,500 automobile, useful life of four years, would be in the capital budget. Dollar limits will differ, but some limit will usually be encountered. Such arbitrary rules are a common factor in any decision process.

Third, availability of funds can distort the priority ranks. As Howard observes: "Despite the fact that how a project is financed does not change the need for it, there is a strong tendency for differences in the availability of capital outlay funds to skew priority decisions."[14] The appropriate approach in establishing final priorities should involve a

---

[13]Ibid., p. 256.
[14]Ibid.

general comparison of the cost of the project with the return to the community from the project—the source of money doesn't matter in that comparison. Some projects can get favored, however, because earmarked funds are available (a special tax creates a fund pool which can be spent only on one class of project); because they produce revenue which can be pledged to repayment of revenue bonds without direct tax burden or need to satisfy restrictions placed on general debt; or because federal or state assistance is available for particular projects. The purpose of many grants is to bend local priorities, so that influence is excusable. The other influences, however, are inappropriate and show why most analysts oppose such fiscal constraints.

Fourth, capital budgeting can bias toward acquisition of items by borrowing. Borrowing may not always be desirable, as with items which are acquired on a regular flow basis. Furthermore, during inflation the bias can add to macroeconomic pressures if state and local governments all operate in about the same fashion. Thoughtful fiscal analysis, however, should prevent that bias—if political pressure can be withstood.

Finally, there is the standard problem in all public decisions. That is the problem of establishing priorities in the capital improvement program. How do items get put into the capital improvement program, and which ones finally enter the capital budget? Benefit-cost analysis, to be examined next, gives some assistance, but as with ordinary items, there are no final answers.

BENEFIT–COST ANALYSIS

The constant problem in public program choice is the judgment whether a particular program is worth its cost, because society cannot afford to waste its scarce resources. Benefit-cost analysis provides a way of organizing information about a program under consideration so that priorities may be reasonably established. A private firm considering a major project, say, the purchase of a new delivery truck to replace an older and smaller one, compares the anticipated increase in revenue from the new truck with the anticipated increase in cost, after making adjustments for the time the costs and revenues are received. If the revenue exceeds cost, the purchase of the truck is a wise use of the firm's scarce resources; if not, the purchase is unwise.

Benefit-cost analysis is the governmental analogue to that process described for the firm: governments can and have used it for assistance in making decisions as diverse as decisions on word processing equipment acquisition, vehicle fleet modernization, water resource development, communicable disease control programs, development of a supersonic transport plane, and license plate reflectorization. It has also been applied to evaluate the worth of numerous governmental regulations.[15] For capital budget purposes, however, its application is much like that of private firm choice: the analysis estimates whether the gain to society (benefit) from the project is greater than the social sacrifice (cost) required to produce the project. If so, the project is worthwhile; if not, then the project is not worthwhile. Worthwhile projects improve the total economic affluence of society because they direct resources where their use provides a greater return than would other alternative use.

Skeptics point out that political bargaining characterizes the public decision process; it is not an exercise in rational consideration by nonpolitical administrators.[16] So what service can benefit-cost analysis provide in that environment? First, the analysis informs that bargaining because it can augment the political influence of underrepresented potential beneficiaries or identify the position of cost bearers. A display of costs and benefits makes it more difficult for the unrepresented to be ignored in political bargaining. In some instances, it can be a valuable weapon in the "it pays for itself" budget strategy. Second, economic efficiency—the guiding force of benefit-cost analysis—is but one of several public goals. Even though a decision may not be based primarily on those grounds, the potential gains sacrificed in the selection of a particular public policy is important information. And finally, benefit-cost analysis forces public decisions to focus on the value of competing alternatives. Valuation and the accompanying process of competing priorities are the keys to sound decision making, so benefit-cost analysis directs attention to vital questions.

Elements in Benefit-Cost Analysis

Five steps make up formal benefit-cost analysis: (1) categorization of project objectives; (2) estimation of the project impact on objectives; (3) estimation of project costs; (4) discounting of cost and benefit flows at an appropriate discount rate; and (5) summarization of findings in a fashion usable for choices. Their exact content varies according to the type of project considered; the following discussion focuses on common elements and their application in selected situations.

Project Objectives

The project analysis should identify the benefits that the project will produce. What desirable results will happen because of the project? The relationship between the project and the objective must be traceable to establish a sound foundation for the analysis. Some examples: a

---

[15]James C. Miller III and Bruce Yandle, *Benefit-Cost Analyses of Social Regulation* (Washington, D.C.: American Enterprise Institute, 1979).

[16]Federal water resource projects have one of the longest histories of cost-benefit applications. Even here, Schenker and Bunamo indicate that these projects are strongly influenced by purely political factors when examined across regions in the United States. [Eric Schenker and Michael Bunamo, "A Study of the Corps of Engineers' Regional Pattern of Investments," *Southern Economic Journal* 39 (April 1973), pp. 548–58.]

rapid transit system could increase travel speed (saving time for travelers), reduce accident costs, and reduce private vehicle operation costs. A water project might reduce flood damage, provide water for residential and other use, and improve effluent dilution conditions for water quality management. A new fire station may reduce operating costs of an older facility and reduce prospective fire loss in a service area. A word processing system may reduce labor and material costs and filing expenses. It is critical, however, that the analysis embody the principle that decisions focus on the factors that are different in the options under consideration. Nothing can be gained by examination of factors that are not changed by the decision. The principle seems too simple to matter, except that much policy argument does take place around elements that will not change regardless of the choice selected.

The benefit-cost logic is not limited to complex projects, but can be particularly useful in more narrow public management decisions about alternative methods of accomplishing a particular task. Among the applications are repair-replace and lease-purchase decisions, fuel conversion, modernization choices, EDP equipment acquisitions, and so on. In these decisions, the objective is simply to perform a task at least cost, often when one option involves a capital expenditure and others do not.

Benefit Estimation and Valuation

A Senate guide to water project evaluation defines benefits as "increase or gains, net of associated or induced costs, in the value of goods and services which result from conditions with the project, as compared with conditions without the project."[17] The same logic applies to any project. Thus, the analyst must estimate for the life of the project both physical changes from the project and the value of these changes. No standard method applies for all projects: techniques used to estimate benefits of a personnel training project would not be the same as those used in water projects. Regardless of the project, however, the decision must be made from estimates, not facts, because facts in economic or social relationships can only be historical. Present decisions cannot change what has already happened. One observer points out: "No amount of sophistication is going to allay the fact that all your knowledge is about the past and all your decisions are about the future."[18] The analysis must proceed with best estimates; it cannot be paralyzed by lack of complete information because complete information only is available when it is too late to make a decision.

---

[17]*Policies, Standards and Procedures in the Formulation, Evaluation and Review of Plans for Use in Development of Water and Related Land Resources,* 87th Congress, 2d sess., Senate document 97, approved May 1962.

[18]J. H. Wilson, quoted in *MBA Magazine,* November 1975.

An initial step estimates the physical size of the change that can be expected from the project. Sometimes a controlled experiment on a sample can estimate probable effects before resources are committed to the entire program. For instance, the state of Virginia estimated the likely benefits of reflectorized motor vehicle license plates by comparing accident frequency among a random sample of cars equipped with these plates with frequency in the remainder of the population.[19] The controlled experiment results could be used to estimate accident reduction from reflectorized plates for the entire state.

Controlled experiments are, however, seldom possible. More often, models developed from the social, physical, or engineering sciences are used to estimate that change. For water resource projects, hydrological models can yield estimates of influences of reservoirs, canals, channelization, etc., on water flows and levels. From that information can be derived the effects on navigation, probability of flooding, water supply, and so on. Gravity models from economic analysis and marketing can indicate likely drawing power of various public facilities. Trip generation models can suggest traffic flows from transportation facility changes. Any model allows the analyst to apply experiments from other environments to predict the results of projects under consideration, so that these changes can be valued: they are the key to linking government inputs to government outputs. Hovey strongly presents the importance of models:

> To analyze any program . . . requires a model, which describes the relationship between what we put into the activity (inputs) and what we expect to get out of it (outputs). Good models explain what exact relationships are, not just that a relationship exists . . . To require that the model be made explicit is one of the greatest potential contributions of systematic analysis to government. An explicit model can be studied, criticized, evaluated, and improved. Too often, decisions are made without explicit models. The result can never be better than if the model is explicit, it can frequently be worse.[20]

When the project impact has been estimated, the worth of that impact must then be estimated. Such valuation permits comparison of project cost to project returns to establish whether the undertaking increases the net well-being of the region. Money values are used, not because of any glorification of money, but simply because exchange values provide a standard yardstick to compare how individuals value the project with how they value the resources used by that project. For example, one million tons of concrete applied to highway construction

---

[19]Charles B. Stoke, *Reflectorized License Plates: Do They Reduce Nighttime Rear-End Collision?* (Charlottesville: Virginia Highway Research Council, 1974). Drivers were not told and could not control the type of plates they received. The plates did not make a difference in the incidence of such collisions.

[20]Harold A. Hovey, *The Planning- Programming-Budgeting Approach to Government Decision-Making* (New York: Praeger Publishers, 1968), p. 23.

may prolong by one year the useful life of 5,000 automobiles: resources of one type are used to save resources of another. Will the community be better off with that use of its scarce resources? A direct comparison is impossible because units being measured (cars and concrete) aren't the same. Our only meaningful alternative is to estimate the relative value individuals place on cars and concrete: how much general purchasing power individuals are willing to give up to acquire each. Those purchasing power units provide the measuring standard.

The particular valuation approach chosen depends on the project, but the task is always easiest when values can be connected to a private market. For instance, river navigation projects may reduce shipper costs: the estimated difference between cost of river shipment and that of the cheapest available alternative can indicate project value of an increased volume of shipping. The value of employment training projects can be estimated from differences in anticipated pre- and post-project incomes of trainees, allowing for differences in employment prospects.[21] Many capital expenditure items purchased by governments may reduce operating cost, the primary benefits in those instances.

For some projects, however, project outputs are not linked to goods or services sold in private markets: the output is desired for its own sake (relaxation in a city park), not because it contributes to another production process.[22] When the product or service is of this type, or when prices of marketed commodities change as a result of the project, a different approach is used. That is the estimation of consumer's surplus—the difference between the maximum price consumers would willingly pay for given amounts of a commodity and the price that the market demands for the commodity (which would be zero for public services provided at no direct charge). The underlying logic of the consumer surplus approach is relatively simple, although its application is anything but simple: points along an individual's demand curve for a product or service represent the value that the person places on particular amounts of the product in question. The individual would voluntarily exchange any amount up to the level on the demand curve rather than not have the product. He will not pay more, so the price on the curve represents the individual's valuation of the product. Refer to Figure 5–3, a representation of an individual's demand for visits to a park: for 10 visits to the park, the maximum that individual would pay is $5. If the price actually charged is above $5, the individual would visit fewer times (if at all); if the price is below $5, the individual receives a consumer sur-

---

[21]Joe N. Nay et al., *Benefits and Costs of Manpower Training Programs: A Synthesis of Previous Studies with Reservations and Recommendations* (Washington, D.C.: Urban Institute, 1973).

[22]Economists distinguish these as final products and intermediate products. See Richard A. Musgrave, "Cost-Benefit Analysis and the Theory of Public Finance," *Journal of Economic Literature* 7 (September 1969).

FIGURE 5-3 Individual Demand for a Park

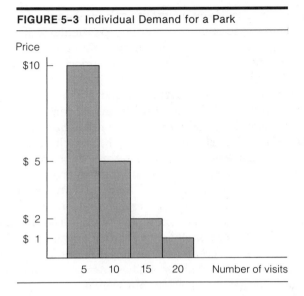

plus—he receives the service at less than the price he would have will-ingly paid. Consumer surplus then equals the difference between the maximum price the individual would have paid less the price he actual-ly pays multiplied by the number of units purchased. If the price were zero (the park has no admission charge), the total consumer surplus here would equal $90, computed by: ($10 × 5) + ($5 × 5) + ($2 × 5) + ($1 × 5). That is the entire area under the demand curve for the service.

Public services are seldom sold, so how is it possible to consider quantities demanded as a function of price? The demand curves are constructed by recognizing that implicit prices have to be paid to use most free services. Thus, individuals must pay transportation cost to use even a free facility—they bear the cost of getting from where they live to where the facility is. This cost is the implicit price; analysis of user patterns allows estimation of a demand curve. Use (quantity de-manded) usually is greater by those who are closest to the facility (travel cost, or implicit price, is lower), following the configuration of a conven-tional demand curve.[23] The approach is not without its problems, but it really is the only feasible technique for that class of public services.

Estimation of Project Costs

An estimate of the resource cost of the project includes construc-tion cost and operating cost for the life of the project. Obviously the

[23]An interesting application of the technique to estimate benefits from visits to histori-cal sites using the consumer surplus approach is Richard J. Cirre, *Estimating User Bene-fits from Historic Sites and Museums* (Ithaca, N.Y.: Program in Urban and Regional Studies, Cornell University, 1977).

preparation of these estimates requires the close cooperation of engineers and accountants skilled in costing, particularly if heavy public works facilities are involved. The analyst must recognize, however, that the important cost for society is the opportunity cost of the resources used in the project: "By the opportunity cost of a decision is meant the sacrifice of alternatives required by that decision . . . [O]pportunity costs require the measurement of sacrifices. If a decision involves no sacrifices, it is cost free."[24] The cost that matters for decisions is the value of paths not taken; that is the true cost of any decision. That complication can produce three types of adjustments to cost estimates based initially on resource purchase prices. First, ordinary project cost estimates included only private or internal costs. Many public projects, however, can create undesirable effects on others, or negative externalities. Examples include the damage done to surrounding properties by pollutants produced by a municipal incinerator or the traffic delays created when streets are blocked by construction of a government office building. These are costs inflicted upon parties outside the market transaction, but they are just as real to society as wages or payment for construction materials. These adjustments are made using the same indirect methods applied in benefit estimation—these impacts are, logically, negative social benefits.

Second, adjustments are appropriate if the project uses completely unemployed resources or resources for which there is no alternative use. If such is the case, there is nothing sacrificed in consuming those resources in the project being considered. Thus, the actual social opportunity cost of the resource to the project is zero, not the financial cost involved in paying the resource's owner. For that reason, it can be sensible to undertake programs in areas with massive unemployment when that program ordinarily would not be economically justifiable: putting the idle resources to work adds a desired product without the loss of any other product.

Finally, many public projects use property already owned by the government. Property acquisition brings no out-of-pocket cost; when sites for a new highway, incinerator, and so forth, are being compared, the site using public property has lowest financial cost. The real social cost of that site for the proposed project is the site's value in its existing (or other possible) use because that is what the community loses if the site is selected for the new use. There is no justification for valuing already-owned properties at zero. Furthermore, the amount paid for the resource (its historical cost) may not be a usable guide. For example, if a municipality invests $1.5 million in a new incineration plant

[24]William Warren Haynes, *Managerial Economics* (Plano, Tex.: Business Publications, 1969), p. 32.

that will not burn the refuse mix generated by the city, the value of the plant clearly is less than $1.5 million and, unless there is some salvage value for the facility, approximates zero. Decisions are appropriately based on opportunity costs, not historical costs.

Selection of a Discount Rate

The costs and benefits of most public projects, particularly those long-life, high-price projects proposed in a capital budget, do not occur in any single year. More often than not, an initial capital expenditure is made in one year and both operating cost and program returns accrue over a long project life. In that event, special attention must be given the timing of the flows, recognizing that a return available only at some point in the future has less value than an equal return available now.

The approach for comparing such impacts in personal, business, and public finance is discounting, a process of converting a stream of returns or costs incurred over time to a single present value. The present value takes account of both the absolute size and the timing of impacts of a proposed action.

Why is a payment of $100 received at the end of one year not equivalent to $100 received now? If inflation's erosion of purchasing power and the uncertainty of the future seem to make the answer obvious, assume that the $100 is certain to be received and has been adjusted for price level changes: the reason for discounting is related neither to inflation nor to uncertainty. The reason is simply that the $100 available now can yield a flow of valuable services (or interest) through the year. At the end of the year, the holder could have $100 plus the flow received from use of the $100 during the year. Therefore, $100 now has greater value than does $100 received at the end of the year. Furthermore, as the date of receipt is more distant, the present value of a given dollar amount is lower: the flow of services between now and then would be greater.

While the principle of time value applies to any resource or service, the mechanics most often are done using market exchange equivalents (dollar values) of those returns and the analysis uses investment for interest as the earned service flow. Thus, $X available now (the principal) will become $X plus $X times the rate of interest (the principal plus interest earned on that principal) at the end of one year. The mechanics of discounting are easier to understand after working through the more familiar process of compounding. Suppose the rate of interest is 10 percent: if $1,000 is invested today, it will accumulate to $1,100 at the end of the year. Thus

$$\$1,100 = \$1,000 + (\$1,000 \times 0.10)$$

or

Amount at end of year = Original principal + Interest earned

Algebraically, if r = the rate of interest, PV = the present amount, and FV_1 = the amount at the end of a year, then

$$FV_1 = PV + PV r \text{ or } FV_1 = PV(1 + r)$$

FV_1 equals the original principal (PV) plus accumulated interest ($PV r$).

Many policy and management questions involve multiple-year decisions—where the returns are permitted to compound over several years. In other words, the principal plus accumulated interest is reinvested and allowed to accumulate. An example would be calculation of the amount to which $1,000 would accumulate at the end of five years with 10 percent annual interest. Annual account balances are shown in Table 5–1. Obviously there must be an easier way to compute compound interest than going through all the year-end computations. Using the symbols previously introduced for values now and values at the end of a year,

$$FV_1 = PV(1 + .10) = PV(1.10)$$

At the end of the second year, the account balance would increase from interest earned:

$$FV_2 = FV_1(1.10) = PV(1.10)(1.10) = PV(1.10)^2$$

The same increase from interest earned occurs at the end of the third year:

$$FV_3 = FV_2(1.10) = \{[PV(1.10)](1.10)\}(1.10) = PV(1.10)^3$$

For the fourth year:

$$FV_4 = FV_3(1.10) = (\{[PV(1.10)](1.10)\}(1.10))(1.10) = PV(1.10)^4$$

The same process applies, regardless of the number of years. In general, if PV = the present amount, r = the appropriate interest rate, n = the number of periods of compounding, and FV_n = the account balance at the end of the periods,

$$FV_n = PV(1 + r)^n$$

From the previous example,[25]

$$FV_n = 1,000(1.10)^5 = 1,610.51$$

Interest often compounds more frequently than once a year. The compounding formula can easily be adjusted to allow for semiannual,

---

[25]For electronic calculators, use the y^x key: y = 1.10 and x = 5. Thus, $(1.10)^5$ = 1.61051.

TABLE 5–1

	Interest Earned (interest rate × previous balance)	Account Balance
Initial deposit, $1,000		
End of year:		
1	$100.00	$1,100.00
2	110.00	1,210.00
3	121.00	1,331.00
4	133.10	1,464.10
5	146.41	1,610.51

quarterly, or any other regular scheme of paying interest. For example, suppose interest is paid twice a year. With an annual rate of 10 percent, that system would mean that 5 percent interest is paid for the first half of the year and 5 percent is paid for the second half year. Thus, principal plus interest amounts at the end of the half years would be

$$FV_1 = PV(1.05) \text{ (Balance at end of one half year)}$$
$$FV_2 = PV(1.05)^2 \text{ (Balance at end of two half years)}$$
$$FV_3 = PV(1.05)^3 \text{ (Balance at end of three half years)}$$

and so on. Thus, at the end of n years,

$$FV_n = PV(1.05)^{2n}$$

In general, if interest is added x times per year, and other definitions are as before,

$$FV_n = PV\left(1 + \frac{r}{x}\right)^{nx}$$

Discounting simply adjusts sums to be received in the future to their present-value equivalent, the amount which will accumulate to that future sum if invested at prevailing interest rates. Recall that FV, the accumulated balance at the end of one year, equals $PV(1 + r)$, the balance at the start of the year multiplied by one plus the rate of interest. That formula can be arranged to become

$$PV = \frac{FV_1}{(1 + r)}$$

The amount PV invested at interest rate r will grow to FV_1 at the end of the year.

Suppose $1,000 will be received at the end of one year ($FV = 1,000$): if the interest rate that could be earned is 10 percent, what sum today (PV) would accumulate to $1,000 at the end of the year? That present value emerges from operation of the present-value formula:

$$PV = \$1,000/(1 + 0.10) = \$909.09$$

That means that $909.09 now plus 10 percent interest earned for one year ($909.90 × 0.10) equals $1,000: the present-value equivalent of $1,000 received at the end of one year when the prevailing interest rate available is 10 percent is $909.09. That prevailing rate is called the discount rate.

What happens if the return is received more than one year into the future? The same logic of adjusting for interest which could have been earned still applies, but the computations look messier because the interest earnings would compound. In other words, interest earned during the first year would be able to earn interest in the second year, and so on through the years. The general formula for compounding, $FV_n = PV(1 + r)^n$, may be rearranged in the same way that the single-year compounding formula was to produce the general present-value formula:

$$PV = \frac{FV_n}{(1 + r)^n}$$

where PV = the present-value equivalent, FV_n = a value received in the future, r is the discount rate, and n is the number of years into the future that the sum is received. For example, $800 received 10 years in the future, assuming a 10 percent discount rate, would have a present value of $308.43 (or $800/(1 + r)^n$).

In many situations, the income stream to be discounted may be constant for several years. For instance, a new maintenance garage might reduce cost by $20,000 per year for 25 years and that cost saving is to be compared with the construction cost of the garage. The flow in each year could be discounted back to the present; a quicker approach entails use of an annuity formula to compute the present value of the income stream in a single computation. If S equals the amount of the annual flow and other variables are as previously defined,

$$PV = \frac{S}{r}\left[1 - \left\{\frac{1}{1 + r}\right\}^n\right]$$

All rules about more frequent compounding (quarterly, semiannually, monthly) apply in this formula as well. In the example here, the present value of those garage cost savings if $r = 10\%$ would equal

$$PV = \frac{20,000}{0.10}\left[1 - \left\{\frac{1}{1.1}\right\}^{25}\right] = \$181,540.80$$

This formula will be used later in determination of bond prices (Chapter 13).[26]

The choice of discount rate has an important impact on the present value of a project. Suppose a project has construction cost of $10,000

---

[26]This formula also can be used to determine the level mortgage payment (principal and interest) needed to pay off a loan and is often used by engineers to convert a capital cost into an annual cost equivalent (annualization). An example of the former: suppose an

TABLE 5-2 The Impact of Discount Rates on Project Present Values

Year	Cost Outlay	Benefit Received	Present Value of Benefits, Alternative Discount Rates		
			8 Percent	10 Percent	15 Percent
1	$10,000	$1,500	1,389	1,364	1,304
2	—	1,500	1,286	1,240	1,134
3	—	1,500	1,191	1,127	986
4	—	1,500	1,103	1,025	858
5	—	1,500	1,021	931	746
6	—	1,500	945	847	648
7	—	1,500	875	770	564
8	—	1,500	810	700	490
9	—	1,500	750	636	426
10	—	1,500	695	578	371
Present value total	$10,000		10,065	9,218	7,527

and no operating cost. Its benefits of $1,500 per year start at the end of the year and continue for nine years. The project ends with no salvage values. Table 5-2 summarizes the project data and computes present values, using different discount rates. An 8 percent discount rate shows the project to produce a return slightly greater than its cost, a 10 percent discount rate shows the project to be slightly more costly than its value, and a 15 percent rate shows the project to have substantially higher cost than its value. The discount rate selected clearly influences the economic evaluation of the project.

There is, however, no single discount rate which is immediately obvious as the appropriate rate for analysis—market imperfections and differences in risk cause a broad spectrum of interest rates in the economy. Several candidates have, however, been proposed for such use. Two important candidates proposed for such use are the cost of borrowed funds to the government (the interest rate the government must pay) and the opportunity cost of displaced private activity (the return that private resources could earn). There are conditions under which either may be appropriate.

The cost of borrowed money provides the closest analogue to private project analysis—it is an interest rate which, presumably, must be paid by a borrower. Because most public programs are financed at least ultimately by tax revenues, use of the rate at which a government can

---

$80,000 mortgage is taken for 20 years at a 12 percent interest rate. The monthly payment would be computed as follows:

$$80,000 = \frac{X}{\frac{0.12}{12}}\left[1 - \left\{\frac{1}{1 + \frac{0.12}{12}}\right\}^{20 \times 12}\right]$$

$$80,000 = \frac{X}{0.01}\left[1 - \left\{\frac{1}{1.01}\right\}^{240}\right]$$

$$X = 880.86$$

borrow would not direct resources to their best-yield uses because absence of default risk on (federal) government debt makes that rate abnormally low. Allocation using that rate would pull resources away from higher-yielding private activities to prospectively lower-yield public use. For state and local government decisions, the borrowing rate could be particularly misleading because the exclusion of this interest from the federal income tax allows these governments to borrow at much below the appropriate market rate.[27] Public authorities which generate their revenue from sales of product or service might use that rate, as that does estimate the market attitude toward the prospects of the enterprise, but even here the interest excluded from income taxes complicates the analysis. The borrowing rate is generally not a good test for a social discount rate.

The return which could have been achieved in displaced private spending is generally more appropriate for the logic of benefit-cost analysis, an analysis aimed at discovering actions which increase the welfare of the community. It is a rate which the analyst must estimate—there is no defined interest rate being paid that can be looked up. Baumol lucidly expresses the essential argument:

> If the resources in question produce a rate of return in the private sector which society evaluates at r percent, then the resources should be transferred to the public project if that project yields a return greater than r percent. They should be left in private hands if their potential earnings in the proposed government investment is less than r percent.[28]

The problem is to estimate what the rate of return would have been on these displaced resources, because that is the opportunity cost a public project must exceed if it is not to misallocate resources of the community. In general, this rate can be estimated according to the formula:

$$P = k_1r_1 + k_2r_2 + \ldots + k_nr_n$$

where P = rate of return on displaced resources (the project discount rate), r = return on investment in a particular private sector, k = fraction of project cost extracted from a particular sector (usually the percentage of total taxes collected from it), and n = the number of private sectors with displaced resources. This weighted average provides a workable estimate of the private opportunity cost of the displaced resources and the resulting discount rate is applied to the estimated benefit and cost flows.

---

[27]An individual in the 30 percent federal tax bracket would receive the same after-tax rate of return on a taxed corporate bond yielding 15 percent or an untaxed municipal bond yielding 10.5 percent.

[28]William J. Baumol, "On the Discount Rate for Public Projects," in *Public Expenditures and Policy Analysis,* ed. Robert H. Haveman and Julius Margolis (Chicago: Markham Publishing, 1970), p. 274.

Decision Criteria

The final stage in project analysis applies a decision criterion to the discounted cost and return flows to summarize the economic case for the project. The summarization can be either to identify whether a project is economically justifiable or to establish rankings among projects to be fitted into a limited budget. Two criteria often used are the benefit-cost ratio (the present value of benefits divided by the present value of costs) and the net present value of the project (the present value of benefits less the present value of costs). If the ratio exceeds 1 or if the net present value is positive, the project passes the test of economic efficiency: resource use for the project will increase economic well-being because alternative use of those resource will produce a lower return for the community. Application of these criteria will ignore politics, desires for wealth redistribution, regional problems, and other side concerns, but both will capture the economics of the project.

Two additional measures sometimes proposed should be mentioned briefly. These are the internal rate of return and the payback period. The payback period method divides the estimated net annual flow of project returns into the capital cost of the project to obtain the number of years it would take to fully recover (pay back) the capital cost. Thus, if $2,000 is the net annual return from a project with a capital cost of $8,000 the payback period is four years. The shorter the period, the more attractive the project. This measure is defective because it ignores both the time profile of returns (proceeds available only late in project life are valued equal to earlier returns) and proceeds after the payback point. For example, consider the projects in Table 5–3. By payback-period reasoning, the project ranks (best to worst) would be A, B, C: if a discount rate of 10 percent were appropriate, the net present value of A = -909; of B = -909; and of C = $+1,292$. Payback periods are simply not reliable as a project guide.

The internal rate-of-return method "is to find a rate of interest that will make the present value of the cash proceeds expected from an investment equal to the present value of the cash outlays required by the

TABLE 5–3

Project	Capital Cost	Annual Net Benefits (end of year)			Payback Period
		Year 1	Year 2	Year 3	
A	10,000	10,000			1 year
B	10,000	9,000	1,100		1+ years
C	10,000	3,000	4,000	7,000	3+ years

investment."[29] That return is compared with the discount rate: the project passes the economic efficiency test if its rate of return is higher than the discount rate. The present value methods are "simpler, safer, easier, and more direct"[30] because of the adaptability of multiple discount rates during investment life, the problem of multiple internal rates of return which can emerge in computation, and the need for additional tests to determine the validity of a computed rate of return. If conditions are right, however, internal rate of return will give the same results as present-value (or benefit-cost ratio) computations.

Project analysis may require not just an evaluation of the economics of a number of projects but also selection of particular projects from several alternatives. Two ranking indexes are available: rank by ratios of benefit to cost or by net present value.[31] Project rankings are often the same with either criteria, but sometimes—especially when project sizes are substantially different—the ranks are substantially different. Which ranking should apply: that produced by net present values or the ratio of benefit to cost?

Table 5–4 presents the discounted cost and benefit data for two capital projects. If $500 is to be budgeted, should project X or project Z be undertaken? Project Z has a higher net present value while project X has the higher benefit/cost ratio. Each criterion supposes particular facts about the projects. Ranking by the ratio assumes that either project can be increased in any proportion without changing the return relationships. In the present comparison, ranking by ratio presumes that project X can be expanded three and one third times its present size at the same benefit rate (to $667), yielding a net present value of $167. That expansion must be technically and economically possible if ratios are the guide to the decision. Ranking by net present value presumes that the alternative investment streams are the size indicated, without the possibility of increase or decrease with returns constant.

In many situations, of course, neither presumption is met entirely. When such is the case, the decision must rely on comparison of present value of benefits from the use of available funds in feasible combinations of all project sizes. If the concern is with indication of economically feasible projects, not with allocation within a fixed budget, either method will be proved satisfactory: if net present value is positive, the benefit-cost ratio will be greater than 1. Conflict emerges only with rankings.

---

[29]Harold Bierman, Jr., and Seymour Smidt, *The Capital Budgeting Decision* (New York: Macmillan, 1975), p. 28.

[30]Ibid., p. 57.

[31]The ratio of excess benefit to cost (benefit minus cost divided by cost) provides no additional information, as project ranks are the same as with the benefit-cost ratio: $B/C = [(B - C)/C] + 1$.

TABLE 5-4 Projects with Ranking Criteria Conflict

Project	Cost	Benefit	Net Present Value	Benefit/Cost Ratio
Z	$500	$600	$100	1.20
X	150	200	50	1.33

Some Special Problems

Multiple objectives. Benefit-cost analysis provides information about the economic impact of projects. Overall economic impacts may not, however, be the sole or even the most important objective of some programs, particularly those concerned with redistribution of income in society. If redistribution is important, benefits received by some groups in society will be more important than benefits received by others. Market values will not measure this objective, so benefit values would need explicit adjustment to encompass redistribution concerns.

Normal benefit-cost analysis accepts all portions of the economy as equal; gaining and losing groups are not considered. It accepts the "hypothetical compensation" criterion of theoretical welfare economics: a public decision will be regarded as sound if those gaining from a public action receive sufficient benefits to compensate any losses, with some surplus gain remaining.[32] The principle ignores distribution of gains and losses across society and can be defended by these arguments: (1) that changes resulting to income distributions can be viewed as negligible,[33] (2) that public investment is not a proper tool for redistributional change because other fiscal policies are superior and can easily correct for any investment-related maldistribution; or (3) that many projects over time will have benefits randomly distributed, causing the overall effect to "average out" at no redistributional change. On these grounds, distribution effects may be ignored with some theoretical justification. The view has been growing, however, that such treatment assumes away too many issues.

Two general techniques have emerged to deal with this distributional concern. Some analysts have allowed for distribution effects by weighting benefits by a measure of the societal importance of the recipient. Values received by meritorious groups (those society wants to help) count more than values received by others. Selection of weights is obviously a problem. Weisbrod has applied weights implied in past public project decisions that have not followed strict benefit-cost

---

[32]J. G. Head, "The Welfare Foundations of Public Finance Theory," *Rivista di diritto finanziaro e scienza della finanze* 24 (September 1965); pp. 379–428.

[33]Otto Eckstein, *Water Resource Development* (Cambridge, Mass.: Harvard University Press, 1958), pp. 36–37.

ranks.[34] This approach does not, however, attack the problem of how the distribution ought to be changed, but would weight analysis in the historical pattern. Besides, the pattern may measure clout of congressional delegates, not social goals. Krutilla and Eckstein approach the problem by using marginal rates of federal taxation as weights, presuming that these rates roughly measure the importance of redistribution to society.[35] The technique does focus directly on income distribution, but it, too, has political pressure problems. Furthermore, it ignores the difference between statutory rates (those in tax law) and effective rates (those applicable after loophole). Other approaches would apply specific weights supplied by the analyst. All bend the general rule that the analyst be an impartial observer in the analytic process. Decision makers may not recognize (or accept) the value system assumed by the analyst.

An alternative, the display technique favored by McKean, would supplement general cost and benefit totals with a tabulation of how costs and benefits are divided among the population.[36] Many distributions could be important: income, age, race, sex, geographic area, etc. By providing such a display, the analyst need not weight the social importance of groups. Decision makers could supply their own weights to each recipient group as desired. The number and type of displays provided would not likely be the same for all projects. If the goal of analysis is to provide information for decision makers and consumers and not to yield conclusive, social-maximizing decisions, such displays seem a prerequisite.

Valuing life-saving projects. A sticky problem occurs when public projects seek to reduce the loss of human life, as with transportation safety, cancer research, nutrition education, or fire protection. Decisions can save or endanger lives: life or death can rest on government allocation of resources to particular projects. Those decisions are distasteful, but they have been and will continue to be made. The important question is not whether a value has been placed on the saving of human life. The real question is whether decision makers know what they are assuming about that value. Any set of decisions that denies resources to activities which have a life-saving element have implicitly

[34]Burton A. Weisbrod, "Income Redistribution Effects and Benefit-Cost Analysis," in *Problems in Public Expenditure Analysis,* ed. Samuel B. Chase (Washington, D.C.: Brookings Institution, 1968).

[35]John V. Krutilla and Otto Eckstein, *Multiple-Purpose River Development* (Baltimore: Johns Hopkins Press, 1958).

[36]Roland McKean suggests the importance of using exhibits to indicate the impact of projects on the distribution of wealth, and demonstrates its use in water resource project evaluation: *Efficiency in Government through Systems Analysis* (New York: John Wiley & Sons, 1958), pp. 131–33, 208, 242.

placed a value on life: they imply that the value is less than the cost of the rejected activity. Is that implicit value reasonable?[37]

A number of methods, none flawless but some better than others, have been proposed to value life saving. Historically, the first was average life insurance face values outstanding, under the logic that this was a value on loss of life that individuals placed on themselves. The obvious problems are that individuals buy life insurance for varied motives, including some—for example, forced saving—which have nothing to do with death potential, and that individual holdings vary substantially by family characteristics. These influences render insurance values generally inappropriate for this use.

A second technique, the earnings loss method, views the human as something equivalent to a machine. Thus, the value of a life saved is estimated at the present value of lifetime earnings less subsistence cost through the work career of the individual. That, it is alleged, equals the contribution of the individual to the economy and is the value of a life saved. There are questions both about what earning pattern to use and about whether that narrow production view truly gauges the social worth of an individual; this approach is seldom used in benefit-cost analysis today.[38] However, the judicial system does use this approach in wrongful-death cases: one element in awards to families is estimated net lifetime earnings of the individual killed.

The third technique uses evidence generated by labor-market response to higher risk of death across occupations. A number of occupations (logging, off-shore drilling, etc.) have greater death risks than other occupations with similar skills. The wage premiums necessary to recruit workers to that work provides an estimate of the value of life in the labor market. Thus, life-saving values emerge directly from the choices of individuals. There are some logical questions about the method—for one, the values may be artifically low because those jobs apparently appeal to individuals whose attitudes toward risk are different from those of others (they may actually enjoy extreme danger)—but it apparently gives the soundest estimates generally available.[39]

Government decisions do generate implicit values for life saving. That valuation cannot be avoided. Benefit-cost analysis must ensure that these valuations are conscious and consistent. It can hope for little else.

---

[37]A questionnaire to 435 adult Americans asked the question "How much, in dollars, is the average human life worth?" The average response was $28,000. [Leonard C. Lewin, "Ethical Aptitude Test," *Harpers* 253 (October 1976), p. 21.] The methods examined here have substantially stronger logical basis than this.

[38]A close variant is reportedly used in military pilot safety decisions: the value used is the cost of training a replacement. Safety feature costs are balanced against that value estimate.

[39]W. K. Viscusi, "Wealth Effects and Earnings Premiums for Job Hazards," *Review of Economics and Statistics* 60 (August, 1978); pp. 408–16.

A Final Note on Benefit-Cost Analysis

Benefit-cost analysis can supply decision makers valuable information about government activities. The analysis can estimate whether a particular project improves the efficiency of resource allocation. Supplemental displays, where relevant, can indicate its distributional impact across income classes, regions, races, sexes, and so forth, depending on the classifications deemed relevant.

The relationships and variables in the computations are estimates based on assumptions made by the analyst. Those making project choices must know what those assumptions are and how the analysis would differ with other reasonable assumptions. At minimum, the public decision maker must comprehend the structure of benefit-cost analysis to safeguard against deception from self-interested parties.

Public choices are political. No computerized, sterile analysis can substitute. Benefit-cost analysis is, however, an invaluable information tool and merits expansion as such, in spite of its possible weaknesses and potential misuses. As John Krutilla has observed:

> Since the alternative is not to retire to inactivity but, rather, to reach decisions in the absence of analysis, we may take some comfort from the belief that thinking systematically about problems and basing decisions on such analysis are likely to produce consequences superior to those that would result from purely random behavior.[40]

Questions and Exercises

1. Roachdale has a population of 22,000 more or less. Several of its important features appear on the map. The city eagerly awaits the full operation of the Intercontinental Widget Plant early in 19X3. While the plant has few employees now, it will have a work force of around 900. The plant has caused a shift in city population to the south. Many people are moving to the Wonder Hills subdivision (45 percent developed now), although a good number are located along SR4 outside of town.

   The data presented here, along with departmental project proposals, should be used to prepare a capital improvement program for the years 19X0 to 19X4 and a capital budget for 19X0. Financial conditions suggest that the city will be unable to pay more than $900,000 for capital investment in any year, so one part of the exercise requires that priority criteria be established if all requests cannot be included in the budget.

---

[40]John Krutilla, "Welfare Aspects of Benefit-Cost Analysis," *Journal of Political Economy,* July 1961, p. 234.

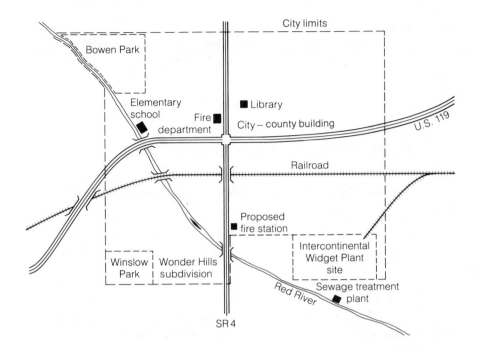

The city has two special capital asset problems. First, the main sanitary sewer at Westside Elementary School near the Red River has suffered structural failure and must be replaced. Second, the SR4 bridge over Red River is unsafe. The bridge replacement will take two years. During the first year, traffic will have to be detoured. The state will pay 90 percent of the bridge cost.

Projects Proposed:

These projects have been proposed by city department heads.

Streets, roads, and bridges:

SR4 bridge replacement—19X0, $350,000; 19X1, $250,000 (costs are totals).

Street upgrading, Wonder Hills subdivision—19X0, $600,000; 19X1, $50,000; 19X2, $20,000.

Street sign replacement—19X0 to 19X9, $18,000 per year (high visibility, break-away signs).

Parks and recreation:

Bowen Park pool—19X0, $300,000 (construction of new above-ground aluminum pool).

Winslow Park Recreation complex—19X1, $25,000; 19X2, $125,000; 19X3, $300,000; 19X4, $300,000; 19X5, $85,000 (pool, ice skating rink, baseball diamonds).

Libraries:

Air-condition building—19X0, $45,000; 19X1, $20,000.

Water and sewer:

Water line upgrading, Wonder Hills—19X2, $725,000.

Storm sewer installation, Wonder Hills—19X3, $850,000.

Sanitary sewer replacement (structural failure)—19X0, $150,000.

Fire department:

New fire substation—19X3, $450,000; 19X4, $65,000.

Fire equipment:

    a. Pumper (main station)—19X0, $25,000.

    b. Pumper, hook and ladder (substation)—19X0, $130,000.

2. My son informed me that a comic book I purchased for 10 cents in 1948 is worth $55 today. What has been the average annual compound rate of return on that valuable asset? (See Chapter 2.)

3. Dr. Rubin has $10,000 to invest for three years. Two banks offer an 8 percent interest rate, but bank A compounds quarterly and bank B compounds semiannually. To what value would his money grow in each of the two banks?

4. The Penn Central Railroad had not paid local taxes since 1969, under federal bankruptcy court protection. Some years later, the court required Penn Central to offer municipalities a choice of two payment options to clear this liability. (Penn Central, of course, has been absorbed by Conrail, so there were no future tax liabilities involved.) The choices were: (*a*) immediate payment of 44 percent of total liability or (*b*) immediate payment of 20 percent of the liability, 10 percent paid at the end of each of the next three years, and 50 percent paid at the end of 10 years. Which alternative would you recommend to a municipality and why?

5. "A logical estimate of the current opportunity cost to the community of destroying the Parris-Dunning House (a structure built in the early 1800s and lived in by an early governor of Indiana) for construction of a traffic corridor in Bloomington, Indiana, could be prepared by using the formula: $C_p = C_o (1 + r)^n$ where C_p = current opportunity cost, C_o = the original construction cost of the house, r = the appropriate interest rate available on investments over a period, and n = the number of years between construction and the present." Do you agree? Explain.

6. The irrigation system a farmer uses cost $10,000 eight years ago. It will last another 25 years without additional investment. With that system, he produces crops valued at $3,000 per year at a cost of $1,000 per year. A new system would cost $15,000 to install, but would increase production to $7,000 per year. Operating cost would be $2,500 per year. The farmer would have to refurbish the new system 12 years after installation at a cost of $5,000. Assume that investment in the new system occurs at the start of the first year, that revenue and operating cost occur at the end of each year and do not change over the 25 years, and that both systems have a salvage value of $1,000 at the end of 25 years. Assume a 10 percent discount rate. Should the farmer replace his existing system?

7. "When the Nuclear Regulatory Commission wanted to consolidate its 10 buildings in the Washington area into a single headquarters, the GSA (General Services Administration) calculated the annual rent required at $15 million and the construction cost at $113 million, or more than double what it would cost to build." (Monica Langley, "Government's Staggering Leasing Expense Stirs Debate on Whether to Rent or Buy," *The Wall Street Journal*, September 4, 1982.) Compute the net present value of the lease expense at a discount rate of 9.0 percent. Assume a 20-year building life. How does it compare with the cost of construction?

8. What problems appear in the following statements involving benefit-cost analysis?

   a. A public power project uses a discount rate of 8.5 percent, the after-tax rate of return for electric utilities in the area.

   b. Evaluation of a new municipal fire station uses a discount rate equal to the rate at which the city can borrow long-term funds.

   c. Evaluation of a new four-lane highway to replace an older two-lane highway shows saved travel time for truckers and for private vehicles, the value of increased gasoline sales, and increased profits of trucking firms.

   d. A cost-benefit analysis of removal of architectural barriers for the handicapped from commercial buildings produced these benefit estimates for a 202,000-square foot shopping center: Economic benefit during 50-year useful life of center (1975–2024) = $4,537,700 cumulative gross revenues from leasable area. (This increase in gross revenue per year attributable to new accessibilty to handicapped persons is calculated by multiplying gross revenues per year by the ratio of handicapped to nonhandicapped persons in the area. The estimate is based on gross revenue per leasable area experienced nationally in 1969, brought forward to 1975 by the rate of consumer price index increase, and extended through the 50-year life of the building according to the compounded rate of growth in sales revenue experienced by community shopping centers, 1966 to 1969. A 7 percent discount rate is employed.)

e. The Big Walnut Creek reservoir proposed for central Indiana has been estimated to cost $92.4 million (land acquisition and preparation, dam, construction, etc.). A 1972 Task Force report indicated that total annual benefits from the reservoir would exceed total annualized costs by $2.9 million. A committee of area farmers, using 1973 production figures, calculated that 16,000 acres of cropland, pasture, and woodland in the "reservoir area" would net $3.4 million annually. An opponent of the dam declared: "This is a beautiful area. It should be preserved—especially if farmland is producing more than reservoir benefits."

9. *The Chronicle of Higher Education** reported that the Kent State University athletic and alumni associations, in an effort to stimulate attendance at its homecoming football game, had sponsored an appearance at the game by the Dallas Cowboy Cheerleaders. For that game, 21,053 tickets were sold, compared to 7,186 the year before. A letter to *The Chronicle* editor sometime later questioned the sexist overtones of the promotion and wondered whether the event had even been profitable.

"*The Chronicle* article did not say whether revenue from the 52 percent increase in ticket sales offset the cost of bringing 32 cheerleaders from Dallas," a cost which the writer estimated to be about $13,000. An official of the University provided information that the athletic department paid $5,000 toward the travel expenses, with another $5,000 provided by outside donors. Further, gate receipts were $23,902. Another letter to the editor, six weeks later, provided a "rudimentary" cost-benefit analysis:

> If one makes the assumption that the 52 percent increase in ticket sales represented a 52 percent increase in dollars from ticket sales, and the university realized $23,902 in gate receipts at the game, it is simple to conclude that previous gate receipts amounted to $15,725.
>
> Since the Dallas Cowboy Cheerleaders cost a total of $10,000, $5,000 of which was paid by the athletic department and $5,000 provided by outside donors, a total of ($10,000–[23,902 - 15,725]) = $1,823 was lost on the stunt.
>
> Now, it's true that the university only paid $5,000 to recoup $8,177 in gate receipts, but they may also have otherwise been able to use the outside donation for some other (more educational) purpose, and thus would have been better off soliciting the funds for some other endeavor.

---

*Material from *The Chronical of Higher Education,* October 21, 1981; December 9, 1981; and January 20, 1982.

Questions:

a. How does this analysis differ from cost-benefit analysis?

b. Rework the analysis of financial effect, making any necessary corrections and taking full account of the principle of opportunity cost.

Cases for Discussion

A   The federal government has no formal capital budget and, as discussed earlier, may well not need one. Federal agencies do, however, have substantial capital assets and do need some systematic method for managing that capital. The following selection examines capital investment in four federal agencies—the U.S. Postal Service, the General Services Administration, the Veterans Administration, and the Corps of Engineers. Although dramatically different in services rendered, all have significant capital investment.

The material is excerpted from a General Accounting Office report. Not only is it a useful case study of capital acquisition practices in four federal agencies, but it also nicely illustrates the work done by the GAO.

Consider These Questions

1. *Do the agencies use capital budgeting as described in the chapter?*
2. *What agency does the best job of managing its capital investments? Why?*
3. *How do funding mechanisms influence the process? Should they?*

General Accounting Office Report

The U.S. Postal Service, the General Services Administration, the Veterans Administration, and the Corps of Engineers (civil works) invest directly in capital assets, which means they acquire and manage federally owned physical capital. Organizations (whether they are federal, state, or local governments or private industry) possess certain

Source: U.S. General Accounting Office, "Federal Capital Budgeting: A Collection of Haphazard Practices" (PAD-81-19, February 26, 1981).

TABLE 1

| Element | Does element enhance capital investment program? | | | |
	USPS	GSA	VA	CORPS
Agency management attitude enhances long-term capital investment.	Yes	No	Yes	Yes
Agency prepares long-term capital investment plan.	Yes	No	Yes	Yes[a]
Congressional authorization process encourages planning for capital acquisition.	Yes[b]	No	Yes	No
Agency has sufficient funds to execute capital program.	Yes	No	Yes[c]	Yes[c]
Agency controls and monitors capital project execution.	Yes	Yes	Yes	Yes
Agency uses economic analyses to justify projects.	Yes	Yes[d]	Yes[e]	Yes
Agency performs postcompletion study to determine if project accomplished its objectives.	Yes	No	Yes	No

[a]Corps annually prepares a five-year investment program that identifies projects likely to be started during the next five years, given probable funding constraints. The Corps has the capability of formulating a range of alternative five-year investment programs responsive to alternative funding levels.

[b]The Congress has granted the Postal Service broad authority over capital investments. The authorizing committees do not participate in the selection of projects.

[c]Subject to appropriated amounts.

[d]Analysis focuses on identifying the least costly way of meeting a need.

[e]Analysis focuses on demographics and identifying the least costly way of meeting a need.

elements that determine the success of their capital investment process. The elements that can enhance or hamper successful capital budgeting in the four agencies discussed in this chapter are shown in Table 1.

Of the four federal agencies discussed in this chapter, we believe that the Postal Service is the closest to what we have defined as a successful organization; however, we are not advocating that its flexibility (off-budget status and freedom from congressional authorization of capital projects) be extended to the other federal agencies. The Postal Service is unique among the agencies we examined in that it operates like a business, selling well-defined services to the public. We cite it as an organization with a capital budgeting process that has many desirable planning, budgeting, and control features that could be readily adapted by other federal agencies.

Although the Postal Service has many good capital budgeting features, it operates under a cloud of criticism because of capital investment decisions made before the effective date of the Postal Reorganization Act of 1970 and before its current capital investment system was established.[1] Today, the Postal Service's capital investment process seems sound, but we are planning to review some of USPS' more recent investments and will report our findings to the Congress.

Postal Service management recognizes that capital assets are important to productivity. USPS is an independent, off-budget agency and is not required to seek congressional authorization for individual projects. This independence makes it relatively free of the Congress as a source of funds for its operating and capital investment programs. USPS does not have to compete with other federal programs for capital investment funds. The Postal Service prepares five-year capital investment plans and performs extensive economic and cost analyses before it funds capital investment projects. Once capital programs are under way, USPS tightly monitors and controls them for cost and time of completion. After a project is completed, a postaudit analysis is done to find out if proposed results were achieved and to identify any trends that need management attention or action.

In contrast to the Postal Service, GSA is subject to strong congressional control. It must first obtain authorization committee approval for each project over $500,000 before it can request funds from congressional appropriations committees. While this requirement does not specifically restrict GSA planning, it does not encourage it either. GSA's funds are generated from user charges that finance lease payments, purchase contract payments, operations, repairs and alterations, program management, and new construction. Because of legal obligations (lease and purchase contract payments) and other priorities, new construction is the last budget item to receive funds, and the remaining funds are not sufficient to execute a successful capital investment program. Because funds are insufficient, and to keep the budget down, the executive branch has preferred to meet capital building needs by continuing GSA's leasing program. These factors do not encourage capital planning. The result is that GSA management does not have a long-term capital investment program at the moment. However, the agency is now developing a management planning system that sets forth long-range policies for public buildings acquisition, leasing, and major repair. The system is scheduled to be fully operational in early 1981. GSA says it is trying very hard to plan effectively for the future.

MANAGERS HAVE DIFFERENT VIEWS OF CAPITAL INVESTMENTS

In successful organizations, managers recognize and understand the long-term effects of capital investment. We found that managers in the four federal agencies had different views of capital investment. Postal Service officials place a very high priority on acquiring and maintaining physical capital. Corps officials told us that they consider

---

[1] U.S. General Accounting Office, "Grim Outlook for the United States Postal Service's National Bulk Mail System" (GGD-78-59, May 16, 1978).

capital investment and operations and maintenance decisions separately. VA places highest priority on operations, which are to provide medical services to veterans, and a lower priority on nonrecurring maintenance. GSA, on the other hand, for years has been preoccupied with meeting its capital investment needs by leasing and rehabilitating existing space rather than constructing new federal buildings.

U.S. Postal Service

Postal Service management wants to keep costs low and increase productivity. Officials believe they can accomplish this only by mechanizing and improving their physical capital. Through its 11-member Board of Governors, USPS can make independent decisions about capital investment, and since the Congress has granted it borrowing authority (up to $1.5 billion annually to finance capital acquisition), USPS management has sufficient funds to invest in needed capital assets.

Since 1972, the Postal Service has committed over $4 billion to capital investment, an average of about $532 million per year over the last eight years. This is considerably higher than the average of about $200 million per year for the six years (1966 to 1971) before the Postal Service became an independent agency. (In constant 1972 dollars, these averages would be, respectively, about $438 million and $233 million.)

Corps of Engineers

Since the 1960s the Corps has planned and budgeted capital investments and operations and maintenance separately. The Congress appropriates these items separately, too; thus, funds cannot be transferred from one account to the other. Traditional budget practice has been to prepare separate justifications for capital investments and operations and maintenance, and to handle priorities separately as well. Corps officials said that the Congress generally specifies funding increases or decreases by category, and only if there were an unspecified, across-the-board, appropriation increase or decrease, would there be any choosing of priorities between capital and operations and maintenance.

Veterans Administration

Like the Corps of Engineers, VA's capital and operations and maintenance are planned, budgeted, and funded separately. Priorities within each account are handled separately and funds cannot be transferred from one account to the other.

To protect its priorities, VA sets a high priority on operations essential to its mission, which is to provide medical care to veterans, and a lower priority on nonrecurring maintenance. VA officials said they understand the long-term effects of capital investments and strive to balance construction projects by selecting those compatible with their mission.

General Services Administration

For years GSA has met its capital investment building needs primarily by leasing rather than by constructing new federal buildings. From 1968 to 1979 federally owned space decreased about 23 million square feet (from 160.4 million to 137.4 million), while leased space increased by 45.1 million square feet (from 48.2 million to 93.3 million). GSA continues to rely on leasing, despite the concerns of the House and Senate Committees on Appropriations and Public Works about the increasing amount and cost of leased space. The Committees have advocated direct federal construction as the most economical way to provide space for federal agencies. GSA said it would prefer to meet more space needs by new construction, but budgetary constraints have limited its ability to do so.

We have reported that from the standpoint of the budget for the Federal Buildings Fund, the best way to finance space is to build new buildings.[2] This means large initial cash outlays for construction, but over the long term less of the Fund's resources would be used and a larger budget surplus would result. A study of eight buildings showed that under the purchase-contract method it would take 27 years to recover their costs. Had these buildings been new construction, their costs would have been recovered in 14 years. Leasing buildings provides a positive cash flow from the start, but over the entire building life direct federal construction provides a larger positive cash flow than either leasing or purchase contracting.

For years GSA's management has not been committed to an aggressive capital investment program for several reasons: its current authorization process does not encourage long-range capital planning, it does not have enough funds to implement an effective capital program, and recently it has received adverse publicity about fraud and mismanagement. In addition, during the last five years the top management of GSA's Public Buildings Service has changed six times and the agency has been criticized by the Congress and the media about kickbacks to GSA employees from contractors.

GSA recognizes the shortcomings of its capital investment plan. It is currently developing a management planning system that delineates long-range policies for physical capital. According to GSA, the system proposes to closely link planning and budgeting and to provide information on facility planning, prospectus review, resources availability, and assessment of accomplishments against planned targets.

---

[2]U.S. General Accounting Office, "Costs and Budgetary Impact of the General Services Administration's Purchase Contract Program" (LCD-80-7, October 17, 1979).

LONG-RANGE PLANNING IS NECESSARY FOR EFFECTIVE CAPITAL INVESTMENT PLANNING

A successful capital investment program depends heavily on long-range planning.[3] Every organization that we identified as successful prepares long-range plans, usually for a five-year period. These organizations understand the many advantages of gauging future trends and developments. They know that long-range planning:

> Encourages early review of priorities and capital investment objectives.

> Serves as a vehicle for coordinating projects and fostering short-term planning.

> Helps determine future funding requirements.

> Informs other agencies and the executive and legislative branches of its capital investment needs in relation to its mission.

U.S. Postal Services

The Postal Service prepares a five-year capital investment plan which, when approved by its Board of Governors, becomes the financial plan for the budget year. The plan is developed "bottom-up" by the field offices and undergoes various reviews by headquarters. Priorities are then set in the plan for the projects to be undertaken.

Each regional office is sent an approved financial plan based on the approved capital investment plan. The regions then implement their plan within the established dollar limits. Before funds are committed, the requesting regional office must prepare a cost analysis for each procurement over $2,000 and a full economic analysis for each project over $30,000.

Veterans Administration

The VA prepares a five-year medical facility construction plan, which is also developed from the bottom up. The plan lists all construction projects that exceed $2 million by year, categories of construction, and location. Public Law 96–22, Section 5007, requires the VA to submit its plan to the congressional authorizing committees for approval.

VA's 1980–84 plan contains 16 different categories of construction such as boiler plants, general projects, medical facility improvements, replacement and modernization, safety and fire. The plan also includes a list of 10 hospitals most in need of construction, replacement, or major modernization.

---

[3]Part of OMB Circular A-109, issued in 1976, directs federal agencies that acquire major systems to (1) relate capital investment needs to agency mission and goals, and communicate this relationship to the Congress early in the planning cycle and (2) identify and explore alternative concepts through early contractual competition and continue competition as long as economically feasible.

Corps of Engineers

Each year the Corps prepares a five-year investment program that lists the projects available for initiation during that five-year period, given the probable funding constraints. The selection of individual projects is based on national and regional needs within the region's allocated share of the total probable funding level. The five-year investment program does not set individual project priorities but does list, by region, the status of a project's availability for initiation.

Annual recommendations for new starts are made from categories in the five-year plan that have a high priority. Right now, the Corps is emphasizing projects that satisfy the need for hydroelectric power, urban flood control, municipal and industrial water supply, and commercial navigation.

General Services Administration

Right now GSA does not prepare any long-range capital investment plans. Officials said they used to prepare them, but since there have been so few funds for new construction in recent years they feel it is a waste of time to prepare long-range plans for construction projects. However, GSA is currently working on a five-year plan for housing its federal customers. This plan is expected to be ready for use for the 1983 budget cycle.

The lack of capital plans by GSA has recently come to the attention of the Senate Environment and Public Works Committee. Committee members introduced S. 2080, which passed the Senate on June 20, 1980. Among other things, the bill requires GSA to prepare and submit to the Congress each year a program for construction, renovation, and acquisition, along with a five-year plan for accommodating the public building needs of federal agencies.

The Committee has also expressed concern about the piece-meal authorization of individual projects throughout the year. Right now the committee approves or disapproves individual projects without the benefit of knowing the relative priority of projects, or how a particular project fits in the building program. In testimony before the Committee in January 1980, GAO said that S. 2080 is an improvement over the current authorization and planning procedure. We also discussed the need for long-range plans in our report "Foresighted Planning and Budgeting Needed for Public Buildings Program," (PAD-80-95, September 9, 1980). GSA acknowledges that it now has no cohesive, prioritized plan for all construction projects. However, such a plan is in the development stage and would be required by S. 2080.

THE CONGRESSIONAL AUTHORIZATION PROCESS CAN ADVERSELY AFFECT FEDERAL GOVERNMENT PLANNING

Today the Congress must authorize many projects individually before they can be funded. We think that planning and executing capital

TABLE 2 Requirements for Congressional Authorization of Individual Capital Investment Projects

U.S. Postal Service	No approval required
General Services Administration	All projects over $500,000
Veterans Administration	All projects over $2 million
Corps of Engineers	All projects over $2 million*

*Some projects have lower authorization levels.

investment programs can be more effective if the authorization process focused more on an agency's mission and related capital investment needs. Authorizing legislation is the basic substantive legislation that sets up or continues the legal operation of a federal agency or program. Such legislation sanctions a particular type of obligation or expenditure. It is a prerequisite for the subsequent appropriation of funds to carry out a program. The four agencies we studied have diverse requirements for congressional authorization of individual projects, ranging from no control, as in the case of the Postal Service, to almost absolute control, as in the cases of the Corps of Engineers and the General Services Administration.

Each agency has general legislative authority to acquire, operate, and maintain certain types of physical capital. For GSA, VA, and the Corps, the Congress determines (by authorizing individual projects) the location, scope, and timing of capital investments. These requirements are designed to maintain congressional authorization control (in addition to the appropriation control) of individual projects. In practice, however, such requirements, though not necessarily by design or desire, can sometimes lessen congressional control, or at least divert attention from the agency's mission. Without benefit of adequate long-range plans, these requirements force committees and the agencies to make decisions about projects without knowledge of overall needs or priorities in relation to authorized missions.

Only the Postal Service is not required to have individual projects authorized by the Congress. Since it became an independent agency in 1971, the Postal Service prepares five-year capital plans. It has also averaged two to three times more capital investment than it did as a cabinet department under more direct congressional control. In contrast, GSA, which has the strongest congressional authorization requirements, has no long-range capital plans. It has averaged significantly less than USPS in capital investment because of lack of funds in recent years. VA has authorization requirements similar to GSA's, but unlike GSA, its authorizing legislation requires that five-year plans be developed and forwarded to the authorizing committees.

U.S. Postal Service

When the Post Office Department was changed to an independent agency by the Postal Reorganization Act of 1970, it was given general authority to construct, operate, lease, and maintain buildings, facilities, equipment, and other improvements without further authorization from the Congress. Since it has become an independent agency, investment in capital assets has increased dramatically.

Veterans Administration

Only recently has the Veterans Administration been required to seek authorization of individual medical facilities before requesting appropriations for their acquisition. From 1931 to 1979, the authority to establish VA hospitals and health care facilities rested solely with the president, subject to the appropriation of funds by the Congress. The location and need for facilities was determined by the Administrator of Veterans Affairs, subject to presidential approval. The only restraint put on the VA by the Congress was the funds made available in the annual appropriation acts.

This procedure was changed in 1979 by the Veterans' Health Care Amendments of 1979 (P. L. 96–22, June 13, 1979). Title III of this Act provides that no appropriation to construct, alter, or acquire a medical facility costing over $2 million can be made unless it is first approved by a resolution of the Committees on Veterans' Affairs of the House and the Senate. These provisions also apply to leased facilities with an annual rental of more than $500,000. The VA must now submit a prospectus to both committees showing a detailed description of the project, its location, its general costs, and the cost of the equipment to operate it.

The Act also requires that VA submit to the committees a five-year plan for constructing, replacing, or altering facilities; a list of 10 hospitals most in need of construction, replacement, or major modernization; and general plans (costs, location) for each project in the five-year plan.

General Services Administration

Section 7 of the Public Buildings Act of 1959, as amended, says that no appropriation in excess of $500,000 shall be made to construct, alter, purchase, or acquire any building to be used as a public building until it has been approved by the Committees on Public Works of the Senate and House of Representatives. This section also applies to leases with an average annual rental exceeding $500,000.

The GSA Administrator submits case-by-case prospectuses to the committees since there is no legal requirement to submit an annual or multiyear plan. The prospectus authorization by each of the committees is a separate action and is not subject to the committee conference process. Thus, GSA's proposed projects are submitted to the Public Works Committees without regard to available appropriations and without explanation of relative priorities. Senator Moynihan, in a statement in the December 5, 1979, Congressional Record on S. 2080, said that:

Other than a pro forma declaration asserting the importance of each to the efficient functioning of the Government, we have no idea of the relative priorities among the proposals, nor do I believe that the GSA itself has any notion of the priorities. We can—and do—authorize projects without knowing whether there will later be an appropriation sufficient to undertake them. Some authorized projects languish unfunded for years, and some are never carried out at all.

Senator Stafford, then ranking minority member of the Environment and Public Works Committee stated that "the prospectus process may no longer be adequate or appropriate." He added: "the current prospectus process leads to piecemeal approvals without program review or oversight of the policies, and procedures inherent in project proposals."

GSA officials told us that even though they cannot get funds from the appropriations committees until the authorizing committees approve their prospectuses, 40 or 50 prospectuses are pending approval. We have reported that the authorizing committees may take several months to well over a year to approve some alteration and major repair prospectuses.[4] For example, GSA asked for $180 million for FY 1980 alterations and major repairs, but the appropriations committees reduced the request to slightly less than $146 million because several proposed projects had not yet been authorized. According to GSA officials, delays in prospectus approvals have hampered their plans for funding projects. GSA said it is trying to limit its budget requests to only those projects previously approved, but the agency points out that often it is forced to add projects for which prospectuses have not been approved because of critical repair work and the space needs of other federal agencies.

Corps of Engineers

The Corps of Engineers has the most complex and lengthy authorization process of the four agencies studied. The conception, authorization, and construction of a Corps flood control project travels through several phases of congressional authorization. In 1978, we reported that of 77 flood control projects studied, an average of 26 years had elapsed since initial authorization and start of construction.[5] Planning and design consumed 12 years of this 26-year period; reviews and the appropriations process took most of the remaining time.

Authorization of Corps projects is at the sole discretion of the Congress. There are three basic phases—study, design, and construction—

---

[4]U.S. General Accounting Office, "Repairs and Alterations of Public Buildings by General Services Administration—Better Congressional Oversight and Control Is Possible" (LCD-78-335, March 21, 1979).

[5]U.S. General Accounting Office, "Corps of Engineers Flood Control Projects Could Be Completed Faster through Legislative and Managerial Changes" (CED-78-179, September 22, 1978).

and Congress must authorize the study and construction phases. Public Works Committees authorize the conduct of studies, usually after local interests make their desires known through their elected representatives. Congress must then appropriate funds for the study. After the study is completed, the Secretary of the Army (after review by the administration) makes a recommendation to the Public Works Committees. If the project is viable and funds are available for planning, preliminary planning is done. Before detailed plans can be completed and construction permitted, the Congress must pass substantive legislation authorizing the construction. However, some projects under $2 million can be initiated by the Secretary of the Army without Congress' authorization, if they meet statutory dollar limits.

FUNDING METHODS INFLUENCE CAPITAL INVESTMENT

The source and type of funds, and an agency's ability to control its funds can hinder or facilitate the acquisition of capital assets. Funding methods affect priorities and the extent to which agencies are able to execute a viable capital investment program.

GSA and generally VA construction projects are fully funded. Postal Service projects are funded incrementally from operating receipts and/or borrowing, and Corps projects are incrementally funded by congressional appropriation. Full funding means that all of the estimated costs of a project are appropriated in the first year. Incremental funding is the appropriation of funds yearly for the estimated costs of the project for that year. As a matter of budget policy, we favor the full funding concept. However, not considering lease commitments for all future years clearly understates leasing costs and diverts decisions away from construction and acquisition to constantly escalating leases which are justified on the next year's cost only.

VA and Corps projects are funded from general fund appropriations. Their funds are placed in accounts to be used exclusively for specific capital construction projects and/or acquisition projects. GSA and the Postal Service, on the other hand, are funded through revolving funds set up by the Congress—the Federal Buildings Fund and the Postal Service Fund. These two funds are similar in that receipts from them finance expenditures, which in turn generate receipts. There are, however, important differences in the way the revenues are collected and the funds are controlled.

Activities of the Postal Service are financed by congressional appropriations and by receipts from (1) mail and services revenue, (2) reimbursements from federal and nonfederal sources, (3) interest on investments, and (4) proceeds from borrowing. These receipts are deposited into the Postal Service Fund and are used to pay for operating expenses, retirement of obligations, investments in capital assets, and investment in obligations and securities as determined by USPS. The Postal Service has a distinct advantage over GSA because it does not have to compete with other federal programs for capital investment funds and it can borrow up to $10 billion. A net increase of up to $2 billion in any one year can be used for either capital investment (no more than $1.5 billion) or operating expenses (no more than $500 million). The borrowing authority of the Postal Service greatly increases its flexibility to finance operations and capital investment.

The Federal Buildings Fund, authorized in 1972 and begun in 1975, obtains receipts from rates charged to federal agencies occupying GSA-controlled space. According to law these rates are to approximate commercial charges for comparable space and services. Collections are deposited into the Federal Buildings Fund and used, subject to annual appropriation act limitations, to finance GSA's real property operations, which consist of six program categories: (1) new construction, (2) alterations and major repair, (3) purchase contract payments, (4) lease payments, (5) real property operations (utilities, cleaning, etc.), and (6) program direction and centralized services. GSA is also reimbursed from federal agencies for space and improvements that are in excess of those covered by the standard level user charge.

New construction is a low priority in GSA's real property operations. GSA officials told us that new construction gets what funds remain after other program needs are met. Since the Federal Buildings Fund began operating in FY 1975, it has not generated enough money for new construction. Only $386 million was available in FY 1975 through 1980, an average of $64 million a year. In addition, because of language in the appropriations acts from 1975 through 1979, about $2.4 million in excess fund receipts related to the new construction program were deposited in the Treasury as miscellaneous receipts.[6] Beginning with the 1979 appropriation act, the language was changed to provide that the excess receipts remain in the Fund.

GSA's current annual average of $64 million for construction projects contrasts sharply with the $115 million annual average during the years (1959–71) before the Fund was established. Even then, GSA considered the $115 million inadequate. In 1971 GSA had a backlog of 63 projects, with estimated construction costs of $750 million, that had been authorized but not funded. GSA pointed out during hearings on the 1972 purchase-contract legislation that with annual appropriations averaging only $115 million, it would take at least 10 years to eliminate the backlog of construction already approved but unfunded by the Congress.

To reduce that backlog, the Public Buildings Amendments of 1972 (P. L. 92–313) was passed to give GSA a three-year, stop-gap authority to enter into purchase-contract agreements to construct the unfunded projects. Since then, GSA has arranged for the construction and financing of 23 projects for which it makes semiannual payments to contractors for interest, real estate taxes, and amortization of principal. At the end of the contract period, title to the buildings vests with the government.

GSA also used a dual method for constructing and financing 45 building projects. Construction contracting under the dual method

---

[6] A total of $13 million for the entire Fund were deposited in the Treasury.

was made the same as under direct federal construction, but the projects were financed by the sale of participation certificates and by borrowing from the Federal Financing Bank.

Today GSA is again faced with a backlog of projects of about $737 million. The Senate Environment and Public Works Committee recognized that direct construction funds from the Federal Buildings Fund will not put a dent in this backlog over the next several years. The Committee reported out a bill (S. 2080) that passed the Senate on June 20, 1980, authorizing GSA to borrow construction funds from the Treasury and to repay the Treasury from user charges.

In October 1979,[7] we recommended to the Congress that any new financing authority for GSA be limited to direct loans from the Treasury or the Federal Financing Bank. In January 1980 testimony before the Senate Environment and Public Works Committee, we concluded that federal construction is the best alternative for acquiring space and that borrowing money for direct federal construction is the most practical current alternative due to the limited funds generated from the Federal Buildings Fund.

B   Air travel to England through Heathrow or Gatwick, the airports serving London, can be complicated and slow. Projections done in the 1960s indicated that those airports would be unable to handle future traffic loads. A commission was established to recommend sites for a third London airport. (The concern was *where* to locate the airport, not whether the airport was needed. Thus, the effort was a cost-effectiveness analysis, not a benefit-cost analysis.) The case presented here, reproduced from the *The Wall Street Journal,* provides an interesting illustration of the problems created in valuing public losses and gains.

Consider These Questions

1. *What problems do you see with valuation according to fire insurance values?*
2. *What is wrong with the antiquarian's approach?*
3. *Can you propose an alternate approach?*

As a postscript, a third London airport has not been built, and none is currently under serious consideration.

---

[7]U.S. General Accounting Office, "Cost and Budgetary Impact of the General Services Administration's Purchase Contract Program" (LCD-80-7, October 17, 1979).

Fight Over an Old Church Raises a Tough Question

By a WALL STREET JOURNAL *Staff Reporter*

What's in a number? It seems inevitable that corporations will try to assign numerical values to elusive social values, but in so doing they may run a risk of absurdity.

Professor C. West Churchman, professor of business administration at the University of California, gives an example from the search for a site to build a third airport to serve London. One spot under serious consideration would have required demolishing the 12th-century Norman church of St. Michael's in the village of Stewkley.

It was disclosed that a cost-benefit analysis had calculated in monetary terms just what would be lost by tearing down St. Michael's. The calculations had used the face value of the fire insurance of the church—the equivalent of a few thousand dollars.

When the calculation was made public, an outraged antiquarian wrote to the *London Times* to urge another, perhaps no less plausible, method of calculation: Take the original cost of St. Michael's (perhaps 100 pounds sterling or about $240), and assume the property grew in value at a rate of 10 percent a year for 800 years. That would put the value of St. Michael's at roughly one decillion pounds. A decillion is a one followed by 33 zeroes.

St. Michael's was spared after a public outcry arose. But to Professor Churchman it was striking how glibly either side could pin a numerical value on the church. "Only a modicum of plausibility is needed to convince people that the numbers represent reality," he says. "I don't think the need is for more numbers at all. The need is for justifying the numbers"—for some rationale that "tells us what difference the numbers make."

Revenue Sources, Structure, and Administration

6

Taxation: Evaluation Criteria

Governments in the United States collect most of their own-source general revenue from taxes on income, sales, or property. Own-source general revenue excludes (1) revenue from intergovernmental aid and (2) revenue from liquor stores, utility operations, or insurance programs (social security or unemployment compensation, for instance). The first exclusion makes revenue own-source; the second, general. Charge and miscellaneous revenue play a very small role in government finance, as Table 6–1 shows. Special revenue at the bottom of the table includes the substantial collections from the payroll tax that funds federal insurance programs. This federal payroll tax, mostly for social security, is the second largest revenue producer among all sources at all levels; only revenue from federal individual income tax is larger.

The table reflects a distinct separation of revenue sources by level of government. The federal government relies predominantly on income taxes, individual and corporate, for revenue and raises more money from those taxes than state and local governments raise from all taxes combined. Federal dominance in income taxation is still greater because of the payroll tax for social security which, for individuals receiving only wage and salary income, amounts to a second federal income tax. State governments apply income taxes as well (40 states levy broad individual income taxes and 45 states tax corporate income), but their aggregate collections do not approach that of the federal government. A number of states, however, do receive more revenue from income taxes than from any other source. State income taxes often copy the federal tax; the state tax return copies data directly from the federal return. A number of cities levy local income taxes, but the overall revenue from them is inconsequential and, in many cases, the taxes are simply taxes on employee payroll, not taxes on income from all sources.

231

TABLE 6-1 Governmental Revenue by Source and Level of Government: 1982–83

	All	Federal	State	Local
Total General Revenue:	878,782	483,733	290,456	298,542
Intergovernmental revenue	—	1,846	72,704	119,399
From federal	—	—	68,962	21,021
From state	—	1,846	—	98,378
From local	—	—	3,742	—
General revenue, own sources	878,782	481,887	217,752	179,143
Taxes	665,764	381,179	171,440	113,145
Property	89,253	—	3,281	85,973
Individual income	344,067	288,938	49,789	5,340
Corporation income	51,280	37,022	13,153	1,105
Customs duties	8,727	8,727	—	—
General sales gross receipts	64,890	—	53,639	11,250
Selective sales and gross receipts	71,101	35,744	30,255	5,102
Motor vehicle and operators licenses	6,732	—	6,289	443
Death and gift	8,598	6,053	2,545	—
All other	21,117	4,695	12,490	3,932
Current charges	113,172	50,547	23,182	39,443
Miscellaneous general revenue	99,846	50,161	23,130	26,555
Special revenue:				
Utility revenue	34,033	—	2,390	31,643
Liquor store revenue	3,311	—	2,819	492
Insurance trust revenue	264,294	195,930	61,971	7,393

SOURCE: U.S. Bureau of Census, *Governmental Finances in 1982–83*, GF83 no. 5 (Washington, D.C.: U.S. Government Printing Office, 1984).

Sales taxes in their several forms are the largest single source of state revenue, and states are the largest overall users of that source. All states receive revenue from sales or gross receipts taxes and only five (Delaware, New Hampshire, Montana, Oregon, and Alaska) do not use a general sales tax. Of these five exceptions, only Oregon has shown any recent movement toward adopting the tax and voters there overwhelmingly reject referenda proposals to adopt the tax. Many local governments levy general sales taxes as well; they are second only to property tax as a tax revenue source to localities. While the sales tax shows no sign of eclipsing the property tax in local importance, there are some communities in which it is the major tax revenue producer. Contrary to the local income tax which is typically locally adminis-tered, local sales taxes are usually administered by the state govern-ment in conjunction ("piggybacked") with the state tax. The U.S. Con-stitution prohibits the states from levying customs duties (selective excises on imported items) and of total federal revenue such taxes yield only a minor proportion.

The property tax remains the major own-source revenue producer for local government. Despite continued popular and academic attacks on the tax, it remains the predominant local tax, possibly because it is the only major tax generally within the means of independent local administration. State property taxes continue their decline—a path which began during the Great Depression, when widespread property tax delinquency and declining property values, combined with a growing demand for state spending, produced a switch to other sources, particularly the sales tax. The U.S. Constitution makes adoption of a federal property tax politically difficult because it requires apportionment of any direct tax:

> No Capitation, or other direct, Tax shall be laid, unless in Proportion to the Census or Enumeration herein before directed to be taken (Article I, Sec. 9[4])

A state with $1/20$ of the national population, by that provision, would have to pay $1/20$ of the tax. To produce that apportionment, a federal tax would require high tax rates in poor states and low rates in wealthy states. Any state-by-state difference in federal tax rates would be politically impractical—as the writers of the Constitution surely knew. In his economic analysis of the Constitution, Charles Beard sums up:

> indirect taxes must be uniform, and these are to fall upon consumers. Direct taxes may be laid, but resort to this form of taxation is rendered practically impossible, save on extraordinary occasions, by the provision that they must be apportioned according to population—so that numbers cannot transfer the burden to accumulated wealth.[1]

These are the taxes which will be analyzed in the next chapters. The remaining sections of this chapter will provide a framework for evaluation of taxes in general. The following chapters will outline the structure of the major taxes and will examine the process of administering these taxes.

Although a popularity contest among taxes may seem remarkable, it is important to see that public attitudes toward taxes have changed over the last dozen or so years. Since 1972, the Advisory Commission on Intergovernmental Relations has commissioned a survey of public attitudes toward tax fairness. Some results from those surveys appear in Figure 6–1. They show that, in public opinion, the federal income and local property taxes have consistently rated as the worst, with the former currently viewed as least fair. State income taxes, despite the fact that they typically are patterned after the federal income tax, although at lower rates, are "least worst." State sales taxes are in an intermediate portion, although closer to the state income tax than to the two

---

[1]Charles Beard, *An Economic Interpretation of the Constitution of the United States* (New York: Macmillan, 1960), p. 176. The federal government has levied property taxes twice, in 1798 and in 1813. Each was apportioned, as directed by the Constitution. Dall W. Forsythe, *Taxation and Political Change in the Young Nation 1781–1833* (New York: Columbia University Press, 1977).

FIGURE 6-1 Public Opinion of Tax Fairness, 1972–1984

Question: Which do you think is the worst tax, that is the least fair, ...

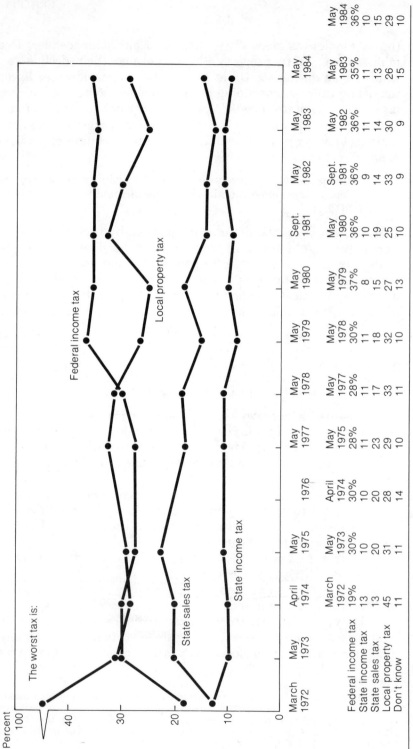

	March 1972	May 1973	April 1974	May 1975	April 1974	May 1975	May 1977	May 1978	May 1979	May 1980	Sept. 1981	May 1982	May 1983	May 1984
	March 1972	May 1973	1976	April 1974	May 1975	May 1977	May 1978	May 1980	May 1979	Sept. 1981	May 1982	May 1983	May 1984	
Federal income tax	19%	30%	30%	30%	28%	28%	30%	37%	36%	36%	36%	35%	36%	
State income tax	13	10	10	11	11	11	8	10	9	11	11	10		
State sales tax	13	20	20	23	17	18	15	19	14	14	13	15		
Local property tax	45	31	28	29	33	32	27	25	33	30	26	29		
Don't know	11	11	14	10	11	10	13	10	9	9	15	10		

SOURCE: ACIR Surveys reported in *Public Opinion* 8 (February/March 1985), p. 23.

particularly "bad" taxes. It is not clear what elements cause these popularity rankings; it would be indefensible to build tax policy on them, in any case.

CRITERIA

Economists George Break and Joseph Pechman succinctly describe the fundamental principle behind the evaluation of tax policy:

> The primary goal of taxation is to transfer control of resources from one group in the society to another and to do so in ways that do not jeopardize, and may even facilitate, the attainment of other economic goals.[2]

Those transfers include (1) shifts of purchasing power among groups in the private sector and (2) shifts of control over purchasing power from the private sector to the public sector. A tax *intends* to move resources away from private use; tax policy seeks to achieve that movement with as little other economic or social harm as possible.

Taxes are the normal source of revenues for purchase of resources used to provide public services. When public goods are financed, the involuntary nature of the tax is essential. Otherwise, rational actions of nonpayers—who could fully enjoy the public good provided without financial payment—would keep the system from producing expected revenue. Regardless of other attributes, a tax may be distinguished from other ways of raising revenue by its compulsory nature: if a potential taxpayer possesses the tax base, the tax is paid without regard to utilization of services provided by the taxing unit. Absence of voluntarism distinguishes taxes from the user charges—recreation admissions, tolls, and so on—that many governmental units collect. The tax is neither a price for service received nor a voluntary contribution. Governments do not rely on "fair share" contributions because fairness is susceptible to widely different individual definitions, particularly in regard to what one's own fair share would be.

Criteria for judging taxes and tax systems have been proposed by many observers, but there has been a substantial degree of conformity in those standards. Thus, in *Wealth of Nations* (1776), Adam Smith proposes four maxims that should be followed in taxation:

> I. The subjects of every state ought to contribute towards the support of the government, as nearly as possible, in proportion to their respective abilities; that is, in proportion to the revenue which they respectively enjoy under the protection of the state..

> II. The tax which each individual is bound to pay ought to be certain, and not arbitrary. The time of payment, the manner of payment, the quantity

---

[2]George F. Break and Joseph A. Peckman, *Federal Tax Reform, The Impossible Dream?* (Washington: Brookings Institution, 1975), p. 4.

to be paid, ought all to be clear and plain to the contributor, and to every other person.

III. Every tax ought to be levied at the time or in the manner, in which it is most likely to be convenient for the contributor to pay it.

IV. Every tax ought to be so contrived as both to take out and to keep out of the pockets of the people as little as possible, over and above what it brings into the public treasury of the state. A tax may either take out or keep out of the pockets of people a great deal more than it brings into the public treasury, in the four following ways. First, the levying of it may require a great number of officers whose salaries may eat up the greater part of the produce of the tax, and whose prerequisites may impose another additional tax upon the people. Secondly, it may obstruct the industry of the people and discourage them from applying to certain branches of business which might give maintenance and employment to great multitudes. Thirdly, by the forfeitures and other penalties which those unfortunate individuals incur who attempt unsuccessfuly to evade the tax, it may frequently ruin them and thereby put an end to the benefit which the community might have received from the employment of their capitals. Fourthly, by subjecting the people to the frequent visits and the odious examination of the tax-gatherers, it may expose them to much unnecessary trouble, vexation, and oppression: and though vexation is not, strictly speaking, expense, it is certainly equivalent to the expense at which every man would be willing to redeem himself from it.[3]

While the language of those standards has changed somewhat over the years, and emphasis has shifted somewhat with the development of a more complex economy, modern reform still concerns questions of tax bearing ability, collection costs, and dislocation of the economy. A cynic might suggest that the second criterion has become certainty of tax for others, negotiability of tax for oneself—but that clearly would not be a standard for use in public debate!

Ability to Pay or Benefits Received

Given that a specific amount of money is to be raised by a system, how ought the revenue burden be distributed? Two general standards are available: (1) burden allocated according to the benefits from the public service and (2) burdens distributed according to taxpayer capabilities to bear the burden. Choice of approach must finally be partly philosophic and partly pragmatic.

The logic of the benefit-received approach is an appealing adjunct to the exchange economy for private goods. In a quasi-market arrangement, individuals would pay for a public service if and only if they benefit from the public service. If the individual benefits, he pays an

---

[3]Adam Smith, *An Inquiry into the Nature and Cause of the Wealth of Nations*, Modern Library Edition. (New York: Random House, 1937), pp. 777–79.

amount consistent with that benefit; if he doesn't benefit, he doesn't pay. There are neither the dangerous over-supplies of public services that can result when individuals receive a service at artificially low cost nor the equally dangerous underprovision that can emerge when individuals perceive a payment greater than the value of services expected to be received. A taxpayer receiving 1 percent of the benefits of a public service would pay 1 percent of the cost of providing that service; there will be no cross-subsidization among taxpayers.

Problems prevent wholesale application of a benefit-received approach, as even the staunchest support of a social contract version of government recognizes. For one thing, pure public goods, by their very nature, produce benefits for the general community. No individually apportionable unit of service can be unambiguously bought by the citizen, so there is no divisable exchange in the public good transaction. Furthermore, modern governments are typically involved in redistribution—the provision of services directly aimed at transfer of affluence from one group to another. In this circumstance the benefit approach fails: the objective of the action is subsidization, not exchange. When circumstances of measurement and redistribution do not prohibit, however, the benefit base has strong logical support.

The ability-to-pay approach eschews the market exchange philosophy. The argument is, in simplest form, that appropriability (and its absence) make public services and private goods different by nature and only the latter are susceptible to market approaches. The decision to provide public services can be considered separately from the choice of financial burden distribution, so the distribution may be set according to concepts of fairness or equity. Unfortunately, scientific tools do not provide the analytic references to establish fairness measures. If individual satisfaction levels could be measured and compared among individuals, tax systems might be designed to yield revenues for public use at least satisfaction loss to society. There remains no calibration method, so the hope of scientific burden distribution seems beyond reach. Distribution is a matter of political opinion, not science.

Application of the ability approach has two decision elements: selection of an ability measure and choice of the manner in which tax payments should vary with that measure. The appropriateness of alternative ability measures varies with the economic circumstances of development. In an agrarian society—possibly 18th-century American—a usable measure of ability might be property ownership, particularly land, buildings, carriages, and cattle. Present-day conceptions lean toward current income—the corporate form of business and development of debt forms make gross property values an unreliable measure of ability. While most public discussion about ability to pay concentrates on income as the appropriate measure, a more comprehensive measure would encompass net wealth as well (possibly on an annuity basis), because both income and wealth figure into the real affluence of an individual.[4] The major danger in the ability-to-pay approach is the problem of clearly tying down taxable capacity. Legislative deliberations about the distribution of tax burden too often hinges on the principle: "Don't tax you, don't tax me, tax that other guy behind the tree—but tax the eyeballs off him."[5]

The second choice is the extent to which households with different abilities ought to pay different taxes. Suppose current income has been selected as the appropriate measure of ability to pay. A household with $20,000 income presumably should pay more tax than a household with $10,000 income. Should the payment by the higher income household be twice that of the other, somewhat more than twice, or somewhat less than twice? Will the distribution of income after tax be different from the distribution of income before tax and, if so, in favor of what income group should redistribution occur? This decision is an important element of social policy. It is, however, significant only for the ability-to-pay approach; it is not a major factor for a benefit-base approach.

Equity in Taxation—Horizontal and Vertical

Consideration of equity of the distribution of tax payments from households has both horizontal and vertical components. The former considers equal treatment of taxpayers who have equal capability to pay taxes: if two taxpaying units are equivalent in all relevant aspects, but one unit pays significantly greater tax, the tax structure lacks horizontal equity. Such a condition may emerge when taxes vary by individual taste and preference, as with taxes levied on commodities that are used by a narrow segment of the population. It may also occur when tax administration is haphazard or capricious. An obvious problem here is defining equivalence of taxing unit condition: the behavior that creates the failure of horizontal equity may be regarded as evidence of elevated taxpaying capability. In sum, the concept of horizontal equity may have problems in application, but the principle is strong. Equal treatment, after all, is a principle implicit in the equal protection requirements of the U.S. Constitution.

Vertical equity concerns the proper relationship between the relative tax burdens paid by individuals with *different* capability to pay taxes. The comparison is between unequals and the question is by how

---

[4] Some observers have argued for taxation primarily on consumption, because consumption represents a withdrawal of resources from social use. Ignoring some definition problems, one must still handle the fact that investment likewise involves resource utilization. For a defense of the consumption view, see Nicholas Kaldor, *The Expenditure Tax* (London: George Allen and Unwin, 1958).

[5] Senator Russell Long quoted in *People & Taxes,* May 1976.

much tax payments should differ. No scientific guides indicate what the proper differentiation might be, but most would argue that those with more capacity ought to pay more taxes. This simple observation, however, provides minimal guidance for tax policy. What needs to be determined further is whether the tax structure should be proportional, progressive, or regressive. Table 6–2 illustrates the three distributions, assuming a simple community with only three taxpayers in it.

The vertical equity concept gauges the relationship between income and effective rates (tax paid divided by the relevant affluence measure, often current income). A structure is **regressive** if effective rates are lower in high ability groups than in low, **progressive** if effective rates are higher in high ability groups than low, and **proportional** if effective rates are the same in all groups. Effective rate behavior distinguishes the structures. Notice that the proportional structure leaves the after-tax income percentages exactly as they were before tax, the regressive structure improves the share of the high-income taxpayer, and the progressive structure improves the share of the low-income taxpayer. The effective rate behavior described for each structure produces the redistribution, which is the essence of vertical equity. The choice of distribution consequences establishes whether public policy should seek progressive, proportional, or regressive tax structures, and that is basically an ethical judgment. Any equity comparison must use the effective rate not the statutory or nominal rate (the rate legally defined as applicable to the tax base). Effective and statutory rates are not the same because tax bases are not the same as affluence measures. Thus, a nominal 4 percent tax on consumption would equal an effective 2 percent tax on income if half of income is consumed. Much tax analysis concerns the relationship between tax bases and affluence measures.

Table 6–2 also illustrates measures which do not reliably indicate whether a structure is progressive or regressive. For instance, a comparison of total tax paid by high- and low-income groups will not produce meaningful information about vertical equity. For each structure here, tax paid rises with income, despite the dramatic differences in relative burden. Therefore, simply comparing total taxes paid by income groups does not provide an appropriate comparison. Neither will a comparison of the proportion of total taxes paid by an income group with that group's proportion of total population. In the example, the highest-income taxpayer represents one third of community population and the regressive tax structure causes that taxpayer to pay 62.5 percent of community taxes, so that comparison is not useful. If holding of the tax base per taxpaying unit is unequal among income groups (as it certainly must be), proportional or regressive taxes will cause high-income groups to pay a disproportionately high share of taxes and low-income groups, a low share. Thus, effective rate comparisons or their logical equivalents are the only reliable guide to vertical equity of a structure.

TABLE 6-2 Regressivity, Proportionality, and Progressivity in Tax Systems

Taxpayer Income	Percent of Pretax Income	Regressive System			Proportional System			Progressive System		
		Tax Paid	Effective Rate	Percent of After-Tax Income	Tax Paid	Effective Tax Rate	Percent of After-Tax Income	Tax Paid	Effective Tax Rate	Percent of After-Tax Income
$ 1,000	0.9	$ 100	10%	0.8	$ 100	10%	0.9	$ 100	10%	1.0
10,000	9.0	500	5	8.7	1,000	10	9.0	1,500	15	9.5
100,000	90.1	1,000	1	90.5	10,000	10	90.1	20,000	20	89.5
$111,000	100.0			100.0			100.0			100.0

Because vertical equity is so significant for decisions about taxes levied on the ability-to-pay principle, analysts often must estimate whether a particular new tax or a revision in an old tax will be progressive, regressive, or proportional. There are some standard approaches to presenting such information, although none is completely satisfactory. Fiscal administrators should understand the approaches, which all follow the same general pattern in application.

Preparing Measure of Vertical Equity

The initial stage in the analysis is identification of data on taxpaying units which contains, by unit or by typical unit within affluence classes, information on all economic behavior needed to construct (1) the level of income (or whatever measure of taxpaying capacity is seen as appropriate) and (2) the tax base being considered for each taxpaying unit. Widely used sources include Bureau of Labor Statistics, *Survey of Consumer Expenditures*; U.S. Internal Revenue Service, *Statistics of Income*; and special microdata files on taxpayers which have been constructed for tax analysis by many states and the U.S. Treasury.

The second step estimates, from that data base, the tax which would be paid by each taxpaying unit in the data file. With a sales tax, for instance, each identifiable consumption category which would be taxed is added for each taxpaying unit to estimate the individual tax base. That base multiplied by the sales tax yields the sales-tax-paid estimate. Thus, when this construction is completed, tax-paid and ability-to-pay estimates will be available for each observed taxpaying unit.

Finally, vertical equity conditions are summarized, following one of three general methods. First, a table or chart may display the effective rate for each ability-to-pay class. Table 6–3 is such a display, a very effective and complete presentation of the data. Sometimes, however, the data need to be collapsed into a quick index for comparison, a need not met by tabular detail. A second method computes a progressivity/regressivity index by dividing the effective tax rate in the highest-income class by the effective rate in the lowest-income class. Regressive structures have an index below 1.0; progressive structures, above 1.0; and proportional structures, equal to 1.0. Thus the 0.95 index (31.0 divided by 32.5) computed from incidence variant 1c of Table 6–3 indicates that the structure is mildly regressive. That index can be the means of comparing this structure with other structures. Other problems, however, often overwhelm this ease of summarization. For one thing, the index ignores patterns of effective rates in all income classes but the highest and lowest. An index computed for the structure charted in Figure 6–2 would indicate a regressive structure, even though the tax is progressive for most groups. Furthermore, the index

TABLE 6-3 Effective Rates of Federal, State, and Local Taxes under Divergent Incidence Assumptions, by Adjusted Family Income Class, 1980

Adjusted Family Income ($ thousands)	Variant 1c*	Variant 3b†
0–5	32.5	57.7
5–10	20.3	26.7
10–15	20.5	24.9
15–20	21.5	25.0
20–25	22.7	25.6
25–30	23.2	25.9
30–50	24.5	26.6
50–100	26.5	26.9
100–500	27.3	24.1
500–1,000	27.0	19.8
1,000 and over	31.0	20.7
All classes‡	25.2	26.3

*Incidence assumption 1c: individual income tax to taxpayers, sales and excise taxes to consumption of taxed commodities, corporation income tax half to dividends and half to property income in general, property tax to general property income, payroll tax (employee and employer) to employee compensation.

†Incidence assumption 3b: as above, except corporation income tax half to general property income and half to consumption, property tax on land to landowners, property tax on improvements to shelter and consumption, and payroll tax on employers half to employee consumption and half to consumption. (Among several reasonable tax incidence assumptions, 1c is most progressive and 3b is most regressive. The actual pattern likely lies between these extremes.)

‡Includes negative incomes not shown separately.

SOURCE: Joseph A. Pechman, *Who Paid the Taxes, 1966–1985* (Washington, D.C.: Brookings Institution, 1985), pp. 35, 46.

is computed from data for only a small portion of the population. Because most taxpayers are in neither the highest nor the lowest group, it ignores the structural conditions applicable to the bulk of the population. A third approach attempts to summarize the pattern of effective rates in all classes in a single index. This index, pioneered by David Davies, computes the index by running a simple regression for the taxpaying unit data by income groups:

$$w\ln\overline{T} = \ln a + b(w\ln\overline{Y}) + \ln e$$

where $\overline{T}$ = the mean tax base for each ability class, $\overline{Y}$ = the mean affluence level (probably income) for each ability class, w = the share of the total population in the ability class, b = the regressivity index, a = the

FIGURE 6-2 Effective Rates of a Hypothetical Tax, by Adjusted Family Income

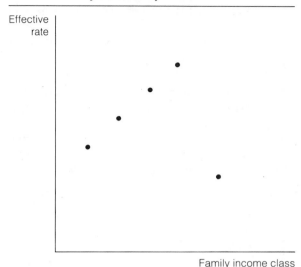

intercept, and e = a random error term.[6] If b is greater than one, the tax is progressive; if less than one, regressive; if equal to one, proportional. The index identifies whether tax paid increase more or less rapidly than does income classes. If it does, effective rates must be increasing. Thus, the regression approach seeks the average relationship between income and effective rates to summarize from all income classes.

Progressive rate structures will redistribute affluence within society. At one time, public finance economists sought scientific support for this structure through reference to diminishing marginal utility of income: those with higher affluence gain less satisfaction from income (increments to affluence) than do those with less affluence. Thus, total utility loss to society to obtain a given revenue would be minimized by applying higher tax rates to those with greater affluence. The argument of diminishing marginal utility of income has not been provable, at least partly because it may be wrong, so progression remains unscientific.[7] There continues, however, a general feeling that tax systems

[6]David G. Davies, "Progessiveness of a Sales Tax in Relation to Various Income Bases," *American Economic Review* 50 (December 1960). Population weights were added by Jeffrey M. Schaeffer, "Clothing Exemptions and Sales Tax Regressivity," *American Economic Review* 59 (September 1969). Recall that "ln" means natural logarithm.

[7]See Walter J. Blum and Harry Kalven, Jr., *The Uneasy Case for Progressive Taxation* (Chicago: University of Chicago Press, 1953).

should redistribute. The evidence in Table 6–3 shows that the U.S. systems in practice are not strongly progressive.

Estimates of vertical equity will not be made simply from the rates specified by tax law. Two conditions cause trouble: shifting of tax burdens and the statutory base/affluence measure relationship. Accounting records and/or surveys can compute the distribution of payments to the government by income class (the tax impact). This distribution will not necessarily show whose real income (or purchasing power) the tax reduces because both businesses and individuals make economic responses to imposition of a tax. Those bearing the initial impact of the tax may respond in such a way that a portion of the real burden of the tax is shifted to others. For example, the payroll tax to finance social security has two components, one paid by the employer and one paid by the employee. Some analysts argue that both components reduce the real income of the employee: the payroll tax paid by the employer represents wages, salaries, and fringe benefits that would have been paid to employees in the absence of the tax. Hence, the real burden, or incidence, is on the employee. As a general principle, laws define tax impacts but market forces (preventing or permitting shifting) define incidence; to legislate incidence is about as effective as legislating against snowfall! The shifting process is not simple to sort out, but is necessary to determine the vertical equity of a tax. The note at the bottom of Table 6–3 illustrates this by presenting the shifting assumptions used to construct that table.

The second complication in measuring vertical equity emerges because taxes are levied against convenient handles, not measures of taxpaying capacity. As an example, most states have taxes on the sale of consumption goods, with constant tax rates. The rate does not vary between consumers or levels of consumption, so the tax appears proportional by statute. Vertical equity, however, hinges on other considerations. Consumption studies, like those done by the Bureau of Labor Statistics, show that the percent of income (a normal measure of true capacity) consumed on items in the sales tax base declines as income is greater, so the effective tax rate declines as income is higher. Suppose a state applies a 5 percent sales tax to many purchases of items of consumers. Two families which are generally representative of similar units in the state have the characteristics shown in Table 6–4. The statutory (legal or nominal) rate paid by each family is 5 percent. However, the effective rate on income is 3.9 percent for family A and 2.7 percent for family B. (Full shifting of the tax to the purchaser is assumed.) The difference emerges because of the different percentages of income spent on taxable items by the two families. In this example, the effective rate falls as income is higher, so the tax has a regressive burden— even though the statutory rate is constant and even though the higher-income family pays more than twice as much sales tax than does the

TABLE 6-4

	Family A	Family B
Income	$5,500	$22,000
Family size	3	4
Purchase of taxed items	4,300	12,000
Sales tax paid	215 (4,300 × 5%)	600 (12,000 × 5%)
Effective rate	3.9% (215/5,500)	2.7% (600/22,000)

lower-income family. Thus, the rate which was proportional by statute is regressive in effect. But what if consumption or even consumption of items identified for consumption in the tax base is really seen as the appropriate measure of taxpaying capacity?[8] Conclusions about the tax change and disagreement among both expert and amateur policy results.

Business and Individual Shares

Analysts occasionally estimate the relative share of taxes paid by businesses and individuals, especially at the state and local level of government, as a guide to tax policy. Business taxes are usually defined to include taxes on business property, corporate net income taxes, business gross receipt taxes, corporate franchise taxes, miscellaneous business and occupation taxes, licenses, severance taxes, document and stock transfer taxes, and the like. Taxes on individuals include property taxes on residences and personal property, individual income taxes, retail sales taxes, and selective excise taxes. Special classification problems arise with taxes on agricultural property (what portion of a farmer's property tax bill is individual and what portion is business?), with taxes on unincorporated business income (the business is taxed through the individual income tax system), and with sales tax paid on business purchases, but those complexities can usually be resolved by allocations based on a sample of taxpayers.

There is, however, some question about the usefulness of these share measurements, even though none can question their importance and frequency of citation in political discussions. The final incidence of any tax is on individuals, regardless of its initial impact. A business may respond in three ways to a tax levied on it: the business may increase its prices to reflect the tax, the business may reduce the price it pays to owners of resources it purchases, or the business may return a lower profit to its owners. What actually occurs depends on the form of

---

[8]If that truly is the appropriate capacity measure, it ought to be the standard applied for consideration of other taxes as well.

the tax and on the market conditions the firm faces, but it can be expected to respond in whatever fashion will leave its owners with greatest profit after tax.[9] With each possibility, however, the business tax reduces the real income of individuals, either by causing customers to pay higher prices, by causing workers or other resource owners to receive lower income for what they sell to the firm, or by leaving owners of the business with lower profit from the business. The business/individual tax share question is usually less significant for tax policy than the patterns of individual tax burdens after business response (tax shifting) has occurred. The business is merely a conduit between the tax-collecting government and the burden-bearing individual.

State and local governments are interested in relative business/individual shares, however, for reasons other than fairness of the burden distribution. In many instances, the individuals ultimately bearing the burden of business taxes live out of state.[10] A higher business share thus means that a greater amount of the cost of state and local government will be exported to nonresidents. That exporting is politically attractive, even if the extent of exporting attempted may not always be logically justified. While those businesses do receive services provided by the host community, the appropriate amount of payment is always subject to dispute between businessses and the government. Furthermore, states must take care that out-of-state businesses are not treated more harshly than are domestic businesses because differential treatment would violate the commerce clause of the U.S. Constitution.[11]

The capability to use taxes with initial impact on business as a means of exporting the cost of government to nonresidents does, however, have an important limitation. That is the concern that the taxes will adversely affect the competitive positions of business in the state. As John Bowman observes:

> If firms in states A and B compete in the same market, and state A raises all its revenue from industry (100 percent business share) while state B raises none of its revenue from industry (zero business share), it may well be that state taxation will place the firms in State A at a competitive disadvantage.[12]

---

[9]The responses are carefully analyzed in Richard A. Musgrave, *The Theory of Public Finance* (New York: McGraw-Hill, 1959), chap. 13.

[10]Note that certain individual taxes may be substantially exported in special circumstances: residental property taxes in second-home communities, lodging taxes in tourist areas, etc.

[11]"The Congress shall have Power . . . to regulate Commerce with foreign Nations and among the several States and with the Indian Tribes." (Article 1, Sec. 8[3]). Differential treatment by a state involves a power reserved to Congress.

[12]John H. Bowman, "What is the Business Share of Taxes?" *Bulletin of Business Research* 47 (January 1972), p. 3.

Share data must be tempered with evaluation of the overall level of taxes in the competitive states (all of a very low absolute tax would have less influence on competitive position than a moderate share of a very high absolute tax), but the concern with competitive balance does influence the quest for cost exporting. Thus, states frequently trade exporting for competitive balance in policy deliberations because relative shares, in addition to vertical and horizontal equity, make up part of the fairness criterion for them.

Adequacy or Revenue Production[13]

A tax levied for revenue is worthwhile only if it can generate meaningful revenue at socially acceptable rates. Some taxes may be levied for reasons other than revenue—punitively high rates to stop an undesirable activity or taxes applied simply to keep track of a particular activity—but revenue is the prime objective of most taxes. One aspect of adequacy—absolute adequacy or the capacity of the source to fund functions of the levying unit—can best be understood using an analytic device called the Laffer or rate-revenue curve.[14] This curve, illustrated in Figure 6–3, relates revenue collected for a specific tax base and tax rates applied to that base (all other influences held constant) and shows that a given amount of revenue, R_z, can be collected at two rates, one high (t_a) and one low (t_o). No revenue would be collected from a particular tax base if no tax is applied to that tax base or if a rate is applied which is so high that the taxed activity ceased to exist (except for bootleg transactions). There is for each tax base a rate (t_1) which produces the maximum possible revenue (R_1) from the base. Efforts to obtain more than that amount will be futile, because higher rates will discourage the taxed activity sufficiently to cause revenue collections to decline. Studies of the relationship between tax rates and revenues, at least for major state taxes, show that states are on the lower portion of the curve.[15] That is, a tax rate increase of 1 percent produces a collection increase of something less than 1 percent, but it is an increase. It is quite likely that some selective excises (cigarette or liquor taxes) may

---

[13]Recall that Adam Smith did not include revenue production among his maxims.

[14]The Laffer curve, after Arthur Laffer, as described by one of its early and strong proponents, Jude Wanniski, hinges on shifts of economic activity between the money economy and the barter economy: when tax rates on transactions in the former reach some level, transactions switch to the latter, where they are difficult or impossible to trace and tax (Wanniski, "Taxes, Revenues, and 'Laffer Curve'," *The Public Interest*, Winter 1978, pp. 3–16.) Wanniski also maintains that U.S. tax rates certainly are on the upper half of the function. That presumption has not been demonstrated; further, the relationship can hinge on more than evasion.

[15]Gerald E. Auten and Edward H. Robb, "A General Model for State Tax Revenue Analysis," *National Tax Journal* 29 (December 1976), pp. 422–35.

FIGURE 6-3 Illustration of Laffer (or Rate-Revenue) Curve

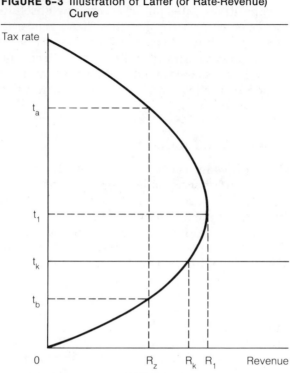

be on the upper portion in some areas, but the only portion discovered to date is that which slopes upward.

The problem of absolute adequacy is more substantial when state restrictions interfere with local actions. For instance, a state legislature may establish a special district to provide services financed only from a single excise tax base or may impose restrictive property tax rate ceilings on local governments. These circumstances may be illustrated again in Figure 6–3. The legally limited rate would be t_k, producing revenue level R_k for the taxing unit. If revenue needs of the special district or local government exceed R_k, then the modern absolute adequacy problem exists and there is little that decision makers for the affected unit can do, except scrimp and seek other revenues.

Adequacy also considers revenue patterns across both cyclical (short-run) and secular (long-run) time dimensions. Efforts to manage the national economy have not eliminated economic fluctuations, particularly in states and smaller economic regions, some of which suffer from episodes of unemployment approaching depression levels. Governmental functions continue during depressed economic activity and may grow because of social tensions in these periods. A revenue source with good cyclical adequacy will not fall dramatically with declining economic activity, but will remain reasonably stable. Such stability is vital for state and local governments, because they lack the borrowing flexibility and money-creating powers that accommodate federal deficits. In general, taxes on corporate profits will be particularly unstable because of the volatility of that base. Some states historically were reluctant to rely on that source for that reason. Property taxes have great stability, except for delinquency problems in deep depression. General sales taxes are somewhat less stable than individual income taxes, probably because business equipment purchases constitute a sizable share of the former tax base.[16]

Revenue stability, however, is a problem for government when economic growth continues with little interruption. Demand for many government services increases more rapidly than the increase in economic activity. The demand pattern can be examined using the income elasticity of service expenditure, a measure which estimates the percentage increase in expenditure resulting from a 1 percent increase in income. Those services for which expenditure increases more rapidly than does income have an income elasticity greater than one: an increase in income of 1 percent generates an increase in government spending greater than 1 percent. Governments lacking revenue sources with similar growth characteristics face the prospect of increased debt, increased tax rates (or new taxes), or unmet demand for government services. Each of these options is politically unpleasant, so there is a general preference for responsive taxes, those whose revenue increase more rapidly than does income (the income elasticity exceeds one). Table 6-5 reports income elasticities by individual tax bases as found in

TABLE 6-5 Compilation of Selected Tax Income Elasticities as Found in Various Tax Studies

	Median	High	Low
Personal income tax (9 studies)	1.75	2.4	1.3
Corporate income tax (9 studies)	1.1	1.44	0.72
General property tax (12 studies)	0.87	1.41	0.34
General sales tax (10 studies)	1.0	1.27	0.80
Motor fuels tax (10 studies)	0.73	0.80	0.43
Tobacco tax (8 studies)	0.26	0.54	0.00

SOURCE: Compiled from ACIR (Advisory Commission on Intergovernmental Relations), *Significant Features of Fiscal Federalism, 1976-1977*, vol. 2, *Revenue and Debt*, p. 254.

---

[16]John L. Mikesell, "Cyclical Sensitivity of State and Local Taxes," *Public Budgeting and Finance* 4 (Spring 1984), pp. 32–39.

several recent tax studies.[17] Overall, the income tax bases show greatest responsiveness (caused both by rate graduation and sensitivity of the base), while motor fuel and tobacco taxes—taxes generally applied on a specific (volume or unit) basis, rather than on a value (volume times price) basis—have the least responsiveness. The general sales tax is in an intermediate position. The property tax elasticity estimates are probably artificially high, as some studies reported do not separate out the revenue effects of increased property tax rates, so the elasticity result is not purely the outcome of automatic base growth.[18] Because responsive taxes may not be stable, the appropriate choice for adequacy over time will depend on whether problems of growth or problems of decline are most likely and whether the government has access to debt markets and the ability to raise rates during periods of economic decline.

Collectibility

A tax must be collectible at reasonable cost to society. Resources used in the collection of revenue provide no net service to society: the revenue, not its collection, is valuable. In general, taxes and tax provisions ought to be designed to keep total collection cost as low as is feasible within the constraint of satisfactory equity. Unfortunately, there is frequently an equity-collectibility trade-off. For instance, taxes on payrolls represent the income tax format with least collection cost: collection is made by employers (there are far fewer of them to keep track of than there are employees), the problem of checking on interest and dividend income is avoided, and special questions about rents and capital gains do not arise. Unfortunately, self-employed individuals and those with interest, dividend, rental, and capital gain income tend to be more affluent than those receiving only payroll income. Thus, the tax which is simple to administer has equity problems. As a rule, collection complexity with broad-based taxes (property, sale, and income) results from attempts to improve the equity of the particular tax. That is the critical trade. Narrow-base taxes—particularly selective excises—often simply cannot be collected at low cost and are good candidates for elimination. The resources used in their collection can be more profitably used in administration of other taxes. A more detailed analysis of

---

[17]These elasticities are typically computed from a time-series regression of the form $\ln B = a + b\ln Y$ where B is the tax base analyzed, Y is the measure of economic activity, and b is the income elasticity of the tax. Other influences on the base—for instance, statutory tax rate changes—may also be included as independent variables.

[18]A study which extracts out both rate changes and general reassessments of property found a property tax base elasticity of 0.27 in one state (Indiana). This measure is more comparable to those reported for sales and income taxes bases because it extracts all statutory and administrative sources of base change. [John L. Mikesell, "Property Tax Assessment Practice and Income Elasticities," *Public Finance Quarterly* 6 (January 1978), p. 61].

the tax collection process, along with collection costs, appears in Chapter 10.

Economic Effects

A final criterion used in evaluation of taxes is the extent to which the tax distorts economic activity. There are philosophic differences in the interpretation of such distortions. Some argue that a tax should be neutral in its effect: market systems can be trusted to function well without intervention, so the most that one should expect from a tax is that it disturbs such functioning as little as possible. Others argue that a tax should have favorable economic effects: the outcome from market operations can be improved by using taxes to alter private behavior in some desired fashion. Regardless of view about the appropriateness of such distortion, it is clear that taxes do influence economic behavior and that influences differ among taxes. Most would agree that taxes ought not harm economic welfare, even if they ought not be used to stimulate desired behavior.

Efficiency effects—the economic dislocations induced by taxes—seldom will be the primary influence on selection of financing mechanisms. As McKie observes, "Failure of efficiency is not a slogan that brings men cheering into the street."[19] The imposition of taxes, however, can have important effects on economic activity. Whenever a tax wedge produces a difference in the return which can be gained between two or more competing economic activities, individuals and businesses can be expected to respond toward the alternative leaving a greater after-tax return. That wedge can influence many different choices:

1. Work versus leisure. High taxes on extra income earned may induce workers to choose more leisure time instead of working more hours with much of the extra income taken by government.
2. Business operations. Firms ought not be induced to undertake strange business practices solely to avoid tax. Thus, a state property tax on business inventory held on particular date can induce firms to ship inventory out of state on that date for return later.
3. Consumption choice. High tax rates on cigarettes and liquor in some states induce their residents to purchase those items from nearby states with lower taxes and lower prices.
4. Personal management. Because travel expense to professional conventions can be subtracted from income subject to the federal individual income tax, such conventions frequently are held in

---

[19]James W. McKie, "Organization and Efficiency," *Southern Economic Journal* 38 (April 1972), p. 451.

resort locations. Those attending can thus combine vacation and business while reducing their tax obligation.

5. Productive investment. High-income entities may direct investable funds to municipal bonds, the interest on which is tax-free, rather than to the purchase of productive capital equipment, the return on which would be taxed.

There are many other examples of each type of distortion. Overall, taxes should not discourage employment or economic growth or encourage inflation more than the minimum needed to extract resources for government operation. Undesirable distortions should be minimized.[20]

CONCLUSION

The number of handles available to governments seems almost without end. In general, the many possible handles eventually translate into taxes on incomes, taxes on ownership and ownership exchange, and taxes on purchase or sales. Taxes require an involuntary payment; they are not collected for services received on a normal exchange basis. Because of separation of service receipt and payment, it is possible to evaluate taxes on the basis of planning criteria. Those criteria are equity (vertical and horizontal), adequacy, collectibility, and economic effects.

Questions and Exercises

1. Patterns and structure of revenue for state and local government are important policy concerns because they establish the distribution of the burden of public service provision. Revenue revision can only begin with a clear understanding of where revenue policy leaves the state and its localities now, and what options available have not been selected. Furthermore, it is useful to understand what conditions are like in surrounding areas. Evidence for such discussions can be drawn from sources like the Department of Commerce's *Survey of Current Business* (monthly); the Census Bureau's *Census of Governments* (quinquennially), *Governmental Finances* (annually), *State Tax Collections* (annually), and *City Finances*; the Advisory Commission of Intergovernmental Relations' *Significant Features of Fiscal Federalism* (biennially); and state tax handbooks published

---

[20]Some taxes intend distortions. For instance, the Canadian federal government has applied a $100 tax on automobile air conditioners—an extra inducement to convince automobile purchasers to skip an accessory which reduces fuel economy in that climate.

annually by Prentice-Hall and Commerce Clearing House. From those and similar sources, prepare answers to these questions about the revenue system in your state:

a. How does the burden of state, local, and state-local taxation in your state compare with that of the nation and region? (Comparisons are often made as percentages of state personal income and per capita.) How does the local share of state and local taxes compare?

b. Prepare an estimate of the relationship between business and individual tax shares for your state. Where are there allocation problems?

c. How rapidly have state and local taxes grown in your state during the past five years? Is that faster or slower than growth in state personal income and the rate of inflation? Have there been tax rate increases (decreases) affecting that growth?

d. What are the major revenue sources used by governments in your state? How does relative use of those sources compare with the nation and the region? Does your state have any major taxes not common to other states (severance, business and occupation, local income, etc.)? Are some typical taxes not used?

Case for Discussion

The governor of Pennsylvania created a commission in 1979 to review the structure of state and local taxes in that state. After considerable research by professionals recruited from universities around the state, the commission released its final report in 1981.

The following selections from the report outline the goals of a tax system, as viewed by the commission.

Consider These Questions

1. *Does the commission see an appropriate balance between income, sales, and property taxes?*
2. *Is the commission concerned with vertical and horizontal equity?*
3. *Do the criteria used by the commission match those described in the chapter? Where are there differences? What might cause those differences?*
4. *How does your state compare on the burden measures reported in the table?*

Overall Considerations: Goals for Pennsylvania's Tax System

The objective of this commission has been to examine the totality of the Pennsylvania Tax System. While total tax revenue collected and the number of taxes levied have grown significantly over the last 100 years, the tendency has been to meet the revenue needs of the moment with ad hoc taxes. As a result, the system has too many taxes which lack a clear rationale. The system lacks a clear set of objectives and fails to display a set of criteria which are met by the various taxes.

In this *Report,* we will specify objectives for the tax system and attempt to develop a system that will meet these objectives. In addition, we will articulate the criteria that individual taxes should meet in order to be used as part of the system. Our long-run objective is to establish a model tax system for state and local governments with the hope that such an accomplishment will influence tax policy throughout the country.

A. GOALS

It is common to state goals to achieve unanimous approval by reducing the content within them. That is not our desire. The goals we state are to be used as standards that will aid in the reform of the system. We also recommend that these goals be utilized in any future examination of the tax system.

1. Simplicity

In order for a tax to be accepted, the individual paying the tax must understand it. As the complexity of a tax increases, understanding decreases and, as a result, resistance to the tax increases. The Federal Individual Income Tax is an excellent example of this proposition. As Congress has tried to influence taxpayer behavior with respect to certain economic and social objectives, it has created a myriad of provisions that define income, taxpayers, and tax rates, and provided many exceptions from the general rules. The Pennsylvania Personal Income Tax, on the other hand, has been kept simple and is much better understood. Simplicity of structure is important in the long run in a democratic society to maintain positive attitudes by the electorate toward government.

2. Certainty

The tax system should be stable, predictable, and relatively permanent so that the taxpayer, whether an individual or a corporation, can determine his tax bill at any time. This characteristic also serves the

Source: Selections from Section I of the *Final Report of the Pennsylvania Tax Commission* (March 1981).

Commonwealth since budgeting is facilitated when revenue estimates are accurate. Uncertainty leads to different opinions as to taxpayer liability and such differences lead to litigation. In turn, litigation increases the cost of collection and also increases hostility toward government. For individuals and businesses considering the decision to move to Pennsylvania, or to stay in Pennsylvania, certainty can be an important ingredient in the final decision, and thus indirectly affect Pennsylvania's potential for economic growth. When state and local taxes are uncertain or ambiguous in application, individuals and firms may find other states more attractive.

3. Equity

The tax system and the individual taxes must be viewed as fair and equitable if taxpayers are to comply voluntarily with it. Attempts to evade and avoid the payment of taxes increase when the system is perceived to be inequitable. A system that is fair is one in which all persons (or firms) with the same economic situation are treated equally. Also, a system that is fair is one in which all persons or firms in different economic situations contribute resources through the tax system in a manner that the electorate finds consistent with its social values. Balanced against the need to redistribute income to achieve social justice must be a concern for the impact such sacrifices have on various segments of society. As we will show later, the property tax, as currently assessed in Pennsylvania, does not meet the equity standard. The large amount of subjective judgment involved in property appraisal leads to differential taxes for taxpayers with property of equal market value in the same jurisdiction. As the lack of equity becomes apparent in a tax, taxpayers become disillusioned with their government.

4. Economy of Administration

Different taxes may require different collection systems and costs. In general, a tax system should contain taxes that can be collected as inexpensively as possible. When the cost of collection, including costs to the taxpayer, is a high percentage of the revenue (3 percent or more), the desirability of the tax must be questioned.

5. Impact of Taxes on Economic Efficiency

From the standpoint of resource allocation, the goal of economic efficiency is central. The objective of neutrality, which enhances economic efficiency, is to avoid distortions of economic choices which can be induced by taxes. When price and output decisions by firms or the decision to work or not to work by individuals are modified as a result of a tax, the tax is not economically efficient. For example, a specific sales or excise tax can have the effect of a price increase. As a result, for those products being taxed, there will be a reduction in demand for the commodity. Consumers will make new sets of decisions with respect to their expenditures as a result of the changes in price due to the sales tax. In this sense, then, such a specific sales tax is not economically efficient because it affects economic decisions. Similarly, relatively high rates of taxation on personal income can dissuade individuals from working, and relatively high rates of taxation on the wealth of business can discourage necessary capital accumulation by business. A tax system should be neutral with respect to the allocation of resources.

6. Revenue Adequacy

The commission is committed to the principle that the overall burden of state and local taxes should not increase over time as a percent of personal income. As a corollary, it believes that public expenditures should be financed with a system of taxation that meets these needs with a minimum of change from year to year. To the extent that tax receipts at given tax rates fail to grow in relation to economic growth, legislators are forced constantly at the state and local level to revise tax rates and in turn cause uncertainty about the future course of tax policy. This revenue adequacy, generally determined by the level of growth elasticity, is most problematical at the local level where such taxes as the property tax and various per capita taxes grow much more slowly than the economy.

7. Efficiency and Effectiveness of Tax Expenditures

Despite a preference for neutrality, it is sometimes necessary to use the tax system to achieve social goals. The use of the tax system to subsidize or support various types of activities is usually referred to as tax expenditure policy. The commission recognizes the utility of tax expenditures, especially in light of the efficiency of tax expenditures in establishing automatic incentives which affect individuals or businesses with a minimum of governmental interference. When the General Assembly appropriates public funds through tax expenditures, however, the same caution should be applied which is customarily employed in making direct appropriations from the public treasury. Tax expenditures should be clearly tied to socially desirable new activities and should not subsidize activities which would occur regardless of tax expenditures. Such tax expenditures should be made for a fixed period of time, following which a detailed evaluation of the efficiency and effectiveness of the tax expenditure should be carefully conducted prior to continuing authorization for the tax expenditure. All too often millions of dollars of potential public funds are lost because of ineffective tax expenditures which continue far beyond their initial rationale.

B. IMPLICATIONS OF GOALS

There are certain important inferences that can be drawn from the goals discussed above for the type of tax system we recommend for Pennsylvania. It should be clear that we cannot develop a tax system in which each tax meets each goal. Moreover, Pennsylvania already has a tax system in place which must be taken into account in making recommendations for change. We do not propose to eliminate every tax in existence and develop an entirely new system. Many taxes that do not meet all the goals are functioning effectively and meet certain goals successfully. They compensate for their weakness vis-a-vis other goals. Thus, the sales tax, as applied in Pennsylvania, has much to recommend it even though it may not meet the economic efficiency criterion. On the other hand, taxes which do not achieve any of these goals are candidates for elimination in the view of the commission. Resultant revenue losses must be made up by greater reliance on taxes that are successful in achieving these goals.

It is also clear the the more broadly based the tax is, the better it is. By broadly based, we mean that the tax base permits few exemptions in the definition of income or in the definition of taxpayer and does not easily permit avoidance. Pennsylvania's personal income tax is a good example. Broadly based taxes are generally simple to understand and calculate and are also stable and predictable. Such broadly based taxes are often viewed as most fair by taxpayers.

* * * * *

Looking at the total system in terms of these goals, it seems reasonable to question the differential taxation Pennsylvania imposes on various industries. In particular, the banking and insurance industries are both exempt from the Corporate Net Income Tax (CNI). Other taxes have been devised to tax the firms in those industries. Uniform taxation for business as a whole on the basis of net income would increase the fairness of the system, contribute to simplification, and result in lower costs.

We believe application of these goals can be effective in ensuring that Pennsylvania improves its tax system over time, eliminates the tendency to pass new taxes on an ad hoc basis to meet present revenue problems of the moment, and adequately finances government. Any proposed new taxes should be analyzed in relation to these goals to see how well they meet the goals before being admitted to the system.

C. CRITERIA FOR A TAX

One of the striking features of Pennsylvania's current system of taxation is the tremendous range of taxes that compose the system. The justification for many of the taxes comes from the necessity of meeting a particular revenue deficiency at a point in time rather than from a well-defined criterion. We have attempted to solve this problem by emphasizing the importance of goals that should be met by the various taxes. Nothing has yet been said, however, about the basic criteria justifying particular taxes.

The literature on public finance is replete with discussions on the criteria justifying a particular tax. The two basic criteria are the ability to pay and the benefit received. Thus, an income tax is justified on the basis of ability to pay. The federal income tax with its progressive features is justified by that criterion, as is an income tax, such as Pennsylvania's, that uses proportional taxation. On the other hand, property taxes and gasoline taxes are justified on the benefits-received crite-rion. Property owners receive police and fire protection, rubbish collec-tion, and other services of local governments; it is widely believed that the benefits of many municipal services are in proportion to the prop-erty they serve. The gasoline tax is paid by automobile owners and the revenue is channelled into road maintenance and improvement. Again, the benefit criterion justifies the tax. We propose to justify every tax in the system that we propose on the basis of one of these two criteria. Where the tax cannot meet one of these two criteria, it will be rejected as a candidate for the system.

* * * * *

D. CHARACTERISTICS OF THE SYSTEM

It can be argued that the ideal tax structure would be one in which there was a single tax, and that tax would be on income. The income tax could meet the goals that we have established and could be justi-fied on the ability-to-pay criterion. Since income, broadly defined, is the ultimate objective of the economic system, a good argument could be made for such a tax system.

However, even if one accepted that argument intellectually, it does not make sense operationally. The interdependence among states is an important factor to be taken into account when developing a tax sys-tem. The ease with which capital and human resources can move to other states means that states must have tax systems that are roughly comparable both in types of states in the system and in the level of rates applied by each tax. Obviously, no two systems are exactly the same, but there will be difficulties if one state attempts to establish a radically different system. Thus, we conclude that one characteristic of the system is that it must be a portfolio of taxes rather than a single tax system.

A second characteristic relates to the social justice or the distribu-tive effects of a tax. At the federal level, the personal income tax and gift and estate taxes are strongly progressive and materially affect the distribution of income and wealth. The federal system attempts to reduce the inequality in income both by applying a progressive tax rate structure to income and wealth and by using transfer payments. Because of the mobility of human and physical resources, and in view of the Commonwealth's constitutional impediments to progressivity, the commission believes that major income redistribution across all income classes through the tax system must be obtained at the federal level.

However, the commission also believes that the state should seek to achieve through its tax system certain distributional objectives which are consistent with the constitutional framework. Within the current constitutional framework, this means that the tax system should seek to alleviate tax burdens on the poor, elderly, and infirm, and as such, should seek progressivity in the tax system for these groups of per-sons. Also, in viewing the state's role in achieving progressivity, the commission believes that both state and local taxes, to the extent possible, should be taken into account.

There are, in addition, other objectives of the system that we want the system to achieve. We want a tax system that is consistent with economic development in the state. There is increasing evidence that the tax structure is not the crucial factor in determining the location of new business. Many other factors, such as the labor climate and other intangible factors relating to the physical and economic conditions of the area, seem to be more important to the location decision than the tax system. Nevertheless, it is still important to make certain that the tax system keeps Pennsylvania competitive with its neighboring states.

E. ASSUMPTIONS AND ADDITIONAL CONSIDERATIONS IN THE REPORT

1. Overall Tax Burden

In reviewing Pennsylvania's current tax system, certain assumptions about the overall revenue needs of the Commonwealth and the constitutional framework had to be made. The governor charged the commission to devise tax reform proposals which do not increase the level of overall taxation. To implement this, the commission presents in this *Report* a set of recommendations which do not increase or decrease materially the percent of total Pennsylvania personal income dedicated to the public sector. Only in this manner can proper attention be focused on the effective rate of taxation.

The effective tax rate measures taxes as a percent of an indicator of resources available to pay taxes, usually personal income. These rates measure the true "burden" of taxes on the economy, in contrast to nominal or statutory rates which may fail to be responsive to economic activity. For example, the commission finds that the flat cent-per-gallon motor fuel tax is really a tax with a decreasing effective rate despite a fixed nominal rate, because the price of motor fuel has risen so much over the past few years. Moreover, higher fuel prices and more fuel-efficient vehicles have meant that total motor fuel taxes have not kept pace with the increasing cost of road repair. Therefore, the commission recommends changes in the structure of motor fuels taxes which will increase nominal tax rates, but which will not lead to any long-term growth in the size of the public sector. In the short run, Motor License Fund revenues will increase to finance the needed restoration of our roads and bridges.

Table 1 shows the pattern of overall effective tax rates in Pennsylvania, U.S. average, and several other major states. While per capita taxes have risen since 1968–69, the effective tax rate in Pennsylvania has generally been below the U.S. average, below that of New York, about the same as New Jersey, and somewhat higher than Ohio. The commission has sought to keep the overall effective rate of taxation at about 11.9 percent of personal income in connection with its recommendations.

TABLE 1 State and Local Tax Burden: 1968–1979 in Pennsylvania and Other States

State and Local Taxes as a Percent of Personal Income

Year	Pennsylvania	U.S. Average	California	Illinois	Michigan	New Jersey	New York	Ohio
1968–69	9.992%	11.220%	11.341%	9.411%	11.688%	10.349%	14.049%	8.839%
1969–70	10.963	11.658	13.480	11.428	11.547	10.576	14.260	9.107
1970–71	11.394	11.887	13.733	11.467	12.237	11.000	14.538	9.253
1971–72	12.710	12.694	14.942	12.118	12.976	11.617	15.788	10.071
1972–73	12.994	12.947	14.909	11.911	12.960	12.042	16.952	10.436
1973–74	12.247	12.358	14.010	12.002	12.308	11.639	16.552	9.790
1974–75	11.675	12.284	14.591	11.728	11.665	11.591	16.653	9.694
1975–76	11.540	12.472	14.892	11.418	12.064	11.826	17.329	10.017
1976–77	11.880	12.805	15.493	11.726	13.039	12.606	17.683	10.004
1977–78	12.254	12.753	15.799	11.803	12.668	12.419	17.188	9.933
1978–79	11.887	12.031	12.042	11.261	12.395	12.095	16.697	9.768

Per Capita State and Local Taxes

Year	Pennsylvania	U.S. Average	California	Illinois	Michigan	New Jersey	New York	Ohio
1968–69	$339.52	$379.94	$ 539.99	$ 372.80	$ 428.26	$ 406.06	$ 575.51	$305.77
1969–70	401.40	427.14	559.33	486.78	455.54	447.25	652.32	343.24
1970–71	444.37	460.47	603.22	513.48	491.33	498.55	688.60	363.87
1971–72	525.93	522.49	687.11	575.19	569.36	554.25	788.68	418.76
1972–73	581.34	577.08	738.84	613.03	635.11	630.51	893.61	475.42
1973–74	614.95	618.39	762.25	699.03	679.15	683.19	952.29	496.70
1974–75	636.43	663.77	868.62	730.27	681.77	725.48	1025.09	533.82
1975–76	683.91	730.52	964.20	769.42	749.04	792.83	1139.94	585.79
1976–77	770.01	813.01	1088.92	860.29	878.17	931.45	1252.22	640.74
1977–78	861.77	888.00	1227.47	916.99	958.84	993.06	1308.28	700.52
1978–79	921.47	933.93	1379.80	1003.75	1049.32	1060.37	1372.71	768.55

SOURCE: U.S. Bureau of the Census, Governmental Finances, 1968–79. Series GF-78 (Washington, D.C.: U.S. Government Printing Office).

2. Balance of Taxes between Business and Personal Sectors, Capital and Labor

In testimony before the commission, reference was made repeatedly to the importance of maintaining a balance between business and personal taxes. The 1968 Tax Study and Revision Commission recommended that 70 percent of taxes be derived from personal taxation and 30 percent from business; these figures were cited before this commission by public witnesses and representatives of industry and organized labor. This commission believes its recommendations have not materially altered the current balance; in main, recommendations have substituted personal income taxes for occupation taxes and business income taxes for other types of business taxes.

While the commission has observed the importance of this dichotomy, it also believes that such distinctions can be somewhat mechanical and misleading for a number of reasons. First, the commission believes that the issue of balance is more properly the issue of the taxation of labor income vis-a-vis the taxation of income from capital. Business per se does not pay tax, but does so on behalf of the individuals who own the firm or its capital. By the same token, the local property tax, while collected from individuals is, in fact a tax on the ownership of capital. The local wage tax is, on the other hand, clearly a tax on labor income. Second, in trying to ascertain what the "balance" of taxation is between labor and capital income it is important to examine the actual incidence of the tax as contrasted with the nominal impact of the tax. Thus, while the utilities literally write a check to the Department of Revenue for the gross-receipts tax, it is clear that consumers pay the tax through higher prices that include the tax. Unfortunately, the limitations of time and resources prevented the commission from performing such incidence analysis and from measuring the current balance of taxes on labor and capital under current law and under its recommendations. The commission believes that this is an important topic for future analysis.

With regard to overall revenue needs, the commission assumed that the current expenditures financed by the Personal and Corporate Net Income taxes would be continued although their rates are scheduled to decline in 1982 from 2.2 percent to 2.0 percent and 10.5 percent to 9.5 percent, respectively. Thus, the commission has assumed that the current personal and corporate tax rates would be continued.

3. Tax Reform in Pennsylvania versus Tax Reform in Other States

In reviewing the history of effective Pennsylvania tax rates, the commission feels an obligation to caution the public and the General Assembly that tax reform in Pennsylvania has a different meaning than the term has generally been given in other states in recent years. Nationally, state and local governments have been experiencing overall budget surpluses of better than $20 billion as reflected in the U.S.

Department of Commerce's national income accounts. These surpluses arise because of the inflation dividends generated by progressive income taxes, or because of the fortuitous location of certain energy resources.

Higher wages and prices have placed taxpayers into higher tax brackets despite relatively stable real personal income. As a result, in other states a type of tax reform has been possible in which across-the-board rate reductions were achieved. Because the Uniformity Clause of Pennsylvania's Constitution prohibits progressive nominal tax rates, Pennsylvania has not experienced the budget surpluses of the other states. Because of Pennsylvania's tax structure, Pennsylvania cannot approach tax reform with a tax-reduction perspective, but must use a balanced budget approach. Any tax reductions in one area must be counterbalanced by revenue generating proposals in some other area. The commission has sought to achieve this balance in its recommendations.

7

Major Tax Structures: Income Taxes

Because governments rely on taxes as the ultimate source of funds to buy resources for use in service delivery, an understanding of the structure of taxes is important. While structures differ among the states and localities and the federal taxes do not remain unchanged over time, a common logic and language defines tax bases and the manner in which rates are applied to the chosen base. Furthermore, there are common issues of tax design that arise wherever a particular base is considered. The following three chapters examine the general nature of the three predominant tax bases: income, consumption, and property. Taxes on income and consumption typically apply to current transaction values; property taxes apply to the value of holdings, not transactions. In many respects, that difference makes property taxes more difficult to administer, although problems of the underground economy have complicated operation of the other two taxes in recent years.

One important point to be emphasized at the outset: all taxes labeled "income" (or sales or property, for that matter) do not operate in the same fashion, and statements about the elasticity, progressivity, or other properties of a particular tax must carefully define what the structure of the tax actually is. Thus, the federal individual income tax has a generally progressive burden distribution; many local income taxes have a generally proportional or slightly regressive burden pattern because of their limited coverage of income, and the way they apply rates to that income. It would be incorrect to observe that income taxes have progressive burden distributions. Some do, some do not: it depends on the structure of the particular tax.

INCOME TAXATION

Governments apply taxes to the income of individuals and/or corporations.[1] Unincorporated business (partnership, proprietorship) income will ordinarily be taxed by the individual income tax. Because individual income taxes yield so much more revenue than do corporate income taxes, most of the consideration here will focus on the former. Many of the structural elements of individual taxation also apply to the corporate form as well; many other corporate tax questions are too arcane for coverage here. One important issue to which there may be no answer will be considered: how should corporate income taxes be related to the income tax of individual corporate stockholders? Otherwise, the coverage will emphasis the individual tax.

Some Background

Before the Civil War the federal government relied on excises (customs duties, liquor taxes, etc.) to finance its limited activities. War was too expensive to finance with that revenue, however, so the federal government enacted a low-rate (3 percent of income above $800) income tax in 1861. The tax reached a rate and revenue peak in 1865 and expired in 1872 after making a significant contribution to war finance. There remained an important legal question. As noted in Chapter 6, the Constitution requires direct taxes to be apportioned among the states, and it was not clear whether an individual income tax was legally direct or indirect.[2] If the tax were direct, the tax would have to be divided among the states according to population and each state's share then raised from its population according to income. A state with lower per capita income would have to apply higher income tax rates than would a state with higher per capita income. The U.S. Supreme Court, however, held in *Springer* v. *United States* (1880) that the income tax was, for purposes of the Constitution, indirect and hence valid. By the time of the ruling, the tax was no longer in force, so the ruling had minimal immediate importance.

In 1894, the federal government again enacted an individual income tax, this time in a package with reduced tariffs (a tariff is simply a tax on imported items). The low-rate tax (2 percent of income above $4,000) affected only a small portion of the population but it was challenged on constitutional grounds. This time, the U.S. Supreme Court,

---

[1] A corporation is an entity created by a government (state or federal) which grants it legal powers, rights, privileges, and liabilities of an individual, separate and distinct from those held by the individuals who own the entity. Each owner has a liability equal only to his investment in the corporation.

[2] Corporate income taxes were never regarded as direct taxes on individuals and, thus were never subject to apportionment. The federal corporate income tax began some years before the federal individual income tax.

in *Pollock* v. *Farmer's Loan and Trust* (1895), ruled that the income tax was direct and, hence, subject to the apportionment requirement. The decision left the federal government with no broad-based revenue source and without a means of financing the increased international role the nation was taking in the early part of the 20th century. This problem was resolved by the 16th Amendment (1913): "The Congress shall have power to lay and collect taxes on incomes, from whatever source derived, without apportionment among the several States, and without regard to any census or enumeration." That provided the financial base for defense and an expanded federal role in domestic affairs.

Many regard an income tax as a fair source of revenue because of the nature of the base and the method of its administration—and it certainly is productive. Why do many believe that the income tax is a satisfactory source, despite poor showings in the previously cited Advisory Commission on Intergovernmental Relations polls? First, income is an important measure of capacity to bear the burden of financing government. Economic well-being is largely determined by current income. An exception is the person with substantial wealth and minimal current income, so a better measure would include current income and net wealth converted into an income equivalent. Such logic does not appear in tax codes, however. Current income remains for most people the most reliable single indicator of relative affluence. Second, the income tax can be made to take account of individual taxpayer conditions. Any tax not based on individual filing will not easily be adjusted to such conditions: a package of cigarettes is taxed regardless of the economic status of the purchaser. Adjustments that can be made with income tax filing allow a more equitable distribution of burdens. Third, the size of the income base permits significant revenue at socially acceptable rates and growth of that base keeps pace with general economic activity. Governments with income taxes need not seek rate increases as often or apply such high nominal rates as those with narrower bases. And, finally, the resource distortion with the general income tax may be less than with narrower taxes.[3]

Individual Income Taxation

The following sections describe the logical construction of the federal individual tax. Many states link their tax to this tax. For instance, some use adjusted gross income or taxable income as the initial computation point for their tax. Some even define their tax as a specified percentage of federal liability. For that reason, an understanding of this

---

[3]Income taxes may distort work and investment decisions made by individuals and businesses. Thus, the resource distortion basis for general income taxation is unclear at best.

FIGURE 7-1 Elements of U.S. Individual Income Tax Structure

Total income
less
Adjustments
equals
Adjusted gross income.
Subtract
Zero bracket amount or (excess) itemized deductions*
and
Personal exemptions
to obtain
Taxable income.
Apply
Rate schedule or tax tables
to calculate
Tax.
Subtract
Credits
to obtain
Total tax.
Subtract
Withholding
to obtain
Tax refund or tax due.

*Itemized deductions over the zero bracket amount: $2,300 for single taxpayers, $1,700 for married taxpayers filing separate returns, and $3,400 for married taxpayers (1984 filing year).

system is thus important for all governments. (Local governments generally do not link their income taxes to the federal tax, but use independent and much narrower income measures.) Figure 7–1 provides a schematic overview of the federal structure, as will be described in later sections. That schematic represents the pattern of the federal individual return forms shown in Figure 7–2 and Figure 7–3. Figure 7–2 is the basic form 1040; Figure 7–3 is the form for reporting itemized deductions, dividends, and interest income. The itemized deduction form (schedule A in Figure 7–3) was used by only 43.9 percent of taxpayers in 1982, but those filers included almost 62.5 percent of adjusted gross income less deficit returns.[4] The remainder used the simpler 1040A or 1040EZ, taking only the standard deductions folded into the zero bracket amount. These elements capture the heart of the federal revenue system and, because many states base their income tax on the federal system, they are vital at that level as well.

---

[4]Internal Revenue Service Preliminary Report, *Statistics of Income—1982, Individual Income Tax Returns* (Washington, D.C.: U.S. Government Printing Office, 1984).

FIGURE 7–2

Form **1040** Department of the Treasury—Internal Revenue Service
U.S. Individual Income Tax Return 19**84** (O)

| For the year January 1-December 31, 1984, or other tax year beginning | , 1984, ending | , 19 | OMB No. 1545-0074 |

Use IRS label. Other- wise, please print or type.	Your first name and initial (if joint return, also give spouse's name and initial)	Last name	Your social security number
	Present home address (Number and street, including apartment number, or rural route)		Spouse's social security number
	City, town or post office, State, and ZIP code	Your occupation	
		Spouse's occupation	

Presidential Election Campaign
Do you want $1 to go to this fund? . . . . Yes ☐ No ☐   **Note:** Checking "Yes" will not change your tax or reduce your refund.
If joint return, does your spouse want $1 to go to this fund? . . Yes ☐ No ☐

For Privacy Act and Paperwork Reduction Act Notice, see Instructions.

Filing Status

Check only one box.

1 ☐ Single
2 ☐ Married filing joint return (even if only one had income)
3 ☐ Married filing separate return. Enter spouse's social security no. above and full name here.
4 ☐ Head of household (with qualifying person). (See page 5 of Instructions.) If the qualifying person is your unmarried child but not your dependent, write child's name here.
5 ☐ Qualifying widow(er) with dependent child (Year spouse died ▶ 19   ). (See page 6 of Instructions.)

Exemptions

Always check the box labeled Yourself. Check other boxes if they apply.

6a ☐ Yourself   ☐ 65 or over   ☐ Blind
b ☐ Spouse   ☐ 65 or over   ☐ Blind
c First names of your dependent children who lived with you _____

Enter number of boxes checked on 6a and b ▶ ☐
Enter number of children listed on 6c ▶ ☐

d Other dependents: (1) Name	(2) Relationship	(3) Number of months lived in your home	(4) Did dependent have income of $1,000 or more?	(5) Did you provide more than one-half of dependent's support?

Enter number of other dependents ▶ ☐

e Total number of exemptions claimed (also complete line 36). . . . .

Add numbers entered in boxes above ▶ ☐

Income

Please attach Copy B of your Forms W-2, W-2G, and W-2P here.

If you do not have a W-2, see page 4 of Instructions.

Please attach check or money order here.

7	Wages, salaries, tips, etc.	7	
8	Interest income (also attach Schedule B if over $400)	8	
9a	Dividends (also attach Schedule B if over $400) _____ , 9b Exclusion _____		
c	Subtract line 9b from line 9a and enter the result	9c	
10	Refunds of State and local income taxes, from the worksheet on page 9 of Instructions (do not enter an amount unless you itemized deductions for those taxes in an earlier year—see page 9)	10	
11	Alimony received	11	
12	Business income or (loss) (attach Schedule C).	12	
13	Capital gain or (loss) (attach Schedule D)	13	
14	40% of capital gain distributions not reported on line 13 (see page 9 of Instructions)	14	
15	Supplemental gains or (losses) (attach Form 4797)	15	
16	Fully taxable pensions, IRA distributions, and annuities not reported on line 17	16	
17a	Other pensions and annuities, including rollovers. Total received 17a _____		
b	Taxable amount, if any, from the worksheet on page 10 of Instructions	17b	
18	Rents, royalties, partnerships, estates, trusts, etc. (attach Schedule E)	18	
19	Farm income or (loss) (attach Schedule F)	19	
20a	Unemployment compensation (insurance). Total received . . . 20a _____		
b	Taxable amount, if any, from the worksheet on page 10 of Instructions	20b	
21a	Social security benefits. (see page 10 of Instructions) . . . 21a _____		
b	Taxable amount, if any, from the worksheet on page 11 of Instructions	21b	
22	Other income (state nature and source—see page 11 of Instructions) _____	22	
23	Add lines 7 through 22. This is your **total income** . . . . ▶	23	

Adjustments to Income

(See Instructions on page 11.)

24	Moving expense (attach Form 3903 or 3903F)	24		
25	Employee business expenses (attach Form 2106)	25		
26a	IRA deduction, from the worksheet on page 12	26a		
b	Enter here IRA payments you made in 1985 that are included in line 26a above ▶			
27	Payments to a Keogh (H.R. 10) retirement plan	27		
28	Penalty on early withdrawal of savings	28		
29	Alimony paid	29		
30	Deduction for a married couple when both work (attach Schedule W)	30		
31	Add lines 24 through 30. These are your **total adjustments** . . . . ▶	31	

Adjusted Gross Income

| 32 | Subtract line 31 from line 23. This is your **adjusted gross income**. If this line is less than $10,000, see "Earned Income Credit" (line 59) on page 16 of Instructions. If you want IRS to figure your tax, see page 12 of Instructions. . . . . ▶ | 32 | |

FIGURE 7-2 (concluded)

Form 1040 (1984)   Page **2**

Tax Compu-tation	33	Amount from line 32 (adjusted gross income)	33
	34a	If you itemize, attach Schedule A (Form 1040) and enter the amount from Schedule A, line 26 . . . . . **Caution:** If you have unearned income and can be claimed as a dependent on your parent's return, check here ▶ ☐ and see page 13 of the Instructions. Also see page 13 if: • You are married filing a separate return and your spouse itemizes deductions, OR • You file Form 4563, OR • You are a dual-status alien.	34a
(See Instruc-tions on page 13.)	34b	If you do not itemize deductions, and you have charitable contributions, complete the worksheet on page 14. Then enter the allowable part of your contributions here	34b
	35	Subtract line 34a or 34b, whichever applies, from line 33	35
	36	Multiply $1,000 by the total number of exemptions claimed on Form 1040, line 6e	36
	37	Taxable Income. Subtract line 36 from line 35.	37
	38	Tax. Enter tax here and check if from ☐ Tax Table, ☐ Tax Rate Schedule X, Y, or Z, or ☐ Schedule G	38
	39	Additional Taxes. (See page 14 of Instructions.) Enter here and check if from ☐ Form 4970, ☐ Form 4972, or ☐ Form 5544	39
	40	Add lines 38 and 39. Enter the total . . . . ▶	40

Credits	41	Credit for child and dependent care expenses (attach Form 2441)	41	
	42	Credit for the elderly and the permanently and totally disabled (attach Schedule R)	42	
(See Instruc-tions on page 14.)	43	Residential energy credit (attach Form 5695)	43	
	44	Partial credit for political contributions for which you have receipts	44	
	45	Add lines 41 through 44. These are your total personal credits		45
	46	Subtract line 45 from 40. Enter the result (but not less than zero)		46
	47	Foreign tax credit (attach Form 1116)	47	
	48	General business credit. Check if from ☐ Form 3800, ☐ Form 3468, ☐ Form 5884, ☐ Form 6478	48	
	49	Add lines 47 and 48. These are your total business and other credits		49
	50	Subtract line 49 from 46. Enter the result (but not less than zero). . . . . ▶		50

Other Taxes	51	Self-employment tax (attach Schedule SE).	51
	52	Alternative minimum tax (attach Form 6251)	52
(Including Advance EIC Payments)	53	Tax from recapture of investment credit (attach Form 4255)	53
	54	Social security tax on tip income not reported to employer (attach Form 4137)	54
	55	Tax on an IRA (attach Form 5329)	55
■	56	Add lines 50 through 55. This is your **total tax** . . . . ▶	56

Payments	57	Federal income tax withheld	57	
	58	1984 estimated tax payments and amount applied from 1983 return .	58	
	59	Earned income credit. If line 33 is under $10,000, see page 16 .	59	
Attach Forms W-2, W-2G, and W-2P to front.	60	Amount paid with Form 4868	60	
	61	Excess social security tax and RRTA tax withheld (two or more employers)	61	
	62	Credit for Federal tax on gasoline and special fuels (attach Form 4136) .	62	
	63	Regulated Investment Company credit (attach Form 2439) . . .	63	
	64	Add lines 57 through 63. These are your **total payments** . . . . ▶		64

Refund or Amount You Owe	65	If line 64 is larger than line 56, enter amount **OVERPAID** . . . . ▶	65
	66	Amount of line 65 to be **REFUNDED TO YOU**. . . . . ▶	66
	67	Amount of line 65 to be applied to your 1985 estimated tax . . . ▶ 67	
	68	If line 56 is larger than line 64, enter **AMOUNT YOU OWE**. Attach check or money order for full amount payable to "Internal Revenue Service." Write your social security number and "1984 Form 1040" on it . ▶	68
		(Check ▶ ☐ if Form 2210 (2210F) is attached. See page 17 of Instructions.) $	

Please Sign Here	Under penalties of perjury, I declare that I have examined this return and accompanying schedules and statements, and to the best of my knowledge and belief, they are true, correct, and complete. Declaration of preparer (other than taxpayer) is based on all information of which preparer has any knowledge. ▶ Your signature Date ▶ Spouse's signature (if filing jointly, BOTH must sign)
Paid Preparer's Use Only	Preparer's signature ▶ Date Check if self-employed ☐ Preparer's social security no. Firm's name (or yours, if self-employed) and address ▶ E.I. No. ZIP code

☆ U.S.GPO:1984-0-423-073 ☆ E.I.#430814328

FIGURE 7–3

SCHEDULES A&B (Form 1040)	**Schedule A—Itemized Deductions**	
Department of the Treasury Internal Revenue Service (1)	(Schedule B is on back) ▶ Attach to Form 1040. ▶ See Instructions for Schedules A and B (Form 1040).	OMB No. 1545-0074 19**84** 07

Name(s) as shown on Form 1040 — Your social security number

Medical and Dental Expenses (Do not include expenses reimbursed or paid by others.) (See Instructions on page 19)	1 Prescription medicines and drugs; and insulin	1	
	2 a Doctors, dentists, nurses, hospitals, insurance premiums you paid for medical and dental care, etc.	2a	
	b Transportation and lodging	2b	
	c Other (list—include hearing aids, dentures, eyeglasses, etc.) ▶............................	2c	
	3 Add lines 1 through 2c, and write the total here	3	
	4 Multiply the amount on Form 1040, line 33, by 5% (.05)	4	
	5 Subtract line 4 from line 3. If zero or less, write -0-. **Total** medical and dental . ▶	5	
Taxes You Paid (See Instructions on page 20)	6 State and local income taxes	6	
	7 Real estate taxes	7	
	8 a General sales tax (see sales tax tables in instruction booklet)	8a	
	b General sales tax on motor vehicles	8b	
	9 Other taxes (list—include personal property taxes) ▶.........	9	
	10 Add the amounts on lines 6 through 9. Write the total here. **Total** taxes . ▶	10	
Interest You Paid (See Instructions on page 20)	11 a Home mortgage interest you paid to financial institutions .	11a	
	b Home mortgage interest you paid to individuals (show that person's name and address) ▶........................	11b	
	12 Total credit card and charge account interest you paid	12	
	13 Other interest you paid (list) ▶..........................	13	
	14 Add the amounts on lines 11a through 13. Write the total here. **Total** interest . ▶	14	
Contributions You Made (See Instructions on page 20)	15 a Cash contributions. (If you gave $3,000 or more to any one organization, report those contributions on line 15b.) . . .	15a	
	b Cash contributions totaling $3,000 or more to any one organization. (Show to whom you gave and how much you gave.) ▶..........................	15b	
	16 Other than cash (attach required statement)	16	
	17 Carryover from prior year	17	
	18 Add the amounts on lines 15a through 17. Write the total here. **Total** contributions . ▶	18	
Casualty and Theft Losses	19 Total casualty or theft loss(es). (You must attach Form 4684 or similar statement.) (see page 21 of Instructions) . . . . ▶	19	
Miscellaneous Deductions (See Instructions on page 21)	20 Union and professional dues	20	
	21 Tax return preparation fee	21	
	22 Other (list type and amount) ▶	22	
	23 Add the amounts on lines 20 through 22. Write the total here. **Total** miscellaneous . ▶	23	
Summary of Itemized Deductions (See Instructions on page 22)	24 Add the amounts on lines 5, 10, 14, 18, 19, and 23. Write your answer here.	24	
	25 If you checked Form 1040 { Filing Status box 2 or 5, write $3,400 / Filing Status box 1 or 4, write $2,300 / Filing Status box 3, write $1,700 }	25	
	26 Subtract line 25 from line 24. Write your answer here and on Form 1040, line 34a. (If line 25 is more than line 24, see the Instructions for line 26 on page 22.) . . . ▶	26	

For Paperwork Reduction Act Notice, see Form 1040 Instructions.   Schedule A (Form 1040) 1984

FIGURE 7-3 (concluded)

Schedules A&B (Form 1040) 1984 **Schedule B—Interest and Dividend Income** 08 OMB No. 1545-0074 Page **2**

Name(s) as shown on Form 1040 (Do not enter name and social security number if shown on other side.) | Your social security number

Part I
Interest
Income

(See Instructions on pages 8 and 22)

Also complete Part III.

If you received more than $400 in interest income, you must complete Part I and list ALL interest received. If you received interest as a nominee for another, or you received or paid accrued interest on securities transferred between interest payment dates, or you received any interest from an All-Savers Certificate, see page 22.

Interest income		Amount
1 Interest income from seller-financed mortgages. (See Instructions and show name of payer.) ▶	1	
2 Other interest income (list name of payer) ▶		
	2	
3 Add the amounts on lines 1 and 2. Write the total here and on Form 1040, line 8 . . ▶	3	

Part II
Dividend
Income

(See Instructions on pages 8 and 22)

Also complete Part III.

If you received more than $400 in gross dividends (including capital gain distributions) and other distributions on stock, or you are electing to exclude qualified reinvested dividends from a public utility, complete Part II. If you received dividends as a nominee for another, see page 22.

Name of payer		Amount
4		
	4	
5 Add the amounts on line 4. Write the total here	5	
6 Capital gain distributions. Enter here and on line 15, Schedule D.*	6	
7 Nontaxable distributions. (See Schedule D Instructions for adjustment to basis.)	7	
8 Exclusion of qualified reinvested dividends from a public utility. (See page 23 of Instructions.)	8	
9 Add the amounts on lines 6, 7, and 8. Write the total here	9	
10 Subtract line 9 from line 5. Write the result here and on Form 1040, line 9a . . . ▶	10	

*If you received capital gain distributions for the year and you do not need Schedule D to report any other gains or losses, do not file that schedule. Instead, enter 40% of your capital gain distributions on Form 1040, line 14.

Part III
Foreign
Accounts
and
Foreign
Trusts
(See Instructions on page 23)

If you received more than $400 of interest or dividends, OR if you had a foreign account or were a grantor of, or a transferor to, a foreign trust, you must answer both questions in Part III. | Yes | No

11 At any time during the tax year, did you have an interest in or a signature or other authority over a bank account, securities account, or other financial account in a foreign country? (See page 23 of the Instructions for exceptions and filing requirements for Form TD F 90-22.1.) . . . .
If "Yes," write the name of the foreign country ▶

12 Were you the grantor of, or transferor to, a foreign trust which existed during the current tax year, whether or not you have any beneficial interest in it? If "Yes," you may have to file Forms 3520, 3520-A, or 926. . . .

For Paperwork Reduction Act Notice, see Form 1040 Instructions.   Schedule B (Form 1040) 1984

Problems of income tax structure: defining income.   Tax statutes do not define income, but rather list types of transactions which produce income for tax purposes. Items on the list include wages, salaries, interest, stock dividends, royalties, and so on. There is no general definition for use in cases of doubt. (Instructors usually receive a copy of this book at no charge: would its value be income for them?) Many analysts favor the Haig-Simons income definition as a standard. The version proposed by Simons defines personal income for tax purposes as "the algebraic sum of (1) the market value of rights exercised in consumption and (2) the change in the value of the store of property rights between the beginning and end of the period in question."[5] In other words, income equals consumption plus any increase in net wealth during the year.

This definition can yield results that differ from application of existing tax law, as three examples illustrate. Suppose Mr. Smith owns shares of a corporate stock that increase in value by $10,000 during the year, but he does not sell the stock during the year. The Haig-Simons concept views that as income—this increase in Smith's net wealth adds to his total potential command over the economy's resources. The existing tax system would not tax that gain; the system taxes such gains only as they are realized, that is, when the higher value stock is actually sold. Second, suppose Ms. Jones lives in a home that she owns. She thus consumes the services provided by that structure. These services are part of Jones's consumption and would be part of Haig-Simons income. The current tax system taxes no imputed incomes, thus providing a significant incentive for use of assets to produce noncash flows of return to the owner. Finally, suppose Mr. White's great aunt gives him $50,000. That clearly will increase his net wealth (or permit increased consumption) so would be part of Haig-Simons income. Because that transaction occurred without any work by White, however, the current system does not regard that as part of income. It could be taxable under the gift tax, but White's aunt's economic circumstance, not his, would determine tax liability.[6] Tax structures avoid general definitions of income, particularly Haig-Simons. They avoid taxation of accrued or imputed values with that policy. At the same time, however, the less broad income concept can distort individual choice and can create equity problems because it favors certain incomes over others. Furthermore,

---

[5] Henry C. Simons, *Personal Income Taxation: The Definition of Income as a Problem of Fiscal Policy* (Chicago: University of Chicago Press, 1938), p. 50. A similar concept appears in Robert M. Haig, "The Concept of Income—Economic and Legal Aspects," in *The Federal Income Tax*, ed. R. Haig (New York: Columbia University Press, 1921), p. 7.

[6] That means the tax on the gift to White (who has an annual income of $3,000) is the same as the tax on her similar gift to his brother (who has an annual income of $60,000). Same aunt, same gift, same tax—regardless of recipient's economic status.

the broad base reduces the administrative problems of determining whether a particular income falls into the taxed or untaxed category. And finally, breadth permits the psychological (and possibly economic) advantage of low rates to produce a given yield.

Adjustments to income.   The general philosophy of income taxation is that the tax should apply to net income. It ought not apply to gross receipts, as such a tax would apply to the cost of earning an income, as well as the income itself.[7] Those costs do not contribute to individual well-being, so they should be subtracted from income. That is the logic behind the adjustments.

Current federal law (which is copied by many states) allows adjustment for moving expenses, job-related education costs, and certain expenses of salesmen, for example. It is, however, difficult to distinguish between some costs of earning personal income and ordinary consumption expenditures. There simply is no clear and logical line between the two. For example, commuting expenses apparently are a cost of earning an income: if one does not get to work, income is not earned. This expenditure, however, results from choice of residence (commuting expense can be reduced by choosing to live closer to the point of employment) and is thus a consumption choice. To change this approach would provide a further incentive to urban sprawl. Moving expenses incurred to follow a changed place of employment, on the other hand, are considered a cost of earning income and are subtracted from income to obtain the tax base. The presumption is that such expenses are necessary for the job, not expenses from consumer choices. Of course, many people seek jobs elsewhere because they prefer different climate, different cultural activities, and so on—personal consumption choices, not costs of employment—but our tax system chooses to err in favor of enhancing labor mobility.

Similar considerations apply for other income adjustments. Advanced education is primarily a cost of earning income for many, while a consumption (noninvestment) expenditure for others. The problem is one of drawing a clear line; once the line is drawn, many people will soon rearrange their expenses to qualify for the adjustment. The line between job cost and consumption will remain indistinct. Choices must finally hinge on the question of what side the error is best made on.

Exclusions from income.   Exclusions from income simply do not show up on the tax return (and do not appear on Figure 7–1), but appear

---

[7]For ease of collection, numerous locally administered taxes apply to payrolls (wages and salaries) almost exclusively. Rental, income, dividends, interest, capital gains, etc., do not get included in the base and adjustments to estimate net income are not made. These taxes are classifiable as income taxes only by tradition.

to be income by popular or Haig-Simons concepts.[8] Among the exclusions are interest received from state and local government debt, government transfer payments (food stamps, welfare, etc.), social security payments, gifts or inheritances, employer-paid insurance premiums and related fringe benefits, insurance settlements, retirement pay, and so on. Several exclusions seem reasonable, particularly those directed to low-income individuals: it is not sensible to assist individuals because of their poverty and then tax away part of that assistance. Some assistance categories, however, are not limited to the poor and eligible recipients may have sizable income from other sources. Thus, if one desires to apply tax according to net well-being, there is a case for including retirement pay, social security, unemployment compensation, and similar payments not strictly conditioned on current income or wealth.

The exclusion of interest received on state and local government debt historically stems from principles of reciprocal immunity of governments. The federal government cannot destroy state or local governments (and vice versa). Because "the power to tax involves the power to destroy," the federal government does not tax instruments of state and local governments.[9] Nondiscriminatory taxation of such interest might not be ruled unconstitutional by present courts, but the exclusion continues as a valuable subsidy to state and local government—it allows these governments to borrow at interest rates substantially below current market rates. To demonstrate the influence of exclusion on these interest rates, suppose an individual pays 30 percent of any additional income as federal income tax (the 30 percent bracket). A tax-exempt municipal bond paying 10 percent yields the same after-tax income as would a taxable bond paying about 14 percent.[10] Thus, the state or local government borrower automatically receives an interest subsidy through the federal tax system and can borrow at artificially low rates. These bonds are a favorite avenue of tax avoidance for higher-income individuals and the value of interest subsidization to state or local government must be balanced against the damage done to the progressivity of the tax system by the exclusion. The provision remains largely because it is a federal subsidy received entirely at the control of state and local governments. Those governments are reluctant to surrender that subsidy for any other unknown structure and, accordingly, fight aggressively against any change.

---

[8]Some federal tax preferences were subjected to a minimum tax in the Tax Reform Act of 1969, particularly some capital gains income, some depletion deductions, accelerated depreciation on real property, and stock options. But much remains excluded.

[9]*McCulloch* v. *Maryland* 4 Wheat. 316 L. Ed. 579 (1819) is the source of John Marshall's famous "power to tax" quote. The reciprocal immunity doctrine, however, is enunciated in *Collector* v. *Day* 11 Wall. 113 20 L. Ed. 122 (1871).

[10]The taxable bond at 14 percent would leave the investor 70 percent (100% − 30%) of its yield after tax. Thus, 14% × 70% = 9.8%.

Another category which can be troublesome is the exclusion of fringe benefits provided by employers as a portion of employee compensation. While benefits like office Christmas parties would be difficult to value, many others (insurance, etc.) would not because they are available for purchase on the open market. This exclusion can induce individuals with higher incomes to choose untaxed fringes instead of pay increases simply to avoid tax burdens, thus distorting both production and consumption decisions. Further, it may artificially increase production costs as in-kind payment seldom is valued as highly by individuals as are cash payments: the cash can be used for anything, the in-kind payment cannot. Taxation of fringe benefits, while sensible and probably feasible, has made little headway because a fringe benefit costing $1,000 per worker will be valued differently by different recipients. Just as we are reluctant to impute values to services from owner-used assets, we are reluctant to value fringes. The policy, however, promises continued mischief.[11]

Personal deductions.   Personal deductions adjust the measured ability to pay the tax to the circumstances of the individual taxpaying unit. They may improve both horizontal and vertical equity of the tax by allowing individuals with such deductions to subtract them from adjusted gross income and hence lower their tax base. There are three logical categories of deduction. First, uncontrollable forces can require particular expenditures which reduce the taxpayer's capacity to bear the tax below that of units with similar income. The deduction for selected state and local taxes, for casualty and losses, and for medical expenses fall into this category. In each instance, individuals—through little fault of their own—must bear these special expenses that more fortunate individuals do not incur. Thus, an adjustment to measured tax-bearing ability is permitted. Second, some expenditures are deductible because the federal government has decided that private spending in those areas is meritorious and ought to be encouraged by reducing the after-tax cost of those actions. Thus, charitable contributions are directly deductible. This spending is optional (not like state taxes or medical bills), but the federal government seeks to encourage private contributions—thus, the deduction. And third, special circumstances produce deductibility of interest payments (included partly to subsidize certain activities and partly to exclude business interest

---

[11]Similar exclusions from the general income measure apply to gifts and inheritances. The problem appears here because there is often little difference between maintaining dependents and providing gifts. If it is a true gift, there is a separate tax; if the transfer occurs on death there are inheritance taxes that apply. One of the difficult problems is the delineation of fellowships and assistantships received by university graduate students. The fellowship is regarded as a gift and not taxed if there is no work requirement; assistantships require work, there is an exchange, and the income tax does apply, unless the degree program requires such work.

costs), professional expenses (dues, professional travel, special equipment, etc., deducted because of the business cost problem if not removed), and alimony payments.

Each was inserted for reasons which seemed to improve the equity of the system or to encourage desirable individual actions. Because each has greater tax impact on high-income individuals (a charitable deduction of $100 has an after-tax cost of $60 to an individual in the 40 percent bracket and a cost of $80 to someone in the 20 percent bracket), there is a special incentive for such individuals to arrange their affairs so that their expenses fit in these deductible categories. Thus, professional meetings are timed to double as vacations, property settlements in divorce are converted to alimony, and so on. As a result, these provisions can reduce the overall progression of the tax system.

Not all taxpayers, however, use the personal deduction. Since 1944 there has been an optional standard deduction—now called the zero bracket amount—that permits individuals to subtract from their adjusted gross income base a specified deduction amount, regardless of itemized totals. This deduction eliminates the need for recordkeeping of deductible expenses. (Tax revision in 1981 allows charitable deduction even if the zero bracket approach is taken.) The initial idea was to make the tax simpler for the many people who became taxpayers for the first time during World War II as effective rates for lower-income classes rose dramatically. Furthermore, the optional deduction for people not having high itemized deductions may have some psychological advantage. When all taxpayers have a general deduction, however, tax rates must be higher for everyone, diluting the relief for the deserving and the undeserving alike.

Personal exemptions. The personal exemptions—per capita subtractions from the tax base—increase the progressivity of the system because the flat number of dollars removed from taxable income has a greater relative effect for low-income individuals than for high-income people. (An exemption of $1,000 is 20 percent of $5,000, but only 5 percent of $20,000.) In fact, a high personal exemption combined with flat income tax rates can cause overall rate progressivity in the system. Table 7-1 demonstrates that impact. The reason for personal

TABLE 7-1 Effective Rate Impact of a Flat Rate Income Tax (10 percent) and a Large Personal Exemption ($1,500 per person) on Selected Families of Three

	Before-tax Income	Exemption	Taxable Income	Tax	Effective Rate
Family A	$20,000	$4,500	$15,500	$1,550	7.75%
Family B	10,000	4,500	5,500	550	5.5
Family C	5,000	4,500	500	50	1.0

exemption in most systems, however, is generally not to increase progressivity. Their role is to adjust for tax capacity across family sizes: on a given income—say, $10,000— a family of four has substantially less tax capacity than does a family of one. The personal exemption adjusts for these differences in arriving at the taxable income level. Systems may not treat all exemptions the same—say, $1,000 for the first two and $800 for any additional—depending on revenue needs, whether large family incentives are seen as desirable, etc. The U.S. system uses equal exemptions, but not all other countries do. The personal exemption likewise excludes small-income families to cut collection costs generated by low-yield returns.

The present system of special exemptions for the blind and elderly has a special problem when integrated with rate graduation. If the exemption is $1,000, an individual who is blind and in the 14 percent marginal tax bracket has a net tax saving from this blindness equal to $140. A blind individual in the 50 percent marginal tax bracket, however, receives a tax saving of $500. The higher the marginal rate bracket, the more valuable in tax saving is the reduction in taxable income received. Persons with no taxable income receive no assistance at all from an exemption. The logic of the exemption would seem better served if aid did not increase with income, as occurs with the present system. Credits, as will be discussed shortly, seem more appropriate to this problem.

Tax rates.   Federal individual income tax rates increase in steps as income increases. At each step, the rate applicable to additional income is slightly higher than the rate on lower income. Figure 7–4 presents the tax rate schedules applicable in 1984; the several possible family patterns that tax legislation recognizes are reflected in the Schedules X (single taxpayers), Y (married), and Z (unmarried heads of households). Taxpayers with taxable incomes less than $50,000 are directed to tax tables with precomputed taxes; see Figure 7–5 for a tax table illustration. The rate schedule is graduated upward, as shown in Figure 7–6. The rate on additional income earned gradually increases, from 11% on the $1,100 from $2,300 to $3,400, 12% on the $1,000 from $3,400 to $4,400, and so on to 50% on income earned above $81,800 (for a single taxpayer). An individual with say, $55,000 taxable income thus has part of that income taxed at 11%, part at 12%, part 14%, and so on. That individual is in the 42% marginal rate bracket, paying a tax of $16,394, i.e., [10,319 + 0.42 (55,000 − 41,500)]. The average rate—tax liability divided by taxable income—always lies below the marginal rate—the increase in tax liability resulting from one dollar additional income. With that structure, an individual always ends up with greater

FIGURE 7-4

1984 Tax Rate Schedules Your zero bracket amount has been built into these Tax Rate Schedules.

Caution: You must use the Tax Table instead of these Tax Rate Schedules if your taxable income is less than $50,000 unless you use **Schedule G,** Income Averaging, to figure your tax. In that case, even if your taxable income is less than $50,000, use the rate schedules on this page to figure your tax.

Schedule X
Single Taxpayers

Use this Schedule if you checked **Filing Status Box 1** on Form 1040—

If the amount on Form 1040, line 37 is: Over—	But not over—	Enter on Form 1040, line 38	of the amount over—
$0	$2,300	—0—	
2,300	3,400	.......11%	$2,300
3,400	4,400	$121 + 12%	3,400
4,400	6,500	241 + 14%	4,400
6,500	8,500	535 + 15%	6,500
8,500	10,800	835 + 16%	8,500
10,800	12,900	1,203 + 18%	10,800
12,900	15,000	1,581 + 20%	12,900
15,000	18,200	2,001 + 23%	15,000
18,200	23,500	2,737 + 26%	18,200
23,500	28,800	4,115 + 30%	23,500
28,800	34,100	5,705 + 34%	28,800
34,100	41,500	7,507 + 38%	34,100
41,500	55,300	10,319 + 42%	41,500
55,300	81,800	16,115 + 48%	55,300
81,800	....	28,835 + 50%	81,800

Schedule Z
Unmarried Heads of Household
(including certain married persons who live apart—see page 5 of the instructions)

Use this schedule if you checked **Filing Status Box 4** on Form 1040—

If the amount on Form 1040, line 37 is: Over—	But not over—	Enter on Form 1040, line 38	of the amount over—
$0	$2,300	—0—	
2,300	4,400	.......11%	$2,300
4,400	6,500	$231 + 12%	4,400
6,500	8,700	483 + 14%	6,500
8,700	11,800	791 + 17%	8,700
11,800	15,000	1,318 + 18%	11,800
15,000	18,200	1,894 + 20%	15,000
18,200	23,500	2,534 + 24%	18,200
23,500	28,800	3,806 + 28%	23,500
28,800	34,100	5,290 + 32%	28,800
34,100	44,700	6,986 + 35%	34,100
44,700	60,600	10,696 + 42%	44,700
60,600	81,800	17,374 + 45%	60,600
81,800	108,300	26,914 + 48%	81,800
108,300	....	39,634 + 50%	108,300

Schedule Y
Married Taxpayers and Qualifying Widows and Widowers

Married Filing Joint Returns and Qualifying Widows and Widowers

Use this schedule if you checked **Filing Status Box 2 or 5** on Form 1040—

If the amount on Form 1040, line 37 is: Over—	But not over—	Enter on Form 1040, line 38	of the amount over—
$0	$3,400	—0—	
3,400	5,500	.......11%	$3,400
5,500	7,600	$231 + 12%	5,500
7,600	11,900	483 + 14%	7,600
11,900	16,000	1,085 + 16%	11,900
16,000	20,200	1,741 + 18%	16,000
20,200	24,600	2,497 + 22%	20,200
24,600	29,900	3,465 + 25%	24,600
29,900	35,200	4,790 + 28%	29,900
35,200	45,800	6,274 + 33%	35,200
45,800	60,000	9,772 + 38%	45,800
60,000	85,600	15,168 + 42%	60,000
85,600	109,400	25,920 + 45%	85,600
109,400	162,400	36,630 + 49%	109,400
162,400	....	62,600 + 50%	162,400

Married Filing Separate Returns

Use this schedule if you checked **Filing Status Box 3** on Form 1040—

If the amount on Form 1040, line 37 is: Over—	But not over—	Enter on Form 1040, line 38	of the amount over—
$0	$1,700	—0—	
1,700	2,750	.......11%	$1,700
2,750	3,800	$115.50 + 12%	2,750
3,800	5,950	241.50 + 14%	3,800
5,950	8,000	542.50 + 16%	5,950
8,000	10,100	870.50 + 18%	8,000
10,100	12,300	1,248.50 + 22%	10,100
12,300	14,950	1,732.50 + 25%	12,300
14,950	17,600	2,395.00 + 28%	14,950
17,600	22,900	3,137.00 + 33%	17,600
22,900	30,000	4,886.00 + 38%	22,900
30,000	42,800	7,584.00 + 42%	30,000
42,800	54,700	12,960.00 + 45%	42,800
54,700	81,200	18,315.00 + 49%	54,700
81,200	....	31,300.00 + 50%	81,200

Page 42

FIGURE 7–5

1984 Tax Table
Based on Taxable Income
For persons with taxable incomes of less than $50,000.

Example: Mr. and Mrs. Brown are filing a joint return. Their taxable income on line 37 of Form 1040 is $25,325. First, they find the $25,300–25,350 income line. Next, they find the column for married filing jointly and read down the column. The amount shown where the income line and filing status column meet is $3,646. This is the tax amount they must write on line 38 of their return.

At least	But less than	Single	Married filing jointly *	Married filing separately	Head of a household
					Your tax is—
25,200	25,250	4,633	3,621	5,770	4,289
25,250	25,300	4,648	3,634	5,789	4,303
25,300	25,350	4,663	(3,646)	5,808	4,317
25,350	25,400	4,678	3,659	5,827	4,331

If line 37 (taxable income) is— / And you are—

At least	But less than	Single	Married filing jointly *	Married filing separately	Head of a household
					Your tax is—
$0	$1,700	$0	$0	$0	$0
1,700	1,725	0	0	a1	0
1,725	1,750	0	0	4	0
1,750	1,775	0	0	7	0
1,775	1,800	0	0	10	0
1,800	1,825	0	0	12	0
1,825	1,850	0	0	15	0
1,850	1,875	0	0	18	0
1,875	1,900	0	0	21	0
1,900	1,925	0	0	23	0
1,925	1,950	0	0	26	0
1,950	1,975	0	0	29	0
1,975	2,000	0	0	32	0
2,000					
2,000	2,025	0	0	34	0
2,025	2,050	0	0	37	0
2,050	2,075	0	0	40	0
2,075	2,100	0	0	43	0
2,100	2,125	0	0	45	0
2,125	2,150	0	0	48	0
2,150	2,175	0	0	51	0
2,175	2,200	0	0	54	0
2,200	2,225	0	0	56	0
2,225	2,250	0	0	59	0
2,250	2,275	0	0	62	0
2,275	2,300	0	0	65	0
2,300	2,325	b1	0	67	b1
2,325	2,350	4	0	70	4
2,350	2,375	7	0	73	7
2,375	2,400	10	0	76	10

At least	But less than	Single	Married filing jointly *	Married filing separately	Head of a household
					Your tax is—
2,400	2,425	12	0	78	12
2,425	2,450	15	0	81	15
2,450	2,475	18	0	84	18
2,475	2,500	21	0	87	21
2,500	2,525	23	0	89	23
2,525	2,550	26	0	92	26
2,550	2,575	29	0	95	29
2,575	2,600	32	0	98	32
2,600	2,625	34	0	100	34
2,625	2,650	37	0	103	37
2,650	2,675	40	0	106	40
2,675	2,700	43	0	109	43
2,700	2,725	45	0	111	45
2,725	2,750	48	0	114	48
2,750	2,775	51	0	117	51
2,775	2,800	54	0	120	54
2,800	2,825	56	0	123	56
2,825	2,850	59	0	126	59
2,850	2,875	62	0	129	62
2,875	2,900	65	0	132	65
2,900	2,925	67	0	135	67
2,925	2,950	70	0	138	70
2,950	2,975	73	0	141	73
2,975	3,000	76	0	144	76
3,000					
3,000	3,050	80	0	149	80
3,050	3,100	85	0	155	85
3,100	3,150	91	0	161	91
3,150	3,200	96	0	167	96
3,200	3,250	102	0	173	102
3,250	3,300	107	0	179	107
3,300	3,350	113	0	185	113
3,350	3,400	118	0	191	118

At least	But less than	Single	Married filing jointly *	Married filing separately	Head of a household
					Your tax is—
3,400	3,450	124	c3	197	124
3,450	3,500	130	8	203	129
3,500	3,550	136	14	209	135
3,550	3,600	142	19	215	140
3,600	3,650	148	25	221	146
3,650	3,700	154	30	227	151
3,700	3,750	160	36	233	157
3,750	3,800	166	41	239	162
3,800	3,850	172	47	245	168
3,850	3,900	178	52	252	173
3,900	3,950	184	58	259	179
3,950	4,000	190	63	266	184
4,000					
4,000	4,050	196	69	273	190
4,050	4,100	202	74	280	195
4,100	4,150	208	80	287	201
4,150	4,200	214	85	294	206
4,200	4,250	220	91	301	212
4,250	4,300	226	96	308	217
4,300	4,350	232	102	315	223
4,350	4,400	238	107	322	228
4,400	4,450	245	113	329	234
4,450	4,500	252	118	336	240
4,500	4,550	259	124	343	246
4,550	4,600	266	129	350	252
4,600	4,650	273	135	357	258
4,650	4,700	280	140	364	264
4,700	4,750	287	146	371	270
4,750	4,800	294	151	378	276
4,800	4,850	301	157	385	282
4,850	4,900	308	162	392	288
4,900	4,950	315	168	399	294
4,950	5,000	322	173	406	300

*This column must also be used by a qualifying widow(er).

a If your taxable income is exactly $1,700, your tax is zero.
b If your taxable income is exactly $2,300, your tax is zero.
c If your taxable income is exactly $3,400, your tax is zero.

Continued on next page

FIGURE 7-6 Graduation in 1984 Federal Individual Tax Rates, Single Taxpayers

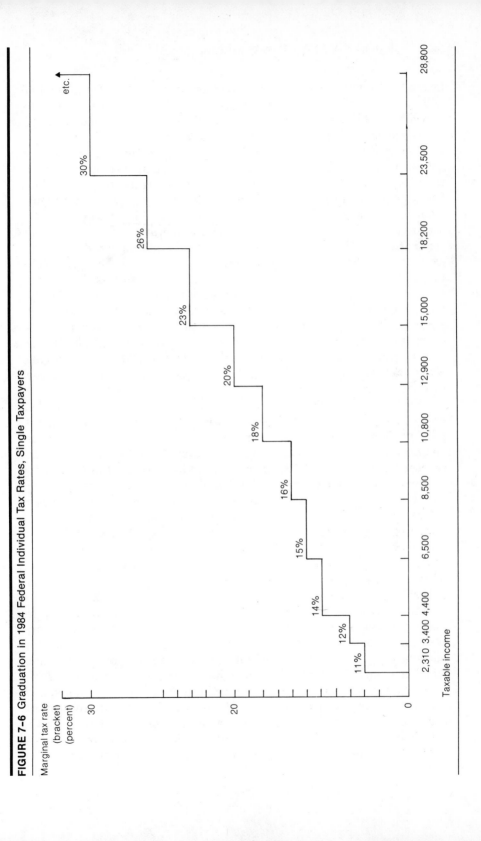

income after tax when more income has been earned. The individual will never have greater after-tax income by having less income. The percentage of income going to federal tax does increase as income rises, but the absolute income left over will not decline.

The statutory, or nominal, rates appearing in the rate schedule of course are not the same as the effective rates. Analysis of the income tax system usually is conducted by looking at the relationship between taxes paid and adjusted gross income, the federal tax system equivalent of net income. This rate is the average effective rate. The statutory rates are reduced substantially by the operation of tax provisions removing individual income from the base (adjustments, deductions, exemptions, and exclusions) and forgiving tax owed (credits). These elements can be regarded as the work of tax loopholes or as the work of tax policy designed to correct inequities or to encourage socially desirable behavior. Figure 7–7 illustrates what the nature of these differences has been in recent years. Note particularly the extent to which exemptions increase the steepness of the effective rate profile, the degree to which deductions and capital gains treatment reduce progressivity, and the substantial overall difference between nominal and actual rates at all income levels.

Statutory rate graduation brings the phenomenon called "bracket creep" during inflation. Suppose a family has an income of $13,000, pays $150 in income tax, and is in the 14 percent marginal tax bracket. In two years, its income has increased to, say, $15,600 (a 20 percent increase), but the cost of living has increased by 20 percent as well, so its real income has not changed. The family will, however, pay taxes on that higher money income—additional income will be taxed at increasing marginal rates through the brackets—even though its living standard has not really changed. Thus, it may now pay $195, an increase of tax liability of more than 20 percent because of the upward rate graduation. While this graduation historically has been viewed as an automatic stabilizer in the economy, accelerating tax collections during inflation to provide a macroeconomic brake and slowing tax collections during recession to provide a macroeconomic stimulus without requiring legislative action, recent observers have suggested that this process has become excessive. One solution is indexation, a technique for automatically adjusting tax liabilities downward to allow for inflation which has moved individuals into higher tax brackets without increasing their real income. Personal exemptions, standard deductions, and bracket starting points are adjusted annually for inflation to prevent the creep of liability. Nine states (Arizona, California, Colorado, Iowa, Minnesota, Oregon, Wisconsin, Montana, and South Carolina) have systems of indexation; indexation of the federal income tax began in 1985.

FIGURE 7-7 Influence of Various Provisions on Effective Rates of Federal Individual Income Tax, 1985

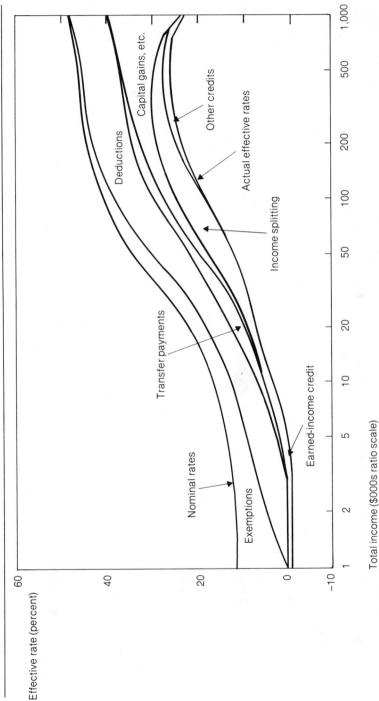

Effective rate (percent)

Total income ($000s ratio scale)

SOURCE: Joseph A. Pechman, *Federal Tax Policy,* 4th ed. (Washington, D.C.: Brookings Institution, 1983), p. 76

TABLE 7-2 History of Federal Individual Income Tax Exemptions (dollars) and Lowest and Highest Bracket Rates (percent)

Year	Personal Exemption[a]			Lowest Rate	Highest Rate
	Single	Married	Dependents		
1913–15	3,000	4,000	—	1	7
1916	3,000	4,000	—	2	15
1917	1,000	2,000	200	2	67
1918	1,000	2,000	200	6	77
1919–20	1,000	2,000	200	4	73
1921	1,000	2,500[b]	400	4	73
1922	1,000	2,500[b]	400	4	56
1923	1,000	2,500[b]	400	3	56
1924	1,000	2,500	400	1.5	46
1925–28	1,500	3,500	400	1.125	25
1929	1,500	3,500	400	3/8	24
1930–31	1,500	3,500	400	1.125	25
1932–33	1,000	2,500	400	4	63
1934–35	1,000	2,500	400	4	63
1936–39	1,000	2,500	400	4	79
1940	800	2,000	400	4.4	81.1
1941	750	1,500	400	10	81
1942–43	500	1,200	350	19	88
1944–45	500	1,000	500	23	94[c]
1946–47	500	1,000	500	19	86.45
1948–49[a]	600	1,200	600	16.6	82.13
1950	600	1,200	600	17.4	91
1951	600	1,200	600	20.4	91
1952–53	600	1,200	600	22.2	92
1954–63	600	1,200	600	20	91
1964	600	1,200	600	16	77
1965–67	600	1,200	600	14	70
1968	600	1,200	600	14	75.25
1969	600	1,200	600	14	77
1970	625	1,250	625	14	71.75
1971	675	1,350	675	14	70[d]
1972–78	750[e]	1,500[e]	750[e]	14[f]	70
1979–80	1,000	2,000	1,000	14	70
1981	1,000	2,000	1,000	13.825	69.125
1982	1,000	2,000	1,000	12	50
1983	1,000	2,000	1,000	12	50
1984	1,000	2,000	1,000	11	50
1985[g]	1,080	2,160	1,080	11	50

[a]From 1948, additional exemption for taxpayers blind or over 65 years old.
[b]Married exemption was $2,000 if net income above $5,000.
[c]For 1944–1963, there were maximum effective rate limitations.
[d]For 1971–1981, lower maximum marginal rate on earned income.
[e]Plus per capita credit of $30 in 1975 and $35 (or 2 percent of first $9,000 of taxable income) in 1976–78.
[f]From 1975 on, reduced by earned income credit.
[g]Indexation applies.
SOURCES: *The Federal Tax System: Facts and Problems, 1964.* Materials assembled by the Committee Staff for the Joint Economic Committee, 88 Cong. 2 session (1964): 22 and 23; Internal Revenue Service, *Statistics of Income, Individual Income Tax Returns* (various years); and federal tax return materials.

Credits.   In recent years, the federal government has made increasing use of a powerful device to stimulate certain private activities deemed desirable. That is the tax credit, direct forgiveness of taxes owed when eligible activities are undertaken. Thus, spending of $100 on the encouraged activity can be substituted for $100 income tax owed. To the prescribed limit of the credit, spending on that activity has no after-tax cost to the individual. Partial credits reduce by the credit percentage the cost of the activity. Among the recently supported credit activities have been new home purchases, household energy saving installations, child care,[12] and political contributions. Because of their high power, credits are expensive to the government and often could effectively be replaced by direct government spending.

History of Rates and Exemptions.   The federal individual income tax structure as defined by marginal rates and personal exemptions has shifted over the years in response to revenue needs and political initiatives. Table 7-2 shows what that pattern has been since the enactment of the 1913 tax.

Tax Computation.   The nature of income taxation can best be understood by working the mechanics of the tax. Figure 7-8 provides an illustration of such a manipulation. It applies the general schematic of the federal income tax to demonstrate deductions, exemptions, and credits, as well as the computation of average, marginal, and average

---

FIGURE 7-8 Illustration of Income Tax Computation

Mr. and Mrs. Gross have two children. Their adjusted gross income is $67,000. They have personal deductions of $9,500. They contributed $20 to a political campaign, with a tax credit of $10.00. Mr. Gross's employer has prepaid $14,230 of their tax liability through withholding. They file a joint return.

Adjusted gross income = $67,000
   Less (excess) itemized deductions (9,500–3,400)
   Less personal exemptions (4 × 1,000)
   Taxable income = $56,900

From rate schedule Y:
   Tax equals 9,772 = 38% (56,900 – 45,800) = 9,772 + 4,218
   Less credits ($10)
         13,980
   Less withholding (14,230)
   Refund   250

Average rate = Tax/Taxable income = 13,980/56,900 = 24.6%
Marginal rate = ~~Tax/Taxable income~~ = 38%   change in tax / Change in Taxable Income
Average effective rate = Tax/Adjusted gross income = 13,980/67,000 = 20.9%

---

[12]Child care logically would be an adjustment, as it is a cost of earning income.

effective tax rates. The calculations are based on 1984 tax rates and exemptions levels. Neither rates nor exemptions have been constant over the years, as Figure 7–8 shows.

Corporate Income Taxation

The corporate income tax applies to the net earnings of a corporation. The tax lacks the personal exemptions, personal deductions, and credits for dependents found in the individual income tax, but it does allow for deductions of charitable contributions and operating costs. The tax applies to total corporate profit including both earnings retained by the firm and those paid in dividends to stockholders. The individual income tax treats dividends in the same fashion as it does other income except the taxpayer and spouse may each exclude up to $100 of dividend income. Above that level, dividend income is fully taxed to the individual.

The basic federal corporation rate is 46 percent of income above $100,000. Rates from 15 to 40 percent (in four brackets) apply to lower income. The lower rates are intended as assistance to small business, but around 80 percent of taxable corporate income is subject to the highest rate.[13] The lower rates may reduce the drain on retained earnings for growing firms.

Only five states (Nevada, South Dakota, Texas, Washington, and Wyoming) do not have corporate income taxes currently, but the state taxes do create some special problems. Foremost is the complication created because corporations conduct business in more than one state and often in more than one country. Some income may be clearly defined as originating from a single state but much can not be so identified. For instance, a particular corporation may have retail outlets in 45 states, warehouses in nine states, and factories in two states. How much of that firm's profit should be taxable in any one state? To handle this problem most states have adopted what is called the three-factor, or Massachusetts, formula for allocation of multistate corporation profits. That formula computes the average percentage of total property, total payroll, and total sales in a particular state to define the percentage of total profit taxable by any one state. Thus, if state A has 50 percent of the firm's total property value, 25 percent of the firm's total payroll, and 60 percent of the firm's sales, that state would apply its corporate tax rate to 45 percent [(50 + 25 + 60) 0.3] of the firm's total profit. Some states, however, do not use the Massachusetts formula and create measures especially favorable to their in-state corpora-

---

[13]Joseph A. Pechman, *Federal Tax Policy.* 4th ed. (Washington: Brookings Institution, 1983), p. 134.

tions.[14] Because most states lack sufficient audit staff to verify the factor computed by all corporate filers, they must accept the calculations done by many corporate filers. This problem of profit allocation makes local taxes impractical.

A major question in the structure and operation of the corporation income tax is whether the corporation income tax reduces the real income of the stockholders of the corporation, whether it produces higher prices for the products of corporations, or whether it causes the real income of labor and other resources used by the corporation to be lower. Neither theoretical nor empirical evidence is clear but certainly there is no support for complete or predominant shifting of the corporate income tax to consumers of corporate products.

The corporate income tax is the third largest source of federal revenue and that revenue would be difficult to replace from other sources, even though its relative significance has fallen in recent years. However, there are problems with the corporate income tax that must be considered. First is the problem of equity. If corporate stockholders bear the tax, why should dividend income be taxed more heavily than other kinds of income? Furthermore, there is much variation of dividend income received among individuals in particular income classes, so the special tax on that income obviously violates the equal treatment of equals rule of appropriate tax burden distributions. The corporate income tax does, however, fill a gap: without it, the portion of corporate income not distributed would go untaxed. In addition, the corporate income tax probably increases the progressivity of the system because dividend income tends to be more concentrated in higher income groups. At the state level, the corporate income tax is a way for the state to extract compensation for benefits that the state provides to corporations whose owners may be largely out of state. The major problem currently with the corporate income tax is, however, its effects on saving and real investment. The corporate income tax probably constitutes a double tax on dividends and thus reduces the rate of savings, with undesirable effects on capital formation. Those capital formation effects add to the productivity problems of the nation, so some change might be appropriate.

Many of the undesirable economic and equity effects would be reduced if individual income and corporate income taxes were integrated either partially or completely. Complete integration would logically treat the corporation in the same way as partnerships. The tax would not apply to corporate income at all but the owners of the corporation

---

[14]The U.S. Supreme Court, in a case involving Moorman Manufacturing Company, upheld the Iowa formula using only sales. ("New Flexibility on Business Tax Granted State," *The Wall Street Journal,* June 16, 1978.)

would be taxed according to their proportionate shares of dividends and retained earnings. That treatment would eliminate the traditional difficulties with the corporate income tax but it would create some additional sticky issues. Those issues are as follows:

1. The tax would apply to income not realized. Individuals would be taxed according to income received as dividends and on income that the corporation retains. There is some question whether this would encourage greater corporate payout of earnings and thus might even lower the rate of real investment.

2. Many holders of corporate stock are tax-exempt entities. Under this integrated structure those entities would not pay individual income tax on their dividends and retained earnings and there would be no collection of tax at the corporate level either. How could that revenue loss be replaced?

3. Sizable amounts of U.S. stock are held by foreign entities. How would that income be treated? What country would be entitled to tax those U.S. dividends and retained earnings? And if it is a country other than the United States, how would that federal revenue loss be made up?

4. Corporations do not have single classes of stock. Corporations frequently have common stock, preferred stock, and possibly other varieties of equity ownership representations. How would corporate income be divided equitably among those various classes of stock?

The alternate approach is partial integration. Partial integration would provide relief only on the share of corporate earnings that are distributed as dividends, either by giving some special credit to dividend recipients to take account of the corporate income tax already paid on the flow or by applying the corporate income tax only to undistributed corporate profit. That relief would cut tax collections substantially and there is the fear that it would appear to be an unwarranted tax break for business. Those two factors have kept interest in such reform low, although there is a revival in connection with the slow growth rate of the American economy and the slow rate of capital formation which has worked to produce that slow growth.

Income Tax Reform?

Analysts, politicians, and the general public had grown uncomfortable about the federal income tax, both individual and corporate, by the mid-1980s. Among the perceived maladies were the following:

1. The taxes were too complicated, causing some people to fail to file because of confusion and allowing others to take advantage of complexity to avoid tax.

2. The taxes had been stuffed with so many provisions to stimulate socially desired actions that many apparently profitable entities were able to pay no taxes at all.
3. The individual tax had such steep graduation that some of the most productive people, i.e., those in high-income brackets, were discouraged from earning extra income, by either work or investment.
4. Personal deductions, while allowing the tax system to recognize certain taxpayer attributes that would diminish tax bearing capacity, had expanded to such an extent that they dramatically added to horizontal inequity and allowed many abuses of the system. They complicated the system, provided an avenue of tax avoidance for the sophisticated and allowed some people to profit handsomely at public expense, without particular gain for the general public.
5. Corporations and businesses in general did not pay a high enough tax burden, in comparison to the tax paid by individuals.
6. Industrial compensation programs were often warped by the tax system, because most fringe benefits were not taxable income to the employee. Those employees able to receive such benefits thus paid lower tax than did people of similar affluence who received their compensation as wages and salary. The inequity and distortion of economic decisions were obviously a problem.

The two income taxes were seen as distorting investment, distorting wages and salaries, distorting saving, penalizing work, being unnecessarily complex, and causing an unfair distribution of tax burdens. The system appeared to be both inequitable and inefficient. Furthermore, it failed to produce sufficient federal revenue. (Recall the history of federal deficits previously reported.)[15]

In response to these concerns, a major review and reform effort was started by President Reagan's 1984 State of the Union message when he directed the Department of the Treasury to perform a major tax reform analysis. His order: "Let us go forward with an historic reform for fairness, simplicity, and incentives for growth." The call followed substantial public discussion, plus Congressional proposals, most notably the FAIR plan proposed by Senator Bill Bradley and Representative Richard Gephart (S. 409, H.R. 800) and the FAST plan proposed by Representative Jack Kemp and Senator Robert Kasten (S. 325, H.R. 777), both of which would broaden the tax base and flatten (and lower) the rate structure while reducing the number of brackets. The Treasury

---

[15]Henry Aaron and Harvey Galper, *Assessing Tax Reform* (Washington, D.C.: Brookings Institution, 1985), chap. 1.

reform proposal released in November 1984[16] followed a related pattern for base and rates, as did the President's tax reform message in May 1985. While the final outcome of the program cannot be estimated, it would not be surprising to find a new federal income tax structure in the near future. Elements may well include:

1. Fewer individual income tax brackets than currently applied, with lower marginal rates in upper-income levels than presently employed.
2. A higher personal exemption and zero bracket amount.
3. Some reduction in preferences for business investment and reduced deductibility of some business expenses.
4. Some expansion of tax coverage of fringe benefits.
5. Possibly some revision in the way corporate dividends are taxed to the shareholder.

CONCLUSION

The income tax is the heart of the federal revenue system, providing sizable revenue for global responsibilities. While achieving progressivity, the tax does have problems of economic inefficiency and horizontal inequity. Reform is in the winds.

Questions and Exercises

1. Identify the important elements of the income tax in your state: what governments levy the tax, does the tax apply to individuals and corporations, how is the tax linked to federal income taxes, are the rates graduated, and is the tax indexed?

2. A midwestern state aids its institutions of higher education by giving a credit against its income tax equal to 50 percent of any gift to such institutions (subject to a limit of $50 credit per person). Two residents of that state, Mr. Blue (in the 20 percent federal tax bracket) and Ms. Jones (in the 40 percent federal tax bracket), each contribute $100 to an eligible state university.

   a. How much will state tax liabilities of each change as a result of their gifts?

   b. State income tax payments and contributions to charitable organizations (such as universities) are both currently deductible from the base used to compute federal tax liability. How much

---

[16]U.S. Department of Treasury, *Tax Reform for Fairness, Simplicity, and Economic Growth* (Washington, D.C.: Department of Treasury, 1984).

will federal tax liability change for Mr. Blue and Ms. Jones as a result of their contributions?

c. Considering both changes in federal and state tax liability, what is the net after-tax cost of their gifts to Mr. Blue and Ms. Jones? (Hint: subtract the changes in state and federal liability from $100.)

d. Suppose the state program changed from a credit to a deduction. If the state tax rate were a flat 3 percent, how much would state liability for Mr. Blue and Ms. Jones change?

e. From the above computations, which approach (credit or deduction) do you suppose universities in the state would favor? Why?

3. Mr. Brown is in the 20 percent federal income tax bracket and wants to invest $8,000 in interest earning assets. Mr. Black is in the 38 percent bracket and wants to invest $15,000. The current rate on a typical high-quality municipal bond is 12 percent and on a similar quality corporate bond is 15.5 percent. You are the financial adviser to both. Which investment would you recommend to each individual?

4. The Millers, a family of three filing joint returns, have the following information to prepare their federal income tax. Use the current federal tax forms (available at the local Internal Revenue Service office) to make your computation.

Salaries	35,000
Interest income, corporate bonds	1,000
Interest income, municipal bonds	1,500
Individual Retirement Account payment	3,500
State and local income taxes	800
Real estate taxes	450
General sales taxes	750
Home mortgage interest	3,350
Cash contributions	250
Contribution to political party	50

Calculate the following:

a. Adjusted gross income

b. Taxable income

c. Tax

d. Tax liability

5. Mr. and Mrs. Busch have adjusted gross income of $136,200 and taxable income of $109,900. They file a joint return. Use the rate schedule in the text to answer these questions.

a. What is their average rate?

b. What is their average effective rate?

    c. What is their marginal rate?

    d. Their accountant discovers a previously omitted personal deduction of $800. By how much does their federal tax liability fall with that addition?

    e. Amazingly enough, the accountant now discovers a $250 credit omitted from previous calculations (but after he discovered the $800 in part d). By how much does their federal tax liability fall because of this credit?

6. A taxpayer has adjusted gross income of $53,200 and taxable income of $36,520. The taxpayer is married and files a joint return. Use this tax table:

If taxable income is—		And you are—			
At Least	But Less Than	Single	Married Filing Jointly*	Married Filing Separately	Head of a Household
			Your tax is—		
36,500	36,550	8,429	6,711	10,325	7,835
36,550	36,600	8,448	6,728	10,346	7,852
36,600	36,650	8,467	6,744	10,367	7,870
36,650	36,700	8,486	6,761	10,388	7,887
36,700	36,750	8,505	6,777	10,409	7,905
36,750	36,800	8,524	6,794	10,430	7,922
36,800	36,850	8,543	6,810	10,451	7,940
36,850	36,900	8,562	6,827	10,472	7,957
36,900	36,950	8,581	6,843	10,493	7,975
36,950	37,000	8,600	6,860	10,514	7,992

Compute the taxpayer's average tax rate and average effective tax rate; determine the marginal rate bracket in which he falls.

8

Major Tax Structures: Consumption Taxes

Governments in the United States collect much revenue from taxes levied on the sale or purchase of goods or service. While such taxes are a poor third in revenue importance for the federal government (behind individual income, social security payroll, and corporate income taxes), they did produce over $38 billion in fiscal 1984 (see Table 8–1 for the major excises). At the state level, their yield was over $95 billion, better than 48 percent of state tax revenue (Table 8–2). When these revenues are considered in aggregate, they amount to the second largest revenue pool used for government finance in the United States, after the direct taxes on income in their various forms.

ALTERNATIVE FORMS OF CONSUMPTION TAXES

Some observations should be made on the basis of data in Tables 8–1 and 8–2. First, much of the revenue collected by excises is earmarked into special funds for expenditure only for specific purposes. Most motor fuel tax revenue, for instance, goes to highway trust funds for use in transportation work and the federal hazardous waste tax collections (superfund) are used for cleaning dangerous waste sites. Unfortunately, such fund earmarking creates excessive rigidity in the budget process. While it has political appeal, the procedure has weak logical foundation. Second, the selective excise taxes grow slowly. In most instances, substantial revenue increases require higher statutory rates. When rates have not increased, the share of total revenue from that excise has declined. Notice that, from 1970 to 1984, selective sales tax revenue grew at a 6.9 percent rate, compared to a 10.6 percent rate for all taxes. And finally, state general sales tax yield is significantly greater than selective sales tax yield. The federal government has no general

TABLE 8-1 Revenue from Federal Excise Taxes, 1970 and 1984

	Taxes Collected by Fiscal Year ($ million)		
	1970	1984	Average Annual Compound Rate of Growth 1970–84
Alcohol taxes, total	$4,746.5	$ 5,402.5	0.9
Distilled spirits	3,501.5	3,566.5	0.1
Wine	163.3	319.9	5.9
Beer	1,081.5	1,516.1	2.4
Tobacco taxes, total	2,094.2	4,663.6	5.9
Cigarettes	2,036.1	4,623.3	6.0
Cigars	56.8	30.4	− 4.4
Manufacturers excise taxes, total	6,683.1	10,097.2	3.0
Gasoline and lubricating oil	3,517.6	9,020.4	7.0
Tires, tubes, and tread rubber†	614.8	423.3	− 2.6
Motor vehicles, bodies, parts	1,753.3	− 14.8	—*
Recreational products	53.4	132.4	6.7
Black lung taxes	No tax	525.4	—*
Special fuels, and retailers taxes, total	257.8	2,619.6	18.0
Diesel and special motor fuels	257.7	1,571.4	13.5
Trucks and buses	No tax	932.6	—*
Miscellaneous excise taxes, total	2,084.7	13,290.2	14.1
Telephone and teletype	1,469.6	2,035.0	2.4
Air transportation	250.8	2,034.7	17.7
Highway use tax	135.1	175.1	1.9
Foreign insurance	8.6	56.0	14.3
Exempt organizations net investment income	No tax	146.8	—*
Crude oil windfall profit	No tax	8,120.3	—*
Environmental taxes (superfund)	No tax	275.4	—*

*Cannot compute meaningful rate.
†Tax on tubes and tread rubber repealed January 1, 1984; dealers assessed one-time floor stock tax.
SOURCE: Internal Revenue Service, *Statistics of Income Bulletin* 4 (Spring 1985), p. 88.

sales tax; selective sales tax collections amounted to only about 6 percent of federal tax collections.

Much state revenue in the United States (and a substantial amount of major city revenue) comes from taxes applied to consumption, either by general sales or selective excise taxes. The difference between the two taxes hinges on the logic of coverage. A sales tax applies to all transactions at, say, the retail level except for those enumerated as exempt (food purchases, for example); excises apply only to those transactions which are enumerated. Sales taxes were derived from fractional rate general business receipts taxes in Mississippi and West Virginia during the early 1930s when existing state revenue sources (predominantly property taxes) were unable to finance the spending activity of the period. Such taxes gradually became the dominant state

TABLE 8–2 National Summary of State Tax Revenue, 1970 and 1984

Tax source:	Amount 1970	Amount 1984	Annual Compound Rate of Growth 1970–84	Percent Distribution 1984
	($ millions)			
General sales and gross receipts	$14,127	$ 62,563.6	11.2	31.8
Selective sales and gross receipts	13,071	33,237.4	6.9	16.9
Motor fuels	6,277	12,395.6	5.0	6.3
Public utilities	918	5,875.0	14.2	3.0
Tobacco products	2,308	4,149.0	4.3	2.1
Insurance	1,182	3,973.7	9.0	2.0
Alcoholic beverages	1,420	2,900.0	5.2	1.5
Other	965	3,944.0	10.6	2.0
Total, all taxes	47,905	196,795.0	10.6	100.0

SOURCE: U.S. Bureau of Census, *State Tax Collections in 1984.*

revenue source. By 1985, all states but five (Alaska, New Hampshire, Delaware, Oregon, and Montana) levied such taxes, using rates from 3 percent in a handful of states to 7 ½ percent in Connecticut. Local sales tax rates piggyback on sales tax rates in several areas, causing the total applicable rate to be higher. The selective excises generally are limited to taxes on motor fuels, nuisance items (tobacco product, alcoholic beverages, etc.), and transactions of special vulnerability (insurance premiums, public utilities).

A consumption-based tax can be applied to sales by a manufacturer, wholesaler, or retailer. Some are applied at more than one of these levels, as is the case with turnover (cascade) taxes and value-added taxes. Single-stage, retail-level taxes have strongest logical support.[1] First, the tax paid by the customer likely will be the amount received by the government. Ordinarily multistage taxes and preretail taxes, however, tend to pyramid: the tax gets included in merchant markups, causing the price of the product to increase by more than the tax. Thus, the customer pays more than the government receives. Second, multistage taxes strike with each transaction. Integrated firms (those which manufacture, wholesale, and retail for instance) have fewer transactions and, hence, lower tax embedded in product cost. Single-stage application (particularly at retail) eliminates that effect. And third, retail application will cause no incentive for the production process to move to a stage of trade above the point taxed to reduce the base to which the tax applies. In general, the more of total product value produced after the point the tax is levied, the lower the tax will be. Retail application leaves no point for escape. The retail application does, however, require somewhat greater administrative effort as there are more retailers

[1]The special circumstances of value-added taxes will be examined later.

than there are manufacturers or wholesalers and, hence, more taxpayers to keep track of.

Selective Excise Taxation

Many state and local governments levy excise taxes on commodities or services, including such items as motor fuels, hotel and motel lodging, public utilities, admissions, restaurant meals, alcoholic beverages, tobacco products, soft drinks, and so on. The federal government also uses a few excise taxes (as illustrated in Table 8–1) although not nearly as many as before a major restructuring in 1965. With the exception of lodging and restaurant taxes, the excises tend to be applied at the manufacturer or wholesaler level. This eases administration, but can produce pyramiding. With those exceptions, plus utility and insurance taxes, the excises tend to be specific (per unit), not ad valorem (on exchange value). Again, this eases administration, but can cause relative revenue declines during periods of inflation as unit consumption does not keep pace. That pattern is amply shown in Table 8–2: compare the growth of alcoholic beverage, tobacco, and motor fuel taxes (all specific) with growth of the others. The taxes have logical antecedents which permit division into three groups: luxury, sumptuary, and benefit base. Each will be examined separately.

Luxury excises.   These excises are applied for revenue to commodities the purchase of which presumably reflects extraordinary taxpaying ability. Effective rates on those excises may be high because purchase of the taxed item demonstrates taxpaying ability beyond ability to pay as measured by other indices. If the luxury excise produces substantial revenue, it may ease rate pressure on other taxes. Unfortunately it seldom does.

The objections to luxury excises are several. First, such taxes distort producer and consumer choices: because the tax establishes a difference between the resource cost ratios in production and the price ratios to which consumers respond, there will be unnecessary loss of economic welfare in the economic system.[2] Second, and pragmatically more important, the tax will distribute burdens on the basis of personal preferences for the taxed items, a potential equity violation. The tax will impose higher effective rates on people within an income class who have high taste for the taxed commodities or services. Further, low-income people will buy the taxed items, because there are few products with no low-income purchasers at all. Finally, there are administrative problems with these excises. Because retailers would have difficulty separating the sales of the taxed luxury items from other sales, these excises typically apply to the manufacturer or wholesaler level. They

---

[2]John A. Tatom, "The Welfare Cost of an Excise Tax," *Federal Reserve Bank of State Louis Review* 58 (November 1976); pp. 14–15.

thus fall prey to the objections to any nonretail levy. But another administrative problem emerges in the definition of the taxed commodity. For example, the old federal excises taxed jewelry. Are watches jewelry? A definition either way will create injustices. The several state soft-drink taxes produce similar trouble. Are powdered drinks mixes, imitation orange juice, bottled chocolate drink, and so forth, to be taxed? In each case, a difficult administrative problem in interpreting and applying the tax may well be handled only by separate, brand name determinations, a process which needlessly clutters the tax department rule makers.

The case for luxury excises is weak at best. There are better devices for reaching tax capacity, especially when the excises produce little revenue relative to administrative cost. Efforts of revenue departments are better directed to taxes of greater fiscal significance.

Sumptuary excises.   Sumptuary excises attempt to discourge consumption of selected items. Because demand for these items usually is rather insensitive to price, consumption does not change much with the tax and substantial revenue may be generated. Seldom do legislatures propose truly prohibitive tax rates because they want revenue. These taxes include excises on alcoholic beverages and tobacco products; they are among the oldest taxes in the United States. Generally increases in their rates elicit minimal protest from consumers, although sellers complain about illegal (nontaxed) competition. Bootlegging is a continual problem; the typical enforcement procedure uses stamps applied to units upon which tax has been paid at the manufacturer level. Sizable rate differences among states swamp control structures with evasion.[3]

Two substantial advantages favor the sumptuary excises. First, they produce relatively high revenue with little public protest. There remains the feeling that people consuming those goods may be somewhat shady, so there is little political advantage for people who seek to reduce or eliminate these taxes. Consumers are likewise reluctant to make any direct protest. And second, there may be substantial social cost involved in the use of some of these commodities. For instance, excessive liquor consumption can lead to drunken driving, accidents on highways, and substantial cost to society. The excise may extract compensation for these social costs.[4] It is not clear, however, that there is any meaningful link between the tax rate and the amount of social cost.

There are three primary objections to sumptuary excises. First, the demand for the products taxed is often highly price-inelastic, so the tax will have little effect on the amount of the product purchased. It may

---

[3]For a review of the problem, see Advisory Commission on Intergovernmental Relations, *Cigarette Tax Evasion: A Second Look.* Report A–100 (Washington, D.C.: ACIR, 1985).

[4]Tobacco taxes have sometimes been earmarked for cancer research, a grim linkage to an associated social cost.

Not too likely issue

divert consumption from desirable or beneficial activities to pay the tax. (The extreme example sometimes quoted: the alcoholic who fails to buy milk for his children because of the tax he pays on liquor!) Second, the absolute burden of these taxes may be particularly heavy on low-income families and may even involve higher effective tax rates on lower-income than higher-income families. The tax is applied, after all, on the basis of personal preferences, so the teetotaling millionaire will pay less liquor tax than the whiskey-drinking working man. And finally, a problem results from the specific (not ad valorem) nature of these excises. While that construction is logical because any social cost involved would be related to the amount of consumption, not its value, it does discriminate against lower-priced brands and those who purchase them. If the tax is $10 per gallon on distilled spirits, the effective rate is much higher on liquor sold for $6 a fifth than on liquor sold for $10 a fifth. This is a special problem if users of the lower-priced brands come from low-income groups. Furthermore, the specific nature of the tax obscures the actual ratio of the tax to the net price, which frequently turns out to be high.

In sum, the sumptuary excises tax something that people are judged to be better off without and, possibly, compensate society for problems created by that consumption. In spite of any logical problems with these justifications, revenue from these taxes is reasonably high (especially for states) and extracted with little protest. They are not likely to be eliminated.

Benefit base excise.   Benefit base excises, primarily motor fuel taxes, operate as a quasi price for a public good. Highway use involves consumption of motor fuel, so a tax on fuel purchase approximates a charge for the use of the highway. These taxes allocate cost to road users and are clearly more economical than the system of direct user charges (tolls) for streets, roads, and highways. The motor fuel tax thus operates as a surrogate for price. It does have difficulties for the truck-to-car relationship because differences in incremental costs of providing highways are difficult to calibrate and relate to motor fuel use. The tax typically applies at the wholsale level, thus reducing the number of firms, subject to review for proper compliance. In September 1984, state motor fuel taxes ranged from 14.9 cents per gallon in Nebraska (15.5 in the District of Columbia) to 4 cents per gallon in Florida.[5] These taxes apply in addition to the federal tax.

There are the additional questions whether motor fuel tax revenues ought to be segregated for highway construction and maintenance only, whether these funds should be spent for any transportation (highway or mass), and whether motor fuel tax revenue should receive the

---

[5]U.S. Bureau of Census, *State Government Tax Collections in 1984*, GF84, no. 1 (Washington, D.C.: U.S. Government Printing Office, 1985), p. 8.

same budget treatment as other revenue, with no earmarking for transportation. These questions are not yet answered, but if revenues from the gasoline tax do not go to transportation projects, then they are probably subject to the complaints made against luxury excises. They sacrifice their benefit base logic and must be evaluated on ability-to-pay grounds. On the other hand, if revenue from the gasoline tax goes exclusively to highways, there is a substantial bias for highways in the total transportation system.

The benefit base logic of highway or motor fuel taxes suggest that the tax should be specific because the number of units of motor fuel used is related to the use of the service. At the same time, however, the specific nature of the tax means that, in times of inflation, there will be significant pressures placed on the motor fuel tax fund because of highway operation and construction cost increases. Some states have attempted to avert the need for legislated rate increases by tying the specific tax rate to the prevailing price of gasoline, so that as the price of gasoline is higher, the specific gasoline tax rate is higher.[6] This strategy may not succeed over the long run—historically, the price of gasoline has seldom kept up with inflation, with the exception of a couple of recent episodes. Highway finance and motor fuel taxation continue as problem areas for all levels of government.

General Sales Taxes

General sales taxes in the United States are the largest single source of state tax revenues. They cover all transactions at a given level of exchange (usually retail, although some states extend coverage to wholesale or manufacturing as well) unless a particular transaction is explicitly excluded. Payment is typically made by the seller in a taxable transaction; returns like that in Figure 8–1 cover all such transaction for a specified period (quarter, month, year). While impact is on the seller, incidence usually is on the purchaser.

More often than not, computation of sales tax owed by multiplying sales price times the tax rate will yield fractional cents: a selling price of $1.65 multiplied by a 5 percent tax rate yields a tax of 8 ¼ cents, an amount not collectible with current U.S. coinage. State and merchants handle that problem by use of bracket systems to define the tax to be collected in exact cents for any transaction. Sometime the brackets coincide with conventional rounding or major fraction rules (round at the ½ cent). The Massachusetts 5 percent nominal rate brackets in Figure

---

[6]An extensive review of state gasoline tax problems and of variable-rate structures may be found in John H. Bowman and John L. Mikesell, "Recent Changes in State Gasoline Taxation: An Analysis of Structure and Rates," *National Tax Journal* 36 (June 1983).

FIGURE 8-1

FIGURE 8-1

01-100 [redacted]
(Rev. 10-84/8)

PL06 1. T Code ■ 03200

2. ■

TEXAS SALES AND USE TAX RETURN—STATE AND CITY

Page 1 of________

3. Taxpayer Number ■

DO NOT STAPLE OR PAPER CLIP

4. Filing Period

5. ■

Taxpayer Name and Mailing Address

6.

If Taxpayer name or address or trade name and location are incorrect, mark out incorrect item and write in correct information.

If ownership changes, new owner must make application for Sales Tax Permit.

Corporation name changes must first be filed with office of Secretary of State

7. ■

Write in white areas only.

IF TRADE NAME OR LOCATION IS INCORRECT, WRITE IN THE CORRECT INFORMATION — ENTER AN AMOUNT IN ITEMS 10 THROUGH 13 EVEN IF THE AMOUNT IS ZERO — REPORT ONLY WHOLE DOLLARS

8. Outlet No ■	9. Trade name and location →			
10. Gross sales ■ .00	Minus 11. Deductions ■ .00	Plus 12. Taxable purchases ■ .00	Equals 13. Amount subject to 4⅛% State Sales tax .00	14. Amount subject to 1% tax for this city only ■ .00
Outlet No	Trade name and location →			
Gross sales .00	Minus Deductions .00	Plus Taxable purchases .00	Equals Amount subject to 4⅛% State Sales tax .00	Amount subject to 1% tax for this city only .00
Outlet No	Trade name and location →			
Gross sales .00	Minus Deductions .00	Plus Taxable purchases .00	Equals Amount subject to 4⅛% State Sales tax .00	Amount subject to 1% tax for this city only .00
Outlet No	Trade name and location →			
Gross sales .00	Minus Deductions .00	Plus Taxable purchases .00	Equals Amount subject to 4⅛% State Sales tax .00	Amount subject to 1% tax for this city only .00

TYPE OR PRINT — *Please read instructions.*

PL07 15. T. Code ■ 03400 COMPUTATION OF TAX DUE	Col A STATE TAX ■ 02	Col B CITY TAX ■ 04
16A Total Amount Subject to State Tax *(Total Item 13 this pg. & Item 18 all supplement pgs.)* 16B Total Amount Subject to City Tax *(Total Item 14 this pg. & Item 19 all supplement pgs.)*	16A ■ .00	16B ■ .00
17A Total state tax due *(Multiply Item 16A by .04125 (4⅛%))* 17B Total city tax due *(Multiply Item 16B by .01 (1%))* ENTER DOLLARS AND CENTS	17A	17B
18 Enter prepayment credit STATE → If filed CITY → on time — If filed late	18A	18B
19 Enter prior overpayment by prepayment *(Enter ONLY overpayments for which you have received a notice and NOT filed a refund claim. ENCLOSE NOTICE WITH RETURN)*	19A	19B
20 Tax due after prepayment credit(s) *(Item 17 minus Items 18 and 19)* *(If this amount is a credit see instructions BEFORE completing return)*	20A	20B
21 DISCOUNT: IF RETURN IS FILED AND TAX PAID ON OR BEFORE DUE DATE, enter 1% of Item 20	21A	21B
22 Enter prior overpayments *(ONLY overpayments not deducted in Item 19 and for which you have received a notice and NOT filed a claim. ENCLOSE NOTICE WITH RETURN)*	22A	22B
23 Tax due *(Item 20 minus Items 21 and 22)*	23A	23B
24 PENALTY: IF RETURN IS FILED OR TAX PAID AFTER DUE DATE, enter penalty *(Minimum $1 each tax)* 1-30 days late-5% of Item 23, More than 30 days late-10% of Item 23	24A	24B
25 INTEREST IF ANY TAX DUE IS UNPAID 61 DAYS AFTER DUE DATE, enter interest at rate of 10% per annum on Item 23	25A	25B
26 TOTAL AMOUNT DUE AND PAYABLE *(Item 23 plus Item 24 and Item 25)*	26A ■	26B ■

PAY TOTAL AMOUNT DUE IN FULL FOR BOTH TAXES

27 Due date	28 Total payment *(Item 26A plus 26B)*	
29 ■	30	31

Pay amount in Item 28 in one check payable to STATE TREASURER
Mail to BOB BULLOCK
COMPTROLLER OF PUBLIC ACCOUNTS
Capitol Station Austin, Texas 78774

FIELD SERVICE OFFICE
No
Date
T.R. Name

I declare that the information contained in this document and any attachments is true and correct to the best of my knowledge and belief.

32 sign here ▶ Taxpayer or Duly Authorized Agent

Business phone — Date

For Sales Tax assistance please contact your Texas State Comptroller's Local Office.
You may also call 512/475-1931 OR call 1-800-252-5555 toll free from anywhere in Texas.

FIGURE 8-2 Brackets for Collection of 5 Percent (nominal) Sales Taxes in Maryland and Massachusetts

Sales Tax Collected	Maryland Bracket	Massachusetts Bracket
0	0–19¢	0–9¢
1¢	20¢	10–29¢
2¢	21–40¢	30–49¢
3¢	41–60¢	50–69¢
4¢	61–80¢	70–89¢
5¢	81¢–$1.00; then 5¢ on each $1.00 plus 1¢ for each 20¢ or fraction thereof above $1.00	90¢–$1.09; same breaks continue

---

8-2 represent that system. Other states use different rules: the Maryland 5 percent nominal rate brackets in the same figure increase to the next cent before the Massachusetts brackets do. Although both sales taxes have the same nominal rate, the brackets established in Maryland will generate greater collections at a given level of vendor sales. Tax on the $1.65 transaction would be eight cents in Massachusetts and nine cents in Maryland.

How the collections from the brackets at purchase translate into vendor liability to the tax department differs among the states. Some states define vendor liability to be the tax rate multiplied by total taxable sales, regardless of the amount the brackets produce from individual transactions. The vendor keeps (or makes up) any differences between what the brackets generate and liability, the difference being called "breakage." Major fraction brackets normally cause breakage to be small. Other states, like Maryland, require payment of collections produced by the brackets on individual transactions. Compliance is easier with the former, but revenue will be greater with the latter.

A number of states also discount sales tax owed by the vendor to compensate for the cost of complying with the tax. (Note line 21 of the Texas return in Figure 8-1.) Discounts can reach 5 percent of collections, but many states provide none. Cooperation of vendors is clearly necessary for successful operation of sales tax, but discounts represent a high price to pay for that help. Furthermore, there is little reason to believe that compliance cost is closely related to sales volume: the discounts will cause some firms to profit handsomely while giving trivial assistance to others. Because other major taxes do not attempt to compensate for compliance, sales taxes probably ought not either.

The typical U.S. sales tax applies to purchases by the final consumer of tangible personal property. Most do not extend to purchases of services, but do apply to numerous purchases made by business. These latter purchases are hardly consumption, but they constitute about 25 percent of many sales tax bases.[7] The tax will often exempt some commodity purchases, particularly food and drugs, to reduce the burden of the tax on low-income families. To protect in-state retailers, states apply use taxes which apply to items purchased out-of-state and brought into the state for consumption. That prevents purchasers from avoiding the high rate in their state by purchase in a low-rate state. Use taxes cannot be effectively enforced on most items, but do work for major business purchases and for registered consumer items (motor vehicles).

Two special evaluation standards apply to sale tax structures beyond those important for all taxes. Those are *uniformity* and *neutrality*.[8] The first standard holds that the tax should produce a uniform tax on consumer expenditures. If the tax intends to do anything else, it ought not be a sales tax. Thus, the structure should ease shifting to ultimate consumers, it should apply at a uniform rate to all consumption expenditures unless there is reason otherwise, and it should apply to the amount actually paid by the consumer. Second, in order to avoid loss of economic efficiency the tax should not create competitive disturbances among types of distribution channels, methods of doing business, or forms of business organization. Choices ought not be distorted because of the tax. Structures as currently applied do not always conform to these standards, as the following design elements will illustrate.

Exclusion of producers' goods.   Business purchases are a tempting target for addition to the tax base. The overall sales tax base is greater with their inclusion, so a given statutory tax rate raises more revenue when business purchases are taxed. A large piece of the tax burden is hidden. If businesses must pay tax on their equipment purchases, their costs are higher. Their prices will be higher because of that cost, but customers will be unable to detect the embedded effect of the producer sales tax on the price they pay. If producers' goods are not excluded, the tax will not be a uniform percentage of consumer expenditures (some consumption items require use of more producers' goods than others), the tax will affect choices among methods of production (it makes capital more expensive), and it may delay the replacement of

---

[7]Richard F. Fryman, "Sales taxation of producers' goods in Illinois," *National Tax Journal* 22 (June 1969), pp. 273–81.

[8]John F. Due, *Sales Taxation* (Urbana, Ill.: University of Illinois Press, 1957), pp. 351–52.

old equipment by increasing the after-tax price of new equipment. Further, the firm has an incentive to produce goods for its own use, rather than purchasing the goods, because their internal cost of production would not be subject to sales tax, as purchases would be. Thus, it is clear that logic suggests producers' goods should be excluded from the tax.

States have developed two general rules for business purchase exemption: the component part/physical ingredient and the direct-use rules.[9] The former rule regards an item as being resold and hence not taxable if it becomes a physical ingredient or component part of a good which itself is being sold (flour sold to a bakery, or gasoline tanks sold to a lawnmower manufacturer). If the good does not become a physical part of the product, then its sale is taxed as a retail sale. This rule predominantes, probably because it gives a larger tax base, although it also is somewhat clearer to administer. The direct-use rule exempts both physical ingredients and machinery and equipment used in the production process (a stamping machine that forms lawnmower gasoline tanks, or an oven in a bakery). This rule produces a smaller tax base, but the base comes closer to consumer expenditures. No existing sales tax, however, is limited exclusively to final consumption expenditure.

Coverage of services.   Many state taxes include virtually no services sold to consumers; others provide only partial coverage of services. If services are not taxed, the tax does not cover consumption uniformly, as it applies only to tangible personal property purchases. Initial objections to taxing of services were that the tax on services is a tax on labor income. Of course, labor constitutes much of the production cost of tangible personal property, so the argument lacks merit. A more important reason for exempting services is the frequent absence of a clear line between the worker/client relationship or the worker/employer relationship, for example, an accountant doing personal tax returns versus an accountant working for a business firm. The latter, a producer-good relationship, ought not be taxed. Furthermore, there are some services—medical, and possibly legal, for instance—which probably should not be taxed as a matter of social policy. Consumers purchasing these services have enough trouble as it is without adding the sales tax to their bill. The pragmatic difficulty of taxing services is not surprising, even though the logical case is sound. Only a few states apply broad coverage of consumer services, but the realities of modern society cause an extension to many services to be virtually inevitable.

---

[9]Daniel C. Morgan, Jr., *Retail Sales Tax, An Appraisal of New Issues* (Madison, Wis.: University of Wisconsin Press, 1964), chap. 2.

Commodity exemption. Sales taxes typically exempt some items of tangible property which are clearly consumption expenditures. The most frequently exempt are purchases of food for at-home consumption and of prescription drugs. There is a logical reason for these exemptions based on the standard evaluation criteria for taxes. Purchases of these items constitute a higher percentage of the income of low-income families than they do of high-income families. Thus, if these items remain in the tax base, the sales tax will be strongly regressive. Exclusion of them from the base will reduce that regressivity. Hence, there is strong logical reason for excluding these items, even though their exclusion makes the sales tax more difficult to collect (the state must define what items are exempt—food stores selling both food and taxed items must maintain segregated accounting records and audits will be more complex) and the tax rate must be higher to yield a given amount of revenue on the smaller base (food constitutes around one third of a prospective sales tax base). A group of six states (Connecticut, Massachusetts, Minnesota, New Jersey, Pennyslvania, and Rhode Island)[10] have extended commodity exemption to purchases of clothing under the apparent logic of freeing from tax a base of necessities. Unfortunately, clothing expenditures are less concentrated among low-income groups than is the ordinary sales tax base, so the exemption provides greater relative relief to the more affluent and adds to the regressivity, complicates compliance and administration, and causes higher rates for given revenues.[11]

Some states use the tax credit or rebate as an alternative to commodity exemption to control sales tax regressivity. Rather than provide exemption for all purchasers of selected commodities, the credit systems return to taxpayers at year's end a fixed sum, usually equal to estimated payment of sales tax on food purchases by individuals in the lowest-income class. If the prevailing sales tax rate is 4 percent and per capital food purchases by individuals in the under-$3,000-annual-income class are about $600, the amount returned would be $24. Return of $24 to all individuals—either by rebate application or as a credit on a state income tax return—would effectively eliminate the sales tax on food purchases by very low-income purchasers. The rebate amount would not increase, however, as food consumption increases through the higher-income classes. (High-income people do spend more on food than do low-income people; the food exemption works because the percentage of income spent on food declines with higher income.) Thus, the rebate concentrates assistance where assistance is most needed as well as eliminates the need for vendors to account for taxed and exempt

---

[10]John F. Due and John L. Mikesell, *Sales Taxation, State and Local Structure and Administration* (Baltimore: Johns Hopkins Press, 1983), p. 70.

[11]J. M. Schaefer, "Clothing Exemptions and Sales Tax Regressivity," *American Economic Review* 59 (September 1969), pp. 596–99.

sales. Overall, the rebate effectively reduces (or even eliminates) regressivity at lower loss of revenue than commodity exemption. The rebate requires that individuals file returns with the state and that the state make cash payment to individuals, but these would seem small disadvantages relative to the other efficiencies of the device.

Value-Added Tax

A final form of consumption taxation is the value-added tax (VAT), a tax levied on the value added in *each* stage of the production/distribution process. It is simply an alternate way of collecting a tax on consumption expenditure; it does not tax a base different from consumption. While it is not used by the United States today, some have proposed it as a means of financing the social security system, as a way to stimulate saving and investment through reduced reliance on the income tax, as a way to stimulate U.S. exports, or, during the Nixon administration, as a replacement for the property tax in the finance of public schools. Around two dozen countries levy value-added taxes. It produces an average of 17 percent of government revenue for nine members of the European Economic Community—the EEC selected the VAT as the consumption tax to be used by all members as a means of tax harmonization.[12]

The VAT is a multistage tax that produces a burden equivalent to that of a single-stage retail-sales tax. In other words, the tax will be a constant proportion of the retail price of the product; it will not vary according to the number of transactions in the production process, as is normally the case for multistage taxes. The reason for the lack of pyramiding is that the tax at each stage depends on value added at that stage, not the total transaction price at that stage. The mechanics of the tax are described in Figure 8–3, an illustration of the value-added tax applied in the making of a table, from tree to final sale. At each stage in exchange, the tax rate applies to the transaction price. All such tax paid on the product to that stage in the process is a credit, however, against tax owed to the government (the sale from sawmill to furniture maker carries a tax of $15 - $150 \times 10\%$, but $10 of that tax is simply a credit representing tax already paid in the exchange between logger and sawmill), so the net tax paid is really only on value added at that production stage.

If a consumption tax is desirable, why should the VAT form be chosen? There are two circumstances in which the VAT can be appropriate. First, the VAT is appropriate if tax evasion and lack of vendor cooperation is a problem. The VAT induces every purchaser to want a documented receipt from every vendor for taxes paid, because that receipt

---

[12]Henry J. Aaron and Harvey Galper, *Assessing Tax Reform* (Washington, D.C.: Brookings Institution, 1985), p. 108.

FIGURE 8-3 Application of a Value-Added Tax (10 percent rate)

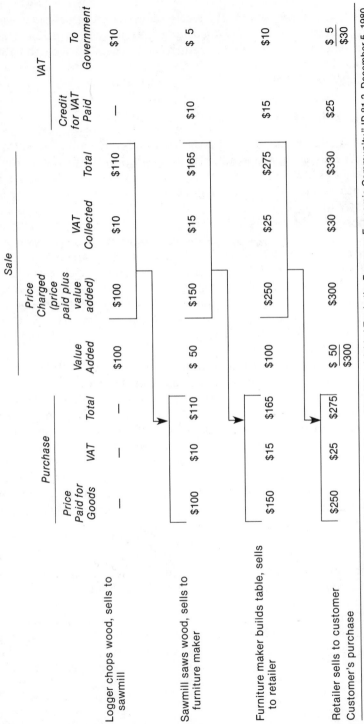

| | Purchase | | | Sale | | | | VAT | |
	Price Paid for Goods	VAT	Total	Value Added	Price Charged (price paid plus value added)	VAT Collected	Total	Credit for VAT Paid	To Government
Logger chops wood, sells to sawmill	—	—	—	$100	$100	$10	$110	—	$10
Sawmill saws wood, sells to furniture maker	$100	$10	$110	$ 50	$150	$15	$165	$10	$ 5
Furniture maker builds table, sells to retailer	$150	$15	$165	$100	$250	$25	$275	$15	$10
Retailer sells to customer Customer's purchase	$250	$25	$275	$ 50 / $300	$300	$30	$330	$25	$ 5 / $30

SOURCE: Adapted from Comptroller General's Report to Congress, "The Valued Added Tax in the European Economic Community," ID-81-2, December 5, 1980.

will be used to pay part of the tax he will owe when he makes a sale. He will pay the tax because the person purchasing the item will demand a tax receipt for credit purposes, and so on through the exchange channel. The self-enforcing nature of VAT thus makes it attractive when the tax compliance climate is not good. Second, nations sometimes choose to remove their domestic taxes from items which will be sold in international trade. The chain of tax documentation produced by VAT makes this extraction simple, although it does not extract any taxes except VAT. It is not clear that these circumstances currently apply in the United States, although they do exist in other countries to greater or lesser degree.

CONCLUSION

Taxes on consumption are at the heart of state revenue systems. While questions of structure persist for each base, there is no doubt concerning the serviceability of these taxes. The case for general sales taxes is much stronger than it is for the selective excises. The key problem with consumption taxation remains regressivity; no perfect solution exists.

Questions and Exercises

1. Identify the important elements of the general retail sales tax in your state: What governments levy the tax? What commodity sales are exempt? Are credits used? Are services taxed? What is the nominal rate? What are the brackets? *figure new*

2. According to the brackets presented in Table 8–2, is it possible in Maryland to make a single purchase of a taxable item with a quarter and receive five cents change? Explain.

3. Suppose a state applies a 5 percent sales tax to consumer purchases of many items. Table 1 presents data about the purchasing characteristics of two families which are generally representative of similar consumer units in the state. The tax applies to food purchases.

TABLE 1

	Low-Income Family	High-Income Family
Income	$5,500	$22,000
Family size	3	4
Purchases of taxed items	4,300	12,000
Purchases of food for at-home use	2,500	5,000

a. What is the statutory sales tax rate paid by each family?

b. What is the effective sales tax rate on income paid by each family?

c. Is the tax progressive, regressive, or proportional? Why?

d. Suppose the state now decides to exempt food purchases for at-home use from the tax. What will be the effective rate for each family? Does the exemption change the progressivity or regressivity of the tax? Explain.

e. Suppose the state provides a rebate or credit of $40 per person, instead of exempting food. (Notice that $40 per person is about equal to the sales tax paid by the lower-income family.) Answer the questions of part d. Compare the impact on state revenue of the two approaches.

4. The *Consumer Expenditure Survey: Interview Survey 1980–81* gives the following data:

Income before Taxes	Average Income before Taxes	Average Annual Expenditure	
		Alcoholic Beverages	Tobacco
Less than $5,000	$ 2,512	$117	$ 89
$ 5,000– 9,999	7,384	191	141
$10,000–14,999	12,279	237	182
$15,000–19,999	17,367	286	195
$20,000–29,000	24,414	332	212
$30,000 and over	44,152	454	218

Analyze the likely vertical equity of selective excises on alcoholic beverages and tobacco products.

Cases for Discussion

A   Large amounts of total sales and use tax collections typically result from sales of automobiles. The sales tax in each transaction is often substantial, so gains from avoidance or evasion can also be large. As a result, states often devise special taxes to replace the ordinary sales tax on such purchases. The Kentucky automobile usage tax considered in the following excerpt from an article in the *Lousiville Courier-Journal* is such a tax.

Consider These Questions

1. *How is the tax supposed to be computed? What variants do the dealers use? How are dealers alleged to profit?*

2. *Does the tax base coincide with the standard used in evaluation of sales taxes? Explain.*
3. *Can you propose a system better able to eliminate abuses?*
4. *Kentucky collected sales tax on the original sale of most cars sold by used-car dealers. Should there be any tax at all on their resale by used-car dealers? Explain.*

Probe Finds Some Dealers Overcharging in Used-Car Sales Taxes

By Larry Werner

A major investigation by the attorney general's Consumer Protection Division into Kentucky's retail automobile industry has uncovered instances of "substantial" overcharging of consumers on the sales tax for used cars.

The investigation, which could result in thousands of dollars in refunds for the state's used-car buyers, has angered the powerful Kentucky Automobile Dealers Association (KADA), which is claiming that the attorney general has embarked on a "fishing expedition" to harass legitimate businessmen.

To this, Attorney General Ed W. Hancock replied: "If we are (fishing), we've got the right bait, I would say."

* * * * *

What the attorney general's investigators are looking for are deviations by the dealers from the method of charging sales tax set out in Kentucky Revised Statute 138.450, the state officials said.

According to that statute, the 5 percent state sales tax must be assessed on the "retail value given in the automotive reference manual prescribed by the Department of Revenue" after deducting "a trade-in allowance equal to the value of the vehicle taken in trade."

The "automotive reference manual prescribed by the Department of Revenue" is the "National Automobile Dealers Association (NADA) Official Used Car Guide."

The statute also says that the trade-in allowance, which is sworn to by the seller on the bill of sale, shall not exceed "the fair market value of the vehicle taken in trade." Although the law doesn't spell out what the "fair market value" of the trade-in is, an attorney general's opinion has defined it as "in the area of" the NADA book value.

The attorney general's investigation has been aimed at the practice of certain dealers' charging used-car buyers more sales tax than is remitted to county clerks for payment to the state. There are several ways in which this is done, according to Hancock and [Assistant Attorney General Robert] Bullock.

One method of overcharging the sales tax is outlined by former Asst. Atty. Gen. David R. Vandeventer in a memo to KADA on the investigation.

In the memo he wrote asking KADA to cooperate in the investigation. Vandeventer states that the overcharging "can be done in a number of ways."

The memo continues:

"For example, by charging the consumer 5 percent of the lot sale price for a used car and remitting 5 percent of the NADA guide book if, as usual, the sale price exceeds the NADA guide price."

Hancock and Bullock explained that if a dealer charges 5 percent of the sales price to the consumer and then gives the county clerk only 5 percent of the lower NADA book value, the dealer is "pocketing" illegally obtained income.

In other cases, they said, dealers seemed to be simply charging the consumer a "lump sum" for sales tax regardless of the NADA book price of the car. When the bill of sale is registered with the county clerk, they said, the proper sales tax is calculated and paid.

For example, a dealer might be charging buyers a uniform $150 for sales tax. But if the NADA price on the car is $2,500, only 5 percent of that amount—or $125—is paid to the county clerk, resulting in a $25 bonus for the dealer.

Hancock and Bullock emphasized that this "lump-sum" method of charging sales tax also results in undercharges in cases where the actual amount of tax due exceeds the lump sum charged the buyer.

In other cases, Hancock said, the investigators have been unable to determine how dealers have arrived at the sales tax they have charged buyers.

"In some instances, there seems to have been no rhyme or reason to the basis for the tax charged," Hancock said. "You can't tie it into any computation."

Bullock and his staff have been visiting auto dealers and asking to see both purchase orders—which are filled out at the time the sale is made—and the bills of sale that are registered with the county clerks.

In many cases, Bullock said, the sales tax figure on the purchase order—which is the amount of tax the buyer paid to the dealer—exceeds 5 percent of the "total" price that is recorded on the bill of sale and on which the tax paid by the dealer is based.

Examples provided by the attorney general's office included:

1. A case in which the purchase order indicated that $93.40 was charged the consumer, but in which the bill of sale indicated only $70 was paid by the dealer to the county clerk.
2. A case in which the purchase order indicated that $75 sales tax was paid by the consumer, but in which the bill of sale indicated only $39.15 was paid by the dealer to the county clerk.
3. A case in which the purchase order indicated that $143.75 was charged the consumer for sales tax and other incidental fees, but in

which the bill of sale indicated only $62.50 was paid by the dealer to the county clerk.

Hancock and Bullock suggested that consumers who have purchased used cars since June 16, 1972, check to see if they have been overcharged for sales tax.

They said this is done by checking the amount of sales tax listed on the purchase order. This should amount to 5 percent of "total" purchase price listed on the "motor vehicle bill of sale" that is sent to the purchaser by the county clerk.

The "total" listed on the bill of sale is equal to the "average retail as shown in NADA Book," less the trade-in value of the car. These figures are listed on the bill of sale in a section entitled "Used Vehicles Valuation of Motor Vehicle for Computation of Usage Tax."

Hancock said the Consumer Protection Division was alerted to the overcharging practice by a former credit manager for a Kentucky dealer.

In a February 22 letter from Hancock to attorneys for KADA, Hancock states that the investigation was begun last November by members of the consumer division staff.

"After bringing it to my attention, I suggested that they contact representatives of KADA, for the purpose of asking for their help in investigating this matter. . .," Hancock's letter states.

However, after Bullock met with the KADA board of directors on December 18 and requested assistance from the trade association, KADA reported to Bullock's staff that the members of KADA "would be opposed to such cooperation and, therefore, no cooperation would be given. . ," the letter says.

The "cooperation" requested of KADA by the attorney general's office was that the trade association ask each of its members to supply the Consumer Protection Division with "complete sets of records on every sale during July and August 1973," according to Vandeventer's memo to KADA.

Vandeventer states in his memo that this would enable the consumer agency to determine whether overcharging was going on and which dealers were doing it.

When KADA refused cooperation, Hancock said, "There was no choice left to me but to authorize the investigation on a dealer-by-dealer basis."

When asked about KADA'a alleged refusal to cooperate with the investigation, KADA president [Ernie] Bates said:

"I told Mr. Bullock we can't give him authority to come into a man's place of business and let him go fishing around for a mistake this man has made."

Bates added:

"We don't condone in any case any overcharging or undercharging of the automobile usage tax. It's a pretty complicated thing to compute. Surprisingly enough, there are a lot of people who don't understand it. There have probably been some mistakes made on it. I think they (dealers) are probably computing it to the best of their ability."

Bates said it is his opinion that "Mr. Bullock went on a fishing expedition in Mr. Jones' case, and he has no law to back him up."

USED VEHICLES—VALUATION OF MOTOR VEHICLE FOR
COMPUTATION OF USAGE TAX - (KRS 138.450 & 138.460)

Passenger Cars
    1. Average retail as shown in NADA Book $ 2000.00

    2. Less trade-in per KRS
       Ky. Registration No.   *1400.00* $ 600.00

    3. Total   *X   .05*   ►$ 1400.00

                               $70.00

CASH DELIVERED PRICE OF VEHICLE ►	186 8	.00
SALES TAX	93.	40
DOCUMENTARY FEE	15.	50
TOTAL CASH DELIVERED PRICE	1976.	90

The illustration above contains segments of a bill of sale and a purchase order on an actual used-car sale in which the Kentucky attorney general's office detected an overcharge on sales tax. On top is a section of the bill of sale that lists the $1,400 "total" on which the 5 percent sales tax is computed for payment by the dealer to the county clerk. The "total" is arrived at by subtracting the trade-in allowance from the "book value" of the car being purchased. As the artist's calculation shows, the correct tax due is $70. However, as the purchase order pictured on the bottom, shows, 5 percent of the "cash delivered price of the vehicle" before subtraction of the trade-in allowance, or $93.40, was paid by the consumer to the dealer.

Hancock said: "As far as his (Bates) saying there's now law behind us, that's going to be up to the court to decide. As far as saying, "There's nothing wrong, but you can't see the records," that's about like (President) Nixon saying, " 'There's nothing wrong, but you can't have the tapes.' "

B   Tax policy gets made in a complex flurry of logic, lobbying, and a need for revenue. Consider these questions about the article about the federal tax on beer:

Consider These Questions

1. *Identify the type of groups being mobilized by the lobbyist. Do they differ from those who would be involved in a general sales tax or individual income tax issue?*
2. *Estimate the effective federal and state tax rates for the excise items. Do they seem high or low? (As a sidelight, the federal tax on cigarettes did not return to its lower level on October 1, 1985, and*

the tax on distilled spirits increased on that date, but there was no change for beer.)

Brewing Industry Organizes Lobbying Coalition to Head Off Any Increase in U.S. Tax on Beer

By Brooks Jackson

WASHINGTON—Stanley Brand says he represents legions of voiceless beer drinkers. "They're not organized, they don't have a lobbyist . . . . They need to be spoken for." The message: Don't raise federal taxes on beer.

Actually, Mr. Brand is a lobbyist for the brewing industry, but he doesn't spend much time hanging around House or Senate vestibules. He's organizing beer wholesalers, brewery suppliers and others in the beer industry into a coalition to speak, if not for consumers, at least against a beer-tax boost.

Such industry groups are being used increasingly to sway Congress by stirring up voters to write, call or visit their representatives. As Mr. Brand puts it, "The most effective way to lobby isn't to lobby at all, it's to mobilize the natural constituencies that exist out there in the hinterlands."

A U.S. map in his downtown law offices bristles with colored pins marking the locations, by congressional district, of members' breweries and other facilities. A monthly newsletter reaches a growing membership list that includes beer wholesalers, bottle and can makers, malt suppliers and others whose income is tied to beer sales. Members of House and Senate tax-writing committees regularly drop by

Excise Taxes on Alcoholic Beverages and Tobacco

	Average Retail Price	Federal Excise Tax	Average State Excise Tax	Yield to U.S. Treasury
Cigarettes	97.8 cents per pack of 20	16 cents per pack*	15.35 cents per pack	$4.75 billion
Beer	$9.00 per case of 24 cans	65 cents per case	41 cents per case	1.51 billion
Wine	$2.30 per 750-ml bottle	3.4 cents per bottle	10.9 cents per bottle	320 million
Distilled spirits	$6.59 per 750-ml bottle of 80-proof vodka	$1.67 per bottle†	$1.33 per bottle	3.55 billion

*Goes down to eight cents October 1   †Goes up to $1.99 October 1
SOURCES: *Tobacco Institute, Coalition on Beverage Issues, Distilled Spirits Council*

the coalition's monthly meetings to talk about budget and tax trends, pick up $2,000 appearance fees and see that the brewers are organizing.

United Front Envisioned

The coalition has enlisted the wine industry, and is courting distillers. Potentially, Mr. Brand envisions a vast, united front that could include tavern owners and perhaps even rank-and-file drinkers. There's talk of putting anti-tax tags on every six-pack, unfurling anti-tax "tent cards" on millions of tavern tables, pinning anti-tax buttons on bowling shirts in beer halls everywhere. One member even suggests commissioning a country-and-western song with an anti-beer tax theme.

All this may seem a bit premature, as there hasn't been an increase in the 65-cent-a-case federal tax on beer since the Korean War, and nobody is seriously proposing one right now.

But brewers are worried, because federal levies on beer and wine are the only "sin taxes" that haven't been increased recently. Last year, tax writers raised the federal tax on hard liquor by 19 percent, effective next October 1. And, in 1981, they doubled the federal excise tax on cigarettes, to 16 cents a pack.

More recently, bills have been introduced to increase tobacco and hard-liquor taxes even more, to help finance the troubled medicaid system. Proponents argue that those products cause health problems that medicaid pays for.

Those ideas haven't included beer and haven't yet generated much interest in Congress, but the beer men worry still. "When people talk taxes, certain industries are singled out," says Donald Shea, president of the U.S. Brewers Association. "We want to be prepared."

Among the first tasks was choosing a name. "We didn't want an acronym that sounded too cute, like 'Sixpac'," says Mr. Brand. Among those rejected were "Capet" for "Coalition Against Punitive Excise Taxes," and "Compete," for "Coalition of Manufacturers for the Promotion of Excise Tax Equity." The brewers fiinally settled on "COBI," for "Coalition on Beverage Issues," a misnomer because the group is formed around only one issue, taxes.

Cigarette Tax

As the brewers organize against a tax increase, others are getting ready, too. The tobacco industry has hired a bevy of high-priced Washington lawyers to help ensure that the temporary tax increase on cigarettes, scheduled to end October 1, doesn't become permanent.

Theirs will be an uphill struggle, many say, because going back to an 8-cent-a-pack tax could reduce the government's income by about $2.3 billion a year at a time when Congress is fretting about swollen budget deficits. Meanwhile, some tobacco-state lawmakers have broken ranks with the cigarette makers by proposing to use cigarette-tax income to finance the troubled system of federal price supports for tobacco growers.

The looming tobacco-tax debate could spell trouble for brewers. "Any discussion of tobacco taxes usually opens the door to a discussion of taxes on beer," Mr. Brand says in the coalition's newsletter.

But if any beer-tax proposal surfaces, Congress will start hearing from people such as Robert Snook, vice president of Minnesota Malting Co., which supplies about 5 million bushes of malt—sprouted, dried barley—to brewers each year. He and his 50 employees "would certainly be getting our message to the senators and representatives of the state of Minnesota," says Mr. Snook, who recently joined the coalition.

Just hearing some talk about a beer-tax increase moved another coalition member, George Brown, a Louisiana beer wholesaler, to get his customers, colleagues and employees to write letters to the White House a few months ago. "I generated about 1,200 letters, I think," Mr. Brown says.

There isn't any sign that those letters were why President Reagan let beer taxes alone in his tax-simplification plan. But Mr. Brown says, "It's all a part of our great democracy; let 'em know what you think."

9

Major Tax Structures: Property Taxes

Property taxes are the closest approximation to wealth taxes currently levied in the United States. They are not, however, true net wealth taxes because they typically omit some wealth types (individually owned personal property); they apply to gross, not net, wealth (the debt against a house or car will seldom be completely subtracted from taxable value); and they may apply twice to certain wealth forms (both corporate stock values and land and buildings owned by corporations are often taxed). To the extent that the taxes do reach wealth holdings, they add an element of redistribution from rich to poor otherwise missing from the tax structure. Because they apply to accumulated wealth, not income, they may also have less effect on work and investment incentives than do income taxes. They are, however, not based on values from current transactions (as is usually the case for income and sales taxes), so the tax requires a value-estimation procedure (assessment). That procedure is the primary weakness of property taxation.[1]

Property taxes are extremely difficult to categorize briefly. As Richard Almy observes:

> In the United States, "the" property tax is composed of 51 separate state level property tax systems, each subject to numerous legal and extralegal local variations and each changing in some fashion over time—through constitutional revision, enactment of statutes and ordinances, changes in administrative procedures, court decisions and changes in the capabilities of tax administration.[2]

The following sections introduce several important features of property taxes and examine a group of structural issues about the tax. Because

---

[1] The tax may have development disincentives as well, depending on its structure.

[2] Richard Almy, "Rationalizing the Assessment Process," in *Property Tax Reform,* ed. George Peterson (Washington, D.C.: Urban Institute, 1973), p. 175.

of the wide variation among the taxes, all local characteristics cannot be actually described here.

STRUCTURAL ISSUES ABOUT PROPERTY TAXES

Property within reach of the tax can be categorized several ways. One important distinction is between real property (land and structures or improvements erected on that land) and personal property (property which is not real, a grouping which includes valuables ranging from factory equipment to jewelry and automobiles). Personal property is generally more easily movable than real property, but there is no general dividing line between those groupings. Each state or local government develops its own definitions, usually resorting to lists of property types which fall into one or the other at the borderline.[3] The distinction is crucial because some governments tax personal property more heavily than real property, while others exempt certain personal property.

A second distinction is between tangible and intangible personal property. Tangible personal property is property held for its own sake, including cars, machinery, inventories of raw materials and finished products, household items, etc. Intangible personal property is property valued because it represents an ownership claim on something of value. Thus, intangible properties include stocks, bonds, and other financial assets. Property taxes vary widely in the extent to which they apply to these properties. Many types of tangible personal property are both difficult to locate and, once located, difficult to value (what is the value of a 10-year-old black-and-white television set, after all?); intangible personal property can often be easily valued, but frequently is difficult to locate. Sometimes intangible property is exempt by law; sometimes, by local practice. Seldom is taxation complete.

A third distinction frequently made for taxes is between business ownership and individual or household ownership of property. Business holdings of personal property may be fully taxable (television sets in motels, for instance), while household holdings of that same item are not taxed (a household personal property exemption). The logic of a net wealth tax would suggest that the household possession represents wealth, probably more so than the business holding, but most structures rule in the opposite manner. Within the business class, some types are treated differently, as with public utility property which is often valued as an operating unit, not on an item-by-item basis as is the case in other assessments.

---

[3]One interesting problem concerns the treatment of mobile homes—are they real or personal property? States use rules including permanency of foundation, presence of wheels or axles, highway licensing, etc., but there is no general division.

Property Tax Rate Setting

Most tax rates change only with special legislative action—they are the portion of the fiscal system which is most strictly incremental, in the sense of small changes being made to a permanent base. That is the case with state sales taxes and state and federal income taxes. Property tax rates are established, however, as a part of the annual budget process, as opposed to rates for individual income, general sales, and other major taxes which change only by special legislative action. Budgets heavily dependent on the property tax have rate setting as a normal part of the legislative process. The rate in most circumstances must be annually readopted at a level sufficient to balance the operating budget and yield revenue high enough to cover current costs of servicing budgets financed by debt. This rate setting uses these data:

1. The total of approved expenditure plans (E) included in the appropriation act or ordinance.
2. The total estimate of revenue from nonproperty tax sources, including miscellaneous charge and fee revenue, revenue from nonproperty taxes (sales or income), grants, etc. (NPR). Part of this revenue may be guaranteed state payments, but much will be estimated.
3. The total assessed value (AV) in the taxing unit, as established at the standard assessment date for the jurisdiction. Assessed value is the base upon which the property tax will be levied. For instance, the assessed value total on March 1, 1986, could be the figure upon which taxes were collected for a fiscal year beginning January 1, 1987. Thus, collections lag behind assessment.

The property tax rate (R) would emerge as a residual from the formula

$$R = \frac{E - NPR}{AV}$$

This rate would apply to property assessed on that earlier assessment date. For example, suppose that a village had appropriated $95,000 for the 1989 fiscal year (January 1 to December 31, 1989), estimated that it would receive $15,000 from nonproperty tax sources during that fiscal year, and had an assessed value of $1.75 million on March 1, 1988 (the assessment date). In that village, the property tax rate for 1989 would be 4.58 percent, or $4.58 per $100 of assessed value. A parcel valued at $8,000 for tax purposes would have a 1989 property tax bill of $366.40, possibly payable in equal installments due in May and November of 1989.

Assessment.   Property taxes require a valuation procedure to establish a basis for distribution of the tax burden. This assessment is the heart of the real property tax system because it determines the share of tax burden that will be borne by property parcels within a jurisdiction. When a reassessment changes property values for tax purposes, some properties will pay a higher share of the tax burden; and others, a lower share, compared to their burdens before that reassessment. It is this adjustment of tax burdens to more closely match perceived capability to pay the tax—as measured by property value—that is the objective of assessment.

Governments employ several different assessment schemes across the United States, but three general structures have been identified: annual assessment, mass cyclical assessment, and segmental assessment. With cyclical mass assessment, all properties in a taxing jurisdiction are valued for tax purposes in a particular year; and that value will not change until the next scheduled mass assessment, except for new construction, demolition, or change in use of a property. A recent study found states prescribing mass cyclical assessments at intervals ranging from 2 to 10 years. Examples include Kentucky (2 years), Iowa (2 years), Minnesota (4 years), Indiana (8 years effective in 1987), and Connecticut (10 years).[4]

Segmental assessment is a procedure by which a specified fraction of real property parcels in a jurisdiction is reassessed each year, moving through the assessing unit in sequence. Thus, if a three-year cycle is used, one third of the properties in the area would be reassessed in each year, with all properties reassessed in three years. The last-valued taxpayers can complain about the inflation in their valuations which is absent from earlier-valued parcels, but administrative convenience and the fact that all parcels take their turn as last valued has preserved the method. Examples include a three-year cycle in Maryland and a four-year cycle in Cook County, Illinois. Figure 9–1 shows how reassessment moves through the latter county. The north quadrant was reassessed in 1985 and will not be reassessed until 1989.

The third system is annual assessment, a process which presumes updated values for all real property parcels each year. Such a process is possible with EDP assistance, although revaluation with actual inventory and inspection of all parcels is not likely. More often than not, annual valuation will employ the physical characteristics of properties as identified in earlier parcel inventories with new value weights applied to those characteristics. For instance, in earlier years, a fireplace might add $1,000 to the value of a house; this year, it is estimated to add $1,800. In that fashion, new value estimates would emerge from old physical feature data. Of course, annual reassessment can become no reassessment if last year's values are simply recopied on this year's

[4]U.S. Bureau of Census, *Census of Governments 1982*, vol. 2, *Taxable Property Values and Assessment—Sales Price Ratios* (Washington, D.C.: U.S. Government Printing Office, 1984), p. 26.

FIGURE 9-1 Property Reassessments—
Cook County Quadrennial
Districts

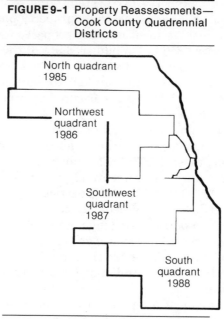

SOURCE: Cook County Assessor. *Chicago Tribune* map, February 24, 1985.

forms. That process destroys the equity of the property tax because no adjustments are made for properties whose value has either fallen or increased. The fiction that properties are reassessed annually prevents any meaningful realignment of parcel values.

The worst mutation of annual assessment is the "Welcome Stranger" system in which properties are revalued only when they are sold, and at the new transaction price.[5] This structure disrupts the property market (prospective buyers would pay a higher property tax than would the prospective seller), creates a property record substructure of sales without recorded deeds as individuals seek to avoid property tax adjustments, and causes completely identical properties to pay widely different property tax.

All assessment systems but "Welcome Stranger" require estimation of values (Welcome Stranger prescribes a perverse value estimation procedure). Three general approaches to estimation of real property values have emerged as offshoots to private property appraisal techniques: (1)

---

[5]This is the system forced on California by Proposition 13 in 1978. Allen Manvel notes the precipitous decline in assessment quality produced by that system: "Assessment Uniformity—And Proposition 13," *Tax Notes* 24 (August 27, 1984), pp. 893–95.

[6]International Association of Assessing Officers, *Assessing and the Appraisal Process* (Chicago: IAAO, 1973), chaps. 5–7.

the market data approach, (2) the cost, or summation, approach, and (3) the income approach.[6] The market data or comparable sales approach uses evidence from the real estate market transactions to estimate values of particular property parcels. Sales of similar parcels are used to gauge buyer and seller attitudes to particular parcels to determine what the value of a parcel would be if it were to sell. A reasonably good comparison is usually possible for residential property (there are many three-bedroom split-level houses with about 2,500 square feet of living space in most cities, after all, and some have probably sold recently), but uniqueness can be a problem for commercial or industrial parcels.

The cost approach estimates the cost to reproduce a particular structure, and then subtracts from estimated reproduction cost the depreciation which has occurred since the building was built. The approach typically proceeds by determining the cost of constructing a standard (average) grade of structure at a particular date, that is, with the labor and materials prices of that time and using the prevailing technology, in the size (square footage and number of stories) of the subject property. That cost is adjusted to account for nonstandard construction materials and workmanship—either higher or lower than standard. To that cost will be added extra features not in the standard unit—extra bathroom fixtures, fireplaces, central air conditioning, etc., for residential units; escalators, sprinkler systems, vaults, etc., for commercial units; and cranes, elevators, air-handling systems, etc., for industrial units. That final cost figure will then be adjusted for depreciation to allow for the fact that the structure is not new, but has suffered physical, technological, and economic forces which have influenced its current value. While the approach can be applied in mass reassessment, it obviously will not apply to land valuation.

The income approach is most applicable to value estimates for income-producing properties (apartments, stores, offices, agricultural land, etc.). The method estimates the sustainable net income flow from the property and capitalizes that income flow at the appropriate interest rate for that investment risk. (Recall the discounting of future income flows from Chapter 5.) The resulting value estimates the amount a willing and knowledgeable buyer would pay for a parcel yielding that income flow.

Each method can yield uniform estimates of values when consistently applied; the first two methods are particularly amenable to the requirements of mass assessment. In some instances, the value of parcels will be estimated using all three approaches so that the assessor will have as much information as possible to form this valuation judgment. These values and the method used in their estimation will be maintained either in EDP record files or on parcel cards. Figure 9–2 presents such a property record card: one side describes the land and the factors used in its valuation; the other side does the same for the structure. The values on such records for all parcels in the jurisdiction,

FIGURE 9-2

Monroe COUNTY Salt Creek TOWNSHIP CORPORATION

OWNERSHIP

SE NE 78-1E 40 A

| PARCEL NUMBER 014 | SECTION & PLAT 007101 | PROPERTY ADDRESS 0071 ROUTING NUMBER | CARD NUMBER 21 01 | PROPERTY CLASS 1101 |

MEMORANDUM

TRANSFER OF OWNERSHIP   DATE

1 AGRICULTURAL
00 vacant land
01 cash grain, gen. farm
02 livestock 01 03 & 04
03 dairy farms
04 poultry farms
05 fruit & nut farms
06 vegetable farms
07 tobacco farms
08 nurseries
09 greenhouses
20 timber
99 other agricultural use

2 MINERAL

3 INDUSTRIAL
00 vacant land
10 food & drink
20 hundreds & heavy mfg
30 medium mfg & assembly
40 light mfg & assembly
50 warehousing
60 mineral
70 ind. truck terminals
72 small shops
80 mines & quarries
90 grain elevators
99 other ind. structures

VALUATION RECORD

ASSESSMENT YEAR	1978	REVALUATION	19 ___	19 ___	19 ___	19 ___	19 ___
REASON FOR CHANGE							
TRUE CASH VALUE LAND		5700					
IMPROVEMENTS		51500					
TOTAL		57200					
ASSESSED VALUE LAND		1900					
IMPROVEMENTS		17170					
TOTAL		19070					

4 COMMERCIAL
00 vacant land
01 04 19 (family apt)
02 20 39 family apt.
10 40 or more (family apt)
11 motels / tourist cabins
12 hotels
14 nursing hms / hospitals
15 mobile home parks
18 Comm. camp grounds
19 other Comm. housing
20 small det. retail (10000)
22 supermarkets
27 discount / dept. stores
24 full line dept. stores
25 neighbrhd. shop. cntr.
26 community shop. cntr.
27 regional shop. cntr.
29 other retail struct.
30 rest. cafe and/or bar
31 franchise food type
35 drive-in restaurant
38 service station
39 other food svc. struct.
40 laundry / drycl. laundry
41 funeral homes
42 med. clinics & offices
44 full svc. banks
45 savings banks
46 office bldg. 1 & 2 story
48 office 3 / 7+ walk-up
48 office c/t elevator
53 auto service station
53 car washers
54 Comm. Garage & service
55 Comm. garage
56 parking lot or struct.
60 theaters
62 golf range, min. course
62 golf courses
63 bowling alleys
80 Comm. warehouse
80 Comm. mini-warehouse
81 Comm. truck terminals
90 marine svc. facilities
90 reg'l. lt. svc. facil.
99 other Comm. structures

5 RESIDENTIAL
0 one family dwelling
1 two family dwelling
2 three family dwelling
3 condominium unit
4 mobile home
5 apartment
L (unplatted) 0-9.99 acs.
L (unplatted) 10-19.99 acs.
2 (unplatted) 20-29.99 acs.
4 (unplatted) 30-39.99 acs.
5 (unplatted) 40+
99 other res. structures

LAND DATA AND COMPUTATIONS

LAND TYPE	SOIL I.D.	ACTUAL FRONTAGE	EFFECTIVE FRONTAGE	EFFECTIVE DEPTH	DEPTH FACTOR	BASE RATE	ADJUSTED RATE	EXTENDED VALUE	INFLUENCE FACTOR	TRUE CASH VALUE
F FRONT LOT		•							%	
R REAR LOT		•							%	
1 PRIMARY IND/COMM SITE		•							%	
2 UNDEVELOPED			SQ FT	FACTOR					%	
3 OPEN TILLABLE			ACREAGE						%	
4 OPEN NON-TILLABLE	7	1.00	1.00		3.000X 100	3.000	3.000		%	3.000
5 WOOD/WASTELAND	5	1.00	15.00	57	450	257	3.860	-60 %		1500
61 PUBLIC ROAD	6	1.00	24.00	57	450	257	6.170	-80 %		1200
HOME SITE									%	
									%	
									%	
									%	
									%	

| | TOTAL ACREAGE | 40.00 | | | | | | TOTAL TRUE CASH LAND VALUE | | 5700 |

TOPOGRAPHY / PUBLIC UTILITIES / STREET OR ROAD / NEIGHBORHOOD

TOPOGRAPHY		PUBLIC UTILITIES	
LEVEL		WATER	✓
HIGH		SEWER	
LOW		GAS	
ROLLING	✓	ELECTRICITY	✓
SWAMPY		ALL	

STREET OR ROAD		NEIGHBORHOOD	
PAVED		IMPROVING	✓
UNPAVED	✓	STATIC	
PROPOSED		DECLINING	
SIDEWALK			
ALLEY		BLIGHTED	

INFLUENCE FACTOR
1 CORNER INFLUENCE
2 ALLEY INFLUENCE
3 TOPOGRAPHY
4 UNDER IMPROVED
5 EXCESS FRONTAGE
0

6 SHAPE OR SIZE
7 MISIMPROVEMENT
8 RESTRICTIONS
9 VIEW
0

PRESCRIBED INDIANA PROPERTY RECORD CARD 1978

FIGURE 9-2 (concluded)

IMPROVEMENT DATA AND COMPUTATIONS

RESIDENTIAL BUILDINGS

OCCUPANCY		STORY HEIGHT	ATTIC	BSMT	CRAWL
1 SINGLE FAMILY	✓	2.0 [ ]	1 NONE	0 NONE	0
2 DUPLEX			1 UNFINISHED	1 ¼	1
3 TRIPLEX			2 ¼ FINISHED	2 ½	2
4 4-4 FAMILY			3 ¾ FINISHED	3 ¾	3
0 ___			4 FINISHED	0 FULL	4

CONSTRUCTION		FLOOR LEVEL	FIN LIVING AREA	ATTIC	BSMT	CRAWL	VALUE
		BASE AREA	1836				
		1.0	1836		24500		
		2.0	1344	1344	13800		

1 FRAME OR ALUM	
2 STUCCO	
3 TILE	
4 CONCRETE BLOCK	
5 METAL	
6 CONCRETE	
7 BRICK	
8 STONE	
9 FRAME W/MAS	

		VALUE
ATTIC		6000
BSMT/CRWL		
TOTAL BASE	3180±	44300
ROW-TYPE ADJUSTMENT		%
SUB-TOTAL		44300
UNFINISHED INTERIOR		
EXTRA LIVING UNITS		
REC ROOM		+1400
FIREPLACE		6000
NO HEATING		
AIR CONDITIONING		+3500
NO PLUMBING		
BASE PLBG [-]		
BASE PLBG [+] 0 2		+900
SUB-TOTAL, ONE UNIT		50100
SUB-TOTAL, ___ UNITS		
GARAGES & CARPORTS		+2500
EXTERIOR FEATURES		+1600
SUB-TOTAL		54200
GRADE & DESIGN FACTOR C [+]		100 %
REPRODUCTION COST		54200
COST FACTOR		
REPRODUCTION COST		

ROOFING: ASPHALT SHINGLES / SLATE OR TILE

METAL / FLOORS / EARTH / SLAB / SUB & JOISTS / NO WOOD OR FIR / PARQUET / TILE / CARPET / UNFINISHED ½ / INT. FINISH / PLSTR OR DR W / PANELING / FIBERBOARD / UNFINISHED ½

ACCOMMODATIONS
NUMBER OF ROOMS 7 / BEDROOMS 4 / FAMILY ROOM / FORMAL DINING ROOM

REC. ROOM TYPE 2 SIZE 600
FIREPLACE STACKS / OPENINGS
HEATING BASE
NO HEATING / CENTRAL WARM AIR / H W OR STEAM
CENTRAL AIR COND / PLUMBING BASE / NO PLUMBING / WATER ONLY / FULL BATHS / HALF BATHS / W C & LAVS

REMODELING & MODERNIZATION: EXTERIOR / INTERIOR / KITCHEN / BATH FACILITIES / PLUMBING SYSTEM / HEATING SYSTEM / ELECTRICAL SYSTEM / EXTENSIONS

COMMERCIAL / INDUSTRIAL BUILDING

WALLS	ROOFING		A			B		
BRICK	BUILT UP	1 PRICING KEY						
STONE	METAL	S.F. AREA						
CONCRETE	SLATE TILE	EFF. PERIMETER	L/F			L/F		
W/O MTL	SHINGLE	PERIM AREA RATIO						
CB/TILE		NUMBER OF UNITS						
		AVE. UNIT SIZE						

FRAMING / WOOD JOIST / FIRE RESISTANT / FIRE PROOF / FLOORS CONCRETE / WOOD / TILE / FINISH TYPE / UNFINISHED / SEMIFINISHED / FINISHED OPEN / FIN DIVIDED / USE / STORE / OFFICE / APARTMENT / VACANT / ABANDONED / HEATING & A.C. / NO HEATING / CEN WARM AIR / H W OR STEAM / UNIT HEATING / CENTRAL AIR / PKG/UNIT AIR / PLUMBING / FULL BATHS / HALF BATHS / OTHER FIXT / SPRINKLER

BASE PRICE / B.P.A. % / SUB-TOTAL / UNIT FINISH / INTERIOR FINISH / DIV WALLS / LIGHTING / HEATING & A.C. / SPRINKLER / S.F./C.F. PRICE / AREA CUBAGE / SUB-TOTAL / PLUMBING / SPECIAL FEATURES / EXTERIOR FEAT / TOTAL BASE / G/D FACTOR % / REPRO. COST / COST FACTOR / REPRO. COST

SPECIAL FEATURES FOR COMMERCIAL/INDUSTRIAL BUILDINGS

QTY	ITEM DESCRIPTION	VALUE

TOTAL (TO BE CARRIED TO PRICING LADDER): _____

SUMMARY OF IMPROVEMENTS

I.D.	USE	STORY HEIGHT	CONST	GRADE	YEAR CONST	YEAR REMOD	COND	SIZE	AREA	RATE	REPRODUCTION COST	ACCRUED DEPRECIATION			TRUE CASH VALUE
												NORM	OBSOL	TOTAL	
	DWELLING	—	—	—	1977	—	A	—	—	—	54200	5	—	5	51500
	GARAGE														

TOTAL TRUE CASH IMPROVEMENT VALUE 51500

DATA COLLECTOR/DATE   APPRAISER/DATE

INDIANA 1978

when summed, constitute the property tax base for the taxing unit; the record information likewise is used for computation of individual tax bills from that rate, after subtraction of whatever exemptions are applicable. Figures 9–3 and 9–4 show an assessed value notice (prepared from the parcel card of Figure 9–2) to inform the property owner, and the resulting tax bill.

Exemption.   Property tax systems almost always include provisions which subtract a portion of assessed value from the taxable holdings of certain individuals or institutions. Thus, if an individual holding property with assessed value of $8,500 qualifies for a veteran's exemption of $1,500, that person's tax bill would be computed on a net assessed value of $7,000. The exemption reduces the tax base; it is not a direct credit against tax owed. In most instances, the exemptions are additive, so if a parcel holder qualifies for exemption because of age and veteran status, for example, the property tax base would be reduced by the sum of both exemptions.

Individuals qualify for many different classes of exemption. Some of the more important in terms of use by states and size of value exemption are homestead, veterans, and old-age exemptions. Homestead exemptions allow homeowners a given assessed value base before any

FIGURE 9-3

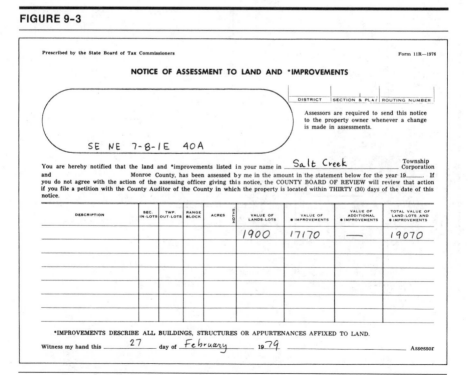

FIGURE 9-4

SPRING REAL ESTATE TAX STATEMENT	MONROE	COUNTY, INDIANA

RETURN BOTH "A" COPIES WHEN PAYING FIRST INSTALLMENT AND BOTH "B" COPIES WHEN PAYING SECOND INSTALLMENT. ENCLOSE SELF-ADDRESSED STAMPED ENVELOPE WHEN PAYING BY MAIL.

EXEMPTIONS	NET VALUATION	TAXING UNIT	TAX ACCOUNT NUMBER
R 1,000	R 17,170	SALT CREEK	53 10 05300 000
NR	NR 900		BANK CODE 00

GROSS TAX FIRST INSTALLMENT	ST. PROPERTY & HOMESTEAD CR.	NET TAX EACH INSTALLMENT
R 444.10	124.35	319.75
NR 23.28	4.66	18.62

TAX RATE	DELINQUENT TAX & PENALTY	TOTAL PAY THIS AMOUNT
5.173		338.37

When paying full year's tax on or before May 10 double net tax for each installment. First installment delinquent after date indicated on "A" statement.

LEGAL DESCRIPTION

SE NE 7-8-1E   40A

THE LETTER "R" INDICATES "RESIDENTIAL" TO WHICH HOMESTEAD CREDIT HAS BEEN APPLIED. THE LETTERS "NR" INDICATE "NON RESIDENTIAL" REAL ESTATE.

DATE AND AMOUNT PAID

This is a valid receipt when stamped paid or validated by the County Treasurer

A 1980   PAYABLE IN 1981   DELINQUENT AFTER

MAY 10, 1981   ADD 10% PENALTY

NOTICE   TAX STATEMENT FOR BOTH INSTALLMENTS ARE ENCLOSED. NO SEPARATE STATEMENT WILL BE SENT IN ADVANCE OF THE DUE DATE OF THE SECOND INSTALLMENT

MAKE CHECK PAYABLE TO: TREASURER OF MONROE   COUNTY
AND MAIL TO: COURTHOUSE   BLOOMINGTON, IN   47401

property tax bill will be levied against property. Veterans and old-age exemptions provide similar partial exemption of properties from the tax. These exemptions can dramatically reduce the base on which the tax can be applied: in Louisiana and Mississippi, 24.2 and 21.9 percent of gross assessed value were exempt because of homestead exemptions in 1981; in Hawaii, homestead and disability exemptions subtracted 15.7 percent of the gross base; in Alabama, homestead and other exemptions eliminated 19.7 percent of the gross value. Nationwide partial exemptions reduced gross assessed value by 4.1 percent.[7] The potential revenues are not trivial.

Such exemption programs are politically popular because of their apparent tax savings and burden redistribution, but they have a number of important problems. First, the programs usually have a statewide purpose, but because property taxes primarily support local government, the revenue loss is local. They are thus a way for state legislatures to win favor with the electorate without loss of state revenue. Second, the programs do not focus tax relief on the needy. All people falling into the specific categories (homeowner or veteran) receive aid regardless of their specific needs, as there is no income test for receipt of exemption. Despite trials and tribulations, homeowners probably are better off than renters and not all homeowners are equally well-(or poorly) situated. Third, if the exemption program is sufficiently widespread, as in the case of general homestead exemption programs, the

---

[7]U.S. Bureau of the Census, *Census of Governments 1982*, vol. 2, *Taxable Property Values and Assessment—Sales Price Ratios* (Washington, D.C.: U.S. Government Printing Office, 1984), p. 49.

effect may be substantially higher property tax rates to recover lost revenue. For properties not completely exempted from the base, actual relief may be more psychological than real as the owner pays a higher rate on a smaller base, with about the same total tax bill. And finally, individual exemption programs ordinarily do not reach renters, many of whom are much less affluent than are property owners. This must be seen as an inherent defect in the structure of exemption programs. Overall, the political popularity of exemption programs does not reduce their substantial flaws in application.

Exemptions also apply to selected types of commercial and industrial property.[8] The exemption for a parcel may be complete and permanent, or it may abate all or a portion of property tax for a specific period of time. It may also exempt portions of an otherwise taxable parcel, such as pollution control equipment or solar energy equipment. Some areas also provide special exemption for rehabilitated property. The idea is to stimulate economic activity of particular types at defined locations. It is, however, not clear that such property tax reductions are an effective industrial incentive. Evidence suggests things other than tax levels, particularly accessibility to markets, resource availability, transportation networks, and environmental amenities are much more significant in determining the location of commercial and industrial facilities. Thus, the expected return from such exemption is low. An even greater problem than low return from the exemption, however, may be the effect on existing property in the area. The new industries do create a demand for public services (police protection, fire protection, planning, etc.) and new people in the area will likely demand more services than can be covered by the tax base they bring. With exemption of that new industrial property, those costs must be borne by the existing tax base. This is, at a minimum, discriminatory and, at a maximum, may eliminate some marginal businesses. Those properties not qualifying for the exemption will be facing artificially high property tax rates because of the assistance provided the new arrivals.

A final exemption group includes properties which are fully exempt because of the religious, governmental, educational, or charitable nature of the owner. An accurate estimate of the total amount of the potential tax base removed by these exemptions is not available—where the law requires assessment of these properties, officials are often cavalier about the process because they recognize that no tax collections will result. Observers maintain that the taxes forgiven are substantial. The revenue loss is a particular problem because of the unequal distribution of such property among localities. Cities or counties with major state installations, for example, universities and state parks, can be

---

[8]The best general source of information on these programs: Steven Gold, *Property Tax Relief* (Lexington, Mass.: D. C. Heath, 1979).

particularly affected: they must provide for the peak, and special, service demands created by users of that facility without the power to include that facility in the tax base. Thus, the taxpayers of that locality must subsidize the citizenry of the state. The problem is reduced somewhat when exemptions are conditioned on both ownership and use of the facility (a university classroom building may be exempt, but not a university-owned hotel), but the dual requirement is neither universal nor applied without interpretation problems. The federal government does make in-lieu-of-property-tax payments to state and local units hosting certain federal installations, but states seldom provide similar relief to their local governments. As will be discussed in a later chapter, user charges may well be an attractive option in such instances.

Circuit breakers.   Property tax exemptions to individuals fail to target property tax relief to those individuals most in need. That problem can be reduced by conditioning property tax assistance on individual income levels, as done by property tax circuit breakers. State circuit breakers, used by 32 states and the District of Columbia, pinpoint relief of property tax overload (defined in terms of the ratio of property tax payment to current family income) through integration of the local property tax and the state individual income tax structure. On the income tax return, the taxpayer reports the amount of property tax paid for the year for comparison with the taxpayer's income. If the ratio of property tax to income is excessive as defined in the circuit breaker law (an "overload"), some portion of that excess is returned by the state to the individual as an addition to income tax refund, as a reduction in income tax owed, or as a direct cash payment. Thus, the circuit breaker eliminates the property tax overload at state expense.

Critical structural elements for circuit breakers include age restrictions, income definition and limits, treatment of renters, and benefit formulas. Many programs limit overload relief to elderly, at least partly to reduce program cost. Elderly individuals may, however, be especially susceptible to overload because the property tax bill on property they accumulate during their work careers does not fall as their income falls with retirement. The property tax bill that was reasonable in relation to salary consumes an excessive chunk of the pension. The circuit breaker can reduce the need for forced sale and can ease retirement. A number of states thus restrict their programs to elderly taxpayers who meet other circuit breaker criteria. Nonelderly low-income homeowners, however, may face similar overloads as well, particularly in the early years of homeownership or when a family income earner becomes unemployed. Exclusion of these homeowners is hardly defensible, but certainly does reduce the cost of the overall program.

Income limitations for the circuit breaker program are another design question. These limits imply that, beyond some income level, the state will not relieve any property tax burden. The limitation both reduces program cost and concentrates assistance at the lower end of the income spectrum. For these purposes, however, income must be defined more broadly than federal or state taxable income to include nontaxed retirement income sources. If it does not, individuals who are reasonably well-off because of pension, social security, and other nontaxed incomes would qualify, reducing aid available for the truly unfortunate.

Renters pose a third design problem, under the presumption that they pay a portion of the property tax on units they occupy. A circuit breaker limited to homeowners would provide them no assistance, even though many renters are much less affluent than the poorest homeowners. Renter relief, where given, presumes a property tax equivalent as a specified percentage of rent paid. The share is not scientifically determined because analysts have been unable to estimate the extent (if any) to which property tax is shifted to renters. With reasonable income limits, however, the program can be seen as a part of general assistance, regardless of property tax conditions.

The final design element is the choice between threshold and sliding-scale relief formulas. The former approach defines a threshold percentage of income as the overload level. Property tax payments above that overload level are subject to partial relief. Relief computation follows the formula $R = t(PT - Ik)$ where R = relief to be provided (subject to a lower limit of zero), t = the percentage of the overload which will be relieved, k = the overload threshold percentage, I = family income, and PT = property tax payment. Suppose a family has an income of $8,000 and pays property tax of $900. If it lives in a state which defines the overload threshold as 10 percent and grants 90 percent overload relief, the family would receive circuit breaker relief of $900. Some states further reduce their costs by reducing the threshold percentage as income increases—a further effort to economize and focus aid.

The second formula is the sliding-scale approach. In this formula, relief is computed as a percentage of property tax payment with the percentage falling as family income increases: $R = zPT$ where z is the percentage of property tax relieved for the income class and R and PT are as previously defined. Unless the relief percentage falls to zero at high incomes, all taxpayers receive assistance under this approach, so it is more like general property tax relief than specific relief of the property tax overload. It does differ, however, from general property tax relief because (1) there is usually an upper limit to circuit breaker relief available to a parcel holder, (2) taxpayers must file to obtain this relief, (3) only homeowner property receives the circuit breaker relief (although some states extend the assistance to farm property), and (4) relief is conditioned on income of the property owner.

Circuit breakers are flexible and easily administrable in conjunction with the state income tax. They can be focused on families in greatest need of relief and, furthermore, are financed from state, not local, revenue. They do, however, provide no incentive for improved property tax administration and may encourage greater use of local property taxes as some property tax costs are shifted to the state. Those problems are probably swamped by the contribution the circuit breaker makes to the equity of the property tax.

Deferrals.   An additional relief device applicable to the special property tax problems of elderly property owners and to farmers on the borders of metropolitan areas is tax deferral. With this mechanism, individuals whose property values have risen dramatically through no fault of their own are permitted to pay tax on the basis of old values, with records kept on the difference between that payment and what it would have been at full property value. That difference is not forgiven, but rather is deferred to a later time. In the case of the agricultural property, it is collected when the farmland converts to a different (higher value) use. In the case of the elderly individual, the deferred tax becomes a claim against that individual's estate. These recaptures can be complete or partial and interest may or may not be charged; state approaches vary. The tax deferral relieves special property tax burdens without creating the problems that circuit breakers and special exemptions can often create; they can relieve without special subsidization—a rare combination in tax policy.

Fractional assessment and assessment uniformity.   The heart of the property tax is assessment, the determination of a property value for distribution of total tax burden. Valuation may or may not be tied to current market value (defined as the transaction price for a parcel that would emerge in exchange between a willing and knowledgeable buyer and a willing and knowledgeable seller) by the prevailing property tax law and, even where it is tied to current market value, prevailing assessment practices may cause substantial difference between market and assessed values. For example, according to the 1982 Census of Governments the national median area assessment ratio (assessed value to market value) for single-family (nonfarm houses) was 36.9 percent in 1981.[9] State median area ratios ranged from a high of 86.8 percent in Idaho to a low of 0.6 percent in Vermont.[10]

Under normal circumstances the overall assessment ratio has little impact on absolute property tax burdens, because assessment levels can be counteracted by differences in the statutory tax rate. For instance, suppose a municipality seeks $5 million from its property tax

---

[9]The single-family, nonfarm home is used as a benchmark for assessment evaluation because almost every assessing district contains several of that class and that grouping tends to be more homogeneous than other property types.

[10]U.S. Bureau of Census, *Census of Governments 1982*, vol. 2, *Taxable Property Values and Assessment—Sales Price Ratios* (Washington, D.C.: U.S. Government Printing Office, 1984), p. 50.

and that the market value of taxable property is $80 million. If the assessment ratio is 100 percent, a property tax rate of $6.25 per $100 assessed value will yield the desired revenue. If the assessment ratio is 50 percent, a property tax rate of $12.50 per $100 assessed value will produce the desired levy total. Low assessment ratios will produce compensating statutory rate adjustments.

Fractional assessment, assessment at less than market value, creates inequities and other complications, not inadequate revenue.[11] These problems are, in fact, the major practical problems with the property tax. First, low assessment ratios increase the likelihood of unfair individual assessments, because an individual parcel holder will probably be unaware of any overassessment. Suppose the legal assessment standard is one third of market value, but the prevailing practice is 20 percent. If a parcel worth about $40,000 is assessed at $10,000, an unwary owner would believe that he has a favorable assessment: the tax assessor has valued the property far below the market value and, should the parcel owner know about legal standards, even below the one-third value standard. In fact, the parcel is overassessed—a 25 percent ratio compared to the prevailing 20 percent—so the parcel will bear an artificially high effective tax rate. Unless the parcel owner is sophisticated about the ways of property taxation, he will never realize the inequity.[12] As John Shannon puts it, "the lower the assessment level, the larger becomes the administrative graveyard in which the assessor can bury his mistakes."[13]

A second general problem is the impairment of overall fiscal legislation that fractional assessment can bring. Fractional assessment can make state-imposed property tax rate ceilings and debt limits linked to assessed value more restrictive than intended. Many states limit local debt to, for instance, 2 percent of assessed value. If assessment ratios have fallen over time, as is often the case, that limit becomes artificially restrictive and creates extra incentive to avoid those debt limits. Further, the practice can cause uneven distributions of any state property tax rate across local areas with differing assessment ratios. The effective state property tax rate is higher in areas with high assessment ratios than other areas. Finally, state grant assistance is frequently distributed in formulas keyed to local assessed value: the lower the assessed value in an area, the greater the amount of state aid. Fractional

---

[11]Rigid statutory rate ceilings may, however, combine with fractional assessment to create inadequate revenue.

[12]There is an extra pitfall in the process. The legal standard is 33 ⅓ percent; the parcel is valued at 25 percent. Some appeal mechanisms suggest that the appropriate action is an increase in assessed value to the legal standard.

[13]John Shannon, "Conflict between State Assessment Law and Local Assessment Practice," in *Property Taxation—USA*, ed. Richard W. Lindholm (Madison, Wis.: University of Wisconsin Press, 1969), p. 45.

assessment can obviously distort that distribution, so states typically develop equalization multipliers to get assessed values to a common assessment level for aid purposes: if an area has an assessment ratio of 25 percent and the statewide standard is 50 percent, its assessed value would be doubled for aid formula calculations. These equalization multipliers may or may not be applied to individual parcel values for tax bill computation. If rates are flexible and all parcels in a taxing area receive the same multiplier, the process makes no difference for those bills.

The major difficulty with fractional assessment occurs, however, when assessment ratios of parcels within a taxing area differ. When this occurs, as it does to some extent in all systems, the effective tax rate is no longer uniform and similarly situated properties bear different property tax burdens solely because of the assessment system. Thus, if property A is assessed at 30 percent of value, and property B is assessed at 20 percent, a property tax of $10 per $100 of assessed value translates into an effective rate of $3 per $100 of value on property A and $2 per $100 on property B. No tax should be so capricious. Unfortunately, property taxes do show such dispersion in actual operation. The coefficient of dispersion (CD) provides a measure of the extent of dispersion (or the absence of uniformity) in assessment ratios and, hence, the extent to which effective property tax rates vary within a taxing unit. The CD—the average percentage by which individual assessment ratios deviate from the median assessment ratio—equals

$$CD = \left[\frac{\sum\limits_{i=1}^{n} |A_i - M|}{n} \div M \right] \cdot 100$$

where A_i = the assessment ratio for an individual property parcel, M = the median assessment ratio for all parcels sampled; and n = the number of parcels in the sample. Table 9–1 illustrates CD computation.

TABLE 9–1

Parcels	Assessed Value	Market Value	Assessment Ratio	Absolute Dispersion
A	$15,000	$ 30,000	0.50	0.10
B	20,000	30,000	0.67	0.07
C	8,000	20,000	0.40	0.20
D	30,000	40,000	0.75	0.15
E	15,000	25,000	0.60	0.00
Total	$88,000	$145,000		0.52

Median assessment ratio = 0.60
Sum of absolute dispersions = 0.52
Average absolute dispersion = 0.104
Coefficient of dispersion = 17.3

TABLE 9-2 Distribution of Selected Local Areas by Coefficients of Intra-Area Dispersion Based on Median Assessment Sales-Price Ratios, for Previously Occupied Single-Family (Nonfarm) Houses: 1966, 1971, 1976, and 1981 (cumulative percentages)

Coefficients of Intra-area Dispersion (percent)	All Selected Areas				Area Population 50,000 or More				Area Population Less than 50,000			
	1966	1971	1976	1981	1966	1971	1976	1981	1966	1971	1976	1981
Less than 10.0	7.6	6.7	6.9	12.3	4.4	3.7	3.5	8.7	9.8	8.8	9.1	15.0
Less than 15.0	28.2	24.6	22.1	29.4	30.2	22.7	15.7	23.2	26.8	26.0	26.1	34.1
Less than 20.0	53.4	48.9	42.3	47.3	60.8	52.1	36.5	42.3	48.4	46.6	45.8	51.1
Less than 25.0	69.1	67.0	59.4	59.5	76.7	72.3	59.0	56.1	64.0	63.2	59.6	62.2
Less than 30.0	80.4	79.1	71.2	71.1	88.0	84.4	70.8	70.5	75.4	75.3	71.4	71.6
Less than 40.0	90.2	90.9	86.3	83.0	94.7	94.4	88.8	84.0	87.3	88.4	84.7	82.2
Less than 50.0	95.7	96.1	93.4	89.2	98.2	98.3	94.3	90.4	94.1	94.6	92.8	88.2
50.0 or more	4.3	3.9	6.6	10.8	1.8	1.7	6.7	9.6	5.9	5.4	7.2	11.8

SOURCE: 1982 Census of Governments, vol. 2, *Taxable Property Values and Assessment Sales-Price Ratio*, p. 41.

If all parcels were assessed at the same ratio, the *CD* would be zero. The *CD* of 17.3 means that the average parcel is assessed 17.3 percent above or below the median assessment ratio. In practical terms, it means that equally situated properties will pay substantially different effective tax rates. In the above example, property D will pay an effective tax rate which is 87.5 percent higher than the rate paid by property C, simply because of lack of uniformity in the assessment process. The higher the *CD*, the greater the difference of effective rates in the jurisdiction.

Fluctuations in property market conditions make it impossible to maintain complete uniformity of assessment ratios. A national investigation of property assessment by the International Association of Assessing Officers suggested performance standards:

> Coefficients of dispersion for residential properties should generally range between 5 and 15 percent. In areas of similar single-family residential properties, coefficients closer to 5 percent are attainable. In older, dissimilar areas, a coefficient at the upper end of this range might indicate good performance. A similar range in coefficients of dispersion should be attainable for multifamily and other income-producing properties. The market for vacant land, however, is much more volatile and, therefore, difficult to predict. Coefficients of dispersion in the area of 20 percent may therefore indicate good performance.[14]

The most recent federal survey of assessment quality, however, shows that this standard is not regularly achieved, as Table 9–2 shows. In fact, success in attaining the quality goal has declined in recent years. The percentage of areas with the CD below 20 declined from 53.4 in 1966 to 47.3 in 1981. Small declines in quality appeared for larger areas. In 1966, 60.8 percent of those areas had CDs better than 20; by 1982, that percentage had declined to 42.3. In 1981 the national median area coefficient was 21.3 percent; states ranged from 10.3 in Wisconsin to 52 percent in Alabama. Only 17 states (Alaska, Connecticut, Florida, Idaho, Maine, Maryland, Massachusetts, Michigan, Nebraska, New Hampshire, New Jersey, Oregon, Rhode Island, Vermont, Virginia, Washington, and Wisconsin) had median CDs below 20 in that year.[15] This lack of uniformity is the greatest problem for operation of the property tax.

Classification.   Several state property tax laws are structured to apply different effective rates to different types of property: their tax rates are classified, rather than uniform.[16] Classification presumes that

---

[14]Research and Technical Services Department, International Association of Assessing Offices, *Understanding Real Property Assessment—An Executive Summary for Local Government Officials* (Chicago: IAAO, 1979), p. 8.

[15]U.S. Bureau of Census, *Census of Governments 1982,* vol. 2, *Taxable Property Values and Assessment-Sales Price Ratios,* (Washington, D.C.: U. S. Government Printing Office, 1984), p. 51.

[16]These taxes still presume uniformity within property classes.

TABLE 9-3 Illustration of Property Classification by Statutory Rates and Assessment Ratios

	Rate Classification			Ratio Classification		
Classes of Property:	Statutory Rate	Assessment Ratio	Effective Rate	Statutory Rate	Assessment Ratio	Effective Rate
Owner-occupied housing	2.00	50%	1.00	4.00	25%	1.00
Farms	1.00	50	0.50	4.00	12.5	0.50
Commercial and industrial	4.00	50	2.00	4.00	50	2.00
Public utilities	8.00	50	4.00	4.00	100	4.00

TABLE 9-4 Property Tax Control Structures and Their Effects

		Limit Effects On		
Type of Limit	Example	Property Tax Rate	Property Tax Levies	Expenditures
Statutory property tax rate limit.	Cities limited to rate of $5/$100 assessed value.	Same ceiling statewide.	Can increase with assessed value or with rate increase for units not at ceiling.	Same as levies, plus depends on other revenue sources.
Property tax rate freeze.	Cities limited to rate applicable in 1978.	Ceiling varies across state.	Can increase only with assessed value.	Same as above.
Property tax levy limit.	Cities' 1981 property tax levy cannot exceed 105% of their 1980 levy.	Depends on assessed value change.	Constrained to limit.	Depends on use of other sources.
Local expenditure lid.	City total appropriations in 1980 cannot exceed 110% of 1979 appropriations.	Depends on assessed value change and changes in other revenue.	Depends on extent of other revenue sources.	Explicitly controlled (new sources of revenue reduce property tax levy.)

SOURCE: Based on Advisory Commission on Intergovernmental Relations, *State Limitations on Local Taxes and Expenditures*, A-64, February 1977 (Washington, D.C.: U.S. Government Printing Office), p. 36.

certain property classes have superior taxpaying capability than other classes. Any validity this presumption contains has small significance for tax design because tax-bearing capability varies dramatically within classes, often to a greater extent than variation between classes. Thus, there are affluent and not-so-affluent homeowners, prosperous and poor farmers, and profitable and bankrupt businesses. The classification systems, however, treat each ownership class or property type as if all units in that class were alike. Furthermore, the basis of classification is more likely to be political clout or the expected ease of shifting the tax to someone else than any reasonable basis for allocation of appropriate tax burdens. Thus, agricultural and residential property receive favorable treatment while public utilities are harshly treated. There is little logic to the pattern.

Classification can be accomplished by either variation in assessment ratios or variation in statutory rates. They both can produce the same effective rate pattern, as Table 9–3 shows. Classification by statutory rate variation is more straightforward and interferes less with the assessment process. If classification is to be adopted, that approach is probably preferable.

Limits, controls, and property tax relief. A final element in the structure of property taxes is the set of extraordinary limits and controls—beyond the normal process of rate setting—which establish a special structure for property tax operation. A categorization of controls appears in Table 9–4. A number of the special controls date from the 1970s, although several have more lengthy heritages. The "tax revolt," especially Proposition 13 in California and related referenda in other states from 1978 through 1980, was partly the product of high and rising effective property tax rates on owner-occupied housing created by demands for local public service, waste in local government, and special exemptions provided other property types. A large part of that rebellion, however, surely reflected irritation with government in general and the feeling of powerlessness to do anything about federal or state taxes—those taxes rose without any statutory rate increase for which elected representatives were responsible. The property tax was another matter: the rate had to be established each year, so it presented an ideal focal point for those concerns. It became the lightning rod for government finance nationwide during the periods of taxpayer discontent.

Property taxes have been subject to extraordinary limitations at least since the Great Depression of the 1930s. Those limits were, however, traditionally controls on statutory tax rates. These controls appeared ineffective as assessed values increased dramatically, both in total and for individual property parcels, during the inflationary 1970s. Governments could adopt property tax rates no higher than those of the prior year—certainly no higher than the legal ceilings—and obtain dramatically increased revenue because of higher assessed values. Property owners could face increased property tax bills at the stable property tax rate if their property had been reassessed to reflect the higher property values which inflation and the demand for real estate brought. Thus, the rate limit and freeze approach seemed powerless to control such increases.

The approach taken in the 1970s was the levy or expenditure limit, a control device which capped collections, not the rate applied to the tax base. That approach does constrain the growth of government activity and prevents increases in assessed value from automatic translation into higher tax collections and individual tax bills. With a levy freeze, a general assessed value increase will require a reduction in tax rates to be consistent with that freeze. For example, suppose a control law permits 5 percent levy growth from one year to the next and that assessed value increases by 8 percent. Rate computations might look like Table 9–5. With this control structure, property tax levy ceilings will dominate the budget process: maximum growth in the levy establishes the budget size and total budget requests must keep within the limit. As soon as assessed value figures are known, property tax rates may be computed because law establishes the total levy. The only unknown is the manner in which the total will be appropriated among operating units. In this case the budget total is not made up of its operating components, rather, the budget total is divided among the operating components, and one extra dollar provided one agency is truly a dollar not available to any other agency. The total budget cannot expand to accommodate any additions.

Limits of the 1970s are obviously more stringent than the earlier rate controls.[17] They have led local governments to adopt a rather consistent set of responses when they are applied. First, governments have reacted by trying to get other governments to take over services they have been providing or to get nonprofit organizations to accept those burdens. If the approach succeeds, the service in question will be provided, but the controlled government will retain the previously

TABLE 9–5

	Assessed Value	Levy	Property Tax Rate
Budget year 1	$5,000,000	$250,000	$5/$100
Budget year 2	$5,400.000	262,500	$4.86/$100

---

[17]The exception is for governments experiencing assessed value decline. A levy control for these units permits the accommodating rate increases which rate control would prevent.

committed resources for other activities. Second, governments have sought increased intergovernmental aid (grants, shared taxes, etc.) to continue services without the use of increasingly scarce local resources. This search is particularly intense to finance mandated services, that is, services which the government provides largely because it has been required to do so by another government. If that government both restricts taxing powers and mandates new expenditure, the intergovernmental strain is especially intense. The quest for grants is particularly accelerated when spending from such revenue is placed outside any control structure, as is often the case. And finally, governments search for charge and nonproperty tax revenues outside the limits. In some instances, the charges are merely disguised property taxes (fire or police protection fees based on property characteristics, for instance), but they can be welcome additions which improve both the efficiency and the equity of service finance. Expanded use of legitimate charges is, in fact, the most attractive side effect of the new limitation movement.

CONCLUSION

Almost by default, the property tax is the predominant tax source to local government. While it represents an opportunity to tax accumulated wealth not offered by levies on other bases, that advantage is overshadowed by haphazard and capricious assessment of items in the tax base. Because the tax applies to values defined by the application of a regulation, not values from a market transaction, assessment will be troublesome and will require special attention. Most problems with the property tax outside of valuation can be largely resolved by circuit breakers, deferrals, and the like, so it would be unfortunate if the advantages of the tax were sacrificed solely because of unwillingness to improve administration.

Questions and Exercises

1. Identify these elements of the property tax in your state: Who assesses property? What valuation standard is used? When was the latest reassessment of real property? What classification system (if any) is used? What circuit breaker type (if any) is used?

2. Randolph County includes four townships (Lincoln, Madison, Wayne, and Indian Creek) and one city, Fairview. It is served by two independent school districts: Tecumseh United (Lincoln and Madison Townships) and Randolph Southern (Wayne and Indian Creek

Townships). The county assessor reports the following fair cash values for the units in the county:

Wayne Township	$ 48,500,000
Indian Creek Township	76,680,000
Lincoln Township—in city	69,250,000
Lincoln Township—remainder	44,720,000
Madison Township—in city	45,000,000
Madison Township—remainder	35,500,000
County total	319,650,000

Each government in the county levies a property tax to finance its activities and no other revenue sources are available. Rates are applied to assessed value, defined to be 50 percent of fair cash value. The county tax does apply within Fairview. The following table presents the amounts that each taxing unit seeks to finance from its property tax.

Randolph County	$5,885,000
City of Fairview	4,500,000
Lincoln Township	800,000
Madison Township	750,000
Wayne Township	450,000
Indian Creek Township	775,000
Tecumseh United Schools	3,500,000
Randolph Southern Schools	1,800,000

a. Determine the property tax rate for each taxing unit. Compute the rate in dollars per $100 of assessed value.

b. The Jones family owns property with a fair cash value of $40,000 in the Madison Township part of Fairview. Prepare an itemized tax bill for them. The Smith family owns $40,000 of property in Wayne Township. Prepare an itemized tax bill for them.

c. There are 5,500 pupils in the Randolph Southern school district and 15,000 pupils in the Tecumseh United district. How many dollars per pupil would a tax rate of $1 per $100 yield in each district?

d. A factory with an estimated fair cash value of $2.5 million may be built in Wayne Township. If the factory has no impact on spending by any local government and there are no other changes in county assessed values, what total property tax bill would the factory face?

3. The state owns 16,500 acres of state forest land in a county. Forest and untilled open areas (the kind of land largely within the boundaries of the state forest) is valued at $60 per acre on average when in

private ownership. Assessed value is one third of that value. The forest area is in two townships of the county; 60 percent is in a township with a tax rate of $5.15 per $100 and the remainder is in a township with a rate of $4.90 per $100. According to the aid formula for compensating local governments containing substantial amounts of untaxed state property, the county receives in lieu of property tax payments of $18,000 per year for division among the affected taxing units of the county. Is the state payment about right in comparison to the equivalent property tax the land would bear? Explain.

4. Mr. and Mrs. Woodard, an elderly couple with no dependents, have total income from taxable sources of $7,000 and $4,000 from social security. The state income tax is imposed at 3 percent on taxable income (equal to taxable source income less $500 per person). They own property assessed at $18,000 (current market value of $55,000) and are subject to a property tax rate of $5/$100 assessed value. They each receive an old age property tax exemption of $500. They are eligible for the state property tax circuit breaker. The relief threshold is 6 percent of total money income; 25 percent of any overload is returned by the state as an income tax credit. Maximum relief paid is $600 per couple.

a. What property tax would they pay without circuit breaker relief?

b. For how much circuit breaker relief are they eligible?

c. What is their state income tax liability, after circuit breaker relief?

5. There have been complaints about assessment practices in Garfield County. Each of the three townships in the county assesses property independently, using an elected assessor. State law dictates that assessed value equal one third of true cash value; the state constitution contains a clause requiring uniform property tax rates. The state agency of which you are an employee judges assessment quality in counties, recommends multipliers to produce overall balance among townships, and can recommend general reassessments where needed.

You have obtained a random sample of assessed values and selling prices of the residential properties that have sold during the last quarter in the county. All prices are arm's-length transactions, none involve special financial arrangements, and none involve substantial amounts of personal property. Table 1 presents these data.

a. Prepare a preliminary opinion of assessment quality in Garfield County. Compute all important statistics.

TABLE 1

Parcel	Assessed Value	Selling Price
Coolidge Township:		
1–1	$ 6,730	$ 38,500
1–2	13,020	65,000
1–3	22,230	120,000
1–4	4,610	28,000
1–5	13,240	67,000
1–6	7,850	75,000
1–7	5,550	29,500
1–8	5,290	27,700
1–9	10,970	36,900
1–10	7,020	34,750
1–11	6,580	23,000
1–12	9,540	39,500
1–13	4,640	24,900
1–14	6,790	37,000
1–15	6,430	30,500
1–16	4,000	16,900
Arthur Township:		
2–1	$ 4,730	$ 20,500
2–2	19,900	15,500
2–3	3,130	15,000
2–4	6,720	38,500
2–5	6,420	28,750
2–6	3,140	27,000
2–7	4,740	22,000
2–8	3,280	15,500
2–9	3,920	19,500
2–10	3,240	18,500
2–11	4,670	17,500
2–12	4,500	27,100
2–13	3,790	25,000
2–14	2,640	12,724
2–15	3,770	26,000
2–16	2,930	15,500
2–17	5,120	28,500
Buchanan Township:		
3–1	$13,360	$ 62,400
3–2	8,720	45,000
3–3	5,680	28,500
3–4	13,080	54,600
3–5	3,400	15,000
3–6	3,460	18,000
3–7	5,040	23,600
3–8	6,850	36,000
3–9	8,180	41,900
3–10	3,580	20,500
3–11	4,590	21,900
3–12	5,050	33,000
3–13	5,470	29,000

    b. The Garfield County Board of Equalization wants multipliers to get each township AV/MV ratio up (or down) to the state-required one-third ratio. What multipliers would you apply in each township? Will the application of these multipliers increase or reduce measured equality of assessment in each township? What would their impact be on measured equality in the county?

    c. Total property tax rates by township are:

Buchanan Township	$6.15 per $100 AV
Arthur Township	$6.00 per $100 AV
Coolidge Township	$5.75 per $100 AV

    (1) What properties pay the highest and lowest nominal tax rates?

    (2) What properties pay the highest and lowest effective tax rates?

6. The following data are for the town of Paragon in the fiscal year staring January 1, 19X6:

Budgeted town expenditures	$ 18,000,000
Estimated revenue from grants, fees, and licenses	6,000,000
Assessed value of property	142,000,000

    a. What is the town property tax rate in dollars per $100 of assessed value?

    b. The Wooden family has property with a fair cash value of $45,000. The assessment ratio is one third. The family is entitled to a mortgage exemption of $1,000. That is taken against assessed value. What is their property tax bill from Paragon?

    c. Suppose that for 19X7 properties in Paragon are not reassessed but that new construction increases total assessed values by 5 percent. The state institutes a levy control, allowing 19X7 levies to increase by 6 percent over their 19X6 level. Nonproperty tax revenue is estimated to be $6.5 million. What is the maximum 19X7 property tax rate permitted, what is the maximum town expenditure, and what property tax bill would the Wooden family face?

    d. Suppose that for 19X8 properties in Paragon are not reassessed but that new construction increases total assessed value by 9 percent. The state enacts a new property tax control: the 19X8 rate can increase by $1.80 per $100 over the 19X7 level. Nonproperty tax revenue is estimated to be $6.75 million. What is the maximum town property tax rate permitted, what is the maximum town expenditure, and what property tax bill would the Wooden family face?

Cases for Discussion

A   The state of Kentucky provides a special assessment basis for farmland for the property tax. In essence, such land is valued not at current market value, the standard there for other property, but at its agricultural use value. The following article, excerpted from the *Louisville Courier-Journal*, describes problems with that special treatment.

Consider These Questions

1. *Why did the state prescribe a special assessment basis for farmland?*
2. *What valuation approach would the proposed agricultural assessment process use? Why not one of the other two?*
3. *How did the process become a loophole? Was that surprising?*
4. *Can you find a computational error?*

Panel Tries to Decide How to Define Farmland and How to Assess It Fairly

By James R. Russell

FRANKFORT, Ky.—A legislative subcommittee struggled yesterday to assure farmers that they won't be taxed off their land and to close loopholes for the rich hobby farmer.

But two basic questions remain unanswered: What is farmland, and how do you assess it?

"Some people," said state Senator John M. Berry Jr. (D-New Castle), "are receiving the benefits of farmland assessments who don't deserve it, and we're trying to protect those people who are trying to make a living out of it (farming)."

And Revenue Commissioner Maurice P. Carpenter, who sat in the subcommittee meeting, added: "Frankly, I think some (farm assessments) are to high, but we took it on ourselves to implement the consti-

---

tutional amendment and many PVAs (property valuation administrators) are using their own judgments, and you can imagine that out of 120 counties, what you'll come up with."

Carpenter also said, "I believe that there are no pure agricultural sales anymore—there's an investment thought in all of them."

And therein lies the problem. The constitutional amendment, passed in 1969 and implemented by the 1970 Kentucky General Assembly, made special provisions for assessing agricultural land. Its intent was to prevent farmland from being taxed for anything other than agricultural uses, as long as it was indeed, a farm.

The amendment supposedly protected farmers from artificially high land values caused by speculators, developers, weekend hobby farmers and sideline investments by wealthy professional people.

The intent of the amendment is not being carried out, Berry said yesterday, noting that fair market value based on comparable sales is being used to assess farmland. And that defeats the purpose of earlier constitutional and legislative efforts.

The "income producing capability" of farmland should be the basis for tax assessment, members of the subcommittee agreed. "And we need a law to require that it be used to determine the value of farmland," Berry said.

*   *   *   *   *

Working over a rough bill draft yesterday, agricultural land was defined—tentatively—as 10 contiguous acres, including improvements which are necessary to produce farm income. The residence would not be included in this portion of the farm assessment.

The draft also would define farmland as yielding at least $1,000 per year during the two years immediately preceding the tax year. For horticultural land, the requirements are the same, except only five acres are needed to qualify.

Tentatively—and apparently very tentatively—value would be figured this way:

Each year on January 1 the University of Kentucky College of Agriculture would determine a five-year average net farm income per acre on each county and give that information to the Department of Revenue.

The Revenue Department would "capitalize the new farm income per acre at a rate equal to the average interest cost for money during the previous five years." (Thus, if the average interest rate were 8 percent and the average per acre net income were $40, the land value would be $320 per acre.)

This information would be sent to the county PVAs, who would multiply the average net farm income per acre by the number of acres in a farm.

But because a county can have farmland ranging from excellent to poor, the local PVA will have discretionary power to adjust the average net farm income figure to coincide with the individual farm.

This adjustment would be determined by a number of factors, including the type of land—tillable, pasture, woodland—and the land's fertility and its risk of flooding.

But the business of getting a true picture of land value through a formula of income-producing capability is still complex and unresolved.

B   The following case describes some conditions often found in urban areas.

Consider These Questions

1. *According to the standard criteria, how is this assessment system doing?*
2. *What sort of city program would you develop?*
3. *What information would you gather and how would you use it?*
4. *Where would you get your information?*
5. *What political factors must be considered?*
6. *What would you emphasize about the program?*
7. *How would you handle inquiries from the press?*

The city of Western Hills is an extremely wealthy suburb with a population of approximately 40,000. It is primarily a "bedroom community" in that most workers residing in Western Hills commute seven miles to downtown Adel which is a major industrial center of the mideastern United States. Both cities are in Steele County.

Since Western Hills has long been considered a prestigious place to live, settlement came early and the city is currently 95 percent developed. This development is primarily single-family dwellings with very few retail establishments. The community borders Adel and is otherwise surrounded by other suburbs. Consequently there is almost no chance of substantial new growth.

During the past half century, Western Hills has prided itself on its good municipal government. The city operates under the council-manager system and the current city manager has served for the past 15 years. His municipal staff is primarily young, well trained, and experienced. The finance director is quite competent.

Western Hills receives half of its revenue from the property tax. The specific breakdown follows:

Source	Percent of Total Revenue
1. Real estate tax revenue	50%
2. Earned income tax	20
3. Transfers from other governments	15
4. Interest licenses, fees, service charges, etc.	12
5. Real estate transfer tax (1 percent of the sale price. All sales must be reported for proper deed transfer.)	3

The city council, city manager, and finance director are concerned with the lack of growth in the city's assessed valuation. The reason for their concern is illustrated in the following table:

Fiscal Year	Total Assessed Valuation	Percent Increase in the Consumer Price Index
19X1–X2	$158,400,493	5.7%
19X2–X3	159,444,545	2.5
19X3–X4	159,705,525	4.1
19X4–X5	165,573,670	7.4
19X5–X6	165,250,000	12.6 (estimated)

This table indicates that the consumer price index is increasing at a substantially faster pace than the city's assessed valuation. With Western Hill's heavy reliance on the real estate tax, that could result in severe financial constraints.

Further investigation shows that the tax millage for the 19X5–X6 budget was increased from 13.15 mills to 16.15 mills. (The state ceiling is 20 mills per dollar of assessed value.) The 19X2 Census of Governments reports a coefficient of dispersion for single-family housing of 22.0 and a median assessment sales price ratio of 39.8 for Steele County; data for Western Hills are unavailable.

Western Hills is not suffering from any form of urban blight. Instead, property values seem to be increasing. Real estate agents maintain that Western Hills is still *the* place to live in the Adel area, and home prices have been increasing accordingly.

The county performs the assessment function for all units of government. Each parcel of property is reassessed every third year. The current market value is the assessment standard; by law, assessments are required to be at 50 percent of that value. Any property that sells is immediately revalued on the basis of that price, regardless of the reassessment cycle. The County Assessor's Office tries to do a good job, but it lacks skilled manpower. The office uses no electronic data processing equipment. The entire county assessment system is not likely to radically change; the assessors apparently will cooperate in any city program.

The city manager and finance director will provide reasonable funds for a program designed to improve the city fiscal structure. Temporary summer employees (college students) are available.

Consider These Questions

1. *How might inflation influence the uniformity of assessment produced by a system like that applied in Cook County? Are there ways to mitigate the problem?*

2. *How could one judge Quinn's claim that assessment quality in surrounding counties is better?*
3. *How would you assess property in Cook County if you had Hynes's position?*

Assessment Game: One Man's Feast

By R. Bruce Dold and Ray Gibson

For Paul Byron, the word from Cook County that the assessed value of his 54-unit North Side apartment complex increased by almost 140 percent could mean financial disaster.

For Larry, the word that the units in his Gold Coast condo building declined about 15 percent in assessed value could mean a lower tax bill. The news is so good that he's afraid to publicize his last name for fear the assessor will change his mind.

The assessor, Thomas Hynes, boasts that his office has entered the computer age, and even his harshest critics credit Hynes with streamlining and professionalizing the delicate job of determining property values—the first step in levying property taxes.

But the recent howls of home and business owners that greeted the quadrennial reassessment of Chicago's North Side and northern suburbs indicate that the process of reassessing one-fourth of the property in Cook County every four years still has some chinks in its microchips.

Cook County's complicated system of tax assessment has prompted complaints from business owners that they are subsidizing residential owners, complaints from condominium owners that they are more closely scrutinized than their brethren in single-family homes, and complaints from the homeowners that the assessor is trying to rectify oversights by boosting their assessments to intolerable levels.

Hynes, who took office in 1978, has been credited with wide-ranging improvements in the assessor's office that have been implemented since several critical studies of its practices were released in 1979 and 1980.

His office has computerized information on close to 1 million pieces of residential property among 1.4 million parcels countywide. As part of what he calls a "massive expansion" of taxpayers' services, he has added a taxpayers advocate to help residents; conducted hundreds of "town hall" meetings to explain how to prepare appeals; and begun providing detailed information to homeowners about their properties in an attempt to update the assessor's files.

But, Hynes says, "we know we're going to make mistakes."

It's not difficult to find someone who will agree with him.

Source: From article in the *Chicago Tribune,* February 24, 1985.

Patrick Quinn, the maverick member of the Cook County Board of (tax) Appeals, charges that Hynes' office has failed to assess residential and commercial property equitably. Although assessments alone don't raise tax bills, if one homeowner's property is assessed higher than another's, the former will pay a greater share of property taxes.

"The basic problem is a lack of uniformity," said Quinn, whose office hears challenges to assessments. "Cook County doesn't measure up to our neighbors such as Lake and Du Page. There is a problem of nonuniformity in every township in Cook County."

Paul Byron, who was notified by Hynes' office that his building's assessed value had increased to $2 million from $837,500, complained that surrounding apartment buildings of comparable value were assessed at one-half to one-third less than his complex.

Byron, who has hired an attorney to appeal the proposed reassessment, says that 75 percent of the $225,000 in rents he collects each year would go to pay his real estate tax bill. "All I'm asking is, I want to be fairly assessed," he said.

"There is no alternative" if his appeal is denied, he said. "Let's face it, if the bank wants it, it's theirs."

A spokesman for Hynes said it appeared that Byron's building was overassessed, compared with nearby property, because of an error in the office. "He should definitely file [an appeal]," said Richard Vanecko. "It is a prime example of the complaint process and why we consider appeals an integral part of the whole process," he said.

Hynes, the 19th Ward Democratic committeeman and former Illinois Senate president, has a powerful sphere of political influence and is viewed as likely to seek higher office.

His recent proposal to offer inducements to a General Motors Corp. subsidiary to build an assembly plant here was supported by the mayor and governor. One of Hynes' more controversial decisions, refusing to give a break to the Hilton Hotel for the North Loop development project, was seen at the time as a political decision to harm Mayor Jane Byrne. The project, however, was also troubled by high financing costs.

Though some businessmen credit Hynes' office with lowering assessments when income and expense figures indicate the property is less valuable, others complain that the assessment system has traditionally put an unfair tax burden on them.

Real estate attorney Thomas McNulty and others cited a 1982 property sales study by the Illinois Department of Revenue and other reports that said Hynes and his predecessors have traditionally assessed business property close to its actual value. But assessors have taken a politically popular road of assessing homes, where the voters are found, well below actual market value, the studies contended.

Hynes, in an interview last week, rejected those conclusions, saying government bodies seeking higher tax levies have provoked anger in taxpayers.

Hynes said his office has also been sympathetic to condominium owners, tempering assessment increases for condominiums to reflect a softening of their market. But some condominium owners contend that their property also has been assessed more closely to market value than single-family homes, largely because condos' faster turnover rate creates more complete sales figures on which to base assessments.

"They treat condominiums differently," said Al Lefkovitz, a Chicago attorney representing several condominium owners who face reassessments ranging from a 10 percent decrease to a 20 percent increase. "They don't argue the change in assessment. But I've looked at sales that show condominiums are assessed much closer to [market value] than homes. If you talk to homeowners, you don't hear them complaining [about increases] because they're still underassessed."

Nevertheless, homeowners have joined condominium and business owners in what this year is likely to top the record 24,000 complaints received by the assessor's office in 1982.

Hynes hasn't released figures on the overall increase in assessed value for the newest reassessed area.

In the north suburbs, most of the seven township assessors say there are indications that assessment increases will run a little higher than sales price increases, with assessments ranging from a 1 percent decrease to a 100 percent increase.

Residential increases will average 30 percent in New Trier Township and 15 to 20 percent in Northfield Township, according to local officials. If those figures hold up, they will be close to or slightly higher than the actual sales price increases in those townships in the last four years.

Price increases for a typical home in the villages of New Trier Township have ranged from 14.4 to 22.3 percent and in the villages of Northfield Township from 8.1 to 24.7 percent, according to a price market study developed by Roger Drew, North Shore regional manager for Merrill Lynch, Pierce, Fenner & Smith.

Carol Burnside, executive director of the River North Association, a homeowners group on the Near North Side, where housing and commercial rehabilitation has been widespread, said reassessments of the area were greeted with "abject horror."

"It presents hardships to some longer-term residents of the area who have not been part of the purchase and rehabilitation of lost buildings. This may force some of them to leave," she said.

Ald. Burton Natarus [42d], whose ward includes the area being reassessed, said he wasn't seeing any more complaints than in the past, "but the feelings of the people, because of the amount of the increase, is stronger. People are very, very angry. . . . People are being assessed at inflated [market] values."

A half-dozen tax attorneys said that about 50 percent of their clients decide not to file an appeal when they learn the assessments reflect only the actual growth in the market value of their properties.

Site inspectors have been trained to avoid increasing the estimated value of unimproved housing in "gentrified" areas, but Hynes conceded that the Near North Side and Lakeview neighborhoods are the toughest to assess because of extremely diverse values in property.

Hynes also said assessments have been made more uniform by the computer analysis of properties. The program, using a formula to compute the value of homes, can consider more than a dozen characteristics, from central air conditioning to fireplaces.

The computer is just a step in the assessment process. Appraisers double-check computer findings and overrule one out of four assessments suggested by the computer.

For some, the increasing professionalism of the assessor's office has left them to grin and bear a hefty assessment increase. Attorney William Parks said he can't complain, because the 150 percent assessment increase on his Evanston home brought it closer to its actual market value.

Four years ago, when Parks's home was last assessed, appraisers counted his land and his garage, but missed his house.

10

Tax Administration

THE COLLECTION PROCESS

Collection of revenue uses resources without directly improving the condition of society. The objective in revenue administration is thus to extract the desired revenues at minimum collection cost, while maintaining fair and uniform tax administration. In other words, the tax system should be applied so that collection cost is as low as possible, subject to the constraint of a nonsystematic distribution of accidental and intentional tax error rates. This collection cost includes both that of administration (the cost to government of collecting the tax) and of compliance (the cost to private firms and individuals of complying with the law). Focus on either portion of cost alone will not produce socially desirable results if the ratio between the cost elements differs among taxes, as it normally does. Those differences can be highlighted more clearly after consideration of the general steps involved in tax administration.

Administration

Tax administration includes six general steps: (1) inventory preparation, (2) base valuation, (3) tax computation and collection, (4) audit, (5) appeal-protest, and (6) enforcement.[1] While the specific activities in any step vary according to the nature of the particular tax, the common elements will be considered here. The initial step is preparation of an inventory of tax eligibles. For a real property tax system, the physical inventory identifies the land and structures within the taxing area

---

[1]These operations are part of a larger system described in John L. Mikesell, "Administration and the Public Revenue System: A View of Tax Administration," *Public Administration Review* 34 (November/December 1974).

and determines who owns each block of property. Particular properties are called parcels; the list of parcels (the tax roll) is the basis for assessment and, eventually, for tax bill distribution. The inventory process for sales and income taxes involves the development of a mailing list for tax forms. That list later serves as a master file for comparing the list of those who have paid against the master list of those from whom payment is expected, as the starting point for delinquency control. The inventory list may be on cards, on microforms, or in machine-readable form (tape or disk); modern revenue systems typically use computer storage of account or property parcel data. The inventory of eligibles provides the foundation for the administration of any tax structure. A government without such an inventory has no basis for delinquency control and probably administers a system of contribution, not taxation.

Second, individual holdings of the tax base must be valued for assignment of tax. For some taxes, particularly individual income and sales taxes, base evaluation involves a compilation of transactions (purchase or sale of goods, services, or resources) over the tax period, largely a gathering of accounting records. Property tax valuation, however, is much more complex as it requires construction of an estimated exchange value for parcels of property which have not been sold in the taxing period: all values are estimates made according to some valuation standard. The process is clearly the most difficult and most critical step in the administration of a real property tax system.

Computation and remittance or collection of tax due is the third step in tax administration. For taxes following the sales or income pattern (taxpayer-active or self-assessed taxes), this step requires the taxpayer (or the taxpayer's agent, for example, employer, accountant, etc.) to apply a statutory rate schedule to the tax base previously valued and then submit a tax return, including any payment due, to the revenue collector. Returns are required at intervals ranging from annually to monthly, depending on the tax involved and, often, on the size of payment expected (large taxpayers must file returns more frequently than do small taxpayers). The cash flow profile of the collecting unit may be manipulated to increase the opportunity for idle fund investment (see Chapter 14). Processing these returns to record and promptly deposit revenues received, ensure that return information is appropriately managed, operate delinquency control systems, and maintain account history is a critical activity for revenue departments. Figure 10–1 illustrates the general flow of returns in the collection stage. The revenue authorities compare returns received against the master file of tax eligibles to determine what accounts are delinquent; those accounts are contacted to obtain returns and, ultimately, any tax due. Initial account contacts are often made by telephone (called "phone power" by state tax administrators). Those contacts have proven highly

FIGURE 10-1 Illustration of Tax Return Processing Flow

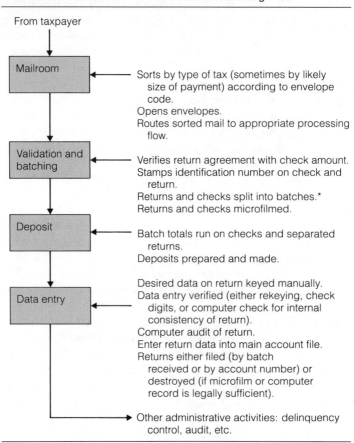

From taxpayer

Mailroom — Sorts by type of tax (sometimes by likely size of payment) according to envelope code.
Opens envelopes.
Routes sorted mail to appropriate processing flow.

Validation and batching — Verifies return agreement with check amount.
Stamps identification number on check and return.
Returns and checks split into batches.*
Returns and checks microfilmed.

Deposit — Batch totals run on checks and separated returns.
Deposits prepared and made.

Data entry — Desired data on return keyed manually.
Data entry verified (either rekeying, check digits, or computer check for internal consistency of return).
Computer audit of return.
Enter return data into main account file.
Returns either filed (by batch received or by account number) or destroyed (if microfilm or computer record is legally sufficient).

Other administrative activities: delinquency control, audit, etc.

*A batch is simply a group of returns (usually 50 or 100) which goes through the processing system together. For record control, each return has a batch and item number stamped on it: number 1050-04 might refer to the 4th return in the 1,050th batch processed.

successful, but later contacts are usually made in person by field representatives.

The computation-collection process for the real property tax is substantially different.[2] Rates are computed in the balance between expenditures to be financed and the available assessed value base, as described in the rate-setting process, covered in Chapter 9. The property

---

[2]Personal property taxes often have taxpayer-active elements, including valuation, recordkeeping, and returns filed by the taxpayer.

tax rate thus established applies to all property parcels within the taxing jurisdiction. Tax authorities compute tax bills and submit the completed bill to the taxpayer; the taxpayer simply pays the tax owed in one or two specified installments. In many instances, the owner of a residential parcel does not even see the tax bill; the mortgage lender receives the tax bill and makes payments from a tax escrow account into which the owner has made monthly payment. Thus, in the real property tax system, the taxpayer is passive. Administration by the taxing authorities minimizes compliance effort. Delinquency problems with the property tax do not involve failure to file, but rather are failure to pay a submitted bill. Delinquency thus immediately becomes an enforcement problem.

Audit, the fourth administrative stage, seeks to ensure substantial taxpayer compliance with the tax law in a voluntary compliance system. It thus protects honest taxpayers, taxpayers who have voluntarily complied with tax liability. If there were no audit process for self-assessed taxes, taxpayers who do not submit taxes would have a clear competitive advantage over any taxpayers who were paying liabilities due. Audit maintains the balance between honesty and dishonesty by making it likely that the dishonest will be caught and appropriately punished. Accounts may be selected for audit for three general reasons: to obtain revenue, to enforce the voluntary compliance principle, and to measure administrative effectiveness. Substantial revenue can be obtained in audits because of taxpayer misinterpretation of complex tax laws, and administrators are often tempted to select accounts solely on revenue production. Unfortunately, that practice will typically lead to audit of the same accounts over and over because the same accounts remain large and complex. That predictability can reduce voluntary compliance by other accounts. Thus, accounts can appropriately be selected to gain notoriety for the audit, a process which could reduce direct audit recovery somewhat but which should improve voluntary collections by deterring taxpayer evasion. Finally, some accounts may be randomly selected for audit, partly to induce voluntary compliance, partly to evaluate the success of tax administration, and partly to improve the criteria used for the selection of returns for audit.[3] Such is the nature of the Tax Compliance Measurement Program (TCMP) of the Internal Revenue Service. There is no normal audit process in real property taxation: the real property tax system involves no voluntary compliance effort by the taxpayer. There may be performance reviews of assessment uniformity (for instance, state

---

[3]Ann Witte and Diane Woodbury demonstrate the effect of audit and other enforcement actions on voluntary compliance in "The Effect of Tax Laws and Tax Administration on Tax Compliance: The Case of the U.S. Individual Income Tax," *National Tax Journal* 37 (March 1985).

preparation of coefficients of dispersion), but this is different from the audit logic.[4]

The fifth step in the tax administration is appeal or protest. Tax statutes typically contain many uncertainties (gray areas), some because the legislature slipped up and some because the legislature felt that tax administrators could better define technical points than it could. Appeals and protests help clarify these uncertainties, so they do play a valuable role in the lawmaking process. Property tax appeals, however, typically occur at a different point in the flow of administration than do appeals of other taxes. Property tax appeal is on the valuation of the property tax base, because that is the sole point ordinarily open to objection. Thus, property tax appeal follows valuation and comes before computation of liabilities and collection. Appeal after a property tax bill has been submitted to a taxpayer ordinarily is too late. Other taxes are appealed on the basis of a tax payment, either proposed or after disagreement with the payment made. Because the principal actor in these taxes is the taxpayer, not the taxing authority, appeal or protest must occur after the taxing authority objects to the manner in which the taxpayer has performed his portion of the collection process.

The final step in the process is enforcement, the step used when other remedies have not produced an appropriate payment of tax due. Most taxpayers will not reach this step, as it is the last resort for protection of the voluntary compliance system. Enforcement of sales and income taxes involves action against the income or wealth of the taxpayer: seizure and sale of assets, attachment of wages, attachment of individual or business bank accounts, closure of business establishments, and so on. Real property taxes are, however, traditionally enforced by action against the property upon which the tax is levied, not the owner of the thing (the tax is *in rem*). The enforcement remedy is sale of property. Tax sales are politically unattractive, so many governments are understandably reluctant to conduct such sales. As a consequence, areas of older cities may contain substantial blocks of property which no one clearly owns because of substantial delinquent taxes. If assessment systems do not keep up with neighborhood decline and if tax sales are infrequent, the delinquent taxes may even exceed current market value of the property. In that case, no one will acquire the property at a tax sale because the amount required for sale is greater than the value of the property. This orphan property thus adds to the general decline of already depressed areas as it becomes a haven for derelicts, a deteriorating eyesore, and a constant fire hazard.

---

[4]Property taxes could be operated on a self-assessed basis. Some states, furthermore, operate their personal property tax on a self-assessment basis with audit to ensure appropriate self-valuation. An operating concept is described in D. Holland and W. Vaughn, "An Evaluation of Self-Assessment under a Property Tax," in *The Property Tax and Its Administration*, ed. A. D. Lynn, Jr. (Madison, Wis.: University of Wisconsin Press, 1969), pp. 79–118.

Total Collection Cost

The total cost of tax collection includes both the cost incurred by the government in administering the tax and the cost incurred by taxpayers and their agents in satisfying legal requirements of that tax (excluding tax actually paid). Because both components of collection cost use resources, neither can be ignored. While a tax agency may reduce its budget problems by shifting greater collection cost to individuals (as with requiring individuals to pick up return forms from revenue agency offices instead of mailing them to tax eligibles), there is no reason to believe that such practices reduce collection cost. In fact, loss of specialization and scale with such practices may actually cause total collection cost to increase. The decision focus properly is on collection cost, the combination of administrative and compliance activities.

The combined costs are particularly critical when comparing real property taxes and the major nonproperty taxes. The nonproperty taxes are largely taxpayer-administered: the individual or firm maintains records of potential taxable transactions, tabulates the tax base, computes appropriate liability, and makes payments at appropriate times. Government agencies concentrate on partial coverage audits to ensure substantial compliance with the law, not direct agency collection. The taxpayer bears the bulk of total collection cost. Administration for voluntary compliance would have low administrative cost and high compliance costs.

The real property tax, on the other hand, does not rest on voluntary compliance. A government agent maintains parcel records, values these property parcels for tax distribution, computes the liability for each parcel, and distributes tax bills to parcel owners; the taxpayer is passive. Moreover, when property taxes are used by overlapping units of government (city, county, special districts, school districts, etc.) the taxpayer typically receives a single bill for all property taxes, to reduce even further the compliance requirement. Unless the taxpayer appeals an assessment, payment is the only taxpayer activity. In the normal scheme, total collection cost equals administrative cost. Thus, it is not appropriate to compare the cost of administering a real property tax with the cost of administering a nonproperty tax.

Table 10–1 presents administrative cost data for a selection of taxes administered in the United States. Table 10–2 illustrates similar data for a handful of other countries. Because most revenue agencies administer more than one tax and, in fact, undertake some nonrevenue functions, the joint cost allocation problem makes completely accurate cost estimates impossible. The data here must thus be viewed as simply estimates prepared through reasonably consistent allocation schemes. None of these broad-based taxes show administration costs above 1 percent of revenue produced. In comparison, the cost of administering a good quality property tax system has been estimated at

TABLE 10-1 Administrative Cost Estimates for Major Taxes

Tax Base (fiscal year)	Administrative Cost as Percent of Net Revenue
Individual income tax:	
Federal (1978)	0.70%
Colorado (1983)	0.81
Michigan (1978)	0.64
Corporate income tax:	
Federal (1978)	0.12
Michigan (single business) (1978)	0.42
Sales and use:	
Colorado (1983)	0.98
Michigan (1978)	0.37
California (1984)	0.76
Twenty-two state average (1979–81)	0.73

SOURCES: California State Board of Equalization, *Annual Report,* 1983–84; Colorado Department of Revenue, *Annual Report,* 1983; Michigan State Treasurer, *Annual Report,* 1977–78; U.S. Internal Revenue Service, *Annual Report,* 1978; and John F. Due and John L. Mikesell, *Sales Taxation, State and Local Structure and Administration* (Baltimore: Johns Hopkins University Press, 1983). Federal estimates are computed by allocating costs to taxes according to returns filed, audits done, or—where available— directly to the tax (printing Form 1040, for instance). The reported overall federal cost to net revenue percentage is 0.49.

around 1.5 percent of collections, substantially more than the cost estimates presented for taxes.[5]

There is, however, a critical distinction between the property tax and the other major taxes. That difference is the extent to which voluntary compliance generates revenue with minimal direct government action. For the major nonproperty taxes, most revenue comes from taxpayer actions alone; very little money comes from enforcement, audit, or related revenue department actions. This pattern is illustrated in the following compilation of 1979 New Jersey data, Table 10–3.[6] That pattern is not unusual. Thus, 2 percent of total Michigan collections, 1.69 percent of California sales and use tax collections (1975), and 1.67 percent of Internal Revenue Service collections come from direct enforcement actions, including audits, penalties and interest, delinquency collection, etc.[7] Most of the revenue comes from voluntary compliance;

[5]Ronald B. Welch, "Characteristics and Feasibility of High Quality Assessment Administration," in *Property Tax Reform,* ed. IAAO (Chicago: International Association of Assessing Officers, 1973), p. 50.

[6]New Jersey Department of Taxation, *Annual Report 1979,* and unpublished materials.

[7]Same sources as Table 10–1 and California State Board of Equalization, Taxable Sales in California (sales and use tax) during 1975.

TABLE 10-2 International Comparison of Tax Administration Costs as Percentage of Collections

	1973	1976–1977
United Kingdom	1.71%	— %
Canada	0.91	1.01
Sweden	1.00	—
Japan	1.87	—
Philippines	—	1.10
Australia	—	0.96
United States	0.48	0.56

SOURCE: U.S., Congress, House Committee on Ways and Means, Subcommittee on Oversight, *Underground Economy, Hearings,* 96th Cong., 1st sess., July 16, September 10, October 9 and 11, 1979 (Washington, D.C.: U.S. Government Printing Office, 1980), p. 125.

TABLE 10-3 Sources of Tax Revenue in New Jersey

Source	*Percent of Collections*
Taxpayer accounting (billings for penalty/interest, bad checks)	0.30%
Contacts (delinquency phone calls, letters)	0.05
Field (delinquency investigations)	0.33
Special procedures (bankruptcies, liens, etc.)	0.68
Office audits	0.52
Field audits	0.89
Voluntary compliance	97.23
	100.00%

taxpayers—not government agencies—bear the bulk of the total collection cost (recordkeeping, return preparation, accounting and legal fees, etc.). Those compliance costs vary substantially among taxpayers, and estimates are hazardous. It is not unreasonable to expect that, for most taxpaying units, compliance cost is at least twice as large as administrative cost.

For the property tax, however, administrative cost is virtually the total collection cost. After allowance for the difference between taxpayer-active and taxpayer-passive characteristics, the real property tax does not appear to be an unduly expensive tax to collect. Relative cost of collection—compliance plus administration—does not appear to be a deterrent to better quality administration. To summarize, a comparison of administrative costs across taxpayer-active and taxpayer-passive-type tax systems will not provide useful information for public policy consideration. The focus must be on total collection cost.

ADMINISTRATIVE STRUCTURE

The administrative structure compartmentalizes responsibility for parts of the collection process. Administration will be structured in different ways in different environments. The particular structure should fit its environment; different does not automatically mean inefficient or wrong. Two structural choices are particularly significant and will be examined here: the extent of agency centralization and arrangements for collection of several taxes by a single agency.[8]

Centralization

Several revenue agency functions may appropriately be dispersed to regional branches of that agency.[9] Regional offices establish a useful local presence for taxpayer contact and can be vital when there are concentrations of taxed entities at several locations around the taxing area. In general, regional offices appear in major cities to service those areas. The keys to dividing functions are operating efficiency of the agency, convenience for the taxpayer, and uniformity of administration. Taxpayer convenience is especially important for taxes relying on voluntary compliance; there should be no artificial barriers to the taxpayer's collection role. Following that guide, centralized activities logically include: legal interpretations (to ensure that the effective tax structure is same everywhere), selection of accounts for audit (to ensure equal geographic treatment), return processing (to obtain scale economies), record maintenance and retention (to ensure that the effective tax structure is the same everywhere), and provision of technical specialists for assistance with special enforcement or audit tasks beyond the ordinary capacity of decentralized offices. As travel costs rise and communication technology expands, centralized activities may increase—as with the use of a central telephone bank to make initial delinquency contact (called "phone power" by tax administrators), use of similar systems to provide taxpayer assistance during the peak income-tax filing period, or CRT terminals in regional offices to permit direct access to taxpayer files. Penniman observes that, for these general areas, "There is little conflict between taxpayer convenience and operating efficiency."[10] Decentralized activities should include those requiring taxpayer contact or special local information. Thus, regional offices may provide full-time taxpayer assistance and information; they may

---

[8]More on administrative structure appears in John L. Mikesell, "The Structure of State Revenue Administration," *National Tax Journal* 34 (June 1981).

[9]States increasingly establish out-of-state regional offices to serve as bases for audit operations.

[10]Clara Penniman, *State Income Tax Administration* (Baltimore: Johns Hopkins Press, 1980), p. 91.

provide offices for auditors when preparing reports or for meetings with taxpayers; and they may be duty stations for enforcement agents dealing with recalcitrant taxpayers. The need for numbers and distribution of district offices will depend on population, area, and transportation geography of the taxing government.[11]

Integration of Activities

A second organizational question is whether the taxing department will be organized on a tax-by-tax basis or on a functional basis. That is, will there be independent divisions responsible for all administration of a particular tax (return distribution, processing, auditing, enforcement, etc.) or will those functions be the organizing units with a particular step in administration of all taxes to be done by that unit? Figure 10-2 illustrates the two forms. Staff functions (personnel, data processing, research and statistics, purchasing, etc.) are almost always integrated, as there are almost always technical or financial economies of scale to be achieved here; the critical decisions are about the line operations in the collection of tax revenue, including return processing, delinquency control, auditing, and enforcement. Penniman observes that the case for integration "rests frequently on the grounds that there is (1) a large overlap of taxpayer clientele—the same taxpayers pay several taxes, and (2) a large overlap in the records that constitute the basic audit information. The argument goes on to assert that auditing is auditing, collecting is collecting, without regard to the particular tax.."[12] Thus, administrative and compliance cost savings logically would result by combining processes for various taxes.

On a more specific basis, the following claims for functional organization of tax department line operations are made: (1) personnel can be better used because peak times for return filing seldom are the same for all taxes; (2) taxpayer irritation can be reduced if there is a single audit for all taxes, if the taxpayer registers once for all taxes, etc.; (3) specialization can emphasize and develop general skills of personnel; and (4) audit unification will save travel costs, permit use of the same taxpayer records in audit of more than one tax, and reduce time lost in gaining access to taxpayer files.

There are, however, several important disadvantages of the functional structure: (1) no one is responsible for operation and overview of

---

[11]The central office of the Maryland Sales Tax Division is in Baltimore, not the capitol (Annapolis). This is a reasonable placement in light of the economic geography of the state.

[12]Penniman, *State Income Tax Administration*, p. 75. Some advocates forget, however, that clientele overlap breaks down with the spread of individual, as opposed to business impact, structures.

FIGURE 10-2 General Forms of Organization

A. Tax - by - tax organization

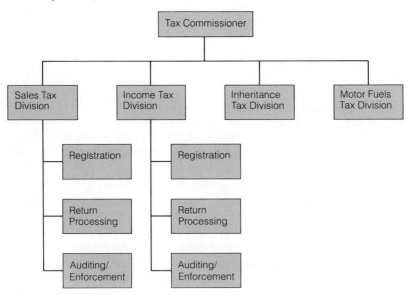

B. Functional organization

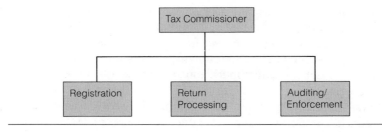

particular taxes, particularly the way individual sections of the administration process and legal structure of the tax fit together; (2) operating data (including the cost of administration) for individual taxes are frequently lost; and (3) audits are seldom truly integrated (audit selection criteria are logically and practically not the same for all taxes, audit emphasis in record systems is not the same for all taxes, and cross-training of auditors is particularly difficult). Because full audit integration has proven so difficult—and may even be logically impossible—there are major questions about the appropriateness of process integration. Nevertheless, the Internal Revenue Service is functionally integrated and states are currently shifting heavily to that structure.

Because of the differences between property and nonproperty administration, local governments are less likely to make that merger.

REVENUE ESTIMATION

The budget process requires an estimate of revenue to be received during the budget year. That revenue figure is never certain because the economic behavior which produces revenue is not easily predictable. Best available estimates are, however, critical for budget preparation and consideration because state and local governments generally must balance their budgets and the federal government must develop stabilization policy plans. In addition to their budget development use, revenue estimates are crucial inputs in development of both long-range fiscal plans and short-term cash-flow forecasts for idle funds management. For each use, the revenue estimates must be operationally accurate, recognizing that the length of the forecast and the distance of the forecast period from the present reduces the expected accuracy of the estimate. As well as providing a forecast, the methods employed may provide insights into the functioning of the economy and may be adapted to simulate alternate public policies.

Revenue departments, as repositories of the basic data for such estimates, are the natural place for such work, but, at state and local levels, these departments seldom have the appropriate technical staff (economists and econometricians) to develop these estimates. Accordingly, the revenue agency role often is provision of usable data for those making the estimates. Openness of process and method of estimation can focus policy debates on *policy*, not on arguments about competing estimates of revenue. Many argue that the agency implementing tax policy ought not be involved in policy formation: policy formation should not be burdened by routine administration and should rise above absorption by details.

Revenue estimation uses several different approaches; seldom will all revenue sources for a single government be estimated using the same approach. The more important approaches include (1) simplistic models, (2) multiple regression techniques, (3) econometric models, (4) microsimulations, and (5) input-output models.[13] Each method has its appropriate place and applications.

Simplistic models include trend extrapolation and pure judgment or intuition. Extrapolations may be by constant increments (collections increased by $5,000 in each of the last five years, so they are estimated to increase by $5,000 this year), constant percentage change

---

[13]James R. Nunns and James A. Papke, "A Critical Survey of State Revenue Estimating Practices and Prospects," *National Association of Tax Administrators Conference on Revenue Estimating* (1973), pp. 28–38.

(collections increase by 5 percent in each of the last five years, so they are estimated to increase by 5 percent this year), and linear or nonlinear time trends.[14] Thus, revenue for the budget year may be estimated as an arithmetic function of time ($R = a + bt$) or as a logarithmic function of time ($\ln R = a + bt$), where R = collections from the revenue source and t = time index. The choice would depend on which is judged most likely to produce a reasonable estimate. Many local governments use this approach because they lack the data on the local economy requisite for the development of more complex models. States often use the approach for minor revenue sources when improved estimates make no impact on the overall fiscal pattern. A second simplistic approach, judgment, involves informed guesses made by experienced observers of the particular revenue system. These estimates, actually based on complex but unspecified intuitive models, are often amazingly accurate. Unfortunately, most governments have more than one such "old hand" and the old hands will frequently disagree. Because there is no structure for evaluating their numbers until after the forecast year is over, their estimates often needlessly confuse budget consideration.

The multiple regression model, the most widely encountered forecasting device, estimates revenue as a function of one or more independent variables. Each equation used to estimate a part of revenue is independent of the others. Thus, retail sales tax collections and individual income tax collections for the fiscal year could both be estimated as functions of calendar year personal income, each in separate and unrelated equations. Other independent variables (the tax rate, demographic features of the economy, etc.) could also be in the equation. For use of this approach, estimates of the independent variable must be available for the forecast period: an estimating equation for sales tax collections which uses the consumer price index will not be usable if the necessary consumer price index measure is not available until three quarters of the way through the budget year. For budget preparation, the revenue estimate has to be presented well before the start of the year.

The estimating equation fitted by multiple regression will ordinarily be selected on the extent to which estimates from the equation coincide with actual revenue collections in prior years. Because many alternative specifications yield similar fit to historic data, trial predictions for earlier years are also prepared: suppose data are available for 1960 to 1985—an estimate is being prepared for the 1987 budget year (the estimate is being prepared during 1986). Possible equations can be devel-

---

[14]Box-Jenkins and similar time series techniques would, technically, fall in this grouping, although they are not simple to apply. The causation linkages, however, are not well developed. Their applicability to revenue forecasting may be limited by the need for lengthy data series; revenue forecasting seldom has available data series that extend for long periods with change in neither tax rate nor base.

oped from 1960 to 1984 data and test "predictions" made for 1985. The alternative equation coming closest to the known 1985 result is selected. Ordinarily, separate equations are prepared for each major revenue category to allow for different responses to changes in independent variables. Careful application of multiple regression models should produce overall predictions within 1 to 3 percent of actual collections.

Econometric modeling estimates revenue within a simultaneous system of interdependent equations.[15] These models are particularly important when revenue sources are not truly independent (as when the state personal income tax allows a deduction for the state sales tax) and may provide useful insights into the way state economies operate and the way in which they respond to external shocks. As a practical matter, however, states have generally found that the revenue predictions from them are little (if any) more accurate than the estimates that multiple regression models produce at lower cost and smaller data requirement.[16]

A promising third approach is microsimulation from sample data files, an approach used by the U.S. Treasury and experimentally by some states.[17] Individual tax return data from a sample of returns are stored in computer file. From this information, the effect of changes in selected fiscal parameters can be estimated as the impact in the sample is expanded to the entire taxpaying population. The approach is particularly valuable in the analysis of policy changes, but it can also be employed in regular estimation. Much effort is involved in selection and preparation of the microfile, so uses beyond revenue estimation improve the economic viability of such an effort. One important other use is in fiscal note preparation: the estimation of the revenue consequences of legal changes in the tax structure.

The final approach uses input-output models for estimation. An input-output table, a model of interindustry sales and purchases, shows how much each industry (steel, for instance) sells to other industries for use in products made by those industries (automobiles, etc.) and to final purchasers (government, households, etc.) and how much that industry purchases from other industries (coal, etc.) and from final

---

[15]The independent variables used in the multiple regression approach (possibly state personal income or U.S. gross national product) often are the product of larger econometric models of the region or the nation. State and local governments obtain these estimates from numerous sources, including proprietary economic forecasting companies, universities, committees of technical advisers, and government economists.

[16]C. Kurt Zorn, "Issues and Problems in Econometric Forecasting: Guidance for Local Revenue Forecasters," *Public Budgeting and Finance* 11 (Autumn 1982).

[17]A federal approach is described in Howard Nester, "The Corporate Microdata File Employed by the Office of Tax Analysis," *Proceedings of the National Tax Association-Tax Institute of America* 70 (1977), pp. 293–306 and Roy A. Wysecarver, "The Treasury Personal Individual Income Tax Institute of America," *Proceedings of the National Tax Association-Tax Institute of America* 70 (1977), pp. 306–10.

purchasers (government, households, etc.).[18] The table provides great detail about operations of an economy and can provide usable estimates of revenue impacts of particular economic shocks and estimates of revenue changes emerging from specified final demand changes. However, the I–O model must exist before it can be used (the preparation of the model is too costly for just revenue estimation) and it must be kept up to date in the face of changes in economic structure.

Regardless of the approach taken, there are some general observations about revenue estimation. First, the hardest task in state and local government revenue estimation—amazingly enough—is collection of a consistent series of revenue data. Messy little transactions (tax redefinition or restructuring, failure to properly record receipts for an unspecified period, failure to open mail bags at the end of a fiscal year, loss of revenue reports, inconsistent revenue accounting, etc.) confuse almost every revenue series, causing the revenue estimator to spend many hours working to obtain a clean data series. Many adjustments are possible to remedy problems with independent variables, but estimation based on a series of wrong dependent variables is nearly hopeless. Furthermore, the estimate is always subject to sabotage through a repeat of the episodes which messed up the initial data. That set of problems will haunt every revenue estimator.

Second, openness in the estimating process is a clear virtue. Both legislative and executive branches occasionally will seek to have artificially high or low revenue estimates as a part of a budget strategy to increase or reduce expenditure for political gain. An open estimation process prevents such manipulation and is quite desirable. The general public seldom wins when several different revenue estimates are strategically unveiled during budget sessions. A wrong consensus estimate will probably lead to better budget making than will a number of competing estimates, one of which is accurate.

And third, the approach selected will often depend on the tasks to be served by the model. If one seeks revenue estimates for the annual budget process, the multiple regression approach will ordinarily yield good results. If one seeks the impact of a structural change in the tax, microsimulation or input-output analysis may be more appropriate. If estimates are needed for long-range plans, trend extrapolations—sometimes adjusted for forecasted structural changes—are probably as good as anything. In sum, no single approach is ideally suited for all revenue estimation uses.

A related revenue estimation problem is that of fiscal impact statement preparation. In many instances, legislation to change tax structures must be accompanied by the amount of revenue increase or de-

---

[18]Input-output analysis is described in William Miernyk, *The Elements of Input-Output Analysis* (New York: Random House, 1966).

crease produced by that action. These estimates may be either *static*, presuming that taxpayers do not alter their behavior in the face of the new fiscal conditions, or, less frequently, *feedback*, adjusting revenue impacts for taxpayer response to the changed after-tax return brought by the new structure. Such statements are difficult to prepare with any accuracy because the data required are unavailable and the size of response by taxpayers is neither known nor has been estimated by others. Because of the many estimation problems and the need for an estimate for policymaking, standard procedure requires that such statements include, along with the dollar estimate, the following additional information: the nature of the data used in the estimate; the basic estimation procedure used, including assumptions made about the level and trend of economic activity; and an appraisal of the limitations of the estimate. About all that can realistically be expected is an estimate of the relative magnitude of the revenue change. (The Appendix includes a static fiscal impact statement as an illustration.)

Tax Expenditure Analysis

The Congressional Budget and Impoundment Act of 1974 (P.L. 93–344) requires that the president's budget report "tax expenditures" for the revenue plans contained in that budget. The act defines tax expenditures to be "revenue losses attributable to provisions of the federal tax laws which allow a special exclusion, exemption, or deduction from gross income or which provide a special credit, a preferential rate of tax, or a deferral of tax liability." The concept treats tax preferences as a mechanism for pursuit of government objectives, an alternative to budget outlays, credit assistance, and other policy instruments. Existing federal tax expenditures encourage selected economic activities (investment, housing, municipal borrowing, support of charities, etc.) or reduce the liability of taxpayers in special circumstances (deduction of medical expenses, casualty loss deduction, exemption for the blind and aged, etc.). Full tax expenditure budgets are limited to the federal level, but there is no theoretical reason why the concept could not be extended to state and local taxes. Fiscal notes prepared by states to estimate the revenue consequences of specific tax changes require similar estimating techniques, but there has been no demand for full tax expenditure budgets at that level.

The analysis involves estimation of revenue loss from tax provisions which differ from the "normal structure" of the tax. Legislation does not define what is normal, although the section of the president's budget message devoted to tax expenditure does carefully define the concept it uses. Because the concept involves computations of what the government does not collect from individuals and corporations, some observers object to the concept on philosophical grounds. Irving Kristol capably makes the point:

> The conversion of tax incentives into "tax subsidies" or "tax expenditures" means that "in effect" a substantial part of everyone's income really belongs to the government—only the government, when it generously or foolishly refrains from taxing it away, tolerates our possession and use of it.[19]

Tax expenditure analysis is a tool—we hope it can be divorced from its philosophical implications because it is important to gauge the extent of the alternative system of supporting public objectives. Normal structure definition is a problem: tax expenditures would fall to zero if the current structure were taken as normal.[20]

Measurement of tax expenditures is important for public policy-making because many special interests prefer them to direct cash assistance. There are two major reasons why. First, elements of the tax structure are permanent unless there is a specific expiration date attached; direct expenditure must ordinarily go through an annual budget process. While programs once included in the approved budget usually have a higher probability of inclusion in later budgets, they still lack the permanence of tax provisions. Furthermore, tax provisions seldom are subject to the sunset reviews that public programs sometimes are.

Second, the size of tax provisions is hidden. In most instances at the state and local level, decision makers will have only the vaguest idea of how much money is actually involved in tax provisions being considered—and voters have no idea at all. As a result, tax relief is granted in amounts far greater than would be approved if the assistance were in the form of direct expenditure. Federal tax provisions are better measured, thanks to the Budget Act requirements, but the relative size of tax expenditures to outlays in some areas raises similar questions about the advantages of hidden tax provisions. Table 10-4 illustrates the relative size of tax expenditures and outlays for health, as reported in the 1986 budget. Would Congress approve outlays as large as the tax expenditure?

In sum, tax expenditure analysis provides a tool for evaluation of pursuit of public policy objectives through the tax structure. It is easier to agree that a tax expenditure budget is worth calculating than it is to prepare one because of the importance of defining the normal structure for comparisons.

---

[19]Irving Kristol, "Taxes, Poverty, and Equality," *The Public Interest* 37 (Fall 1974), p. 15.

[20]An example of the definition quirks: the personal exemption for individuals is part of normal structure, the extra personal exemption given the blind and aged is not. Why should they be regarded differently?

TABLE 10-4 Outlay Equivalent Estimates for Tax Expenditures for Health ($ millions)

Description	Fiscal Years					
	Corporations			Individuals		
	1984	1985	1986	1984	1985	1986
Health:						
Exclusion of employer contributions for medical insurance premiums and medical care	—	—	—	25,335	28,200	31,555
Deductibility of medical expenses	—	—	—	3,190	3,470	3,850
Exclusion of interest on state and local debt for private nonprofit health facilities	1,090	1,425	1,790	—	—	—
Deductibility of charitable contributions (health)	245	255	275	1,415	1,580	1,855
Tax credit for orphan drug research	25	25	25			
Total (after interactions)	1,360	1,705	2,090	30,240	33,585	37,635

Budget outlays for health:
1984 Actual	30,400
1985	33,900
1986	34,900

SOURCE: *Special Analyses G. Budget of the United States Government, 1986,* and *Budget of the United States Government, 1986.*

CONCLUSION

Tax collection usually requires effort by both the taxpayer (compliance cost) and the collecting government (administrative cost). Both elements are true costs to society; government decisions must not ignore either portion. For the major nonproperty taxes, in fact, voluntary compliance—effort by the taxpayer—produces far more revenue than does direct government collection and enforcement. That points out the predominant objective of direct collection: not revenue for itself, but rather protection of the voluntary compliance system.

Revenue estimation, a portion of administration particularly vital for budget preparation, has two significant divisions: estimation of collections in future fiscal years, and calculation of revenues currently collected (or sacrificed) by existing or proposed elements of the tax law. The former activity normally produces excellent accuracy (1 to 3 percent error) when professionally done; there are few tests available for the latter.

Questions and Exercises

1. A state intangibles tax is levied on the holders of intangible personal property in the state. The tax base is market value of the item of property on the last day of December; for most taxpayers, intangible holdings in December will establish tax due by April 15 of the next year (paid with the annual income tax return). Tax rates have been 0.0025 percent, but a phase-out of the tax begins in calendar year 19Y2. In that year, the rate will be 0.00233 and in the following year, 0.00217.

   Fiscal year (July 1 to June 30) collections for the tax from 19X3 through 19Y0 follow, along with estimates previously prepared for fiscal 19Y0 and 19Y1 and calendar year data on state personal income. Both income and collections are in millions.

Year	Collections	Personal Income
19X3	$15.6	$26,158
19X4	17.8	27,776
19X5	15.7	29,816
19X6	17.1	33,206
19X7	16.6	37,132
19X8	18.4	41,487
19X9	22.2	46,279
19X0 (estimated)	18.0	n.a.*
19X1 (estimated)	18.5	n.a.

   *n.a. = Not available.

   Estimate revenue from the tax for fiscal years 19Y1, 19Y2, and 19Y3, using any method that is appropriate. (An independent commission has estimated Indiana personal income for the three years to equal $52,660 million in 19Y1, $59,800 million in 19Y2, and $67,500 million in 19Y3.) Describe the method you use and indicate why it is better than other alternatives available.

2. The Indiana General Assembly is considering a bill to permit Marion County (Indianapolis) to impose a 1 percent tax on sales by restaurants and bars. The tax would be collected with the 4 percent state sales tax. The lawmakers need to know the amount of revenue the tax would generate. Furthermore, the city intends to use the revenue as support for a bond issue to construct a domed stadium and will require a revenue estimate for that issue. The following data are available:

Sales Tax Data for SIC Code 58—Eating and Drinking Places (4 percent state tax)		
	Calendar 19X6	*Calendar 19X9*
Marion County		
Taxable sales	$ 228,962,065	$ 325,478,215
Receipts	9,110,890	13,066,175
State		
Taxable sales	1,352,036,319	1,929,639,993
Receipts	54,207,562	77,516,374

Sales Data from 19X2 and 19X7 Census of Retail Trade		
	19X2	*19X7*
Marion County		
SIC 58: eating and drinking places	$181,237,000	$ 289,238,000
State of Indiana		
SIC 58	904,181,000	1,519,522,000

Census definitions of sales seldom coincide with the base for sales tax purposes. Indiana uses consolidated reporting of sales tax collections: all outlets of a restaurant chain would report their sales through the single home office county.

Use the data provided here to estimate the yield for the tax in calendar 19Y1 and 19Y2. Clearly describe your estimation procedure and indicate each assumption you make in the derivation.

Minnesota Department of Revenue Fiscal Note

The following fiscal note prepared by the Minnesota Department of Revenue illustrates both the method of presentation and analytic approach.

STATE OF MINNESOTA
DEPARTMENT OF REVENUE
CENTENNIAL OFFICE BUILDING
SAINT PAUL, MINNESOTA 55145

General Fund
Revenue Gain (or loss):
F.Y. 1984: $0.7 to $2.8 Million
F.Y. 1985: $0.8 to $3.5 Million

March 29, 1983

Department of Revenue
Analysis of a Proposal
        to Impose the Sales Tax
        on All Clothing Items with
        a Sales Price over $150.

Revenue Analysis Summary
Enactment of this proposal, assuming an effective date of July 1, 1983, and a 5 percent sales tax, would result in an estimated revenue gain of $1.5 million to $5.8 million in the 1984–1985 biennium.

Source: Minnesota Department of Revenue Research Office.

Explanation of Proposal:
  Current Law: Clothing sales, except for some athletic and fur items, are exempt from the sales tax.
  Proposed Law: The sales tax would be imposed on all items of clothing with a sales price greater than $150.

Revenue Analysis Summary
Clothing sales in Minnesota for fiscal years 1984 and 1985 were estimated from the *1977 Census of Retail Trade—Merchandise Line Sales* by assuming that sales would increase from 1977 to 1985 by an average annual rate of 6.9 percent. From data provided in the 1977 Census concerning the type of clothing sales, it is estimated that about 30 percent of clothing sales fall into categories that would include the more expensive items, such as coats, suits, dresses, and boots. Within these categories of clothing, it is assumed that between 2.5 percent to 10 percent of the sales represent items selling for over $150. Thus, it is assumed that between 0.8 percent and 3 percent of all clothing sales represent items selling for over $150. The table below displays the estimated taxable sales and revenue gain.

	Estimated Taxable Sales Assuming 0.8 Percent (millions)	Revenue Gain[1] (millions)	Estimated Taxable Sales Assuming 3 Percent (millions)	Revenue Gain[1] (millions)
F.Y. 1984	$14.6	$0.7	$58.6	$2.8
F.Y. 1985	15.7	0.8	62.8	3.0

[1]Effective date of July 1, 1983, with 5 percent sales tax rate. Includes accelerated payment and income tax offset.

Addendum: According to the Massachusetts Department of Revenue, they are unable to estimate the amount of revenue the state receives from imposing the sales tax on clothing items selling for more than $175, but it is believed to be negligible.

11

Revenue from Public Prices: User Charges, Traditional Government Monopolies, and State Lotteries

Government normally obtains its revenue from taxes, compulsory payments that do not presume the purchase by the taxpayer of any good or service. Taxes are paid because governments possess the power of coercion as a means of financing publicly desirable services; tax payments are not part of a normal exchange relationship. In some instances, however, governments do sell services to any willing buyer and the public may purchase those services or decline them, according to its tastes, preferences, and affluence. This financing concept based on free will and market exchange has important advantages, along with some important limitations, as the following chapter will demonstrate.

The range of goods or services sold by governments in the United States is diverse. Although alternate classifications are possible, this introduction will break the sources into three groups:

1. User charges—prices charged for voluntarily purchased, publicly provided services that, while benefiting specific individuals, are closely associated with pure public goods.
2. Government monopoly revenues—revenues that a government receives from exclusive sale of a private or toll good or service, including government operated utilities and state monopoly liquor stores.
3. Lotteries—proceeds from government operated games of chance.

Table 11-1 presents the level of such types of revenue in fiscal year 1983. While relatively small compared with taxes, the flows are large enough to require some attention.

USER CHARGES

User charges are a tantalizing source of revenue for all levels of government. They can be a lucrative source of additional revenue outside public resistance to increased tax burden. Furthermore, and more importantly in less agitated fiscal conditions, they can improve both the efficiency of government resource allocation and the equity of the distribution of public service cost. Table 11-1 shows that governments continue to raise only a small percentage of their revenue from this source. Only 12.9 percent of own-source general revenue for all governments came from current charges in 1982–83. The share for local governments, 22 percent, is the highest of the three levels, largely because local governments probably provide more services amenable to charge finance as will be illustrated later and because the forces of tax revolt in the late 1970s and early 1980s placed local governments under great fiscal stress. Local use may be expected to increase, a shift that ought to be generally encouraged.

For its statistical compilations, the Bureau of Census defines charges as

> amounts received from the public for performance of specific services benefiting the person charged and from sales of commodities and services . . . including fees, toll charges, tuition, and other reimbursement for current services, rents and sales incident to the performance of particular government functions, and gross income of commercial-type activities (parking lots, school lunch programs, and the like).[1]

Their tabulations exclude municipal utility (water, electric, gas, etc.) and state liquor-store revenue, a distinction that will be continued here because of the generally private nature of the good or service involved.

License taxes imposed to regulate specific activities for the benefit of the general public (massage parlor licenses might be an example) are also correctly excluded from the Census definition; these are not charges or public prices at all. A license tax is a fee—flat rate, graduated by type of activity, related to business receipts, or whatever—levied by a government as a condition for exercise of a business or nonbusiness privilege. Without the license, one or more governments forbid the activity. The license is a necessary condition for operation, but it does not

---

[1] U.S. Bureau of the Census, *Governmental Finances in 1982–83*, series GF83, no. 5 (Washington, D.C.: U.S. Government Printing Office, 1984), p. 84.

TABLE 11-1 Revenue from User Charges, Traditional Government Monopolies, and Lotteries, 1982–83

Sources:	All Governments	Federal Government	Amount (millions of dollars) State and Local Governments		
			Total	State	Local
Total Revenue	1,181,420*	679,663	593,586	357,637	338,070
Revenue from own source	1,181,420	677,817	503,603	284,933	218,670
General revenue from own sources	878,782	481,887	396,895	217,752	179,143
Taxes	665,764	381,179	284,585	171,440	113,145
Charges and miscellaneous general revenue	213,018	100,310	112,310	46,312	65,998
Current charges	113,172	50,547	62,625	23,182	39,443
National defense and International relations	7,122	7,122	—	—	—
Postal service	22,679	22,679	—	—	—
Education	18,829	—	18,829	13,126	5,703
School lunch sales	2,363	—	2,363	9	2,354
Institutions of higher education	14,808	—	14,808	12,964	1,844
Other	1,658	—	1,658	152	1,505
Hospitals	19,320	76	19,244	5,309	13,935
Sewerage	5,816	—	5,816	7	5,809
Sanitation other than sewerage	1,644	—	1,644	—	1,644
Parks and recreation	1,778	67	1,711	403	1,308
Natural resources	13,227	12,326	901	637	264
Housing and urban renewal	3,116	1,473	1,643	147	1,496
Air transportation	2,559	24	2,535	235	2,300
Water transport and terminals	1,468	482	986	284	702
Parking facilities	453	—	453	—	453
Other	15,161	6,298	8,863	3,035	5,827
Lotteries†	2,050	—	2,050	2,026	24
Other miscellaneous general revenue	47,796	50,161	47,635	21,104	26,531
Utility revenue‡	34,033	—	34,033	2,390	31,643
Liquor stores revenue‡	3,311	—	3,311	2,819	492
Insurance trust revenue§	265,294	195,930	69,364	61,971	7,393

Note: Because of rounding, detail may not add to totals. Local government amounts are estimates subject to sampling variation.
—Represents zero or rounds to zero.
*Net of duplicate intergovernmental transactions.
†Lottery revenue equals proceeds available from ticket sales. Local lottery revenue is from the District of Columbia.
‡In keeping with Census concepts for taxes and other current charges (but not lotteries), these are total receipts, not net over production cost.
§Unemployment compensation, public employee retirement, OASDHI, veterans' life insurance, railroad retirement.
SOURCE: U.S. Bureau of Census, *Governmental Finances in 1982–83*, GF83 no. 5 (Washington: U.S. Government Printing Office, 1984); D.C. Lottery and Charitable Games Control Board, *1983 Annual Report*, and U.S. Bureau of Census, *State Government Finances in 1983*, GF83 no. 3 (Washington, D.C.: U.S. Government Printing Office, 1984).

"purchase" any specific government service. It may thus be distinguished from a user charge, which may be avoided if an individual or firm chooses not to purchase the supplied item or service and the payment of which entitles the individual or firm to a commodity or service, and from fees that are indirectly related to particular privileges.

The license tax must also be distinguished from franchise fees. The latter involve contracts detailing rights and responsibilities of both franchisee and the issuing municipality, entail requirement of service to all in the servicing area, and bring a presumption of rate and quality of service regulation. A license simply permits a holder to undertake an activity otherwise forbidden and involves no contractual or property rights.[2] In general, franchises are provided in very limited numbers, while licenses are made available to virtually all applicants.

The definitions usually do not differentiate between licenses for revenue and for regulation. Both varieties are based on the inherent authority of a state to exercise all elements of police power, with state delegation of this power to municipalities by constitution, statute, or city charter grant. Revenue and regulation motives may often be hopelessly entangled. Nevertheless, a tentative separation may be suggested: a license ordinance which does not require inspection of the business or of the articles sold or fails to regulate the conduct of business in any manner is a pure revenue license, particularly if license applications are never denied. If such controls apply or if licenses are difficult to obtain (not just expensive), the license is of the regulatory variant. While the differences may not always be sharp, the distinctions are serviceable. Some states require that license charges be reasonably related to the cost of issuing, policing, or controlling the thing or activity being licensed. When that stipulation applies, it is especially important to review cost and adjust charges frequently.

Both user charges and fees attempt to relieve burdens placed on the general revenue system by extracing greater contribution from service beneficiaries, but the former more closely resembles private enterprise pricing. Fees can compensate government for extra costs incurred in the provision of special services to identifiable entities or for administrative paperwork done for individuals. Thus, governments often apply fees for traffic direction or crowd control and charge fees for many legal filings. Fees, however, seldom involve the direct sale of a good or service, but involve payment for some privilege granted by government. The exercise of that privilege may cause government to incur a cost which the fee seeks to recoup in part or in total.

User charges apply prices for services provided so that only those receiving the service bear the cost of its provision. The charge is voluntary: an individual can choose not to receive the service and, accordingly,

---

[2]Charles S. Rhyne, *Municipal Law* (Washington, D.C.: National Institute of Municipal Law Officers, 1957), p. 655 further develops this logic.

not to pay for its finance. Thus, there is no burden on the general public or on the general tax system. The individual would receive no service if the user charge were not paid. Taxes are by their nature compulsory and are not linked to any government services, individually or separately. A dramatic difference of individual choice divides taxes and user charges and can influence all resulting attributes of agency operation. Sometimes, individuals are given no right to refuse a service—a city may require all to pay a garbage collection charge. Whether this finance structure is a true user charge is doubtful. It may better be viewed as a residential unit tax with proceeds dedicated to garbage collection. It clearly lacks the incentive effects of true user charges.

Necessary Conditions for User Charge Application

User charges can induce production and consumption efficiency while gauging citizen preferences and demand for government services. Unfortunately, they can function only when activities financed have two necessary conditions: benefits separability and chargeability. These are the features absent from pure public goods (Chapter 1); the farther a good or service departs from publicness and the closer it approximates a private good, the more feasible are user charges.

First, user charges are feasible when identifiable individuals or firms, not the community as a whole, benefit from the service. Services to a narrow segment of the community financed by general revenues provide an opportunity for that segment to profit at the expense of others. Those using the service will benefit, but pay no more than similarly situated citizens who do not benefit. A user charge would prevent that systematic subsidization. If recipients of benefits cannot be identified or if the community in general benefits, a user charge is neither feasible nor desirable. Thus, charges for elementary education would be inappropriate; they would be quite desirable for an adult auto mechanics course. Voluntarism in the first instance would be foolish—Milton benefits if his neighbor's children receive an elementary education because they help choose his government, they read traffic signs, they do not go on welfare which Milton must help provide, and so on. In the latter instance, the mechanic does help the community, but that help is for a fee: if Milton's car is repaired, he directly pays the bill—there are no uncompensated community benefits.

Second, user charges require an economical method for excluding from service benefits those who not pay for the service. If exclusion cannot be accomplished, the charge cannot be collected. Furthermore, resource allocation gains will be greatest if service use can actually be metered, as with water meters, toll booths, and the like. Thus, heavy users would pay more than light users, although both pay more than nonusers. Some discretion is needed here, however, because everything that can be gauged may not be worth gauging: city street use could be metered using the tollgate technology of turnpikes and toll bridges. The costs involved, including the time waiting in lines, make that option untenable. Administrative cost—measurement of customer service use (metering), calculation of charges according to service cost, and billing and collection of computed charges—and compliance cost must not be excessive. Many services can, however, be gauged and controlled by meters, fences, turnstyles, decals, and the like. Others may be indirectly measured—many cities gauge residential sanitary sewer use by water use, a reasonable proxy for volume in the drain. Without enforceable charge barriers, user charges are inappropriate.

Charges are particularly appropriate when substantial waste would occur if the individually identifiable service were unpriced. Such would undoubtedly result if, for instance, water were provided through property tax financing. Under that system, efforts to economize on water use would yield the individual consumer no direct return. Payments for water would be determined by property holdings, not the amount of water used. Usage would be much inflated. Investment in supply facilities would have to be abnormally great and artificially expanded amounts of water would have to be treated. Appropriate user charges could substantially reduce water waste and total water supply cost.

Advantages of User Charges

When a user charge can be applied, it has advantages beyond the naked pragmatism of additional revenue for government functions. These strengths include both the important efficiency effects of appropriately designed charge structures and improved equity from direct pricing. First, user charges can register and record public demand for a service. Suppose a city is considering support of extensive summer softball leagues for adults. If these leagues are financed by user charges (either team sponsors or individual participants), the city receives important information for choices about service type, quality, and quantity. Without charge finance, there will be continual—and inconclusive—debate about program advisability and structure. That need not occur with appropriate charges. Furthermore, a program which, through user charges, covers its costs of provision is not likely to be eliminated and places no burdens on other governmental activities. Not incidentally, citizens who do not want the service do not have to receive it and do not have to pay for it. Thus, a user charge system not only provides a tangible way for citizens to register their preference for particular services but also provides some funds for provision of the services.

Those extra funds can be a problem, however, when the program does not cover all costs it generates, but does provide some revenue.

During periods of tight finances, decision makers are tempted to expand revenue-generating activities, often reasoning that any revenue will help with the fiscal problem. Unfortunately, such expansion can actually increase the total subsidy required for that service and worsen the overall budget condition. For example, a city may expand its summer tennis instruction program because it generates $25 per person in charge revenue. If recreation department cost increases by $30 per person enrolled in the program, the expanded revenue produced will actually increase any city deficit. The difficulty is prevented if the design of the charge system ensures that program charges at least cover the additional cost caused by the program, an important condition for the demand—registering advantage attributed to user charges.

Second, the user charge can dramatically improve equity of financing selected services. If the service is of a chargeable nature, its provision by general tax revenues will undoubtedly subsidize the service recipient group at the expense of the general taxpaying public. User charges can obviously prevent that problem. Less obvious but equally significant are two related equity problems that direct pricing can reduce: the problems created by nonresident service recipients and by tax-exempt entities. Many urban services, particularly cultural and recreational, can easily be used by anyone in the region. General revenue finance permits a subsidy to any nonresident consumer; a user charge prevents that subsidy. The approach is a simple and direct way to reduce burdens placed on one government by citizens of neighboring governments. A user charge similarly provides a mechanism for obtaining financial support from tax-exempt institutions. Many cities, for example, finance refuse collection with property tax revenue. Charitable, religious, or educational institutions exempt from property tax would contribute nothing to finance refuse collection, even though they receive the refuse collection service. The cost of this service must be borne by the general taxpaying body. If, however, refuse collection were financed by user charges, that cost shifting would not occur. Just as these entities must pay for gasoline purchased from a private firm, they would pay the refuse collection charge: tax exemption does not exempt institutions from paying for goods or services obtained on the open market. For both nonresidents and exempt institutions, the user charge allows governments to extract revenue from entities outside their tax network; if they use, they pay.

Third, a user charge program may improve operating efficiency, as agency staff must respond to client demand. Agencies usually operate with funds obtained by request to, and justification prepared for, a legislative body. That justification will elaborate needs as determined by the agency staff and defended according to performance criteria established by the staff. User charge finance, however, requires a shift to preferences articulated directly by consumer demand. The agency must provide services which are desired by consumers or it will fail the financial test for survival. It cannot define what clients should want in its budget defense: it must provide the services which clients do want or it will not survive.

Finally, a user charge may correct cost and price signals in the private market. Suppose a manufacturing plant placed extraordinary demand on traffic control in a neighborhood. That special demand requires additional police officers to be assigned to traffic direction duties at a handful of intersections in that area during shift changes at the factory. The way the plant operates thus produces substantial extra costs for the community. If the plant must pay for the extra traffic control costs its operations require, its management has a direct financial incentive to consider whether the current operating pattern (with attendant traffic control charges) or patterns with lower peak flow traffic produced by staggered shifts, van pooling, subsidies for mass transit use, and so on (and no traffic control charge) are less expensive. The user charge makes the decision unit recognize and respond to the true social cost of its action. In the example cited, without the user charge the additional traffic control costs the plant nothing; no one can be expected to conserve a resource which appears to be free. This is exactly the same logic which applies in the application of effluent charges to the discharge of environmental pollutants.

The efficiency arguments are most important in the continuing federal effort to apply substantial deep draft and inland waterway user fees. David Stockman made that case as director of the Office of Management and Budget:

> When the federal government renders a service directly to economic enterprises at less than cost, the service amounts to a subsidy. Subsidies not only increase the size of the federal budget, but almost inevitably distort the workings of our free market economy. Such distortions decrease economic efficiency.
>
> The imposition of user fees will increase overall national economic efficiency. If a plant locates in one region rather than another because the decision was biased by the presence of a subsidy, the nation's overall economic efficiency is reduced and the nation's output is smaller. Because the decision maker does not consider the cost of the subsidy when he makes a decision—only his own costs—he may locate where it costs him less, but you and I, the taxpaying public, end up paying the difference.[3]

User charges closely tied to the cost of providing a service thus prevent the misallocation of resources which can result from general tax financing of specific services.

---

[3]Testimony before the Senate Subcommittee on Environment and Public Works, reported in *Rail News Update*, no. 2327, July 29, 1981.

Limitations of User Charges

User charges cannot be substituted generally for taxes in the finance of government services because many public services, in fact most services provided by most governments, simply do not fit the full requirement for finance by price. First, activities which have substantial benefits extending beyond the principal recipient are not candidates for user charge finance. Basic fire protection in an urban area could not, for example, be considered for charge finance because fire tends to spread; extinguishing a fire in one building will protect those surrounding units. Thus, protection financed by one individual will automatically protect others; nonpayers are not excludable, so the service cannot be financed by charges. There is a corollary to the external benefit problem: the ability to charge for particular services can distort agency decision making. Thus, there is the scenario of magnanimous resources for a high school football team, because gate receipts are sizable, while the girls' volleyball team gets hand-me-downs. The question for resource allocation is contribution to the purposes of the community (or social benefits); simple cash flow should not be the determining factor in such an instance.

Second, services may intentionally subsidize low-income or otherwise disadvantaged recipients. Charges for these services could be counterproductive.[4] Beneficiaries ought not pay if the service has welfare elements. In a related fashion, some have argued that user charges in general are unfair because they often produce a regressive burden pattern, taking a larger percentage of a low-income consumer's income than from higher-income consumers.[5] That argument is not a convincing attack on user charges for several reasons. For one thing, not all low-income families would use many priced services, even if the services were tax-financed and priced at zero. They would thus share in the payment for the service without receiving any benefits from it. Thus, low-income families not using the service clearly are better off with the user charge system. A further reason is that tax financing devices may have a more regressive burden than user charges, even if the service is widely used by disadvantaged citizens. Local revenue systems often are very regressive, so it is not unlikely that a shift to charges could reduce regressivity from its level with general tax finance. Finally, it may be possible to design "payability" tests for the charges, because the services are received by identifiable individuals.[6]

---

[4]There are, of course, more efficient ways of redistributing income in society than providing government services. But once that method is selected, it ought not be thwarted by charges.

[5]Willard Price, "The Case against the Imposition of a Sewer Use Tax," *Governmental Finance* 4 (May 1975), pp. 38–41.

[6]Mushkin and Vehorn coined the "payability" phrase. Selma J. Mushkin and Charles L. Vehorn, "User Fees and Charges," *Governmental Finance* 6 (November 1977), p. 46.

Suppose a city charges an admission fee to swimming pools: benefits are primarily individual (to the swimmer and family), prices can be enforced using fences and turnstyles (safety requires access control, regardless of financing technique), and overcrowding may otherwise result when children are dumped at the facility for "free" babysitting. Charge opponents argue that free pools are a significant recreation option for low-income families; a charge would harm that redistributive function. Charges can, however, function equitably and efficiently if disadvantaged families receive season passes at no cost or if pools located in low-income areas are free while charges apply at other pools. In general, protection of the disadvantaged ought not be an excuse for subsidizing the well-to-do.

Guidelines

Governments differ in the extent to which they charge for services, partly because of the different services they provide (national defense, welfare, and highway patrol are, for instance, hardly priceable), and partly because of political attitude toward pricing of public goods. Outside those constraints, there are some guides for charge preparation and manipulation. Any service showing the features described earlier (individual benefit, susceptibility to excluding nonpayers, an absence of redistributive elements) are reasonable candidates for charge finance. The short list in Table 11–2 provides some suggestions. Bird and Mushkin nominate for charge (1) household support functions (water, refuse collection, sewerage); (2) industrial development support (airports, parking, special police or fire services, etc.); (3) "amenities" (specialized recreation facilities, cultural facilities, etc.); and (4) services provided to tax-exempt entities.[7] The list and its classification should give ample direction.

Some governments, often in response to property tax limits, controls, or freezes, have applied general police or fire protection charges based on the value of property protected. These are not true charges because they are not voluntary; they are simply an escape mechanism around the control. A related charge does have greater logical appeal. That is the assignment of service costs in relation to physical characteristics of a property, according to an estimate of how those characteristics produce demand for a service. There has been more discussion of this approach than actual adoption, but—as a response to the reduction in property taxes required by California's Proposition 13—Inglewood, California, adopted a "fire-flow assessment fee" in 1978. The fee was "based on the relative risk of each structure and the

---

[7]Selma J. Mushkin and Richard M. Bird, "Public Prices: An Overview," in *Public Prices for Public Products,* ed. S. J. Mushkin (Washington, D.C.: Urban Institute, 1972), pp. 8–9.

TABLE 11-2 Selected Government Services Amenable to Public Pricing

---

Special police work—service for stadium or auditorium events, alarm servicing.
Parking—garage, meters.
Refuse management—collection, disposal.
Recreation—golf courses, tennis courts, swimming pools, park admissions, concessions.
Health and hospitals—ambulance charges, inoculations, hospital rates.
Transportation—transit fares, bridge and highway tolls, airport landing/departure fees, hangar rentals, lock tolls.
Education—rentals of special books, equipment, or uniforms; college or technical school.
Resource management and development—surveys, extension service inquiries, tree nursery stock.
Sewerage
Utilities—water, electric, gas, transit.

---

amount of water, personnel, and equipment that would be needed to extinguish a blaze there."[8] Single-family residences with some simple fire protection device (a smoke detector) paid no levy. Other structures (multiple family dwellings, commercial/industrial units, etc.) paid an assessment based on service need criteria, including construction type, structure use, and fire protection equipment sprinklers.

The Inglewood fee survived only one year. A court challenge questioned whether it was a tax and, hence, adopted by means in violation of Proposition 13; the city council repealed the fee. It was not a good revenue raiser, possibly because of the challenges to it, and state assistance substantially restored lost property tax revenue. Citizen response at a public hearing also halted plans for a similar assessment for street maintenance based on property foot frontage and street type (neighborhood, commercial, thoroughfare, etc.).

That variety of fee should not be considered a true user charge because it cannot be voluntary. Because unchecked fires in urban areas will spread, voluntary decisions about purchase of fire protection are untenable. Protection for one unit will protect its neighbors and an unprotected unit will endanger its neighbors. Thus, these financing devices must be structured as taxes (nonvoluntary), but they are taxes based on a concept other than the ability of an economic unit to afford the designated tax burden. The burden of financing that municipal service is allocated among economic units according to the physical attributes of those units which require service cost to be incurred. As such,

---

[8]Stephen J. Sansweet, "Californians Discover Tax-Cut Mania Has a Corollary: Fee Fever," *The Wall Street Journal* 59 (June 1, 1979), p. 16. Fire service fees in Inglewood increased from $188,000 in fiscal 1978 (pre-Proposition 13) to $911,000 in fiscal 1979. Over that same period, property taxes fell from around $3.5 million to about $1.4 million, because of Proposition 13. (California State Controller, *Financial Transactions Concerning Cities of California, 1978–79 Annual Report* and *1977–78 Annual Report*.).

it could have desirable development effects; it could provide structure owners an extra financial reward for installing private fire control devices (smoke alarms, sprinklers, fire walls, etc.) in older units and could also cause owners of particularly deteriorated structures to raze them. The fees, of course, would not be related to firm profitability: some marginal business housed in deteriorated, high-fire-risk structures could face substantial fees. On the whole, however, a rigid structure of fire-risk fees could significantly accelerate the process of structural modernization and, over time, could reduce the total cost of fire protection, even though they are not user charges.

When a government does decide that a particular service can be financed by a charge, the question of appropriate level of that charge remains. Answering that question is not simple. Stocker reports:

> Evidence suggests that pricing policies used by municipal governments are often fairly unsophisticated, perhaps understandably so in light of the difficulty of determining price elasticities, marginal costs, distribution of benefits and other things that enter into economic models of optimal pricing.[9]

The municipality, may, however, derive reasonable, if not optimal, prices with fairly simple concepts about service cost.[10] In particular, the government should separate its service costs into two categories: those that change as a result of the service being provided (incremental cost) and those that do not change with provision of that service. The latter include any cost which would continue, regardless of decisions concerning that service. The pricing objective can then be, at least initially, recovery of those costs incurred because of the particular service. If that price is collected, the provision of the charge-financed service is no burden for the normal functions of government.[11] Prices above that

[9]Frederick D. Stocker, "Diversification of the Local Revenue System: Income and Sales Taxes, User Charges, Federal Grants," *National Tax Journal* 29 (September 1976), p. 320.

[10]Downing maintains that an appropriately designed user charge would have three components: a portion which reflects the short-run cost of production and varies with output consumed, a portion which reflects the cost of plant and equipment used in production (possibly allocated as an individual's share of its designed capacity), and a portion based on the cost of delivering the service to a specific customer location. The first portion may vary by time of day, depending on whether the system is at peak utilization or not. If so, the charge would be increased. These principles are particularly important for utility operation. [Paul Downing, "User Charges and Special Districts," in *Management Policies in Local Government Finance*, eds. J. Richard Aronson and Eli Schwartz (Washington, D.C.: International City Management Association, 1981), pp. 191–92.]

[11]Johnson has identified six elements in existing municipal sewerage service charges: water use (a volume proxy), flat charges, number of plumbing fixtures used by the customer, size of water meter or sewer connection, property characteristics (assessed value, square footage, front footage), and sewage strength. Water use is the most frequently encountered charge element. [James A. Johnson, "The Distribution of the Burden of Sewer User Charges under Various Charge Formulas," *National Tax Journal* 22 (December 1969), pp. 472–85.]

level are possible, subject to the demand for the service and the con-
science of the government as reflected in its desire to subsidize other
governmental activities. There is no reason why a charging government cannot experiment with different prices for its service to see what
happens to demand and its net revenue; there is no special virtue in stable prices.

A final consideration about user charges concerns their method of
application. Alfred Kahn writes, in an analysis of public utility pricing:
"The only economic function of price is to influence *behavior*. . . . But of
course price can have this effect on the buyer's side only if bills do indeed depend on the volume of purchases. For this reason, economists in
the public utilities field are avid meterers."[12] A similar principle applies
in the application of user charges: buyer behavior will not change unless changes in behavior will influence payments owed. If a refuse collection customer pays $25 per year for that service, regardless of
whether 2 or 15 cans of trash are collected per week, the customer cannot be expected to change the number of trash cans he sets out for collection. A charge sensitive to usage, however, will induce behavior
changes by some customers. To obtain the full benefits of user charge
finance, then, the service must be metered and made usage-sensitive:
dividing estimated total cost by the number of entities served and presentation of a bill to each entity will not produce the desired effects of a
user charge.

GOVERNMENT MONOPOLY REVENUE

Government power to own and operate business enterprises, to sell
private goods, is extensive. The limits are generally public opinion as
expressed through the legislature, not through constitutions. Nevertheless, government ownership is the exception, not the rule in the
United States; presumably the arguments identifying the enterprise
and efficiency of private ownership have substantial convincing power
here. When a public interest is identified that competitive pressures
cannot handle, the normal approach is to regulate the private firm, not
for government to own the enterprise.

In spite of the tendency toward private ownership, for some services there is widespread use of municipal ownership.[13] The major areas
are in water supply, electric power, public transit, and gas supply. The
great majority of cities over 5,000 population are serviced by municipal
water utilities. Municipal electric power systems, usually distributors

---

[12]Alfred E. Kahn, "Can An Economist Find Happiness Setting Public Utility Rates?"
Public Utilities Fortnightly, January 5, 1978, p. 15.

[13]Martin T. Farris and Roy J. Sampson, *Public Utilities: Regulation, Management, and
Ownership* (Boston: Houghton Mifflin, 1973), part 4.

TABLE 11-3 Utility and Liquor Monopoly Revenue, 1982-83

	State and Local Government Revenue	City Revenue
Total Utility Revenue	34,033	22,270
Water supply	9,528	6,894
Electric power	17,823	11,544
Transit	3,635	1,436
Gas supply	3,047	2,396
Liquor store	3,311	273

Note: the Federal government has neither utility nor liquor store revenue.
SOURCE: U.S. Bureau of Census, *Governmental Finances in 1982–83,*
GF83 no. 5 (Washington , D.C.: U.S. Government Printing Office, 1984) and
U.S. Bureau of Census, *City Government Finances in 1982–83,* GF83 no. 4
(Washington, D.C.: U.S. Government Printing Office, 1984).

of power produced by others, operate mostly in small communities, however, and gas supply is predominantly through private ownership. Public transit has made something of a resurgence with the failure of private systems, but the public systems have been as unprofitable as their private predecessors. Table 11–3 reports the extent to which state and local governments in total and in cities generated utility revenue in fiscal 1983. In the tradition of census statistics, revenues are gross from the utility; they do not net out expenditures made by the utility in producing the service sold to generate that revenue. In point of fact, expenditures in the utility categories often exceed the revenue taken in by the utility. When that happens, the general government may have to subsidize the operation of the utility.

Why should a municipality choose to operate a utility, rather than allow a private firm to do it? Surely government has pressing public concerns and can better allocate time to those decisions than to focus on the mundane questions of utility management. Motivation is, not surprisingly, a bit unclear. In some instances, the governing body believes that it can obtain profits from utility operation that can be used to subsidize the operations of the general government. In fact, some decades ago, some cities were able to be "tax free towns," because of profits from electric utility systems. That era has passed, however, and the best that one could hope for is some assistance from the utility to the city, but not a fiscal bonanza.

In other instances, the government owner may be more interested in keeping the price of the service as low as possible, possibly even providing the service at less than cost. That policy requires some subsidization of the utility by the tax base, either directly or through payments from government to the utility. This practice can be politically appealing—the low-cost service can be an important element in reelection strategy—but the government decision makers must be quite certain that other important city services are not shortchanged by the

TABLE 11-4 State Lottery Performance, 1983

State	Lottery Ticket Sales ($ thousand)	Net to State ($ thousand)	Lottery Net as Percent of State Own Source General Revenue	Percent of Lottery Sales not Available to State	Percent of Lottery Sales Used for Administration*
Arizona	74,893	23,086	0.91	69.17	20.61
Colorado	128,704	46,995	1.92	63.49	8.68
Connecticut	177,990	73,848	2.24	58.51	5.83
Delaware	27,627	9,968	1.05	63.92	7.33
Illinois	461,486	214,899	2.40	53.43	3.28
Maine	13,075	3,759	0.37	71.25	22.12
Maryland	444,036	198,236	4.33	55.36	4.15
Massachusetts	216,916	84,346	1.34	67.80	8.61
Michigan	512,819	214,727	2.38	58.13	5.61
New Hampshire	14,540	5,652	0.97	61.13	14.94
New Jersey	654,319	295,367	3.65	54.86	2.85
New York	578,518	268,814	1.39	53.53	4.35
Ohio	377,785	146,502	1.69	61.22	7.20
Pennsylvania	825,049	354,805	3.48	57.00	3.68
Rhode Island	38,451	14,377	1.24	62.61	5.37
Vermont	3,847	1,053	0.20	72.63	18.66
Washington	166,801	69,688	1.40	58.22	13.22
Mean			1.82	61.31	9.21
Median			1.40	61.13	7.20

*Not including commission to sellers.

SOURCE: U.S. Bureau of Census, *State Government Finances in 1983*, series GF83 no. 3. (Washington, D.C.: U.S. Government Printing Office, 1984).

drains to the subsidized utility. Otherwise, the practice can contribute to fiscal decay of the city.

A second, and radically different, sort of monopoly is maintained in 17 states. In these states, some if not all alcoholic beverage sales are made in state-owned liquor stores. The state establishes a markup over inventory cost sufficient to cover its operating cost as well as to return a profit for other state operations. In some instances, the state will add an excise to the price, although the practice is not frequent. Table 11–3 reports liquor store revenues, again following the census practice of not netting out cost. In contrast to the utility case, however, liquor stores do return a profit to their parent government. Only in New Hampshire, however, do these profits constitute a large relative portion of state revenue (in 1983, liquor store revenue exceeded expenditure by $30 million; all general revenue totaled only $875 million).[14]

STATE LOTTERIES

The final government sales item considered here is the state lottery. New Hampshire in 1964 initiated the first state lottery since the demise of the Louisiana lottery in 1894 and was followed by New York in 1967. Both states experienced disappointing proceeds, however. Greater success came with better merchandising and attention to customer tastes, the approach pioneered by New Jersey in 1970, to generate remarkable revenue totals and substantial public excitement. That approach featured "(a) lower priced tickets; (b) more frequent drawings; (c) more numerous outlets; (d) numbered tickets in lieu of recording purchasers' names and addresses; (e) somewhat better odds; and (f) energetic promotion."[15] Through 1984, 17 states plus the District of Columbia had lotteries in operation. At November 1984 elections, voters in California, Missouri, Oregon, and West Virginia approved referenda to allow lotteries. Iowa instituted a lottery in 1985. Table 11–4 indicates the amount of lottery revenue generated in 1983, a tiny amount in comparison with taxes, but larger than some user charge categories.

There are four general types of lotteries:

a. *Passive*—The customer receives a prenumbered ticket with a winner selected at a periodic drawing. This type has largely been superseded by other games.

b. *Instant*—The player buys ticket and rubs off a subtance to reveal whether the ticket is a winner.

---

[14]U.S. Bureau of Census, *State Government Finances in 1983*, GF83 no. 3 (Washington, D.C.: U.S. Government Printing Office, 1984), p. 5.

[15]Frederick D. Stocker, "State Sponsored Gambling as a Source of Public Revenue," *National Tax Journal* 25 (September 1972), p. 437.

c. *Numbers*—The player selects a 3- or 4-digit number and places a bet on an on-line computer terminal regarding whether the number will be drawn.

d. *Lotto*—A pari-mutuel game in which the player selects 6 out of 36 or more numbers.[16] If no one holds the number selected in a weekly drawing, a portion of the total amount wagered rolls over to next week. Total prize money can grow quite rapidly, producing multimillion dollar prizes.

Lotteries appear to be a painless and possibly enjoyable approach to government finance. Why have so many states not taken the lottery plunge? Table 11–4 helps with some of the answers. In the first place, lottery revenue, while absolutely large in some states, is a small contributor to overall state finances. The 4.3 percent of own-source revenue in Maryland is the highest, but the median contribution is only 1.4 percent of own-source general revenue. Too much attention to the lottery can distract revenue administration from more lucrative pursuits. Second, lottery revenue is expensive revenue. If evaluated on roughly the same grounds as a tax would be, the 7.20 median percent of lottery sales taken up by administration would be astronomical. (As a percent of revenue available to the state, the median administration percentage is 18.6.) One could argue with some truth that the money spent on lottery administration would yield the state more revenue if it were placed in better tax enforcement, not in running the lottery. Finally, evidence suggests that low-income families spend a higher percentage of their income on lottery tickets than do high-income families, thus producing a cost burden distribution that is regressive. Although it is a voluntary burden, it does remain a burden that makes corrective action by other parts of the tax or expenditure system more difficult.[17]

CONCLUSION

Public prices can be an attractive alternative to tax finance. They avoid citizen resistance to taxes and can improve both equity and efficiency of service provision. Of the various governmental levels, cities make greatest use of charges currently. Charges have the advantages of voluntarism not found with taxes, but only services with some degree of benefit separability and chargeability are reasonable candidates for charge finance. Services provided by government usually lack

---

[16]The pari-mutuel system is one in which those backing the winner divide, in proportion to their wagers, the total pool bet, after a percentage has been removed by those conducting the event.

[17]Some have suggested that lotteries can cut into the profits of gambling operated illegally. Unfortunately, lotteries typically offer worse odds than do illegal operations, so the competition presented by state systems is not likely to be effective.

those features. Most governments could increase their user charge revenues, but seldom can true charges (not disguised taxes) constitute a major portion of financial support. A similar conclusion is warranted for municipal utilities and state liquor monopolies; it is not clear why, if a government operates such, it would not seek roughly the same objectives as a private owner. Lotteries in recent years have produced, relatively speaking, more public attention and acclaim than revenue.

Questions and Exercises

1. The Fernwood Wastewater District—at the gentle insistence of both state and federal agencies—is changing methods of financing the operating and maintenance costs of its system. Presently, all users of the system (residential, commercial, agricultural, industrial, etc.) pay for the system by a property tax: payments to the district are assigned according to individual holdings of property value. If a car wash constitutes 0.0001 of total property in the district, the car wash pays 0.0001 of the operating and maintenance cost of the system. The proposed effluent charge system would assign cost on the basis of estimated toxic waste quality and quantity introduced into the system. The structure could easily be applied, because a federal agency has data on the amount and type of waste that production and consumption processes generate annually, based on national data. These data would then be used to assign an annual effluent charge to each user, based on the total costs of the system.

   How do the two systems differ in terms of incentive to reduce wastewater quantity and toxicity?

2. The following describes the manner in which a public library sets its library card fee.

Nonresident Library Card Fee
1984

The South Bend Public Library issues free library cards to anyone residing or paying property taxes within the boundaries of Centre, Clay, Greene, German, Liberty, Portage, or Warren Townships of St. Joseph County, Indiana—those townships which provide property tax support to the public library. For those who do not reside or pay property taxes within any of these townships, the South Bend Public Library offers an annually renewable nonresident fee card. The annual fee for this card is equal to approximately the annual property taxes paid for library services by the average household within the library's taxing district. At its January 1984 board meeting, the

TABLE 1 Public Libraries in St. Joseph County: Selected Operating Data, 1981

| | | | | | | Percent of Operating Expenditures on | | |
	Registered Borrowers	Total Circulation	Total Books	Total Periodicals	Total Operating Income	Operating Income Property Tax	Personal Services	Library Materials	Supplies
Mishawaka	20,116	299,519	111,760	240	$ 617,446	$ 486,882	51.6	19.5	2.7
New Carlisle	4,630	28,110	25,026	98	70,086	57,039	50.3	19.6	1.9
South Bend	64,546	1,434,789	323,631	386	1,967,760	1,623,839	54.0	16.0	2.4
Walkerton	1,077	22,071	18,009	28	21,776	17,505	52.9	14.2	2.2

board of the library trustees passed a resolution to set this fee on a schedule approximating the cost per family in the library's service area, as indicated below.

Formula for Determining Nonresident Library Card Fee:

$$\frac{\text{1984 Library Budget}}{\text{Population}} = \frac{\text{Average Cost}}{\text{per Capita}} \times \frac{\text{Average Number of}}{\text{Persons per Household}} = \frac{\text{Cost per}}{\text{Family}}$$
$$\text{(per latest census)}$$

$$\frac{\$3,153,753}{168,000} = \$18.77 \times 2.7 = \$50.00$$

Some other details about the area for your use:

a. In the most recent census, the seven townships paying property tax to the library constituted almost 69 percent of St. Joseph county population; in the prior budget year, those townships made up 70 percent of the property tax base of the county.

b. The card is required to check books from the library. One can consult available materials in the library without a card.

c. The property tax base includes farm, residential, commercial, industrial, and utility real estate, and personal property owned by businesses.

d. A large share of total library cost is independent of year-to-year circulation.

e. Operating information for all public libraries (each operated by an independent library district) in the county are found in Table 1.

Consider the following questions:

a. Does the method of computing the charge produce a figure roughly equal to the property tax paid for the library service by the typical resident of the taxpaying townships?

b. Does the computation likely approximate the user charge that would emerge from the principle of efficient charging?

c. For efficiency, is the charge likely too low or too high? Who loses, in your estimation?

d. Can you suggest an alternative financing structure?

3. In mid-1985, the U.S. Customs Service proposed a user charge system for partial support of its services. The system would charge $2 for every arriving passenger on an international flight, $0.25 for passengers arriving by train from a foreign destination, and $2.50 for arrivals by boat. Fees to inspect airplanes would be $32 and to check

passenger and freight carriers, up to $397. The customs system currently is financed by general revenue.

Does the proposal seem reasonable? Discuss its logic, advantages, and disadvantages.

Case for Discussion

California voters approved a dramatic reduction in property taxes in 1978. While a state surplus provided substantial funds to replace reduced local property tax revenue, many local governments had to seek additional revenue sources to continue services desired by the public. As the following selection from *The Wall Street Journal* reports, many localities sought to replace property tax revenue with user charges and fees.

Consider These Questions

1. *What distinguishes user charges and fees from taxes? Do any of the charges and fees described here seem to be taxes? Explain.*
2. *Does the logic of user charge finance (pricing for public services) require a link between cost of service and level of the charge? Explain.*

Californians Discover Tax-Cut Mania Has a Corollary: Fee Fever

By Stephen J. Sansweet

Students in Glendale, California, who need to brush up on their skills at summer school this year will have to pay as much as $110 for the sessions. Last year they were free.

Los Angeles art and nature lovers put up with recently imposed administration charges of up to $1.50 for once-free visits to county museums and botanic gardens.

Builders in the San Diego suburb of La Mesa find that the cost of fees and permits for an average house has rocketed to $1,283 from just $43 in early 1978.

In the year since Californians voted themselves a deep cut in property-tax payments under Proposition 13, they have been increasingly confronted with new or rapidly escalating fees, charges and other costs for services and programs local governments previously paid for from general revenue. So far, the average homeowner is still coming out ahead, but the gap is narrowing. And the non-tax-deductible fees are a particular blow for the large number of renters in the state who received little, if any, benefit from last year's initiative.

Prostituting 13

"The real meaning of Proposition 13 is being prostituted right and left by local government," charges Paul Gann, cosponsor of the initiative that ignited national tax-cutting fever when California passed it last June 6. "We got the property taxes cut, but they immediately took the dough back in another way."

Mr. Gann's response has been to join in several suits challenging fees, as well as to sponsor a new initiative, the "Spirit of 13," that would limit spending by the state and local governments. The measure will be on the ballot by June 1980 at the latest, and political observers think it has a good chance of enactment.

But regardless of whether the "Spirit of 13" passes, the original "13" has wrought a fundamental and probably irreversible change in the way Californians pay for services, programs, and facilities provided by the state's 58 counties, 417 cities, and 4,750 special districts. While many have praised the new "pay as you go" approach, others fear its possible negative effects on such groups as low or fixed-income people and first-time home buyers.

Cities Recoup 19 Percent

Proposition 13, which limited property taxes to 1 percent of the 1975–76 assessed market value and restricted assessment increases, cut about $550 million from city revenues. According to the latest available statistics, compiled last fall, the cities made up 19 percent of this, or $103 million, from new or higher fees and service charges in the months just before and after Proposition 13 took effect. (Much of the rest was made up by bail-out legislation that distributed surplus state revenue.)

Counties, which lost nearly $1.5 billion in property-tax revenue, added only $22 million in fees. An incomplete survey of special districts, each of which is set up to raise money for a purpose such as sewers or hospitals, showed higher fees and charges of around $70 million, compared with a property-tax loss of $291 million.

Most observers believe that the initial rush to impose fees was only the beginning. "If state bail-out funds decrease as projected . . . local government officials will be increasingly tempted to raise existing fees and create new ones," a state task force that studied the situation predicts. "Fees are one of the few mechanisms open to local governments for raising added revenues."

Fees for Sidewalk Repair

After lengthy debate and several changes of mind, the Los Angeles city council recently passed a residential trash-collection fee ranging from $1.50 to $5 a month. There wasn't any agonizing earlier when the city imposed or raised fees for such things as dog licenses, use of recreation facilities, emergency ambulance transportation, fire-safety inspections and repair of cracks in sidewalks, to name a few.

Besides Mr. Gann's "Spirit of 13" and the numerous lawsuits, other attempts are being made to stem the upward spiral of fees. Several bills pending in the California legislature would restrict the kinds of fees that could be levied and limit each fee to the cost of the service provided. Also, state attorney general George Deukmejian has just issued an advisory opinion that several new fees are actually special taxes and thus require approval of two thirds of the electorate under terms of Proposition 13.

The residential-construction industry has been hit with an especially large number of fee increases. Prior to Proposition 13, existing homeowners in a community, in effect, partially subsidized new development, because their property taxes helped pay for such things as sewer hookups and new streets. With the taxes reduced, localities have switched the cost of new developments to builders, who, in turn, have passed it on to home buyers. Fees are up in more than a dozen items, ranging from filing of plans to on-site inspections.

* * * * *

The California Building Industry Association says the median bill for construction related fees and service charges across the state has risen 26 percent in the last year, but the range is all the way from zero to $3,000 for an average three-bedroom house. "Builders are in a difficult position," says Norman Jachens, spokesman for the trade group. "We don't want to be blamed for local governments being unable to fund improvements for new housing. But we don't want to be easy pickings to make up for Proposition 13 losses either."

Even simple modifications or additions to existing homes "have become a rich man's game," says Donald E. Cunningham, Los Angeles land-use consultant. "It costs $1,200 to $1,500 in fees before you even walk up to the counter with your final plans, and the city and county are about to raise the fees again."

Focus on Sales Taxes

Some communities are using the fund crunch to further their "no-growth" policies. One state survey concludes that many localities aren't any longer interested in luring residential or industrial development because of the low property-tax revenue relative to the cost of capital improvements and services. Instead, they are competing more vigorously for commercial establishments, which generate sales-tax revenue.

Raymond Jallow, senior vice president and economist at United California Bank, is concerned at what he sees as a rush to impose or raise business and licensing fees without knowing the consequences. Beverly Hills businessmen, for example, are faced with business-fee increases of up to 1,800 percent, and Los Angeles County is raising license fees for everyone from weed eradicators to "massage technicians."

"While the economy is still expanding, there might not be much impact," says Mr. Jallow. "But in any slowdown, many of the fees will prove detrimental because they will drive away business and professional people. Some fees haven't been changed in 100 years and certainly should be raised, but others are going up without any direct justification, just to raise revenue."

Effects on the Poor

Many officials concede that tying the level of a fee to the cost of the service performed would often be guesswork. Because of archaic accounting and bookkeeping systems and the difficulty in allocating overhead expenses, service charges frequently bear little relation to service costs, UCLA's Professor [Fred] Case says. "They usually err on the high side, and the money just goes to the general fund anyway," he says. "Los Angeles raised building-permit fees but still laid off people in the department, so we're paying more money for less service."

A major concern of a state Commission of Government Reform, appointed by Gov. Edmund G. Brown, Jr., to suggest ways to cope with Proposition 13, is the effect of new and higher fees on the quality of life, particularly that of the lower-income groups that tend to use public facilities the most.

"Low-income residents may find fees prohibitive to the enjoyment of a park or a community swimming pool as these fees are increased," a commission task force warns. Attempts to set a rate structure subsidizing such groups would require a bureaucracy that in itself would lead to even higher costs, the report adds.

"We don't want to turn parks and swimming pools into country clubs for the middle-class and the rich," says Larry Naake, executive director of the California Park and Recreation Society, a professional group. "Fees may increase total revenue, but already attendance is down everywhere, from the Sacramento zoo to inner-city pools and parks." Mr. Naake says a recent survey by his group shows that 85 percent of the park and recreation agencies in the state have raised fees, the boosts ranging from 30 percent to 400 percent.

Money-Raising Strategies

Fees have been instituted at previously free museums, while charges at beaches and campgrounds are up substantially and fines for overdue library books have doubled or tripled in many cases. Community colleges, almost wholly dependent on property-tax revenue, have started charging for formerly free classes and services. As a result, attendance at noncredit courses—mainly recreation, crafts and courses for senior citizens—dropped 26 percent this past semester. Some 20 percent of 4,600 noncredit courses were shelved.

Localities have come up with some innovative ways to replenish their coffers. Oakland enacted an employe [sic] license fee based on salary earned in the city. Inglewood has instituted a fire-service fee based on the relative fire risk of each structure and the amount of water, personnel, and equipment that would be needed to extinguish a major blaze there. Pasadena's board of directors enacted an ordinance that will adjust all taxes, fees, and charges annually based on the preceding year's consumer price index. The directors retain the option to veto any particular increase.

Theoretically, communities could raise fees and charges to cover all their property-tax losses. But political realities, strong lobbying by interest groups and public opinion have helped to mitigate the increases. When put to the test of advisory or actual votes, proposed fee increases have failed in cities ranging from San Francisco to Palos Verdes Estates.

The ultimate tool of the angry taxpayer, the recall election, also has been used successfully. Voters recalled two members of the Simi Valley city council who were identified as leaders of the move that raised the annual sanitation service charge to $96 a home from $60. And voters in Sacramento County recalled four members of the San Juan United School District who had voted to contribute $1,000 in district funds for a lawsuit challenging Proposition 13.

12

Intergovernmental Fiscal Relations: Diversity and Coordination

Federal, state, and local governments provide and finance public services in the United States, sometimes independently, sometimes cooperatively. No level operates as a regional department of another, although the extent of control and independence varies by level (as considered in Chapter 1). Each level is distinct and separate from the others, each with prescribed powers and authorities. Governments of each level are selected by their own electorates; even though local electorates sum to a state electorate and state electorates sum to the federal electorate, the balance of choices differs among localities in a state and among states in the nation. Because of that diversity of choice possible in a federal system, state and local governments have an important role in provision and finance of government services.

In spite of the important role performed by state and local governments, completely independent operation of these levels would, most argue, produce unacceptable results. Such a posture would undoubtedly leave the public without desired and affordable services, would inflict severe burdens on some unluckily placed individuals and businesses, and would leave some lower-level governments in chronic fiscal crisis outside their control. Those problems create the importance for fiscal interrelationships among governments.

DIVERSITY

Subnational governments provide what Justice Louis Brandeis called "insulated chambers of experimentation" for public action, but this diversity itself requires an allocation of the government functions among operating levels, an allocation which includes both questions of delivery and of financing that delivery. While only the federal government provides national defense in a meaningful sense,[1] few other public services show dominance by only one level. What establishes the appropriate level for predominant provision and how should intergovernmental financing be arranged?

Spillovers

The initial and probably the most important factor involved in choosing the level of government for service delivery is the extent of benefit spillover. Because governments exist to provide collective, or public, goods, there is logic behind the attempt to match the extent of spillover with the jurisdictional scope of the government making decisions about that activity. This structural idea is called the *correspondence principle*.[2] Making the spillover area and the decision unit coincide serves to concentrate the government attention on the matters of most importance and prevents the convoluted patterns of decisions which otherwise occur when beneficiaries do not pay for a service.

A mismatch of spillover extent and government jurisdiction can produce significant misallocation of public resources. Suppose a city can construct a local sports complex which would cost $1 million with only $50,000 of its own resources, the difference being financed by the federal government. The city will reasonably behave as if the full cost of the project is $50,000, even though the project uses $1 million of resources. If the project has minimal beneficial impact beyond the city, there is no significant spillover which the project financing from the federal government corrects. Thus, the lack of correspondence causes the city to behave as if $1 million of resources have a value of only $50,000. Had the city been required to finance the project itself, it would have been unwilling to pay the $1 million. (The project wasn't worth $1 million to the community.) Resources get wasted and costs get exported to federal taxpayers only because of correspondence principle failure.

For analysis of the intergovernmental system, one can draw out a hierarchy of public services by the geographic extent of primary spillovers. A completely private good would have no spillovers; no distortions result from permitting private individuals decisions on the provision of purely private goods. Local recreation facilities—neighborhood parks—involve benefit spillovers extending beyond the family unit but certainly seldom involve spillovers far outside the immediate geographic area. Police and fire protection both involve some spillover beyond neighborhoods through movement of individuals requiring safety

---

[1] In spite of state names, the various National Guard units are federally financed.

[2] Wayland Gardner, *Government Finance* (Englewood Cliffs, N.J.: Prentice-Hall, 1978), p. 276.

and the flow of commerce that requires protection of the production process. Provision of these services purely at the individual or neighborhood level would generally lead to underprovision, as significant service spillovers would be ignored in decisions. Primary and secondary education, at least through welfare drains created by interregional mobility, involves concerns over a fairly wide area. At the furthest extreme is national defense, with a range of spillover extending throughout the geographic extent of the nation, and possibly even beyond. Failure to match spillover range and provision range can produce substantial misallocations. These can be reduced by either reallocation of responsibility for decisions to other governments or through construction of intergovernmental aid programs which compensate lower governments for benefits spilled over to other units. Such corrections represent a major focus of fiscal federalism.

Under different circumstances, broader financing (federal or state) can correct misallocations from spillovers. Consider a situation in which the sewage treatment plant of a city dumps partially treated waste into a river. That river flows past another city, the latter city drawing water from it for the municipal water utility. The more complete the treatment of sewage by the first city, the less the cost of water treatment for the second and the more attractive is the river to the residents of the second. The primary beneficiaries of treatment done by the first city are thus residents of the other. Without some intervention by geographically larger government—an assistance program designed to relieve the city of treatment plant expense incurred primarily for the benefit of those downstream—actions desirable for society as a whole probably will not be undertaken. The city decision would be made on the comparison of returns to its residents (only a small portion of total returns) against the full cost of the complex. In this case, federal (or state) financing of a large share of project cost is justified. That financing would allow the city to pay only to the extent its residents receive benefits, while federal taxpayers pay for returns received by outsiders.

Fiscal Imbalance

A second influence in intergovernmental service delivery questions is fiscal imbalance between governments of a given level. Within the nation, per capita income of states ranges significantly—from $8,098 in Mississippi and $8,967 in Arkansas to $14,895 in Connecticut and $17,194 in Alaska in 1983.[3] Similar differences occur among local units in any state. While there is no one-to-one relationship, similar differences occur in the tax base available to governments.[4] If there is a

---

[3]"State Personal Income," *Survey of Current Business* 64 (August 1984).

[4]A formal approach to comparing fiscal capacity and effort is the Advisory Commission on Intergovernmental Relations' representative tax system: ACIR, *1981 Tax Capacity of the Fifty States,* Report A–93 (Washington, D.C.: ACIR, 1983).

disparity of fiscal resources among governments, equally situated individuals will be treated differently because of the affluence of the government in which they are located. Possibly the simplest method for demonstrating the problem uses the property tax as an example. Suppose Smith and Jones each own houses assessed at $10,000 for the property tax. Smith lives in a community with a property tax base of $40,000 per pupil; Jones lives in a community with a property tax base of $20,000 per pupil. If a quality education uses resources costing $1,500 per pupil, Smith's community need only levy a property tax of $3.75 per $100 assessed value to meet that cost while Jones's community would require a tax of $7.50 per $100. When both communities spend the same amount per pupil, the Jones property must pay property tax twice as high as the Smith property for the quality education previously described ($750 versus $375). Thus, services rendered from a given tax rate—or level of tax effort—will be greater where the capacity endowment is greater. Because there often is a mismatch between need for government service and capacity to finance those services, higher governments intervene by providing various fiscal assistance.

COORDINATION

Revenue Relationships

Fiscal relationships between levels of governments can involve adjustments in revenue structures to provide both financial and administrative assistance. Revenue side assistance will not bring new resources into a government but it can improve access to resources already there. That can be a valuable help, as it can reduce higher-level involvement in the affairs of the unit, permitting substantial local freedom in government decisions. The two general classes of revenue relationship are relief in use of the tax base and assistance in lower-level revenue administration and compliance.

Revenue relief includes both deductions and credits granted the taxes of one unit in tax computations made for another unit. The two devices are both significant, but their operation and power are different. Deductibility means that the tax base for one tax is reduced by the amount of tax paid to a supported unit. For example, the federal individual income tax currently permits deduction of selected state and local taxes in computing the base upon which the federal rates are levied. Not only does this procedure free tax capacity for the lower units, but it also serves as an incentive for the adoption of the deductible taxes. The power of deduction may be demonstrated: suppose a taxpayer is in the 30 percent federal tax bracket. If his state income tax increases by $100, the taxpayer's net tax burden will increase by only $70 because the deduction of that state tax will reduce his federal liability by $30.

Thus, the deduction provides both an incentive to coordination and aids lower units of government. In the pre-1964 tax reduction period—when federal marginal rates were as high as 90 percent—deductibility prevented taxpayers from encountering marginal rates above 100 percent. Of course, the coordination effects are not extraordinarily strong (states continue to use nondeductible taxes) and deductibility will not equalize wealth between lower units.

Deductibility creates a curious effect on state tax reductions—the loss of state tax revenue will be greater than the increase in disposable income available to its taxpayers. The other beneficiary is the federal government. For example, an individual pays $1,000 state income tax and is in the 30 percent marginal bracket for federal taxes. If his state tax is cut in half (to $500), his federal tax base will increase by $500 (because his deduction for state income tax is lower) and his federal tax will increase by $150. Thus, the $500 state tax reduction increases his after-tax income by only $350—increased federal income tax accounts for the remainder. Estimates suggest, for instance, a federal revenue increase of $1–1.7 billion in 1979 as a result of California's Proposition 13 property tax reduction.[5]

A stronger device is the tax credit, an arrangement in which the tax levied by one unit of government acts as full or partial payment of the liability owed to another unit of government. One of the best examples is the federal tax on transfer at death: payments under a qualifying state tax act as an 80 percent credit of liability owed on the federal tax.[6] This creates an almost overwhelming incentive for state units to adopt the tax at least up to the maximum credit limit and obviously frees resources for subunit use. The credit does involve loss of revenue for the unit that grants the credit and the credit does not alter the basic distribution of resources among states or localities: affluent units remain affluent and poor units remain poor. In general, the credit does involve substantial implicit control of the lower unit by the higher unit.[7]

Both deduction and credit of lower-level taxes free up resources for lower-level use and provide incentive for use of "approved" tax forms. They do not assist lower levels with administration and do not reduce the burden of compliance with taxes by multiple governments encountered by businesses and individuals. Another set of revenue tools can

---

[5]Report to the Comptroller General of the U.S., *Will Federal Assistance to California be Affected by Proposition 13?*, GGD-78-101, August 10, 1978.

[6]Death taxes (estate and inheritance) are levied on the value of property transferred to another at the death of the property owner. The transfer must be gratuitous, or not in payment for services rendered. Estate taxes apply at the benefactor level; inheritance taxes apply to the heir.

[7]The power of the credit can be easily shown. Property can be transferred on death or during the benefactor's life. There are both federal death and gift taxes, but the credit applies only to the former. While only Nevada has no state death tax, only 15 states apply gift taxes.

assist with that part of the intergovernmental fiscal problem. These devices include source separation, cooperative administration, coordinated tax bases, tax supplements, and centralized administration, arrayed in order of high to low amounts of lower- level government involvement in operations.

Separation of tax sources prevents tax overlapping. Tax overlapping occurs vertically when governments at different levels (say, federal and state) apply a tax to exactly the same base, and horizontally when more than one government at the same level (say, two different states) applies a tax to the same base. Overlapping may merely produce the nuisance of multiple taxpayer filings, but it may also cause distortion of economic activity. If each level of government were guaranteed an exclusive use of particular tax bases, the vertical overlap problem would be effectively eliminated. The federal government, however, would likely continue with the individual income tax—a lucrative, generally viewed as satisfactory, source—which responds well to changes in economic activity. State and local units would be left with their traditional sales and property tax sources, an unhappy bargain for them.

Table 12-1 presents the record on separation of sources over the past 20 years. In 1963, local government dominated the property tax source, as it has for as long as records are available. The federal government has been, for all practical purposes, excluded from the source by the Constitution. State government once obtained a large portion of its revenue from the source (40 percent of state revenue in 1922 came from general property taxes, for example),[8] but the overall state role was small relative to that of local government. As state activity increased, those governments resorted to other sources than the property tax, so the state share of property tax revenue has never been high.

The federal government nearly monopolized the income base in 1963: 93.5 percent of total individual and corporate collections were at

TABLE 12-1 Tax Source Separation, 1963 and 1983

	Federal		State		Local	
Source	1963	1983	1963	1983	1963	1983
Taxes on property	0%	0%	3.42%	3.68%	96.58%	96.33%
Taxes on individual and corporate income	93.54	82.45	6.03	15.92	0.42	1.63
Taxes on sales on gross receipts	49.58	30.73	44.90	57.97	5.45	11.30

SOURCE: U.S. Bureau of Census, *Government Finances in 1963*, G-GF63 no. 2; and *Government Finances in 1982–83*, GF83 no. 5.

---

[8]Bureau of the Census, *Wealth, Public Debt, and Taxation: 1922. Taxes Collected Compiled as a Part of the Deciennial Report on Wealth, Public Debt, and Taxation* (Washington, D.C.: U.S. Government Printing Office, 1924), p. 12.

the federal level. The highest federal marginal rate on individuals was 91 percent at that time, so neither states nor localities were much inclined to add any tax to that rate, even though very few individuals would have been subject to such punitive rates. Several states had corporate income taxes, but they were reluctant to appear to discourage business. In all, the income base was nearly preempted by the federal government. In 1964, the federal government began a substantial reduction in that highest marginal rate, and in lower brackets as well. Those reductions made heavier state and local use of the base palatable; by 1983, the federal share of income taxes had fallen 11 percentage points (to 82.5 percent), the state share had risen almost 10 percentage points (to 15.9 percent), and the local share had increased to 1.6 percent. Federal dominance continues, but source separation is not nearly so complete as it had been 20 years earlier.

The pattern of sales and gross receipts tax separation over the past 20 years is less easily summarized. The federal government collected a slightly larger share (49.6 percent) in 1963, than did state (44.9 percent); local use was minimal (only 5.5 percent). From that time to the present, the federal government has dramatically reduced its use of selective excises (taxes on motor fuel and alcoholic beverages constitute over half of such revenue); state governments have increased their use of general sales taxes; and local governments have added both general sales and selective excise taxes. State use dominates (58 percent), while the federal share has fallen to 30.7 percent and the local share has doubled (to 11.3 percent). General sales taxation has long been dominated by state government. There has never been a federal general sales tax. Some have argued, however, that the federal government should adopt a value-added tax, clearly a movement away from base separation.[9]

Overall, governments show little taste for source separation as a response to vertical coordination problems. Only sources viewed rightly or wrongly as inferior (like the property tax) are likely to be separated to any level of government—and those governments can be expected to seek other sources traditionally used by other levels. While source separation would be an orderly solution, practical problems make its use not especially likely.

The other coordination approaches all entail use of a single tax base by more than one level of government (source separation is not attempted) and leave lower levels of government with varying amounts of involvement in administration. The arrangements include (1) cooperative administration, (2) coordinated tax bases, (3) tax supplements, and (4) centralized administration.[10] Cooperative administration involves

---

[9]It is not clear why any federal consumption tax should not be simply piggybacked on state sales taxes. Certainly that linkage would have the advantage of familiarity in compliance and administration.

[10]George Break, *Financing Government in a Federal System* (Washington, D.C.: Brookings Institution, 1980), p. 34.

continued contact and exchange of information among taxing units. Sales tax administrators may inform their peers when a firm is found to be violating their tax laws in a manner which would generate liability in other states. Income tax administrators may exchange information about audits performed: the Internal Revenue Service may inform a state about audit findings for an individual living in that state. Business tax administrators may exchange information about contractors who should be registered to pay taxes in other states. Coordination is weak, but profitable for the administering parties: work done by one administration can generate revenue for another with little or no additional work. Base, rates, and rates structure need not coincide among governments for this cooperation, but all governments can gain from the exchange.

The next level of tax coordination is the coordinated tax base, an arrangement in which one government begins its tax from some stage in the structure of the tax levied by another government. Thus, several states key their individual income tax to adjusted gross income in the federal system and a number of localities begin their local sales tax ordinances with definitions taken from their state sales tax. Other elements of the tax may differ from that point—different exemptions, rate patterns, rate levels, etc.—but the higher- and lower-level taxes do have common elements. As a result, taxpayer compliance problems are reduced (one set of records can be used for both taxes and some of the computations need not be replicated) and administrative cooperation is simplified. Usually substantial differences between the taxes would, however, prevent the full gains from coordination in compliance or administration.

Greater coordination results with tax supplements, either through application of a lower-level rate on the base used by the higher level (many state sales taxes have supplements added by localities) or application of a lower-level rate as a percentage of tax paid to the higher unit (a few states have determined their tax as a percentage of federal liability). This method dramatically reduces compliance requirements for taxpayers and cuts administration expenses when the supplementing unit refrains from making numerous changes in the tax used by the higher unit. Few units can refrain from at least a few changes and each change cuts the saving to taxpayers.

The final coordination system is central administration of a supplemental, or "piggyback," tax rate: the lower governmental unit applies its own rate on a tax base used by a higher unit of government. Full piggybacking would have the higher unit doing all administrative and enforcement work for the tax—the tax is paid on a single form to the higher unit, which records and remits collections for the lower unit. Lower units must adopt the tax to receive revenue (it is not simply a system of tax sharing), but they cannot select a base different from that used by the higher unit. Administrative economies are possible with single unit administration and the taxpayer can comply with multiple obligations at one time. Supplemental tax rates, however, do not permit a redistribution of resources among lower units. Most local sales taxes are piggybacked on the state sales tax—many times the local tax return consists simply of some extra lines on the state sales tax return—and local income taxes in Maryland, Indiana, and Iowa are similarly supplements to the state return. Most local income taxes are, however, not related to either federal or state taxes. States that continue a state property tax do apply them to the locally administered base, an example of piggybacking from state to local.

Grants

Grants transfer spending power (command over resources) from one government to another. A significant amount of the money spent by state and local government comes from assistance provided by other levels of government. In 1982–83, 20 percent of state revenue and 35 percent of local revenue was assistance (grants) from other levels of government. These funds were raised by other governments for use by the recipient government. The general pattern of intergovernmental aid between 1962 and 1983 appears in Table 12–2. During that period, the growth of intergovernmental assistance to these governments exceeded that of total revenue: in 1962, state and local intergovernmental revenue was 24 percent of total revenue; in 1983, it was 28 percent of total revenue. Within that overall increase are some important developments.

There has been a healthy growth of aid to each level from each providing level. As Table 12–2 shows, the average annual growth rate of aid to each level exceeds the growth rate of total revenue in all instances. Aid growth from each level exceeds total revenue growth in all instances except for assistance by local government and federal aid to school districts. The greatest difference between aid growth and total revenue growth appears with federal aid to local government and to cities only. Those aid growth rates—respectively 18 and 19 percent— are nearly double the total revenue growth rates. Federal aid growth has, however, substantially declined in recent years. From 1982 to 1983, federal aid to states grew at a 4.4 percent rate but aid to localities declined by 1.1 percent and to cities by 3.0 percent.

States continue as the primary source of intergovernmental aid for local government, both overall and to cities and school districts. States provided 82 percent of total aid to local government in 1982–83, compared to 95 percent in 1957. The major increase in federal assistance came in the decade between 1967 and 1977. School districts did not fare well during the expansion: their share of federal assistance to local units fell from 30 percent to 1967 to 6 percent in 1977.

TABLE 12-2 Sources of Intergovernmental Assistance, 1962 to 1983 ($ millions)

Recipients	Total Revenue	Intergovernmental Revenue* Source			
		Total	Federal	State	Local
1962:					
State	37,595	7,480	7,108	—	373
Local	43,147	11,642	763	10,879	—
Cities	16,797	2,674	330	2,134	210
School districts	14,199	5,769	204	5,267	298
1966–67:					
State	61,082	14,289	13,616	—	673
Local	64,608	20,188	1,753	18,434	—
Cities	24,096	5,081	803	4,001	277
School districts	22,787	10,064	522	9,103	439
1971–72:					
State	112,343	27,981	26,791	—	1,191
Local	114,791	39,694	4,551	35,143	—
Cities	42,114	11,528	2,538	8,434	556
School districts	39,364	17,653	749	16,471	433
1976–77:					
State	204,426	169,126	45,890 (2,217)	—	2,737
Local	196,458	76,831	16,554 (4,397)	60,277	—
Cities	73,527	24,062	8,910 (2,390)	14,093	1,059
School districts	62,938	31,501	952 (—)	29,659	891
1981–82:					
State	330,899	69,166	66,026 (—)	—	3,139
Local	315,322	116,619	21,256 (4,576)	95,363	—
Cities	115,493	31,621	10,996 (2,583)	19,003	1,622
School districts	96,326	52,131	987 (—)	49,641	1,503
1982–83:					
State	357,637	72,704	68,962 (12)	—	3,742
Local	338,070	119,399	21,021 (4,571)	98,378	—
Cities	125,000	32,200	10,666 (2,468)	19,729	1,805
1962–1982 average annual growth rate:					
State	11.5	11.8	11.8	—	11.2
Local	10.5	12.2	18.1	11.5	—
Cities	10.1	13.1	19.2	11.6	10.8
School	10.0	11.6	8.2	11.9	8.4

Note: Comparable school district data are not available for 1983.

*Amounts in parentheses indicate revenue sharing.

SOURCE: U.S. Bureau of the Census, *Census of Governments: Compendium of Government Finances.* Censuses of 1962, 1967, 1972, 1977; U.S. Bureau of the Census, *Governmental Finances in 1983;* and *City Government Finances in 1983.*

Overall, intergovernmental assistance plays a significant role in governmental finance. State and local dependence on these revenues is sufficient that their loss would create substantial fiscal pressure if they were stopped. In terms of assistance, at least, things have changed since President Coolidge's observation: "If the federal government should go out of existence, the common run of people would not detect the difference in the affairs of their daily life for a considerable length of time."[11] Recent estimates suggest a "cresting of federal aid flows to states and localities,"[12] and recent growth rates of federal aid clearly do not approach those of the expansion decade before 1977. The (expected) demise of the federal general revenue sharing experiment continues the pattern. The evidence suggests greater attention to intergovernmental revenue relationships as subnational governments seek stronger indigenous tax sources.

In the practice of intergovernmental finance there is a classical conflict between the donor government and the recipient government, a difference in attitude that can never be entirely resolved in structuring the aid system. The donor government raises the revenue distributed, bearing whatever political burdens may be associated with the revenue function. The political benefits associated with service delivery are garnered by the recipient government, but, because the recipient did not have to raise the money, might it be likely that the funds will be mismanaged or misallocated? To prevent such carelessness (or worse!), the donor seeks controls or "strings" on the utilization of the funds. The recipient government, of course, views the situation differently. The granting government is less familiar with local conditions, needs, and priorities. Any controls make service delivery more difficult and reduce the ability to provide needed services. The controls that the donor seeks to insure accountability are viewed by the recipient as barriers to effective response. The existing assistance structure shows the strains produced by that conflict.

The federal grant system has included three types of assistance: (1) categorical grants, (2) block grants, and, from 1972 through 1985 at least, (3) general revenue sharing. State grant systems have some elements similar to the federal, although each state has its own peculiar mix. Overall there is much hybridization of grant styles, making clear classification more and more difficult. In general, federal grants have moved gradually from a narrow categorical grant structure to broader, general-purpose assistance, deflected only by the recent retreat from general revenue sharing. Between 1972 and 1978, the proportion of

---

[11]Quoted in Arthur Schlesinger, *Crisis of the Old Order* (Boston: Houghton Mifflin Company, 1957), p. 57.

[12]Advisory Commission on Intergovernmental Relations, *Significant Features of Fiscal Federalism, 1978–1979* (Washington, D.C.: ACIR, May 1979), p. 1.

TABLE 12-3 Number of Federal Categorical Grants, by Type: FY 1975, 1978, 1981, and 1984

	1975		1978		1981		1984	
	Number	Percent	Number	Percent	Number	Percent	Number	Percent
Formula-based								
Allotted formula	96	21.7	160	21.5	111	20.8	79	20.2
Project grants subject to formula allocation	35	7.9	47	9.6	42	7.9	29	7.4
Open-end reimbursement	15	3.4	17	3.5	20	3.8	18	4.6
Total formula-based	(146)	(33.0)	(170)	(34.6)	(173)	(32.4)	(126)	(32.2)
Project	296	67.0	322	65.4	361	67.6	266	67.8
Total	442	100.0	492	100.0	534	100.0	392	100.0
Three-year change			+50	+11.3	+42	+8.5	−142	−26.6
Percent requiring matching		61.5		57.1		53.4		55.4

SOURCE: Advisory Commission on Intergovernmental Relations, *A Catalog of Federal Grant-in-Aid Programs to State and Local Governments: Grants Funded, FY 1984* (Washington, D.C.: U.S. Government Printing Office, 1984).

block or general grants increased from 8.4 to 14.7 percent of the federal total.[13] State grants have always been for relatively broad purposes, sometimes involving specified percentages of certain state taxes distributed for any local purpose.

Categorical grants.   Categorical grants provide assistance for a particular program purpose, usually limited to spending for certain activities, like construction of a wastewater treatment plant or payment of salaries for special education teachers. These grants intend "to stimulate and support state and local programs in areas of specific national interest."[14] Their intention is to induce the recipient government to behave in a fashion other than the way it would behave without the aid— the grants seek to encourage recipient units to shift expenditures to particular functions or to guarantee provision of certain recipient government services in a manner consistent with national interest. In these areas, narrow local interest and national interest presumably do not coincide. The grant alters local interest by making certain activities more attractive—the federal share makes the aided activity cheaper for the lower government—so that local actions are consistent with national interest.

Categorical assistance has four forms: formula-based, project, formula-project, and open-end reimbursement. The Advisory Commission on Intergovernmental Relations describes the varieties:

> Formula grants are those for which funds are allocated among recipients according to factors specified in legislation or in administrative regulations. Project grants are nonformula grants for which potential recipients submit specific, individual applications in the form and at the times indicated by the grantor. The third or mixed type of categorical grants are project grants for which a formula specified in statues or regulations is used to determine the amount available for a state area. Distribution takes place in two stages, with the first stage involving state area allocations governed by formula and the second entailing project applications and discretionary awards. For open-end reimbursement grants—often regarded as formula grants—the federal government commits itself to reimbursing a specified proportion of state-local program costs, thus eliminating "competition" among recipients as well as the need for an allocational formula.[15]

Table 12–3 reports the distribution of categorical grants by type in recent years, according to the Advisory Commission on Intergovernmental Relations' triennial review of such aid. Project programs

---

[13]Break, *Financing Government in a Federal System*, p. 167.

[14]John Shannon, "Federal Revenue Sharing—Time for Renewal?" *National Tax Journal* 27 (December 1974), p. 496.

[15]Advisory Commission on Intergovernmental Relations, *Summary and Concluding Observations, The Intergovernmental Grant System: An Assessment and Proposed Policies* (Washington, D.C.: ACIR, 1978), p. 3.

represent around two thirds of those grants, even though two thirds of outlays have been for formula-based programs. The overall number of categorical programs declined by 26.6 percent from 1981 to 1984, as a result of the movement toward broader assistance. Only 55.4 percent of the grants had matching provisions, requirements that the recipient spend a specified sum for each dollar spent by the federal government in the grant.

Project grants are the realm of the grantsman, the person assigned by many state and local governments and nonprofit agencies to make application for external assistance. (Formula and reimbursement categories plus the block and revenue sharing assistance to be examined shortly do not require competitive application.) This individual becomes familiar with the activities of federal agencies and private foundations (state government tends not to use project grants) and watches announcements of available funding published in sources such as the Federal Register. When project requirements and the activities of the grantsman's employer coincide, the grantsman manages the preparation of a project proposal. The funding agency awards go to proposals evaluated as best according to the contraints of legislation and regulations. While political influence may sometimes be important, more often the decision will depend on factors like these:

1. Does the project meet goals of legislation?
2. Is the project within restrictions of the legislation?
3. Does the proposer demonstrate capacity to implement the project?
4. Does the project address a significant problem area?
5. Does the project demonstrate creativity?
6. Does the project have results transferable to other local governments?[16]

One peculiarity of the categorical grant must be recognized. For the recipient, the grant is most valuable if it will support an activity the unit was going to undertake even without the assistance. In that case, there is minimal disruption of local interest and resources are released for use in accord with local priorities. For the donor, the grant is most powerful when it supports activities not ordinarily undertaken by the recipient, at least at levels consistent with the donor's interest. Thus there will consistently be some divergence of interest between recipient and donor in a well-designed categorical grant. Many do, in fact, have matching requirements to get greater spending for a granted donor dollar.

Critics of the categorical grant system emphasize three particular difficulties. First is the administrative complexity of the categorical

---

[16]Reported by Charles A. Morrison, "Identifying Alternative Resources for Local Government," *Management Information Service Report* 9 (July 1977).

grant system. In an effort to ensure that federal policy objectives are met as nearly as possible by state and local activities financed by federal funds, federal programs establish elaborate control mechanisms to monitor and shape actions taken by the recipient. Systems usually have different planning, application, reporting, and accounting requirements—none of which coincides with those ordinarily used by the recipient government. Not only are these controls an irritation but they also divert state and local resources to the administrative process.

A second criticism is the program overlap and duplication which has emerged in the federal grant system. An Advisory Commission on Intergovernmental Relations count found, for instance, 24 agencies administering 52 separate grant-in-aid programs related to control and prevention of fires in 1979.[17] That pattern almost inevitably means that some communities will not participate, leaving their residents less well-served than would be desirable, while others will aggressively seek funds, producing extraordinary assistance for their residents. Governments may even use funds from one program to meet matching requirements of another, thus thwarting the intention of matching to stimulate local expenditure.

Finally, critics fault the distortion of local priorities that categorical grants produce. While the recognition of national interest is the predominant logical reason for the existence of such grant structures, the distortion may exceed any justified by the traditional spillover of local action argument. Furthermore, the aid may not be reliable. Aid often is eliminated after a few years, leaving state and local government with a responsibility but no resources. The combination of these criticisms has been instrumental in movement toward block and general-purpose assistance.

Block grants.   Block grants are distributed, usually to general-purpose governments (categorical grants often go to special-purpose governments or nongovernments as well), according to a statutory formula to finance activities in a broad functional area. Much of the expenditure is left to the discretion of the recipient institution. To the early 1980s, the federal government had established five block grant programs:

1. Partnership for Health (Comprehensive Health Planning and Public Health Service Amendments of 1966) consolidated nine grant programs to reduce categorization of public health and improve the quality of health care funded by the programs.
2. Safe Streets (Omnibus Crime Control and Safe Streets Act of 1968) grants established a broad program of assistance for crime prevention and the administration of justice.

---

[17]Cited in Sarah Scott, "Fighting Fires from Washington," *National Journal,* January 3, 1981, p. 8.

TABLE 12-4 Federal Block Grant Programs, 1985.

Budget Subfunction and Title	U.S. Code	Formula Factors*	Recipient	Federal Share	Administering
Ground transportation					
Urban mass transporation capital and operating assistance	49 USC 1608	(P), O	Local	50/80	DOT
Community development					
Community development/entitlement	42 USC 5303–6	P, I, O	Local	100	HUD
Community development/state's program	42 USC 5306	P, O	State	100	HUD
Elementary, secondary, and vocational education					
Improving school programs	31 USC 1243	(P)	State	100	ED
Training and employment					
JTPA, Title IIA: Training services for disadvantaged adults and youth	29 USC 1501–1605	(P)	State	100	DOL
Social services					
Community services	42 USC 9801, 9901	O	State	100	HHS/OCS
Social services	42 USC 1397–1397f	P	State	100	HHS/OHDS
Health care services					
Preventive health and health services	42 USC 300w	P, E	State	100	HHS/PHS
Alcohol and drug abuse and mental health services	42 USC 300x	E	State	100	HHS/PHS
Primary care	42 USC 300y	E	State	100	HHS/PHS
Maternity and child health	42 USC 701	E	State	57	HHS/PHS
Other income security					
Low-income home energy	42 USC 8621	E, (I)	State	100	HHS/SSA

*Formula Factors: E, expenditure or program level; F, equal amount among states; basic minimum to each recipient and remaining funds, if any, distributed according to formula; I, per capita income; (I), per capita income of special segment of population; or income used to modify other formula factor, such as number of children in families under "poverty line"; O, other; P, total population; and (P), special segment of population (urban population, school age population, etc.), SOURCE: Advisory Commission on Intergovernmental Relations, *A Catalog of Federal Grant-in-Aid Programs to State and Local Governments: Grants Funded, FY 1984* (Washington, D.C.: U.S. Government Printing Office, 1984).

3. Comprehensive Employment and Training Program (CETA, 1973) consolidated 17 categorical programs generally related. It did not include all federal manpower programs (47 authorizations administered by 10 federal departments or agencies continued in 1978) and CETA likewise had sizable categorical programs along with the block program.[18]

4. Community Development Block Grants (1974) combined six urban aid programs. The grants, while distributed partly by formula, also have a discretionary funding component and the legislation includes 13 eligible activities for funding. The program thus rests somewhere between a categorical and a block grant.

5. Social Services (Social Services Amendments of 1974) block grants brought together several social service programs that had been troublesome to operate.

A sixth program, the Public Works Employment Act of 1976, sometimes is classified as a block grant: funds were allocated by formula and there was no matching requirement. It was not a true block grant because state and local governments competed on the basis of project application.

The Omnibus Reconciliation Act of 1981 (Public Law 97-35) consolidated 57 existing grant programs into nine block grants. The new programs and the number of consolidated programs in each are social services (2), home energy assistance (1), community development (1), elementary and secondary education (33), alcohol, drug abuse, and mental health (3), maternal and child care (6), community services (1), primary health care (1), and preventive health and health services (9). Since then, Congress has replaced the CETA block grant with another block grant, part of the Job Training Partnership Act, and reduced the 15 CETA categoricals with 6 in the new Act. Another block grant, Urban Mass Transportation Capital and Operating Assistance, has been created. By 1984, the federal government had 12 block grants, accounting for about 15 percent of grant outlays in that year; the programs are listed in Table 12–4.

The Advisory Commission on Intergovernmental Relations states the case for block grants with "well-designed allocation formulas and eligibility provisions" to ensure that funds go to the appropriate units. These grants:

1. Provide aid to those jurisdictions having the greatest programmatic needs, and give them a reasonable degree of fiscal certainty.

2. Accord recipients substantial discretion in defining problems, setting priorities, and allocating resources.

---

[18]ACIR, *Summary and Concluding Observations, The Intergovernmental Grant System*, pp. 10–11.

3. Simplify program administration and reduce paperwork and overhead.
4. Facilitate interfunctional and intergovernmental coordination and planning.
5. Encourage greater participation on the part of elected and appointed generalist officials in decision making.[19]

The block grants should not be expected to stimulate new initiatives by recipient governments and should be confined to activities for which a broad consensus already exists. They are not well designed to bend local choices in a direction more consistent with national interest or to cause local units to change their methods of operation. They can be useful as replacements for groups of similar categorials which have established strong local clienteles during their operation.

General revenue sharing. The third variety of federal grant is general revenue sharing, a formula distribution with few or no restrictions on the use of funds provided. The federal revenue sharing program, started in 1972, distributed, by formula, money appropriated on a multiyear basis to that use. Similar (and older) state tax-sharing programs typically dedicate a given share of selected taxes, for example, one percentage point of the state sales tax rate, to a local aid formula. The federal approach provided some greater certainty of aid during the life of the appropriation (unforeseen changes in federal revenue did not influence distributed shares), but the funds had to be appropriated again when the period of appropriation expired and each renewal raised questions about continuation of the program. States were excluded permanently as of October 1983; the entire program is excluded from the 1986 budget.

Revenue sharing distributed funds to general-purpose governments according to a formula which combined population, percent of population urban, tax effort, income tax effort, and per capita income to distribute the appropriate shares. State governments initially received revenue sharing (one third of the total amount), but were gradually removed: the 1980 extension of the program discontinued the share for any state not giving up categorical grants equal to the allocation received and, as noted previously, the state share ended entirely in 1983. Local general purpose governments (cities, counties, native-American governments, townships, etc.) continued through the life of the program. Checks were sent to each eligible government without application and with only minimal restrictions concerning use (there had to be a publicized appropriation process, there could be no discrimination in hiring or compensation, funds could not be used for grant matching, use had to be subject to external financial audit, etc.).

---

[19]Ibid., p. 24.

General revenue sharing can strengthen local spending power and reduce intergovernmental fiscal disparities (the great differences in fiscal capacity that exist among governments at the same level across the nation). It does not shape local priorities to make them more consistent with national interest, and it is not particularly effective as a way to aid disadvantaged groups. The former results because of the lack of controls placed on the assistance; the latter, because advantaged and disadvantaged tend, with few exceptions, to live in the same political jurisdictions. General aid to the jurisdiction will produce improved capability to provide services (or reduce taxes with no change in services) for anyone—and probably the advantaged will do better because they usually have greater political clout. It is simply not reasonable to expect revenue sharing (or block grants) to achieve the targeting and revision of public action that categorical programs can produce. Revenue sharing is suited for reducing fiscal disparity among governments at a given level and to strengthen the expenditure capability of units with constrained taxing powers. That is its reasonable and appropriate position in the grant system.

Mandates

A mandate is a constitutional provision, statute, administrative regulation, or judicial ruling which places an expenditure requirement on a government, that requirement coming from outside the government forced to take the action.[20] Mandates are much like operating restrictions that governments place on private industry to regulate workplace safety, environmental quality, and so on. A state government can mandate local spending, the federal government can mandate either state or local spending, and the judiciary—the branch of government outside the normal flow of budgeting and appropriation—can mandate spending at any level. Most concern about mandates emerges at the local level because these units typically lack the overall size needed to respond flexibly to external expenditure shocks (few individual mandates would be sufficiently large, relative to overall expenditure, to significantly disrupt the federal or a state government). And these units lack the access to revenue sources of the other levels.

Mandates seek to cause governments to behave in some manner other than the way they would ordinarily behave. This changed behavior can be directed either toward services and programs or toward inputs used (normally personnel). Examples of the former include such things as hours libraries will be open, provision of special education by local schools, jail condition standards, water temperature in hospitals,

---

[20]Advisory Commission on Intergovernmental Relations, *State Mandating of Local Expenditures* (Washington, D.C.: ACIR, July 1978), p. 2.

provision of legal defense for indigents, etc.[21] Each requirement or regulation directs some expenditure, unless existing action already fulfills the requirement. Input use requirements encompass levels of compensation which must be paid, resources acquired, the quality and/or quantity of input to be used, and the conditions under which the input will be employed. All potentially change the cost of providing any given level of service. Examples include state determination of local welfare department salaries; requirement of local collective bargaining or compulsory arbitration; required employee training; funding requirements for pension systems; required participation in unemployment insurance or workers' compensation systems; regulation of wages, hours, and working conditions; and so on.[22] Of course, several of this latter group are simple extensions of requirements applied to private employers.[23]

There are many other state controls on local government action beyond the mandates. States establish the "rules of the game" for localities: election frequency, budget and finance structures, permissible forms of government, due process definitions, etc. Many of these standards cause extra expenditure, but we accept them as reasonable costs of an informed democracy. "Rules of the game" are, however, often designed to reduce local government costs by limiting competition among local units, restricting direct democracy initiatives and elections of officials, constraining salaries of elected officials, or defining tax processes on a statewide basis. They are clearly of a different nature than the earlier group of mandates. Other interventions determine the distribution of tax burdens as the permissible scope of local taxation is defined (e.g., residential electricity may be removed from the local sales tax base). Because these actions directly restrict revenue-raising capability only in conjunction with tax rate limitations, they are not of the same concern as service or input mandates. Furthermore, these controls, along with control of the rules of the game, are best considered with the issue of home rule and the balance between local power and state sovereignty.

The case for mandates has two logical elements. First, the benefit of a lower unit action (or the cost of inaction) may spill beyond the boundaries of the lower unit. Thus, an irresponsible action by one unit can reduce the expenditure of that unit (and the taxes paid by those in

---

[21]*Gideon* v. *Wainwright*, 372 U.S. 335 (1963) and *Argersinger* v. *Hamlin*, 407 U.S. 25 (1972).

[22]In *Garcia* v. *San Antonio Metropolitan Transit Authority* (1985), the Supreme Court held that the federal Fair Labor Standards Act of 1938 standards for overtime pay and minimum wages applied to state and local government. The cost implications are substantial.

[23]Governments also pick up restrictions as a result of accepting grants from federal or state governments. Grant controls create fewer logistical problems than ordinary mandates: the recipient government accepts obligations as a condition of accepting the funds. There is no compulsion to enter the system.

that unit) while producing harm to residents of adjacent units. The state government may choose to mandate correcting service levels to prevent that damage to innocent bystanders. Second, statewide uniformity may be seen as essential by the legislature or the judiciary. The state may require equal expenditure per unit for schools, sanitation, etc., to prevent individuals from having low service levels solely because of their residence. Expenditure correction thus is mandated.

Against these arguments for mandates are strong countercases. First, many argue that the mandating unit should be responsible for financing the mandate. The mandate can become a mechanism for producing political credit for the higher unit while the lower unit bears the burden of finance—a condition not conducive to careful decisions. Second, mandates can threaten other government programs. If limits rest on a government's ability to raise revenue, mandates for certain expenditures can endanger the provision of other desirable services. Third, mandates are characteristically enacted without cost awareness. While the result of the mandate may be desirable, the cost of its achievement may be excessive, particularly when compared with the return from other uses of the government resources. Mandates seldom are imposed in an environment favorable to comparisons of return and cost. This is particularly true when mandates emerge from the judiciary. Twenty-five states estimate in fiscal notes the cost to localities of state mandates,[24] but there is seldom any effort to identify cost to individual units—the point where expenditures must be financed. Finally, mandates restrict any autonomy provided under other legal provisions. They are clearly an uneasy companion where home rule has been provided.

For decisions about mandates, the appropriate comparison would appear to be whether the resource cost created by the mandate is worth the return generated by the mandate. Inflicting costs on other units may not be a likely way to generate that comparison. Some suggest that mandates without financial assistance sufficient to cover their costs are a violation of intergovernmental fair play. Others are skeptical, pointing out that governments do not finance mandated activities for private firms or individuals (minimum wage requirements, safety regulations, etc.), so while mandates may raise questions of appropriate government roles, they do not logically require accommodating fiscal transfers.

CONCLUSION

Multiple levels of government provide public services in the United States. That diversity allows greater individual choice, but service

---

[24]Advisory Commission on Intergovernmental Relations, *Intergovernmental Perspectives* 5 (Winter 1979).

delivery cannot be entirely uncoordinated because of two factors: inter-governmental spillovers and fiscal imbalance. Spillovers occur when an action by one government has impact (good or bad) on its neighbors. Intergovernmental intervention can induce that government to allow for those external effects. Imbalance emerges because fiscal capacity is unevenly distributed across the nation and within states. Without an intergovernmental response, some individuals will be unduly penalized by the public sector simply because of where they live.

Those intergovernmental problems can be reduced by four different varieties of coordination: revenue relief (deductibility, credits), assistance in administration (source separation, coordinated use of a single revenue base), grants (categorical, block, revenue sharing), or mandates. The devices together help retain the advantages of multilevel government without some associated problems.

Cases for Discussion

A   The following selection appeared in *The Wall Street Journal.* No questions about it are necessary.

The Squirrel Memo

Many releases and handouts that cross newspaper desks each day could be offered as prime exhibits for hiking the postal rates on unsolicited mail. But occasionally there's gold in them thar hills, and we offer as evidence a recent item from the news bureau of Washington and Lee University in Lexington, Virginia.

It seems that one Frank Parsons, assistant to the university president, was struggling with a lengthy application for federal funds to be used in building the university's proposed new library. Among other things, HEW wanted to know how the proposed project "may affect energy sources by introducing or deleting electro-magnetic wave sources which may alter man-made or natural structures or the physiology, behavior patterns, and/or activities of 10 percent of a human, animal or plant population." The questions go on and on, but you get the idea.

Assistant Parsons plugged away, dutifully answering as best he could. And then he came to the section on animal populations, where he was asked to list the extent to which the proposed library would "create or precipitate an identifiable long-term change in the diversity of species within its natural habitat."

"There are some 10 to 20 squirrels living, or appearing to live, in the site proposed for the new library," he wrote. "Some trees that now provide either homes or exercise areas for the squirrels will be removed, but there appear to be ample other trees to serve either or both of these purposes. No major food source for the squirrels will be affected. It is likely that the squirrels will find no difficulty in adjusting to this intrusion. . . . They have had no apparent difficulty in adjusting to relocations brought on by nonfederally supported projects."

To the question of whether the proposal will "create or precipitate an indentifiable change in the behavior patterns of an animal population," he assured HEW the squirrels and such would have to make some adjustments but "it will be difficult to tell if they're unhappy about having to find new trees to live in and sport about."

Eventually the application was shipped off to Washington, and lo and behold before long HEW official Richard R. Holden actually wrote the president of the school. He said: "Perhaps bureaucracy will tremble, but I salute Washington and Lee University. . . . The mountain of paperwork which confronts me daily somehow seemed much smaller the day I read about the squirrels in Lexington. May they and your great university coexist in harmony for many, many years." As copies of the correspondence zipped throughout federal agencies, with all the speed of a confidential memo destined for Jack Anderson, bureaucrats from all over telephoned their congratulations to the "squirrel memo man."

We're still not sure exactly what lesson is to be drawn from all this. Our initial reaction was surprise that anyone actually reads these exhaustive applications, and even now we're undecided whether that's cause for comfort or dismay. Yet while we never doubted that HEW possessed a sense of humor—indeed, we've gotten some of our biggest laughs from proposals emanating from the vicinity of 330 Independence Ave., S.W.—it's nice to know that an occupational devotion to red tape has not completely eroded the agency's ability to laugh at itself.

B   State revenue sharing can be a major vehicle for equalizing local government ability to provide services. Such a plan is far superior for that purpose than categorical assistance, an approach appropriate for stimulation of spending on specific local services. The following case, excerpted from an Advisory Commission on intergovernmental Relations report describes the development of state revenue sharing in

Wisconsin, a state providing much heavier general support to local government than is typical in the United States.

Measures of General Support for Local Governments (1978)

	Wisconsin	All States
General state-local support ($000)	$701,598	$6,716,418
Per capita	$149.82	$30.87
Percent of local government general-purpose general revenue	23.3%	5.7%
Percent of total state expenditure	14.8%	3.3%

SOURCE: ACIR, *The State of State-Local Revenue Sharing,* p. 18.

Consider These Questions

1. *Why did Wisconsin revenue sharing drift away from an origin basis?*
2. *Explain the conflict between urban and rural areas on the aid formulas. Would that be a problem in other states?*
3. *How does equalization affect the willingness of localities to accept industries?*

State-local revenue sharing in Wisconsin dates from 1905 when the state legislature exempted utility property (mainly railroad property at that time) from local property taxation. Using a state gross earnings tax instead, part of the proceeds were used to reimburse communities for their lost tax base. These utility aids have continued, in a much altered form, to the present.[1]

In 1911 Wisconsin initiated the first state individual and corporate income taxes. Their primary purpose was to enable the state to exempt all intangible personal property from the local property tax. To compensate localities, 70 percent of the proceeds of the state income taxes went to municipalities, 20 percent went to county governments, and only 10 percent was retained by the state.[2]

Both the utility aids and shared income taxes initially, and for many years, were origin-based revenue sharing. Utility aids went to communities in proportion to their amount of utility property, while personal income tax receipts were disbursed in proportion to the amount of

Source: ACIR, *The State of State-Local Revenue Sharing* (Washington, D.C.: ACIR, 1980).

[1] James R. Donohue, "Local Government in Wisconsin," *Wisconsin Blue Book 1979–1980* (Madison, Wis.: Madison Legislative Reference Bureau), p. 214.

[2] Wisconsin Commission on State-Local Relations and Financing Policy, *The Final Report of the Commission on State-Local Relations and Financing Policy* (Madison, Wis.: 1977), pp. 1–8.

taxes paid by residents of each county and municipality. Since the individual income tax applied only to high incomes, and the exempted property was financial wealth, the new tax base was distributed among localities much like the old base. The origin method of sharing served well as a reimbursement to localities for lost tax base. The proceeds of the corporate income taxes were also distributed according to where corporate income was generated.

As the state's role in the provision of state and local services grew, the proportion of the income tax revenues earmarked for localities was decreased. For example, in 1925 the legislature lowered the shares of income tax from 70 percent to 50 percent for municipalities and from 20 percent to 10 percent for counties. Dollar levels did continue to rise because the income tax base and rates were increased. As other types of personal and business property were removed from the tax roles, the state earmarked new funds to reimburse local governments. A portion of state motor vehicle license charges and highway user taxes was allocated to communities to replace local property taxes on automobiles. A portion of the liquor tax was distributed to cities and towns, based on population.

After 1925, the legislature obtained additional revenues solely for state purposes by attaching surcharges to the income tax and making deductions prior to the local sharing distribution. The state abandoned these subterfuges in 1962 and adopted the principle that the state would receive all the additional revenue that would result from tax rate increases. Localities would continue to benefit from the growth in revenues resulting from increases in income. In order to implement this change, the legislature reduced the percentage of income tax revenues going to local government as the tax rate was increased.[3] Despite the growth in state revenue sharing money, the structure of the sharing continued to reflect the original plan to reimburse localities for property exempted from their tax rolls.

Wisconsin was an innovator not only in revenue sharing, but also with other actions related to property taxes. In 1949 the state introduced an aid formula for school districts that recognized the lack of district property taxing ability compared to a minimum guaranteed valuation per pupil. In the early 1960s Wisconsin instituted a sales tax and used much of the early proceeds to finance a new general property tax relief program. Under this program the state paid a portion of the real estate property taxes for all taxpayers in communities where the mill rate exceeded a state-specified rate. The aid is in proportion to that part of the property tax levy due to a rate in excess of the state-specified rate. A separate, personal property tax relief credit was created for the taxes paid on merchants' stock-in-trade, manufacturers' inventories, and farmers' livestock. A proportional credit was given everywhere, regardless of tax rate. The state also enacted a property tax "circuit breaker" for the elderly called the homestead credit. In

---

[3]Wisconsin Task Force on Local Government Finance and Organization, *The Report of the Task Force on Local Government Finance and Organization* (Madison, Wis.: 1969), pp. vi–1,4.

1973 the homestead credit was extended to include all individuals with low incomes.[4]

1969: THE TARR COMMISSION

Dissatisfaction with the state-shared revenue policy led to creation of the Task Force on Local Government Finance and Organization in 1969. Known as the Tarr Commission for its chairman, Curtis W. Tarr, the main conclusion of this commission's studies was that the then current system of origin-based aids were needlessly complex and inequitable.

The Tarr Commission said that the revenue sharing system was complex because of the various separate funds involved which necessitated the mailing of 8 to 10 checks a year to roughly 1,900 units of local government.

The commission found that the origin-based distribution of corporation income tax receipts was a particular administrative burden. Corporations had to maintain special records of income by municipality. Localities were concerned about the accuracy of these records and the accounting practices used to derive them, since in 1966 shared corporate income taxes amounted to nearly $42 million.

The Tarr Commission emphasized a second weakness in the Wisconsin revenue sharing program: The method of distributing aids led to inequities, as communities that needed aid did not get enough of it and communities that did not need aid received too much. The origin-based system led to local governments with adequate property tax bases being rewarded by disproportionate shared aids, because they were the homes of higher-income families and corporations whose taxes were the primary sources of the aids. The Tarr Commission cited examples of communities that received aid many times the size of their property tax levy and noted that "one municipality has sufficient resources to offer two-year scholarships to all of its young people attending college."[5]

The Local Need Discussion

To remedy the defects of the origin-based formula, the commission considered two different approaches to measuring needs. The commission studied but rejected a local expenditure-related formula that would have provided aid to communities which spent above a certain per capita amount for essential services such as police and fire. The commission rejected this approach because it felt that the theory of causation of expenditure levels was insufficiently developed, and the methods of municipal accounting sufficiently varied, as to make this approach unworkable. Instead, the commission described its preferred alternative—a tax rate—type of formula:

---

[4]Ibid., pp. vi–2–3.

[5]Ibid., pp. vii–1.

A second alternative seems more suitable as a representation of community needs: to assume that the tax rate itself expresses local requirements. This alternative stipulates that a municipality determines its expenditure level, subtracts the revenue it receives from state payments and special charges, and raises the remainder from property taxes. The underlying assumption is that the local elected governing body knows best the requirements of the local government and can balance these against the tax capacity of the community.[6]

* * * * *

The Tarr Commission advocated a consolidated revenue sharing fund from which the new aid distributions would be made and which would replace the general aids then provided on an origin and population basis (that is, personal and corporate income taxes, utility and liquor taxes, and motor vehicle registration fees). The size of the fund was to be based on percentages of the same taxes that were shared before. The system for allocating shared taxes was to have three components. The first part was a payment to communities to be determined by multiplying a state-set mill rate by the value of certain types of utility property. There was to be a maximum or cap put on the amount that could be received under this part of the formula. The logic was that utility property paid no property taxes and yet certain utility property received local services, particularly fire protection. It had been argued that the old origin formula provided excessive aid to communities with utility property.

A second part of the formula was to be a per capita payment to all localities, with the amount determined by the state. The logic here was that need for expenditures is primarily, although not exclusively, a function of population.

The final component was to incorporate the new need measure into the formulas, by providing aid to communities in proportion to the excess taxes caused by having a total tax rate for all purposes higher than a state-specified mill rate. The commission suggested that communities with tax rates below 20 equalized mills should receive no aid; this would have included 7 percent of the communities in the state. This part of the formula was referred to as the "percentage of levies payment." The statewide total payment to offset excess taxes, however, would be limited to the remainder of the revenue sharing money after the special utility and per capita payment had been distributed.

The distribution of aid between counties and municipalities was handled by having each county receive a percentage of what was determined by the formulas for each municipal area in the individual county; the commission suggested 16 percent of the municipal area amount be given to the county. This arrangement roughly preserved the historic county share. To ease transition problems, the Tarr Commission also advocated that the formula be phased in.

---

[6]Ibid., pp. vii–1.

Legislative Response

At the urging of newly elected Gov. Patrick Lucey, the Wisconsin legislature, in 1971, adopted nearly all of the shared revenue recommendations made by the Tarr Commission. One change, however, was that added annual payments for general property tax relief were provided and funded by deductions from the municipal and county shared tax account. When the new redistributive formulas were enacted, "hold-harmless" guarantees were also superimposed on the system to prevent injury to any locality.

This new need-related formula system did not dramatically increase the amount of revenue sharing and it was not intended to. While total property tax relief-related state payments rose after 1971, most of the growth through 1977 came in general property tax relief, which also used an excess tax-type formula.

1975: CLOSER TARGETING FOR THE NEED CONCEPT

During its 1975 session, and again at the urging of Governor Lucey, the Wisconsin legislature further developed its revenue sharing system. The major change was to replace the percentage of levies formula with a new one that better recognized differences in local taxing ability rather than tax effort alone. The new formula also keyed municipal or county government aid to its respective taxing status alone, not including the level of school or other taxes.

The new formula was aidable revenues (a three-year average of most revenues raised by the recipient government) multiplied by a measure of taxing capacity. Taxing capacity was determined by subtracting from one a fraction equal to the ratio of actual full-value local tax base divided by a state standard for per capita property valuation. This latter amount was set at $30,000, over twice the 1976 state average. Communities with per capita property valuation over $30,000 received no aid under this part of the formula, although new hold-harmless provisions prevented actual reductions in aid.

For example, if a community had aidable revenues of $1 million, a local property tax base of $75 million full value, and a population of 5,000, its aid factor would equal $500,000. The formula multiplied aidable revenues by 0.5 because the locality was 50 percent short of the standard set for taxing ability. An otherwise identical community, with a larger property tax base of $100 million would have a smaller aid factor, because it was only 33 percent short of the standard set for taxing ability. The actual aid was subject to proration because the sum of the aid factors exceeded the total available funds.

Also associated with the move from a "percentage of levies" to "aidable revenues" formula was a redetermination of the county share. Rather than having county funds set by the municipal shares, the counties began to compete on their own for aidable revenue aids, although only 25 percent of their aidable revenues were counted in the formula.

CURRENT ISSUES

The Formula

By 1979 the percentage of levies formula had been changed to aidable revenues, the per capita formula aid had been frozen for three years, hold-harmless payments were no longer fully funded, and general property tax relief growth had been stopped in favor of added direct sharing. These circumstances combined to increase rapidly the money to be distributed under the aidable revenues portion of the formula.

The move to aidable revenues and the consequent greater targeting to low tax base urban areas have not been greeted with enthusiasm by officials in many rural areas and suburbs. Table 1 shows why. Rural areas are largely unincorporated and the town is the primary unit of local government. Roughly 59 percent of Wisconsin citizens live in cities, 11 percent in villages, and 30 percent in towns. All three are mutually exclusive.

Towns received over $16 million, or 18.4 percent of the aid allocated in 1975 under the percentage of excess levies portion of the aid formula. They received just over $4 million in 1977 under the aidable revenues portion of the aid formula. The towns' 18.4 percent share had shrunk to 4.8 percent in 1977. The losses in total aids were largely offset by the various hold-harmless elements of the formula. It was originally the intent of the legislature to phase out the hold-harmless clauses, but it has renewed them several times.

Nevertheless, further equalization and aid to cities was recommended in January 1977, by the Commission on State-Local Relations and Financing Policy, empaneled by Gov. Patrick J. Lucey:

> The commission recommends that the shared tax program be revised to more nearly equalize disparities between municipalities in the relationship between their available revenue sources and their financial requirements. The shared tax formula should take into account the burden imposed upon central cities in providing services to commuters.[7]

Members of the Wisconsin legislature representing rural districts who were on the commission took exception to this policy statement. They filed a minority report concerning state-shared revenues which said:

> We do not believe it is equitable to the rural areas of the state that state-shared tax payments emphasize the aidable revenue portion of the formula to the detriment of the per capita payment portion. This, in essence, rewards big spenders and penalizes those municipalities which have been efficient or even frugal. . . .

---

[7]Wisconsin Commission on State-Local Relations and Financing Policy, *The Final Report of the Commission,* p. 19.

TABLE 1 "Percentage of Levies" and "Aidable Revenue" Aids (by type of recipient municipal government, 1975 and 1977)

	Percentage of Levies Aids 1975	Percent	Aidable Revenue Aids 1977	Percent
Cities	$62,704,644	71.2	$73,118,706	86.8
Villages	9,189,917	10.4	7,096,320	8.4
Towns	16,186,354	18.4	4,035,035	4.8
Total	88,080,915	100.0	84,250,061	100.0

SOURCE: Wisconsin Department of Revenue. Bureau of Local Fiscal Information and Analysis, *Taxes, Aids, and Shared Taxes in Wisconsin Municipalities, 1975, 1977* (Madison, Wis.: Department of Revenue, 1977, 1979), p. 103.

We hasten to add that many services in rural areas, e.g., sewage, water, and garbage, are handled by the individual and require little, if any, public expenditures. Nonetheless these persons are entitled to state-shared tax payments inasmuch as they are also a point source of the revenue collected by the state income and sales tax.

If the rural areas are to lose their per capita payments, at the very least those monies should go to expand substantially the homestead tax credit program rather than be consumed by those municipalities which benefit greatly from the aidable revenue portion of the formula.[8]

The change from the percentage of levies to the aidable revenue formula increased aids to urban areas at the expense of rural sectors partly because the aidable revenues for municipalities are based only on revenues raised locally by a municipal government and partly because rural property values rose faster than urban values between 1975 and 1977. The percentage of levies formula gave aids to municipalities based on total county, school, and municipal property tax levies. Since urban areas typically spend much more for municipal services than rural areas, but not much more or equal amounts on schools and county services, switching only to municipal revenues to determine aid acted to the disadvantage of rural areas.

The rural versus city debate illustrates the different aspects of need, and the difficulty associated with its definition. Although schools are aided separately from municipalities in Wisconsin, rural areas feel that school and overall property tax burdens from any given tax rate are more of a hardship than in urban areas. There is more hardship because of lower rural incomes and because the rapid increases in rural property values lowered their share of aid but did not provide increased ability to pay taxes. Urban areas, while acknowledging a relative shift in aid to their favor, could argue that their needs remained inadequately met. Table 2 shows that the average per capita amount of shared taxes from all formulas going to towns declined between 1971 and 1977 relative to the amount going to the city of Milwaukee.

[8]Ibid., p. MR–8.

TABLE 2 Average Shared Taxes Per Capita Indexed to Amount Received by Milwaukee, 1971 and 1977

	1971	As a Percentage of Milwaukee's Allocation	1977	As a Percentage of Milwaukee's Allocation
Milwaukee	$54.27	(100)	$72.19	(100)
Cities*	36.16	(67)	56.44	(78)
Villages	55.70	(103)	53.49	(74)
Towns	40.90	(75)	43.70	(61)
State	50.55	(93)	54.46	(75)

*Excludes Milwaukee.
SOURCE: ACIR staff calculation based on Wisconsin Revenue Department data.

Despite the increase that favored Milwaukee and other cities, the municipal property tax rate difference between urban and rural areas of the state continued between 1971 and 1977 (see Table 3).

One way of measuring the equalizing effect of state-shared revenues is to calculate how much property tax and shared revenues a municipality obtained per person, relative to its property tax effort. Municipalities can be compared by examining these ratios of revenue per person to mills of property tax rate. When this is done (as Table 4 shows), Milwaukee remains disadvantaged in 1977 as well as in 1971. While the relative advantage of towns declined between 1971 and 1977, towns still obtained over three times the tax and shared revenue per capita for each mill of tax effort than was obtained by Milwaukee. Put differently, Milwaukee's 1977 tax rate was nearly 12 times the average for towns, but it obtained less than four times as much revenue per person. The relative advantage of other areas over Milwaukee, and of towns and villages over cities, was still substantial in 1979, but the equalizing trend accelerated in the years 1977 to 1979.

The decision of the legislature to continue to increase the aidable revenues portion of the formula represented a commitment to decrease the difference in revenue raising ability among municipalities.

TABLE 3 Municipal Purpose Mill Rates,* 1971 and 1977

	Municipal Mill Rate Levy 1970 (payable 1971)	Municipal Mill Rate Levy 1976 (payable 1977)
Milwaukee	15.34	14.36
Cities†	7.21	8.48
Villages	4.00	5.14
Towns	1.44	1.19
State	6.34	6.11

*As equalized to adjust to varying levels of property assessments.
†Excludes Milwaukee.
SOURCE: ACIR staff calculations based on Wisconsin Revenue Department data.

TABLE 4 Equalization in Wisconsin, 1971, 1977, 1979

	Levy and Shared Taxes Per Capita Per Property Tax Mill	As a Percent of Milwaukee
1971 total:		
Milwaukee	$10.55	100
Cities*	15.44	146
Villages	22.22	211
Towns	36.61	347
Total state	15.85	150
1977 local:		
Milwaukee	$16.16	100
Cities*	19.78	122
Villages	24.04	149
Towns	54.37	336
Total state	23.14	143
1979 total:		
Milwaukee	$23.78	100
Cities*	28.12	118
Villages	31.84	134
Towns	62.49	263
Total state	32.90	138

---

*Excludes Milwaukee.
SOURCE: ACIR staff calculations based on Wisconsin Department of Revenue data.

In the future, the governor and legislature will be called upon to reconsider this policy in light of rural and suburban complaints that too many state tax dollars have to be taken from them in order to equalize the ability of higher spending cities to obtain local revenue. In 1979 new Governor Lee Sherman Dreyfuss called for a study by the Wisconsin Department of Revenue on the fairness of the aid formulas.

The Impact of Equalization on Industrial Location

The emphasis on equalization, which has characterized Wisconsin public finance not only for general-purpose local government finance but also for school finance, has raised an interesting issue: Does equalization, substantial or otherwise, mistreat communities with industrial property and cause communities not to accept or seek an industrial tax base? That is, are localities now so insulated from tax base changes that they can be indifferent or opposed to attracting new industry?

Wisconsin business groups and legislators from districts with high concentrations of industrial property gave the answer, yes. The 1979 legislature and governor agreed that action was necessary. Manufacturing property, which makes up 5 percent of the state's property tax base, was excluded from calculations of a community's tax capacity in the aidable revenues portion of the shared revenues formula. Roughly

250 communities with high concentrations of manufacturing property gained aid because of this change. The loss was spread among the remaining 1,600 localities, so the loss to any individual community was not significant.

The legislature had passed a bill excluding 50 percent of industrial valuation from the calculation of fiscal capacity, but the governor vetoed the 50 percent clause, thereby excluding all industrial valuation.

The Wisconsin Revenue Department Study

In 1978–79, the Wisconsin Department of Revenue studied the issue of equalization and industrial location and focused on two questions:

1. Are there local government costs associated with concentrated industrial development which are not recognized in the shared revenue formulas?
2. Does the existence of equalization formulas for school and local government aids cause communities not to seek or to oppose industrial development to the detriment of the economic health of the state?[9]

The aidable revenue portion of shared revenues formula is based on the principle that differences among local property tax rates should be a function of service levels, but not tax bases. What this system did not take into account, critics maintained, was that industrial properties cause a need for additional revenue to be raised per resident because of the cost of municipal services for industry. Further, it was contended that the burden was unfairly placed on the community's residents because the aid formula allows their tax rate to be higher, regardless of where the beneficiaries from industry live.

The revenue department found some empirical evidence to substantiate this claim. Using a multiple regression analysis, the department found that higher than average per capita local spending could be statistically explained in part by high industrial concentration when the latter was one independent variable in a statistical model with other explanatory factors such as total tax base wealth and intergovernmental aids. These other factors were included to control for the possibility that higher per capita spending in industrial communities was due to past fiscal advantages rather than industry per se. The revenue department's analysis further found that the aidable revenue portion of the formula could result in higher tax rates for industrial communities than for nonindustrial communities of similar per capita tax base. The additional aid that they would receive through the formula due to higher expenditure was more than offset by the aid they lost due to their having a higher tax base. This would be unfair if the residents of

[9]Wisconsin Department of Revenue, Division of Local Fiscal Analysis, internal department document, "Technical Supplement: Aidable Revenues Formula and Local Cost Impacts from Industry" (Madison, Wis.: March 25, 1978).

industrial communities did not themselves benefit substantially from industry-related government spending.

It is difficult to empirically determine the answer to the second issue—whether formula equalization discourages communities from accepting new manufacturing plants. Wisconsin and Minnesota have gone further than other states in equalization of local government finance. Even in these states, however, equalization is not dollar for dollar. Communities do not lose a dollar in aid for each dollar increase in potential tax revenue that comes from tax base growth. The move in Wisconsin from a pro-industrial area aid system to a partly equalizing aid system was also accompanied in 1974 by a property tax exemption for manufacturers' machinery and equipment and, in 1977, by legislation to also exempt inventories over a five-year period. The end result of the exemptions will be to eliminate nearly two thirds of taxable manufacturing property. Thus, the potential tax base gain from industrial development was considerably diluted over the 1970s. There are no documented cases, however, of a community planning to refuse future permission to industry to build because of a possible adverse effect on state aids.

This problem is in one sense ironic. The intent of state programs to equalize revenue raising abilities has been to create "tax base neutrality," i.e., to make tax rates less influenced by tax base, and to reduce the advantages that high tax base places had in attracting more tax base. As a result some Wisconsin officials now fear that if the local tax base is guaranteed, the willingness of communities to accept industrial development will substantially diminish.

Administration of Public Debt and Idle Fund Management

13

Debt Administration

Public debt, whether federal, state, or local, results when a government borrows money from an individual or institution with the promise of repayment at a later date. Borrowing changes the pattern of purchasing power between the lender and the borrower: the lender forgos purchasing power now for the promise of repayment later, the borrower receives purchasing power now and makes repayment later. The bond representing that debt simply is a long-term promise by the borrower (bond issuer) to the lender (bondholder) to pay the face amount of the bond at a defined maturity date. That contract specifies the interest the borrower will pay the lender for use of the money, typically with interest payment semiannually. This stated or nominal return on a bond is its coupon rate. Thus, a 9 percent coupon rate means that the bond pays $90 interest per $1,000 face value. The actual or current yield on a bond may well be substantially different from the coupon rate, because the current value of the bond itself may differ from the face value. The bond contract will, however, state a coupon rate and a face value to be redeemed at maturity.[1]

Government debt results (1) from the necessity to cover deficits (annual expenditures greater than annual revenues), (2) from the finance of capital project construction, and (3) from coverage of short periods within a fiscal year in which needed disbursements for payment of bills exceeds cash on hand. Governments borrow for different purposes, depending on the level of government. For that reason, those causes will be briefly considered before a more intense examination of debt policy and administration by state and local units.

---

[1]For a bond purchaser, the yield-to-maturity is the total annualized return earned on a bond if it is held to maturity. It includes both the coupon and any difference between the amount paid for the bond and its face received on redemption by the borrower.

TABLE 13-1 Ownership and Maturity of Public Debt of the United States Treasury (billions of current dollars, end of year)

	1939	1946	1960	1970	1975
Total gross public debt	$41.9	$259.1	$290.4	$389.4	$576.6
Held by U.S. government agencies and trust funds	6.1	27.4	55.1	97.1	139.1
Held by Federal Reserve Banks	2.5	23.4	27.4	62.1	89.8
Held by private investors	33.4	208.3	207.9	229.9	347.7
Held by foreign and international investors	0.2	2.1	13.0	20.6	66.5
Average maturity of market ability interest bearing (year/month)				3/8	2/8
Gross national product	90.9	209.8	506.5	992.7	1549.2

SOURCE: Federal Reserve Bulletin (several issues) and *Economic Report of the President,* February 1985. (1984 debt data for end of September and GNP preliminary.)

SOURCES OF PUBLIC DEBT

The federal government debt, compiled in Table 13–1, largely has been the product of war finance and of actions taken to stabilize the macroeconomy of the nation, that is, to deal with problems of unemployment and inflation. Greater deficits are presumed to stimulate the economy, with accompanying boosts to employment and production. The table shows that, over the years, the federal government has seen fit to increase its debt by sizable amounts. There is no meaningful linkage of borrowing to particular federal capital expenditure projects; the debt levels are the accumulated totals of deficit outcomes. This nonproject orientation is reflected in the shortness of maturity of federal debt: at the end of fiscal 1984, 43 percent of privately held federal debt matured within one year and average maturity was 4½ years. The debt is issued for cash, not for projects, and must be regularly refinanced at the same time new borrowing is done. Gross public debt grew at an annual rate of 10.5 percent from 1970–1984. That rate was slightly greater than growth in gross national product (9.8 percent), so the absolute claim from federal debt repayment in 1984 was somewhat greater than it was at the beginning of the 1970s.

Not all the federal debt is, however, a net requirement for resource transfer outside government. Sizable portions of that debt are held by federal agencies or federal trust funds (17 percent of gross debt in 1984) and by Federal Reserve Banks (10 percent in 1984). Trust funds and agencies acquire the debt in their cash management programs—what safer place to invest funds than in U.S. Treasury debt?—so this debt is not truly a net claim on federal government resources. Federal Reserve Banks buy and sell federal debt in the practice of monetary policy (transactions with the public and the commercial banking system to

1980	1981	1982	1983	1984	Compound Annual Growth Rate, 1970–84	Growth, 1983–84
$930.2	$1028.7	$1197.1	$1410.7	$1572.3	10.5%	11.5
92.5	203.3	209.4	236.3	263.1	7.4	11.3
121.3	131.0	139.3	151.9	155.0	6.8	2.0
616.4	694.5	848.4	1022.6	1154.1	12.2	12.9
134.3	136.6	149.5	166.3	175.5	16.5	5.5
3/9	4/0	3/11	4/1	4/6		
2631.7	2957.8	3069.3	3304.8	3661.3	9.8	10.8

change the supply of money in the economy). Because the Federal Reserve Banks legally must return to the U.S. Treasury sizable portions of interest received and because they are, at least loosely, government agencies, this debt likewise is not an outside claim on the government. For most analytic purposes, then, it is the debt held by private investors—that debt outside federal agencies, federal trust funds, and Federal Reserve Banks—that is the major concern for federal debt policy. From 1970 through 1984, debt held by investors did increase as a share of gross public debt (from 59 percent in 1970 to 73 percent in 1984), as agency and trust fund investments were less important (their investable balances were less, as most experienced overall cash outflows).

The amount of debt in private investor hands thus depends on accumulated federal deficits (gross public debt), monetary policy actions by the Federal Reserve, and investable cash balances of trust funds. Investor-held debt grew at a rate somewhat greater than did both gross debt and the economy in the 1970–84 period. Thus, the ratio of investor-held debt to gross national product grew to 32 percent in 1984 from its 1970 level of 23 percent. This increase in relative claim against production is remarkable for peacetime conditions. Probably more significant, however, is the remarkable growth of debt held by foreign and international investors; during the 14 years, ownership grew at a 16.5 percent annual rate, a dramatic increase in the extent to which federal debt holders are outside the United States economy.[2] Thus, repayment of that portion of federal debt and interest represents a transfer of resources outside the economy, and the federal debt can no longer be casually dismissed as a problem because "we owe it to ourselves." About

---

[2] The rate from 1970 to 1980 was 206 percent, so the rate has slowed substantially since 1980.

TABLE 13-2 Indebtedness of State and Local Government, by Type of Government: 1981–1982 (millions of dollars)

	State and Local Governments				Local Governments			
	Total	State Governments	Total	County	Municipal	Township	School District	Special District
Debt outstanding, total	$404,579	$147,470	$257,109	$44,671	$96,421	$5,568	$29,770	$78,680
Long-term	385,786	143,702	242,084	42,090	93,598	4,096	28,251	74,049
Full faith and credit	153,946	51,507	102,439	19,273	38,721	3,414	28,251	12,781
Nonguaranteed	231,840	92,195	139,645	22,818	54,878	682	—	61,268
Short-term	18,793	3,768	15,025	2,581	4,822	1,472	1,519	4,631
Net long-term debt outstanding	302,753	87,047	215,705	36,710	81,295	3,949	26,075	67,677
Debt outstanding, total	26.1%	9.5%	16.6%	2.9%	6.3%	0.4%	1.9%	5.1%
Long-term	100.0	37.2	62.8	10.9	24.3	1.1	7.3	19.2
Full faith and credit	100.0	33.5	66.5	12.5	25.2	2.2	18.4	8.3
Nonguaranteed	100.0	39.8	60.2	9.8	23.7	0.3	—	26.4
Short-term	100.0	20.1	79.9	13.7	25.7	7.8	8.1	24.6

Note: Because of rounding, detail may not add to totals.
SOURCE: 1982 Census of Governments (Compendium, p. 15).

15 percent of debt in private investor hands is owed, not to ourselves, but to foreign individuals and institutions. Servicing that debt transfers resources from American taxpayers to foreign bondholders, a condition with substantially different standard-of-living implications for the United States than the traditional situation of American taxpayers making payment to American bondholders.[3] Only 9 percent was in foreign hands in 1970. As long as foreign entities build up dollar reserves in international trade and world investors regard United States government debt as yielding a high rate of return without significant risk of the sort of political upheaval which leads to debt repudiation and seizure of foreign assets, such investment shall continue.

Debt of state and local governments has likewise grown rapidly since the early 1970s, from $175.2 billion in 1972 to $404.6 billion in 1982, an annual growth rate of 8.7 percent. If one considers only net long-term debt, thus subtracting cash and other assets held specifically for redemption of long-term debt (bond reserve funds, deposits with fiscal agents, balances in refunding bond accounts, etc.), the debt levels are $147.8 billion in 1972 and $302.8 billion in 1983, with a growth rate of 7.4 percent. This debt, the product of borrowing by states, counties, municipalities, townships, school districts, and special districts as shown in Table 13–2, is generically called municipal debt, distinguishing it from corporate or federal issues. The preponderance of this debt is long term (95 percent of the total). That differs radically from the condition with the federal debt and, furthermore, typically is issued for construction of identifiable, long-life assets, such as schools, highways, housing projects, and so on. The purposes are indicated in Table 13–3 on pages 436–37, which shows the heavy state-local debt emphasis on education and electric or gas utilities. Such an identification of purposes would, of course, not be possible for federal debt.

The state-local debt figures distinguish between full faith and credit debt and nonguaranteed, or limited-liability, debt. Full faith and credit obligations "have an unlimited claim"[4] on the taxes (and other revenues) of the issuing unit; nonguaranteed debt issues lack that assurance and are sold on the basis of repayment from revenue proceeds from particular sources. Types of nonguaranteed debt include:

1. Revenue bonds; revenue from the project financed (toll bridge, water plant, etc.) redeem the debt.

---

[3] A compilation of foreign-held debt (November 30, 1978) shows it heavily concentrated in Germany (36 percent), Japan (22 percent), and Switzerland (9 percent). Further, it is heavily concentrated in the under one-year maturity structure: 66 percent of the total holdings mature in less than a year.

[4] Roland I. Robinson, "Debt Administration," in *Management Policies in Local Government Finance*, eds. J. Richard Aronson and Eli Schwartz [Washington, D.C.: International City Management Association (ICMA), 1975], p. 231.

TABLE 13-3 Long-Term Debt of State and Local Governments Outstanding at End of Fiscal Year, by Purpose, 1981–1982

Function	State and Local Governments	State Governments	Local Governments					
			Total	County	Municipal	Township	District	Special district
			Amount ($ millions)					
Long-term debt outstanding total	385,796	143,702	242,084	42,090	93,598	4,096	25,251	74,049
By purpose:								
Education	62,052	24,057	37,995	2,697	3,136	718	28,251	3,194
Higher education	19,867	18,229	1,638	205	26	—	1,407	—
Elementary and secondary education	39,806	3,827	35,981	2,291	3,018	718	26,844	3,111
Other education	2,378	2,001	376	201	93	—	—	83
Hospitals	15,350	9,269	6,082	921	684	—	—	4,477
Highways	17,291	14,645	2,646	747	1,609	—	—	291
Toll highway facilities	5,446	5,446	—	—	—	—	—	—
Other highways	11,845	9,199	2,646	747	1,609	—	—	291
Air transportation	5,763	346	5,418	733	3,016	—	—	1,669
Water transportation and terminals	2,659	676	1,983	183	623	—	—	1,177
Parks and recreation	3,684	1,621	2,063	520	911	—	—	632
Housing and community development	20,941	9,204	11,737	136	4,309	—	—	7,293
Sewerage	11,151	2,176	8,975	1,323	3,354	—	—	4,298
Utilities	68,125	5,508	62,617	2,539	25,637	467	—	33,975
Water supply	23,810	400	23,410	2,424	13,623	430	—	6,933
Electric power	39,048	5,105	33,943	45	10,058	37	—	23,803
Gas supply	688	—	688	3	488	—	—	197
Transit	4,579	3	4,575	66	1,468	—	—	3,041
Other and unallocable	178,770	76,202	102,568	32,292	50,320	2,910	—	17,045

Percent Distribution by Purpose of Debt

Long-term outstanding, total	100.0	100.0	100.0	100.0	100.0	100.0	100.0	100.0
By purpose:								
Education	16.1	16.7	15.7	6.4	3.4	17.5	100.0	4.3
Higher education	5.1	12.7	0.7	0.5	—	—	5.0	—
Elementary and secondary education	10.3	2.7	14.9	5.4	3.2	17.5	95.0	4.2
Other education	0.6	1.4	0.2	0.5	0.1	—	—	0.1
Hospitals	4.0	6.5	2.5	2.2	0.7	—	—	6.0
Highways	4.5	10.2	1.1	1.8	1.7	—	—	0.4
Toll highway facilities	1.4	3.8	—	—	—	—	—	—
Other highways	3.1	6.4	1.1	1.8	1.7	—	—	0.4
Air transportation	1.5	0.2	2.2	1.7	3.2	—	—	2.3
Water transportation and terminals	0.7	0.5	0.8	0.4	0.7	—	—	1.6
Parks and recreation	1.0	1.1	0.9	1.2	1.0	—	—	0.9
Housing and community development	5.4	6.4	4.8	0.3	4.6	—	—	9.8
Sewerage	2.9	1.5	3.7	3.1	3.6	—	—	5.8
Utilities	17.7	3.8	25.9	6.0	27.4	11.4	—	45.9
Water supply	6.2	0.3	9.7	5.8	14.6	10.5	—	9.4
Electric power	10.1	3.6	14.0	0.1	10.7	0.9	—	32.1
Gas supply	0.2	—	0.3	—	0.5	—	—	0.3
Transit	1.2	—	1.9	0.2	1.6	—	—	4.1
Other and unallocable	46.3	53.0	42.4	76.7	53.8	71.1	—	23.0

SOURCE: *1982 Census of Governments, vol. 4 Government Finances, number 5, Compendium of Government Finances* (GC82(4)-5), (Washington, D.C.: U.S. Government Printing Office, 1984), p. 6.

2. Lease-rental bonds: facilities (office buildings, computer equipment, etc.) constructed from the debt proceeds are leased to a government at a rent sufficient to cover debt service and operating cost.

3. Lease-purchase bonds: public works (school, hospital, etc.) constructed by a private firm from debt proceeds are leased to a government (the government receives title to the property when the debt is retired).

4. Industrial development and pollution control bonds: private facilities—ultimately owned by their user—are constructed by the municipal debt with rental payments by the users servicing the debt.

5. Special revenue bonds: projects financed by bonds services from special revenues (parking garages financed by a special property tax on downtown property or sidewalks financed by a special assessment on property owners in the affected area).

6. Tax increment bonds: bonds financing area redevelopment which are serviced from the additional taxes generated in the redeveloped region.[5]

Because purchasers of public debt (the individuals and institutions lending the money to state-local governments) regard the claim on all tax resources as offering greater likelihood that bond principal and interest payments will be made on time, full faith and credit debt bears a lower interest rate than does equivalent nonguaranteed debt. (Later sections will suggest why many governments use nonguaranteed debt, in spite of its greater cost.) Long-term state government debt is almost two-thirds nonguaranteed; long-term local government debt is more heavily full faith and credit. Short-term debt at both levels is almost completely full faith and credit.

Nonguaranteed debt is outside limits frequently placed on municipal government debt by state statute or constitution. Interest on such debt is, however, granted the same exclusion from federal taxation received by municipal debt. That creates a logical inconsistency:

> In order to invoke tax immunity, the agency which issues those bonds must show that they are the obligations of a state or subdivision; but in order to provide that they are revenue bonds and not subject to the usual debt limitations it must show that they are not the obligations of any such unit.[6]

Creating and defending the appropriate distinctions is the source of substantial income for bond counsel. The convenience of having the debt interpreted both ways is usually worth the price. Much revenue

---

[5]Mortgage revenue bonds (state and local borrowing to obtain funds for home mortgage lending at low rates) were prohibited after 1983.

[6]B. U. Ratchford, "Revenue Bonds and Tax Immunity," *National Tax Journal* 7 (March 1954), p. 42.

bond debt is issued by public authorities, entities with public powers outside normal constraints placed on government. Governments form authorities to build a public project (bridges, power projects, highways, etc.) and pay off bonds used to finance the construction with tolls from users. The authority may or may not go out of existence when the bonds are retired.[7]

Table 13–3 provides extensive detail on the nature of local government debt. Of particular importance are the following features. First, municipalities are the largest local user of debt markets. Second, special districts are the heaviest users of nonguaranteed debt. This is not surprising because many special districts (waste management, transit, water, etc.) are established on a semicommercial basis, that is, they are financed by user charges and lack taxing power. Thus, they have revenue generated by capital projects and lack the tax base for guarantee. And third, school districts are heavy users of full faith and credit debt, with no nonguaranteed debt, according to the Census Bureau classification. School districts traditionally have not been operated from user charges, so they have no project revenue available to support borrowing. Tax and intergovernmental aid revenue are the sole sources for repayment, so full faith and credit issues are the fiscal devices used by schools. They do, however, establish separate building corporations that issue debt to finance construction with repayment guaranteed by leases charged a school district. For purposes of avoiding debt limits, these issues may be considered revenue bonds of the building corporation.

Table 13–4 on page 400 identifies the pattern of state-local debt growth since 1960. While all sectors of debt have risen substantially, local nonguaranteed debt shows the greatest increase in relative terms, from 31 percent of the local total to 57 percent. This shift emerges largely from a desire to avoid the legal restrictions placed on full faith and credit issues. The trend is troubling for larger cities: "The economic advantage of cities lies in making the marginal maintenance and repair expenditures that can keep the basic elements of their present infrastructure in adequate working order.[8] Nonguaranteed bonds are not easily adapted to generate financing for reconstruction or maintenance, so the shift indicates special problems to confront those cities. If the infrastructure (streets, water and sewage systems, etc.) is not maintained, the economic advantage of new cities becomes overwhelming. Debt is not, however, the complete answer to public infrastructure deterioration: much work or maintenance is recurring and belongs as part of operating financing.

---

[7]For a fascinating view of public authority operation, see Robert Caro, *The Power Broker: Robert Moses and the Fall of New York* (New York: Vintage Books, 1975), chap. 28.

[8]George E. Peterson, "Capital Spending and Capital Obsolescence—The Outlook for Cities," in *The Fiscal Outlook for Cities*, ed. Roy Bahl (Syracuse, N.Y.: Syracuse University Press, 1978), p. 49.

TABLE 13-4 State and Local Debt Outstanding, by Character of Debt ($ millions)

Year	State Governments				Local Governments			
	Full Faith and Credit	Nonguaranteed	Short Term	Net Long Term	Full Faith and Credit	Nonguaranteed	Short Term	Net Long Term
1960	8,912	9,216	415	15,595	32,738	15,935	2,739	46,001
1965	11,819	14,415	800	22,504	44,598	23,371	4,509	63,438
1970	17,736	21,167	3,104	34,479	57,601	34,911	9,051	87,255
1975	33,736	33,812	4,580	58,388	81,836	52,054	15,206	124,962
1977	42,913	44,271	3,016	67,583	94,837	62,126	10,369	144,750
1979	48,286	61,164	2,291	81,238	97,100	85,753	9,510	167,298
1981	52,582	79,940	2,325	81,538	99,168	116,639	13,237	192,278
1983	55,078	109,617	2,595	94,779	108,043	163,208	15,959	239,178

SOURCE: U.S. Bureau of Census, *Governmental Finances* (various years).

APPROPRIATE DEBT POLICY

Debt yields resources for public use now to be repaid (with interest) in the future. Borrowing thus commits future budgets. Because of the contractual rigidity, debt must be issued with care: improper use can disrupt lives of those paying taxes and expecting services in the future as debt service costs can impair the ability of the borrower to operate normally. The fundamental rule of debt construction is: do not issue debt for a maturity longer than useful life of the project it is financing. If the debt life exceeds useful life, the true annual cost of the project has been understated and people will continue to pay for the project after the project is gone. If the useful life exceeds the debt period, the annual cost has been overstated and people will receive benefits in periods in which no payment is made. The timing of payment question is particularly significant across generations and, at the local level, across a citizenry which is frequently changing.[9]

Long-term borrowing is appropriately done for long-life capital facilities. Economic growth does require expanded public capital infrastructure, often before any associated expansion of public revenue, so a strong case can be made for use of debt: the future revenue stream will be adequate to service debt expansion, to borrow a concept from corporation finance. Some governments have, however, elected to employ "pay-as-you-go financing," paying for capital facilities only from current-year operating surpluses. Such a policy can produce both inefficiency and inequity. First, with population mobility, users would not pay an appropriate charge for those facilities. Those in taxing range would pay when the facility is built; they may not be there when the facility for which they have paid is actually providing services. Second, the high single-year ticket price of a major project may discourage construction, even when the project is sound and feasible. Finally, pay-as-you-go financing can produce substantial tax-rate instability, with artificially high rates during the construction phase and artificially low rates during operation. Such instability is unlikely to be helpful in development of the local economy. Furthermore, debt finance produces annual debt service charges which are fixed by contract. Therefore, when the area tax base grows, the property tax rate for debt service for a project will decline over time.

Debt commits resources for extended periods and can be misused by public officials who seek to postpone the time when costs of public actions are felt. Potential for misuse, however, does not preclude debt finance. When properly handled, debt is an appropriate financing medium.

---

[9]Temporary cash needs should be covered by short-term borrowing liquidated within the fiscal year. Carrying short-term cash borrowing across a fiscal year (rolling over) would violate the fundamental principle.

In fact, strict "pay as you go" can be as unsound as careless use of debt. Both financing methods can be appropriate tools in the fiscal arsenal.

THE MECHANICS OF BOND VALUES

Bond markets involve exchanges in which a lender exchanges payment to a borrower now for the contractual promise of repayment at a later date plus interest. Most bond calculations thus employ the time value of money, compounding, and discounting techniques discussed in Chapter 5. Recall that

$$FV_n = PV(1 + r)^n$$

and

$$PV = FV_n \frac{1}{(1 + r)^n}$$

where FV_n = a value received in the future, PV = a value received now, r = the market rate of interest, and n = the number of years.

The current price of a bond equals the present value of cash flows to which the bondholder is entitled (return of principle plus interest). Therefore,

$$P = \sum_{i=1}^{m} \frac{F \times C}{(1 + r)^i} + \frac{F}{(1 + r)^m}$$

where P = the market value or current price of the bond, m = the number of years in the future until maturity of the bond, F = the face value of the bond, C = the coupon rate of the bond, and r = the market interest rate available on bonds of similar risk and maturity. (Note that for a bond with semiannual interest payment, m would be doubled while r and c would be halved). The first term of the formula requires computing the present value of a constant stream of returns in the future, so the annuity value formula (Ch. 5) provides a quick method of valuation.

To illustrate, suppose a Stinesville Water Utility bond matures in 15 years, pays an 8 percent coupon semiannually, and has a face value of $5,000. The market rate currently available on comparable bonds is 6 percent. The holder receives an interest payment of $(F \times C)/2$ or $200 each six months for 30 periods $(m \times 2)$. At the end of those 30 periods, the holder will receive back the $5,000. The bond price emerges from the formula:

$$P = \sum_{i=1}^{m} \frac{(F \times C)/2}{(1 + r)^i} + \frac{F}{(1 + r)^m} = \sum_{i=1}^{30} \frac{200}{(1 + 0.03)^i} + \frac{5,000}{(1 + 0.03)^{30}}$$

$$= 3,920 + 2,060 = \$5,980$$

It is obvious that the value of a bond can change, causing capital gain or loss for its holder, as market interest rates vary. The value of the

Stinesville bond, will be higher than computed here if the market rate is less than 6 percent and lower if the market rate is above 6 percent. The change would not affect an individual holding the bond to maturity, but would change the return for anyone selling it early.

DEBT STRUCTURE AND DESIGN

After the decision to finance a project by borrowing has been made, a number of debt structure decisions remain. They will be considered here, along with some institutional detail about municipal bond markets. Characteristics should ideally be designed to assure least-cost marketability of the issue, to simplify debt management, and to provide appropriate cost signals to fiscal decision makers.

One initial decision involves the type of security and its term to maturity (i.e., the period for which the money will be borrowed). Markets respond differently to full faith and credit bonds as opposed to revenue bonds. The greater security behind the former debt typically will cause a lower interest rate to be paid on an offering of that type, compared to a generally equivalent revenue issue. The latter form of debt may be desired, however, because of legal restrictions placed on full faith and credit debt[10] or because revenue debt is appropriate as a means for allocating costs to the users of a project. For instance, a city may enter capital markets to obtain funds for pollution control equipment for a private electric utility. There can be no logic to full faith and credit finance here: charges paid by the utility should be the sole service source.

Maturity of the debt should roughly coincide with project life to ensure that the project will be paid for and the debt liquidated before replacement or major repair is required. This maturity-matching principle both prevents debt finance of operating expenditures and permits those financing an improvement to receive benefits from that improvement. Debt service costs along the life of the project roughly represent a rental (or depreciation) charge for the facility: users pay charges or taxes to cover those annual costs. The total charge can thus more accurately reflect annual cost of the service, including both capital and operating costs.

A given bond issue with 30 years overall maturity, for example, can be of either **term** or **serial** nature. A term issue would have all bonds in the issue timed to mature at the end of 30 years. Funds to repay principal

---

[10]Full faith and credit debt may be limited to a maximum total amount, to a maximum percentage of the tax base (usually assessed value), or by a requirement that voters approve the debt at a referendum. Reserve bond debt generally escapes all these limits. Limits are reported by state in tables 61–63 of Advisory Commission on Intergovernmental Relations, *Significant Features of Fiscal Federalism*, 1976–77, vol. 2, *Revenue and Debt* (Washington, D.C.: ACIR, 1977).

would be obtained through the life of the bond issue (along with interest charges along the way) and placed into a sinking fund maintained by the bond issuer. At maturity of the issue, sinking fund accumulations would be sufficient to repay the principal. A serial issue contains multiple maturities in a single issue. Thus, some bonds would be for a 30-year term, some for a 20-year term, and so on. (Issuers often seek to maintain constant total annual debt service—interest plus retirement of maturing bonds—through the length of an issue by gradually increasing the volume of bonds maturing through the life of the issue.) Portions of the project cost would be paid through the overall term of the issue. The serial issue may improve marketability of many municipal issues. Thin secondary markets for municipal debt cause most purchasers of that debt to hold the bond to maturity.[11] With serial issues, the issuing government can sell its debt to purchasers with funds available for several different periods of time. Either term bonds with sinking funds or serial bonds spread the financing of the project over the life of the project and provide financing on a "pay as you use" basis.[12]

Maturity of the debt will play an important role in determining what the ultimate interest cost of the issue will be because there is a relationship between the term to maturity of debt and the interest rate required. This relationship, the "term structure of interest rates," is influenced by economic conditions at the time of borrowing and will often, but not always, be upward sloping. That is, the longer the term to maturity, the higher the interest rate required to borrow for that period of time. Figure 13-1 illustrates the term structure prevailing at the end of 1984. The maturity-matching principle dictates, however, that maturities not be shortened to reduce the overall interest rate paid.

Municipalities can protect themselves from the high cost of borrowing for extremely long periods at a time when interest rates are high. A call provision in a debt issue allows the borrower to repay debt before the normal maturity. The borrower usually refunds the debt, or borrows to cover the repayment, at lower interest rates. If interest rates fall sufficiently before the first call date, the municipality may use advance refunding—borrowing at the lower interest rate and using the proceeds to cover debt service until the call date allows the initial issue to be entirely replaced. Of course, possibility of call reduces the attractiveness of an issue to lenders, so issues with such a provision must compensate the investor (a call premium above face value) to permit marketability of the original issue.

---

[11]Corporate bond purchasers can purchase a bond with reasonable assurance that the bond can be sold to another person if funds are needed prior to maturity: a strong secondary market exists. Thus, these bonds will ordinarily not be serial.

[12] "Pay as you go" would have current payment for purchases with no debt. Payment occurs as facilities are acquired, not as they are used.

FIGURE 13-1 The Term Structure of Interest Rates: Yields of Treasury Securities, December 31, 1984 (based on closing bid quotations)

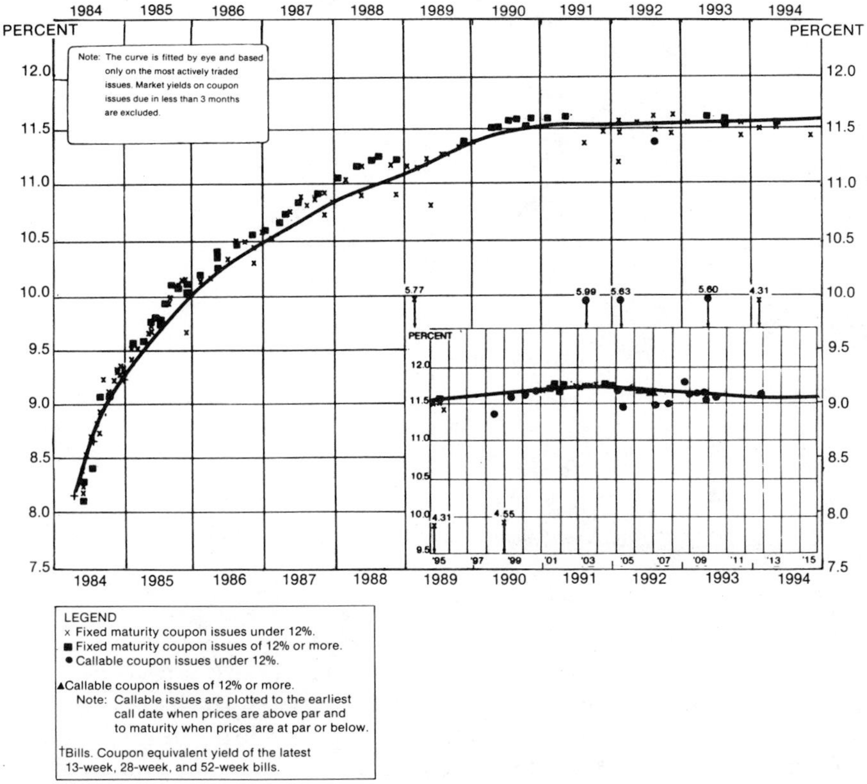

SOURCE: *Treasury Bulletin.*

RATINGS

The extent of risk to lender attached to a particular bond issue will be critical in determining the interest rate paid by the borrowing government. Creditworthiness opinions in the municipal market are prepared by three firms: Moody's Investors Service (a division of Dun and Bradstreet, Inc.), Standard & Poor's (a subsidiary of McGraw-Hill, Inc.), and Fitch Investors Service.[13] The first two are more widely used than the third and Moody's has been doing municipal ratings longer than has Standard & Poor's. These agencies, for a fee paid by the bond

[13]The Securities and Exchange Commission identifies these firms as those whose ratings will be used in valuing bond assets of SEC registered brokers and dealers. Two other identified rating firms, Duff and Phelps and McCarthy Crisanti and Maffei, do not presently rate in the municipal market. Luis Ubinas, "Small Bond Rating Firms Are Competing Aggressively for a Bigger Share of Market," *The Wall Street Journal* (September 10, 1984).

TABLE 13-5 Yield by Moody's Municipal Rating Group, 1940–1982 (end of year)

	Aaa	Aa	A	Baa
1940	1.56	1.78	2.11	2.60
1945	1.11	1.27	1.62	1.91
1950	1.42	1.60	1.92	2.17
1955	2.29	2.46	2.81	3.25
1960	3.12	3.35	3.60	4.03
1965	3.39	3.47	3.60	3.78
1970	5.21	5.33	5.60	5.80
1972	4.91	5.04	5.19	5.39
1974	6.65	6.81	7.14	7.50
1975	6.50	6.94	7.78	7.96
1976	5.07	5.50	6.42	6.73
1977	5.07	5.23	5.46	5.79
1978	5.91	6.01	6.51	6.76
1979	6.50	6.69	6.89	7.42
1980	9.44	9.64	9.80	10.64
1981	11.70	12.16	12.60	13.30
1982	9.34	9.85	10.24	10.80
1983	9.34	9.58	10.08	10.29
1984	9.54	9.88	10.19	10.45

SOURCE: Moody's Investors Service, *Moody's Municipal and Government Manual.*

issuer, prepare an opinion of the credit quality of the borrower (for full faith and credit issues) or of the particular bond issue (for revenue bond debt). These rating opinions are widely distributed to the investment community and are nationally used to form portfolio strategy. An issue without a rating will seldom sell on national markets, but issues can be unrated if local markets will buy them. These ratings have a major influence on borrowing cost, as Table 13–5 shows. Notice that about a full percentage point separates highest grade (Aaa) and lower investment grade (Baa). Grades lower than investment grade fare less well because many financial institutions are forbidden to hold lower-rated securities with a speculative aspect to them. Table 13–6 relates the ratings of the two major services and suggests the general risk factors associated with each rating.

The precise manner in which borrowing-unit characteristics contribute to a rating is not estimable. However, Moody's Investors Service reports that the following information is used in a full faith and credit rating:

1. Debt policy: the uses, purposes, and planning of debt issuance, as well as the type instruments used.
2. Debt structure: adequacy of plans for debt retirement—the relation between rate of retirement and purpose of debt, resources of the community, and existing and future debt needs.

TABLE 13-6 Credit Ratings by Moody's and Standard & Poor's

Moody's Investors Service	Symbol	Symbol	Standard & Poor's Corporation
Best quality, smallest degree of investment risk; referred to as "gilt edge."	Aaa	AAA	Prime: obligation of highest quality and lowest probability of default; quality management and low-debt structure.
High quality; smaller margin of protection or larger fluctuation of protective elements than Aaa.	Aa	AA	Higher grade: only slightly more secure than prime; second lowest probability of default.
Upper medium grade, many favorable investment attributes; some susceptibility to future risk evident	A	A	Upper medium grade: safe investment; weakness in local economic base, debt burden, or fiscal balance.
Medium grade: neither highly protected nor poorly secured; adequate present security but may be unreliable over any great length of time.	Baa	BBB	Medium grade: lowest investment security rating; may show more than one fundamental weakness; higher default probability.
Judged to have speculative elements; not well safeguarded; very moderate protection of principal and interest, over both good and bad times.	Ba	BB	Lower medium grade; speculative noninvestment grade obligation; relatively low risk and uncertainty.
Lack characteristics of desirable investment.	B	B	Low grade; investment characteristics virtually nonexistent.
Poor standing; may be in default.	Caa	CCC	
Speculative in high degree; default or other marked shortcomings.	Ca	CC	Defaults.
Lowest rated class; extremely poor prospects of ever attaining any real investment standing.	C	C	

Note: Moody's designates with 1 those bonds in Aa, A, Baa, Ba, and B groups with the strongest investment attributes, i.e., Aa1. A plus or a minus attached to a S&P rating indicates upper or lower segment of the rating category. Moody's Con. (−) indicates security depends on completion of some act or fulfillment of some condition; rating in parenthesis notes probable statute when condition fulfilled.

3. Debt burden: gross and net debt related to resources and a comparison with other communities—overlapping debt and pyramiding.
4. Debt history and trend: the record as to defaults, refunding of maturing bonds, and funding of operating deficits—rapidity of debt growth relative to purposes for which it has been incurred.

5. Prospective borrowing: authorized and uninsured bonds—adequacy of capital programming—obsolescence or inadequacy of capital plant—existing debt structure.

Financial analysis:

6. The current account: the year-end relation of current liabilities to available cash—promptness in disposing of casual deficits—devices to keep deficits from accumulating—if accounting is revenue accrual, the adequacy of reserves for uncollectible accounts—the liquidity of current account cash and uncollected taxes should equal demand liabilities outstanding.
7. Revenue system: adequacy of property tax base—trend of assessed value, equalization ratio, levy, and collections—other components of revenue system—source, base rates, yields—diversity, cyclical stability and adequacy of aid from other governments.
8. Expenditure analysis: vulnerability to mandated expenditures—relation of debt service to total expenditures.
9. Budget analysis: adequacy of planning—appraisal of past performance on revenue and expenditure estimates—current trend of financial operations.
10. Financial administration: assessment practices—tax collection procedures—financial planning as evidenced by budgeting, reporting, services.
11. History of financial operations: long-term trend of revenues, and expenditures—secular and cyclical patterns.

Government:

12. Organization: diffusion of responsibility—degree of professionalism—sufficiency of powers to discharge functions.
13. Services: provision for essential services to perpetuate economic base.
14. Intergovernmental factors: the pyramid of governmental units, conflicts, and duplications—complementarity—other units which drain off resources or impede planning.
15. Administrative performance: conscientious administrators who promote confidence through standing and experience—availability of audits, budgets, annual reports, capital planning documents, land-use plan.

Economic:

16. Identity and natural resources: geographic and locational advantages—natural catastrophe—natural resources—size and land-use characteristics.

17. Population, wealth, and labor factor: population characteristics—wealth level (family income and per capita full value)—housing characteristics—new construction values.
18. Economic structure and capital: types of employment industry and occupation—major employers—relation to SMSA (Standard Metropolitan Statistical Area)—evidences of industrial decline or population shifts—transportation and its relation to the economic structure.
19. Economic performance and prospects: the secular trends of the economy—cyclical trend—seasonal and random variations.[14]

No explicit formula produces the ratings: they are proprietary house opinions based on forecasts of the borrower's ability and willingness to repay the debt as shaped by the economic, financial, and governmental environment. Accumulations of report summaries are published annually as a guide to investors. Figure 13–2 illustrates with the Moody's report for Big Rapids, Michigan.

Revenue bonds analysis is primarily concerned with the revenue potential of the enterprise and legal protection of bondholders in the covenants in the bond resolution. There is little concern with the government, as there is no precedent requiring bailout of revenue bonds. For instance, in two well-publicized incidents, neither the city of Chicago nor the state of West Virginia prevented default of associated revenue bond issues (Chicago Skyway and West Virginia Turnpike). No government has intervened to assist the Washington Public Power Supply System in its major default, either. Thus, revenue bond analysis presumes the project must stand on its financial merits.

The impact of ratings on borrowing cost for an issuer has been altered recently with the development of third-party guarantees of debt service for new municipal bond issues. These guarantees reduce the risk associated with the bond, enabling the borrower to issue at a lower interest rate. Three such guarantees should be noted: (1) state credit guarantees, (2) bank letters of credit, and (3) municipal bond insurance. Each has the effect of transferring the credit strength of the guaranteeing entity to the borrower to one extent or another and each will be considered in turn.

The state credit guarantees are on "explicit promise by the state to a local unit bondholder that any shortfall in local resources will automatically be assumed by the state. In its strongest form, a state guarantee places the full faith and credit of the state behind the contingent

---

[14]Moody's Investors Service, Inc. *Pitfalls in Issuing Municipal Bonds* (New York: Moody's, 1977), pp. 14–15.

FIGURE 13-2 Illustration of Moody's Credit Report: Big Rapids, Michigan

BIG RAPIDS

County seat of Mecosta County. Area, 5¾ sq. miles.

Population: 1980, 14,361; 1970, 11,995.

Assessed Value, etc. (State equalized) ($000):

Year	All Property	– Tax per $1,000 – City	Total
1983	65,784	5.10	46.99
1982	58,307	5.10	47.87
1981	54,091	5.10	46.70

Bonded Debt, June 30, 1984: General, $4,040,000; water revenue, $80,000; sewer revenue, $323,000; hospital revenue, $435,000.

Tax Collections, years ended June 30 ($000):

Year	Taxes Levied	–Current Collect– (Amt.)	%
1983	547	497	90.9
1982	528	457	86.6
1981	424	389	91.7

Schedule of Bonded Debt, June 30, 1984:

①Water Revenue

5s	'59B	③Ser. to 10-	1-86	A & O1a	$45,000
4⅛s	'61C	③Ser. to 10-	1-90	A & O1a	35,000

④Sewer Revenue

3¼s	'55	⑤Ser. to 10-	1-87	A & O1a	78,000
5s	'67	⑥Ser. to 10-	1-95	A & O1a	245,000

Water

4½s	'68	⑩Ser. to 10-	1-84	A & O1e	35,000
5s	'68	⑩Ser. 10-	1-85-91	A & O1e	290,000
5.05s	'68	⑩Ser. 10-	1-92-93	A & O1e	120,000
5.10s	'68	⑩Ser. 10-	1-94-96	A & O1e	180,000
5⅛s	'68	⑩Ser. 10-	1-97-00	A & O1e	240,000
⑦..	'81	Ser. to 10-	1-04	A & O1	2,725,000

G.O. Wastewater Treatment System

⑪..	'76	Ser. to 10-	1-93	A & O1	450,000

Hospital Revenue

⑧..	'66	Ser. to 10-	1-06	A & O1	435,000

①Payable solely from net revenues of water system.

③Callable inversely at 105 through Apr. 1, 1972; decreasing premiums thereafter.

④Payable solely from net revenues of sewer system.

⑤Callable inversely at 100.

⑥Callable inversely beginning Oct. 1, 1982 through Apr. 1: 1985, 104; 1988, 103; 1992, 102; thereafter, 101.

⑦Bonds are dated Jan. 1, 1981. Interest payable as follows:

Year	%	Year	%	Year	%
1983-91	13.00	1992	12.75	1993-97	11.00
1998-99	11.10	2000-01	11.20	2002-04	11.25

Insured as to principal and interest by Municipal Bond Insurance Association.

⑧Callable inversely on any interest payment date beginning Oct. 1, 1976 at par plus accrued interest.

⑩Callable inversely beginning Oct. 1, 1983, prior to Oct. 1: 1986, 103; 1989, 102½; 1992, 102; 1995, 101½; 1998, 101; thereafter, 100.

⑪Interest payable as follows:

Year	%	Year	%	Year	%
1978-82	6.25	1983	5.70	1984	5.00
1985	5.20	1986	5.30	1987	5.50
1988	5.60	1989	5.75	1990	5.90
1991	6.00	1992	6.10	1993	6.25

Callable in inverse numerical order beginning Oct. 1, 1985 at 102 prior to Oct. 1, 1989 and 101 thereafter.

RATING: General obligations ....**A**
Bonds dated 1-1-81 (MBIA).....**Aaa**

Interest Paid: As follows:
a Comerica Bank-Detroit, Detroit.
e National Bank, Detroit or Citizens Commercial & Savings Bank, Flint.
Other paying agents not reported.

SOURCE: *Moody's Municipal and Government Manual, 1985,* vol. 1, p. 2059–60.

call on state funds."[15] The guarantees may take the form of a state insurance fund into which local issuers make premium payments; the program may guarantee only portions of debt service; the guarantee may not automatically pledge the full faith and credit of the state; or there may be other conditions placed on the backing. In the final analysis, the guarantee can hardly be stronger than the finances of the state itself. That fact, plus the many different shades of the guarantee, make generalizations about this form of third-party credit strengthening particularly hazardous.

A second form of guarantee is the bank letter of credit (LOC), "an unconditional pledge of the bank's credit to make principal and interest payments of a specified amount and term on an issuer's debt. The LOC may be valid even in cases of issuer default, in effect acting as a guarantee of the debt."[16] The LOC may provide a source of liquidity to the municipality, but it can also provide the municipality with the creditworthiness of the bank issuing the LOC. Thus, if the bank has the AAA rating, the LOC held by a municipality with a much lower rating would normally allow the municipality the benefits of that higher rating. The fee for the LOC typically is charged annually, not at the time of initial issue, as is characteristic of bond insurance.[17]

The third bond guarantee is municipal bond insurance. This insurance purchased by the bond issuer guarantees timely payment of principal and interest on that issue. Thus a low-rated issue with insurance can sell at roughly the same interest rate as a higher-quality issue because the insurer adds its resources as pledge to payment of debt service on the issue. Purchase of insurance by a municipal buyer is advisable when the premium paid for insurance at time of issue is less than the discounted interest savings resulting from the greater market acceptance of the insured issue. Not all issues can be insured and not all issues can profit from insurance, but insurance is a growing phenomenon.[18]

There are several insurance programs, with some of the better known shown in Table 13–7 on page 452. The first program, MBIA, started in 1974. Around 3 percent of term issues were insured in 1980;

---

[15]Ronald W. Forbes and John E. Petersen, "State Credit Assistance to Local Governments," in John E. Petersen and Wesley C. Hough, *Creative Capital Financing for State and Local Governments* (Chicago: Municipal Finance Officers Association, 1983), p. 226.

[16]Ibid., p. 22.

[17]The status of LOC backing is currently unclear. The combination of congressional action, a court ruling, and an Internal Revenue Service news release create the possibility that bonds backed by letters of credit from banks insured by the Federal Deposit Insurance Corporation would lose their tax exemption status. The result was not intended and probably will be corrected. Ann Monroe, "Some Bonds Backed by Letters of Credit In Danger of Losing Tax-Exempt Status," *The Wall Street Journal*, June 19, 1985.

[18]Insurance may also be purchased by a bondholder to guarantee scheduled payments on his bond portfolio. That is, however, not the concern of an issuing municipality.

TABLE 13-7 Features of Selected Municipal Bond Insurance Programs (new issue), Summer 1985

Program	Owners/Members	Quality Limitations	Cost of Guaranty* (time of issue)
Municipal Bond Insurance Association (MBIA)	Aetna Casualty & Surety (33%), Fireman's Fund Insurance (30%), Travelers Indemnity (15%), Aetna Insurance (12%), and Continental Insurance (10%).	S&P BBB, Moody Baa, or better.	0.65% to 1% of total principal and interest.
AMBAC Indemnity Corporation†	Citibank N.A., Xerox Financial Services, Stephens, Inc., and AMBAC Management (with reinsurance agreement).	Investment grade only.	0.40% to 1% of total principal and interest.
Bond Investors Guaranty	American International Group, Bankers Trust New York Corporation, Government Employers Insurance Company, Philbro-Salomon Incorporated, and Xerox Credit Corporation.	Investment grade only.‡	0.25% to 1.5% of total principal and interest.
Financial Guaranty Insurance Corporation	General Electric Credit Corporation; Merrill Lynch & Company; General R.E. Corporation; J.P. Morgan & Company; Shearson Lehman/American Express; and Kemper Group.	BBB − or better.	

*Cost depends on issue quality, length, size, and type.
†Merger of American Municipal Bond Assurance Corporation and MGIC Indemnity Corporation.
‡Insures unrated if their analysis finds the issue to be investment grade.
Other municipal bond insurers: Continental Casualty Company; Fireman's Fund Insurance Company; Industrial Development Bond Insurance (Continental Insurance Company); Industrial Indemnity Company (Crum & Forster); Old Republic Insurance Company; and the Travelers Indemnity Company. Not all cover all forms of state and local government bonds.

by 1984, the percentage was approaching 20 percent. It is a market with substantial demand and the development of more suppliers is likely. Both Moody's and Standard & Poor's currently upgrade MBIA-insured issues to their highest rating (Aaa, AAA); the other insurers normally receive Standard and Poor's AAA or AA. The insurance programs normally have quality limits for insurance (AMBAC and MBIA both require S&P BBB or better) and premiums, paid at time of issue, vary by quality, length, size, and type of issue. Premiums range from around 0.25 to 1.5 percent of total principal and interest of the issue. Figure 13–3 illustrates coverage with a sample MBIA insurance policy. By pooling default risk, new issue insurance should improve markets for smaller units and increase the range of markets for many borrowers.

UNDERWRITING

Bond issues are usually too large to be bought by a single investor and the issuer cannot effectively handle marketing of the issue to large numbers of individual investors.[19] Thus, bonds are typically sold to an underwriter, a firm which purchases the entire issue. The borrower receives proceeds of the entire issue quickly, without having to worry about marketing. The underwriter hopes to resell them at a profit to investors.[20] The gross profit (or "spread") equals the difference between the price the firm pays for the bonds and the price the firm receives from their sale to investors. From that spread, the firm will pay all costs of distribution involved in the transaction.

Underwriting firms are selected either by negotiation or by competitive bid. In the former case, the underwriter is selected as the bond issue is being designed. An interest rate is established in negotiation between the borrowing unit and the underwriting firm. The underwriter will be engaged in presale marketing and will assist the borrower with such organization services as preparation of official statements, structuring the bond issue, and securing credit ratings. Negotiated offerings are particularly common with revenue bond offerings, especially when they are large or involve novel uses of bonding. Some states (Vermont is

---

[19]Some experiments with "mini-bonds" sold directly to investors were tried in Massachusetts and East Brunswick, N.J. in 1978. (*The Wall Street Journal*, September 29, 1978, and January 1, 1978.) Among larger cities, Boston and Rochester, New York, are recent direct sellers (*The Wall Street Journal*, September 14, 1984).

[20]The top five underwriters by dollar volume in 1983 were Merrill Lynch Capital Markets (951 issues), E. F. Hutton and Company (724 issues), Salomon Brothers (699 issues), Blythe Eastman Paine Webber, Inc. (579 issues), and Goldman Sachs and Company (366 issues). *Statistical Yearbook of Municipal Finance, The New Issue Market in 1983.* (New York: Public Securities Association, 1984), p. 20.

FIGURE 13-3

Policy Current as of August 15, 1984

MUNICIPAL BOND GUARANTY INSURANCE POLICY

Municipal Bond Insurance Association
White Plains, New York 10601

Policy No.: ....

The insurance companies comprising the Municipal Bond Insurance Association (the ''Association''), each of which participates and is liable hereunder severally and not jointly in the respective percentage set forth opposite its name, in consideration of the payment of the premium and subject to the terms of this policy, hereby unconditionally and irrevocably guarantee to any holder as hereinafter defined, other than the Issuer of the following described bonds, the full and complete payment required to be made by or on behalf of the Issuer to

_____ *

or its successor (the ''Paying Agent'') of an amount equal to the principal of and interest on, as such payments shall become due but shall not be so paid (except that in the event of any acceleration of the due date of such principal, the payments guaranteed hereby shall be made in such amounts and at such times as such payments of principal would have been due had there not been any acceleration), the following bonds (the ''Bonds''):

SPECIMEN

The insurance companies constituting the members of the Association are as follows:

The Ætna Casualty and Surety Company	33%
Fireman's Fund Insurance Company	30%
The Travelers Indemnity Company	15%
Ætna Insurance Company	12%
The Continental Insurance Company	10%

Upon receipt of telephonic or telegraphic notice, such notice subsequently confirmed in writing by registered or certified mail, or upon receipt of written notice by registered or certified mail, by the General Manager of the Association or its designee from the Paying Agent or any holder of a Bond or coupon the payment for which is then due to the Paying Agent, that such required payment has not been made to the Paying Agent, the Association on behalf of its members on the due date of such payment or within one business day after receipt of notice of such nonpayment, whichever is later, will make a deposit of funds, in an account with Citibank, N.A., in New York, New York, or its successor, sufficient for the payment to the holders of any Bonds or coupons which are then due. Upon presentment and surrender of such Bonds or the coupons, or presentment of such other proof of ownership of Bonds registered as to principal or as to principal and interest together with any appropriate instruments of assignment as shall reasonably satisfy Citibank, N.A., Citibank, N.A. shall disburse to such holders or the Paying Agent payment of the face amount of such surrendered and uncancelled Bonds and coupons less any amount held by the Paying Agent for the payment of the principal of or interest on the Bonds and legally available therefor. Upon such remittance and transfer of such uncancelled Bonds and uncancelled coupons or appropriate instruments of assignment to Citibank, N.A., by the holders or the Paying Agent, the members of the Association shall become the owners thereof in proportion to their percentage of participation under this policy. This policy does not insure against loss of any prepayment premium which may at any time be payable with respect to any Bond.

As used herein, the term ''holder'' shall mean the bearer of any Bond not registered as to principal and the registered owner of any Bond registered as to principal or as to principal and interest as indicated in the books maintained by the Paying Agent for such purpose and, when used with reference to a coupon, shall mean the bearer of the coupon.

Any service of process on the members of the Association may be made to the Association, one of the members of the Association or the General Manager of the Association and such service of process shall be valid and binding as to the Association and each of its members. During the term of its appointment, Municipal Issuers Service Company will act as the General Manager of the Association and its offices are located at 34 South Broadway, White Plains, New York 10601.

This policy is non-cancellable for any reason. The premium on this policy is not refundable for any reason including the payment prior to maturity of Bonds.

IN WITNESS WHEREOF, each of the members of the Association has caused this policy to be executed and attested on its behalf by

the general manager and agent of the Association, this .... day of .... 19 ....

MUNICIPAL BOND INSURANCE ASSOCIATION

The Ætna Casualty and Surety Company
Fireman's Fund Insurance Company
The Travelers Indemnity Company
Ætna Insurance Company
The Continental Insurance Company

By MUNICIPAL ISSUERS SERVICE COMPANY

_____
President of Municipal Issuers Service
Corporation, General Partner

Attest:

_____
Secretary of Municipal Issuers Service
Corporation, General Partner

* Insert Name of Trustee or Paying Agent

–7–

an example) have bond banks which underwrite municipal offerings; these sales are also negotiated.[21]

Two important documents must be prepared during the sale of bonds: the official statement and the legal opinion. The official statement, a requirement when the underwriter will be selected by competitive bid, contains two sections providing information prospective underwriters and investors need before committing funds to the borrower. One section provides information about the ability of the borrower to repay its borrowing: a description of the community and its industries, its major taxpayers, debt currently outstanding, a record of tax collections and bond repayments in the last five years, and future borrowing plans. The other section describes the proposed bond issue: purpose, amount, and type of issue, its maturity structure and interest payment schedule, call provisions, date and place of bidding, whether a bond rating has been applied for, the name of the counsel preparing the legal opinion (described later), and where bonds will be delivered. The statement will also indicate any maximum interest rate and discount. Most statements will include a disclaimer indicating a right to refuse any and all bids, even though that right will seldom be used by units intending to maintain good relations with underwriters.

The second document is the legal opinion prepared by a bond counsel, a certification that the bond issuer has complied with all federal, state, and local legal requirements governing municipal debt. Seldom will local law firms do this work; underwriters and large private investors require opinions of specialist law firms. The bond counsel assures that the issuer has legal authority to borrow, that the revenue source for repayment is legal and irrevocable, and that the community is legally bound by provisions of the bond. The counsel also indicates whether interest paid on the debt will, in his opinion, be exempt from federal and state income tax. The counsel offers no judgment about the capacity of the borrower to repay the debt; his concern is with how tight the contract to repay binds the borrower. Without a satisfactory opinion, the bond issue is virtually worthless on the tax-exempt market.

Competitive bid is the typical method of selecting underwriters for full faith and credit bonds and for many revenue issues. In this method, the issuer selects the amount of principal to mature at various years through the life of the issue, and underwriters bid on the interest rate which the issuer would have to pay. The rates, of course, need not be the

---

[21]Bond banks reduce interest costs to local borrowers, but they have been adopted by few states. See Martin T. Katzman, "Municipal Bond Banking: The Diffusion of a Public-Finance Innovation," *National Tax Journal* 33 (June 1980), pp. 149–60; and David S. Kidwell and Robert J. Rogowski, "Bond Banks: A State Assistance Program that Helps Reduce New Issue Borrowing Costs," *Public Administration Review* 42 (March/April 1983), p. 108–12.

same for different maturities but would be the same for all bonds in a single maturity. The issuer chooses the underwriter bidding the lowest interest rate for the total issue.

Two methods are used to evaluate bids, net interest cost (NIC) and true interest cost (TIC). (The complexity emerges because of the serial nature of municipal bonds.) The *NIC* method computes cost according to the formula

$$NIC = \frac{\text{Interest payable (less premium or plus discount)}}{\text{Principal} \times \text{Average maturity}}$$

and produces an average annual cost of the debt as a percentage of the outstanding principal of the debt. *NIC* is computed in the following fashion. First, compute *N*, the total dollar cost of coupon payments over the life of the bond:

$$N = \sum_{i=1}^{n} \left[C_i \times A_i \times Y_i \right] + D$$

where N = Net dollar interest costs
 n = Number of different maturities in issue
 C = Coupon rate on each maturity
 A = Par amount in each maturity
 Y = Number of years to maturity
 D = Bid discount (bid premium is negative discount).

NIC equals N divided by bond year dollars:

$$NIC = N / \sum_{i=1}^{n} (A_i \times Y_i)$$

The TIC (or Canadian) method is more complicated because it takes into account the time profile of interest payment flows. If two bids have the same net interest cost, but one bid involves higher interest payments in the early maturities of the issue and lower interest payments in the later maturities (front loading), then that bid would be less attractive: it requires the issuer to surrender resources earlier and, thus, to lose the return that could have been received from use of those resources. Thus, the other bid is, in present-value terms, lower than this bid. *TIC* is the interest rate which equates the amount of dollars received by the bond issuer with the present value of the flow of principal and interest payments over the life of the issue. The *TIC* formula is:

$$B = \sum_{i=1}^{m} \frac{A_i}{(1 + TIC)^i} + \sum_{i=1}^{m} \frac{I_i}{(1 + TIC)^i}$$

where B = aggregate dollar amount received by issuer; i = number of years to cash payment; m = number of years to final maturity; A_i = annual principal in dollars repaid in period i; TIC = true interest cost; and I_i = aggregate interest payment in period i (assuming one interest payment per year). In a *TIC* computation for municipal bond sale, the bid price or amount to be paid by the underwriter to the issuer (*B*) and the stream of debt service payments (I_t) are specified by the bidder. The number of years to future payments were defined in the offering. The implied interest rate (*TIC*) is solved for. Larger offerings require computer assistance for *TIC* calculation, but smaller issues can be handled using standard methods for approximating the internal rate of return. Table 13–8 illustrates *TIC* and *NIC* computation.

The successful underwriting firm or syndicate (a group of firms) then sells the bonds to investors. Underwriters cover their costs and make any profit from the difference between the price the underwriters pay the issuer and the price they receive from purchasers (the spread). As the previously discussed mechanics of the bond market demonstrated, an increase in market interest rates causes bond values to decline. If

---

TABLE 13-8 Example *TIC* and *NIC* Computation Worksheet

Bonds sold July 1, 1981, and interest payable on July 1 thereafter
(Bid amount = $39,920)

Maturity Dates	Amount	Bid Interest Rate	Annual Interest Paid	Bond Years	Bond Dollar Years
July 1, 1985	$ 5,000	6.00%	$ 300	4	20,000
July 1, 1986	5,000	6.50	325	5	25,000
July 1, 1987	5,000	7.00	350	6	30,000
July 1, 1988	5,000	8.00	400	7	35,000
July 1, 1989	10,000	9.00	900	8	80,000
July 1, 1990	10,000	10.00	1,000	9	90,000
Total	$40,000				

Schedule of payments by dates paid

	Interest	Principal	Total
July 1, 1982	$ 3,275	—	$ 3,275
July 1, 1983	3,275	—	3,275
July 1, 1984	3,275	—	3,275
July 1, 1985	3,275	$ 5,000	8,275
July 1, 1986	2,975	5,000	7,975
July 1, 1987	2,650	5,000	7,650
July 1, 1988	2,300	5,000	7,300
July 1, 1989	1,900	10,000	11,900
July 1, 1990	1,000	10,000	11,000
Total	$23,926	$40,000	$63,926

a. Solving for *NIC*:

$$NIC = \frac{23,926 + 80}{280,000} = 8.573571\%$$

b. Solving for *TIC*:

$$\$39,920 = \frac{3275}{1 + TIC} + \frac{3275}{(1 + TIC)^2} + \frac{3275}{(1 + TIC)^3} + \frac{8275}{(1 + TIC)^4} + \frac{7975}{(1 + TIC)^5} + \frac{7650}{(1 + TIC)^6} + \frac{7300}{(1 + TIC)^7} + \frac{11900}{(1 + TIC)^8} + \frac{11000}{(1 + TIC)^9}$$

$$TIC = 9.00\%$$

TABLE 13-9 Entities Holding State and Local Government (tax exempt) Securities (end of year)

	Holdings as Percent of Total			
	1974	1977	1980	1983
Households	29.8%	26.7%	25.5%	35.9%
Nonfinancial corporate business	2.3	1.3	1.0	0.9
State-local government general funds	1.3	3.0	2.0	2.0
Commercial banking	48.7	43.9	42.4	33.5
Savings and loan associations	0.2	0.5	0.3	0.2
Mutual savings banks	0.4	1.1	0.7	0.5
Mutual funds	—	0.8	1.8	6.5
Life insurance companies	1.8	2.3	1.9	2.1
State-local government retirement funds	0.5	1.3	1.2	0.4
Other insurance companies	14.8	18.8	22.9	17.9
Brokers and dealers	0.3	0.4	0.3	0.3

SOURCE: *Flow of Funds Accounts, Assets and Liabilities Outstanding, 1960–83* (Washington, D.C.: Board of Governors of the Federal Reserve System, 1984).

increases in market rates cause a substantial decline in the value of the issue before the firm has the bonds sold, that spread can be negative.

Table 13-9 reports the type of entities holding municipal bonds. Ownership in any class is concentrated among units in higher tax brackets—those are the purchasers to whom the tax-exempt status of municipal bond interest is especially attractive. From 1974 to 1983, the role of household purchases has increased substantially, while the role of commercial banks has declined. Other shares have been rather stable, except for the development of mutual funds as a financial intermediary. These holdings might properly be added to household holdings.

Questions and Exercises

1. What restrictions are placed on state and local government debt in your state? What methods are used to avoid those limits? Is there a state bond bank?

2. Investigate the debt and debt rating history for a large city of your selection. Have debt issues been full faith and credit or limited liability? Have issues been insured?

3. Indicate which bond in the following pairs of bonds is likely to bear the higher interest rate (yield) and state why. If there is no general reason for a difference, indicate that they would be the same.

    a. A corporate bond rated Aaa—a municipal bond rated Aaa.

    b. A municipal bond rated Baa—a municipal bond rated Aa.

    c. A general obligation bond issued by a city—a revenue bond issued by a city.

    d. A general obligation bond rated Aa issued by a city—a general obligation bond rated Aa issued by a county.

    e. A municipal bond (term) with maturity in 5 years—a municipal bond (term) with maturity in 20 years.

4. A city advertised for bids for the purchase of $2 million principal amount of Sewage Works Revenue bonds. Bonds will be delivered on April 1, 19X0; interest will be payable annually on April 1 of the following years. The bonds mature as follows:

Maturity Date	Amount
April 1, 19X5	$ 50,000
April 1, 19X6	50,000
April 1, 19X7	50,000
April 1, 19X8	100,000
April 1, 19X9	100,000
April 1, 19Y0	100,000
April 1, 19Y1	150,000
April 1, 19Y2	150,000
April 1, 19Y3	150,000
April 1, 19Y4	550,000
April 1, 19Y5	550,000

Two bids were received:

    a. From Five Points Securities:
    Pay $2 million (a 5% premium).
    The interest rates for each maturity:
    19X5 through 19Y3—8.50 percent
    19Y4 through 19Y5—9.25 percent

    b. From Wellington-Nelson:
    Pay $2 million.
    The interest rates for each maturity:
    19X5 through 19X7—8.25 percent
    19X8 through 19Y3—8.75 percent
    19Y4 through 19Y5—9.25 percent

    For each bid, compute the net interest cost (NIC) and the true interest cost (TIC). Which bid is most advantageous to the city?

5. From tables in *The Wall Street Journal* or other papers which carry quotations on U.S. Treasury bonds, notes, and bills, determine the general shape of the term structure of interest rates.

6. An Eminence Water Utility Revenue Bond matures in 15 years, pays an 8.5 percent coupon rate semiannually, and has a face value of $5,000. The market interest rate for similar risk and maturity municipal bonds is 7 percent. What is the current price of the bond? What would be its price if the market rate were 9 percent?

Cases for Discussion

A   The following selection from *The Wall Street Journal* reports on municipal bond insurance.

Consider These Questions

1. *Who gains from municipal bond insurance?*
2. *Explain why the insurers avoid large borrowers.*
3. *If the estimated interest saved over the life of the Dade County issue was $4.3 million and the insurance premium was $920,000, why is the real interest saving listed as only $1 million?*

Insured Issues Attract Top Rating, Buyers, But Not All Borrowers Can Get Coverage

By Byron Klapper

NEW YORK—When Dade County, Florida, needed $43 million last month to buy a water system, it let Wall Street decide whether to bid on revenue bonds backed by certain taxes, or those covered by municipal bond insurance.

Without exception, dealers selected insured bonds carrying Standard & Poor's triple-A rating, instead of the county's uninsured medium grade triple-B credit.

The higher bond rating slashed Dade's borrowing fees by more than $1 million over 20 years based on current-value dollars. And it allowed dealers to avoid a 6¾ percent interest ceiling, above which bids may have been rejected.

The offering had one other distinction. It was the largest issue accepted for coverage since Municipal Bond Insurance Association began guaranteeing tax-exempt bonds in 1974.

A Bitter Reality

Such a program would have enormous benefits for such cities as New York, Detroit, Cleveland, Philadelphia, and Boston. But before their mayors try to sign up for an insurance policy, they should be aware of a bitter reality.

"If they need it badly, we don't want them," said John R. Butler, president of Municipal Issuers Service Corp., the insurance group's managing agent.

Last year, 159 local governments and agencies sold $1.05 billion of insured bonds, up 9 percent from 1977. Insurance premiums jumped 31 percent to $17.5 million. Nevertheless, MBIA reported $2 million of losses, reflecting "substantial underwriting costs associated with conducting the business," Mr. Butler said. Part of that is the way insurance companies account for profits and losses, and certain funds which must be kept in reserves.

As the nation's largest bond insurer, MBIA guarantees $6.6 billion of principal and interest payments. The liability is spread among four underwriters. They are Aetna Casualty & Surety Co., with 40 percent; Fireman's Fund Insurance Co., 30 percent; and 15 percent each by Aetna Insurance Co. and U.S. Fire Insurance Co.

Guaranteed Payment

Holders of insured bonds are guaranteed payment on tax-exempt issues as they come due. The concept attracted investors after default by New York's Urban Development Corp. in 1975, and a moratorium on $1.6 billion of New York City notes. Noteholders waited more than a year for payment while the moratorium bought time for New York to devise a plan to keep from going bankrupt. Currently, insured issues account for just over 2 percent of the $45.9 billion of tax-exempt bonds sold last year. MBIA said there haven't been any missed payments among bonds it insures.

"Insurance throws a security blanket over the issues come hell or high water," says Mr. Butler. "It's an unconditional, irrevocable guarantee that we will make payment. There isn't a Proposition 13, a New York City, or any other disaster for a municipal government which isn't covered."

Such ironclad protection doesn't come cheaply once MBIA's credit tests are met. Last year more than twice as many applicants were rejected as accepted. Those that qualified paid $9 to $20 as insurance premiums for each $1,000 face amount of bonds sold. Fees depend on credit quality and marketability, and are payable when bonds are sold.

Reasons for Rejection

Issues are rejected where revenue sources aren't considered reliable, if there are doubts over certain legal aspects of a security, or where debt service is backed by revenue of a private corporation, to name a few.

Says Mr. Butler: "We're established to assist creditworthy communities with a good history and a promising future who want to obtain money at a lower interest rate."

That goal is largely achieved as a result of the automatic triple-A rating from Standard & Poor's. Moody's Investors Service, another agency, views it differently.

"We choose to rate issuers on their own credit worthiness," said Frieda Ackerman, a Moody's vice president of municipal research. In its credit analysis, Moody's says it recognizes insurance coverage. The service said it won't revise its rating, however, because it doesn't "want to confuse the public" by departing from its accepted rating methods. As a result, insured issuers rarely apply for a Moody's rating.

Absence of Large Borrowers

Of all insured bonds sold last year, 55 percent were general obligations, 42 percent were water, sewer and electric revenue issues, and the remaining 3 percent were other revenue bonds. Most policies were written in nine states, led by Florida, Pennsylvania, New Jersey, Michigan, Kansas, New York, Connecticut, Tennessee, and Georgia. No states or large cities are among the insured. The absence of large borrowers reflects the limits of the municipal insurance industry.

"If we accept major cities which sell substantial volumes of bonds, we'd be insuring very little else," Mr. Butler says. "From an insurance point of view, it would create undue concentration and risk."

Smaller government units with high-grade or premium bond ratings also would find little benefit in insurance. The interest difference on their uninsured bonds and those with MBIA coverage wouldn't justify the insurance fee.

For Dade County, however, the $920,000 insurance premium was more than offset by the $4.3 million interest-rate reduction. That saving, taken over the 20-year average life of the bonds, will be reduced by inflation. After making an up-front payment of the insurance premium, Dade's "present value" interest saving is estimated at about $1 million.

"We advise clients that the difference between insured and uninsured interest should take into account present-value cost and future-value savings," says Arthur L. Greenfield, first vice president of Loeb Rhoades, Hornblower & Co., Dade's fiscal adviser.

B   As Table 13–8 shows, insurance companies—particularly casualty insurers—are heavy holders of municipal debt. This case from *The Wall Street Journal* reports on the investment of one company.

Consider These Questions

1. *Explain why State Farm is in the municipal market when other similar insurers are not.*

2. *Explain how an interest rate increase would create a paper loss for State Farm. Why might the firm, as compared with an underwriter or dealer, be unconcerned about that loss?*

State Farm Bets Day Will Come for Municipals

By David P. Garino

BLOOMINGTON, Illinois—In the long-term municipal bond market, or what's left of it, they call State Farm Insurance Company's financial vice president Rex J. (Jim) Bates the Lone Ranger. That's because other corporate and institutional buyers of new municipal bond issues have become so scarce. Day in and day out, State Farm is one of the few that continues to buy new issues.

On paper, the big insurer's persistence has cost it a bundle. As interest rates have risen and stuck at record levels, the market value of the company's bonds has sunk. The full face value of its portfolio of tax-exempts stands at some $8.4 billion. "Unfortunately," Mr. Bates says, "that's not the market value"—which has fallen to about 70 percent of face value from 98 percent at the end of 1977.

Still, the company is sticking with its strategy of buying high-grade tax-exempts. "We don't plan to change anything," Mr. Bates says. "We'll go on our own naive way." He does concede, "You have to fight the human tendency to leave when things don't work out."

That has made State Farm exceedingly popular among underwriters and dealers in municipal bonds. Last month, only 40 percent of a $105 million offering of revenue bonds by Washington Suburban Sanitary District, Maryland, sold on the first day, and State Farm was practically the only buyer. On some days State Farm's municipal securities departments get more than 200 telephone calls from dealers trying to peddle bonds; often all the department's five direct lines are busy.

Casualty insurers such as State Farm historically bought municipal bonds for the same reason other investors did, to earn tax-free income. But as claims payoffs exceeded premium income in recent years, the insurers' big underwriting losses cut their cash income and made income taxes an academic problem. In addition, institutional investors of all kinds have backed away from the bond market because of the inflationary threat to principal and the market losses created by high interest rates.

But State Farm—which rarely discusses its investment strategy publicly—committed $692 milion to the tax-exempt market in the first

---

half of 1981, compared with $580 million in 1980's first half. For one thing, State Farm had cash. It outperformed the casualty industry last year. Its underwriting ratio—the percentage of premium income paid out in claim losses and expenses—came to 95.3 percent, producing a profit of $269.7 million. For the industry, the ratio was a losing 103 percent. "Fortunately, we had the cash flow for municipals as the markets slid into new depths," Mr. Bates says.

Waiting It Out

For another thing, the company has bought for the long term and isn't greatly concerned about an adverse market meantime. "We've learned you can't outguess the market," Mr. Bates says, although he adds, "We used to think we could."

If interest rates do fall, bond prices will rise, and, a municipal bond analyst says, "They"—State Farm—"will look good. If the rates are 20 percent, they don't look so good. You have to give State Farm credit for sticking its neck out." A trust officer at a Midwest bank says, "Unless they need to liquidate, all they have is a paper loss. If they've selected the right issues, they'll come out all right. In the meantime, they're getting a hell of a yield."

The yield on State Farm's tax-exempt portfolio amounted to 10.15 percent for the first half this year, up from 8 percent a year before, Mr. Bates says.

Only the Best

The company buys only high-grade issues. Clifford F. Steinkraus, vice president of municipal securities, says the average rating on the bonds the company buys is double-A. Such high-grade issues have become relatively more attractive, he says, because the difference in yields between higher-grade and lower-grade issues has narrowed. Thus, the additional reward in yield for buying lower-grade issues is small in terms of the additional risk in those issues. That narrowing in spread has come about largely because of the demand for high-yielding, lower-grade issues by bond funds that pool individual investors' money to buy maximum-yield securities.

State Farm's municipal bond staff does its own research; staffers even drive through communities whose bonds the company may buy, inspecting residential, commercial, and industrial areas to get impressions of the communities' economic health, and tape their observations on recorders. But the company has found state obligations particularly attractive lately. State governments, Mr. Bates says, "have potential resources to make the bonds secure." Of the first half's bond investments, $305 million went into state general obligation bonds.

State Farm is also a big buyer of industrial revenue bonds sold to raise money for pollution control. Such bonds are sold by communities to build nonpolluting facilities that are leased out to corporations. The corporate lease rentals supply the cash to pay interest and principal on the debt. Because interest on the obligations is tax-exempt, interest costs to the corporation are less than they would be on the corporation's own securities.

There are some bonds that the company dislikes. "We don't own any hospital revenue bonds for philosophical reasons," Mr. Steinkraus says. "We don't feel they serve a public purpose, and they're often promoted by investment houses" with little regard for any surplus of hospital beds in a community, he says.

In the bond market, State Farm gets high marks for its accessibility. "The best thing is that they're good people," says a New York municipal bond dealer who complains that many institutional bond investors shut their doors to all but a favored clique.

Mr. Bates says, "Life's too short to be nasty to people, so we try to talk to them." Not long ago, however, a visiting bond dealer kept "telling us how great we were," Mr. Bates says, and complimented the company's "super advertising." The dealer cupped his hand and said, "You're in good hands"—part of the tag line of a commercial for Allstate Insurance Co., State Farm's arch competitor.

14

Cash Management and Investment

Cash management encompasses the collection and disbursement of public money and the use of those funds between the time of receipt and disbursement in a manner consistent with the public interest. Treasury operations should (1) ensure the safety of public resources, (2) maintain liquidity when needed,[1] (3) increase funds available for investment, and (4) obtain the highest feasible yield on public funds. The funds are a valuable public resource which should work for the community. Leaving them idle in a checking account, for instance, provides safety and liquidity but no yield. Such a strategy would increase profits of the favored bank by providing it a low-cost source of short-run investable funds, but would provide the government with no return. Idle deposits apparently neither keep down the loan cost in the community nor stimulate the local economy activity.[2] The government fiscal officer must thus seek investment of these funds in money market instruments to utilize this community resource.

Table 14-1 reports recent patterns of state and local general fund investment. Such governments held almost 40 percent of their financial assets in cash and checking accounts as recently as 1950. While interest rates were far lower than they are now, that cash management policy sacrificed potential interest earnings. Since then, there has been a significant and continuing trend toward interest-yielding assets. Only 12 percent of financial assets were in cash and checking accounts

---

[1]Liquidity is "the ease of converting an asset into money." [Basil J. Moore, *An Introduction to the Theory of Finance* (New York: Free Press, 1968), p. 12.] Some items may be valuable (land or antiques) but their value cannot be used directly to pay bills; they must be sold to obtain money before payment can be made (and market conditions may make it difficult to sell them quickly or at their normal value). Those items are illiquid.

[2]Kerry S. Cooper, "The Economics of Idle Public Funds Policies: A Reconsideration," *National Tax Journal* 25 (March 1972), pp. 97–99.

TABLE 14-1 Financial Assets of State and Local Governments, 1946-1982 (excludes retirement funds)

Year	Demand Deposits Checkable Deposits, (billion)	Time and Saving Deposits (billion)		Federal Funds and Security Repurchase	Credit Market Instruments (billion)	Percent in Demand Deposits on Currency
1946	$ 4.6	$ 0.7			$ 6.5	39
1950	6.5	1.4			9.0	38
1955	8.0	2.4			14.6	32
1960	8.4	4.6			18.8	26
1965	12.1	12.2			23.7	25
1970	12.5	23.2			32.5	18
1975	14.4	48.1			53.7	12
1980	11.1	62.5		14.0	114.4	5
		Small Time and Savings	Large Time			
1981	5.9	3.3	61.0	16.6	140.3	3
1982	5.2	5.0	65.9	16.6	177.5	2

SOURCE: Board of Governors of the Federal Reserve System, Flow of Funds Accounts, 1946-1975 (December 1975) and *Annual Statistical Digest.*

by 1975, but developments in cash management have progressed so rapidly since then that the percentage was 2 percent at the end of 1982. That movement represents several influences, including the lure of higher interest rates, greater sophistication of government fiscal officers, and public demand for better use of government resources.[3] Because idle fund investment provides revenue without additional burden on taxpayers, no government can afford to ignore its potential. The critical problem is the balance between investment yield on the one hand and investment risk and liquidity on the other.

GOVERNMENT CASH BALANCE

A public cash manager will invest cash available from daily flows not simply an annual surplus. The investment opportunity results because governments typically receive revenue inflows in lumps around tax due days, while expenditures occur in relatively smooth outflows. Figure 14-1 illustrates such a cash balance pattern. That government receives major cash inflows at two dates in the year, the start of April and the start of October. These may be property tax due dates, payment dates from vendors collecting a sales tax, receipt dates for intergovernmental assistance, or whatever. The government spends from

---

[3]State and local governments were estimated to have lost $453 million in 1972 because of excess idle cash. [Georege M. Blankenbeckler, "Excess Cash Management at the State and Local Levels," *State and Local Government Reviews* 10 (January 1978), pp. 2-7].

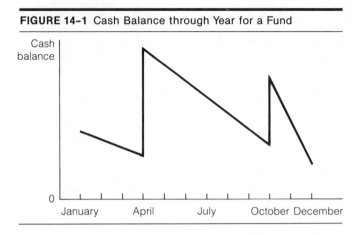

FIGURE 14-1 Cash Balance through Year for a Fund

the fund at a relatively constant rate through the year. The require-ments of the budget-appropriation-disbursement process make these outflows more or less predictable and controllable. (It should be appar-ent that, for the unit depicted in Figure 14–1, the first cash inflow is larger than the second and that spending exceeds receipts during the fiscal year shown here.) The cash manager will invest available lumps as fully as is feasible. Thus, investment is of the daily—not just annual—surplus for as many days as possible.

ELEMENTS OF CASH MANAGEMENT

Government cash management operates within an important policy dilemma. Cash is needed to bridge the gap between daily disbursement outflows and revenue inflows; the two flows are seldom matched. Any cash held above that amount needed for the bridge means lost interest earnings. If the government, however, chooses to minimize those lost interest earnings and fails to hold adequate cash, it will not be able to pay its bills when due. There would be no dilemma if cash flow could be perfectly forecast; exact cash needs to bridge the gap would be known, available cash for investment would be certain with regard to both amount and period of availability, and investments could be made for exactly the period cash would otherwise be idle. All of these are, of course, subject to forecast error, so the process of cash management is more complicated.

The balancing act involves proper allocation of municipal resources between cash and short-term, marketable investments. Cash includes currency on hand and, predominantly, checkable deposits (bank de-mand deposits, NOW accounts, and the like). These assets are liquid be-cause they are immediately available to pay bills. Unfortunately, they earn little or no interest. Short-term investments earn interest but, because they are quickly marketable with little or no loss of value and low transaction cost, allow a liquidity cushion in case of cash emergencies. The balance is between the immediate liquidity for paying bills that cash brings and the earnings produced by short-term investment.

The process of cash management includes three distinct elements: controlling the cash collection and disbursement process, managing the available cash balances, and short-term investment of those balances. For a public manager, each portion of the process is governed by federal, state, or local laws which constrain the government cash manager by "determining when monies can be collected, when obligations must be paid, where deposits can be placed and what securities can and cannot be purchased."[4] Although many of these limits reduce potential earnings from the cash management program, most were introduced to prevent specific abuses of the public trust.

Cash collection and disbursement.   Within the normal taxing and spending functions, the cash manager seeks to control the largest fund pool for as long as possible by speeding collections and slowing outflows. That procedure will maximize the financial pool available for cash management. The three portions of this strategy include (1) acceleration of collection, (2) consolidation of balances, and (3) control of disbursements. In general, the cash manager seeks deposit of all revenues owed to any part of the government as quickly as possible. That presumes a prompt billing for any funds owed, rapid processing of remittances with an accurate accounting of funds to maintain fiscal records and control nonpayment, and immediate deposit of funds into an account controlled by the cash manager.[5]

An acceleration of collection attempts to reduce the period between the time the taxpayer writes a check to the government and the time the government has use of those funds. This collection and deposit float consists of (1) mail time: the time it takes for the check to reach the government, (2) recordkeeping and processing time: the time it takes the revenue agency to process and deposit the check, and (3) clearing time: the time between deposit of the check and the check's clearance at the taxpayer's bank. The flow is outlined in Figure 14–2. The government does not have full use of the check amount until the check has cleared the taxpayer's bank, so actions to reduce the length of any of these three steps improves the cash pool.

---

[4]Frank M. Patitucci and Michael H. Lichtenstein, *Improving Cash Management in Local Governments* (Chicago: Municipal Finance Officers Association, 1977), p. 4.

[5]Cash managers in some large Texas cities fly to the state capital to pick up the check for the state-collected city sales taxes and deposit it immediately. The interest for the extra few days more than covers the travel cost.

FIGURE 14–2 Collection and Deposit Float

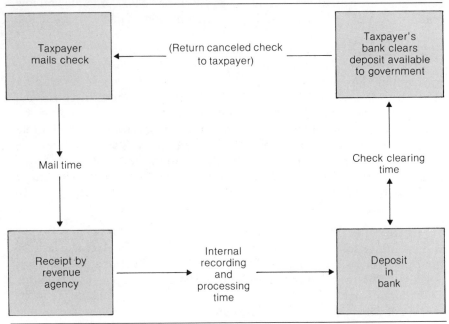

SOURCE: Philip Rosenberg et al., *A Treasury Management Handbook for Small Cities and Other Governmental Units* (Chicago: Municipal Finance Officers Association, 1978), p. 56.

Lockbox systems offer one approach to speeding collection. Figure 14–3 diagrams such a system with regional banks acting as collections agents. Taxpayers mail payments to a local or nearby postal box. A bank in that city promptly empties the box, deposits checks, and transmits details to the government cash manager. Closeness to the taxpayer (and the taxpayer's bank) cuts both mail and clearing time. Furthermore, the bank may handle processing more quickly than a government mail processing unit, but that depends on the specifics of the situation. Other governments use their own postal box system to gain quick control over funds by reducing the need to sort revenue mail from other government mail.[6] High-quality systems have deposits made within 24 hours of receipt; internal recording and processing of returns often lags check deposit, the first goal of the system. Not only does quick collection and control provide longer investment pools, but rapid deposit also prevents questions that taxpayer rightly have about the quality of any administration which leaves checks undeposited for extended periods. Lockbox systems are reputed to cut collection and deposit float by one to four days, depending on the environment.

---

[6]In some instances, banks may arrange to provide direct, over-the-counter collection of municipal utility payments, property taxes, or the like. The arrangement obviously reduces collection/deposit float.

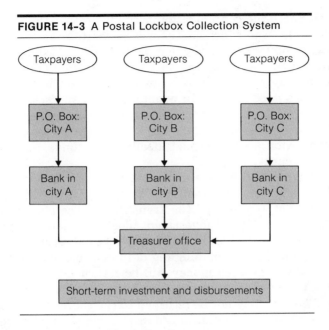

FIGURE 14-3 A Postal Lockbox Collection System

A second method used to improve the investment prospects of cash collection is the concentration account. This approach produces a large investment pool without sacrificing the internal control available from maintaining separate accounts for each major expenditure function. Figure 14-4 illustrates such an arrangement. All revenues are received

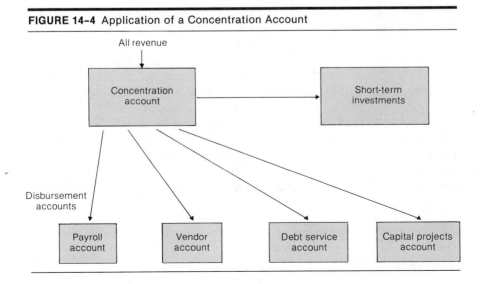

FIGURE 14-4 Application of a Concentration Account

into a cash pool—the concentration account—rather than to the particular accounts from which checks will be written. As cash is needed for payroll, to pay vendors, to cover debt service, or whatever, it gets transferred to that specific account; this central account for investment retains any cash not needed to cover a specific disbursement. This provides a good method for pooling cash balances, the fundamental concern of cash management, because the pool gives longer availability of larger investible dollars, the key to higher interest earnings. The concentration account would ideally cross funds, as well as disbursement accounts.

Financial institutions offer more attractive deposit terms for larger investments and some transaction costs vary with the number of transactions, not the size of the transaction. Therefore, pooling of funds to obtain the largest investment block available for the longest investment period possible should increase the net return to cash management. Pooling is not commingling of funds: sources of the cash are recorded and the invested money will be returned to the originating fund as the investment instruments mature. Interest from the investment pools may or may not be returned to the source fund, depending on state law and local investment orders. The simplest practice returns total interest from the investment pool to the general fund for reappropriation by the legislative body.

The third important element is control of disbursements, the other end of the cash management flow. Among the special features here, beyond the normal internal audit to verify validity of claims before payment, are care to avoid late payment penalties and a balancing of early payment discounts against the interest that could be earned from cash investment. Slow payment, as has been pointed out in an earlier chapter, can be a technique used to conceal budget imbalance. The objective here is not to conceal but rather to maximize return from a public resource.[7] Where the banking relationship permits, the government can gain substantial disbursement control through use of *zero balance accounts*. With such a system, each of the disbursement accounts would contain a zero balance; checks clearing on the account during a banking day would be covered by overdrafts. At the end of the day, sufficient funds would be transferred from the concentration account to cover the overdrafts in each account and return the balance to zero. Transfers would occur only as the checks clear, not as checks are written. The zero balance account eliminates disbursement float and makes the investment pool as large and as long as possible. Unfortunately, local banks

---

[7]Examples of these cash management practices are reported in Executive Office of the President, Office of the Management and Budget, *Report on Strengthening Federal Cash Management* (Washington, D.C.: U.S. Government Printing Office, 1980). Savings available there were estimated at $450 million per year.

may not permit the arrangement and laws may prohibit shopping elsewhere for the service.

Cash balance management.   Collection and disbursement control provides a pool for investment. Balance management seeks to determine the minimum cash balance required in the government checking account (possibly the concentration account demand deposit). That balance may well be imposed by special constraints, like a compensating balance required by the bank as payment to it for services it extends to the government, for instance. There may also be legal constraints or other contractual arrangements that dictate that balance. Such special controls then establish the cash level to be maintained.

Without special limitation, the task of the cash manager involves an evaluation of the trade-off between the opportunity cost of holding too much cash (the interest earnings forgone) and the cost of being short of cash (the transaction costs involved in selling securities to obtain cash). The optimum level of cash holding has declined dramatically over the last decade because of three developments: higher interest rates have increased the cost of cashholding, improved computer technology has made quicker security conversion feasible, and lower computer cost has reduced transaction cost significantly.[8] For marketable security portfolios, the likelihood is that external constraints will apply before cash levels decline to the otherwise optimal level.[9]

Cash management requires the regular preparation of a cash budget to establish the amount available for investment. Although the largest units would operate on a daily forecast, more governments would forecast weekly or monthly. In general, the process works in the following framework:

$$\text{Total cash available in the period} = \text{Beginning period} \\ \text{Cash balance} \\ \text{plus} \\ \text{Cash receipts in} \\ \text{period}$$

---

[8]Michael Dotsey, "An Investigation of Cash Management Practices and Their Effects on the Demand for Money," *Federal Reserve Bank of Richmond Economic Review* 70 (September/October 1984), pp. 3–5.

[9]Two models for determining optimal cash levels: William J. Baumol, "The Transactions Demand for Cash: An Inventory Theoretical Approach," *Quarterly Journal of Economics* 66 (November 1952), pp. 545–56, presents a deterministic model, and Merton H. Miller and Daniel Orr, "A Model of the Demand for Money by Firms," *Quarterly Journal of Economics* 80 (August 1966), pp. 413–35, present a probabilistic model. An application of the logic of each to Honolulu show the latter suggested a much higher optimum balance: Rita M. Maldonado and Lawrence S. Ritter, "Optimal Municipal Cash Management: A Case Study," *Review of Economics and Statistics* 47 (November 1971), pp. 384–88.

$$\text{Investable funds} = \begin{array}{c} \text{Total cash available} \\ \textit{less} \\ \text{Cash disbursements} \\ \textit{and} \\ \text{Required cash balance} \\ \text{(end of period)} \end{array}$$

Uncertainty complicates that simple arithmetic. Both receipts and disbursements must be estimated on the basis of experience, administrative policy, and existing statutes. Some flows, both in and out, will be easier to estimate than others, but all will be uncertain. For most governments, the key elements for successful forecasting may be noted:

1. Make errors on the side of conservatism.
2. Pay most attention to the major items.
3. Keep the forecast simple.
4. Maintain documentation of how the forecasts were prepared.[10]

That approach carried over a number of investment periods will allow forecasting improvements and adjustments to refine the estimated investment pool.

Estimates must consider both what cash is available and for what period of time that cash pool will be available. Money market conditions are often such that longer-term interest rates are higher than short-term interest rates. When the six-month Treasury bill rate is higher than the three-month rate, cash available for six months can profitably be directed to the longer instrument. The manager can invest without fear of actual capital loss from interest rate fluctuations if the manager matches the term of the security to the time that the cash will be available.[11] Matching is possible only if cash flows have been estimated through the fiscal year. Thus, forecasting of revenue and expenditures flow is critical for a cash-management program. Those forecasts will be keyed to experience of recent fiscal years and actions in the current-year budget.

Short-term investment.   Investment of idle cash seeks to maximize yield within the constraint of full safety of principal and liquidity when cash is required. Suitable instruments will provide a sound balance between a return on idle cash and the ability to respond to unexpected cash demands; they will earn interest but will be quickly salable at low cost and be virtually devoid of risk. These constraints indicate

---

[10]The logic of cash forecasting and some general guidelines are discussed in David A. Wismer, "Approach to Cash Flow Forecasting," *Journal of Cash Management* 5 (January/February 1985), pp. 12–16.

[11]Nathaniel B. Guild, ed., *The Public Money Manager's Handbook* (Chicago: Crain Books, 1981), p. 124.

several inappropriate investments. First, default risk—the loss of principal because of failure of the investment activity or of changing market estimates about the prospects of the activity—must be avoided, so cash will not be invested in the acquisition of physical properties or in commercial stocks and bonds. Public pension funds may invest in such assets because of their long-term focus, but they remain inappropriate for cash management. Second, the constraints dictate that credit market risk—loss in the market value of a fixed-dollar return asset which results when market interest rates rise—must be avoided, so long-term debt instruments will not be in the idle fund management portfolio.[12] And third, debt issued by state or local governments will be avoided by the public cash manager because the tax-exempt nature of interest paid by these bodies permits them to bear artificially low interest rates. Governments ordinarily are exempt from the federal income tax on all their activities, so this exclusion is of no value for their cash investment program. The lower interest rate received on state and local bond holdings would simply penalize the investing government for its investment mistake. If rates on such debt are sufficiently high to look like attractive investments, they probably reflect dangerously high risk to principal.

Beyond the constraints established by sound financial management, cash managers must operate within the special limits placed by federal, state, and local laws. Those controls can limit the places where deposits can be held, establish shares of total financial assets which may be placed with a particular depository, establish what securities and maturities can be purchased, define formulas for determining what interest rate will be paid on public fund deposits, limit the funds from which investment can be made, and so on.[13] While the tendency has been toward greater freedom and expanded options, it is unlikely that public cash managers will have all the options available to corporate cash managers because of potential conflict-of-interest problems which can emerge in the management of government resources. Table 14–2 presents some key features of important money market instruments and, where available, the recent yields available from them.

---

[12]A recent violation of that principal occurred when investment officers of San Jose, California, placed an investment pool of $750 million in long-term government bonds which had an average maturity of 17 years. When interest rates rose in early 1984, the value of the bonds fell dramatically, imperiling the capacity of the city to pay its bills. Losses in the portfolio were stopped at $60 million. The problem resulted because long maturity debt was used for short-term investment, violating safety of principal against credit market risk. Harold E. Boldt, "Do You Know the Way to San Jose? or Would You Like to Invest City Funds in Long-term Government Bonds?," *Missouri Municipal League*, September 1984, pp. 17–19.

[13]A list of recent state actions on how governments may manage idle cash appears in Advisory Commission on Intergovernmental Relations, *Understanding State and Local Cash Management* (Washington, D.C.: ACIR, 1977), pp. 47–58.

TABLE 14-2 Features and Yields of Money Market Instruments Available to Governments

Characteristics and Yields of Money Market Instruments

Instrument	Issued by	Denominations	Maturies
U.S. Treasury bills.	U.S. Treasury.	Denominations between $10,000 and $1 million.	91 days, 182 days, 52 weeks
Federal agency issues.	Loan, loan guarantee system	Denominations from $1,000 to $1 million.	Many maturities from several days to more than 10 years.
Negotiable certificates of deposit.	Commercial banks.	$25,000 to $1 million.	1 to 18 months.
Commercial paper.	Major companies.	$5,000 to $5 million or more in multiples of $1,000.	2 or 3 days to 270 days.
Repurchase agreements.	Commercial banks and security dealers.	Vary in amount, no standard denominations.	1 day to several months.
Time deposits.	Commercial banks and savings and loans.	No minimum.	30-day minimum.
Bankers' acceptances.		Vary in amount, depending on the size of the commercial transaction.	30 to 180 days.

*n.a. = Not available.
SOURCE: *Federal Reserve Bulletin,* June 1981 and June 1985.

Special attention should be given the instruments most commonly employed in government cash management:

a. **Treasury bills.** These short-term instruments issued by the U.S. government are the most popular marketable security for cash managers. Federal Reserve Banks sell them in weekly auctions in 91-day, 182-day, and in some auctions, one-year maturities. The secondary market is broad and lively, so they can easily be liquidated if an unanticipated need for cash develops or purchased anytime cash is available. Their yields are normally the lowest of the marketable securities, but that disadvantage is compensated by their safety from default, their short maturity, and easy marketability.

Bills bear no interest in the ordinary sense, although they do yield a return to their holder. Because they are sold at a price less than their face value (i.e., at discount), the holder receives a yield equal to the difference between the purchase price and the price received when the bill matures (or is resold). Thus, the purchaser might pay $9,860 for a bill

Marketability		1978	1980	1982	1984	March 1985
Highly organized secondary market.	Secondary market:					
	3 month	7.19	11.43	10.61	9.52	8.52
	6 month	7.58	11.37	11.07	9.76	8.90
	1 year	7.74	10.89	11.07	9.92	9.06
Fairly good secondary market.	Secondary market:					
	1 month	7.88	12.91	12.04	10.17	8.73
	3 month	8.22	13.07	12.27	10.37	9.02
	6 month	8.61	12.99	12.57	10.68	9.60
Weak secondary market.	1 month	7.76	12.76	11.83	10.05	8.74
	3 month	7.94	12.66	11.89	10.10	8.90
	6 month	7.99	12.29	11.89	10.16	9.23
Good, since borrower agrees to repurchase securities at a fixed price.						
Primary by demand; no secondary.	(Maximum rates:)	7.75	7.75	8	8	Market
Good, although less extensive than for most other instruments.	3 month	8.11	12.78	11.89	10.14	8.88
	6 month	n.a.*	n.a.	11.83	10.19	9.20

with a face value of $10,000; the return at maturity would be $140. The annualized rate of return or yield rate on a bill purchased through the discount mechanism may be computed according to the formula:

$$\text{Investment yield to maturity } (Y) = \frac{(100 - P) \times 365}{P \times H}$$

where P = purchase price paid by the investor for each $100 of the bill's face value and H = the number of days to maturity.[14]

For example, if the auction price is $98.25 per $100 of face value ($9,825 for the $10,000 Treasury bill) for a 91-day bill, the effective yield would equal:

$$Y = \frac{(100 - 98.25) \times 365}{98.25 \times 91} = 0.0714 \text{ or } 7.14\%$$

---

[14]Richard D. C. Trainer, *The Arithmetic of Interest Rates* (New York: Federal Reserve Bank of New York, 1982).

The same approach may be applied to compute the effective yield for a bill purchased or sold on the secondary market, substituting for $100 the price per $100 of face value received on sale.[15]

b. Other federal agency issues.

Federal agencies which make or guarantee loans issue their own securities. They include Government National Mortgage Association, Federal National Mortgage Association, Bank for Cooperatives, Student Loan Marketing Association, Federal Home Loan Bank, Federal Land Bank, and others. These securities are not legal obligations of the U.S. government, but are regarded as extremely low default risk. They normally sell at a yield between the Treasury issues and other money market issues. The same dealers who trade in the Treasury market trade in these issues as well, so they are salable in a strong secondary market. Some state and local government investment statutes are not clear about the legality of purchase of such issues, even though investment in Treasury issues is permitted.

c. Negotiable certificates of deposits.

A certificate of deposit is a time deposit with a commercial bank (or savings and loan association) issued for a specified period at a contracted interest rate. The issue is for a contracted period over which the stated interest rate holds, regardless of other rate changes in the period. Issues of the largest banks are bought and sold by government security dealers. Certificates of deposit usually bear rates above those paid on federal securities and are marketable. Investment statutes often reduce the ability of state or local government to acquire CDs from out-of-state purchasers, so some flexibility may be reduced in many applications. High-denomination certificates of deposit will usually not be fully covered by federal insurance (negotiated rates typically begin with CDs of $100,000, the current insurance limit). Thus, some states require pledging of particular assets by banks to guarantee the security of public funds: if the bank fails, those pledged assets would ensure that the public funds were not lost. Pledging is not popular with banks because it reduces profitability and the amount of credit a bank can extend.[16]

d. Commercial paper.

Large corporations and finance companies sell short-term, unsecured promissory notes directly to investors or through dealers. Maturities range up to 270 days. The secondary market is weak, but commercial paper from large corporate borrowers offers high rates. Higher risk and lower marketability reduce their attrac-

---

[15]The appropriate price of a bill, given a discount rate or desired investment yield, may be computed algebraically from the same formula. Pricing, however, is based on the 360-day financial year.

[16]James A. Verbrugge, "The Effects of Pledging Regulations on Bank Asset Composition," *Journal of Bank Research* 4 (August 1973), pp. 168–76.

tiveness for most public cash management programs. Furthermore, they offer substantially greater potential exposure to political problems than do other money market instruments.[17]

e. Repurchase agreement ("repo") and reverse repurchase agreements.   A repo is an agreement between a bank or security dealer and an investor in which the investor purchases a security, usually a U.S. Treasury security, with the commitment that the dealer will repurchase the security at a later date at a set price. A reverse repo involves sale of the security by investor to the dealer, with an agreed repurchase. Maturity is short, one day to a few months, and flexible to meet the requirements of the investor. The rate is slightly below the rate available on the security itself. The repo should be safe, because a security is available as full collateral on the transaction. Unfortunately, collapse of two large government security dealers in 1985 left many governments with large losses because collateral was missing. The market currently is both unregulated and uninsured.

f. State and local debt.   Most public investment statutes allow the purchase of state and local government bonds. Such purchases are made, but usually to support weak local bond markets and usually because of political pressure, not fiscal judgment. Normally, those acquisitions are unwise because the term of the debt is too long for cash management purposes and because yields are too low. If the yield is sufficiently high to be attractive, risk of default must be excessive.

g. State investment pools.   A number of states, including California, Connecticut, Florida, Georgia, Illinois, Maryland, Massachusetts, Montana, New Jersey, North Carolina, Oklahoma, Oregon, Tennessee, Utah, Virginia, West Virginia, and Wisconsin, have formal local government investment pools to enable local units to combine funds for short-term investment. The pools offer professional management, wider markets for investment, and the return advantages of larger investment blocks. Participation by eligible governments has not been high. Overall, these pools ought to be most attractive for smaller governments; their use should grow with tight budgets and fiscal sophistication.[18]

KEEPING SCORE

The final step of cash management is maintenance of a rolling score card for the program. The score card would contain the data required to

---

[17]Corporate bonds and stocks are to be avoided because of both default risk and credit market risk. Because pension funds are more concerned with long-term investment, public pension funds do frequently acquire high-grade corporate stocks and bonds.

[18]Timothy Q. Cook and Jeremy G. Duffield, "Short-term Investment Pools," *Economic Review of Federal Reserve Bank of Richmond* 66 (September/October 1980), p. 6.

evaluate the success of the program and to improve operation of the program. At a minimum the score card would have on a weekly basis:

1. Estimated total financial assets (cash and investments) held by unit (from the forecast).
2. Actual total financial assets held.
3. Demand deposit and currency total.
4. Interest received to date, this year.
5. Interest received to date, last year.
6. Six-month Treasury bill rate, this week.
7. Six-month Treasury bill rate, same week last year.

A comparison of interest rate profiles is important because substantial differences in investment income can occur from one year to the next from fluctuations in money market conditions, not because of cash management efforts. The data thus can provide feedback to improve forecasting models as well as gauge the benefits from the programs.

CONCLUSION

Idle cash in public accounts should be invested at the highest yield consistent with safety of principal and liquidity. Liquidity matters, because the primary objective is to ensure that the government's bills get paid. While many investment media are legally available to governments, U.S. Treasury bills, certificates of deposit, and repurchase agreements are the heart of most cash management programs. Cash management involves four critical steps: forecasting daily cash balances, pooling available funds to maximize investable balances, investment in the most attractive instruments, and maintenance of a score card for the program. Nationally, state and local governments have made great improvements in cash management over the past 30 years.

Questions and Exercises

1. What controls are placed on state and local cash management in your state? What investment instruments are legal? Is there a state investment pool?

2. What charges do banks in your area apply for services rendered governments?

3. Grantsville is a medium-sized midwestern town, not quite rural, not quite urban, and not quite a willing participant in the 20th century. As the new clerk-treasurer, you are eager to bring new aggressiveness to the city administration, so long as none of the "Old Guard"

gets mad. You suspect that a nonirritating first step would be the development of a cash plan and short-term investment strategy for the city. You further believe that an appropriate start would be with the four largest funds in the city financial structure: general, parks and recreation, motor vehicle, and cumulative capital. The following data emerge from your research. (A 19X7 calendar is shown.)

JANUARY						
S	M	T	W	T	F	S
						1
2	3	4	5	6	7	8
9	10	11	12	13	14	15
16	17	18	19	20	21	22
23	24	25	26	27	28	29
30	31					

FEBRUARY						
S	M	T	W	T	F	S
		1	2	3	4	5
6	7	8	9	10	11	12
13	14	15	16	17	18	19
20	21	22	23	24	25	26
27	28					

MARCH						
S	M	T	W	T	F	S
		1	2	3	4	5
6	7	8	9	10	11	12
13	14	15	16	17	18	19
20	21	22	23	24	25	26
27	28	29	30	31		

APRIL						
S	M	T	W	T	F	S
					1	2
3	4	5	6	7	8	9
10	11	12	13	14	15	16
17	18	19	20	21	22	23
24	25	26	27	28	29	30

MAY						
S	M	T	W	T	F	S
1	2	3	4	5	6	7
8	9	10	11	12	13	14
15	16	17	18	19	20	21
22	23	24	25	26	27	28
29	30	31				

JUNE						
S	M	T	W	T	F	S
			1	2	3	4
5	6	7	8	9	10	11
12	13	14	15	16	17	18
19	20	21	22	23	24	25
26	27	28	29	30		

IMPORTANT DATES

JANUARY
1 New Year's Day
15 Martin Luther King's Birthday

FEBRUARY
12 Lincoln's Birthday
14 Valentine's Day
16 Ash Wednesday
21 Washington's Birthday - Obsvd.
22 Washington's Birthday

MARCH
17 St. Patrick's Day
27 Palm Sunday
29 Passover Begins

APRIL
1 Good Friday
3 Easter Sunday

MAY
8 Mother's Day
21 Armed Forces Day
23 Victoria Day (Canada)
30 Memorial Day

JUNE
14 Flag Day
19 Father's Day

JULY
1 Dominion Day (Canada)
4 Independence Day

SEPTEMBER
5 Labor Day
8 Rosh Hashanah
17 Yom Kippur

OCTOBER
10 Thanksgiving Day (Canada)
10 Columbus Day - Obsvd.
12 Columbus Day
24 United Nations Day
31 Halloween

NOVEMBER
8 Election Day
11 Veterans Day
24 Thanksgiving Day

DECEMBER
1 Hanukkah
25 Christmas Day

JULY						
S	M	T	W	T	F	S
					1	2
3	4	5	6	7	8	9
10	11	12	13	14	15	16
17	18	19	20	21	22	23
24	25	26	27	28	29	30
31						

AUGUST						
S	M	T	W	T	F	S
	1	2	3	4	5	6
7	8	9	10	11	12	13
14	15	16	17	18	19	20
21	22	23	24	25	26	27
28	29	30	31			

SEPTEMBER						
S	M	T	W	T	F	S
				1	2	3
4	5	6	7	8	9	10
11	12	13	14	15	16	17
18	19	20	21	22	23	24
25	26	27	28	29	30	

OCTOBER						
S	M	T	W	T	F	S
						1
2	3	4	5	6	7	8
9	10	11	12	13	14	15
16	17	18	19	20	21	22
23	24	25	26	27	28	29
30	31					

NOVEMBER						
S	M	T	W	T	F	S
		1	2	3	4	5
6	7	8	9	10	11	12
13	14	15	16	17	18	19
20	21	22	23	24	25	26
27	28	29	30			

DECEMBER						
S	M	T	W	T	F	S
				1	2	3
4	5	6	7	8	9	10
11	12	13	14	15	16	17
18	19	20	21	22	23	24
25	26	27	28	29	30	31

1. *Fund balances for January 1, 19X7*

General fund	$520,860
Parks and recreation	52,968
Motor vehicle	104,015
Cumulative capital	739,611

2. *Revenue estimates*
    a. *Property Tax.* Collections are received by the city on May 1 and November 1. Because of a discount for early payment, ⅝ of the collections come in the first installment. Delinquency has historically been about 2 percent of the levy.

Levy: General fund $2,965,200
         Parks and recreation   718,300
         Cumulative capital   385,400

b. *Parking meters* (general fund). Revenues run about $6,000 per month, except September and October (football season) run about 5 percent higher, December about 10 percent higher, and July 15 percent lower.

c. *Building permits, inspection fees* (general fund). Estimated at $130,000 for the year. The Engineer's office transmits collections to you at the end of each quarter. You estimate the seasonals as QI, 85.0; QII, 105.0; QIII, 125; QIV, 85.0.

d. *Traffic fines* (half to general fund, half to motor vehicle). Estimated at $6,500 per month. Court remits at end of month.

e. *Swimming pool admissions* (park and recreation). Estimates based on prior years.

May	$ 800
June	950
July	1,750
August	2,500
September	750

f. *Community auditorium rental* (parks and recreation). Estimates based on prior year.

July 4 Freedom Celebration	$ 400
Labor Day Custom Car Show	1,500
Casual rentals (square dances, Rotary, etc.) bring in about	$150 per month.

g. *State shared tax* (motor vehicles). Data provided by state department of revenue:

March 31	$109,000
June 30	120,000
September 30	110,000
December 31	108,000

3. *Expenditures, as appropriated by city council*
   a. *Payrolls.* Paydays are every other week. The first payday is January 7.

General fund	$95,000 biweekly
Parks and recreation	15,000 biweekly
Also, temporary summer lifeguards, playground supervisors, etc., from May 15 to September 10	20,000 biweekly
Motor vehicle fund	10,200 biweekly

With these data, do the following:

a. Prepare a complete cash plan for 19X7 and include end-of-year balances. Estimate what amounts are available for investment and what your investment strategy will be. Estimate what funds shortages occur and how you intend to cover them. Base your estimates and strategies on current money market conditions and local bank costs and policies.

b. After this work is completed, you wonder what the Utilities Service Board (water and sewerage), which has independent control of its financial affairs, does with its available cash. The USB manager is a registered professional engineer. A bookkeeper does all financial and accounting work. One board member comments, "Oh sure, we try to invest every extra penny we get as soon as we get it. We have a couple of $30,000 CDs, maybe a $40,000, and a $70,000 one, but nothing larger. We also make a few Treasury-bill investments. The banks have been very cooperative and even waived the commission charge. We're happy to see that extra cash come to use." This member is likely to be more familiar with utility finances than any other members. What does your investigation suggest to you about USB cash management? Do you have any recommendations?

c. On the basis of your efforts, do you have any special financial operating reports for the council? What investment income do you suspect that you can generate?

d. How might the success of a municipal cash management program be evaluated?

4. A six-month (182-day) Treasury bill was auctioned at a price of $9,620 per $10,000 face value. What is the investment yield?

5. What is the purchase price per $10,000 face value for a 3-month (91-day) Treasury bill for an 7.5 percent discount rate?

Cases for Discussion

A   The three case histories written by officers of the First National Bank of Chicago illustrate the key points in establishing a public cash management program. That bank was a pioneer in such corporate systems; these cases represent application of similar principles to government operations.

Consider These Questions

1. *What key elements appear in each program?*
2. *What differences in incentives are the driving force behind each?*

CASE HISTORY #1: ARMY AND COAST GUARD BATTLE IDLE BALANCES

In December of 1980, the U.S. Army issued a proposal request for the design of a cash flow system for the Army Morale Support Fund. This fund holds the receipts of the 900 officers' and NCOs' clubs, golf courses, bowling alleys, crafts shops and other recreational facilities on the 260 Army installations in the U.S. These monies are self-generated, not tax dollars. The problem was how to concentrate the receipts from 900 accounts scattered across the United States into one pool so the Army could invest the excess funds. First Chicago's solution freed up an eight-figure dollar amount in idle balances which the fund promptly put to profitable use.

At the core of the Army's concentration system is a master sweep account with 900 local "sub-accounts." Each day, receipts from each individual unit are deposited into a local account. First Chicago, then, electronically sweeps those funds into the master account. Once the funds flow into the bank, the Army's daily investment withdrawals are achieved through a complex system of zero-balance accounts (ZBA). By using this system of ZBAs, the Army dramatically reduced the need for manually monitoring and reconciling the 900 accounts. In addition, the reports that First Chicago generates provide the Army with up-to-date balance and transaction information.

Using these reports, the Army's central investment office seeks the best return for the total of net investable funds that the bank collects each day. Currently the Army Morale Support Fund has an investment portfolio of more than $200 million. Our cash concentration system has freed up an additional $20 million, and the Army hopes to double that figure when its overseas bases become part of the system. The interest earned by the Morale Support Fund's investments is prorated and returned to the 900 participants in a manner similar to a mutual fund.

As the Army has become more comfortable with its new cash management capability, it has begun trying some advanced maneuvers. One of these is managing around a target. This gives them the luxury of meeting their required compensating balance figure on average over specified intervals rather than exactly every day. During leaner periods they are allowed to fall below the required balance so they can keep investments intact. They simply make up the shortfall during peak periods.

First Chicago is also working on enhancements for the system. For example, it soon will provide electronic, same-day reports on balances for all 900 participants rather than relying on slower microfiche.

Source: Patrick E. Rea and Maynard Brandon, "Applying Cash Management Techniques," *Government Accountants Journal* 33 (Spring 1983), pp. 45–49.

The cash concentration system developed for the Army is among the largest in terms of dollar volume in the Federal Government. In size and form, it compares to some of the largest and most sophisticated systems in private industry.

CASE HISTORY #2: CASH MANAGEMENT POSITIONS COMMUNITIES FOR THE FUTURE

Orland Park and Vernon Hills, two Chicago-area suburbs, share a similar revenue blessing—the existence of a major regional shopping center within their corporate boundaries. While the shopping centers provide a much-needed source of revenue for these relatively new communities, they also place an extra burden on city infrastructure and services. This particularly was true for Vernon Hills, since the village collects no local real estate tax and the shopping mall serves as the main source of income. Both communities chose to improve their cash management techniques in order to meet their financial responsibilities of today and the future.

In 1979 when First Chicago conducted the first cash management study for Orland Park, it was a village that had outgrown the capabilities of its paper bookkeeping system. And, despite its healthy tax base, the village faced its first debt-financed capital projects—expansion of municipal buildings including the village hall, public works garage and police department. The village also had to hook up with the city of Chicago's water system (at a cost of about $12 million) because the area's water table is dropping.

First Chicago's examination of Orland Park's cash flow system revealed that the villge needed to consolidate its receivables so it could reduce the processing float. The bank set up a lockbox system to which village residents would mail payments for their water bill and other fees and fines. The lockbox thus reduced the time between when the remitter paid his bill and when available funds were actually credited to the village's account. The bank also created an information system to net reporting of the village's receivables. This system produced a report based on the lockbox receipts that was in the same form as the nightly reports generated by the sophisticated computerized cash register used for in-person payments at the village hall. In addition to reducing reconciling functions, these computer-generated reports gave the village a clearer picture of its cash flows so that it could project future revenues and, thereby, maximize investment potential.

For the village of Vernon Hills, in Lake County north of Chicago, forecasting cash flows also played a part in its investment scheme. This village, however, was more interested in predicting disbursements so that it could utililze long-term rather than short-term investment, thereby getting better rates of return on its funds.

First Chicago completed its first cash management study for Vernon Hills in 1980. This government was not faced with a cash squeeze nor did it anticipate any major capital expenditures in the coming five years. The village's professional staff and elected officials, however, wanted to increase the town's income by pursuing an agressive investment policy. We examined the village's receipts and expenditures, and determined that the town needed to accelerate its receivables while at the same time aging its payables.

Our examination of the village's disbursement practices revealed that it was paying its bills too soon, and that trade terms, where available, were being ignored. Therefore, the bank recommended that the village pay its bills more slowly, taking advantage of trade terms and the 30-day rule often used in government. In addition, First Chicago developed a forecasting system for the village. The purpose of the forecasting system was to better predict cash flows—both receipts and disbursements—and to make longer term, more profitable investments using the enhanced prediction. By aging its payables and employing the forecasting system, the bank predicted that Vernon Hills could increase its investable balances by 10 percent yearly.

CASE HISTORY #3: A CASH MANAGEMENT "CHECK UP" LEADS TO A CURE FOR A DISBURSEMENT AILMENT

Cook County, Illinois, is among the largest governmental units in the nation. By virtue of its population and economic power, it would rank 12th in the Union if it were a state. This past year the Cook County Treasurer's Office collected $2.7 billion in property, inheritance, gasoline, liquor, and cigarette taxes. It distributes these revenues to 659 local taxing bodies such as cities, townships, park and school districts.

To ensure that its already sophisticated cash management system was operating at peak efficiency, the County Treasurer requested First Chicago's cash managment consultants to analyze the system and make recommendations.

Because the bulk of the county's collections are property taxes the consultants initially focused on this area. The bank analyzed how property tax payments are received, how the treasurer's office deposited them, the agency's record keeping processes, how the treasurer disbursed funds back to the taxing bodies, and how the undistributed funds are pooled and invested.

The consultants' immediate objecctive was to profile the clearing patterns of the checks issued to distribute property tax revenue to individual taxing bodies. This information would provide the basis for a forecasting data base to help optimize the time the county could earn interest on those funds. Without good forecasting information the potential existed for either excessive idle balances in the county account or for large overdrafts. By getting a handle on clearing patterns and leveling out the peaks and valleys of account balances, more profitable investment activity could easily be achieved.

Another objective of the study was to develop an overall picture of how the county system currently operates. Essentially everyone involved in both collections and disbursements—management, cashiers, data processors, auditors and accountants—was interviewed.

This information helped the treasurer's office update and redefine its cash management policies and procedures. In addition, it provided the treasurer with the kind of documentation of cash management that bond rating services such as Moody's or Standard & Poor's look at when analyzing a government's credit worthiness. Without such accurate, up-to-date documentation, rating points can be lost. This same information is also an invaluable tool in training new personnel.

Armed with data on current operations, our consultants were able to determine how the treasurer's system should work optimally. Because of the tremendous volume of checks the treasurer's office processes, First Chicago recommended that the county use an automated system for collecting and processing. In addition, the consultants recommended that the treasurer's office use the automated clearing house (ACH) to distribute the $2.5 billion in property taxes to the appropriate taxing bodies. This would help eliminate some short-term borrowing by local governments necessitated by the inefficiencies of the mail system.

The disbursement system created by the bank allows the treasurer's office to use the ACH to electronically deposit property tax payments directly into the accounts of the local taxing bodies. The new electronic system is easier to monitor and eliminates the need for the county to reconcile disbursements. In some instances, it also reduces costs for the taxing bodies because a number of the larger ones used to send armed couriers to pick up their payment from the treasurer's office.

First Chicago is also in the process of developing a sophisticated, integrated information system for the county. Many levels of government agencies could reap benefits from a similar system that would funnel timely, accurate financial information into the waiting hands of management.

B   The following article about state investment pools appeared in *The Wall Street Journal.*

Consider These Questions

1. *What advantages do state pools provide, compared with individual local government investment? What units are most likely to gain from such pools?*
2. *What are the arguments against such pools? What validity are they likely to have?*
3. *Why do banks oppose the pools?*

Cities Earn Extra Interest by Pooling Investment of Surplus Funds, but Banks Fight to Halt Trend

By Byron Klapper

Since the beginning of the year, Robert Schwab, finance director of Milpitas, California, has pulled $4 million of the city's money out of banks paying 4.5 percent interest and put it in a special investment account yielding 5.8 percent.

For the city of 27,000 people, the extra income ($52,000 on an annual basis) doesn't add up to much. But, says Mr. Schwab, "I'd be remiss if I didn't get the highest interest on investments of city funds."

Mr. Schwab put the Milpitas money in California's Pool Money Investment Account, one of a half-dozen cash pools that have sprung up in the past five years to enable cities and public agencies to earn higher interest on surplus funds. The idea behind the pools is simple enough. A small town can't shop for the high interest rates that banks and companies pay on large, short-term investments. But combine the cash from many localities, and the doors open at money centers like New York and San Francisco.

While the state pools aid investment officers like Milipitas's Mr. Schwab, they are heartily disliked by banks fearful of losing deposits. Stiff opposition by bankers has already knocked out one proposed state pool and almost scuttled two others. Moreover, some public officials also are concerned about the idea of sending local funds off to state capitals for investment. "It's a form of state-run bank to bypass other banks," says Elinor M. Ray, treasurer of the island community of Nantucket, in referring to Massachusetts's new Municipal Depository Trust.

Free Service Cited

Bankers contend that they earn the deposits of governmental units with free services like handling city payrolls and giving market advice when treasurers sell bonds and notes. They also argue that large-scale withdrawals would impair a region's fiscal health, particularly in rural areas. "Money drawn out of the community to any degree damages the local economy by reducing funds available for lending," says Truman Jeffers, executive secretary of the Minnesota Bankers Association.

Last spring, two Minnesota state senators, Wayne Olhoft and Earl W. Renneke, drew up a bill to form a state investment pool. But after intensive lobbying by bankers, the two legislators removed their names from their own bill and helped vote it down. Says Senator Olhoft, "My banker in Herman (population 600) saw it as a threat. He didn't like the idea that funds raised locally would be sent off to the big city."

Wisconsin started a cash pool last year over objections of the Wisconsin Bankers Association. It was approved by the legislature only after it was tacked onto a bill to cope with a state cash-flow crisis.

In New Jersey, the legislature passed a bill this summer to create a state Cash Management Fund, but the measure carried in the senate by only a two-vote margin above the 40 necessary for passage due to "considerable opposition from banks," says Roland M. Machold, head of the state's investment division. "Banks were concerned about money leaving the state and were wary of losing deposits," he says. The bill now is awaiting Governor Byrne's signature.

A Warning Sign

The defeat of the state pool in Minnesota and opposition in other states signal trouble for state treasurers willing to lend their market savvy to help local-government units. It also shows that bankers will fight to keep public deposits that might earn higher interest elsewhere (in Minnesota, in fact, about 30 percent of idle local government funds sit in bank accounts paying no interest at all, bank sources say).

Opposition to the pooled funds has continued even in states where they are already operating. Mattoon, a city of 24,000 in central Illinois, won't send surplus cash to the state fund in Springfield regardless of rates. "It's a matter of policy," says City Treasurer Frank McFarland, who also happens to be senior vice president of Central National Bank in Mattoon. "We support area financial institutions and, if possible, keep money invested locally," he says.

Some city officials, such as Theodore L. Scafidi, treasurer of Newton, Mass., don't think the extra return provided by some of the securities in state pool portfolios is worth the risk. While cities and towns often are limited to investing in U.S. government securities and collateralized bank certificates, a state pool may also buy corporate bonds, short-term trade bills (bankers' acceptances) and unsecured corporate IOUs (commercial paper). "If there's another Penn Central, we share the loss," Mr. Scafidi says. (Penn Central Transportation Co. filed for reorganization under federal bankruptcy laws in June 1970 and left investors with nearly worthless commercial paper.)

Pressure from Banks

In states with pooled funds, banks sometimes try to discourage communities from using them. "Make us your bank, and when you need money, we'll bid on your bonds," is the tactic banks commonly use, says Harry V. Keefe Jr., president of Keefe, Bruyette & Woods Inc., a dealer in bank securities. Small towns without access to national credit markets are most vulnerable to such pressures since there are few sources other than local banks to finance projects like school construction and road repair.

Nantucket Treasurer Ray says the community's bank balances help it get favorable terms on its bonds. "My impression from banks is that their willingness to bid is based somewhat on past business relationships," she says. "If we pull out our balances, rates may not be so attractive."

In California, however, banks have taken a benign view of the state's investment pool, according to the state's chief investment officer, Terry A. Brown. "We don't act in lieu of banks," he says. "We help small people without market access or expertise." As a consequence, California municipalities have $1.3 billion on deposit in Sacramento, where the money is commingled with the state's own $6.5 billion of short-term funds.

A typical user is June Stevens, treasurer of Larkspur, just south of San Francisco. "We don't leave funds lying in idle checking accounts over the weekend," she says. "I wire $25,000 to the state pool on Friday, withdraw it on Monday, and get the same interest rate as the state gets on its billions of dollars." In some states, deposits may be as small as $5,000 for periods ranging from one day to a year.

Flexible Operation

Even in states where investment pools are available, city officials don't automatically use them for excess funds. Darien, Conn., City Treasurer Earl Johnson says his state's Short Term Investment Fund (STIF) gives him "flexibility to get the best return on the city's money." But recently, 70 percent of the city's reserves were in Connecticut banks' certificates of deposit, which at the time were yielding half a percentage point more than STIF.

While investment pools are proving to be useful for smaller communities, they are also helping some states manage their funds. With the advent of STIF in 1972, the first such cash pool to get started, Connecticut keeps just enough interest-free deposits, known as compensating balances, to cover banks' costs of services to the state, such as handling payroll, welfare and vendor checks (the state figures $1 million of interest-free deposits is worth about $152 a day to a bank, based on the going rate on U.S. Treasury bills). A monthly cost analysis of the banks' services is sent to the state treasurer's office, which then adjusts state balances in the banks to meet the cost. Excess funds are invested through STIF.

The repurchase agreement has become a favored instrument for public cash management. It offers attractive yields and flexible maturity, high liquidity, and apparent safety of principal. Recent security dealer failures have tarnished the market, however. The following short selection examines the major points about this money market instrument.

Repos and Reverse Repos: A Guide to Government-Securities Markets

By Lee Berton

The government-securities market may seem remote to most investors, but its current problems can cripple savings and loan associations or handcuff towns and cities. That's because thousands of thrifts and local governments depend on this market for their financial health.

In the past two months, two major government-securities dealers—E.S.M. Government Securities Incorporated and Bevill, Bresler & Schulman Asset Management Corporation—have collapsed, causing large losses for dozens of thrifts and cities that traded with the firms. Yet few consumers understand how these dealers and the government-securities market work, and why the market has been under enormous pressure since mid-1982.

The size of the government-securities market and its borrowing and lending activities dwarf any other U.S. securities market. Every day, U.S. financial institutions, securities dealers and local government units trade more than $60 billion of government securities; players estimate that repurchase agreements—or "repos"—and reverse repos made in the market reach a trillion dollars on some days.

A thrift could collapse almost overnight if a government-securities firm it deals with goes sour. If the thrift is federally insured, $100,000 of each depositor's account is protected. For the 10 states in which private funds guarantee money in thrifts, the coverage is sometimes limited, and it may take several days, weeks or months before depositors receive their funds.

City or county governments could have their services and capital projects curtailed because of losses related to failed government-securities dealers. Among government units in danger of losing funds in recent dealers' failures are Allentown, Pennsylvania; Beaumont, Texas; Harrisburg, Pennsylvania; Pompano Beach, Florida; Toledo, Ohio; and Dauphin County in Pennsylvania and Chellan, Clallam, and Jefferson counties in Washington.

To explain the government-securities market and the threat to it, the Journal has interviewed representatives of government, the securities business, and the accounting profession.

Q. What is a repurchase agreement or repo?

A. A repo occurs when one party sells government securities to a second party and agrees to repurchase them later at a higher price that includes interest. For example, a government-securities dealer sells securities, such as Treasury bills or the debt of the Federal National Mortgage Association (called Fannie Maes), to a local government for $10 million. The dealer promises to buy back the securities within 30 days for nearly $10.1 million. In effect, the government is making a loan to the dealer, and the securities are the collateral.

A repo also occurs when a thrift sells securities from its investment portfolio to a dealer and agrees to buy them back later at a higher price.

Q. What is a reverse repo?

A. It's looking at the same transactions from the lenders' point of view. In the first example above, the government is doing a reverse repo with the securities dealer.

Q. How is the dealer paid?

A. The dealer receives the difference between the interest it collects from the thrift and the interest it pays to the city. This spread is usually very small in relation to the size of the transaction.

Q. So the dealer is just a middleman?

A. No, it's more. The dealer seems to act only as a go-between for the parties holding the securities, such as the thrifts, and those wanting to invest their cash, such as the governments. But the dealer is in fact a principal in the transactions; when a deal sours, both the thrift and the city seek redress from the dealer—not from each other.

Q. What actually happens to government securities when they are put up as collateral for a loan?

A. The dealer who takes delivery of them is supposed to keep them with its bank in a custodial account. But more than 80 percent of repo transactions are recorded only through book entries at the Federal Reserve Bank, so they cannot be physically checked.

Q. Why would a thrift borrow from a government-securities dealer?

A. It's cheap money. At current rates, a thrift can use funds from the dealer to make mortgage loans at 12 percent or more while paying the dealer only 8 percent interest. Putting up $10 million in collateral with government securities, a thrift can make at least $3,300 a day in interest.

Q. Why do local governments lend money to securities dealers when they can buy certificates of deposit or government securities at higher rates?

A. Repos are more liquid. For example, if a community has $10 million for new roads but is waiting for construction bids, it can invest with a securities dealer and avoid tying up the funds for a long time.

Q. Why have government-securities dealers failed?

A. Regulators are still trying to figure out the reasons for the latest failures. But in past failures, dealers often used collateral to shore up other businesses, or to make multiple loans. When more than one party sought its collateral, the house of cards collapsed. Dealers were able to perpetuate this fraud because thrifts and municipalities were willing to accept written confirmations of the collateral from dealers without getting added confirmation from the dealers' banks.

Q. How are thrifts hurt by entering repos with securities dealers that collapse?

A. Two ways. First, thrifts often have to put up 5 percent to 8 percent more collateral than the cash they receive from the dealers. If the dealer fails, all of that collateral may be lost.

Second, dealers sometimes convince thrifts to take the money they receive from dealers and lend it right back to the same dealer. So if a dealer collapses, these thrifts can lose everything: their collateral and the money they lent back to the dealer.

Q. How are governments hurt by failed securities dealers?

A. The governments are the biggest and most obvious losers. They have lent money to the dealer—supposedly receiving collateral in return. If the dealer collapses, the governments may not be repaid their loan, and they might find that their collateral doesn't exist or is pledged to other governments as well.

Q. Should the repo market be regulated?

A. Regulators and legislators are divided. Critics of the market say regulation is needed to prevent additional failures and protect thrifts and local governments. They want dealers to have minimum capital requirements and want federal and state agencies to inspect dealers' operations, particularly the existence of collateral. But proponents of the current system warn that too much regulation could stifle a market that has helped the federal government quickly borrow money for its huge operations.

Understanding Financial Data in
*The Wall Street Journal**

——

Any public financial manager must from time to time obtain a feel for general financial market conditions because of public debt or investment proposals. Some administrators, because of their functions, must maintain touch with these markets on a daily basis. While there are several sources for this information, one of the most readily available is *The Wall Street Journal.* The following selection is a guide to interpretation of information in that source (omitted sections provide detail on stock and futures markets, not generally the concern of government finance).

The Wall Street Journal publishes at least 10 pages of data on financial markets every day. These appear regularly in the second section of the paper. They cover trading in stocks, bonds, currencies and certain other financial instruments, including futures and options. Many readers turn first to these pages because they want to find the value of securities they own or plan to buy. Others are looking for data to use in research for business or educational needs.

To the casual reader, these pages may seem a blur of small type and obscure abbreviations. They must look this way because they pack a great deal of information into a relatively small space. This special section attempts to put that information into focus.

——

STOCKS

The majority of the data has to do with stocks. About 42 million Americans own stock, many of them institutional investors who have amassed large blocks of shares. Stocks are at the heart of the U.S. economic system.

Stocks represent shares in the ownership of corporations. Companies issue them to raise money for their activities; investors buy them in hopes that their price will rise as the company's business prospers and that some of the profits will be paid to the investors as dividends. When a company issues new shares of stock, the process of selling them to investors takes place in what is called the primary market.

It helps greatly in selling new issues if investors can easily resell the stock when they wish. This need for marketability has given rise to stock exchanges, called secondary markets. Here, buyers and sellers exchange cash for shares, but none of the proceeds goes to companies that issued the shares.

The New York Stock Exchange, popularly known as the Big Board, is by far the biggest stock exchange and only the soundest corporations qualify for listing on it.

Reputable companies whose stocks, for one reason or another, aren't quoted on the New York Stock Exchange may be traded on the American Stock Exchange, or Amex, in New York, or on one or more of 14 regional exchanges in other cities. Trading results for stocks listed both on the NYSE and regional exchanges are combined on the NYSE page; this is called composite trading. Amex listings also are composite and have a page of their own. An Other Markets table reflects activity in issues traded exclusively on regional or Canadian exchanges. Some foreign stocks are listed in tables called Foreign Markets and Foreign Securities.

Still more stocks aren't listed on any exchange, but a thriving market in them exists nonetheless. This is the inaptly named over-the-counter market, or OTC. Far from being the archaic system its name might conjure, this is a highly sophisticated network of interlocking computers, communications wires and telephones. Stocks traded in this market may be found in the OTC listings.

Some stocks are bought mostly for the dividends they pay, others because they offer good potential for price appreciation. Most offer some combination of these two attractions.

Besides price quotations, a variety of other information about stocks is published. A Stock Market Data Bank appears on the second-to-last page each day. The daily Earnings Digest reports corporate profit or loss figures, which can have an impact on stock prices. Dividend announcements, of interest to all shareholders, are reported in Dividend News. More specialized information on short positions, most active stocks, new highs and lows and other data also is provided regularly.

OPTIONS

A refinement of stock trading is the options market. This permits traders to participate in the capital-appreciation potential of stocks, but not in any dividends. Traders can do this without putting up substantial (currently 50 percent) margin, or down payment, required for stocks themselves.

For a fee, a trader can have an option to buy a stock, or to sell it, at a fixed price for a fixed time period. If the stock's price goes up by an amount greater than the fee, the trader makes a profit. The option to buy is known as a *call;* the option to sell is known as a *put.* A profit on a put is made when a stock's price falls by an amount greater than the fee to buy the put. Because stock prices may not change as much as options buyers may expect, the risk of losing one's entire investment in options is considerably greater than in stocks themselves.

BONDS

In contrast to stocks, bonds don't convey any ownership in the entity that issues them. A bond is a loan. It pays interest to the investor and the loan is repayable after a stipulated period. Bonds are issued by a variety of borrowers, including corporations, governments and agencies of governments, such as highway authorities.

The interest rate on a bond is partly a reflection of the investor's risk of losing his money. Corporations occasionally go bankrupt, for example. Governments are considered the least risky of borrowers, so government bonds such as those of the U.S. Treasury generally pay lower interest rates. The rates also vary according to the maturity, or duration, of the loans. The shortest common borrowings are for about three months, in the form of U.S. Treasury bills, and for about one month, in the form of commercial paper issued by corporations and certificates of deposit issued by banks.

The Wall Street Journal publishes tables of bonds listed on the New York Stock Exchange and the American Stock Exchange as well as listings of government issues and certain other instruments. Interest on some bonds isn't subject to income tax; selected prices of such issues are reported in a Tax Exempt Bonds table.

Numerous funds pool investors' money to buy securities more diversified and in larger amounts than individuals generally could accumulate on their own. Mutual funds concentrate on stocks and bonds; a special table lists their net asset values daily. Money market funds specialize in short-term instruments; their yields are listed weekly.

COMMODITY FUTURES

Commodity futures are contracts that cover the future delivery of raw materials such as wheat, cotton or gold, and of financial instruments such as bonds or stock indexes. These contracts cover stipulated quantities and grades of the commodities, and they specify where, when and at what price the goods are to be delivered. Like stocks or bonds, futures may be bought and sold through brokers. Trading in them takes place on 12 U.S. exchanges, as well as abroad. The largest exchanges are the Chicago Board of Trade, the Chicago Mercantile Exchange and the Commodity Exchange, or Comex, in New York.

People buy futures when they think the price of the underlying commodity will rise; they sell futures when they think the price will fall. There isn't any stigma attached to selling short in commodity markets. These markets, however, are very risky because margin payments—the amount a trader has to deposit with a broker to buy or sell a futures contract—are only about 5 percent of the value of a contract and prices are volatile. The possibility of losing all one's investment in futures is high.

A growing proportion of the commodity business consists of financial futures, which cover debt instruments (bonds and the like), currencies (British pounds, Japanese yen, etc.) and stock indexes (notably the Standard & Poor's 500).

Each provides participants in their respective markets with the same protection against price variance that participants in traditional commodity markets may obtain. They also provide opportunities to speculate on trends in interest rates, foreign exchange and the stock market, with the same high risk and high profit potential in the raw materials futures markets.

The Futures Prices table gives data on futures of all types. A separate Cash Prices table lists prices for immediate delivery of a more extensive group of commodities. There is also a table of oil prices.

ADDITIONAL DATA

Other tables in the Journal's financial pages include Foreign Exchange, the rates at which U.S. dollars may be exchanged for various other currencies. The rates given are for large quantities traded among banks and they vary minute-by-minute. Smaller quantities, especially banknotes, bought or sold by individuals will result in rates that may be different from those printed.

Besides the tables, graphic charts on the second to last page show trends over the last two years in stocks, interest rates and foreign exchange. In addition, texts are provided daily commenting on developments in these markets.

BONDS

Only corporations can issue stocks but bonds can be issued by corporations or government units. "Governments" are bonds issued by the U.S. Treasury or by agencies of the federal government. Direct obligations of the Treasury are considered free of risk that the issuer will default. Agencies such as the Federal National Mortgage Association (called FNMA or Fannie Mae) use the proceeds to finance their activities; the FNMA finances home mortgages.

Another agency, the Government National Mortgage Association (GNMA or Ginnie Mae) issues certificates that are backed by mortgages. In the case of failure, the U.S. government guarantees payment. Some agency obligations are backed by the government and some aren't, but agency defaults are considered unlikely.

The Treasury issues instruments due after various lengths of time, known as maturities. The shortest regularly issued maturities, three or six months, take the form of Treasury bills. These are issued every Monday in minimum denominations of $10,000 and in increments of $5,000 above the minimum. Investors bid for them at a discount, by offering, say $97.50 for every $100 of bills. At maturity, the investor will receive $100 for every $97.50 he paid. Yields are expressed on an annual basis, so in the case of a three-month bill purchased for $97.50, the yield would be the discount ($2.50) divided by the price ($97.50) and multiplied by 4 because there are four three-month periods in a year. In this example, the yield would be about 10.25 percent.

Similar bills due in one year are sold monthly. The Treasury also issues cash management bills on an irregular basis, generally for short periods such as a few days.

Treasury issues maturing in between one and 10 years are called notes. Those maturing in more than 10 years are called bonds. The process of selling these issues to the public takes place in the primary market, with the proceeds going to the issuer.

Secondary markets are made by securities dealers in all maturities of Treasury issues. These permit holders to sell their securities before they mature and they permit purchases even at times when the Treasury isn't making any offerings in the primary market. The Federal Reserve also uses the marketplace to buy and sell Treasury issues as part of its monetary policy.

In the secondary market, the prices of bills, notes and bonds fluctuate according to changes in interest rates. But, in one of the more confusing aspects of financial markets, the prices fluctuate inversely to the interest rates. Thus, when interest rates rise, bond prices go down, and when interest rates fall, bond prices go up.

The rationale for this is as follows. Say the Treasury issues some 30-year bonds with an interest rate of 10 percent, or $10 for every $100.

In time, interest rates may rise to 12 percent. Then, no one in the secondary market will want to pay full price for bonds paying 10 percent interest when they can buy new ones at 12 percent. However, they might be willing to pay less than $100 for every $100 of the old bonds. Tables and calculators exist which show the exact price to pay so the yield to maturity on a 10 percent bond is 12 percent, taking into account the time left to maturity when the purchase is made. Leaving aside the complicating factor of yield to maturity, a price of $83.33 for every $100 face value of a 10 percent bond would result in a current return of 12 percent.

Similarly, when interest rates fall, bond prices will rise because sellers will hold out for a higher price to compensate for the higher-than-market interest paid on their holdings.

These changing prices are the basis of the Journal's tables for bonds and other debt securities. Governments are covered in one table (Figure 1). These issues are traded over the counter by securities dealers. Like the OTC stock market, the bond market is a sophisticated network of interlocking telephones, wires and computer connections among dealers and customers.

For bonds and notes, the price quotations are given per hundred dollars of face value. The first column shows the original interest rate, with an "s" after it for ease of pronunciation. For example, 9 percent bonds due in 1987 are called "nines of eighty-seven." The next two columns give the year and month of maturity. The notation "n" designates notes; the rest are bonds. Bonds issued some time ago may mature sooner than recently issued notes; this list is chronological. Some newer issues, designated "p," are exempt from withholding tax if held by non-U.S. citizens.

The first column to the right of the dots gives that mid-afternoon bid price, at which dealers were willing to buy the issue that day. The second column to the right gives the asked, or dealer selling price. The next column, second from the end, gives the changes in the bid price from the day before. The last column gives the yield, or effective return on the investment. This is a calculation that takes into account the original interest rate, the current asked price and the amount of time left to maturity.

In the bond market, a price of 100 is called par and each one-hundredth of par is called a point. Normally, the minimum price fluctuation is 1/32 of a point. To avoid repeating the figure 32 all the time, and to save space, there is a convention in the bond market that figures after a decimal point in a price represent 32ds. Thus, a quotation of 90.16 means 90 and 16/32 or 90½.

In the Treasury bill section of this table, however, the decimal takes on its customary meaning: 16.50 means 16½. Maturities are given as

FIGURE 1

TREASURY BONDS, NOTES & BILLS

Friday, July 12, 1985

Representative mid-afternoon Over-the-Counter quotations supplied by the Federal Reserve Bank of New York City, based on transactions of $1 million or more.

Decimals in bid-and-asked and bid changes represent 32nds; 101.1 means 101 1/32. a-Plus 1/64. b-Yield to call date. d-Minus 1/64. k-Non U.S. citizens exempt from withholding taxes. n-Treasury notes. p-Treasury note; non U.S. citizens exempt from withholding taxes.

Treasury Bonds and Notes

Rate	Mat.	Date	Bid	Asked	Bid Chg.	Yld.
10⅝s,	1985	Jul n	100.4	100.8	.....	4.37
8¼s,	1985	Aug n	100.2	100.6	.....	5.78
9⅝s,	1985	Aug n	100.5	100.9	– .1	5.79
10⅝s,	1985	Aug n	100.10	100.14	– .1	6.82
13⅛s,	1985	Aug n	100.16	100.20	.....	5.49
10⅞s,	1985	Sep n	100.21	100.25	– .1	6.84
15⅞s,	1985	Sep n	101.24	101.28	.....	6.54
10½s,	1985	Oct n	100.26	100.30	– .2	7.05
9¾s,	1985	Nov n	100.21	100.25	– .1	7.22
10½s,	1985	Nov n	100.31	101.3	– .2	7.40
11¾s,	1985	Nov n	101.10	101.14	– .2	7.17
10⅞s,	1985	Dec n	101.15	101.19	– .3	7.23
14⅛s,	1985	Dec n	103.3	103.7	– .2	6.81
10⅝s,	1986	Jan n	101.17	101.21	– .2	7.45
10⅞s,	1986	Feb n	101.26	101.30	– .4	7.65
13½s,	1986	Feb n	103.7	103.11	– .4	7.54
9⅞s,	1986	Feb n	101.4	101.8	– .2	7.65
14s,	1986	Mar n	104.11	104.15	– .2	7.42
11½s,	1986	Mar n	102.16	102.20	– .2	7.63
11¾s,	1986	Apr n	102.29	103.1	– .2	7.74
7⅞s,	1986	May n	100	100.4	– .2	7.72
9⅜s,	1986	May n	101.4	101.8	– .3	7.80
12⅝s,	1986	May n	103.25	103.29	– .3	7.92
13¾s,	1986	May n	104.21	104.25	– .3	7.72
13s,	1986	Jun n	104.20	104.24	– .1	7.76
14⅞s,	1986	Jun n	106.21	106.25	– .3	7.41
12⅝s,	1986	Jul p	104.15	104.19	– .2	7.95
8s,	1986	Aug n	100	100.4	– .2	7.88
11⅜s,	1986	Aug n	103.10	103.14	– .2	8.00
12⅜s,	1986	Aug p	104.12	104.16	– .2	8.12
11⅞s,	1986	Sep p	104.3	104.7	– .3	8.14
12¼s,	1986	Sep n	104.17	104.21	.....	8.13
11⅝s,	1986	Oct p	104	104.4	.....	8.20
6⅛s,	1986	Nov	97.26	98.26	.....	7.07
10⅜s,	1986	Nov p	102.16	102.20	+ .1	8.32
11s,	1986	Nov n	103.9	103.13	.....	8.26
13⅞s,	1986	Nov n	106.24	106.28	– .2	8.32
16⅛s,	1986	Nov n	109.30	110.2	– .5	8.02
9⅞s,	1986	Dec p	101.29	102.1	.....	8.37
10s,	1986	Dec n	102.1	102.5	– .1	8.40
9¾s,	1987	Jan p	101.20	101.24	– .1	8.52
9s,	1987	Feb n	100.20	100.24	.....	8.48
10s,	1987	Feb p	102.1	102.5	.....	8.55
10⅞s,	1987	Feb n	103.6	103.10	– .3	8.59
12¾s,	1987	Feb n	105.29	106.1	– .2	8.60
10¼s,	1987	Mar n	102.14	102.18	– .1	8.61
10¾s,	1987	Mar p	103.7	103.11	– .3	8.61
9¾s,	1987	Apr p	101.20	101.22	– .1	8.71
9⅛s,	1987	May p	100.18	100.20	– .1	8.76
12s,	1987	May n	105.13	105.17	– .1	8.67
12½s,	1987	May n	106.5	106.9	– .2	8.72
14s,	1987	May n	108.21	108.25	– .1	8.72
8½s,	1987	Jun p	99.17	99.19	– .2	8.73
10½s,	1987	Jun n	102.31	103.3	– .2	8.75
12⅜s,	1987	Aug p	106.11	106.15	– .4	8.91
13¾s,	1987	Aug n	108.26	108.30	– .6	8.95
11⅛s,	1987	Sep n	104.12	104.16	– .3	8.84
7⅝s,	1987	Nov n	97.28	98.4	– .5	8.53
11s,	1987	Nov p	104.4	104.8	– .3	8.94
12⅝s,	1987	Nov n	107.10	107.14	– .4	9.02
11¼s,	1987	Dec n	104.25	104.29	– .4	8.98
12⅜s,	1988	Jan n	107.9	107.13	– .5	9.00
10⅛s,	1988	Feb n	102.6	102.10	– .4	9.10
10⅜s,	1988	Feb p	102.25	102.27	– .3	9.12
12s,	1988	Mar n	106.22	106.26	– .2	9.11
13¼s,	1988	Apr n	109.21	109.25	– .4	9.15
8¼s,	1988	May n	98.13	98.21	– .3	8.80
9⅞s,	1988	May n	101.24	101.28	– .4	9.11
10s,	1988	May p	102.10	102.14	.....	9.01
13⅝s,	1988	Jun n	110.26	110.30	– .7	9.31
14s,	1988	Jul n	111.29	112.5	– .7	9.26
10½s,	1988	Aug n	103.7	103.11	– .6	9.23
15⅜s,	1988	Oct n	116.8	116.16	– .8	9.37
11⅜s,	1988	Sep p	105.11	105.15	– .11	9.36
8¾s,	1988	Nov n	98.27	99.3	– .6	9.07
11¾s,	1988	Nov n	106.12	106.16	– .8	9.43
10⅝s,	1988	Dec p	103.12	103.16	– .6	9.42
14⅝s,	1989	Jan n	114.23	114.27	– .6	9.53
11⅜s,	1989	Feb n	105.13	105.17	– .6	9.52
11¼s,	1989	Mar p	105.10	105.12	– .3	9.50
14⅜s,	1989	Apr n	114.14	114.22	– .4	9.62
9¼s,	1989	May n	99.28	100.4	– .4	9.21
11¾s,	1989	May n	106.17	106.21	– .4	9.63
9⅝s,	1989	Jun p	100.17	100.19	– .3	9.44
14½s,	1989	Jul n	115.19	115.27	– .4	9.63
13⅞s,	1989	Aug n	113.18	113.22	– .4	9.73
11⅞s,	1989	Oct n	107.11	107.15	– .3	9.69
10¾s,	1989	Nov n	103.24	104	– .5	9.60
12¾s,	1989	Nov p	110.8	110.12	– .2	9.76

U.S. Treas. Bills

Mat. date	Bid Discount	Asked Discount	Yield
-1985-			
7-18	7.00	6.76	6.86
7-25	6.81	6.73	6.83
8- 1	6.88	6.82	6.94
8- 8	6.93	6.89	7.02
8-15	6.79	6.75	6.88
8-22	6.87	6.83	6.97
8-29	6.89	6.85	7.00
9- 5	6.98	6.94	7.11
9-12	6.92	6.90	7.07
9-19	6.97	6.95	7.14
9-26	6.99	6.95	7.15
10- 3	7.14	7.12	7.33
10-10	7.09	7.07	7.29
10-17	7.11	7.09	7.32
10-24	7.11	7.09	7.33
10-31	7.13	7.09	7.34
11- 7	7.13	7.11	7.37
11-14	7.15	7.11	7.39
11-21	7.17	7.13	7.42
11-29	7.15	7.11	7.41
12- 5	7.16	7.12	7.43
12-12	7.16	7.12	7.44
12-19	7.17	7.13	7.46
12-26	7.13	7.09	7.43
-1986-			
1- 2	7.17	7.13	7.48
1- 9	7.20	7.18	7.55
1-23	7.22	7.18	7.56
2-20	7.24	7.20	7.59
3-20	7.24	7.20	7.60
4-17	7.32	7.28	7.72
5-15	7.36	7.34	7.81
6-12	7.34	7.30	7.80
7-10	7.33	7.31	7.84

months and dates; 5-28 means May 28. The bid and ask quotations are for discounts, as explained above. The yield, as for longer term issues, represents the effective total return and is used for comparison with other investments.

Quotations for a selection of Government, Agency and miscellaneous securities are given in a separate table (Figure 2) which is displayed much like Treasury bonds.

FIGURE 2

GOVERNMENT AGENCY ISSUES

Friday, July 12, 1985
Mid-afternoon Over-the-Counter quotations usually based on large transactions, sometimes $1 million or more. Sources on request.
Decimals in bid-and-asked represent 32nds; 101.1 means 101 1/32. a-Plus 1/64. b-Yield to call date. d-Minus 1/64.

FNMA Issues					Fed. Home Loan Bank				
Rate	Mat	Bid	Asked	Yld	Rate	Mat	Bid	Asked	Yld
14.10	8-85	100.13	100.17	6.59	12.80	7-85	100.2	100.6	5.70
15.00	9-85	101.2	101.6	6.79	13.90	7-85	100.3	100.7	5.64
7.90	10-85	100.1	100.5	7.08	9.35	8-85	100.4	100.8	6.89
8.80	10-85	100.7	100.11	7.15	11.95	8-85	100.14	100.18	6.67
10.15	10-85	100.17	100.21	7.13	11.70	9-85	100.24	100.28	6.89
13.00	11-85	101.22	101.26	7.13	14.15	9-85	101.7	101.11	6.85
9.75	12-85	100.24	100.28	7.44	11.20	10-85	100.30	101.2	7.12
14.90	12-85	102.25	102.29	7.36	8.10	11-85	100.5	100.9	7.22
13.00	1-86	102.15	102.19	7.46	10.13	11-85	100.29	101.1	7.10
11.70	2-86	102.6	102.10	7.45	14.70	12-85	103.1	103.5	7.35
8.20	3-86	100.9	100.13	7.52	9.20	1-86	100.24	100.28	7.49
9.50	3-86	101.3	101.7	7.52	12.75	1-86	102.19	102.23	7.44
9.95	3-86	101.8	101.12	7.72	13.85	1-86	103.5	103.9	7.45
10.95	4-86	102.4	102.8	7.71	9.55	2-86	101.2	101.6	7.50
9.20	4-86	100.29	101.1	7.70	15.30	2-86	104.15	104.19	7.43
11.00	5-86	102.14	102.18	7.70	10.20	3-86	101.19	101.23	7.58
14.63	6-86	105.20	105.28	7.74	15.75	3-86	105.12	105.16	7.43
7.95	7-86	99.30	100.6	7.75	9.15	4-86	100.29	101.1	7.73
14.30	7-86	105.28	106.4	7.73	10.25	4-86	101.25	101.29	7.65
13.90	8-86	105.21	105.29	8.02	11.70	4-86	102.27	102.31	7.66
7.90	9-86	99.26	100.2	7.83	8.75	5-86	100.22	100.26	7.74
13.25	9-86	105.7	105.15	8.16	15.50	5-86	106.6	106.14	7.65
10.10	10-86	101.26	102.2	8.29	15.35	7-86	107.4	107.12	7.74
12.90	10-86	105.2	105.10	8.26	14.60	8-86	106.20	106.28	7.99
10.95	11-86	102.27	103.3	8.40	16.40	9-86	108.27	109.3	8.22
13.05	11-86	105.12	105.20	8.43	12.25	9-86	104.7	104.15	8.22
7.30	12-86	98.24	99.4	7.96	10.80	10-86	102.21	102.29	8.34
10.13	12-86	102	102.8	8.38	11.00	11-86	103.1	103.9	8.38

Besides the U.S. government and its agencies, bonds may be issued by a variety of other government bodies, which are lumped together under the heading "Municipals" even though they include states, highway authorities and other non-city entities, as well as cities and their agencies. Usually, interest on these issues is exempt from income tax by the federal government and by the state (and sometimes the city) in which the borrower is located. Because of this privilege, the issuer can pay a lower rate of interest and investors have to consider the after-tax yield, based on their own income-tax situation, when comparing yields on these with those of other bonds. These bonds also are known as Tax Exempts.

Most Tax Exempts trade infrequently, in the over-the-counter market, so the Journal prints prices of only a small number of issues that are relatively large. (See Figure 3) These also are listed much like Treasury bonds, although a yield isn't given. On Fridays, an index of municipal bonds is published, along with indexes covering various subgroups. (Figure 4). Revenue bonds are secured by income from specific projects such as airports or hospitals. General obligations are covered by the general revenues of the entities that issue them.

FIGURE 3

Tax-Exempt Bonds

Monday, July 15, 1985

Here are current prices of several active tax-exempt revenue bonds issued by toll roads and other public authorities.

Agency	Coupon	Mat	Bid	Asked	Chg.
Alabama G.O.	8⅜s	'01	97½	99½	....
Bat Park City Auth NY	6⅜s	'14	73	77	− ½
Chelan Cnty PU Dist	5s	'13	69½	72½	+ ½
Clark Cnty Arpt Rev	10½s	'07	103½	106½	....
Columbia St Pwr Exch	3⅞s	'03	84	87	+ ½
Dela River Port Auth	6½s	'11	79	82	....
Douglas Cnty PU Dist	4s	'18	48	51	....
Ga Mun El Auth Pwr Rev	8s	'15	82½	86½	+ ½
Intermountain Pwr	7½s	'18	78	81	....
Intermountain Pwr	10½s	'18	102½	106½	....
Intermountain Pwr	14s	'21	131	135	....
Jacksonville Elec Rev	9¼s	'13	98	101	....
Loop	6½s	'08	70	74	....
MAC	7½s	'92	99½	103½	....
MAC	7½s	'95	98	102	....
MAC	8s	'86	101½	105½	....
MAC	8s	'91	101	105	+ ½
MAC	9.7s	'08	104½	108½	....
MAC	9¾s	'92	103	107	....
MAC	10¼s	'93	108	112	....
Mass Port Auth Rev	6s	'11	73	77	....
Massachusetts G.O.	6½s	'00	81	85	....
Mass Wholesale	6⅜s	'15	50	54	....
Mass Wholesale	13⅜s	'17	99	103	+ 1
Metro Transit Auth	9¼s	'15	100	104	....
Michigan Public Pwr	10⅝s	'18	106½	110½	....
Nebraska Pub Pwr Dist	7.1s	'17	76½	79½	+ ½
NJ Turnpike Auth	4¾s	'06	68½	71½	....
NJ Turnpike Auth	5.7s	'13	71	73	....
NJ Turnpike Auth	6s	'14	73½	76½	....
NY Mtge Agency Rev	9½s	'13	102	106	....
NY State Pwr Escr	5½s	'10	68½	70½	....
NY State Pwr	6⅝s	'10	79½	82½	....
NY State Pwr Escr	9½s	'01	109	112	....
NY State Pwr	9⅞s	'20	105½	108½	....
NY State Thruway Rev	3.1s	'94	75	78	....
NY State Urban Dev Corp	6s	'13	67½	71½	....
NY State Urban Dev Corp	7s	'14	77½	81½	....
NC East Mun Pwr Agcy	11¼s	'18	106½	109½	+ ½
Okla Tpke Auth Rev	4.7s	'06	66½	69½	....
Port of NY & NJ	4¾s	'03	67	70	....
Port of NY & NJ	6s	'06	77	80	....
Port of NY & NJ	7s	'11	85	88	....
Port of NY-Delta	10½s	'08	107½	111½	....
Salt River-Arizona	9¼s	'20	99	103	....
SC Pub Svc Auth	10¼s	'20	104	108	....
Texas Munic Pwr Agcy	9½s	'12	97½	101½	....
Valdez (Exxon)	5½s	'07	67	69	....
Valdez (Sohio)	6s	'07	69	71	....
Wshngtn PPSS #4-5	f6s	'15	5½	9½	....
Wshngtn PPSS #4-5	f7¾s	'18	6	10	....
Wshngtn PPSS #4-5	f9⅞s	'12	6½	10½	....
Wshngtn PPSS #4-5	f12½s	'10	8	12	− 1
Wshngtn PPSS #2	6s	'12	53½	57½	+ ½
Wshngtn PPSS #1	7¾s	'17	65½	69½	+ ½
Wshngtn PPSS #2	9¼s	'11	81½	85½	+ ½
Wshngtn PPSS #3	13⅞s	'18	107½	111½	+ ½
Wshngtn PPSS #2	14¾s	'12	113½	117½	+ ½
Wshngtn PPSS #1	15s	'17	113½	117½	+ 1

f-Trades flat without payment of current interest.

Corporate bonds constitute another major group. There are three main types of them:

Mortgage bonds, which are secured by real property such as buildings.

Debentures, which are backed by a company's earning power rather than by anything specific.

Convertible bonds, which can be exchanged for shares of the issuer's stock. Because of this feature, they carry a lower interest rate than "straight," or nonconvertible bonds.

FIGURE 4

Municipal Bond Index
Merrill Lynch 500
Week ended Wednesday, July 10, 1985

The following index is based on yields that about 500 major issuers, mainly of investment grade, would pay on new long-term tax-exempt securities. The securities are presumed to be issued at par; general obligation bonds have a 20-year maturity and revenue bonds a 30-year maturity. The index is prepared by Merrill Lynch, Pierce, Fenner & Smith Inc., based on data supplied by Kenny Information Systems, a unit of J.J. Kenny & Co.

—OVERALL INDEX—
9.12 +0.04

—REVENUE BONDS—
Sub-Index   9.24 unch

	7-10-85	%Chng In Week
AAA-Guaranteed	9.02	unch
Airport	9.38	+ 0.03
Electric-Retail	9.30	+ 0.04
Electric-Wholesale ...	9.63	+ 0.06
Hospital	9.37	− 0.01
Housing	9.18	+ 0.05
Miscellaneous	9.12	+ 0.08
Pollution Control/ Ind. Dev.	9.18	− 0.23
Transportation	9.32	+ 0.04
Utility	9.21	+ 0.07

—GENERAL OBLIGATIONS—
Sub-Index   8.80 +0.17

	7-10-85	%Chng In Week
Cities	8.90	+ 0.15
Counties	8.80	+ 0.17
States	8.61	+ 0.19
Other Districts	8.97	+ 0.16

The transportation category excludes airports; utility excludes electrics. Other districts include school and special districts.

If a company's stock price rises substantially, the value of a convertible bond can become considerably more than its issue price, regardless of the level of interest rates. The interest rate acts as a floor for the bond's price if the stock's price falls.

Some bonds are issued in bearer form, without any record of the owner's name on it. Registered bonds, like stock certificates, have the owner's name printed on them. Bearer bonds have coupons attached to them that can be clipped and presented to banks for payment of interest on stipulated dates without charge. One common registered bond is the U.S. Savings Bond, for which there isn't a secondary market. Treasury bills, because of their short life, aren't issued in certificate form.

FIGURE 5

NEW YORK EXCHANGE BONDS

Friday, July 12, 1985

Total Volume $42,720,000

SALES SINCE JANUARY 1

1985	1984	1983
$4,934,922,000	$3,645,553,000	$4,541,068,000

	Domestic Fri.	Domestic Thu.	All Issues Fri.	All Issues Thu.
Issues traded	930	965	936	972
Advances	322	381	324	386
Declines	367	395	369	397
Unchanged	241	189	243	189
New highs	85	88	86	90
New lows	6	6	6	6

Dow Jones Bond Averages

–1983– High	–1983– Low	–1984– High	–1984– Low	–1985– High	–1985– Low		–Friday– –1985–		–Friday– –1984–		–Friday– –1983–	
77.84	69.35	72.92	64.81	80.45	72.27	20 Bonds	80.18	–0.27	65.41	+0.19	71.84	–0.43
78.88	65.76	70.31	59.43	78.78	68.62	10 Utilities	77.83	–0.53	60.80	+0.29	70.22	–0.64
77.13	71.51	76.22	69.61	82.61	75.61	10 Industrial	82.53	–0.02	70.02	+0.09	73.47	–0.21

Bonds	Cur Yld	Vol	High	Low	Close	Net Chg.
GEICr 13⅝91	12.	10	110	110	110	– ¼
GFood 8⅞90	9.0	1	99	99	99	– ¼
GFood 14⅜89	13.	11	109¾	109¾	109¾	....
GnHme 15½95	15.	30	103	103	103	.....
GMills 8⅞95	9.9	5	90	90	90	–1⅜
GMills zr88s	..	4	79½	79½	79½	+ ⅛
GMA 4½85	4.6	15	98 31-32	98¾	98¾	+1-16
GMA 4⅝86	4.8	35	96 11-16	96 11-16	96 11-16	–9-16
GMA 4⅞87	5.3	10	92⅜	92⅜	92⅜	+ ⅝
GMA 6¼88	6.8	25	93	91⅜	91⅜	–1⅝
GMA 7⅛90	8.0	91	89⅝	89⅜	89½	+ ⅛
GMA 8s93	9.0	15	88½	88	88½	– ⅛
GMA 7¾94	9.2	21	85⅜	84¼	84¼	+1¼
GMA 7¼95	8.9	4	81½	81½	81½	– ½
GMA 7⅛92	8.4	25	85⅛	84⅜	84⅜	– ¾
GMA 7.85s98	9.9	52	79¼	79¼	79¼	+ ½
GMA 8⅞99	10.	57	85½	84¾	85½	– ⅞
GMA 8¾s00	11.	107	84⅛	83¼	83¼	– ¾
GMA 7.35s87	7.5	15	98	98	98	.....
GMA 8¼06	11.	5	75¾	75¾	75¾	–1¾
GMA 8.2s88	8.4	20	98	97⅞	98	.....
GMA 8⅝88	8.7	15	98⅞	98⅞	98⅞	+ ¼
GMA 9⅝89	9.6	182	100	99⅞	99⅞	– ⅝
GMA 9¾03	11.	16	91½	91½	91½	+ ⅜
GMA 9¼89	9.4	1965	99	98¼	98¼	– ⅞
GMA 9.4s04	11.	23	87¾	87¼	87¼	+ ½
GMA 11⅝90	11.	5	103½	103½	103½	.....
GMA 12s05	11.	12	105⅜	105⅜	105⅜	– ⅛
GMA 11¾00	11.	11	104⅛	104	104	– ½
GMA 14⅜91	13.	10	111⅛	111⅛	111⅛	+ ⅝
GMA d6s11	10.	403	57½	57⅛	57⅜	– ⅛
GMA 14⅝89	13.	5	109⅜	109⅜	109⅜	.....
GMA 12⅝85	13.	7	101	100 7-16	100 7-16	+3-16
GMA 12s86	12.	32	103⅞	103⅞	103⅞	+ ⅞
GMA 11¾89	11.	28	104	103	103	–1¾
GMA zr15	..	18	49	49	49	–6
GMA 10⅜88	10.	10	102⅝	102⅝	102⅝	– ⅜
GTE 4s90	cv	4	92	92	92	.....
GTE 6⅝91	8.3	10	81	79½	79½	.....
GTE 9⅜99	11.	15	86½	85½	86½	.....
GaPac 5¼96	cv	41	90½	90	90	– ½
GaPw 7⅜01	11.	8	69¼	69¼	69¼	.....
GaPw 8⅛01	11.	25	74½	74	74½	.....
GaPw 7⅝01	11.	22	71	70⅝	70⅝	+ ⅜
GaPw 7½02D	11.	10	69¾	68⅝	68⅝	–1⅛
GaPw 7⅞03	11.	15	72⅜	71⅛	72⅜	–1⅜
GaPw 8⅝04	11.	5	77½	77½	77½	– ⅛
GaPw 11⅝00	12.	47	99	98½	99	.....
GaPw 11¾05	12.	15	98⅞	98⅞	98⅞	– ⅛
GaPw 9¾08	12.	28	83¾	83⅛	83⅛	–1⅜
GaPw 10½09	12.	10	89½	89½	89½	– ⅛
GaPw 11s09	12.	14	92¼	92	92¼	–1¾
GaPw 14½10	13.	9	108	108	108	+1
GaPw 16⅛11	15.	38	109⅝	109¼	109¼	+ ⅜
GaPw 16¼11	15.	20	111	110	110	–1½
GaPw 17½91	15.	56	113	113	113	– ½
GaPw 16¼12	15.	15	112	111½	111½	–1⅜
GaPw 16s14	14.	19	114½	114½	114½	.....
GloMar 12⅜98f	..	57	36½	35⅜	36¼	– ⅝
GloMr d16s01f	..	241	38⅜	37⅛	37⅝	– ⅛
GloMar 16⅛02f	..	423	38½	38	38	– ¼
GloMar d13s03f	cv	312	33	32	32⅛	+ ⅝
Grace 4¼90	cv	10	87	87	87	+ ½
GtNoN 9½13	cv	20	120	120	120	+1
GWstFn 8⅞07	cv	8	107¾	107½	107½	– ½
Greyh 6½90	cv	2	158	158	158	–2
Greyh 9⅞00	11.	7	90	90	90	–1
GreyF 9¼92	10.	2	91¾	91¾	91¾	+ ⅝
GreyF zr94	..	5	36½	36½	36½	– ¼

Bonds	Cur Yld	Vol	High	Low	Close	Net Chg.
ITTCB 9¾95	11.	2	87½	87½	87½	–7
ITTF 10½95	10.	20	100½	100½	100½	+3⅜
IllBel 7⅝06	10.	22	72⅝	72⅝	72⅝	– ⅜
IllBel 8¼16	11.	10	75½	75½	75½	–1
IllBel 12¼17	12.	20	105½	104½	105½	– ⅞
IllPw 8⅝06	11.	12	77¼	77	77	– ¼
IllPw 8⅞08	11.	3	78½	78½	78½	–1½
Inco 12⅜10	13.	15	94½	94½	94½	+ ¼
IndBel 10s14	11.	21	90½	90	90	–3
Inexc 8½00	cv	26	64	64	64	+ ¼
IngR 8.05s04	11.	5	75½	75½	75½	+2½
Insilco 9s10	cv	41	108	107¾	108	.....
Intrfst 9¾99	12.	50	83⅛	83⅛	83⅛	– ⅞
Intrfst 7¾05	cv	19	75	75	75	.....
IBM 9⅜04	10.	137	91⅝	91⅛	91¼	– ⅝
IBM 7⅞04	cv	516	108¼	107¾	108¼	.....
IntHrv 9s04	13.	2	69	69	69	.....
IntHrv 18s02	16.	58	112¾	112⅛	112¾	– ¼
IntHrv 13¼95	14.	2	96½	96½	96½	– ⅜
InHvC 8⅝91	11.	52	82¼	81⅞	81⅞	– ⅜
InHvC 7⅝93	10.	2	73	73	73	.....
InHvC 8.35s86	8.6	73	97	96⅜	97	+ ⅞
InHvC 13½88	13.	37	104	103¾	103¾	– ¼
IPap d5⅛12	..	10	50	50	50	.....
Intnr 17½91	15.	26	113½	113½	113½	.....
Intnr 10½08	..	70	104¼	104	104¼	+ ¼
JCP 9¾06	12.	10	82¾	82¾	82¾	– ⅛
vjJnM 7.85s04f	..	5	58½	58½	58½	–1½
vjJnM 9.7s85f	..	20	72½	71	72½	– ½
JonsLl 6¾94	13.	487	53	52¾	52⅞	+ ⅛
JoneL 6¾94	15.	67	50⅞	46⅛	46⅛	–3⅞
JoneL 9⅞95	15.	2	66	66	66	+ ½
K mart 6s99	cv	140	108⅞	108⅜	108⅞	+ ⅜
Kaisr 9s05	cv	3	85	85	85	.....
KaufB 12¼99	13.	15	97½	97	97	–1
KimCl 5⅞91	7.3	19	81	80⅞	81	–1½
KimCl 5⅞92	7.6	5	78⅛	77	77	– ⅛
KogerP 9¼03	cv	10	97	97	97	.....
Kolmrg 8¾09	cv	40	86	86	86	.....
Kraft 8⅜04	10.	5	80½	80½	80½	+ ½
Krogr 9s95	10.	8	86¼	86¼	86¼	– ⅛
Krogr 8.7s98	11.	10	82¼	82¼	82¼	–2¾
LTV 5s88	6.5	1250	77⅝	76¾	77⅛	– ⅛
LTV 9¼97	14.	45	67½	66	66	+1
LTV 11s07	15.	45	71¾	71	71	– ¾
LTV 13⅞02	16.	119	86	85	85	– ¾
LTV 14s04	16.	130	86⅞	85½	85¾	– ⅝
LaQuin 10s02	cv	12	100¼	100¼	100¼	– ¾
LearS 11½98	12.	20	97	95	95	–2
Litton 11½95	11.	737	102	101¼	101¼	– ¾
Litton flt00	..	17	100	100	100	– ⅛
Litton 12⅝05	12.	37	105⅛	104⅝	105⅛	+ ⅜
Loew 6⅞93	8.7	15	79⅛	79⅛	79⅛	– ¼
LomN 9¾08	cv	43	146	145	146	+2½
LomN 9s10	cv	21	114½	114½	114½	.....
LglsLt 12⅝92	13.	2	99½	99½	99½	.....
LglsLt 13½13	14.	35	97½	96¾	97½	.....
Loral 10¾97	11.	10	93½	93½	93½	+1½
LouGs 7½02	10.	18	72½	72½	72½	+1⅝
Lykes 7½94N	14.	194	56	54⅝	54⅝	– ⅞
Lykes 7½94	14.	999	55¾	54½	55	– ½
Lykes 11s00	16.	11	70	70	70	.....
MACOM 9¼06	cv	10	98	98	98	– ½
MCI d14⅛01	14.	53	103	102⅞	103	.....
MCI 12⅞02	13.	8	101⅜	101	101	.....
MGM 10s94	12.	4	86⅞	86⅞	86⅞	.....
MGM 10½s96	12.	8	87	86	86	.....
MGM 9½00	cv	26	105½	105	105½	+ ½
MGMUA 10s93	12.	74	84¾	84	84	– ¾

Bonds	Cur Yld	Vol	High
NJBTl 14⅝21	13.	25	113¾
NYTl 14⅝91	14.	41	107⅛
Newell 8¾03	cv	8	97
Nortek 12½99	13.	5	97
NoNG 9½90	9.6	14	99
NoPac 3s47	4.2	52	71¾
NoPac 3s47r	4.2	50	71½
NwtAir 7½07	cv	65	115½
Norwst 7⅞86	8.0	40	99
Norwst 6¾03	cv	10	92
Nwstl 7½94	11.	3	65¼
Nwstl d7s11	13.	39	52¼
Nwstl 12⅜03	14.	13	88½
NwPipl 10¼91	11.	5	90½
NwnBl 7⅞11	11.	31	73
Norton 9½05	cv	30	98¼
Oakln 10½02	cv	9	59½
OcciP 16s89	14.	50	111½
OccP 9.65s94	11.	191	85⅞
OcciP d8.95s94	11.	4	83
Ogden 5s93	cv	2	92½
OhBIT 7½11	11.	2	67⅝
OhBIT 9s18	11.	10	80
OhEd 9½06	12.	30	79¾
OhEd 9½08	12.	37	80⅞
OhEd 15¼87	14.	38	107
OhEd 11⅞10	12.	40	97
OhPw 15¼88	14.	20	108
OhPw 17⅝88	15.	2	115½
OklGE 3⅞88	4.6	5	84
Orion 10s99	14.	10	73⅝
PPG 9⅜89	9.4	50	99¾
PSA 11⅛04	cv	8	115
PGE 4½s86	4.7	4	94⅞
PGE 4½s90	5.8	5	78⅛
PGE 5s91	6.5	1	77⅛
PGE 4⅜s94	6.6	10	66½
PGE 4½96JJ	7.4	18	61
PGE 4½96KK	7.4	5	61
PGE 7½s03	11.	16	70⅛
PGE 7½s04	11.	5	70
PGE 9⅛s06	11.	73	82½
PGE 9⅝s06	11.	20	85¾
PGE 8¼08	11.	2[illegible]	75
PGE 8½09	11.	44	77
PGE 9⅜11	11.	25	83
PGE 10⅛12	11.	20	89¾
PGE 12¾13	12.	1	106
PGE 16¼14	14.	220	115⅞
PGE 15⅜92	14.	5	113¼
PNwT 8⅝10	11.	5	78
PNwT 8¾08	11.	15	79⅝
PNwT 9s12	11.	20	82
PNwT 10⅛19	11.	12	90⅛
PacSci 7¾03	cv	2	77
PacTT 3⅛87	3.5	32	90⅜
PacTT 4⅜88	5.0	32	88¼
PacTT 8.65s05	11.	122	80⅝
PacTT 8¾06	11.	66	80⅝
PacTT 7.8s07	11.	74	72¾
PacTT 7¼08	11.	5	68⅞
PacTT 7⅝09	11.	2	69¾
PacTT 9½11	11.	27	85⅛
PacTT 8⅞15	11.	26	82⅜
PacTT 8⅜17	11.	5	75⅜
PacTT 9⅝14	11.	39	86⅞
PacTT 9s18	11.	42	81⅛
PacTT 9⅝18	11.	27	86⅞
PacTT 9⅞16	11.	23	89¼
PacTT 9¾19	11.	59	87⅛
PacTT 12.7s19	12.	55	106¾
PacTT 12.35s20	12.	34	104⅝
PacTT 11.35s90	11.	60	102[illegible]
PacTT 15s20	13.	3	113⅞
PacTT 15s91	14.	51	106⅞
PacTT 16⅛21	14.	15	117¾
PacTT 13⅝90	13.	20	104⅝
Paine 11½99	12.	4	95¾
Paine 8¼08	cv	1	92
PalmB 16⅛02	16.	27	104
PAA 4½s86	cv	42	93
PAA 5¼s89	cv	2	78½
PAA 11¼s86	11.	2	100
PAA 11⅛s86	11.	2	100⅜
PAA 11½94B	12.	2	93
PAA d13½03	14.	29	93½
PAA 15s04	15.	27	102
PAA 15s98	cv	248	131¾
PanEP 12s10	11.	28	113½
Pennzl 7½88	8.0	5	93⅝
Pennzl 7⅜88	7.9	1	93¾
Petrie 8s10	6.8	29	118
Pfizer 8¾06	cv	10	183¼
Phelp 8.1s96	11.	4	71
PhilEl 6½93	8.5	10	76½
PhilEl 6⅛97	9.6	24	64

Buyers get a receipt for their money and a record of their holding is kept in a computer. This "book entry" system also is used for newer Treasury notes and bonds.

Prices of a large number of corporate bonds are given in a table called New York Exchange Bonds (Figure 5). This covers bonds traded on the New York Stock Exchange where only a small proportion of trading in these bonds takes place. Most bond trading is over the counter among securities dealers. The first column gives the name of the issuer. The second shows the original interest rate, the one shown on the coupons, and the year of maturity, with an "s" for ease of pronunciation. Thus 9s04 means "nines of oh-four," or 9 percent bonds due in 2004. The third column gives the current yield, or the interest obtained by dividing the original interest rate by the latest price. The fourth column gives the volume of trading, in thousands of dollars. The four columns on the right give the highest, lowest and closing prices of the day, along with the change in the closing price from the previous close, much like stock quotations.

At the top of this table, there is data on the year's volume to date and a market diary. There is also a set of market averages for bond prices. The main index covers 20 bonds. There are component indexes for the 10 industrials and the 10 utilities. The table is followed by a short listing of bonds traded on the American Stock Exchange.

Another small table (Figure 6) shows prices of recent issues that aren't yet listed on a principal exchange.

FIGURE 6

Prices of Recent Issues

Current quotations are indicated below for recent issues of corporate senior securities that aren't listed on a principal exchange.

Issue		Moody's Rating	Bid	Asked	Chg.	Yield %
UTILITIES						
DukePwr	12⅝s '15	Aa2	106¾	107¼	– ⅛	11.74
NY Tel	12¼s '24	A2	104¾	105¼	– ⅛	11.63
PacTel	12¾s '25	A1	106⅞	107¼	....	11.88
SoCalEd	13s '15	Aa2	108¾	109⅛	....	11.88
INDUSTRIALS						
IBM-n	10½s '15	Aaa	98⅝	99⅛	– ⅛	10.60
FordMCred	11⅞s '95	A1	104⅞	105⅜	– ¼	10.96
JCPenney	11s '15	A1	96⅛	96⅝	+ ⅛	11.40
FOREIGN						
Ontario	12½s '94	Aaa	111½	112⅜	....	10.30
PrvQueb	12¾s '94	A1	112⅝	113⅜	....	10.45
QuebHydro	11¾s '12	A1	104	104½	....	11.23

Source: PaineWebber Inc. (Quotes are for round lots)
n-New listing.

Budget Preparation—or—How to Be a Budget Analyst

A new budget analyst may well be overwhelmed by the scope and complexity of the task at hand. Nothing can completely prepare for that first attempt, but most bright, inquisitive, energetic people survive. Here is a memo outlining methods and procedures for analysts in Oregon. Save for references to the particular budget system used there, it could have been written for guidance in any government.

State of Oregon   Interoffice Memo

TO: Budget Analysts   DATE: June 30, 1982

FROM: Jon Yunker, Administrator
           Budget and Management Division

SUBJECT: Budget Preparation—or—How to Be a Budget Analyst

THE ROLE OF THE ANALYST

Budget analysts are key persons in the development of the governor's biennial budget. While others are responsible for development of the broad program and fiscal policies for the state as a whole, it is the individual analysts who must convert these broad policies to balanced, properly financed programs for assigned agencies. In this regard, several points should be emphasized:

1. You must function as an equal with agency heads or other top agency administrative staff. You are expected to have the

maturity necessary to avoid being intimidated by imposing titles, higher-salaried officials, or executives your senior in age. You have a professional assignment and must carry it out with the confidence of a professional.

2. You work primarily for your budget supervisor and the budget and management administrator. Direct relationships with the director, other administrators and staff within the executive department, and governor's assistants are frequently necessary and desirable. However, you should inform the budget and management administrator, *in writing,* in cases where these contacts will significantly influence your recommendations. All reports submitted to other individuals should be routed through your budget supervisor and the budget and management administrator to ensure that they are fully informed about activities of the division. They are responsible for your actions; make sure you are responsible to them.

3. You must be flexible. Don't busy yourself in work related only to your assigned agencies. State government is too dynamic and interrelated and the central staff too small to allow the luxury of specialists within the division. The analyst must be reasonably conversant with the governor's total program and should be constantly aware of the role a particular assignment plays within it.

   During the executive budget preparation season, you will be in an essentially negative posture as far as an agency is concerned. During the legislative session, however, you will be intimately allied with the agency in "selling" approved budget recommendations to the legislature. In some cases, you may be expected to effectively support a program that you originally recommended against.

RESPONSIBILITIES PRIOR TO BUDGET SEASON

The work performed during the budget season represents the culmination of many months of preparation and field work. Prior to receipt of the agencies' request documents, the analyst should be concerned with the following:

1. Budget field work: This phrase simply describes the process whereby an analyst develops a sufficient knowledge of assigned agencies' programs to enable him or her to make informed budget decisions when the time comes. Budget field work may be accomplished in a variety of ways:

   a. Review of items submitted for consideration by the state emergency board.
   b. Execution of special management or fiscal studies affecting your assigned agencies.

      c. Completion of a formal field work program during which you personally visit individual agency activities and discuss them with the person directly responsible for their administration.

      d. Preview of agency budget requests for format and content.

2. Development of the Biennial Budget Preparation Manual. This activity enables the analyst to foresee special problems in format or budget organization which some of his assigned agencies might encounter in meeting executive department requirements. Your knowledge of your assigned agencies enables you to assist in developing budget preparation instructions to be followed by all state agencies. Each analyst *must completely understand all instructions included in the manual and supporting documents.*

3. An analyst frequently assists agencies in the preparation of their biennial budget requests. It is imperative that the analyst *express no opinion about the content or amount,* or the ranking of decision packages, to be included in the request. Your role is that of technical advisor on format and compliance with specific budget instructions. You have neither the authority nor the responsibility to advise the agency on *what* should be requested; you will only assist in ensuring that it is properly presented.

4. As budget season approaches, the analyst should become familiar with the internal procedures to be used by the budget and management division during the biennial budget preparation process. You must *learn and understand* all significant internal procedures performed by the technical staff to enable you to "track" the budget request and related documents through the entire budget season.

5. Based on your field work and knowledge of the internal procedures, specific deadlines for review of each of your assigned agencies should be established. You cannot spend a disproportionate amount of time on one agency and hope to do an adequate job on the entire assignment. You must *assess your assignment* and *plan* your own *individual work schedule* for that assignment. Keep in mind that time must be spent where the money is—minor, stable, low-cost agencies may be fascinating, but should not take time away from those agencies competing for scarce resources.

WHEN THE BUDGET REQUEST IS SUBMITTED

Don't panic! DON'T PANIC! *D O N ' T P A N I C ! ! !*

There will be a few surprises, but generally the request will reflect the same programs you saw during your budget field work. It will look bigger and more complicated than you expected, but bear in mind that it represents all activities of that agency for a two-year period. Several steps are critical at the time of initial receipt of the budget request:

1. Make sure that the budget is given immediately to the coordinating secretary so that internal processing is properly performed. Know where it is at all times.
2. *Read the entire budget request.* Skim the summary reports and other detailed forms. Read all narrative for content. Study the performance measurement forms. Review previous biennia's performance claims and compare them with what was actually accomplished during that biennium. *Finish the job.* You will have plenty of opportunities to go back and review various sections, so plow right through the entire request before taking any steps toward detailed analysis.
3. After reading the request, skim the statutes related to the agency. This will provide you a context in which to assess the programs the agency is proposing to fulfill its legal responsibilities.
4. The analyst should carefully review the objectives and levels of accomplishment upon which the agency has predicated its budget request to make certain they correspond with the agency's statutory responsibilities and executive priorities. These objectives and levels of accomplishment may be modified or augmented by the analysts in the governor's budget to more accurately reflect the executive department recommendations regarding the agency's mission.
5. Identify the major policy issues in the request. A policy issue is a proposed new program or revision in an existing program (either expansion or retrenchment), which represents a significant change in the agency's scope or level of activity.

    The budget analyst must determine which decision packages are major policy issues and if any significant changes are contained in the base budget. In addition, you must determine if the numerical ranking of decision packages represents a major policy shift.

    You should summarize these policy issues (including costs by fund source), develop alternatives, and prepare your recommended course of action. This report, or *policy memo,* should be submitted through your budget supervisor to the budget and management administrator. This memo will be further distributed to other appropriate members of the executive department.
6. You may also prepare a memo to the budget and management administrator outlining the need for an analysis of a particular portion of a budget request which you will not have time to

perform yourself during budget season. In some cases, these analyses can be performed by the management section or by other divisions of the department in time to be considered by you in developing budget recommendations. Their special expertise in the areas of data processing, management analysis, local government relations, personnel administration, or economic analysis can be most helpful to you in arriving at your final recommendations. Bear in mind that *they are advising you; the budget recommendations are yours.*

In other cases, the needed analysis will be beyond the capability of the executive department staff to perform during the executive budget season. In these cases, the proposed analysis will be considered as an "item for future study" and held until staff time becomes available. A special form for these memos will be available on which the budget analyst will be expected to enter his or her recommendations as to whether the study should be performed during budget season or deferred as an "item for future study."

7. Review the request for any proposed programs and interagency transfers of funds which affect other state agencies. These proposals should be described and submitted, *in writing,* to the analyst assigned to the affected agency or agencies. The governor's budget must be internally consistent among agencies.

8. Develop a list of questions about the request you want the agency personnel to answer. . . . You will have many unanswered questions in your mind at this stage (since you are an insatiably curious person), and the easiest way to get answers is to reduce the questions to writing and submit them to the agency. Don't be afraid to ask agency personnel to work for you in this way. You have to do the analysis, but agency personnel can produce needed data for you.

DETAILED ANALYSIS

Only after you have read the document and identified the items listed above are you ready to review the request in detail. Once again, don't spend too much time on one agency. Know where *all* of your assigned budgets are at all times. Detailed analysis should include the following steps:

1. Always contact the agency head first. He or she is responsible for all items in the budget and has the best understanding of how the components interrelate. You should discuss several items during this first meeting.

   a. What approach does the administrator prefer—are you free to meet individually with subordinates on matters in their areas, or does the administrator want to participate in all budget discussions?

    b. What about the role of governing boards or commissions— are they to be involved in the budget review process?

    c. Solicit the administrator's description of the program achievements proposed in the budget request. He or she may have goals or accomplishments proposed in the budget that you missed in your preliminary review.

    d. Explain your personal schedule for review of the request. You may find conflicts which will require revisions in your internal deadlines.

2. Review past approved budgets and Joint Committee on Ways and Means reports and, if possible, talk to analysts previously assigned to the budget. This will acquaint you with past analytical approaches and will highlight executive and legislative decisions of the past few years.

3. Divide the budget into manageable segments. The request may be divided by program or organizational lines—or both. Choose one segment for detailed analysis. Remember that no individual segment should be considered complete until all of your recommendations are prepared.

4. Approach the request with *skepticism, not cynicism.* Your job is *not* to justify the request, nor is it to eliminate the agency (usually). All activities of the agency are subject to question, even those most politically popular or well established. It is important to remember that you must not interject your personal philosophy or biases in your review. You deal with *facts or clearly understood gubernatorial policy, not emotion.*

5. Approach the request with an open mind. You are not responsible for interpreting the governor's political statements or public positions on issues. Don't let the agency tell you that "confidentially, the governor is keenly interested in this program." If he is, you'll find out through normal budget procedures.

6. Don't analyze dollars—analyze programs and decision packages. Dollars are an important item in budgeting. However, it is the program achievements that are budgeted; and the dollars merely provide a common denominator in expressing the resources necessary to provide these programs. Understand the programs and decision packages first, and the dollar levels will follow.

7. When comparing proposed program levels, your base for comparison is the latest legislatively approved level. It is *not the agency request.* The legislatively approved level will be expressed in both dollar and program terms in the latest Joint Committee on Ways and Means report. *Review the performance of the agency during the first year of the biennium and*

compare it with the levels approved by the previous Legislature. You may find areas where we are actually spending more and accomplishing less.

8. In reviewing the budget, use a zero-based conceptual attitude and consider the following questions:

   a. Is the base budget consistent with the existing approved level?
   b. Does the base budget include expenditures which were originally approved on a "one-shot" or nonrecurring basis?
   c. Are there activities in the base budget which are of lower priority than some proposed expansions, new programs, or decision packages? In an austere budget season, program expansions may have to be financed by offsetting program retrenchment.
   d. Are there activities in the budget request which, for various reasons, should be stopped or could better be performed by a different agency? In these cases, prepare a policy memo outlining the issue. Minor reorganizations can be recommended within the governor's budget.

9. In reviewing decision packages based upon increased workload, consider the following questions:

   a. Is the projected workload self-generated? That is, does it represent activity levels controllable by the agency; or does it truly reflect increased demands for service by the public or other beneficiaries?
   b. Is the proposed volume of increased workload consistent with workload patterns of the past few years and supported by adequate justification?
   c. Are the requested levels of staff, support costs, and facilities properly related to the volume of increased workload? Ratios, economies of scale, seasonal peaks and valleys of activities, and the existing capacity to absorb increased workload should be considered.
   d. What is the true program impact of not providing the requested increased volume of service in a particular program?

10. In reviewing program adjustments which have taken place in the interim, consider the following questions:

    a. Was the adjustment approved in the manner and at the level described? (Review emergency board minutes and other relevant documents.)
    b. Was the adjustment intended for continuation into future biennia?

c. Does the adjustment retain sufficient priority for continuation or was it provided to meet an emergency need which is no longer critical to the agency's program?

11. In reviewing requests for operation of new facilities, consider the following questions:

    a. Has the capital project already been approved, or is it contingent on future executive or legislative action?
    b. What is the latest estimate for the building to come on-line and require operational support?
    c. What standards or other empirical justification are available to support the estimated costs to operate the new facilities?
    d. What offsetting savings, such as vacation of rental space, are available, and have they been reflected in the request?
    e. What effect will the new facilities have on basic programs? Is the agency using the new facility as a smoke screen to go into new programs not fully analyzed? What are the future costs and benefits of these new programs?

12. In reviewing decision packages which constitute program improvements, consider the following questions:

    a. What is the true effect or product of the improvement?
    b. What are the bases of the request for the improvement—who originated the demand for expanded or improved services?
    c. What is the impact of the improvement on existing programs?
    d. What criteria were used to develop the staff and support costs of the improvement? Are they valid?
    e. Has the improvement been previously requested and denied? If so, on what grounds?
    f. Is the improvement consistent with agency objectives?
    g. Is the improvement of a higher priority than an existing program or activity?
    h. What are the future costs and benefits of the requested improvement?

13. In reviewing requests for new programs, all items listed for program improvements should be considered. In addition, ask the following:

    a. Is this the appropriate agency to perform this service? Is the service now being provided by another state agency, other governmental units, or private industry?
    b. Are there any revenue sources, such as special fees, available to offset the cost of implementing this program?

14. A note of caution—don't ignore programs simply because no program improvements or new programs are being proposed. The thorough analyst will examine ongoing programs for continued relevance and necessity. This is one of the most lucrative areas of investigation for an economy-minded analyst.

15. Another note of caution—don't get trapped by counting desks—either literally or figuratively. After some frustration in considering the solutions to major social problems, you will be tempted to revert to considering the minor details of bureaucratic operation. Don't yield to the temptation—you'll learn to accept the frustration and maybe even be instrumental in really solving a social problem.

    Conversely, do not become so awed by the social issues that you lose sight of your basic purpose—to produce a responsible budget. Don't get lost in the clouds.

16. Still another note of caution—GET ORGANIZED AND STAY ORGANIZED. Know where you've been, where you are, and where you have to get at all times during the season. If you realize you are becoming disorganized—STOP—get reorganized and then start again.

17. In the course of detailed analysis, you will prepare a variety of memos, worksheets, and other written material. General suggestions:

    a. *Keep them neat.* Most likely the analyst preparing the budget recommendations will *not* be responsible for executing that budget. Give your successor a break—and some useful budget files.

    b. *Identify your worksheets.* Columns of numbers with no headings or other identification are useless to everyone, including the analyst. Each worksheet should be readily identifiable as to content. *Date them! Date them! Date them!*

    c. Keep your files in an *organized manner.* Make sure your secretary knows where you keep certain workpapers (such as memos from governor's assistants or other executive department staff). She may need to find something in your absence—and in a hurry.

18. *You will never have the time to perform as detailed an analysis as you think is necessary.* If you encounter a problem or issue too complex to review in the time available, it may be necessary to prepare a memo recommending an item for future study and move on. This is not a cop out, but a realistic appraisal of the volume of work which can be done in a limited period of time. *Meet your deadlines! Meet your deadlines! Meet your deadlines!*

19. Analyze the agency's revenues as well as the expenditures. *They matter.*

20. After you've completed the detailed analysis of a budget request—step back and "look at the forest." Review the sum of your detailed work to see if the total makes sense and is reasonable.

PREPARING THE RECOMMENDATION

You earn your salary when you tie all of the analytical efforts, alternatives, and mass of data together into one proposed course of action. Remember, that you are *only recommending.* You *don't allow or deny. Use these words around an agency and you'll feel rather silly* when items are restored at the appeal hearing.

Remember that, even though you are to recommend one course of action, you are also to consider and be prepared to implement various alternatives. Presentation of alternatives is required when forwarding a policy memo, and alternatives can be included in the analyst report.

Remember that a good analyst report satisfies all the requirements of "completed staff work." (You should review the completed staff work definition attached to this memo.)

Although you don't have the authority to include or exclude items in a budget, don't expect your boss to make your decisions for you. You are responsible for your recommendations; and you must be in a position to defend them with hard, objective data. You are telling your superiors what you think they should do—they must also consider other factors in arriving at their decisions.

In developing your specific recommendations, consider the following:

1. Recommendations are transmitted through the *analyst report.* This document must be a concise, complete summary of your findings. Keep it understandable; don't try to show off your knowledge of agency jargon. Slang and obscure abbreviations have no place in the analyst report.

2. You are displaying a piece of specific analysis, not presenting a discourse on the theory of the agency. All narrative should directly relate to specific recommendations.

3. Don't devote more than a minimum of discussion to items which you have not recommended. If they are significant in size or content, mention them briefly. Otherwise, concentrate your efforts on what you *are* recommending.

4. The analyst report is an internal document. However, it will be the basic vehicle for transmitting the executive department's recommendations to the agency. Keep it objective. If you have special comments of a confidential nature, attach them as a

special memo which can accompany the analyst report through its internal review; or transmit your ideas orally.

5. In developing final recommendations, remember that an unreasonable budget is useless to everyone. You're not paid on a commission of dollars cut from the request. Unrealistically low recommendations place a burden on your superiors to restore the funds. If an agency has erred in preparing its request, you may find yourself in a position where you'll be *adding* money in a particular area. Don't be alarmed—remember, the goal is a *realistic budget.*

6. Conversely, your job is to recommend the least amount of money and the least number of positions necessary to support the agency at the recommended program level. Let your superiors make most of the generous gestures to agencies.

7. After you have developed your preliminary recommendations, try them out on the agency administrator. (Even though you may have a big ego, you also are an honestly humble person who realizes he doesn't know everything. Besides, the agency may be able to correct some bad work you've done before someone else uncovers it.)

AGENCY APPEALS

We cannot predict accurately how the various levels of appeal will be handled. There is no question but that agencies generally will appeal the decisions and recommendations of the analyst. These appeals will probably take several forms:

1. The pro forma appeals: These include those agencies which have never accepted the legitimacy of the budget staff and are satisfied only after discussing the budget with the director of the department or the governor.

2. Appeals to correct errors: During the course of a budget season, other analysts (not you) will make some arithmetic or reasoning errors. When the agency discovers these, it has every right to request correction.

3. Emotional appeals: These occur most frequently when the analyst has failed to establish good personal rapport and the agency head is convinced that "he just doesn't understand our problems." Stick to the facts and don't get drawn into personal conflicts. When you lose your objectivity, you lose your usefulness.

4. Objective or "legitimate" appeals: These represent judgments by the agency that your recommendations do not adequately support the programs during the coming biennium. Sometimes the agency will produce supplemental data not made available to you during the course of budget review. The technical word

for this is "dirty trick." Most items in this type of appeal, however, deal simply with judgments made by the analyst and questioned by the agency. Be equally objective in analyzing them for your superiors.

In all types of appeals, the analyst is responsible for several actions:

1. Review of the appeal letter and development of specific recommendations *with reasons* for each item included.
2. Detailed minutes of the proceedings of the appeal hearing.
3. An *immediate* update of all appropriate documents as soon as the final decisions are made. Draft a letter summarizing the results of the hearing for distribution to the agency and your superiors.
4. Informing the coordinating secretary and technical support section of the results of the hearing so they can update their master summaries.

WHEN THE NUMBERS ARE FIRM

Don't relax! There is still a lot of work to do. First priority is the final preparation of reproduction copy. Reproduction copy is the narrative and supporting schedules that will be printed in the governor's budget released December 1. Careful editing must be done to ensure that the narrative and fiscal data accurately describe the final budget decisions.

The governor's budget is written primarily for the legislature. It is not the prime working document for the Joint Committee on Ways and Means—that honor belongs to the updated agency request document. The printed budget must be meaningful to the freshman Legislator, who has never seen a state budget, and the most experienced member of Ways and Means.

After repro copy has been prepared and all master summaries have been updated, the analyst still has several responsibilities:

1. Edit your working papers. You'll be using them throughout the legislative hearings, so make sure you're not cluttered with excess baggage. Organized, orderly, neat working papers are essential during hearings.
2. Prepare material explaining the budget for your agencies. Additional analyses can be performed and presented in narrative, graphic, or tabular presentations that can be used in orienting the Legislature, selling the budgets to Ways and Means, and informing the public about the proposals.

   The emphasis in these analyses should be on *program and decision packages,* not dollars. While you should be able to speak very precisely about proposed expenditure levels if asked, don't plan to explain your budgets by accounting for dollars. It's boring—and meaningless.

3. Keep in close communication with your assigned agencies to ensure that they are on schedule in updating their request documents to reflect the governor's recommendations.

There are many things not described in this report. A budget season must be experienced before any level of understanding is possible. Hopefully, these comments will provide some help to those analysts about to participate in their first. Good luck!

Glossary

The following terms are commonly used in public finance and budgeting. A number of the definitions are taken from three publications of the federal government: U.S. General Accounting Office, *A Glossary of Terms Used in the Federal Budget Process and Related Accounting, Economic, and Tax Terms*, 3d ed., PAD-81-27 (Washington, D.C.: General Accounting Office, 1981); Bureau of the Census, *State Government Finances in 1979*, GF79, no. 3 (Washington, D.C.: U.S. Government Printing Office, 1980); and Bureau of the Census, *City Government Finances in 1978–79*, GF79, no. 4 (Washington, D.C.: U.S. Government Printing Office, 1980). Because of language difference from state to state, most definitions stay with the federal system. Terms that fall under general categories are listed under the general category. For example, *Appropriations* follows *Budget authority* under the general heading *Forms of budget authority*.

Ability to pay   The principle that the tax burden should be distributed according to a person's affluence. It is based on the assumption that as a person's affluence increases, the person can and should contribute a larger percentage of his/her affluence to support government activities.

Accounting system   The procedures which record, classify, and report on the finances and operations of a business, government, individual, or other entity.

Accrual basis of accounting   Accounting basis which records revenues when they are earned (whether or not cash is received then) and expenditures when goods and services are received (whether or not cash payments are made then).

Accrued interest   Interest earned on bond issue from its date or last coupon payment date to the date of delivery or settlement date to the purchaser.

Activity   A specific and distinguishable line of work performed by one or more organizational components of a governmental unit for the purpose of discharging a function or subfunction for which the governmental unit is responsible. For example, food inspection is an activity performed in the discharge of the health function.

Ad valorem   A tax computed from the value of the tax base.

Advance appropriation   Budget authority provided in an appropriation act to become available in a fiscal year, or more, beyond the fiscal year for which the appropriation act is passed. The amount is not included in the budget totals of the year in which the appropriation bill is enacted, but it is included in the budget totals for the fiscal year in which the amount will become available for obligation. For examples and further discussion of this term, see Part V of the *Budget of the United States Government, Appendix*.

Advance funding   Budget authority provided in an appropriation act to obligate and disburse funds during a fiscal year from a succeeding year's appropriation. The funds so obligated increase the budget authority for the fiscal year in which obligated and reduce the budget authority of the succeeding fiscal year. Advance funding is a device for avoiding supplemental requests late in the fiscal year for certain entitlement programs should the appropriations for the current year prove to be too low. For examples and further discussion of this term, see Part V of *The Budget of the United States Government, Appendix*.

Advance refunding   The refunding of an issue of securities prior to the date when the outstanding issue of securities can be redeemed. Thus, before redemption both the issue being refunded and the refunding issue are outstanding.

Agency missions   Responsibilities assigned to a specific agency for meeting national needs.

Agency missions are expressed in terms of the purpose to be served by the programs authorized to carry out functions or subfunctions which, by law, are the responsibility of that agency and its component organizations. In contrast to national needs, generally described in the context of major functions, agency missions are generally described in the context of subfunctions. (See also Functional classification; Mission budgeting; National needs.)

Allotment   An authorization by the head (or other authorized employee) of an agency to his/her subordinates to incur obligations within a specified amount. An agency makes allotments pursuant to the requirements stated in OMB Circular no. A-34. The amount allotted by an agency cannot exceed the amount apportioned by the Office of Management and Budget.

Amortization Paying the principal amount of an issue through periodic payments either directly to bondholders or to a sinking fund for later payment to bondholders. Amortization payments include interest and any payment on principal.

Anticipation notes or warrants Short-term debt issued in anticipation of collection of taxes, the proceeds of a bond sale, or other revenue, and retirable from the collections they anticipate.

Antideficiency act Legislation enacted by Congress to prevent the incurring of obligations or the making of expenditures (outlays) in excess of amounts available in appropriations or funds; to fix responsibility within an agency for the creation of any obligation or the making of any expenditure in excess of an apportionment or reapportionment or in excess of other subdivisions established pursuant to 31 U.S.C. 665(g); and to assist in bringing about the most effective and economical use of appropriations and funds. The act is sometimes known as Section 3679 of the Revised Statutes, as amended.

Apportionment A distribution made by the Office of Management and Budget of amounts available for obligation, including budgetary reserves established pursuant to law, in an appropriation or fund account. Apportionments divide amounts available for obligations by specific time periods (usually quarters), activities, projects, objects, or a combination thereof. The amounts so apportioned limit the amount of obligations that may be incurred. In apportioning any account, some funds may be reserved to provide for contingencies or to effect savings, pursuant to the Antideficiency Act; or may be proposed for deferral or rescission pursuant to the Impoundment Control Act of 1974 (Title X of the Congressional Budget and Impoundment Control Act, P.L. 93-344, 31 U.S.C. 1400, et seq.).

The apportionment process is intended to prevent obligation of amounts available within an appropriation or fund account in a manner that would require deficiency or supplemental appropriations and to achieve the most effective and economical use of amounts made available for obligation. In this regard, federal agency obligations may not be incurred in excess of the amount of budget authority apportioned.

Appropriation act A statute, under the jurisdiction of the House and Senate Committees on Appropriations, that generally provides authorization for federal agencies to incur obligations and to make payments out of the Treasury for specified purposes. An appropriation act, the most common means of providing budget authority, generally follows enactment of authorizing legislation unless the authorizing legislation itself provides the budget authority.

Currently, there are 13 regular appropriation acts enacted annually. From time to time, Congress also enacts supplemental appropriation acts. Similar relationships apply to state local governments.

Arbitrage   Investing borrowed funds in higher rate of return investments.

Ascending or positive yield curve   The interest rate structure with long-term interest rates higher than short-term interest rates.

Asked price   The price at which dealers offer securities in the market.

Assessed value   The value placed on property, usually by a government employee, for the purpose of distributing property tax burden. That value may or may not be directly related to market value.

Assets   Property with economic value owned by an entity.

Audit   An examination of evidence, including records, facilities, inventories, systems, etc., to discover or verify desired information. A written report of findings will normally result and findings will normally be based on investigation of a sample of agency operations.

Authorizing committee   A standing committee of the House or Senate with legislative jurisdiction over the subject matter of those laws, or parts of laws, that set up or continue the legal operations of federal programs or agencies. An authorizing committee also has jurisdiction in those instances where backdoor authority is provided in the substantive legislation.

Authorizing legislation   Substantive legislation enacted by Congress that sets up or continues the legal operation of a federal program or agency either indefinitely or for a specific period of time or sanctions a particular type of obligation or expenditure within a program.

Authorizing legislation is normally a prerequisite for appropriations. It may place a limit on the amount of budget authority to be included in appropriation of "such sums as may be necessary." In some instances, authorizing legislation may provide authority to incur debts or to mandate payment to particular persons or political subdivisions of the country.

Average life   Measure equal to number of bond years divided by number of bonds ($1,000 increments).

Backdoor authority   Budget authority provided in legislation outside the normal (appropriation committees) appropriations process. The most common forms of backdoor authority are authority to borrow (also called borrowing authority or authority to spend debt receipts) and contract authority. In other cases (e.g., interest on the public debt), a permanent appropriation is provided that becomes available without any current action by Congress. Section 401 of the Congressional Budget and Impoundment Control Act of 1974 (31 U.S.C. 1351) specifies certain limits on the use of backdoor authority.

Balance sheet   A statement of the financial position of an entity which presents the value of its assets, liabilities, and equities on a specified date.

Ballon maturity   Bond issue with substantially more late maturities than early maturities. Some or all of the late maturities are often callable to allow for early redemption.

Basis point   One 100th of one percent. Ten basis points equal 1/10 of one percent.

Bearer security   A security without owner identification, presumed that its bearer is the owner.

Benefits received   The principle that the tax burden should be distributed according to the benefits an individual receives from government. It is a logical extension of the exchange relationship of private markets.

Bid discount   Amount by which par value exceeds bid price.

Bid price   Price at which a prospective buyer offers to purchase securities.

Bond   Contract to pay specified sum of money (the principal or face value) at a specified future date (maturity) plus interest paid at an agreed percentage of the principal. Maturity is usually longer than one year. Notes have shorter maturities and are issued with less formality.

Bond bank   State institution which buys entire issue municipal bonds from proceeds of state bonds.

Bond discount   The excess of the face value of a bond over its price (or underwriter bid).

Bond fund   See "Debt service fund."

Bond insurance   Insurance purchases to guarantee the timely payment of principal and interest to bondholders.

Bond premium   The excess of the bond price (or underwriter bid) over its face value (excluding any accrued interest).

Bond year   Number of 12-month intervals between the date of the bond and its maturity date, measured in $1,000. Thus, the "bond year" for a $5,000 bond dated April 1, 1985, and maturing June 1, 1986, is 5.830 [1.666 (14 months divided by 12 months) × 5 (number of $1,000 in $5,000 bond)].

Budget A financial plan, including proposed expenditures and estimated revenues, for a period in the future.

Budget authority Authority provided by law to enter into obligations that will result in immediate or future outlays involving federal government funds, except that budget authority does not include authority to insure or guarantee the repayment of indebtedness incurred by another person or government. The basic forms of budget authority are appropriations, authority to borrow, and contract authority. Budget authority may be classified by the period of availability (one-year, multiple-year, no-year), by the timing of congressional action (current or permanent), or by the manner of determining the amount available (definite or indefinite).

Forms of Budget Authority

Appropriations An authorization by an act of Congress that permits federal agencies to incur obligations and to make payments out of the Treasury for specified purposes. An appropriation usually follows enactment of authorizing legislation. An appropriation act is the most common means of providing budget authority, but in some cases the authorizing legislation itself provides the budget authority. (See Backdoor authority.) Appropriations do not represent cash actually set aside in the Treasury for purposes specified in the appropriations act: they represent limitations of amounts that agencies may obligate during the period of time specified in the respective appropriation acts. Several types of appropriations are not counted as budget authority, since they do not provide authority to incur additional obligations. Examples of these include: appropriations to liquidate contract authority–congressional action to provide funds to pay obligations incurred against contract authority; appropriations to reduce outstanding debt–congressional action to provide funds for debt retirement; appropriations for refunds of receipts.

Authority to borrow Also called borrowing authority or authority to spend debt receipts. Statutory authority that permits a federal agency to incur obligations and to make payments for specified purposes out of borrowed monies.

Contract authority Statutory authority that permits obligations to be incurred in advance of appropriations or in anticipation of receipts to be credited to a revolving fund or other account. (By definition, contract authority is unfunded and must subsequently be funded by an appropriation to liquidate obligations incurred under the contract authority, or by the collection and use of receipts.) See also "Backdoor authority."

Determination of Amount

Definite authority   Authority which is stated as a specified sum at the time the authority is granted. This includes authority stated as "not to exceed" a specified amount.

Indefinite authority   Authority for which a specific sum is not stated but is determined by other factors, such as the receipts from a certain source or obligations incurred. (Authority to borrow that is limited to a specified amount that may be outstanding at any time, i.e., revolving debt authority, is considered to be indefinite budget authority.)

Period of Availability

One-year (annual) authority   Budget authority that is available for obligation only during a specified fiscal year and expires at the end of the time.

Multiple-year authority   Budget authority that is available for a specified period of time in excess of one fiscal year. This authority generally takes the form of two-year, three-year, etc., availability, but may cover periods that do not coincide with the start or end of a fiscal year. For example, the authority may be available from July 1 of one year through September 30 of the following fiscal year. This authority is sometimes referred to as "forward funding."

No-year authority   Budget authority that remains available for obligation for an indefinite period of time, usually until the objectives for which the authority was made available are attained.

Extensions of Budget Authority

Reappropriations   Congressional action to continue the obligation availability, whether for the same or different purposes, of all or part of the unobligated portion of budget authority that has expired or would otherwise expire. Reappropriations are counted as budget authority in the year for which the availability is extended.

Continuing resolution   Legislation enacted by Congress to provide budget authority for federal agencies and/or specific activities to continue in operation until the regular appropriations are enacted. Continuing resolutions are enacted when action on appropriations is not completed by the beginning of a fiscal year. The continuing resolution usually specifies a maximum rate at which the obligations may be incurred, based on the rate of the prior year, the president's budget request, or an appropriation bill passed by either or both houses of the Congress.

Timing of Congressional Action

Current authority   Budget authority enacted by Congress in or immediately preceding the fiscal year in which it becomes available.

Permanent authority   Budget authority that becomes available as the result of previously enacted legislation (substantive legislation or prior appropriation act) and does not require current action by Congress. Authority created by such legislation is considered to be "current" in the first year in which it is provided and "permanent" in succeeding years.

Budget calendar   The timetable a government follows in budget preparation and adoption, either by law or by administrative regulation.

Call   Payment of principal before stated maturity, as provided for in the security contract.

Callable bond   A bond which permits the issuer to redeem it before maturity according to terms and price (the call price) stipulated in the bond agreement.

Call premium   Premium paid, stated as percentage of the principal amount called, for the exercise of a call provision.

Canadian interest cost   See "true interest cost."

Capital assets   Assets with a useful life of several years (also called fixed assets).

Capital budget   A plan for investment in capital assets separate from current or operating expenditures.

Capitalized interest   Funds reserved from an issue to pay interest on it for a period of time (often during construction of the project).

Capital improvement program   A plan for future capital expenditures which identifies each capital project, its anticipated start and completion, the amount to be spent in each year, and the method of finance.

Capital outlay   Direct expenditure for acquisition of capital assets by contract or direct construction of buildings, roads, or other improvements, and purchase of equipment, land, and existing structures. The work may be addition, replacement, or major alteration, but not simply repair.

Cash and security holdings   Cash and deposits (including demand and time deposits) and governmental and private securities (bonds, notes, stocks, mortgages, etc.) held by a government.

Cash basis of accounting   Accounting basis which records revenues when received in cash and expenditures when paid.

Cash budget   An estimate of receipts and disbursements during a given period, usually as a cash management guide. The projection usually covers a year with estimates made for periods within the year (month, week, day).

Certificate of deposit   Deposit with a financial institution for a contractual period at a contracted interest rate.

Commercial paper   Unsecured promissory obligations with a maturity of substantially less than a year to support current operations or for interim.

Concurrent resolution on the budget   A resolution passed by both houses of Congress, but not requiring the signature of the president, setting forth, reaffirming, or revising the congressional budget for the United States government for a fiscal year.

Two such resolutions are required before the start of a fiscal year. The first, due by May 15, establishes the congressional budget targets for the next fiscal year; the second, scheduled to be passed by September 15, sets a ceiling on budget authority and outlays and a floor on receipts. Additional concurrent resolutions revising the previously established budget levels may be passed by Congress at any time.

Congressional budget   The budget as set forth by Congress in a concurrent resolution on the budget. By law the resolution includes:

The appropriate level of total budget outlays and of total new budget authority.

An estimate of budget outlays and new budget authority for each major functional category, for undistributed intergovernmental transactions, and for such other matters relating to the budget as may be appropriate to carry out the purposes of the 1974 Congressional Budget and Impoundment Control Act.

The amount, if any, of the surplus or deficit in the budget.

The recommended level of federal receipts.

The appropriate level of the public debt.

Continuing resolution   Legislative resolution to permit government agencies to continue activities requiring authority to spend beyond the end of a fiscal year, even though no appropriation bill has been passed.

Controllability   The ability of Congress and the president to increase and decrease budget outlays or budget authority in the year in question, generally the current or budget year. *Relatively uncontrollable* refers to spending that the federal government cannot increase or decrease without changing existing substantive law. For example, out-lays in any one year are considered to be relatively uncontrollable when the program level is determined by existing statute or by contract or other obligations.

Controllability, as exercised by Congress and the president, is deter-mined by statute. In the case of Congress, all permanent budget au-thority is uncontrollable. For example, most trust fund appropriations are permanent, as are a number of federal fund appropriations and in-terest on the public debt, for which budget authority is automatically provided under a permanent appropriation enacted in 1847. In the case of the president, relatively uncontrollable spending is usually the re-sult of open-ended programs and fixed costs (e.g., social security, medi-cal care, veterans' benefits—outlays generally mandated by law), but also includes payments coming due resulting from budget authority enacted in a prior year, such as entering into contracts.

Corporation net income taxes   Taxes on net income earned by busi-ness organized as a corporation. Net income is gross earnings less ex-penses.

Cost-benefit analysis   An analytical technique that compares the so-cial costs and benefits of proposed programs or policy actions. All losses and gains experienced by society are included and measured in dollar terms. The net benefits created by an action are calculated by subtracting the losses incurred by some sectors of society from the gains that accrue to others. Alternative actions are compared, so as to choose one or more that yield the greatest net benefits, or ratio of bene-fits to costs.

The inclusion of all gains and losses to society in cost-benefit analysis distinguishes it from cost-effectiveness analysis, which is a more limited view of costs and benefits.

Cost-effectiveness analysis   An analytical technique used to choose the most efficient method for achieving a program or policy goal. The costs of alternatives are measured by their requisite estimated dollar expenditures. Effectiveness is defined by the degree of goal attain-ment, and may also (but not necessarily) be measured in dollars. Either the net effectiveness (effectiveness minus costs) or the cost-effectiveness ratios of alternatives are compared. The most cost-effective method cho-sen may involve one or more alternatives.

The limited view of costs and effectiveness distinguishes this tech-nique from cost-benefit analysis, which encompasses society-wide im-pacts of alternatives.

Coupon   Detachable portions of a bond presented by its holder to bond issuer's paying agent to document interest due. The coupon rate is the rate of interest on face value that the coupons reflect.

Coupon rate   Stated rate of interest payable on the principal amount.

Coverage   The number of times by which earnings of a revenue bond-financed project exceed debt service payable in a period. It gauges the margin of safety offered the bondholder.

Crosswalk   Any procedure for expressing the relationship between budgetary data from one set of classifications to another, such as between appropriation accounts and authorizing legislation or between the budget functional structure and the congressional committee spending jurisdictions.

Current charge revenue   Amounts received from the public for performance of specific services benefiting the person charged, and from sales of commodities and services, except liquor store sales. Includes fees, assessments, and other reimbursements for current services, rents, and sales derived from commodities or services furnished incident to the performance of particular functions, gross income of commercial activities, and the like. Current charges are distinguished from license taxes, which relate to privileges granted by the government or regulatory measures for the protection of the public.

Current services estimates   Presidential estimates of budget authority and outlays for the ensuing fiscal year based on continuation of existing levels of service. These estimates reflect the anticipated costs of continuing federal programs and activities at present spending levels without policy changes, that is, ignoring all new initiatives, presidential or congressional, that are not yet law.

These estimates of budget authority and outlays, accompanied by the underlying economic and programmatic assumptions upon which they are based (such as the rate of inflation, the rate of real economic growth, the unemployment rate, program caseloads, and pay increases) are required to be transmitted by the president to the Congress with the president's budget. (For a more detailed discussion of this term, see Special Analysis A of the Special Analyses, *Budget of the United States Government.*)

Death and gift taxes   Taxes imposed on transfer of property at death, in contemplation of death, or as a gift. The death tax may be either on the estate (the undivided holdings of the decedent) or on the inheritance (the share received by the heir).

Debt Comprises long-term credit obligations of the government and its agencies, and all interest-bearing short-term (i.e., repayable within one year) credit obligations. Includes judgments, mortgages, and "revenue" bonds as well as general obligation bonds, notes, and interest-bearing warrants. Excludes noninterest-bearing short-term obligations, interfund obligations, amounts owed in a trust or agency capacity, advances and contingent loans from other governments, and rights of individuals to benefits from employee-retirement funds. Nonguaranteed federal agency debt is excluded from total long-term balances. **Full faith and credit debt** is long-term debt for which the credit of government, implying the power of taxation, is unconditionally pledged. Includes debt payable initially from specific taxes or nontax sources, but representing a liability payable from any other available resources if the pledged sources are insufficient. For the federal government, includes *public debt* (subject to Public Law 94-3 statutory limitations) and *agency debt* (issued outside the above federal statutory restrictions). *Nonguaranteed debt* consists of long-term debt payable solely from earnings of revenue-producing activities, from special assessments, or from specific nonproperty taxes. *Net long-term debt* is total long-term debt outstanding minus *long-term debt offsets*.

Debt, Federal

There are three basic tabulations of federal debt: gross federal debt, debt held by the public, and debt subject to statutory limit.

Gross Federal Debt

Consists of public debt and agency debt and includes all public and agency debt issues outstanding.

Public debt That portion of the federal debt incurred when the Treasury or the Federal Financing Bank (FFB) borrows funds directly from the public or another fund or account. To avoid double counting, FFB borrowing from the Treasury is not included in the public debt. (The Treasury borrowing required to obtain the money to lend to the FFB is already part of the public debt.)

Agency debt That portion of the federal debt incurred when a federal agency, other than the Treasury or the Federal Financing Bank, is authorized by law to borrow funds directly from the public or another fund or account. To avoid double counting, agency borrowing from Treasury of the FFB and federal debt. (The Treasury or FFB borrowing required to obtain the money to lend to the agency is already part of the public debt.) Agency debt may be incurred by agencies within the federal budget (such as the Tennessee Valley Authority) or by off-budget federal entities (such as the Postal Service). Debt of government-sponsored, privately owned enterprises (such as the Federal National Mortgage Association) is not included in the federal debt.

Debt held by the public   Part of the gross federal debt held by the public. (The Federal Reserve System is included in "the public" for this purpose.) Debt held by government trust funds (e.g., Social Security Trust Fund), revolving funds, and off-budget federal entities is excluded from debt held by the public.

Debt subject to statutory limit   As defined by the Second Liberty Bond Act of 1917, as amended, it currently includes virtually all public debt. However, only a small portion of agency debt is included in this tabulation of federal debt.

Under Public Law 96-78, approved September 29, 1979, an amendment to the Rules of the House of Representatives makes possible the establishment of the public debt limit as a part of the congressional budget process.

Debt limit   The maximum debt a governmental unit may incur under constitutional, statutory, or charter requirements, either in total or as a percentage of assessed value. Limits typically encompass only full faith and credit debt.

Debt management   Operations of the U.S. Treasury Department that determine the composition of the federal debt. Debt management involves determining the amounts, maturities, other terms and conditions, and schedule of offerings of federal debt securities and raising new cash to finance the government's operations. The objective of debt management is to raise the money necessary for the government's operations at least cost to the taxpayer and in a manner that will minimize the effect of government operations on financial markets and on the economy.

Debt outstanding   All debt outstanding remaining unpaid on the date specified.

Debt service   Expenditure to pay interest and repay principal to owners of debt issued by an entity.

Decision package   In zero-base budgeting, a brief justification document containing the information that managers need to judge program or activity levels and resource requirements. Each decision package presents a level of request for a decision unit, stating the costs and performance associated with that level. Separate decision packages are prepared for incremental spending levels:

Minimum level—performance below which it is not feasible for the decision unit to continue because no constructive contribution could be made toward fulfilling the unit's objectives.

Intermediate level—performance between the minimum and current levels. There may be more than one intermediate level.

Current level—performance that would be reflected if activities for the budget year were carried on at current-year service or output levels without major policy changes. This level permits internal realignments of activities within existing statutory authorizations.

Enhancement level—where increased output or service are consistent with major objectives and where sufficient benefits are expected to warrant the serious review of higher authorities.

A series of decision packages are prepared for each decision unit. Cumulatively, the packages represent the total budget request for that unit.

Default   Failure to pay a bond's principal and/or interest when due.

Deferral of budget authority   Any action or inaction by an officer or employee of the U.S. government that temporarily withholds, delays, or effectively precludes the obligation or expenditure of budget authority, including authority to obligate by contract in advance of appropriations as specifically authorized by law. Deferrals consist of (*a*) amounts reserved for contingencies pursuant to the Antideficiency Act (31 U.S.C. 665) and (*b*) amounts temporarily withheld for other reasons pursuant to the Congressional Budget and Impoundment Control Act of 1974 (P.L. 93-344; 31 U.S.C. 1403).

Deferrals may not extend beyond the end of the year in which the message reporting the deferral is transmitted and may be overturned by the passage of an impoundment resolution by either house of Congress.

Deficiency apportionment   A distribution by the Office of Management and Budget of available budgetary resources for the fiscal year that anticipates the need for supplemental budget authority. Such apportionments may only be made under certain specified conditions provided for in law [Antideficiency Act, 31 U.S.C. 665(e)]. In such instances, the need for additional budget authority is usually reflected by making the amount apportioned for the fourth quarter less than the amount that will actually be required. Approval of request for deficiency apportionment does not authorize agencies to exceed available resources within an account.

Deficient   The amount by which expenditures exceed revenues during an accounting period.

Demand deposit   Checking account; claims against a bank (or similar financial institution) which may be transferred to another individual or firm by an order to pay (usually check).

Denomination   The face amount of a note or bond.

Deobligation   A downward adjustment of previously recorded obligations. This may be attributable to the cancellation of a project or contract, price revisions, or corrections of estimates previously recorded as obligations.

Direct expenditure   Payments to employees, suppliers, contractors, beneficiaries, and other final recipients of government payments (i.e., all expenditure other than *intergovernmental expenditure*).

Discount   Amount (stated in dollars or a percent) by which the price of a security is less than its face amount.

Document and stock transfer taxes   Taxes on the recording, registering, and transfer of documents such as mortgages, deeds, and securities, except taxes on vehicle titles, which are classified elsewhere.

Double-barreled bond   A bond secured by the pledge of more than one source of repayment, often project revenue and taxing power.

Employee-retirement system   A government-administered contributory plan for financing retirement and associated benefits for government employees. Does not include noncontributory plans.

Encumbrances   Purchase orders, contracts, or salary commitments which must be covered by an appropriation and for which part of the appropriation is reserved. When paid, they are no longer encumbrances.

Entitlements   Legislation that requires the payment of benefits (or entitlements) to any person or unit of government that meets the eligibility requirements established by such law. Authorizations for entitlements constitute a binding obligation on the part of the federal government, and eligible recipients have legal recourse if the obligation is not fulfilled. Budget authority for such payments is not necessarily provided in advance, and thus entitlement legislation requires the subsequent enactment of appropriations unless the existing appropriation is permanent. Examples of entitlement programs are social security benefits and veterans' compensation or pensions. Section 401(b) of the Congressional Budget and Impoundment Control Act of 1974 (P.L. 93-344, 31 U.S.C. 1351[b]) imposes certain limits on the use of entitlements.

Expenditure   All amounts of money paid out by a government—net of recoveries and other correcting transactions—other than for retirement of debt, investment in securities, extension of credit, or as agency transactions. Note that expenditure includes only external transactions of a government and excludes noncash transactions such as the provision of prerequisites or other payment in kind.

The cost of goods received or services rendered whether cash payments have been made or not (accrual basis); payment of cost of goods received or services rendered (cash basis).

Face amount   The par value (i.e., principal or value on maturity) of a security.

Failure of exclusion   An element of nonappropriability; the inability to prevent persons not paying for a service from receiving that service.

Financial administration   Activities involving finance and taxation. Includes central agencies for accounting, auditing, and budgeting; the supervision of local government finance; tax administration; collection, custody, and disbursement of funds; administration of employee-retirement systems; debt and investment administration; and the like.

First concurrent resolution on the budget   The resolution, containing government-wide budget targets of receipts, budget authority, and outlays that guide Congress in its subsequent consideration of appropriations and revenue measures. It is required to be adopted by both houses of Congress no later than May 15, pursuant to the Congressional Budget and Impoundment Control Act of 1974 (P.L. 93-344, 31 U.S.C. 1324).

Fiscal year   The 12-month period at the end of which a government determines its financial condition and the results of its operations and closes its books.

The fiscal year for the federal budget begins on October 1 and ends on September 30. The fiscal year is designated by the calendar year in which it ends; for example, fiscal year 1980 is the year beginning October 1, 1979, and ending September 30, 1980. (Prior to fiscal year 1977, the federal fiscal year began on July 1 and ended on June 30.) The following conventions are followed:

The *budget year* is the fiscal year for which the budget is being considered (the fiscal year following the current year).

The *current year* is the fiscal year in progress.

The *prior year* is the fiscal year immediately preceding the current year.

Float   Value of checks written but not yet presented for payment to the bank upon which the check was written.

Frontloaded   Higher coupon rates on the shorter maturity bonds or larger principal repayments in the early years of a serial bond issue.

Full faith and credit debt   Long-term debt for which the credit of the government, implying the power of taxation, is unconditionally pledged. Includes debt payable initially from specific taxes or nontax sources, but representing a liability payable from any other available resources if the pledged sources are insufficient.

Full funding   Provides budgetary resources to cover the total cost of a program or project at the time it is undertaken.

Full funding differs from incremental funding, where budget authority is provided or recorded for only a portion of total estimated obligations expected to be incurred during a single fiscal year. Full funding is generally discussed in terms of multiyear programs, whether or not obligations for the entire program are made in the first year. For further discussion of this term, see U.S. General Accounting Office, *Further Implementation of Full Funding in the Federal Government*, PAD-78-80, September 7, 1978.

Functional classification   A system of classifying budget resources by function so that budget authority and outlays of budget and off-budget federal entities, loan guarantees, and tax expenditures can be restated in terms of the national needs being addressed.

Budget accounts are generally placed in the single budget function (e.g., national defense, health) that best reflects its major end purpose addressed to an important national need, regardless of the agency administering the program. A function may be divided into two or more subfunctions, depending upon the complexity of the national need addressed by that function.

For budget presentation purposes, each budget function is described in the context of national needs being served, and the subfunctions are described in the context of the major missions devoted to meeting national needs. (For distinction, see Object classification.)

Functions   Public purposes served by governmental activities (education, highways, public welfare, etc.). Expenditure for each function includes amounts for all types of expenditure serving the purpose concerned.

Fund   An accounting device established to control receipt and disbursement of income from sources set aside to support specific activities or attain certain objectives. In the accounts of individual governments, each fund is treated as a distinct fiscal entity.

Fund accounting   The legal requirement for federal agencies to establish accounts for segregating revenues and other resources, together with all related liabilities, obligations, and reserves, for the purpose of carrying on specific activities or attaining certain objectives in accordance with special regulations, restrictions, or limitations. Fund accounting, in a broad sense, is required in the federal government to demonstrate agency compliance with requirements of existing legislation for which federal funds have been appropriated or otherwise authorized.

One of the most important laws requiring federal agencies to adhere to fund accounting concepts is the Antideficiency Act.

Funding   Issuance of bonds or other long-term debt in exchange for, or to provide funds to retire, outstanding short-term debt.

General obligation (GO)   Instrument secured by a pledge of the issuer's full faith and credit.

General obligation debt   Long-term full faith and credit obligations other than those payable initially from nontax revenue. Includes debt payable in the first instance from particular earmarked taxes, such as motor fuel sales taxes or property taxes.

General revenue   All revenue of government except utility revenue, liquor-store revenue, and insurance-title revenue. All tax revenue and all intergovernmental revenue even if designated for employee-retirement of local utility purposes, is classed as general revenue.

General revenue sharing   Funds distributed to states and local general-purpose governments by the federal government under the State and Local Fiscal Assistance Act of 1972.

General sales or gross receipts taxes   Sales or gross receipts taxes which are applicable with only specified exceptions to all types of goods, all types of goods and services, or all gross income, whether at a single rate or at classified rates. Taxes imposed distinctively upon sales or gross receipts from selected commodities, services, or businesses are separate.

Grants   Assistance awards in which substantial involvement is not anticipated between the federal government and the state or local government or other recipient during the performance of the contemplated activity.

Major Forms of Federal Grants

Block grants are given primarily to general-purpose governmental units in accordance with a statutory formula. Such grants can be used for a variety of activities within a broad functional area. Examples of federal block grant programs are Omnibus Crime Control and Safe Streets Act of 1968, Comprehensive Employment and Training Act of 1973, Housing and Community Development Act of 1974, and the 1974 Amendments to the Social Security Act of 1935 (Title XX).

Categorical grants can be used only for a specific program and are usually limited to narrowly defined activities. Categorical grants consist of formula, project, and formula-project grants.

Formula grants allocate federal funds to states or their subdivisions in accordance with a distribution formula prescribed by law or administrative regulation.

Project grants provide federal funding for fixed or known periods for specific projects or the delivery of specific services or products.

Impoundment Any action or inaction by an officer or employee of the United States government that precludes the obligation or expenditure of budget authority provided by Congress.

Impoundment resolution A resolution by either the House of Representatives or the Senate that expresses disapproval of a proposed deferral of budget authority set forth in a special message transmitted by the president as required under Sec. 1013(a) of the Impoundment Control Act of 1974 (P.L. 93-344, 31 U.S.C. 1403).

Whenever all or part of any budget authority provided by Congress is deferred, the president is required to transmit a special message to Congress describing the deferrals. Either House may, at any time, pass a resolution disapproving this deferral of budget authority, thus requiring that the funds be made available for obligation. When no congressional action is taken, deferrals may remain in effect until, but not beyond, the end of the fiscal year. If the funds remain available beyond the end of a fiscal year and continued deferral of their use is desired, the president must transmit a new special message to Congress.

Incremental funding The provision (or recording) of budgetary resources for a program or project based on obligations estimated to be incurred within a fiscal year when such budgetary resources will cover only a portion of the obligations to be incurred in completing the program or project as programmed. This differs from full funding, where budgetary resources are provided or recorded for the total estimated obligations for a program or project in the initial year of funding. (For distinction, see Full funding.)

Indirect cost Any cost incurred for common objectives and which therefore cannot be directly charged to any single cost objective. These costs are allocated to the various classes of work in proportion to the benefit to each class. Indirect cost is also referred to as overhead or burden cost.

Individual income taxes Taxes on individuals measured by net income, including distinctive taxes on income from interest, dividends, and the like.

Industrial development bonds Municipal bonds which finance private industrial plant construction. Lease payments by the private firm service the bonds.

Institutional investor or buyer   A bank, financial institution, insurance company, mutual fund, or similar investment organization.

Insurance trust system   A government-administered program for employee retirement and social insurance protection relating to unemployment compensation, workmen's compensation, old age, survivor's, disability, and health insurance, and the like. *Insurance trust revenue* comprises amounts from contributions required of employers and employees for financing these social insurance programs, and earnings on assets of such systems. *Insurance trust expenditure* corresponds with the character and object category, *insurance benefits and repayments,* and comprises only cash payments to beneficiaries (including withdrawal of contributions). These categories exclude costs of administering insurance trust systems, which are classed as general expenditure. Insurance trust revenue and expenditure do not include any contributions of a government to a system it administers. Any amounts paid by a government as employer contributions to an insurance trust system administered by another government are classed as general expenditure for current operation, and as insurance trust revenue of the particular system and receiving government.

Interest   Price of borrowing money; rate measured by percent of principal borrowed.

Intergovernmental transactions   *Intergovernmental revenue* and *intergovernmental expenditure* comprise, respectively, payments from one government to another as grants-in-aid, shared revenues, payments in lieu of taxes, or reimbursements for governmental services. Excludes amounts for the purchase of commodities, property, or utility services, any tax levied as such on facilities of the payer, and employer contributions by the government for social insurance (e.g., employee-retirement and OASHI insurance).

Inverted or negative yield curve   The interest rate structure with short-term interest rates lower than long-term rates.

Investment   Asset purchased and held to generate interest, dividend, or rental income.

Joint resolution   A joint resolution requires the approval of both houses of Congress and the signature of the president, just as a bill does, and has the force of law if approved. There is no real difference between a bill and a joint resolution. The latter is generally used in dealing with limited matters, such as a single appropriation for a specific purpose.

Joint resolutions also are used to propose amendments to the U.S. Constitution. These do not require presidential signature, but become a part of the Constitution when three fourths of the states have ratified them.

Lease purchase financing   A long-term lease sold publicly to finance capital equipment or real property acquisitions.

Lease revenue bond   Tax exempt bond secured by lease-back by the local entity lessee. Lessee pledges operating revenues to lease payments. Title to the property reverts to the lessee when the bonds are paid off.

Letter of credit   Agreement by a bank or other entity to honor drafts or other demands for payment of debt service.

Level debt service   Serial maturities arranged so that the volume of maturing bonds increases at approximately the same rate as interest payments decline with reduced outstanding debt. Thus, total debt service remains almost constant, even as debt is retired.

License taxes   Taxes enacted (either for revenue raising or for regulation) as a condition to the exercise of a business or nonbusiness privilege, at a flat rate or measured by such bases as capital stock, capital surplus, number of business units, or capacity. Excludes taxes measured directly by transactions, gross or net income, or value of property except those to which only nominal rates apply. "Licenses" based on these latter measures other than those at nominal rates, are classified according to the measure concerned. Includes "fees" related to licensing activities—automobile inspection, gasoline and oil inspection, professional examinations and licenses, etc.—as well as license taxes producing substantial revenues.

Limited liability bonds   Bonds which do not pledge the full faith credit of the jurisdiction, but do usually dedicate a specific revenue source for repayment.

Liquidity   The ease with which an asset can be converted to money.

Long-term debt   Debt payable more than one year after date of issue.

Long-term debt issued   The par value of long-term debt obligations incurred during the fiscal period concerned, including funding and refunding obligations. Debt obligations authorized but not actually incurred during the fiscal period are not included.

Maturity   The date on which the debt principal is to be repaid.

Maturity date   Date on which all or a stated portion of the principal of a security is due and payable.

Maturity schedule   The schedule (dates and amounts) of principal maturities.

Mil   One tenth of one cent.

Millage   Tax rate expressed in mills per dollar, normally in property taxation.

Mission budgeting   A budget approach that focuses on output rather than input and directs attention to how well an agency is meeting its responsibilities. By grouping programs and activities according to an agency's mission or end purposes, mission budgeting makes it easier to identify similar programs. Missions at the highest level in the budget structure then focus more sharply on the specific components of the mission and the programs needed to satisfy them. At the lowest levels are line items—that is, the supporting activities necessary to satisfy the missions. For further discussion of this term, see U.S. General Accounting Office, *A Mission Budget Structure for the Department of Agriculture—A Feasibility Study,* PAD-80-08.

Moral obligation bond   Municipal bond not backed by full faith and credit, but law requires states to replenish its debt service reserve if necessary.

Mortgage revenue bond   A tax-exempt security issued to make or purchase loans for single-family residences.

Multiyear budget planning   A budget planning process designed to make sure that the long-range consequences of budget decisions are identified and reflected in the budget totals. Currently, multiyear budget planning in the executive branch encompasses a policy review for a three-year period beginning with the budget year, plus protections for the subsequent two years. This process provides a structure for the review and analysis of long-term program and tax policy choices.

Municipal bond   A bond issued by a state or local government, including cities, towns, villages, counties, special districts, states, and state agencies.

Municipal Securities Rulemaking Board (MSRB)   An independent self-regulatory organization established by the Securities Act Amendments of 1975 with rulemaking authority over dealers, dealer banks, and brokers in municipal securities.

Net interest cost (NIC)   The percentage rate, from dividing the net interest cost in dollars by the amount borrowed.

Nominal interest rate   The contractual interest rate appearing on a bond and determining the amount of interest to be paid to a holder.

Nonexhaustion   An element of nonappropriability; one person's use of service does not preclude full concurrent use of that service by others.

Nonguaranteed debt   Long-term debt payable solely from pledged specific sources—e.g., from earnings of revenue-producing activities (university and college dormitories, toll highways and bridges, electric power projects, public building and school building authorities, etc.) or from specific and limited taxes. Includes only debt that does not constitute an obligation against any other resources of the government if the pledged sources are insufficient.

Nonrivalry   See nonexhaustion.

Object classification, object-of-expenditure classification   A uniform classification identifying the transactions of the government by the nature of the good or services purchased (such as personnel compensation, supplies and materials, and equipment), without regard to the agency involved or the purpose of the programs for which they are used.

Obligational authority   The sum of (*a*) budget authority provided for a given fiscal year, (*b*) balances of amounts brought forward from prior years that remain available for obligation, and (*c*) amounts authorized to be credited to a specific fund or accounts during that year, including transfers between funds or accounts.

Off-budget federal entities   Certain federally owned and controlled entities whose transactions (e.g., budget authority or outlays) have been excluded from budget totals under provisions of law. The fiscal activities of these entities, therefore, are not reflected in either budget authority or budget outlay totals. However, the outlays of off-budget federal entities are added to the budget deficit to derive the total government deficit that has to be financed by borrowing from the public or by other means. Off-budget federal entities are discussed in Part 6, Perspectives on the Budget, of *The Budget of the United States Government.* Schedules and financial statements are presented in Part 4 of *The Budget of the United States Government, Appendix.*

Offering price   Price at which underwriters offer securities to investors.

Operating budget   A financial plan which presents proposed expenditures for a given period (typically a fiscal year) and estimates of revenue to finance them. Excludes expenditure for capital assets.

Outlays   Obligations are generally liquidated when checks are issued or cash disbursed. Such payments are called outlays. In lieu of issuing checks, obligations may also be liquidated (and outlays occur) by the maturing of interest coupons in the case of some bonds, or by the issuance of bonds or notes (or increases in the redemption value of bonds outstanding).

Outlays during a fiscal year may be for payment of obligations incurred in prior years (prior-year outlays) or in the same year. Outlays, therefore, flow in part from unexpended balances of prior-year budget authority provided for the year in which the money is spent.

Total budget outlays are stated net of offsetting collections, and exclude outlays of off-budget federal entities.

The terms *expenditure and net disbursement* are frequently used interchangeably with the term *outlays*.

Oversight committee   The congressional committee charged with general oversight of the operation of an agency or program. In most cases, but not all, the oversight committee for an agency is also the authorizing committee for the agency's programs.

Par value   The face value of a security. For bonds, the amount that must be paid at maturity. A quotation of 100 means selling at par; below 100, at a discount (95 = $950 for a $1,000 par value bond); above 100, at a premium (105 = $1,050 for a $1,000 bond).

Paying agent   The bank, trust company, etc., at which securities are presented for payment.

Personal services and benefits   Amounts paid for compensation of officers and employees of the government. Consists of gross compensation before deductions for taxes, retirement plans, or other purposes.

Personnel benefits   Comprises cash allowances paid to civilian and military employees incident to their employment and payment to other funds for the benefit of employees. Prerequisites provided in kind, such as uniforms or quarters, and payments to veterans and former employees resulting from their employment are excluded.

Benefits to former personnel   Pensions, annuities, or other benefits due to former employees or their survivors, based (at least in part) on the length of their services to the government, other than benefits paid from funds financed from employer and/or employee contributions and premiums. Includes federal payments to funds that provide benefits to former employees. Excludes benefits provided in kind, such as hospital and medical care, and indemnities for disability or death of former employees.

Personnel compensation   Comprises gross compensation (before deduction for taxes and other purposes) for services of individuals, including terminal leave payments. This classification covers all payments (salaries, wages, fees) for personal services rendered to the government by its officers or employees, either civil or military, and compensation for special services rendered by consultants or others.

Point   One percent.

Poll taxes   Capitation taxes levied as specific amounts, uniform or graded, against persons, as ad valorem taxes on arbitrary valuation of polls.

Premium   Amount by which the price of security exceeds its par value.

Prepayment provision   Provision specifying at what time and on what terms repayment of the principal amount may be made before the stated maturity.

Present value   The sum which, when available now and invested at prevailing interest rates, will equal a given value at a defined date in the future.

Price   Security price, generally quoted in terms of percent of par value (e.g., premium price = 103, discount price = 97) or in terms of annual yield to maturity (e.g., "yielding 10 3/8%").

Principal amount   Total face amount of all securities in the issue. See also "Face amount."

Private placement   The original placement of an issue in the private money market composed of different types of financial institutions (banks, life insurance companies, pension funds, REITs, etc.) with no public offering of the securities.

Program   Generally defined as an organized set of activities directed toward a common purpose, or goal, undertaken or proposed by an agency in order to carry out its responsibilities. In practice, however, the term *program* has many uses and thus does not have a well-defined, standard meaning in the legislative process. Program is used to describe an agency's mission, programs, functions, activities, services, projects, and processes.

Program evaluation   In general, the process of assessing program alternatives, including research and results, and the options for meeting program objectives and future expectations. Specifically, program evaluation is the process of appraising the manner and extent to which programs (1) achieve their stated objectives; (2) meet the performance perceptions and expectations of responsible federal officials and other interested groups, and (3) produce other significant effects of either a desirable or undesirable character.

Progressive tax   A tax with effective rates that are higher for families with high affluence than they are for families with low affluence.

Property taxes   Taxes conditioned on ownership of property and measured by its assessed value. Includes general property taxes relating to property as a whole, real and personal, tangible or intangible, whether taxed at a single rate or at classified rates; and taxes on selected types of property, such as motor vehicles or certain or all intangibles.

Proportional tax   A tax with *effective* rates that do not change across families with different affluence levels.

Public Offering   Sale by an underwriter to the public.

Rating   Grading by analysts or investors' services of quality (safety of principal and interest payment) of a bond.

Reapportionment   A revision by the Office of Management and Budget of a previous apportionment of budgetary resources for an appropriation or fund account. Agency requests for reapportionment are usually submitted to OMB as soon as a change in previous apportionment becomes necessary due to changes in amounts available, program requirements, or cost factors. A reapportionment would ordinarily cover the same period, project, or activity covered in the original apportionment.

Reconciliation process   A process used by Congress to reconcile amounts determined by tax, spending, and debt legislation for a given fiscal year with the ceilings enacted in the second required concurrent resolution on the budget for that year. Section 310 of the Congressional Budget and Impoundment Control Act of 1974 (P.L. 93-344, 31 U.S.C. 1331) provides that the second concurrent resolution on the budget, which sets binding totals for the budget, may direct committees to determine and recommend changes to laws, bills, and resolutions, as required to conform with the binding totals for budget authority, revenues, and the public debt. Such changes are incorporated into either a reconciliation resolution or a reconciliation bill. (See also Concurrent resolution on the budget.)

Reconciliation bill   A bill, requiring enactment by both Houses of Congress and approval by the president, making changes to legislation that has been enacted or enrolled.

Reconciliation resolution   A concurrent resolution, requiring passage by both Houses of Congress but not the approval of the president, directing the clerk of the House or the secretary of the Senate to make specified changes in bills or resolutions that have not yet reached the stage of enrollment.

Refunding   The issuance of long-term debt in exchange for, or to provide funds for, the retirement of long-term debt already outstanding.

Registered securities   Securities registered by issuer as to ownership, the transfer of ownership of which must be registered with the issuer or trustee.

Regressive tax   A tax with effective rates that are lower for families with high affluence than they are for families with low affluence.

Reoffering yields   Interest rates at which underwriters resell individual bonds to investors.

Rescission   The consequence of enacted legislation that cancels budget authority previously provided by Congress before the time when the authority would otherwise lapse (i.e., cease to be available for obligation).

The Congressional Budget and Impoundment Control Act of 1974 (P.L. 93-344, 31 U.S.C. 1402) specifies that whenever the president determines that all or part of any budget authority will not be needed to carry out the full objectives or scope of programs for which the authority was provided, the president will propose to Congress that the funds be rescinded. Likewise, if all or part of any budget authority limited to a fiscal year—that is, annual appropriations or budget authority of a multiple-year appropriation in the last year of availability—is to be reserved from obligation for the entire fiscal year, a rescission will be proposed. Budget authority may also be proposed for rescission for fiscal policy or other reasons. Generally, amounts proposed for rescission are withheld for up to 45 legislative days while the proposals are being considered by Congress.

All funds proposed for rescission, including those withheld, must be reported to Congress in a special message. If both Houses have not completed action on a rescission proposed by the president within 45 calendar days of continuous session, any funds being withheld must be made available for obligation.

Rescission bill   A bill or joint resolution that cancels, in whole or in part, budget authority previously granted by Congress.

Rescissions proposed by the president must be transmitted in a special message to Congress. Under Section 1012 of the Congressional Budget and Impoundment Control Act of 1974 (P.L. 93-344), unless both Houses of Congress complete action on a rescission bill within 45 days of continuous session after receipt of the proposal, the budget authority must be made available for obligation.

Revenue   All amounts of money received by a government from external sources—net of refunds and other correcting transactions—other than from issue of debt, liquidation of investments, and as agency and private trust transactions. Note that revenue excludes noncash transactions such as receipt of services, commodities, or other "receipt in kind."

Revenues represent the increase in assets (or decrease in liabilities) that result from operations. Revenues result from (1) services performed by the federal government, (2) goods and other tangible property delivered to purchasers, and (3) amounts becoming owed to the government for which no current performance by the government is required.

Contingencies that might result in gains should not be recorded in the accounts since to do so would recognize revenue prior to its realization. Contingencies that might result in gains should be carefully explained in financial statements.

The term *revenues* is commonly used interchangeably with the term *collections*.

Revenue anticipation notes   A short-term municipal debt obligation with future revenues pledged for retirement of the notes at maturity.

Revenue bond   Limited liability bond whose debt service requirements are paid only from the earnings of a public project.

Revenue elasticity   A coefficient measuring the percentage increase in revenue from a given source resulting from a 1 percent increase in economic activity.

Roll over   Issuance of new notes to retire outstanding notes.

Sales and gross receipts taxes   Taxes, including "licenses" at more than nominal rates, based on volume or value of transfers of goods or services, upon gross receipts therefrom, or upon gross income, and related taxes based upon use, storage, production (other than severance of natural resources), importation, or consumption of goods.

Scorekeeping   Procedures for tracking the status of congressional budgetary actions. Examples of scorekeeping information include up-to-date tabulations and reports on congressional actions affecting budget authority, receipts, outlays, surplus or deficit, and the public debt limit, as well as outlay and receipt estimates and reestimates.

Scorekeeping data published by the Congressional Budget Office (CBO) include, but are not limited to, status reports on the effects of congressional actions (and in the case of scorekeeping reports prepared for the Senate Budget Committee, the budget effects of potential congressional actions), and comparisons of these actions to targets and ceilings set by Congress in the budget resolutions. Periodic scorekeeping reports are required to be produced by the CBO pursuant to Section 308(b) of the Congressional Budget and Impoundment Control Act of 1974 (P.L. 93-344, 31 U.S.C. 1329).

Second concurrent resolution on the budget   The resolution adopted by Congress containing a budget ceiling classified by function for budget authority and outlays and a floor for budget receipts. This resolution may retain or revise the levels set earlier in the year, and can include directives to the appropriations committees and to other committees with jurisdiction over budget authority or entitlement authority. The second resolution may also direct the appropriate committees to recommend changes in budget receipts or in the statutory limit on the public debt.

Changes recommended by various committees pursuant to the second budget resolution are to be reported in a reconciliation bill (resolution, in some cases) on which Congress must complete action by September 25, a few days before the new fiscal year commences on October 1.

Selective sales and gross receipts taxes Sales and gross receipts taxes imposed on sales of particular commodities or services or gross receipts of particular businesses, separately and apart from the application of general sales and gross receipts taxes.

Serial bond A bond in an issue that contains multiple maturities.

Severance taxes Taxes imposed distinctively on removal of natural products—e.g., oil, gas, other minerals, timber, fish—from land or water and measured by value or quantity of products removed or sold.

Short-term debt Interest-bearing debt payable within one year from date of issue, such as bond anticipation notes, bank loans, and tax anticipation notes and warrants. Includes obligations having no fixed maturity date if payable from a tax levied for collection in the year of their issuance.

Sinking fund Fund used to accumulate periodic payments toward redemption of bonds at maturity: payments on schedule plus interest earnings will accumulate to par value of the bonds.

Special assessment bond Bond services from special assessments; a local tax against certain property to cover the cost of improvements giving special benefit to that property (sidewalks or street paving in an area, for instance). The bonds may be supported either by the special assessment alone or by full faith and credit as well.

Spending authority As defined by Congressional Budget and Impoundment Control Act of 1974 (P.L. 93-344, 31 U.S.C. 1323), a collective designation for appropriations, borrowing authority, contract authority, and entitlement authority for which the budget authority is not provided in advance by appropriation acts. The latter three are also commonly referred to as backdoor authority.

Spending committees The standing committees of the House and Senate with jurisdiction over legislation that permits the obligation of funds. For most programs, the House and Senate Appropriations Committees are the spending committees. For other programs, the authorizing legislation itself permits the obligation of funds (backdoor authority). When this is the case, the authorizing committees are then the committees with spending responsibility.

Spending legislation (spending bill) A term used in the budget scorekeeping of the Congressional Budget Office to indicate legislation that directly provides budget authority or outlays. Spending legislation includes (1) appropriations legislation, (2) legislation that provides budget authority directly without the need for subsequent appropriations action, and (3) entitlement legislation which, while requiring subsequent appropriations action, essentially "locks in" budget authority at the time of authorization (except legislation that establishes conditional entitlements, where recipients are entitled to payments only to the extent that funds are made available in subsequent appropriations legislation).

Spread A bond underwriter's gross profit: the price received by the underwriter on sale of the bonds less the price paid by the underwriter for those bonds.

Substantive law Statutory public law other than appropriation law; sometimes referred to as basic law. Substantive law usually authorizes, in broad general terms, the executive branch to carry out a program of work. Annual determination as to the amount of the work to be done is usually thereafter embodied in appropriation law.

Supplemental appropriation An act appropriating funds in addition to those in an annual appropriation act. Supplemental appropriations provide additional budget authority beyond the original estimates for programs or activities (including new programs authorized after the date of the original appropriation act) in cases where the need for funds is too urgent to be postponed until enactment of the next regular appropriation bill. Supplementals may sometimes include items not appropriated in the regular bills for lack of timely authorizations.

Supplemental summary of the budget (mid-year or mid-season review) A supplemental summary of the budget for the ensuing fiscal year transmitted to Congress by the president on or before July 15 of each year pursuant to the Budget and Accounting Act of 1921, as amended (31 U.S.C. 11[b]). With respect to that ensuing fiscal year, the summary reflects (a) all substantial alterations in or reappraisals of the estimates of expenditures and receipts, (b) all substantial obligations imposed on that budget after its transmission to Congress, (c) the actual or proposed appropriations made during the fiscal year in progress, and (d) the estimated condition of the Treasury at the end of the fiscal year if the financial proposals contained in the budget are adopted. The summary also contains any information the president considers necessary or advisable to provide the Congress, and a complete and current estimate of the functions, obligations, requirements, and financial condition of the government for the ensuing fiscal year.

Syndicate   A group of underwriters.

Tax credits   Tax credits include any special provision of law that results in a dollar-for-dollar reduction in tax liabilities that would otherwise be due. In some cases, tax credits may be carried forward or backward from one tax year to another, while other tax credits lapse if not used in the year earned. Tax credits may result in a reduction of tax collections or an increase in the value of tax refunds.

Tax expenditures   Revenue losses attributable to provisions of the federal income tax laws that allow a special exclusion, or deduction from gross income, or that provide a special credit, preferential tax rate, or deferral of tax liability.

Tax expenditures may be considered federal government subsidies provided through the tax system to encourage certain activities and to assist certain groups. For example, capital information is encouraged for permitting businesses to claim some portion of the cost of an investment as a credit on their income taxes, and the unemployed are aided by excluding employment benefits from taxable income. Tax expenditures involve no transfer of funds from the government to the private sector. Rather, the U.S. Treasury Department forgoes some of the receipts that it otherwise would have collected, and the beneficiary taxpayers pay lower taxes than they otherwise would have had to pay.

Tax expenditures budget   A list of legally sanctioned tax expenditures for each fiscal year which the 1974 Congressional Budget and Impoundment Act (P.L. 93-334, Sec. 601 [e]) requires be part of the president's budget submission to Congress. (See Special Analysis G of the *Special Analyses, Budget of the United States Government.*)

Tax rate limit   The maximum legal rate at which a government may levy a tax. The limit may apply to a single tax applied by a single government for a purpose, to a single tax applied by a single government, or class of governments, or to all taxes applied by any government or class of governments.

Taxes   Compulsory payments to a government based on holdings of a tax base.

Term bonds   Bonds of an issue that have a single deferred stated maturity date.

Treasury bills   The shortest term federal security. Treasury bills have maturity dates normally varying from 3 to 12 months and are sold at a discount from face value rather than carrying an explicit rate of interest.

True interest cost   A method of computing interest cost or rate which recognizes time value of money.

Underwriter   Investment firm that buys an entire bond issue from an issuing government with the intention of reselling to the public.

Underwriting   Purchase of all bonds in a new issue and the marketing of them.

Underwriting spread   Difference between the offering price to the public and the price the underwriter pays the issuer.

Unemployment compensation system   A state-administered plan for compulsory unemployment insurance through accumulation of assets from contributions collected from employers or employees for use in making cash benefit payments to eligible unemployed persons. Does not include distinctive sickness or disability insurance plans carried out in conjunction with unemployment insurance programs by certain states. Unemployment insurance contributions collected by the state are deposited in the U.S. Treasury in a trust account maintained for the state; interest is credited by the U.S. Treasury on balances in state accounts; and funds are withdrawn by the state as needed to make unemployment compensation benefit payments.

Unified budget   The present form of the budget of the federal government adopted beginning with the 1969 budget, in which receipts and outlays from federal funds and trust funds are consolidated. When these fund groups are consolidated to display budget totals, transactions that are outlays of one fund group (i.e., interfund transactions) are deducted to avoid double counting. By law, budget authority and outlays of off-budget entities are excluded from the unified budget, but data relating to off-budget entities are displayed in the budget documents.

Warrant   An order drawn by a government officer directing the treasurer of that government to pay a specified amount to the bearer after a specified date. Some state and local governments issue warrants rather than checks in order to strengthen internal expenditure control.

Workers' compensation system   A state-administered plan for compulsory accident and injury insurance of workers through accumulation of assets from contributions collected from employers for financing cash benefits to eligible injured workers.

Zero-base budgeting   A process emphasizing management's responsibility to plan, budget, and evaluate. Zero-base budgeting provides for analysis of alternative methods of operation and various levels of effort. It places new programs on an equal footing with existing programs by requiring that program priorities be ranked, thereby providing a systematic basis for allocating resources. Formally adopted at the federal level in 1977 and formally abandoned in 1981.

Zero coupon bonds   Bonds that bear no interest, but are marketed below face value amount, to produce a substantial gain on maturity.

Index